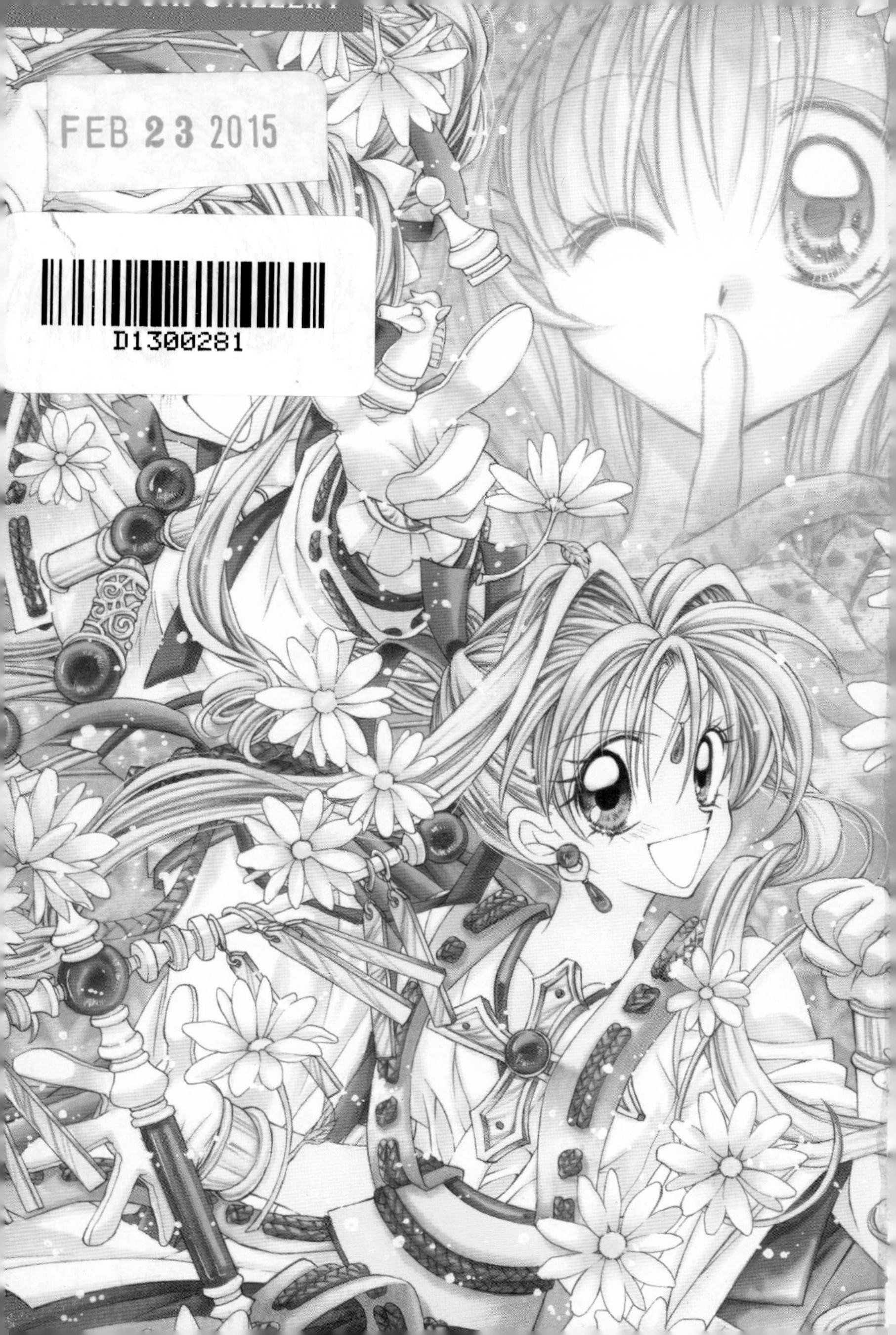

--- ·◦⟩⟨⟨◦·⟩⟨⟨◦⟩⟨⟨◦⟨· ---

COMMENT FROM **CURATOR ARINACCHI**

This is the only illustration I ever drew with
Jeanne in both the old and new outfits. It's a
memorable piece to me because Maron is in
it as well.

PHANTOM THIEF

Jeanne

5

STORY AND ART BY
Arina Tanemura

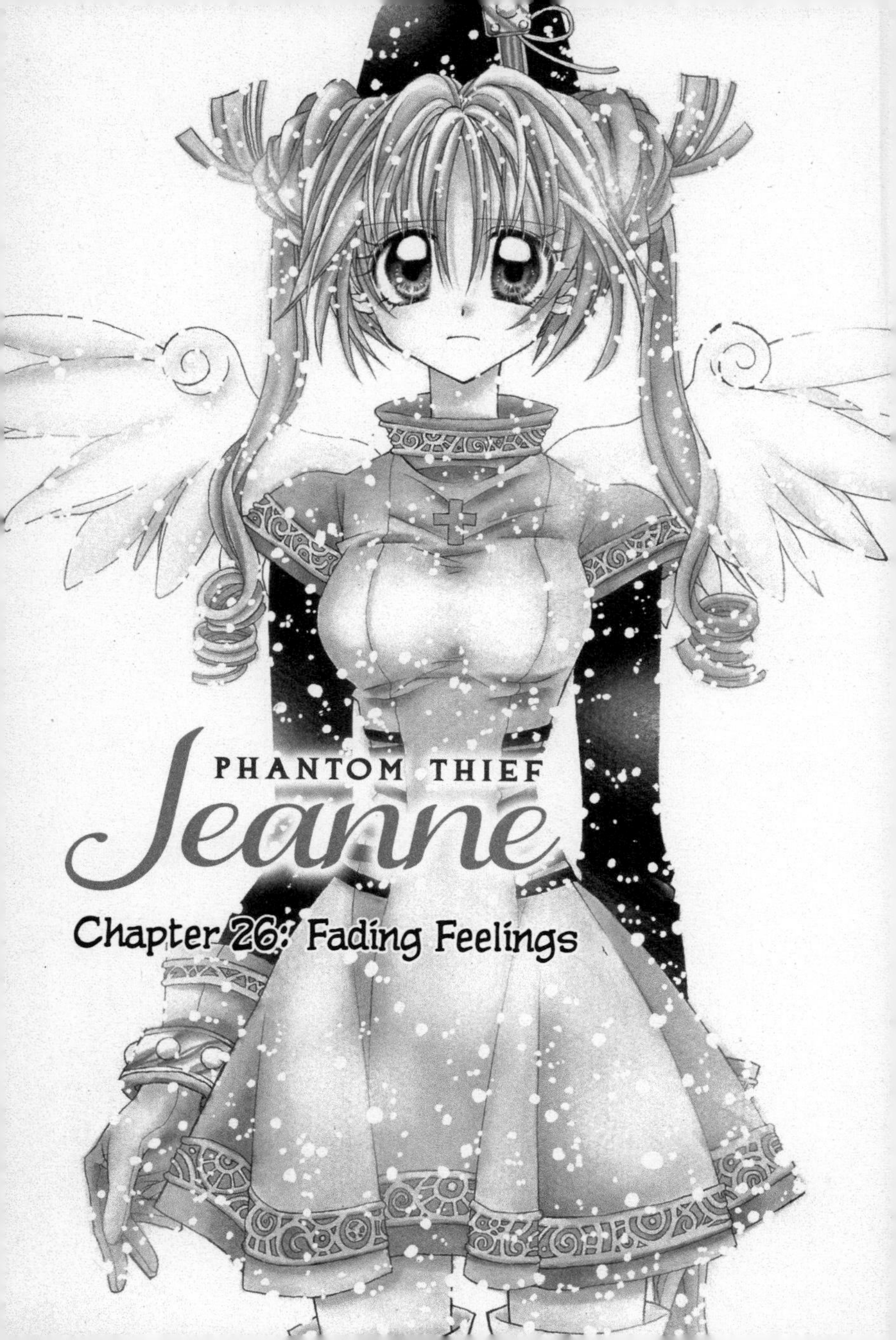
PHANTOM THIEF
Jeanne
Chapter 26: Fading Feelings

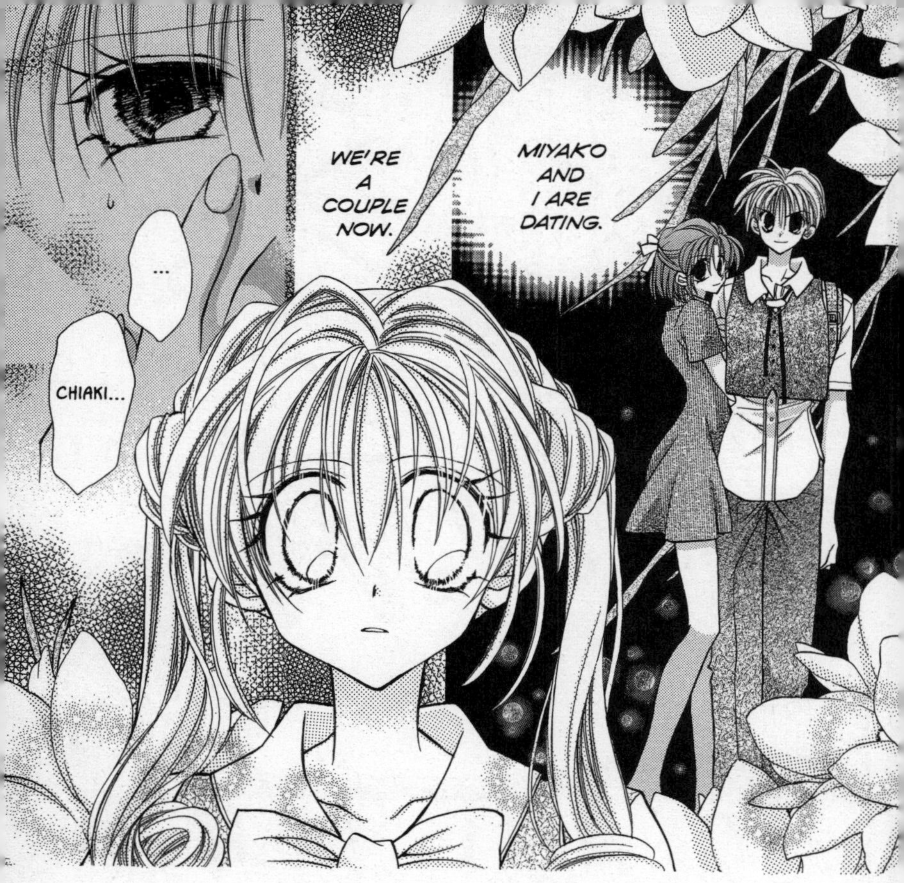
MIYAKO AND I ARE DATING.
WE'RE A COUPLE NOW.
...
CHIAKI...

PHANTOM THIEF JEANNE

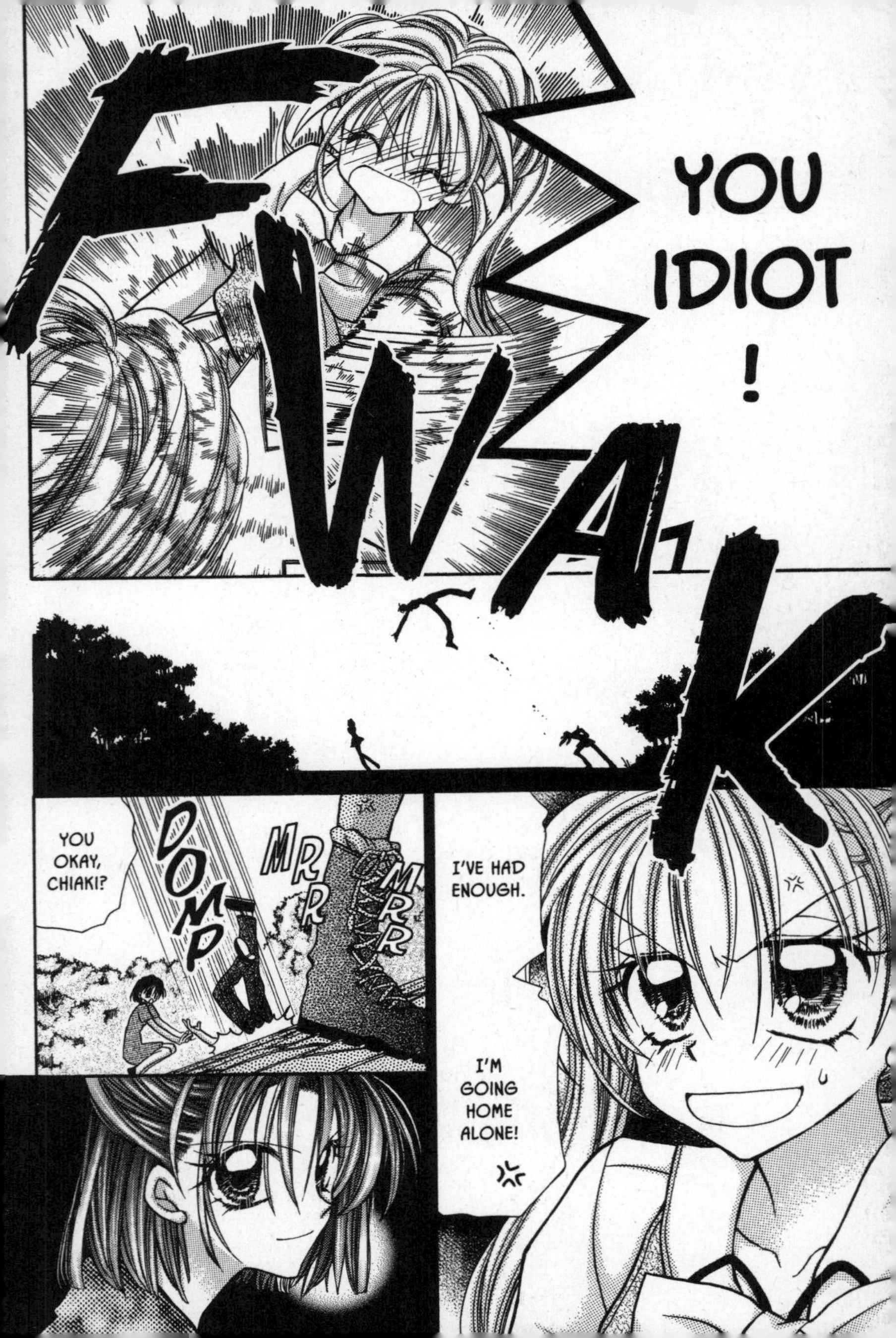
YOU IDIOT!
FWAK
I'VE HAD ENOUGH.
I'M GOING HOME ALONE!
YOU OKAY, CHIAKI?
DOMP
MRR MRR

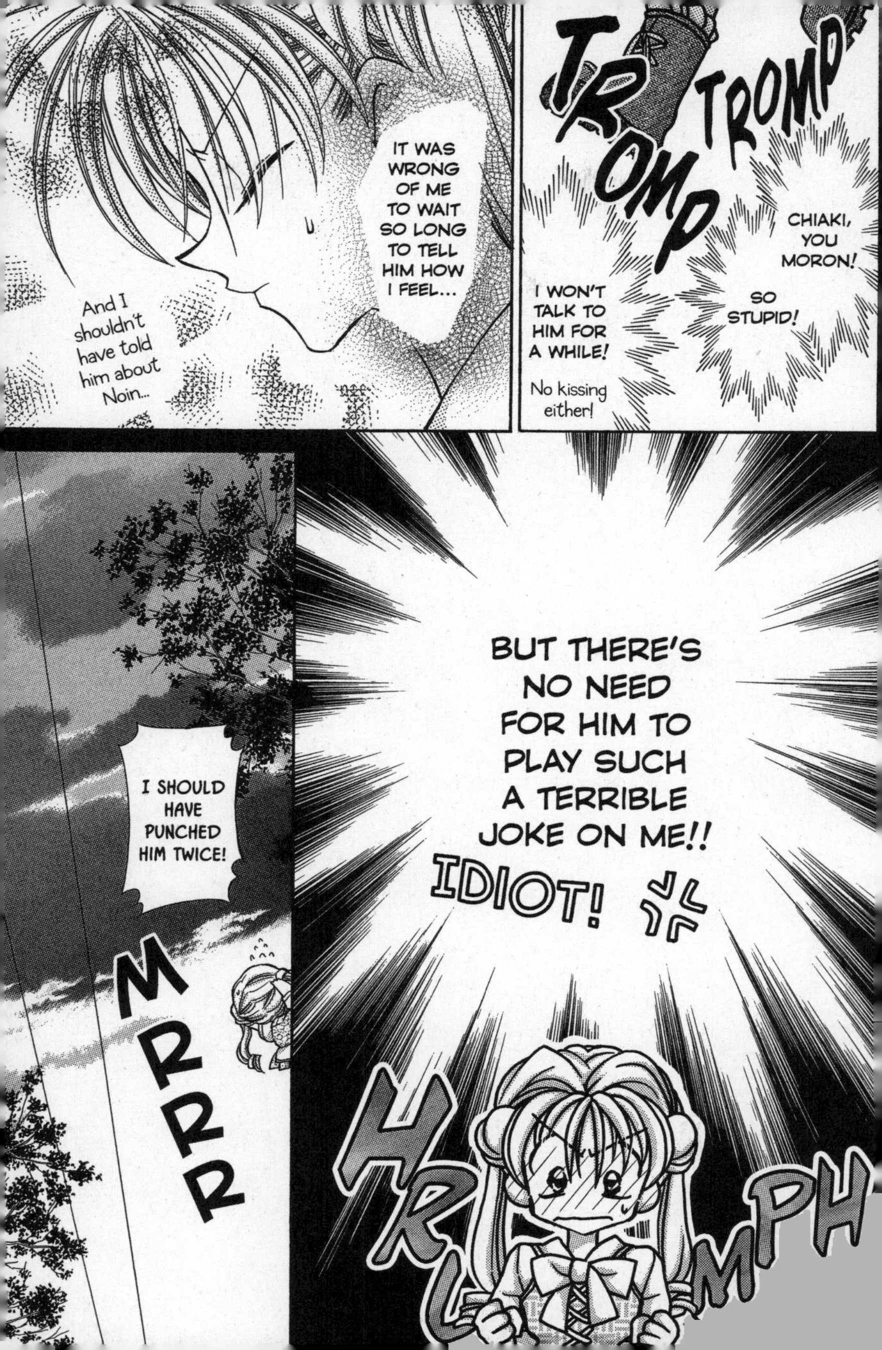
TROMP TROMP
CHIAKI, YOU MORON!
SO STUPID!
I WON'T TALK TO HIM FOR A WHILE!
No kissing either!
IT WAS WRONG OF ME TO WAIT SO LONG TO TELL HIM HOW I FEEL...
And I shouldn't have told him about Noin...
BUT THERE'S NO NEED FOR HIM TO PLAY SUCH A TERRIBLE JOKE ON ME!!
IDIOT!
HRUMPH
I SHOULD HAVE PUNCHED HIM TWICE!
MRRR

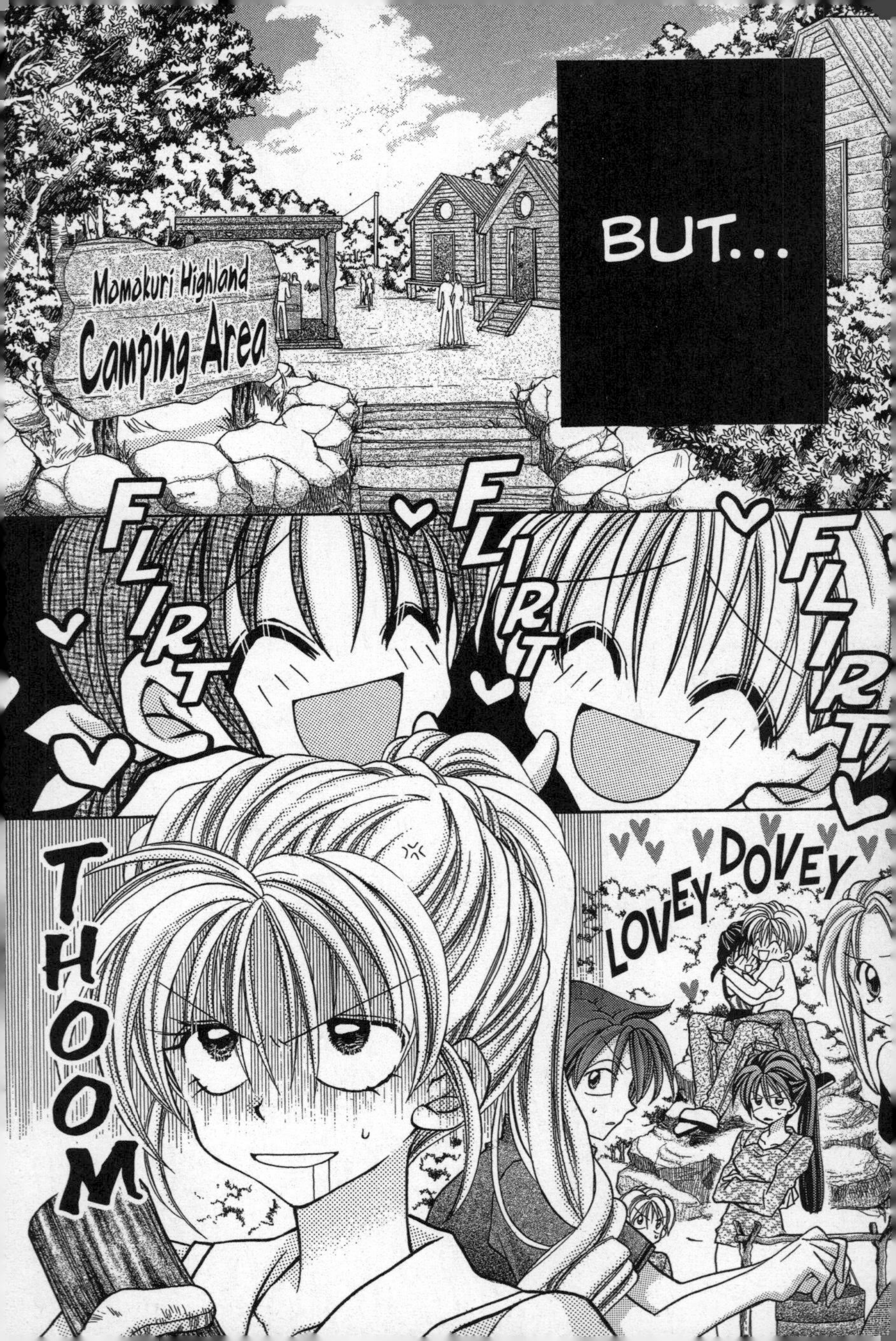
BUT...
Momokuri Highland
Camping Area
FLIRT
FLIRT
FLIRT
LOVEY DOVEY
THOOOM

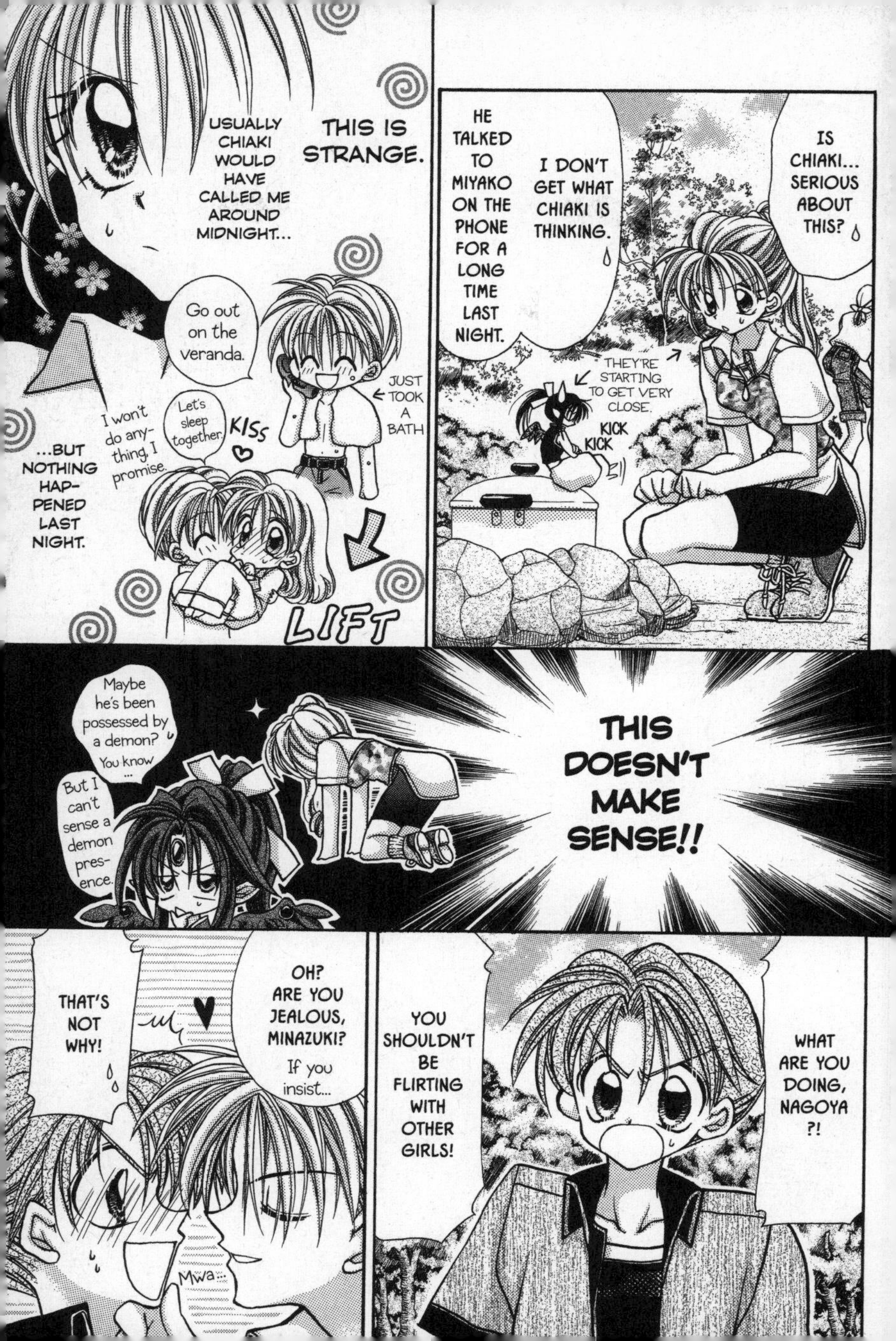
IS CHIAKI... SERIOUS ABOUT THIS?
I DON'T GET WHAT CHIAKI IS THINKING.
HE TALKED TO MIYAKO ON THE PHONE FOR A LONG TIME LAST NIGHT.
THEY'RE STARTING TO GET VERY CLOSE.
KICK KICK
THIS IS STRANGE.
USUALLY CHIAKI WOULD HAVE CALLED ME AROUND MIDNIGHT...
JUST TOOK A BATH
Go out on the veranda.
KISS
Let's sleep together.
I won't do anything, I promise.
...BUT NOTHING HAPPENED LAST NIGHT.
LIFT
THIS DOESN'T MAKE SENSE!!
Maybe he's been possessed by a demon? You know ...
But I can't sense a demon presence.
WHAT ARE YOU DOING, NAGOYA?!
YOU SHOULDN'T BE FLIRTING WITH OTHER GIRLS!
OH? ARE YOU JEALOUS, MINAZUKI?
If you insist...
THAT'S NOT WHY!
Mwa...

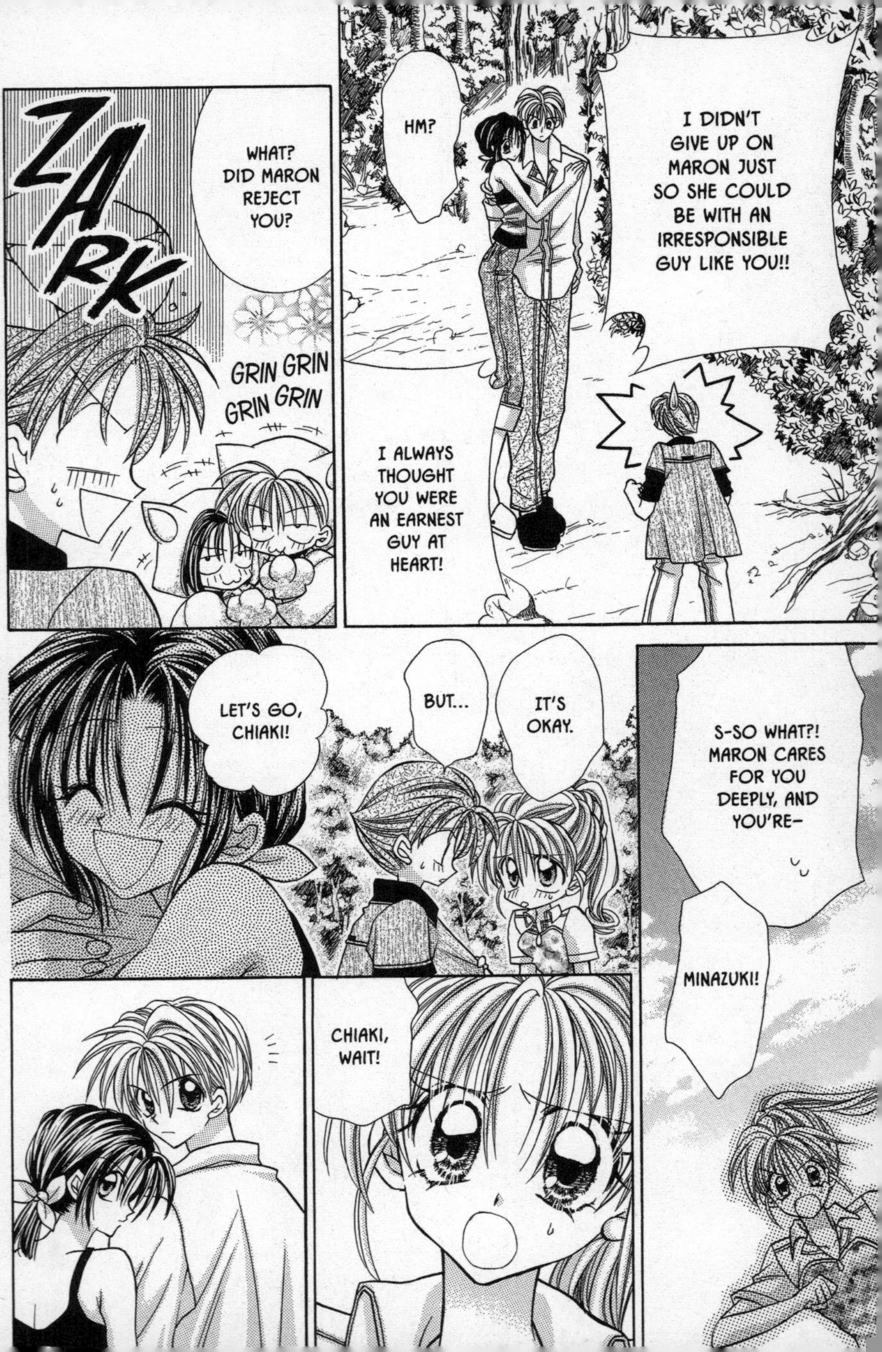
I DIDN'T GIVE UP ON MARON JUST SO SHE COULD BE WITH AN IRRESPONSIBLE GUY LIKE YOU!!
HM?
I ALWAYS THOUGHT YOU WERE AN EARNEST GUY AT HEART!
WHAT? DID MARON REJECT YOU?
ZARK
GRIN GRIN GRIN GRIN
S-SO WHAT?! MARON CARES FOR YOU DEEPLY, AND YOU'RE-
MINAZUKI!
IT'S OKAY.
BUT...
LET'S GO, CHIAKI!
CHIAKI, WAIT!

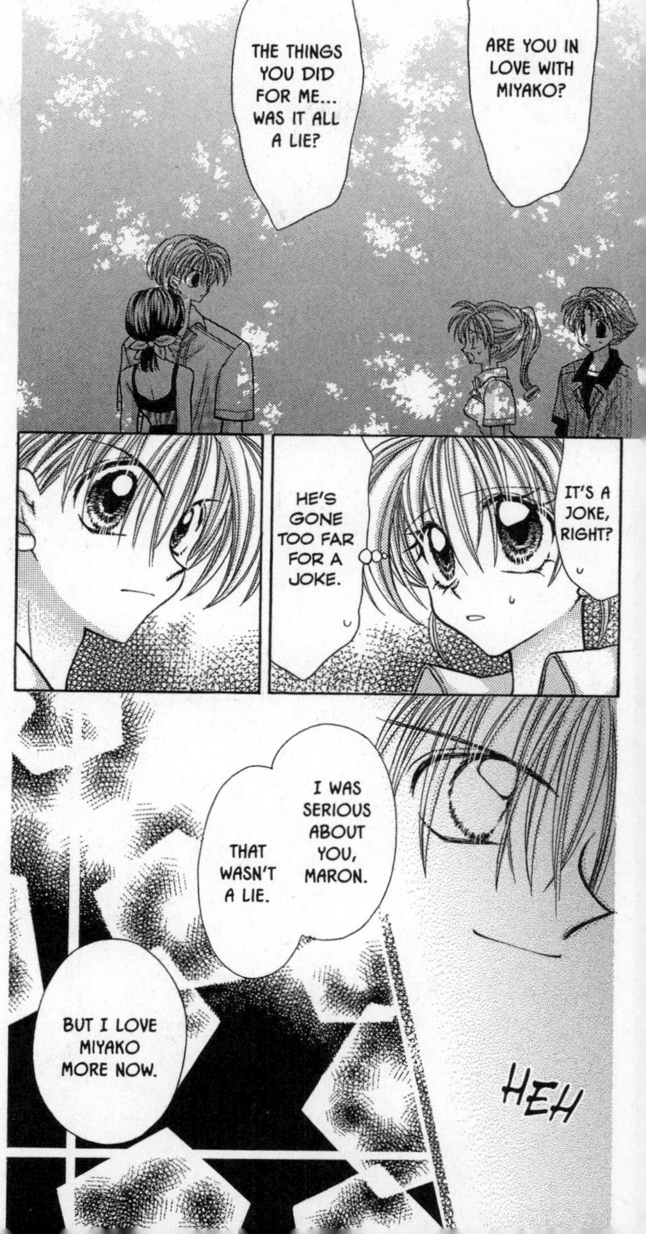
ARE YOU IN LOVE WITH MIYAKO?
THE THINGS YOU DID FOR ME... WAS IT ALL A LIE?
IT'S A JOKE, RIGHT?
HE'S GONE TOO FAR FOR A JOKE.
I WAS SERIOUS ABOUT YOU, MARON.
THAT WASN'T A LIE.
HEH
BUT I LOVE MIYAKO MORE NOW.

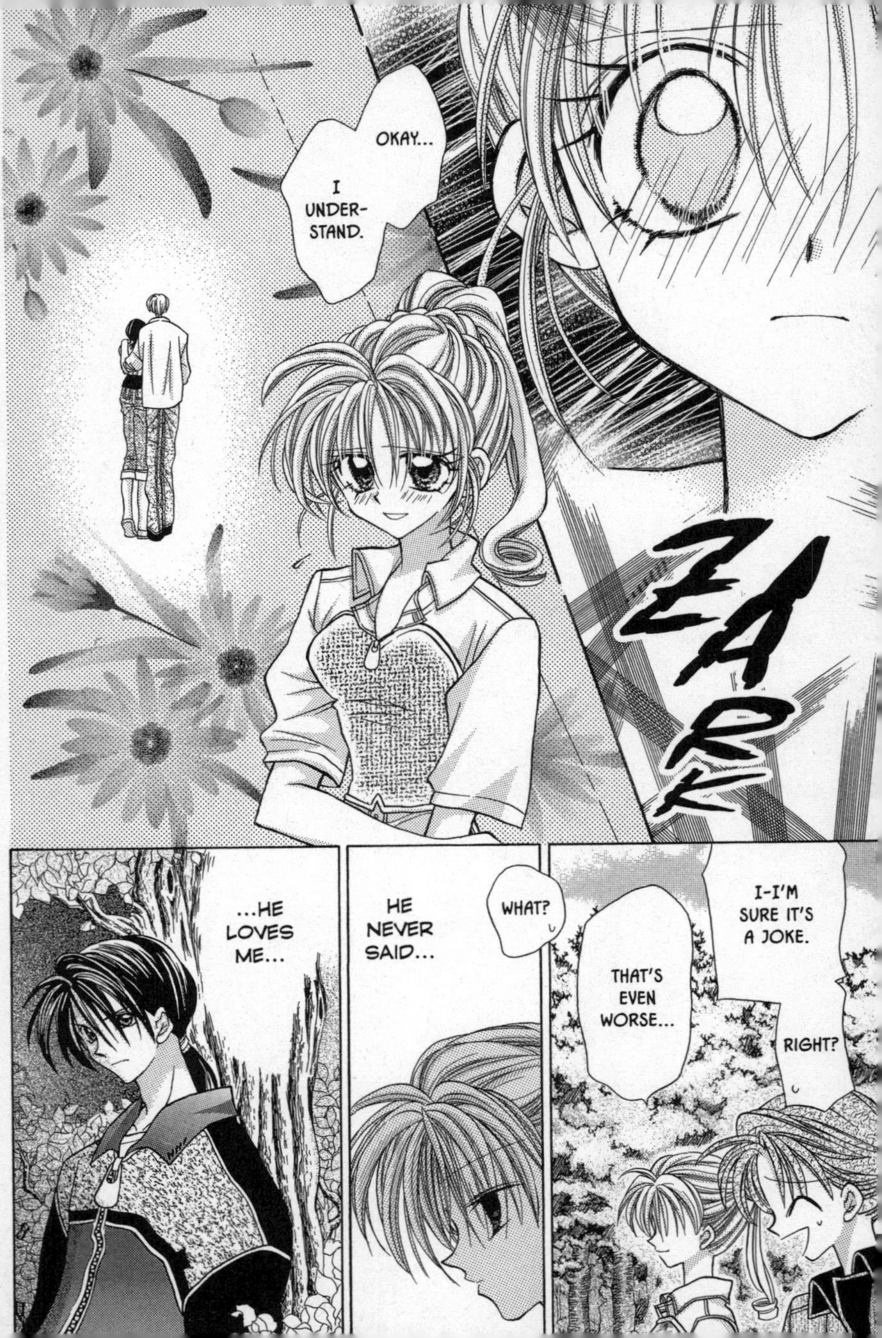
OKAY...
I UNDERSTAND.
ZARK
I-I'M SURE IT'S A JOKE.
RIGHT?
THAT'S EVEN WORSE...
WHAT?
HE NEVER SAID...
...HE LOVES ME...

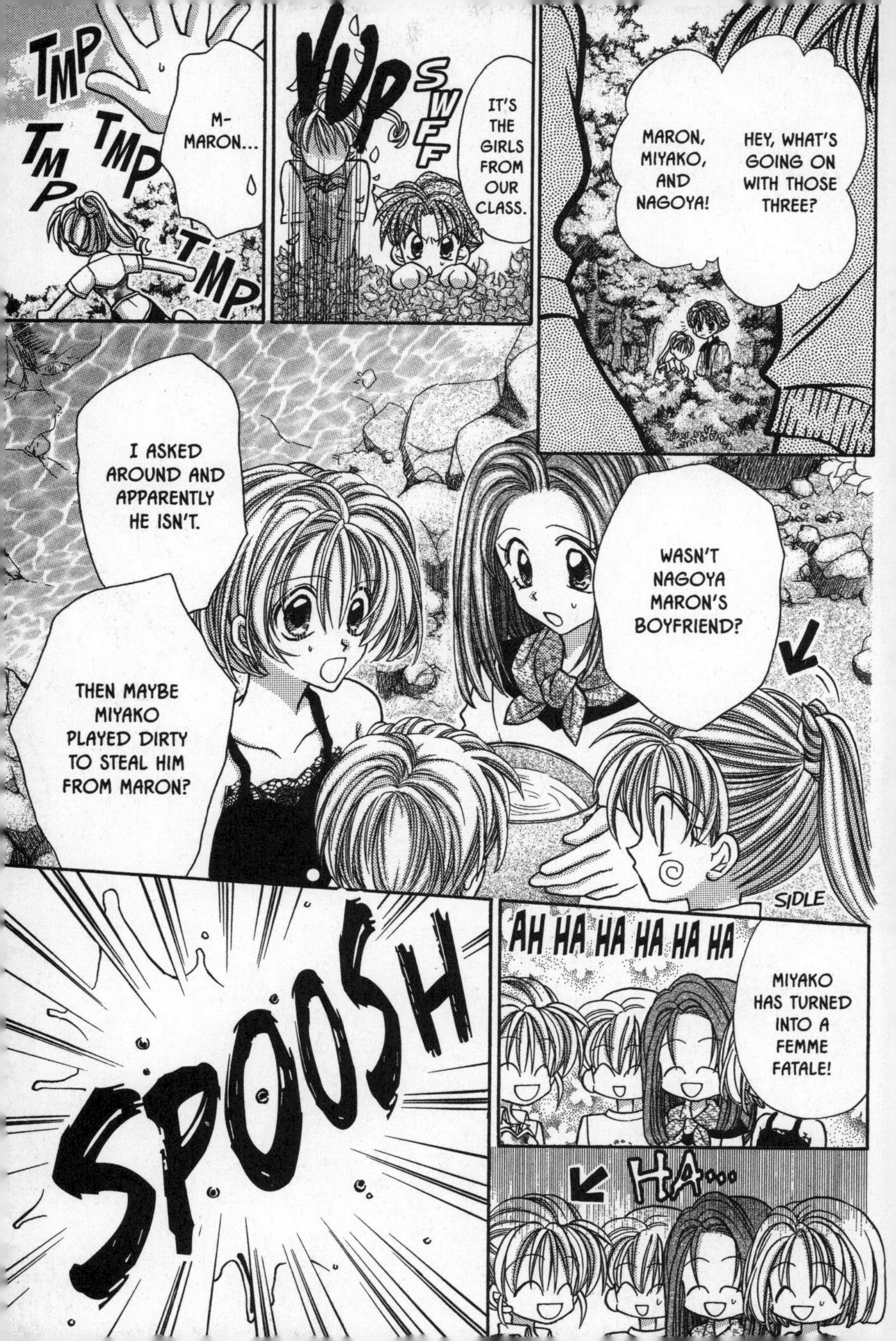
HEY, WHAT'S GOING ON WITH THOSE THREE?
MARON, MIYAKO, AND NAGOYA!
VUP
SWFF
IT'S THE GIRLS FROM OUR CLASS.
TMP
TMP
TMP
TMP
TMP
M-MARON...
WASN'T NAGOYA MARON'S BOYFRIEND?
I ASKED AROUND AND APPARENTLY HE ISN'T.
THEN MAYBE MIYAKO PLAYED DIRTY TO STEAL HIM FROM MARON?
SIDLE
AH HA HA HA HA HA
MIYAKO HAS TURNED INTO A FEMME FATALE!
HA...
SPOOSH

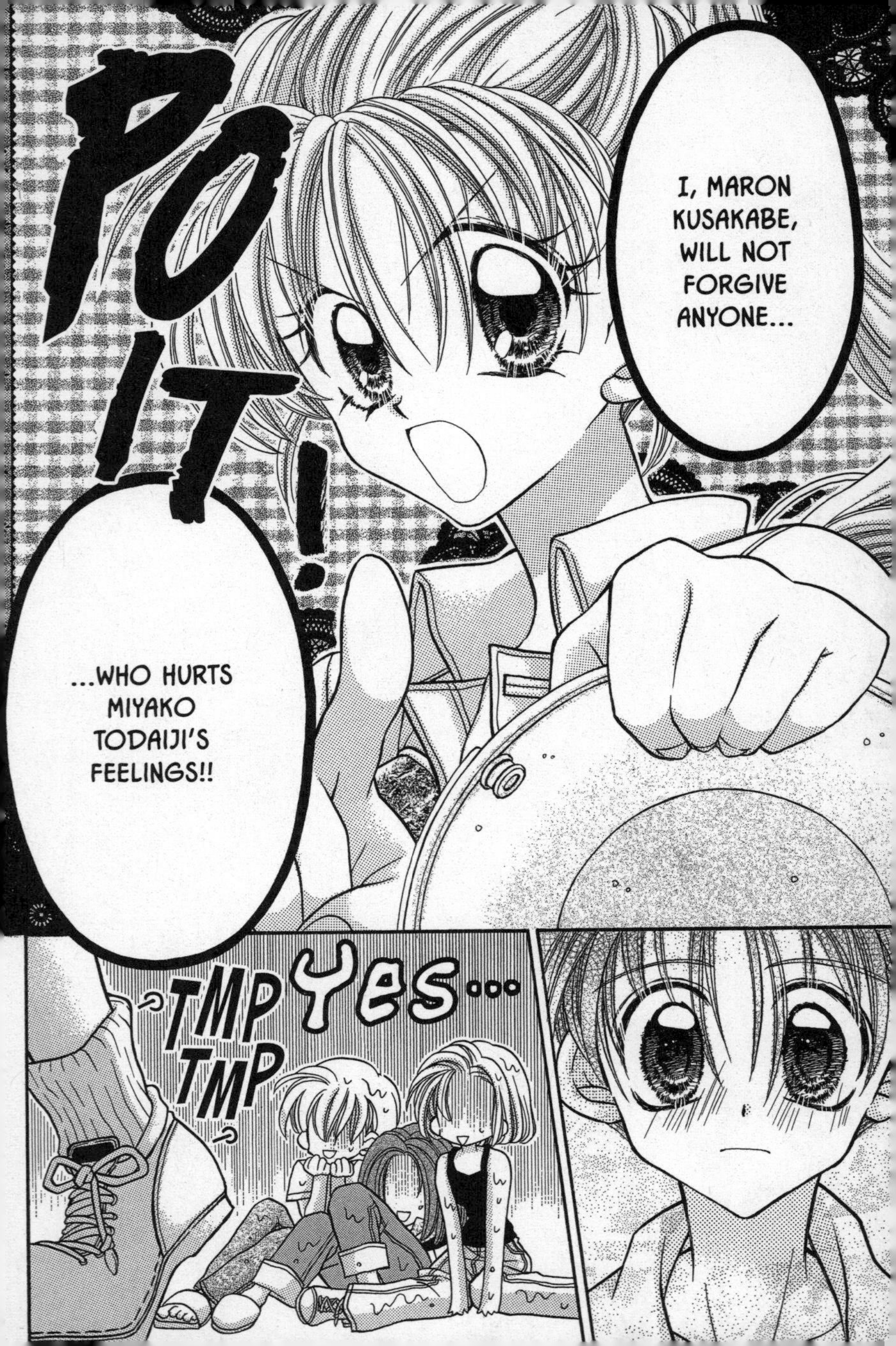
I, MARON KUSAKABE, WILL NOT FORGIVE ANYONE...
POIT!
...WHO HURTS MIYAKO TODAIJI'S FEELINGS!!
Yes...
TMP TMP

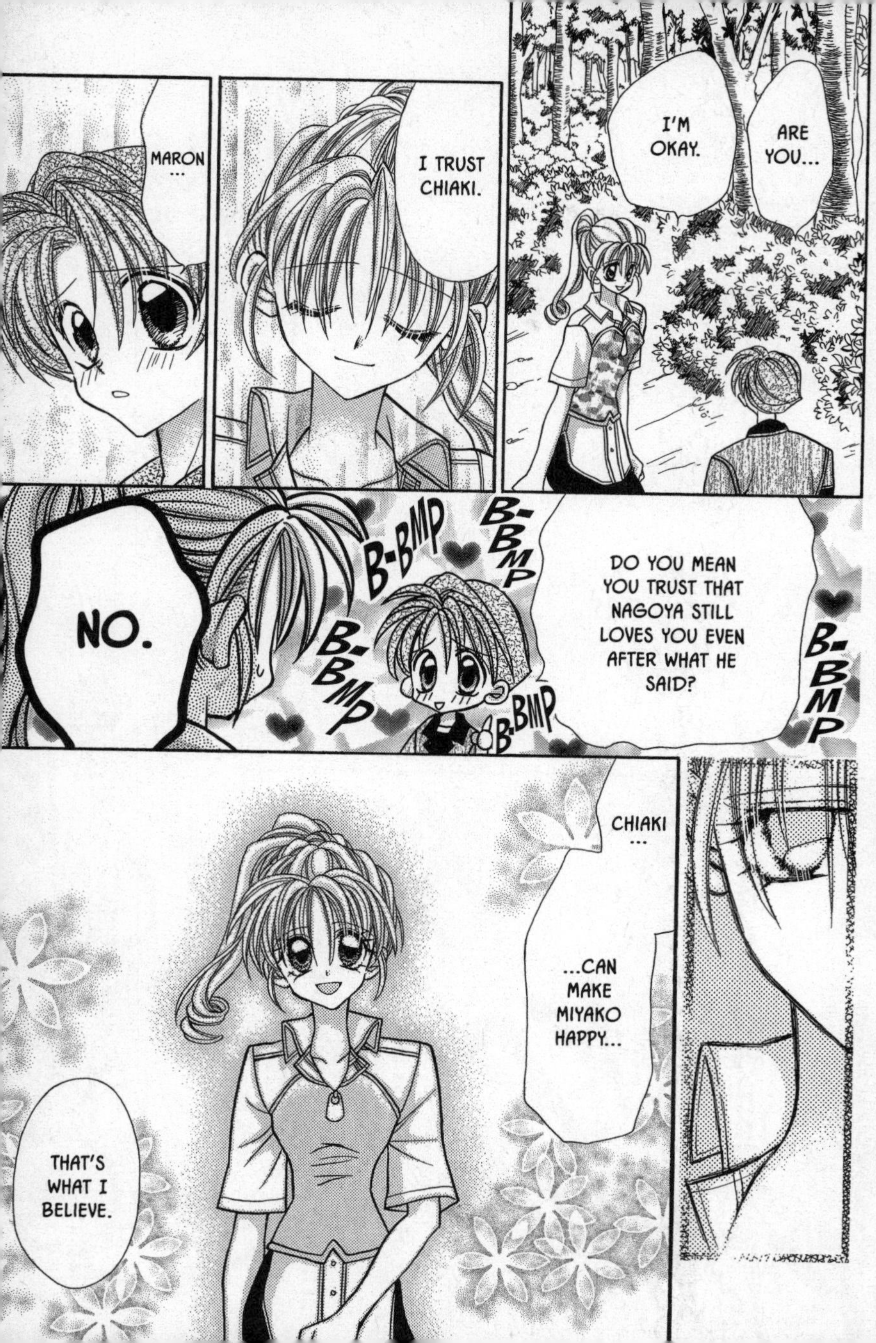
ARE YOU...
I'M OKAY.
I TRUST CHIAKI.
MARON ...
DO YOU MEAN YOU TRUST THAT NAGOYA STILL LOVES YOU EVEN AFTER WHAT HE SAID?
B-BMP
B-BMP
B-BMP
B-BMP
B-BMP
NO.
CHIAKI ...
...CAN MAKE MIYAKO HAPPY...
THAT'S WHAT I BELIEVE.

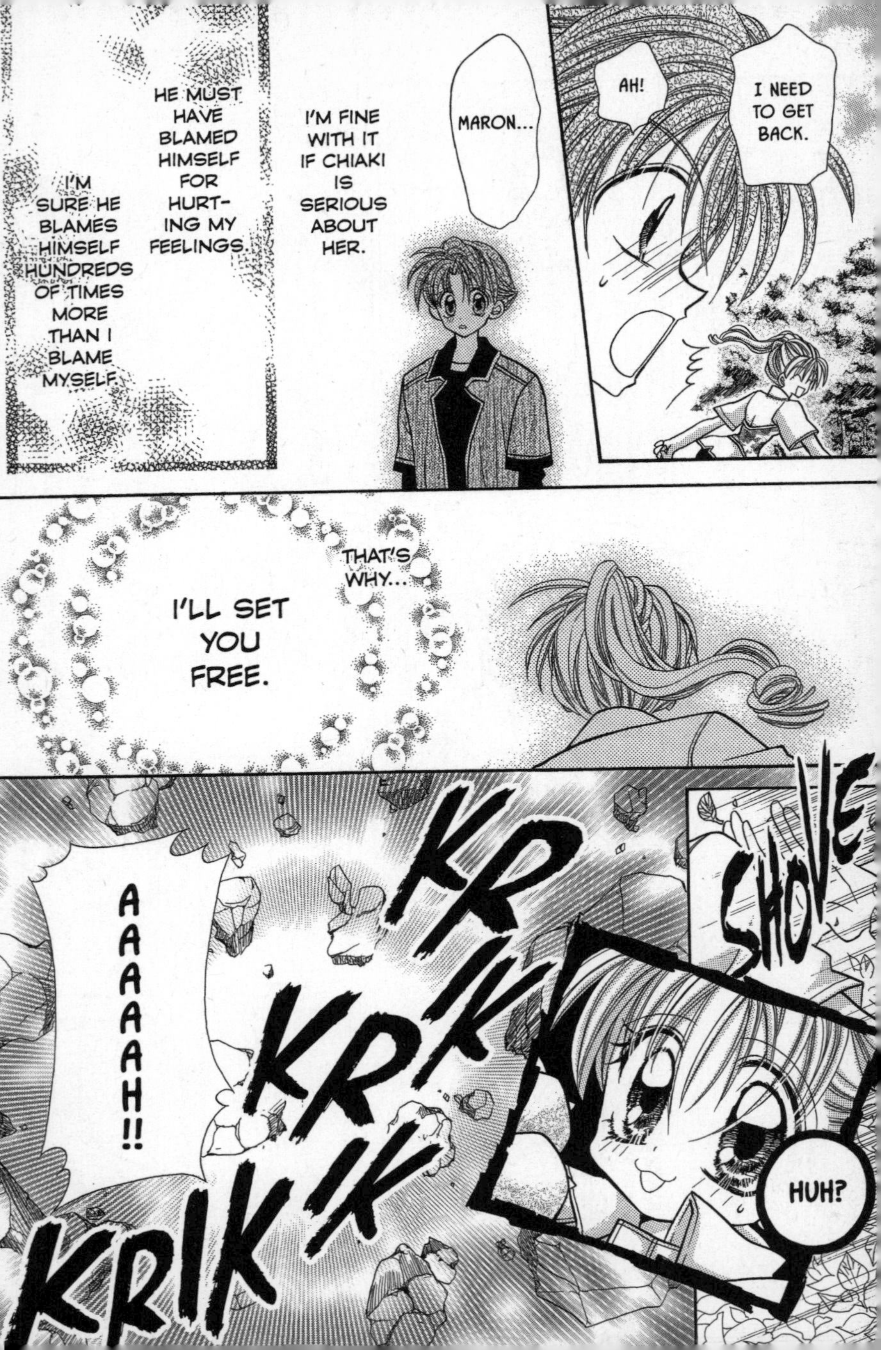
AH!
I NEED TO GET BACK.
MARON...
I'M FINE WITH IT IF CHIAKI IS SERIOUS ABOUT HER.
HE MUST HAVE BLAMED HIMSELF FOR HURT-ING MY FEELINGS.
I'M SURE HE BLAMES HIMSELF HUNDREDS OF TIMES MORE THAN I BLAME MYSELF.
THAT'S WHY...
I'LL SET YOU FREE.
SHOVE
HUH?
KRIK KRIK KRIK
AAAAAAH!!

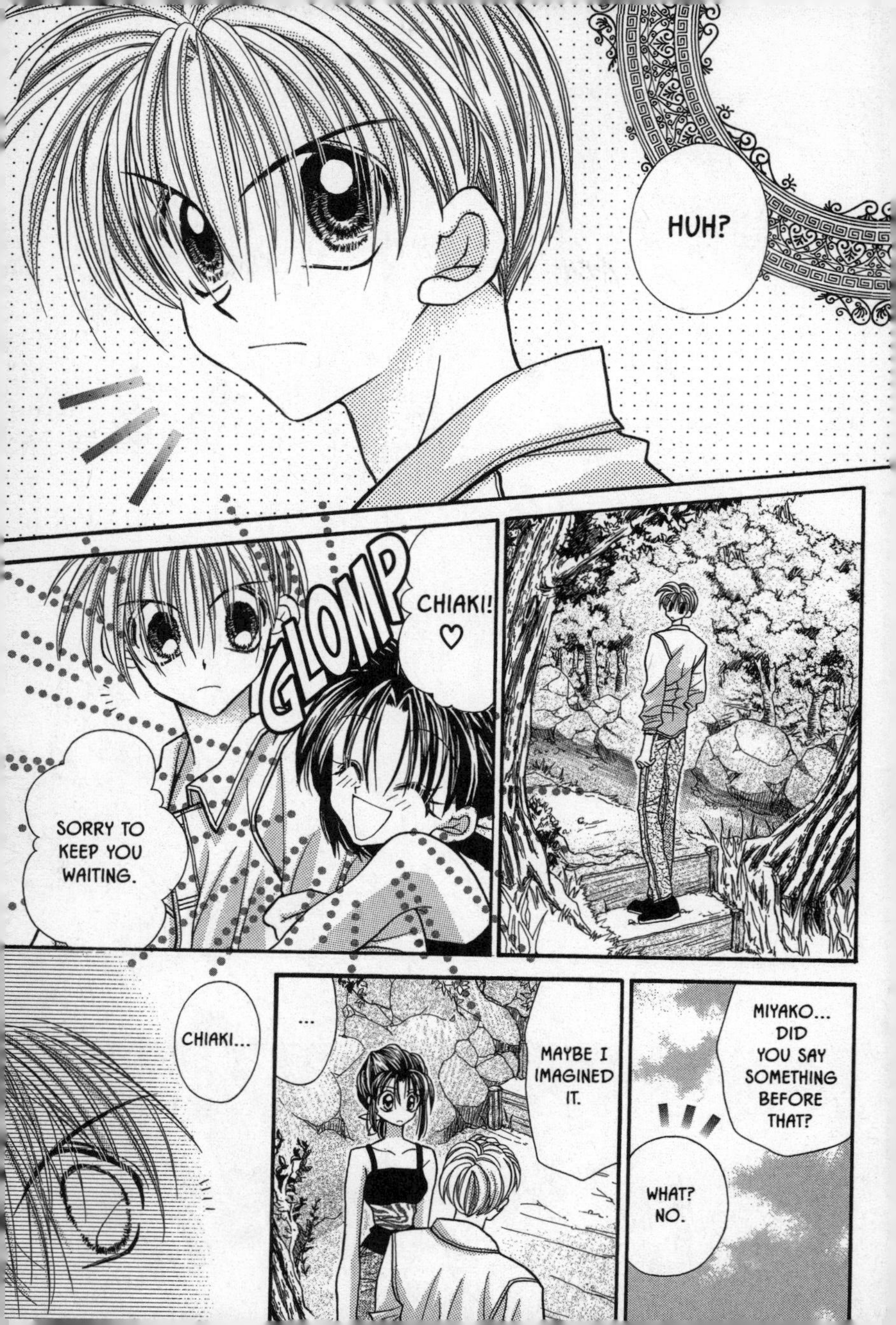
HUH?
CHIAKI! ♡
GLOMP
SORRY TO KEEP YOU WAITING.
MIYAKO... DID YOU SAY SOMETHING BEFORE THAT?
WHAT? NO.
MAYBE I IMAGINED IT.
...
CHIAKI...

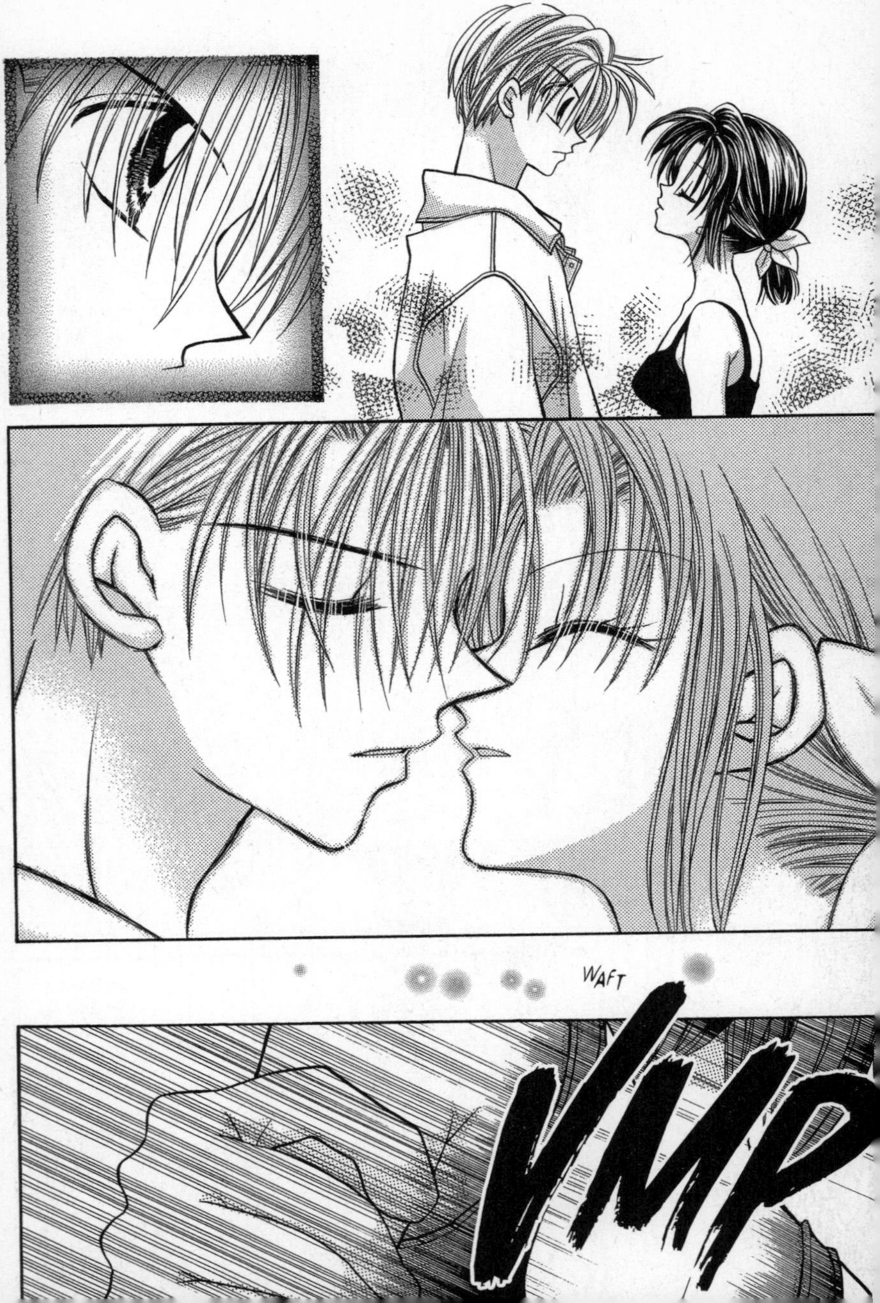
WAFT

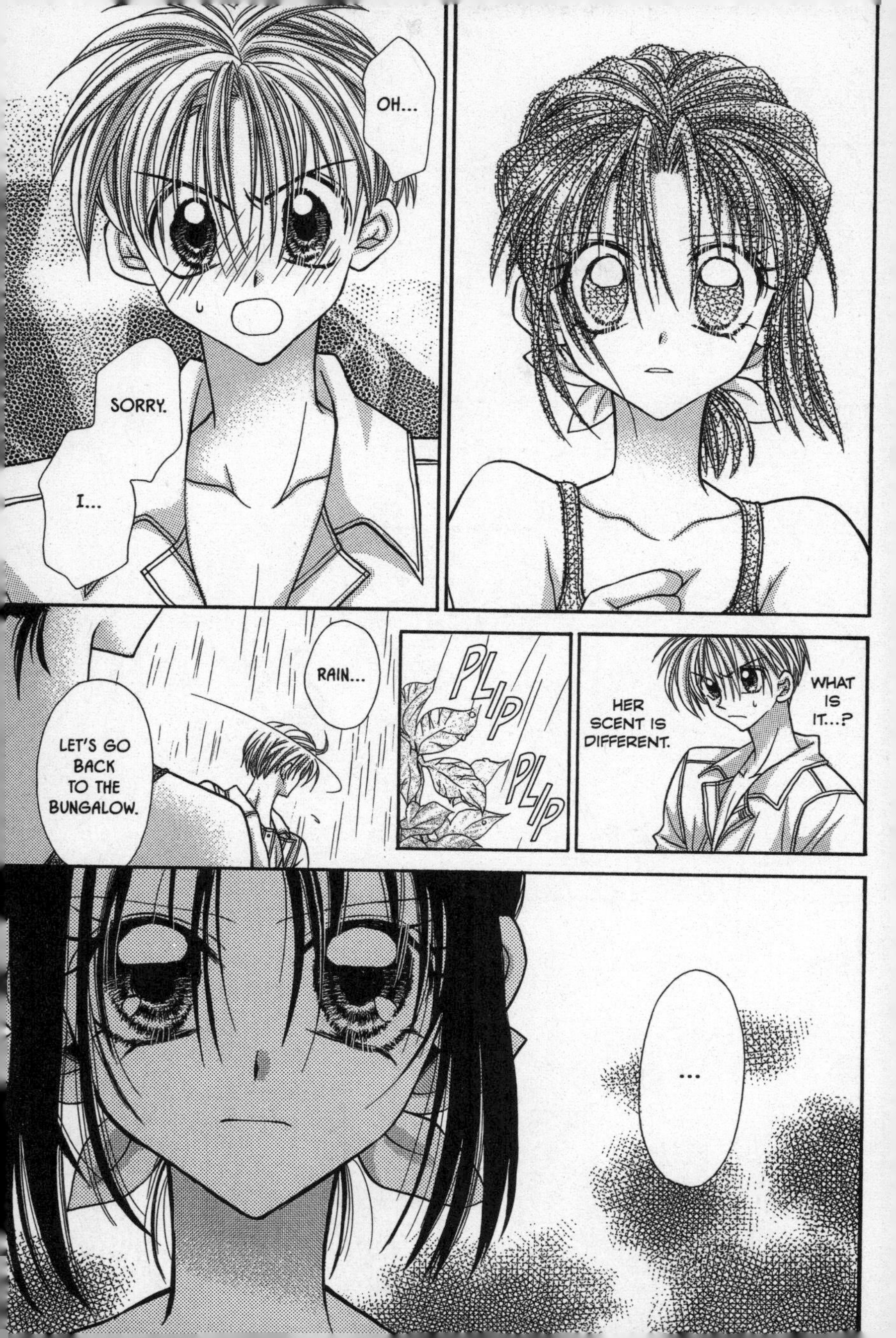
OH...
SORRY.
I...
WHAT IS IT...?
HER SCENT IS DIFFERENT.
PLIP
PLIP
RAIN...
LET'S GO BACK TO THE BUNGALOW.
...

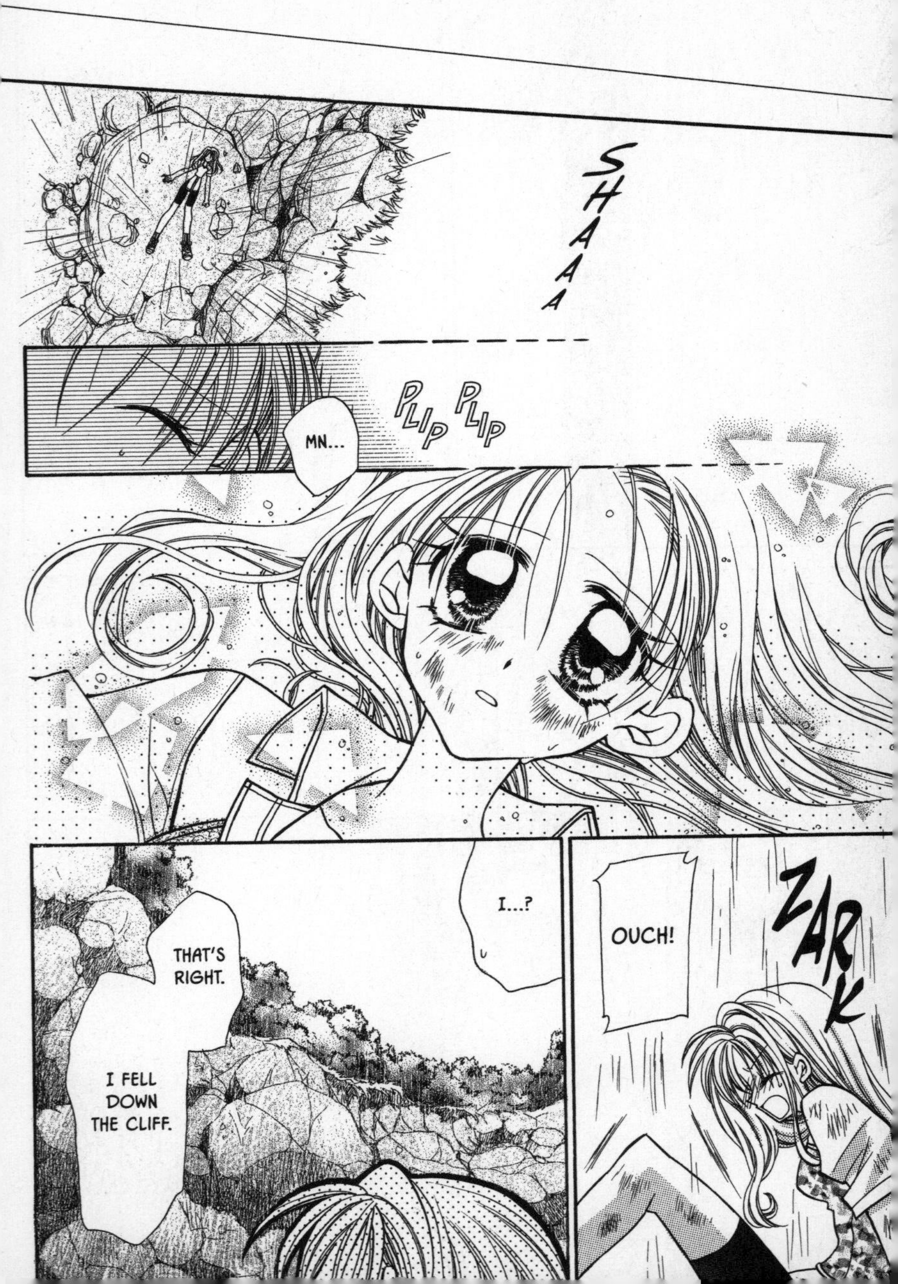
SHAAAA
MN...
PLIP PLIP
OUCH!
ZARK
I...?
THAT'S RIGHT.
I FELL DOWN THE CLIFF.

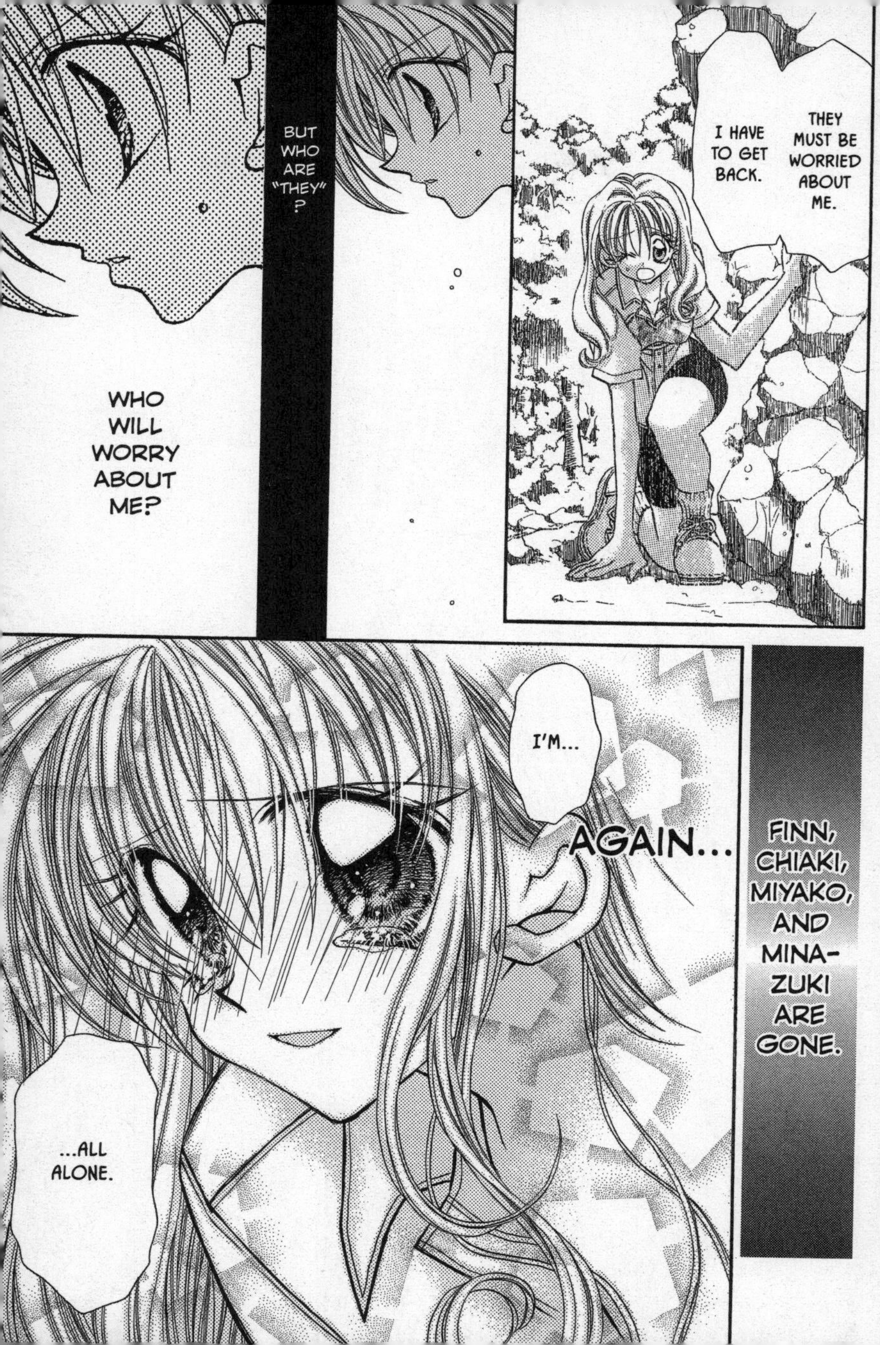
THEY MUST BE WORRIED ABOUT ME.
I HAVE TO GET BACK.
BUT WHO ARE "THEY"?
WHO WILL WORRY ABOUT ME?
FINN, CHIAKI, MIYAKO, AND MINA-ZUKI ARE GONE.
AGAIN...
I'M...
...ALL ALONE.

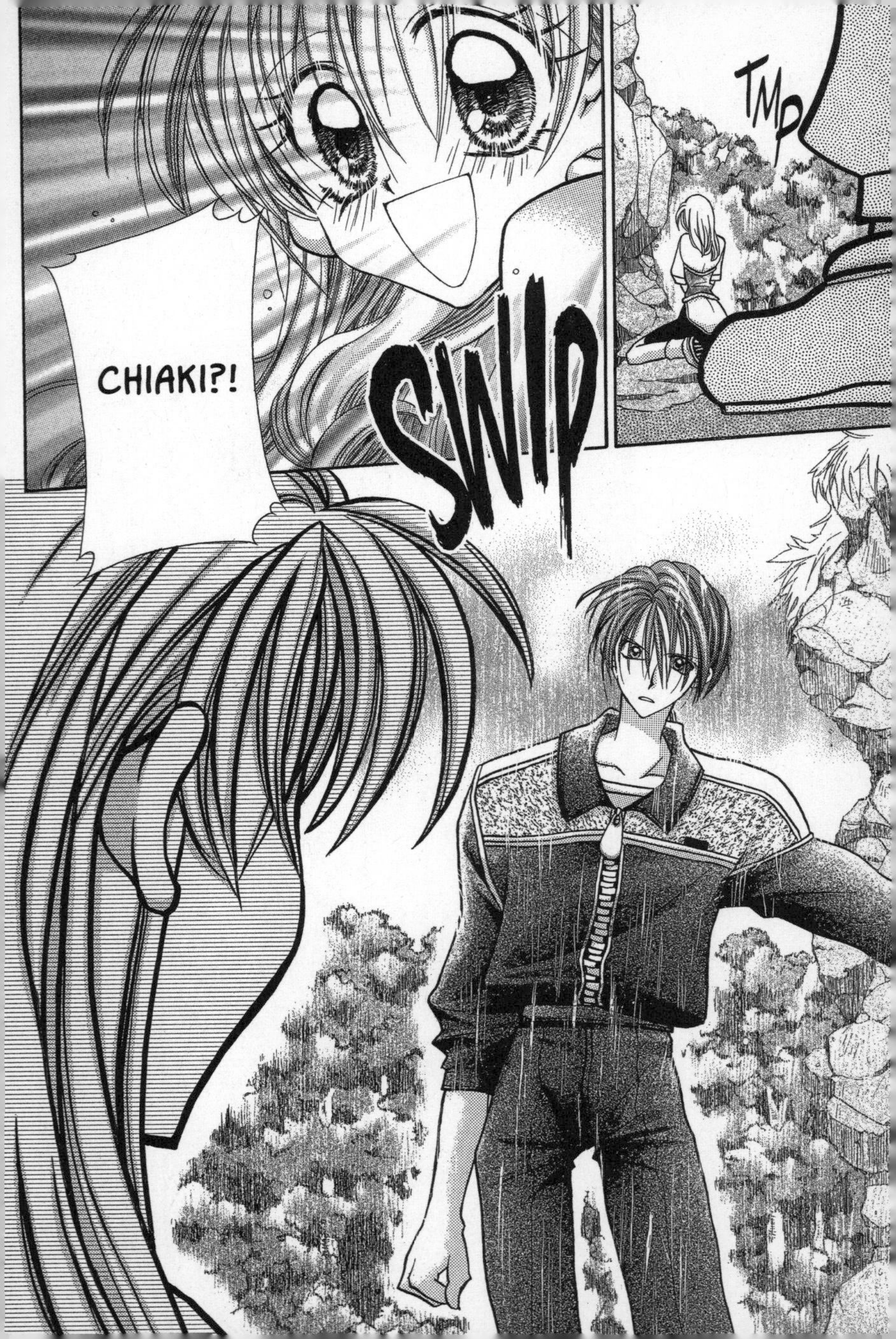
TMP
CHIAKI?!
SWIP

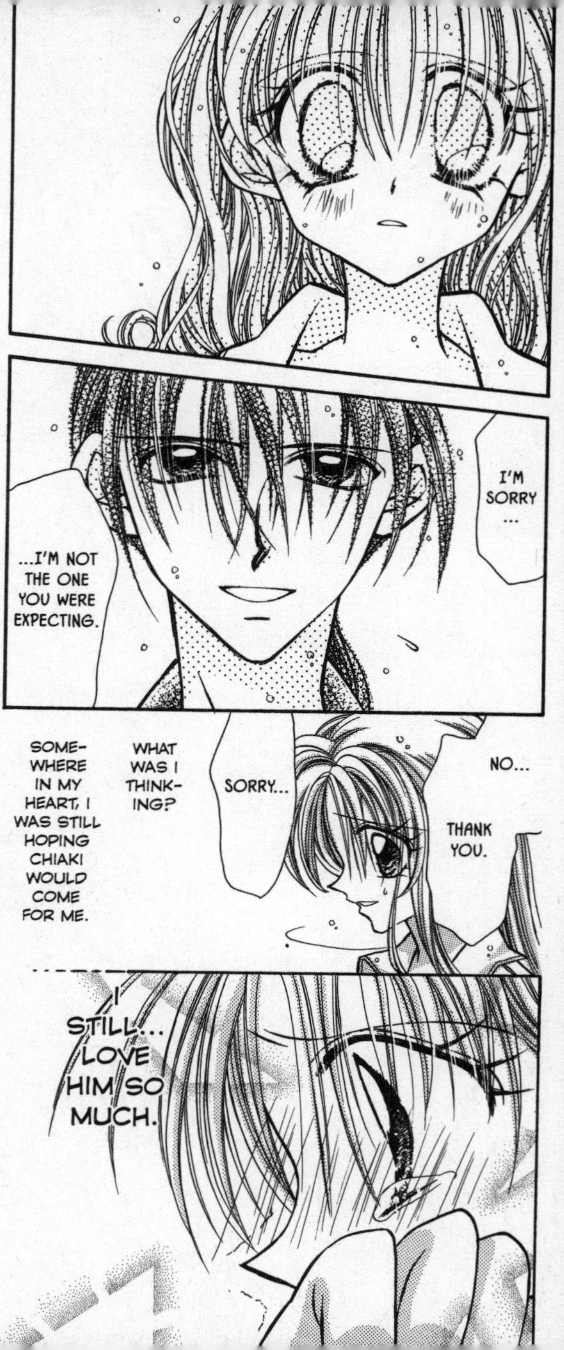
I'M SORRY...
...I'M NOT THE ONE YOU WERE EXPECTING.
NO...
THANK YOU.
SORRY...
WHAT WAS I THINKING?
SOMEWHERE IN MY HEART, I WAS STILL HOPING CHIAKI WOULD COME FOR ME.
I STILL... LOVE HIM SO MUCH.

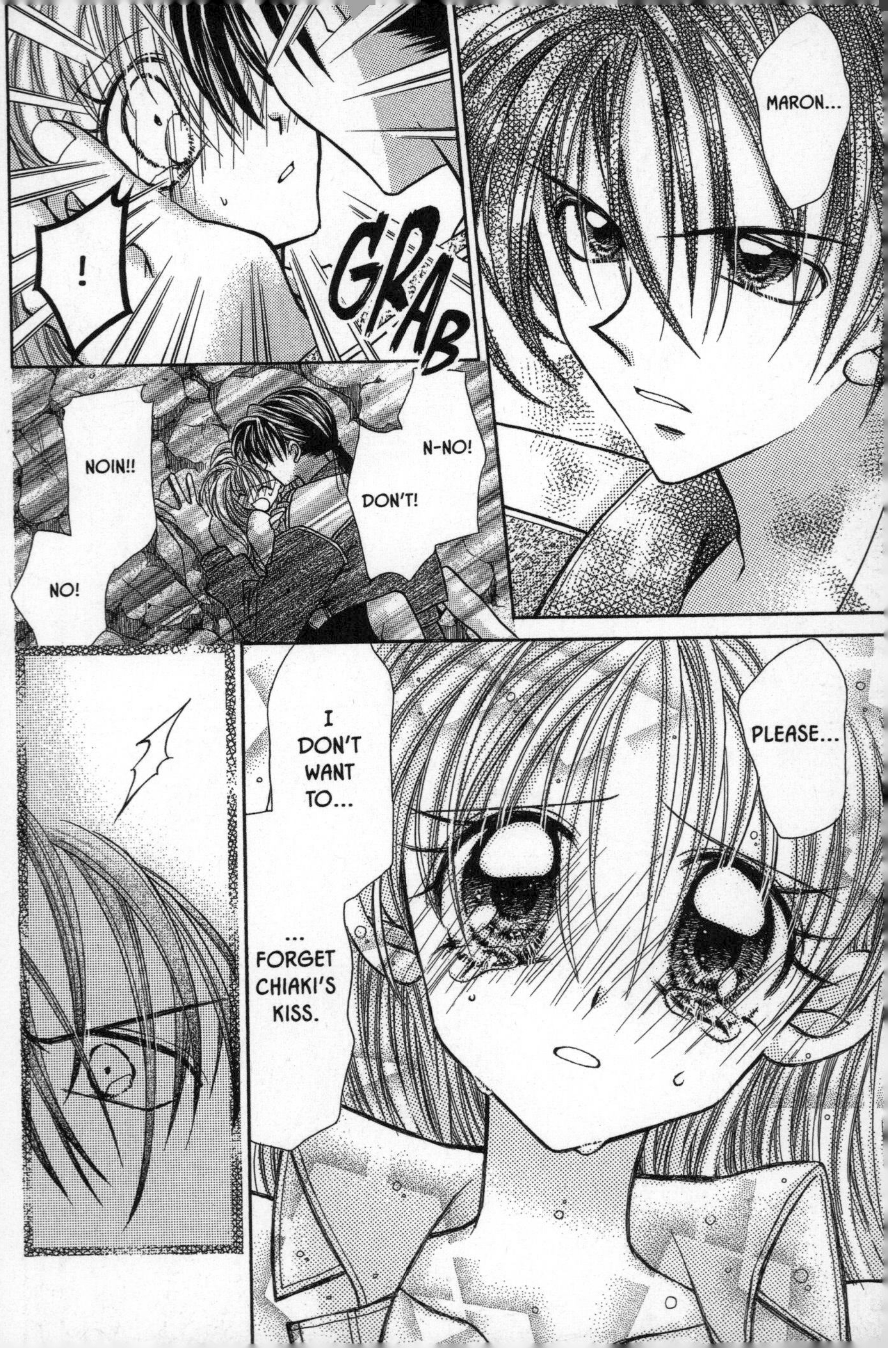
MARON...
GRAB
!
N-NO!
DON'T!
NOIN!!
NO!
PLEASE...
I DON'T WANT TO...
... FORGET CHIAKI'S KISS.

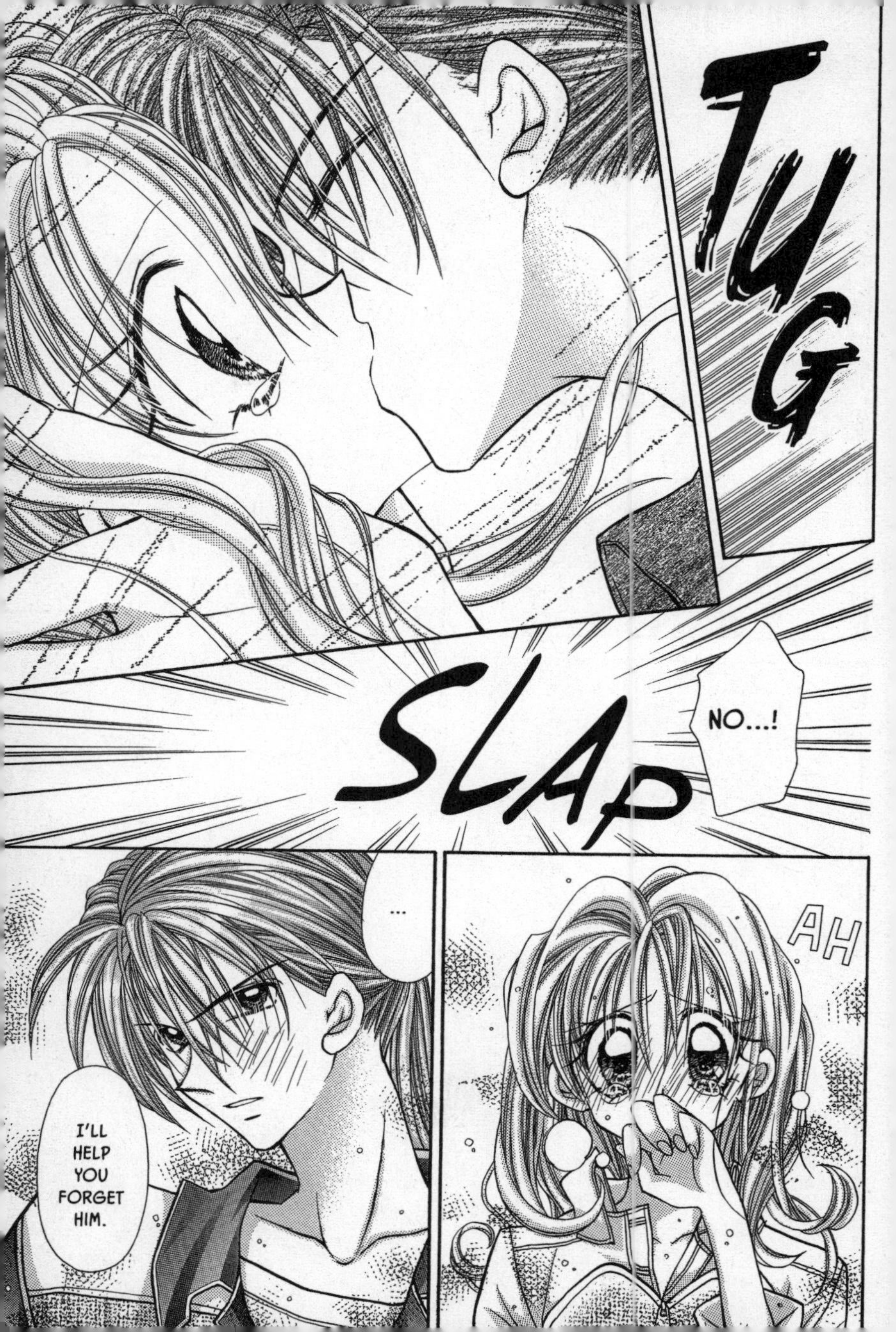
TUG
NO...!
SLAP
AH
...
I'LL HELP YOU FORGET HIM.

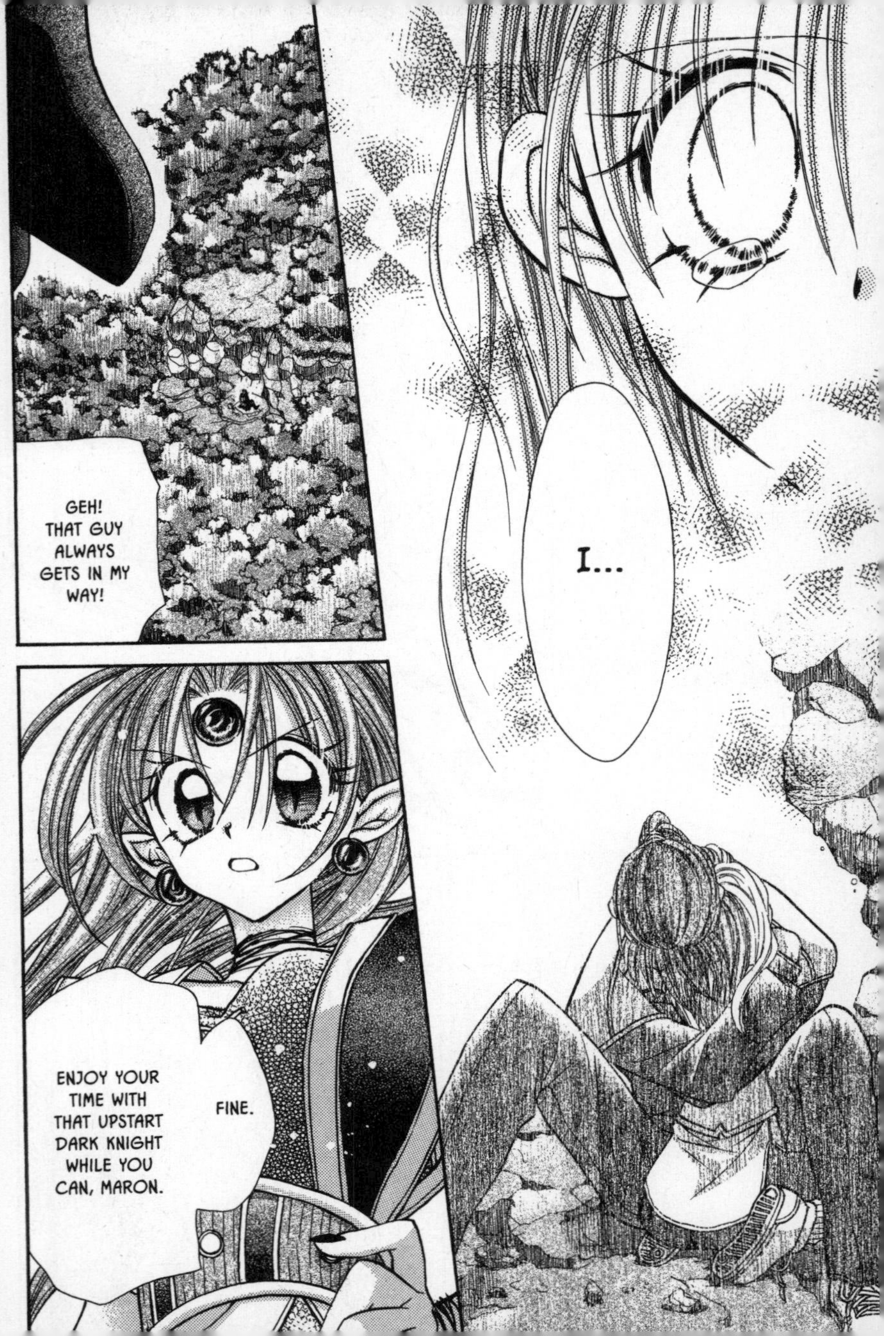
I...
GEH! THAT GUY ALWAYS GETS IN MY WAY!
FINE.
ENJOY YOUR TIME WITH THAT UPSTART DARK KNIGHT WHILE YOU CAN, MARON.

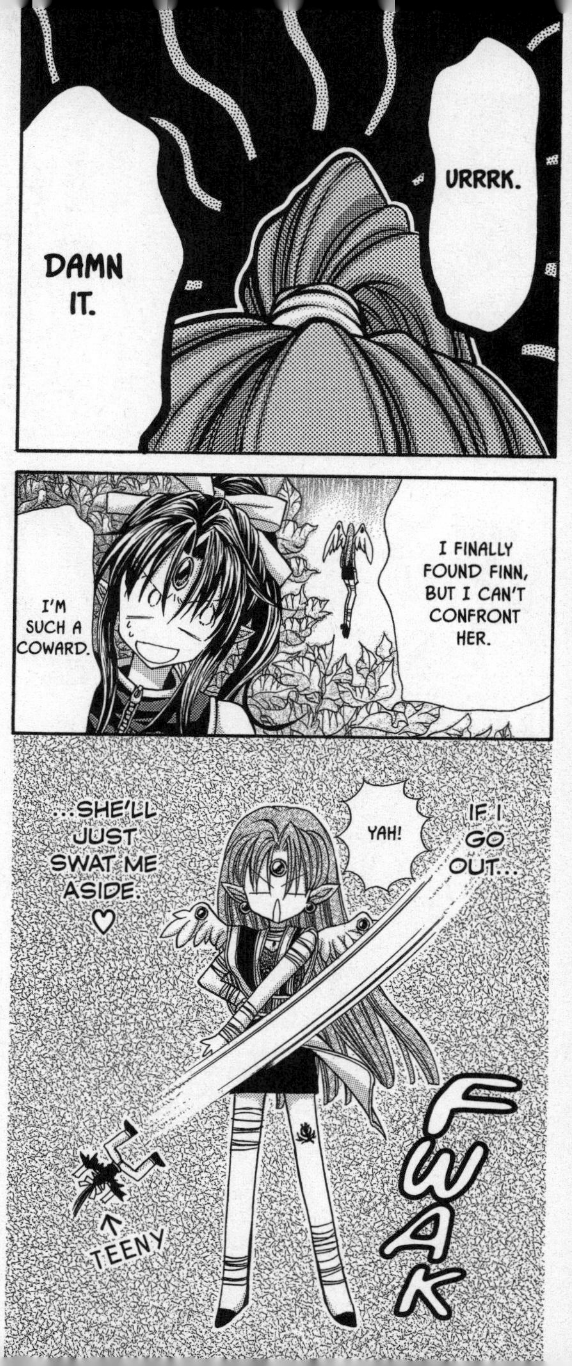
URRRK.
DAMN IT.
I FINALLY FOUND FINN, BUT I CAN'T CONFRONT HER.
I'M SUCH A COWARD.
IF I GO OUT...
YAH!
FWAK
...SHE'LL JUST SWAT ME ASIDE. ♡
TEENY

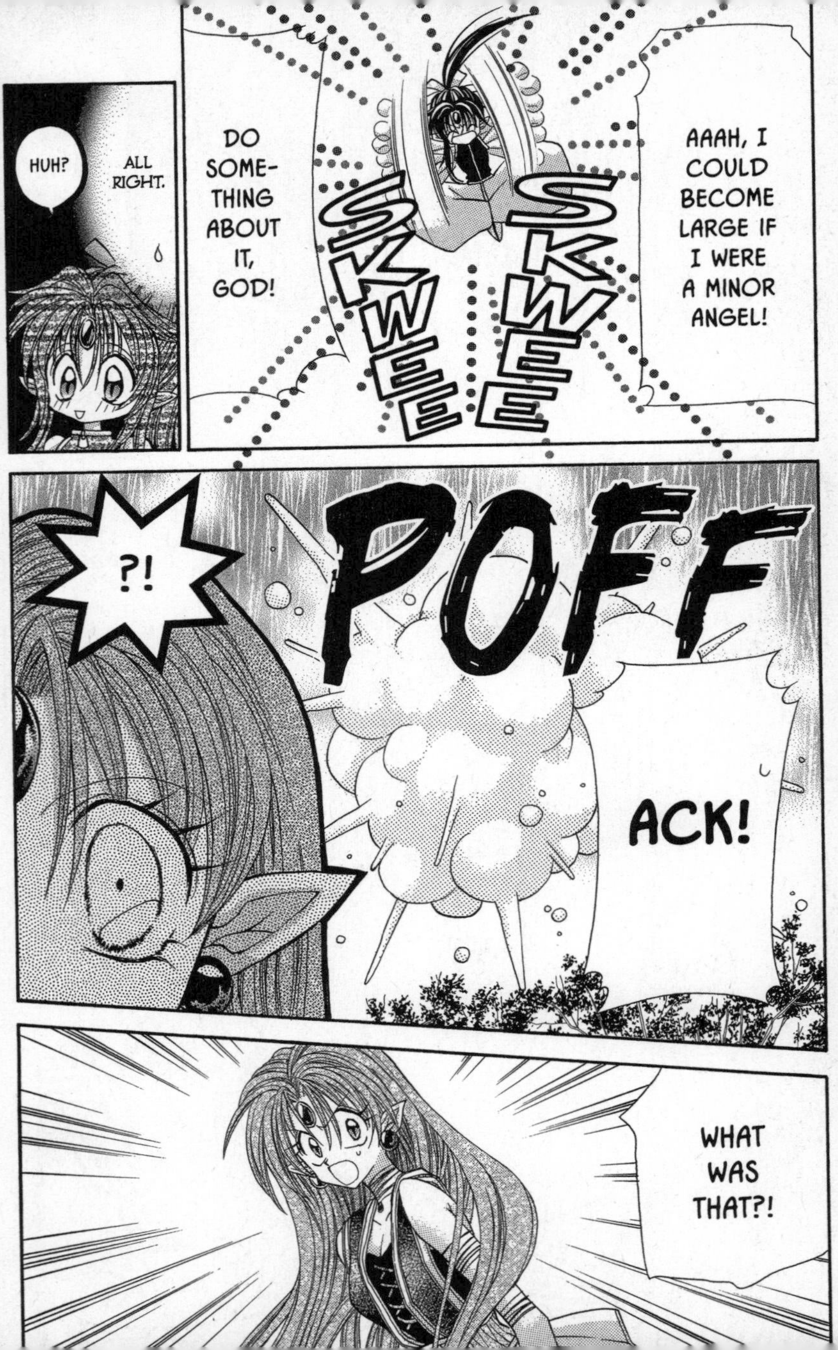
AAAH, I COULD BECOME LARGE IF I WERE A MINOR ANGEL!
SKWEE
SKWEE
DO SOME-THING ABOUT IT, GOD!
ALL RIGHT.
HUH?
POFF
ACK!
?!
WHAT WAS THAT?!

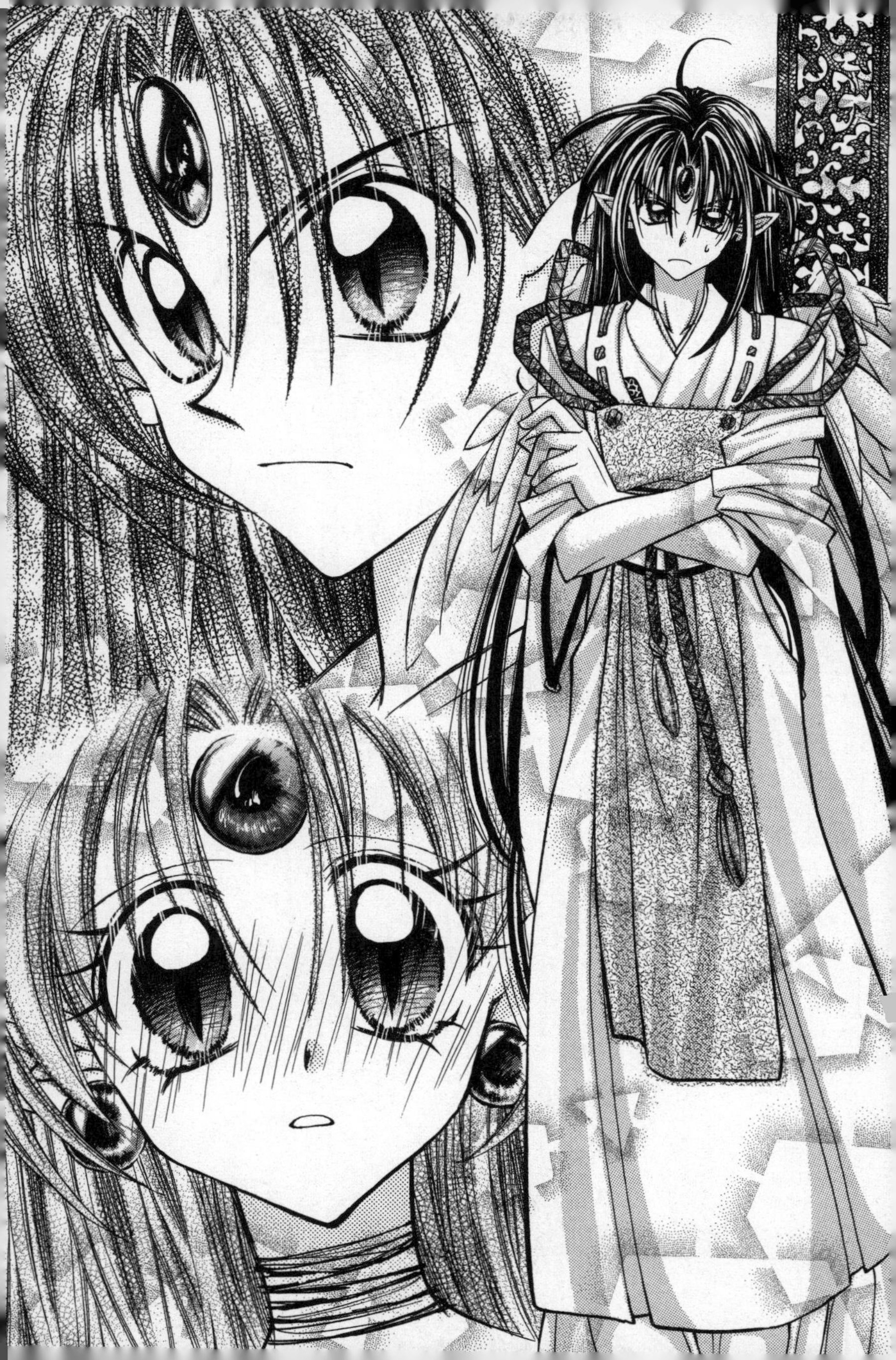

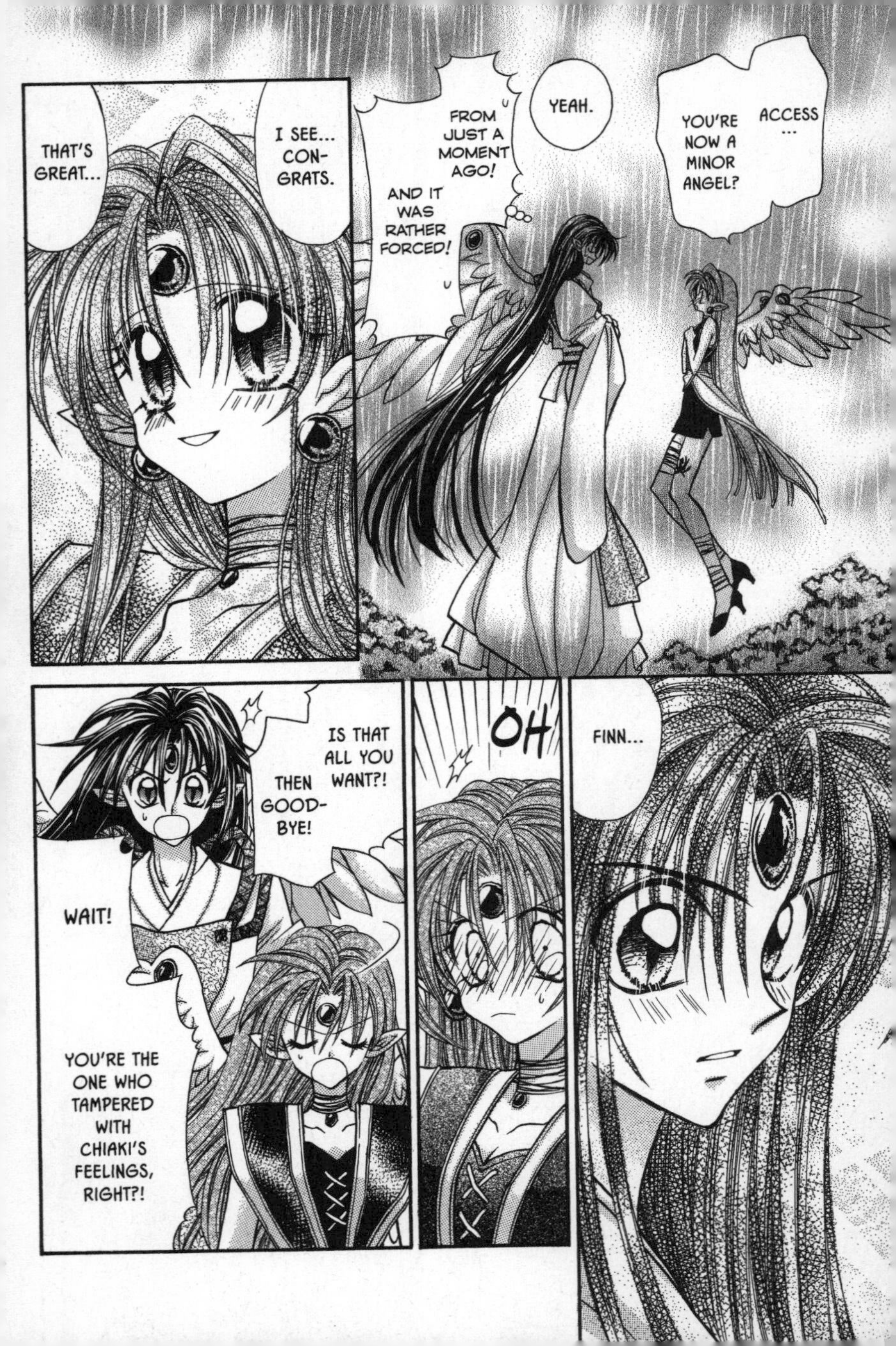
ACCESS ...
YOU'RE NOW A MINOR ANGEL?
YEAH.
FROM JUST A MOMENT AGO!
AND IT WAS RATHER FORCED!
I SEE... CON-GRATS.
THAT'S GREAT...
FINN...
OH
IS THAT ALL YOU WANT?!
THEN GOOD-BYE!
WAIT!
YOU'RE THE ONE WHO TAMPERED WITH CHIAKI'S FEELINGS, RIGHT?!

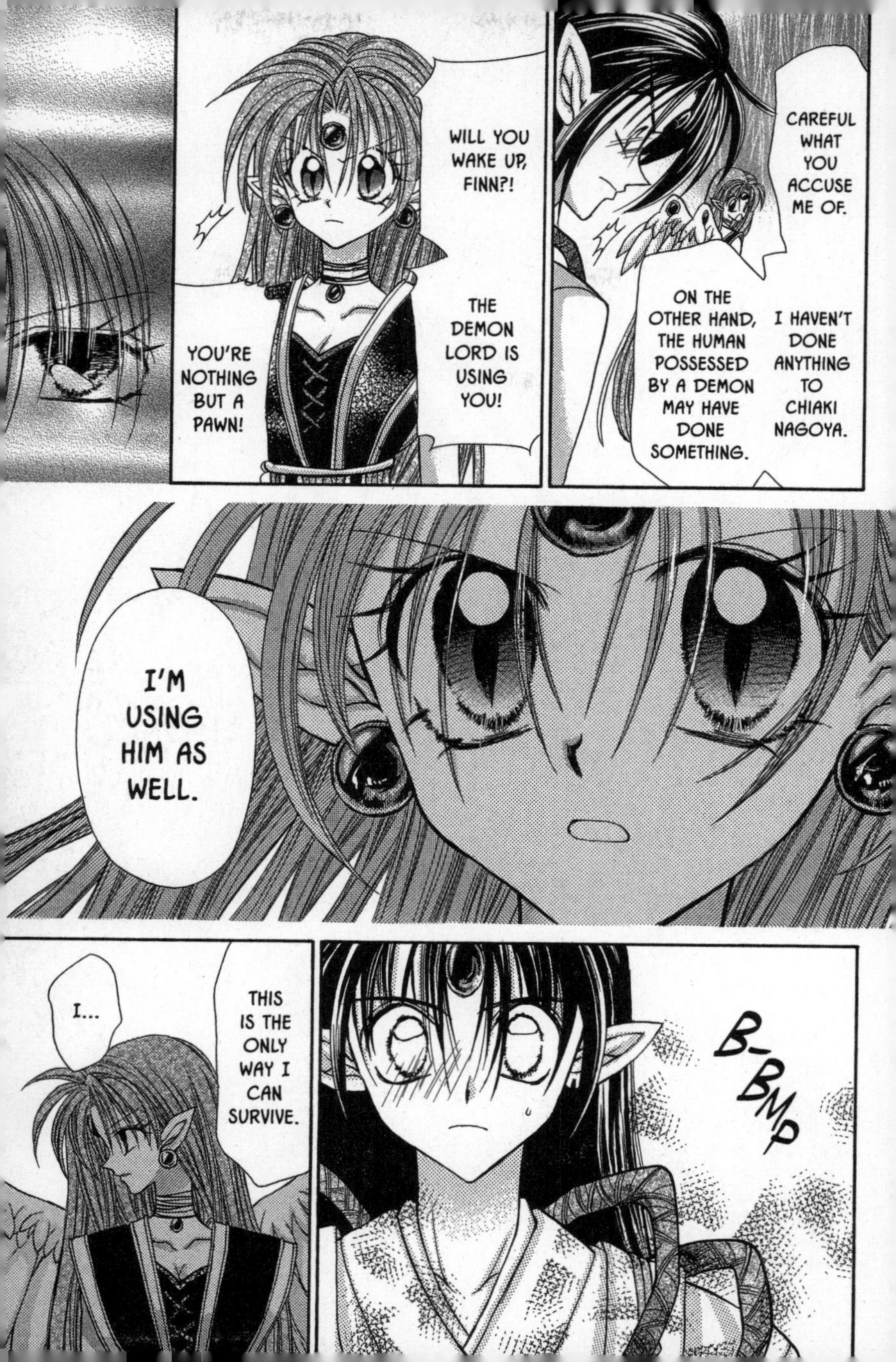

CAREFUL WHAT YOU ACCUSE ME OF.
I HAVEN'T DONE ANYTHING TO CHIAKI NAGOYA.
ON THE OTHER HAND, THE HUMAN POSSESSED BY A DEMON MAY HAVE DONE SOMETHING.
WILL YOU WAKE UP, FINN?!
THE DEMON LORD IS USING YOU!
YOU'RE NOTHING BUT A PAWN!
I'M USING HIM AS WELL.
B-BMP
THIS IS THE ONLY WAY I CAN SURVIVE.
I...

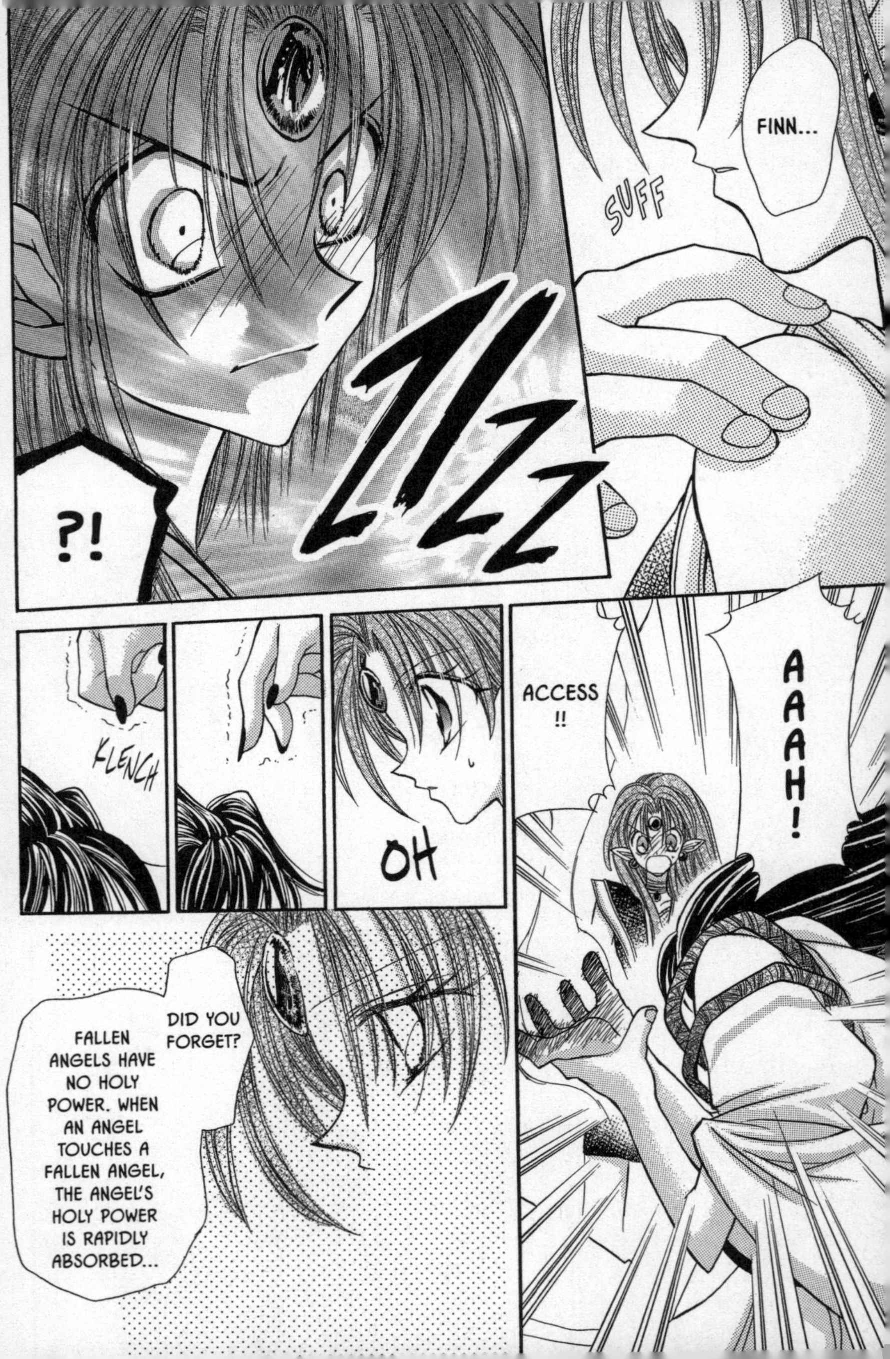
FINN...
SUFF
?!
AAAAH!
ACCESS !!
OH
KLENCH
DID YOU FORGET?
FALLEN ANGELS HAVE NO HOLY POWER. WHEN AN ANGEL TOUCHES A FALLEN ANGEL, THE ANGEL'S HOLY POWER IS RAPIDLY ABSORBED...

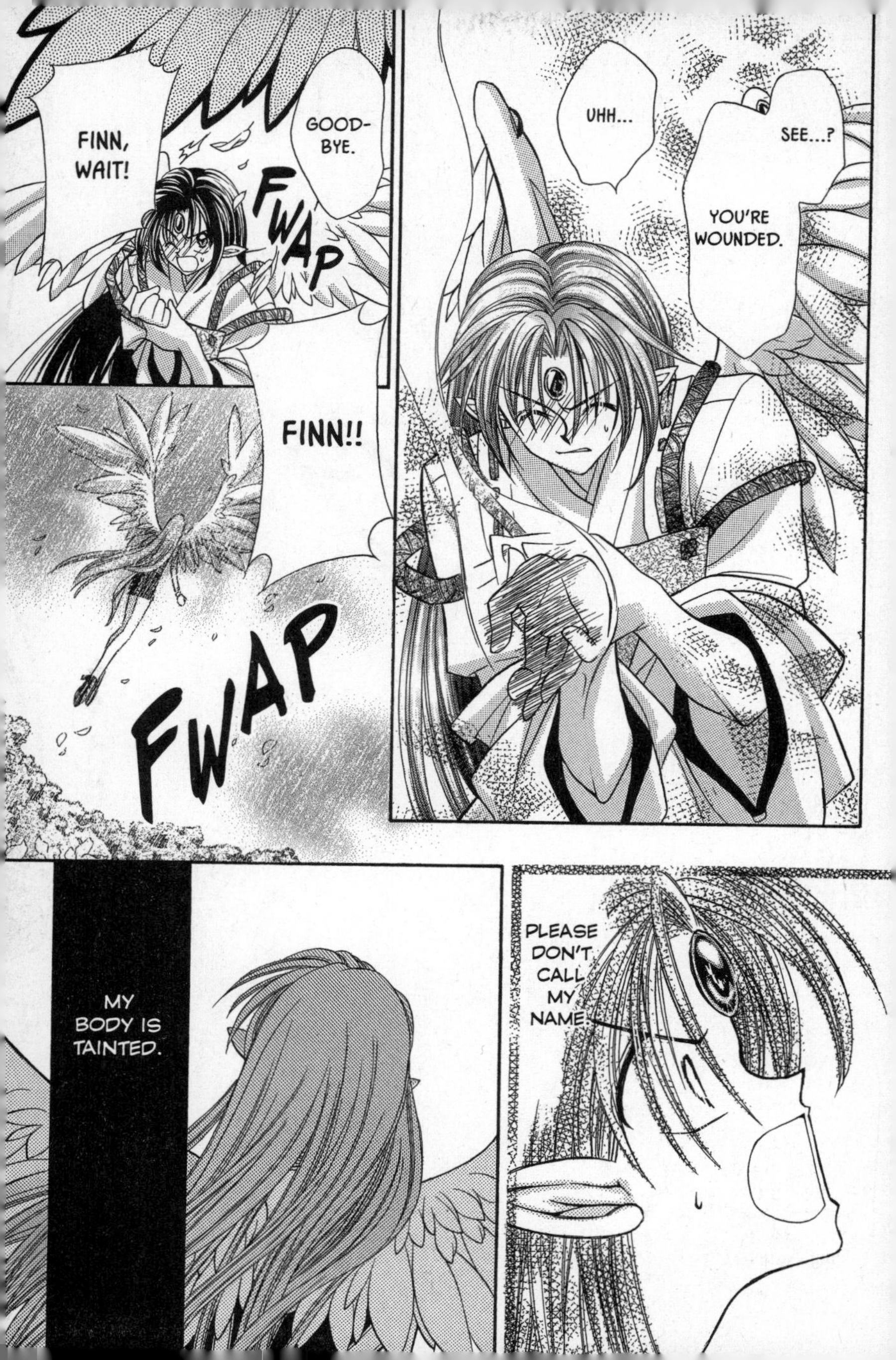
SEE...?
YOU'RE WOUNDED.
UHH...
GOOD-BYE.
FWAP
FINN, WAIT!
FINN!!
FWAP
PLEASE DON'T CALL MY NAME.
MY BODY IS TAINTED.

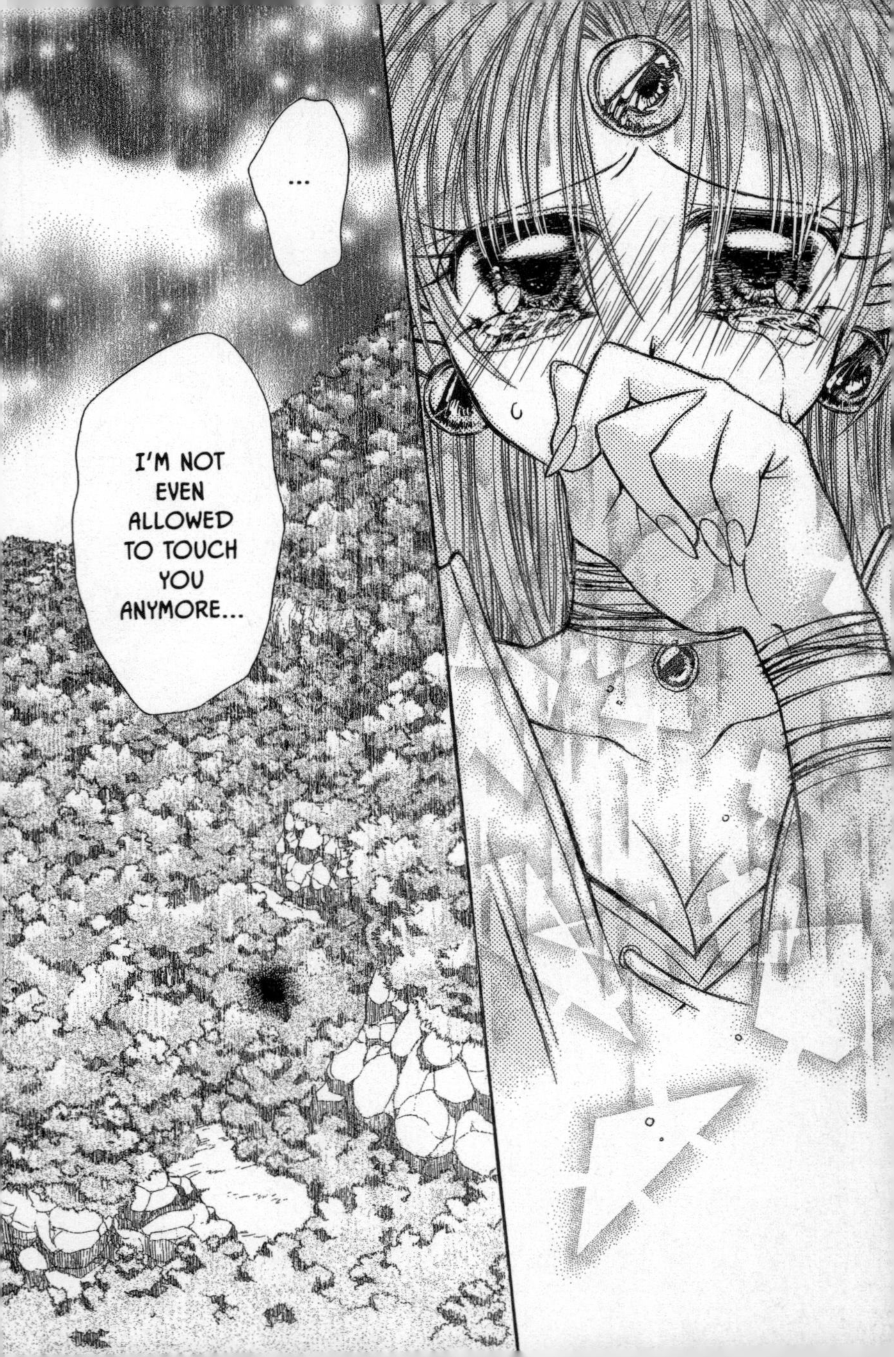
...
I'M NOT EVEN ALLOWED TO TOUCH YOU ANYMORE...

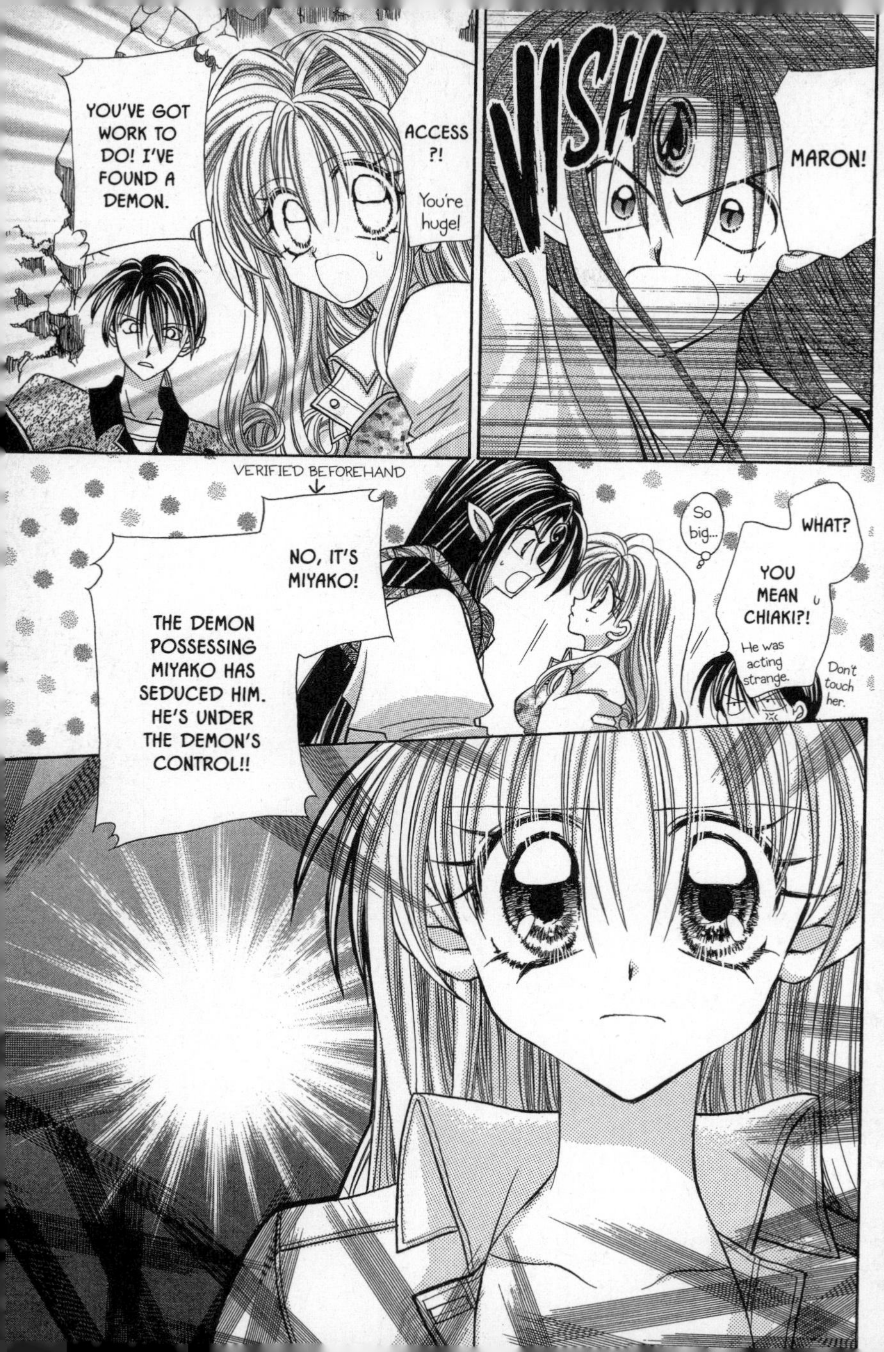
VISH
MARON!
ACCESS?!
You're huge!
YOU'VE GOT WORK TO DO! I'VE FOUND A DEMON.
WHAT?
YOU MEAN CHIAKI?!
Don't touch her.
He was acting strange.
So big...
VERIFIED BEFOREHAND
NO, IT'S MIYAKO!
THE DEMON POSSESSING MIYAKO HAS SEDUCED HIM. HE'S UNDER THE DEMON'S CONTROL!!

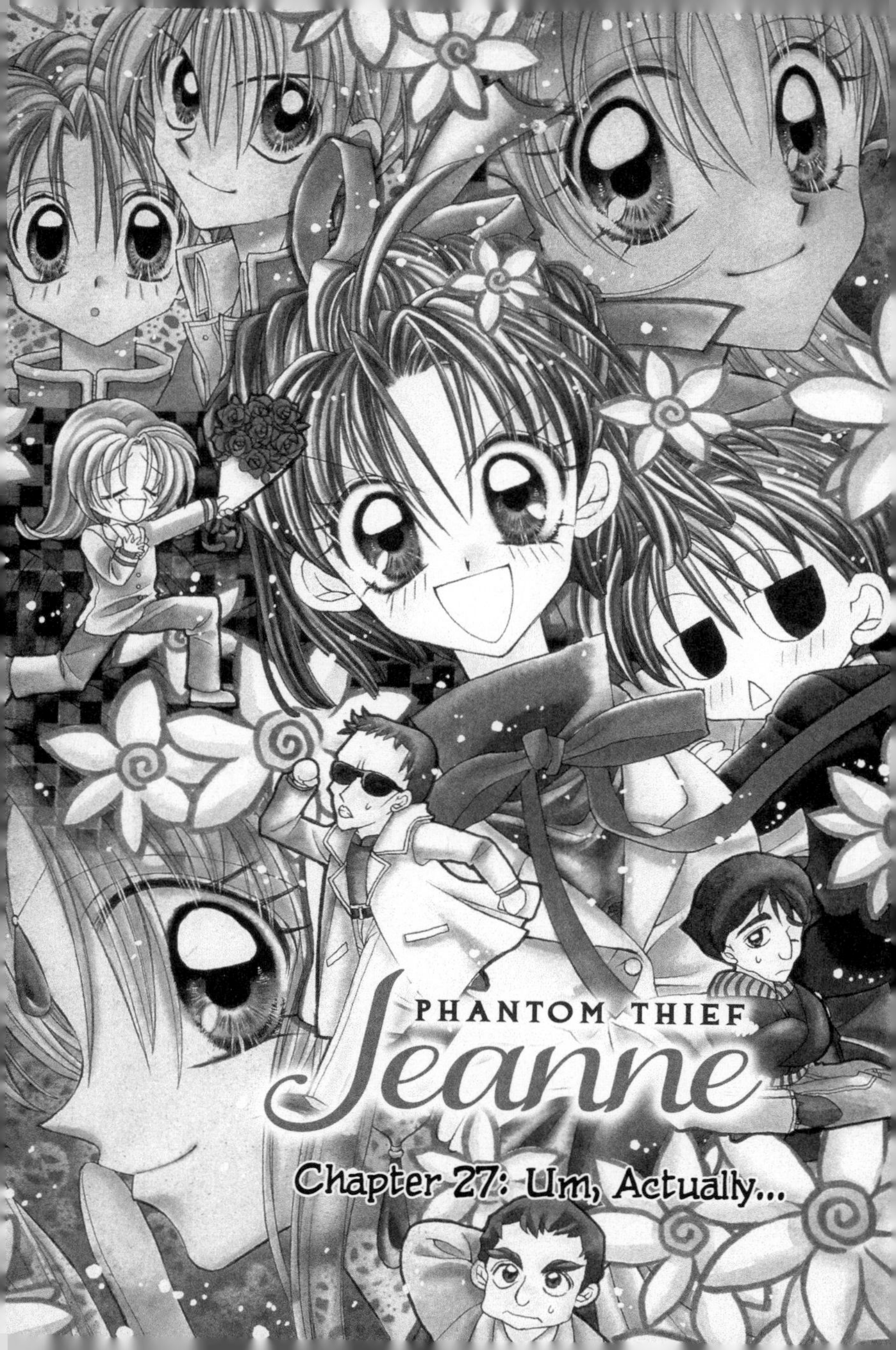
PHANTOM THIEF
Jeanne
Chapter 27: Um, Actually...

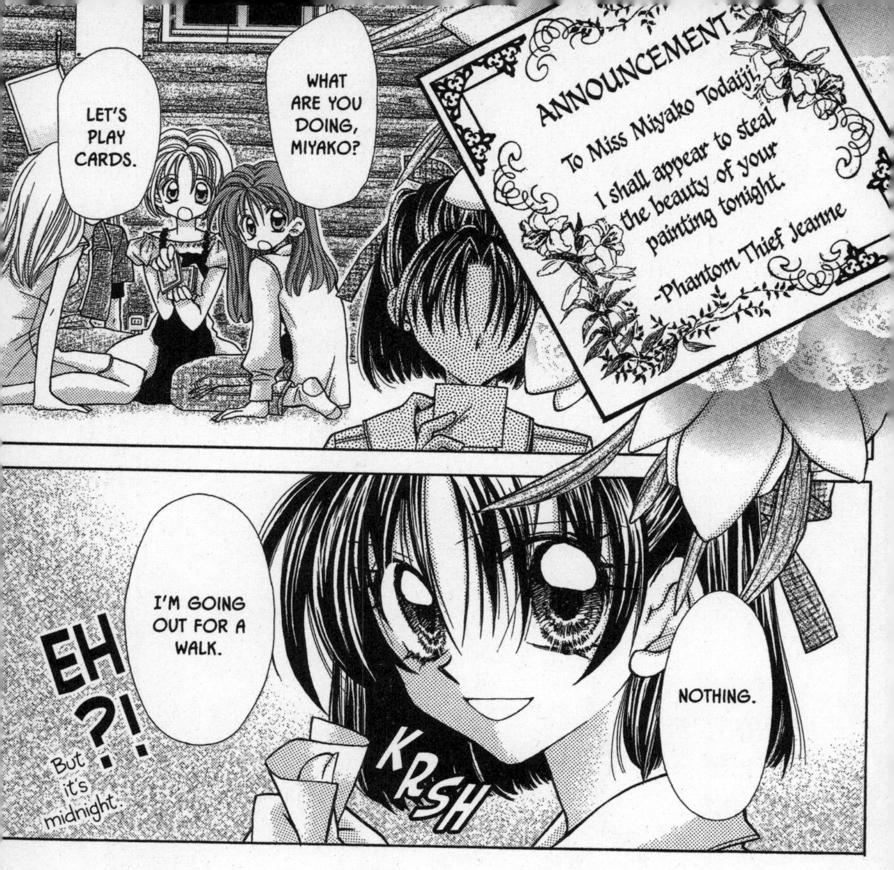
ANNOUNCEMENT
To Miss Miyako Todaiji,
I shall appear to steal the beauty of your painting tonight.
-Phantom Thief Jeanne
WHAT ARE YOU DOING, MIYAKO?
LET'S PLAY CARDS.
NOTHING.
KRSH
I'M GOING OUT FOR A WALK.
EH?!
But it's midnight.

PHANTOM
THIEF
JEANNE

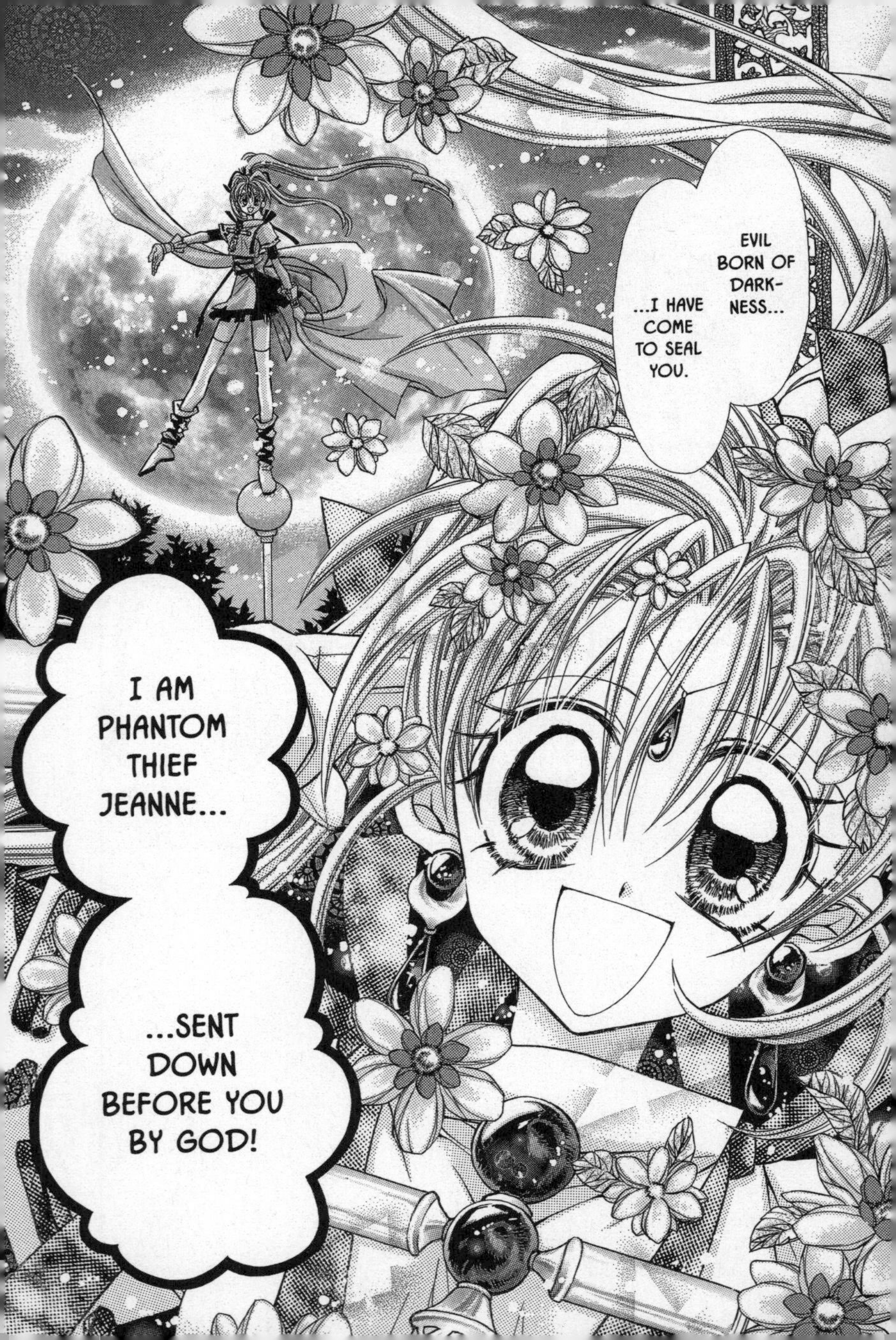
EVIL BORN OF DARK- NESS...
...I HAVE COME TO SEAL YOU.
I AM PHANTOM THIEF JEANNE...
...SENT DOWN BEFORE YOU BY GOD!

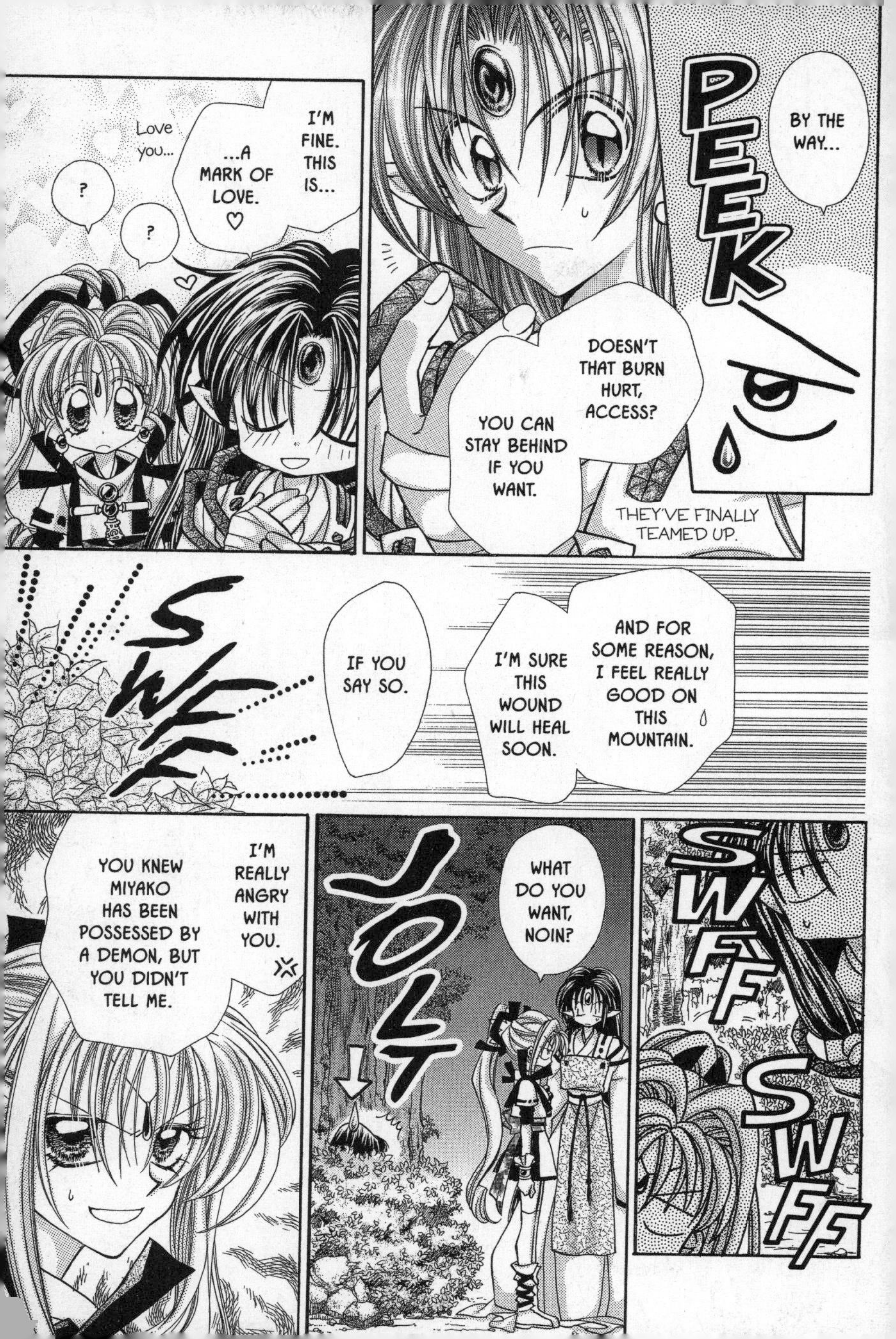
BY THE WAY...
PEEK
DOESN'T THAT BURN HURT, ACCESS?
YOU CAN STAY BEHIND IF YOU WANT.
THEY'VE FINALLY TEAMED UP.
I'M FINE. THIS IS...
...A MARK OF LOVE. ♡
Love you...
?
?
AND FOR SOME REASON, I FEEL REALLY GOOD ON THIS MOUNTAIN.
I'M SURE THIS WOUND WILL HEAL SOON.
IF YOU SAY SO.
SWFF
SWFF
SWFF
WHAT DO YOU WANT, NOIN?
JOLT
I'M REALLY ANGRY WITH YOU.
YOU KNEW MIYAKO HAS BEEN POSSESSED BY A DEMON, BUT YOU DIDN'T TELL ME.

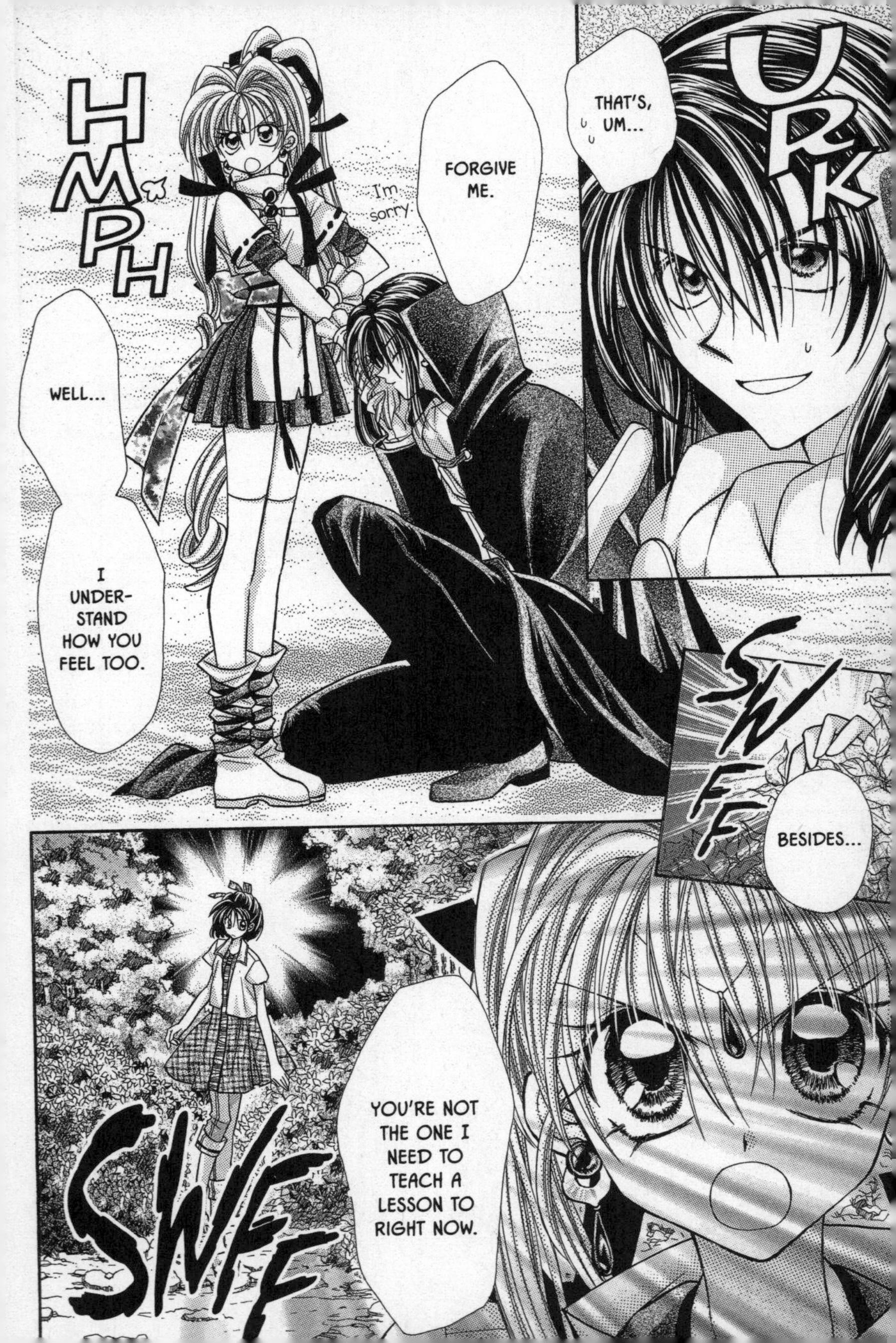
URK
THAT'S, UM...
HMPH
FORGIVE ME.
I'm sorry.
WELL...
I UNDER-STAND HOW YOU FEEL TOO.
SWFF
BESIDES...
YOU'RE NOT THE ONE I NEED TO TEACH A LESSON TO RIGHT NOW.
SWF

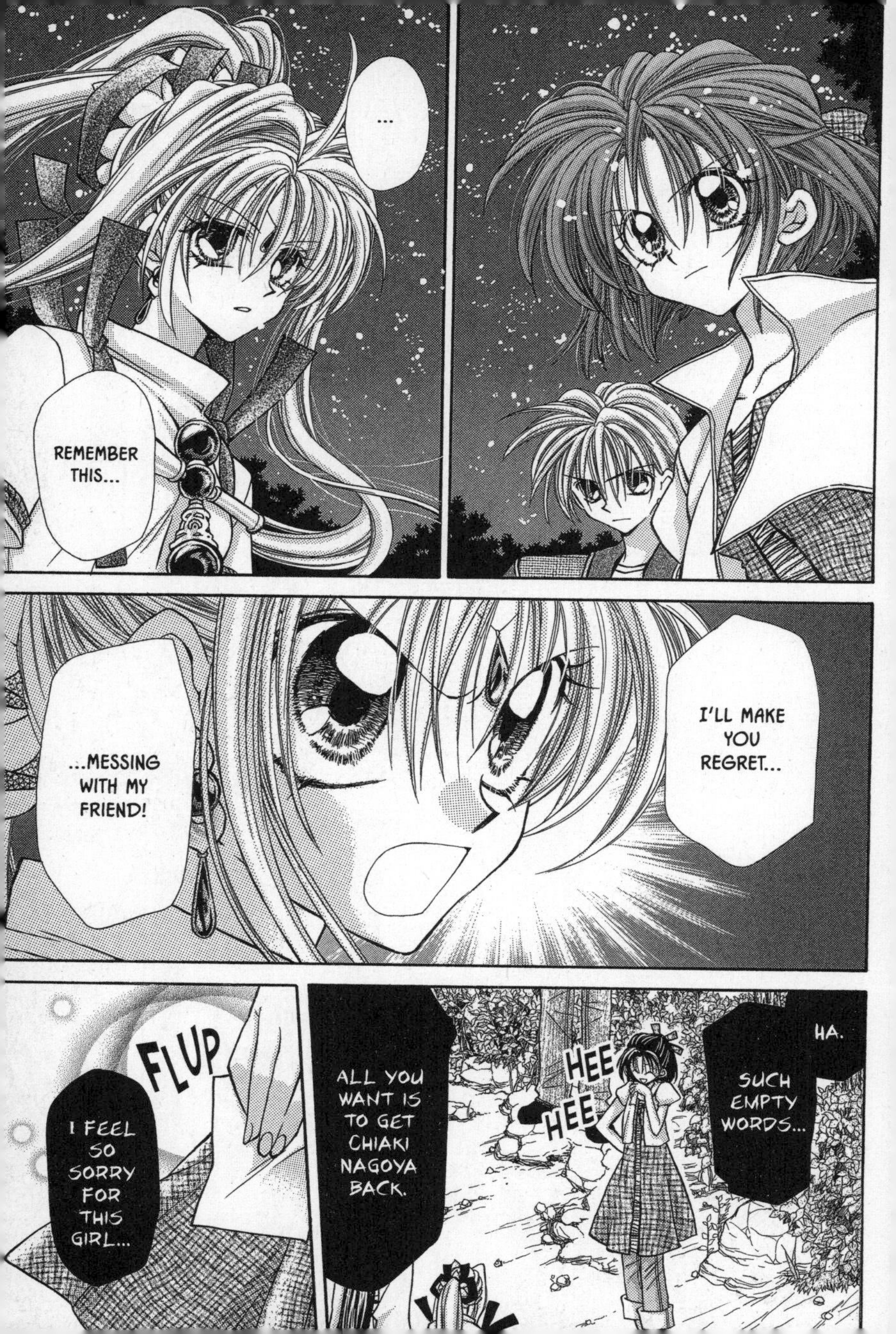
...
REMEMBER THIS...
I'LL MAKE YOU REGRET...
...MESSING WITH MY FRIEND!
HA.
SUCH EMPTY WORDS...
HEE HEE
ALL YOU WANT IS TO GET CHIAKI NAGOYA BACK.
FLUP
I FEEL SO SORRY FOR THIS GIRL...

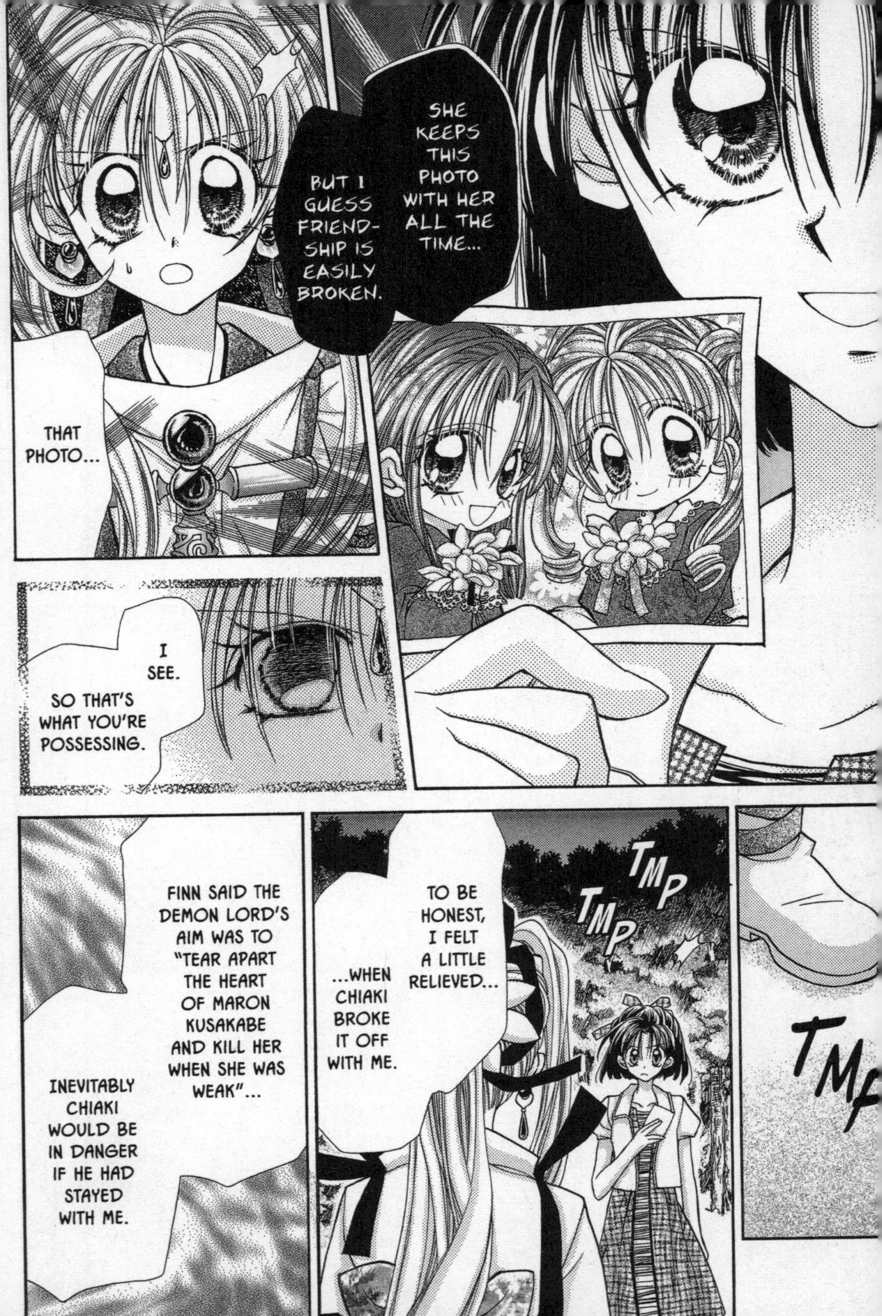
SHE KEEPS THIS PHOTO WITH HER ALL THE TIME...
BUT I GUESS FRIEND-SHIP IS EASILY BROKEN.
THAT PHOTO...
I SEE.
SO THAT'S WHAT YOU'RE POSSESSING.
TMP TMP
TO BE HONEST, I FELT A LITTLE RELIEVED...
...WHEN CHIAKI BROKE IT OFF WITH ME.
FINN SAID THE DEMON LORD'S AIM WAS TO "TEAR APART THE HEART OF MARON KUSAKABE AND KILL HER WHEN SHE WAS WEAK"...
INEVITABLY CHIAKI WOULD BE IN DANGER IF HE HAD STAYED WITH ME.

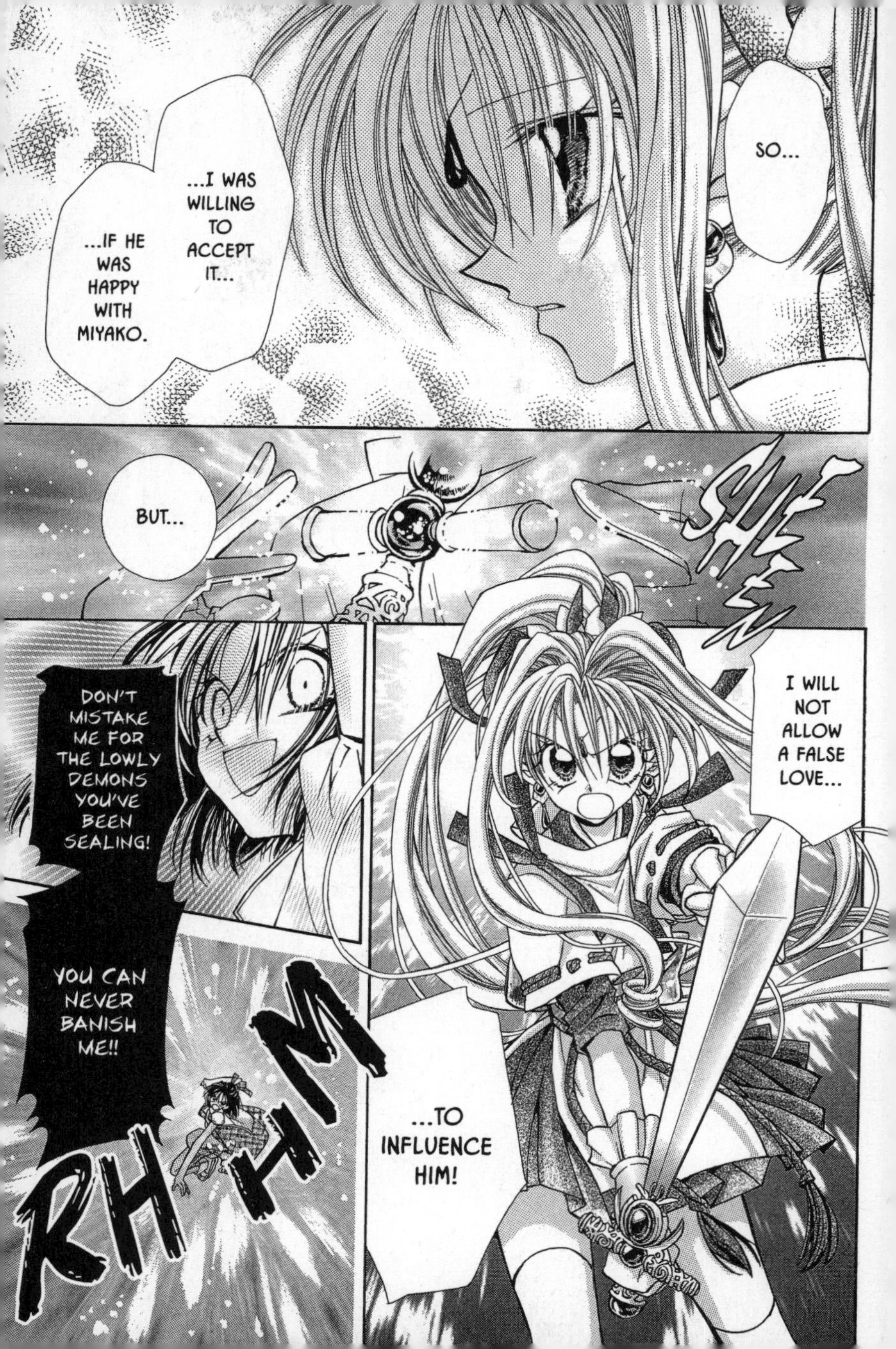
SO...
...I WAS WILLING TO ACCEPT IT...
...IF HE WAS HAPPY WITH MIYAKO.
SHEEN
BUT...
I WILL NOT ALLOW A FALSE LOVE...
...TO INFLUENCE HIM!
DON'T MISTAKE ME FOR THE LOWLY DEMONS YOU'VE BEEN SEALING!
YOU CAN NEVER BANISH ME!!
RHHM

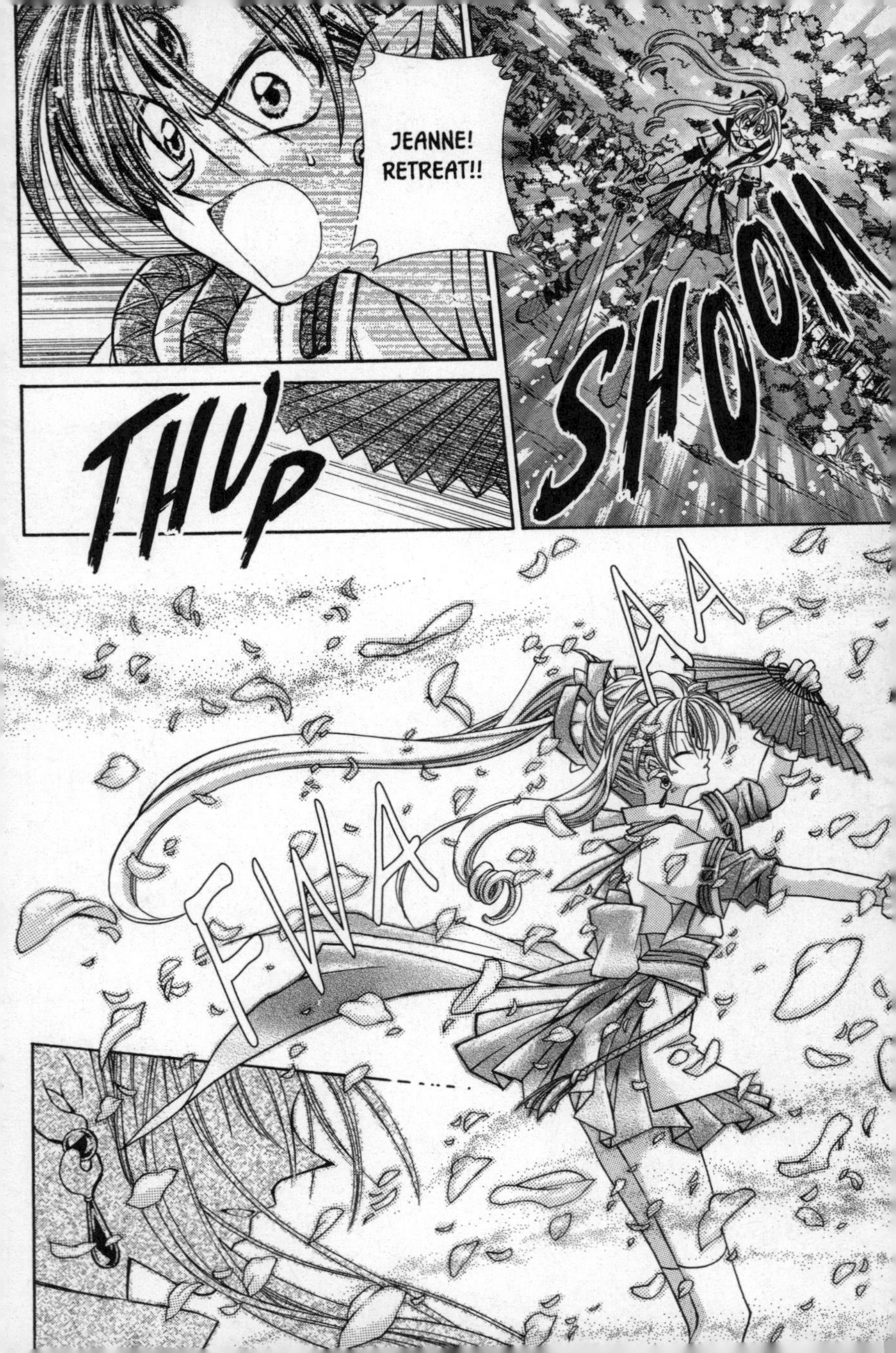
SHOOM
JEANNE! RETREAT!!
THUP
FWAAA

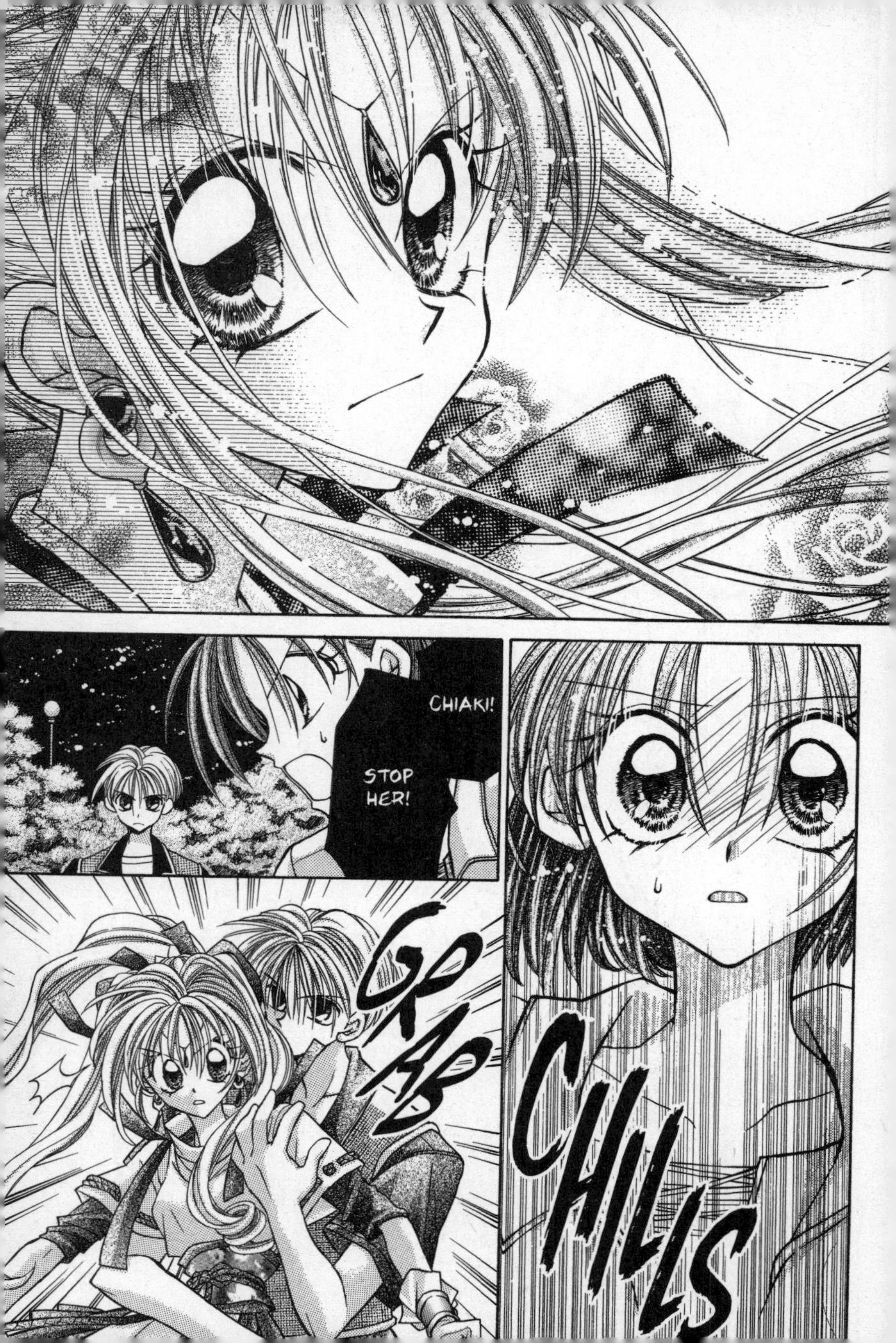
CHILLS
CHIAKI!
STOP HER!
GRAB

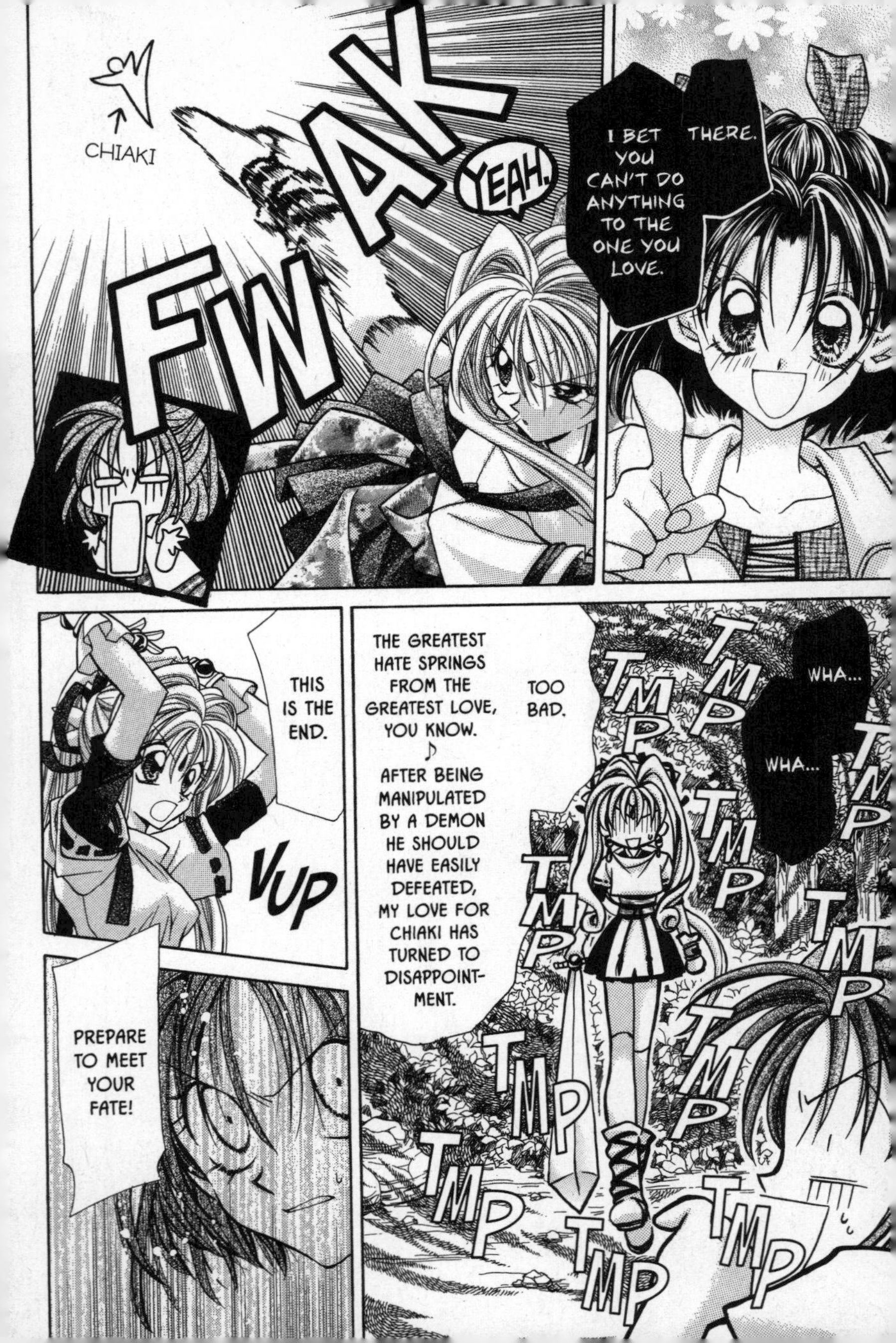
THERE.
I BET YOU CAN'T DO ANYTHING TO THE ONE YOU LOVE.
YEAH.
FWAK
CHIAKI
WHA...
WHA...
TMP TMP TMP TMP TMP TMP TMP TMP TMP TMP TMP TMP
TOO BAD.
THE GREATEST HATE SPRINGS FROM THE GREATEST LOVE, YOU KNOW. ♪
AFTER BEING MANIPULATED BY A DEMON HE SHOULD HAVE EASILY DEFEATED, MY LOVE FOR CHIAKI HAS TURNED TO DISAPPOINTMENT.
THIS IS THE END.
VUP
PREPARE TO MEET YOUR FATE!

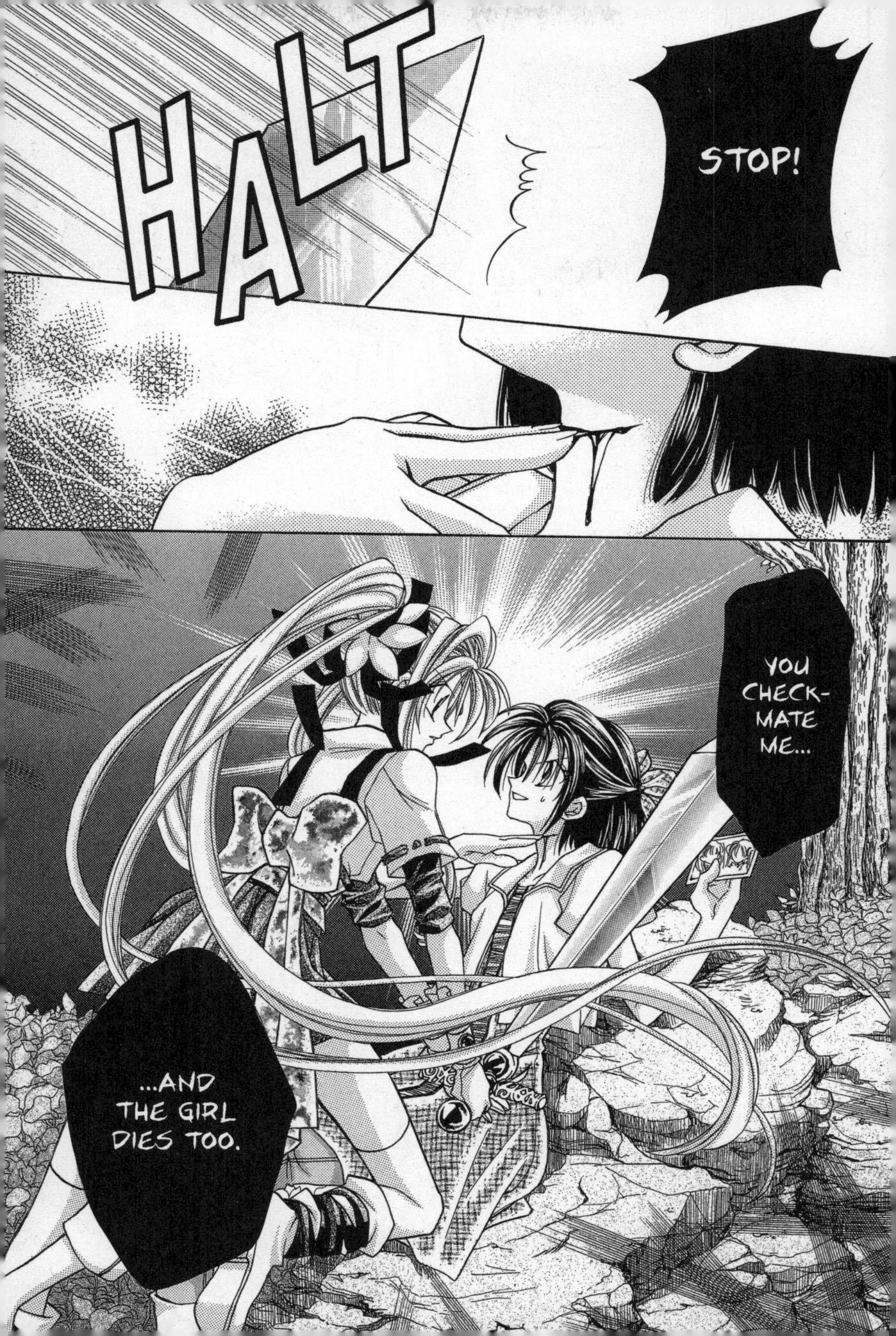
STOP!
HALT
YOU CHECK-MATE ME...
...AND THE GIRL DIES TOO.

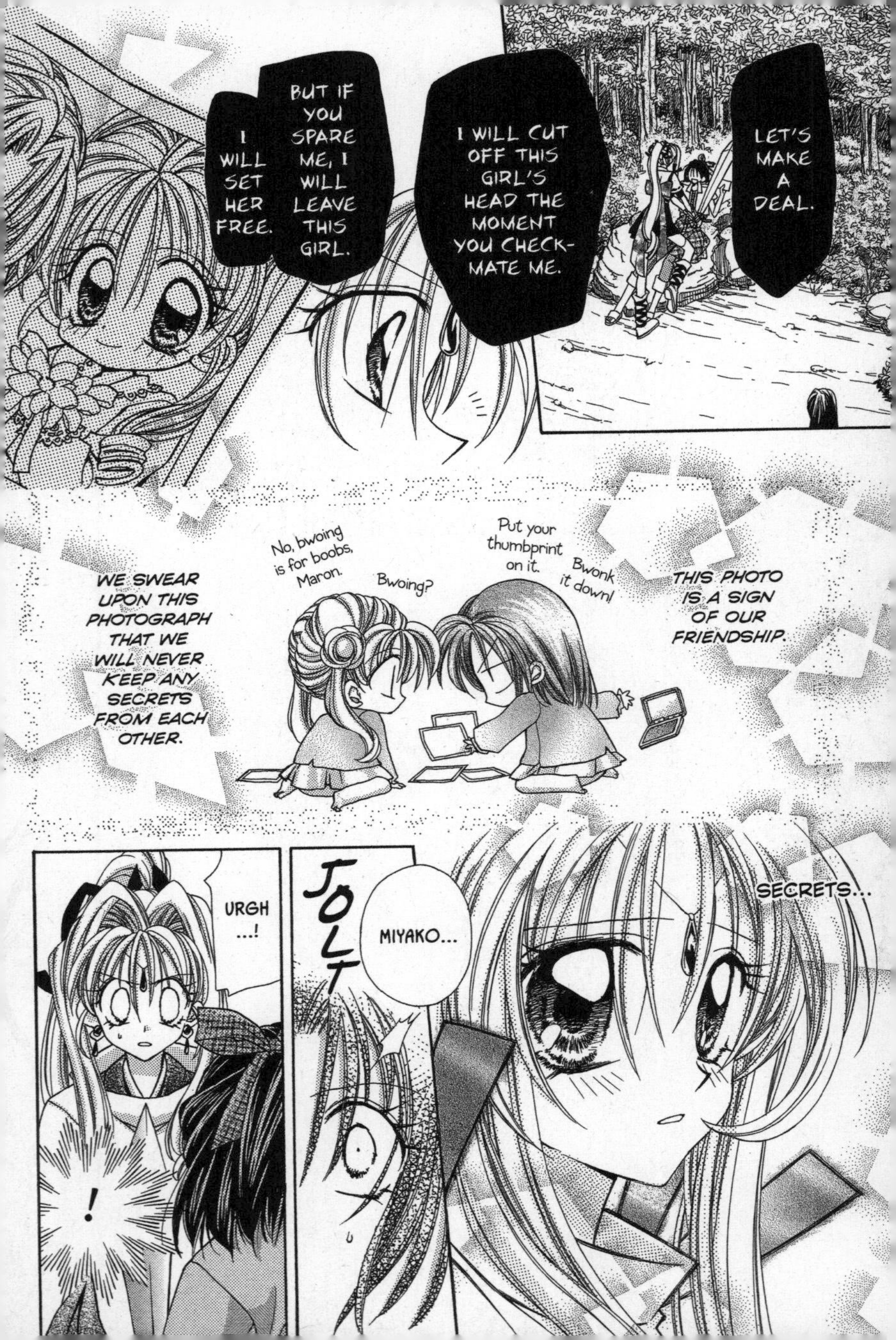
LET'S MAKE A DEAL.
I WILL CUT OFF THIS GIRL'S HEAD THE MOMENT YOU CHECK-MATE ME.
BUT IF YOU SPARE ME, I WILL LEAVE THIS GIRL.
I WILL SET HER FREE.
THIS PHOTO IS A SIGN OF OUR FRIENDSHIP.
Bwonk it down!
Put your thumbprint on it.
Bwoing?
No, bwoing is for boobs, Maron.
WE SWEAR UPON THIS PHOTOGRAPH THAT WE WILL NEVER KEEP ANY SECRETS FROM EACH OTHER.
SECRETS...
MIYAKO...
JOLT
URGH ...!
!

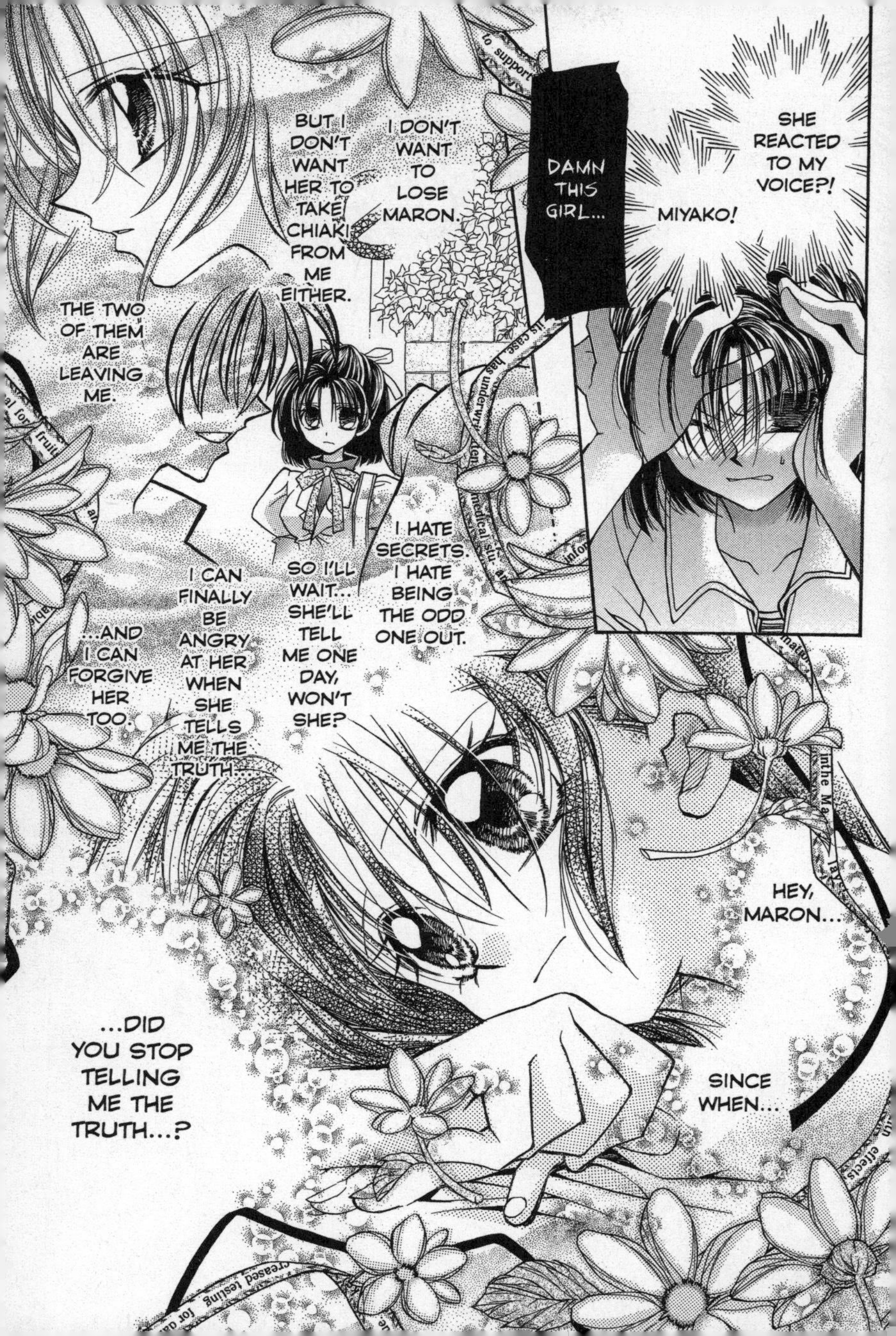
SHE REACTED TO MY VOICE?!
MIYAKO!
DAMN THIS GIRL...
I DON'T WANT TO LOSE MARON.
BUT I DON'T WANT HER TO TAKE CHIAKI FROM ME EITHER.
THE TWO OF THEM ARE LEAVING ME.
I HATE SECRETS. I HATE BEING THE ODD ONE OUT.
SO I'LL WAIT... SHE'LL TELL ME ONE DAY, WON'T SHE?
I CAN FINALLY BE ANGRY AT HER WHEN SHE TELLS ME THE TRUTH...
...AND I CAN FORGIVE HER TOO.
HEY, MARON...
SINCE WHEN...
...DID YOU STOP TELLING ME THE TRUTH...?

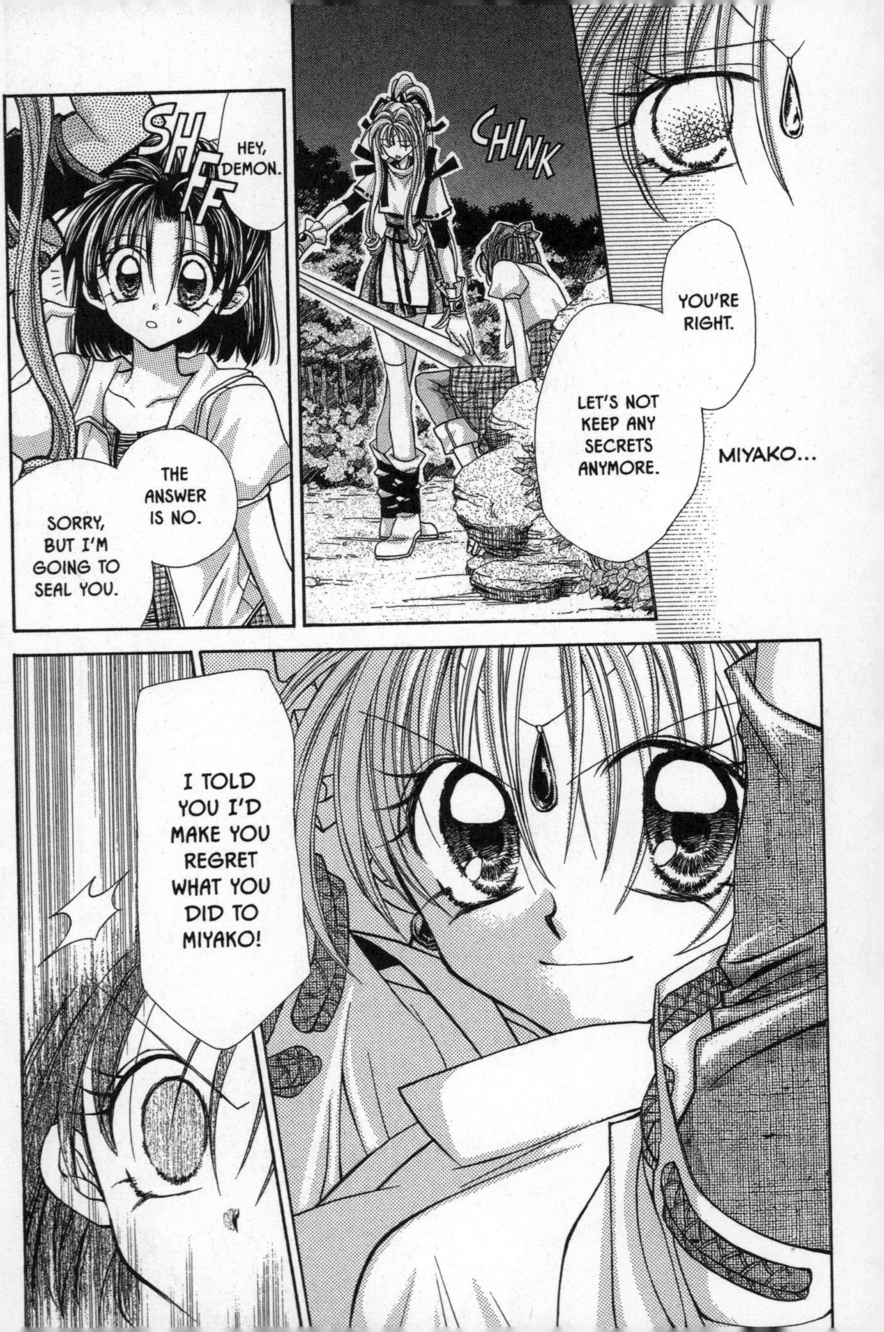

YOU'RE RIGHT.
LET'S NOT KEEP ANY SECRETS ANYMORE.
MIYAKO...
CHINK
SHFF
HEY, DEMON.
THE ANSWER IS NO.
SORRY, BUT I'M GOING TO SEAL YOU.
I TOLD YOU I'D MAKE YOU REGRET WHAT YOU DID TO MIYAKO!

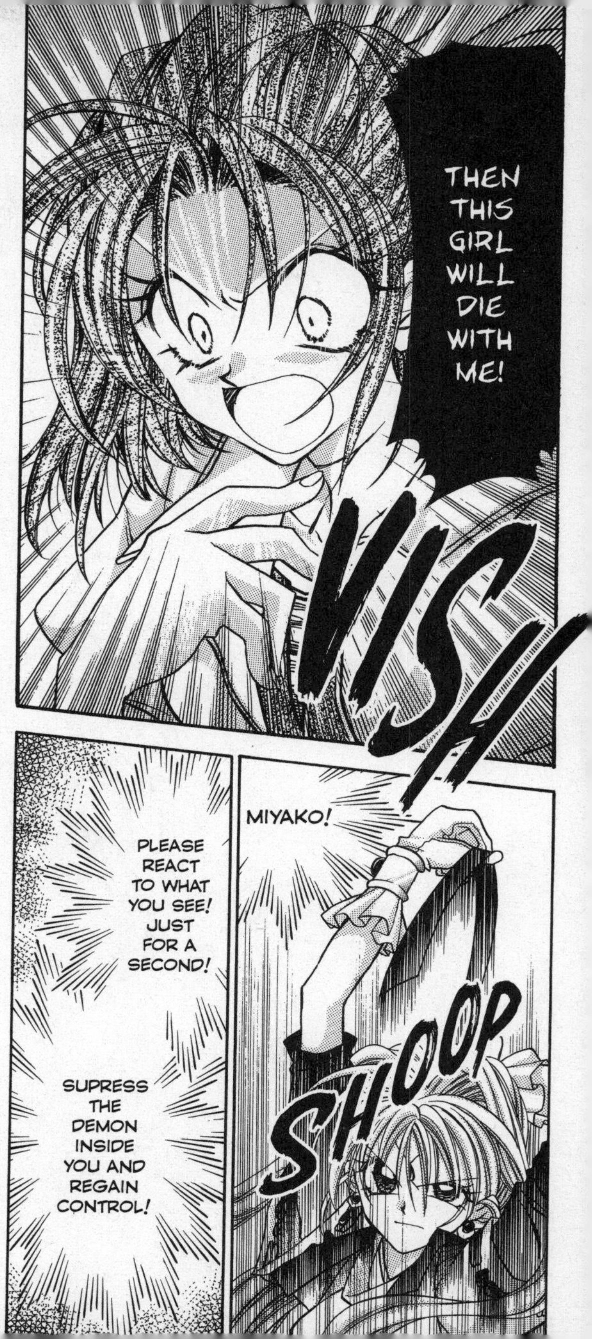
THEN THIS GIRL WILL DIE WITH ME!
VISH
MIYAKO!
SHOOP
PLEASE REACT TO WHAT YOU SEE! JUST FOR A SECOND!
SUPRESS THE DEMON INSIDE YOU AND REGAIN CONTROL!

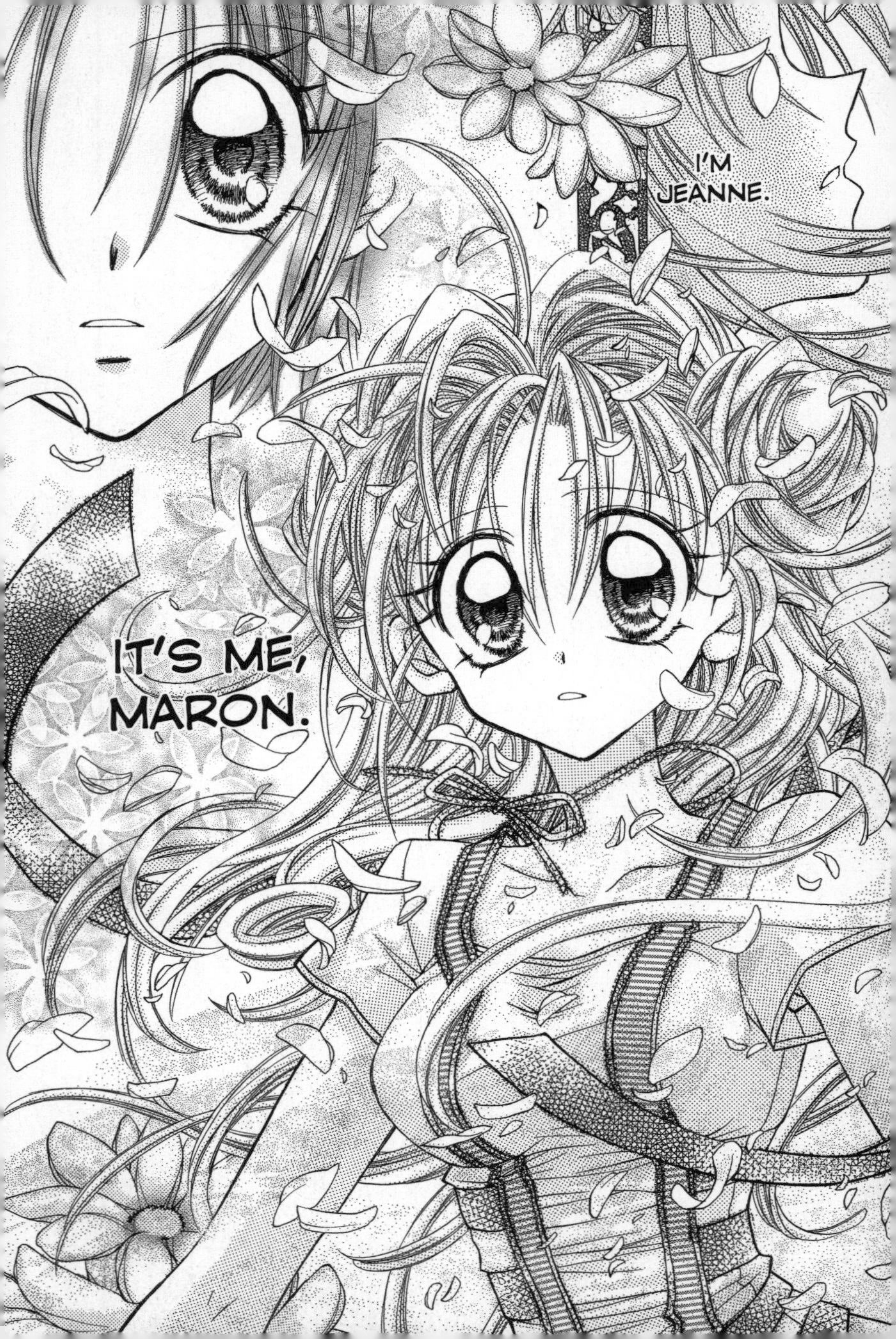
I'M JEANNE.
IT'S ME, MARON.

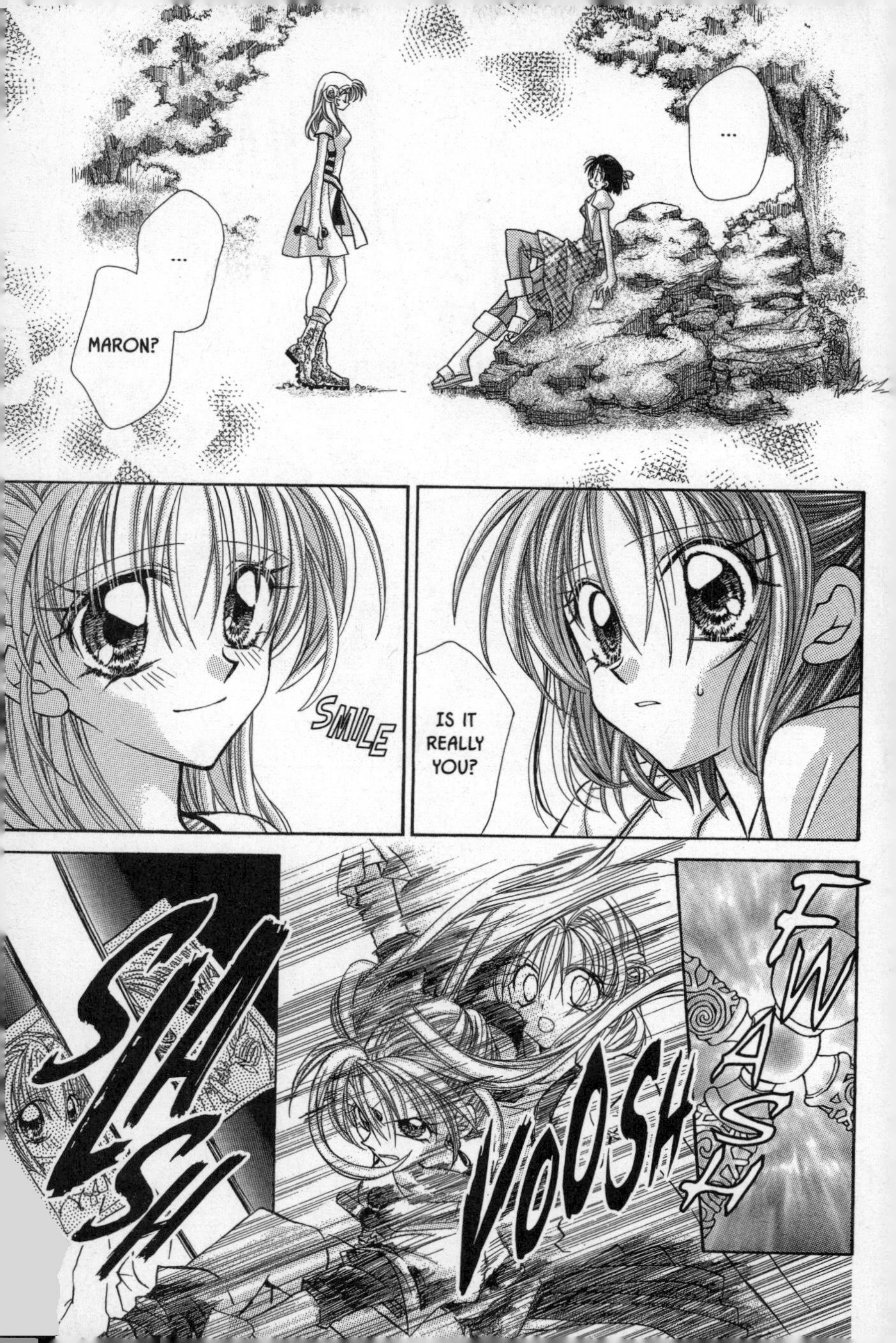
...
...
MARON?
IS IT REALLY YOU?
SMILE
FWASH
VOOSH
SHASH

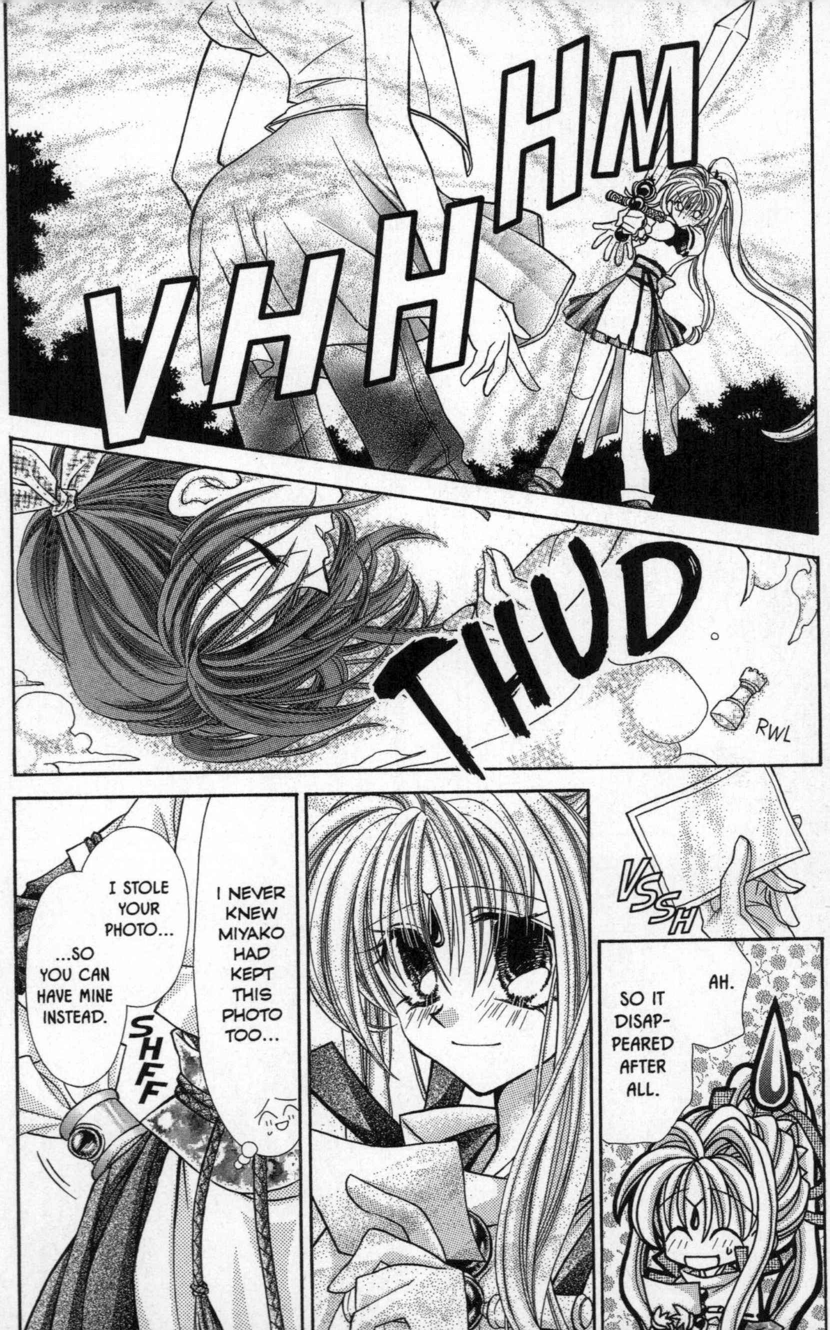
VHHHM
THUD
RWL
VSSH
AH.
SO IT DISAPPEARED AFTER ALL.
I NEVER KNEW MIYAKO HAD KEPT THIS PHOTO TOO...
I STOLE YOUR PHOTO...
...SO YOU CAN HAVE MINE INSTEAD.
SHFF

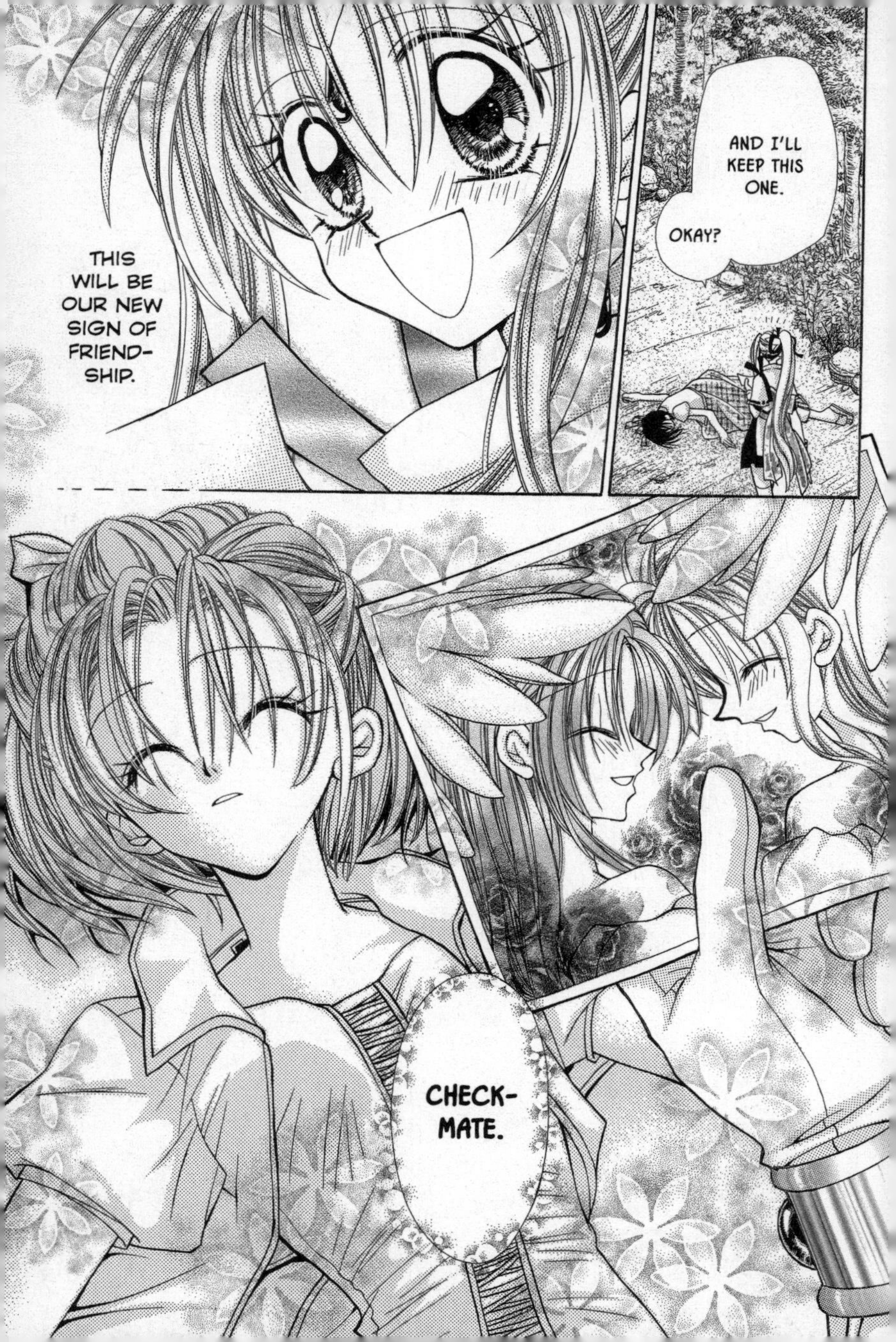
AND I'LL KEEP THIS ONE.
OKAY?
THIS WILL BE OUR NEW SIGN OF FRIEND-SHIP.
CHECK-MATE.

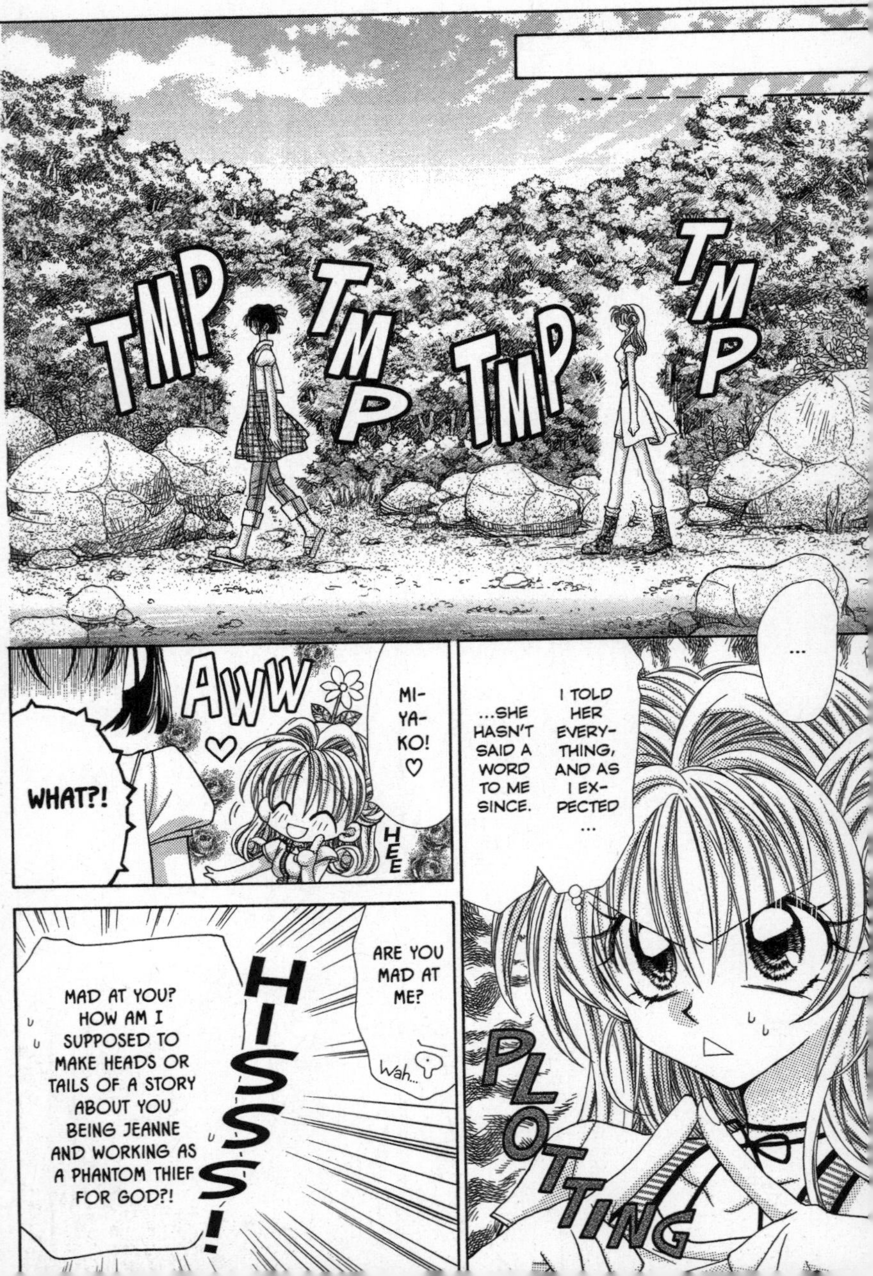

TMP
TMP
TMP
TMP
...
I TOLD HER EVERY-THING, AND AS I EX-PECTED ...
...SHE HASN'T SAID A WORD TO ME SINCE.
PLOTTING
MI-YA-KO! ♡
AWW ♡
HEE
WHAT?!
ARE YOU MAD AT ME?
Wah...
HISS!
MAD AT YOU? HOW AM I SUPPOSED TO MAKE HEADS OR TAILS OF A STORY ABOUT YOU BEING JEANNE AND WORKING AS A PHANTOM THIEF FOR GOD?!

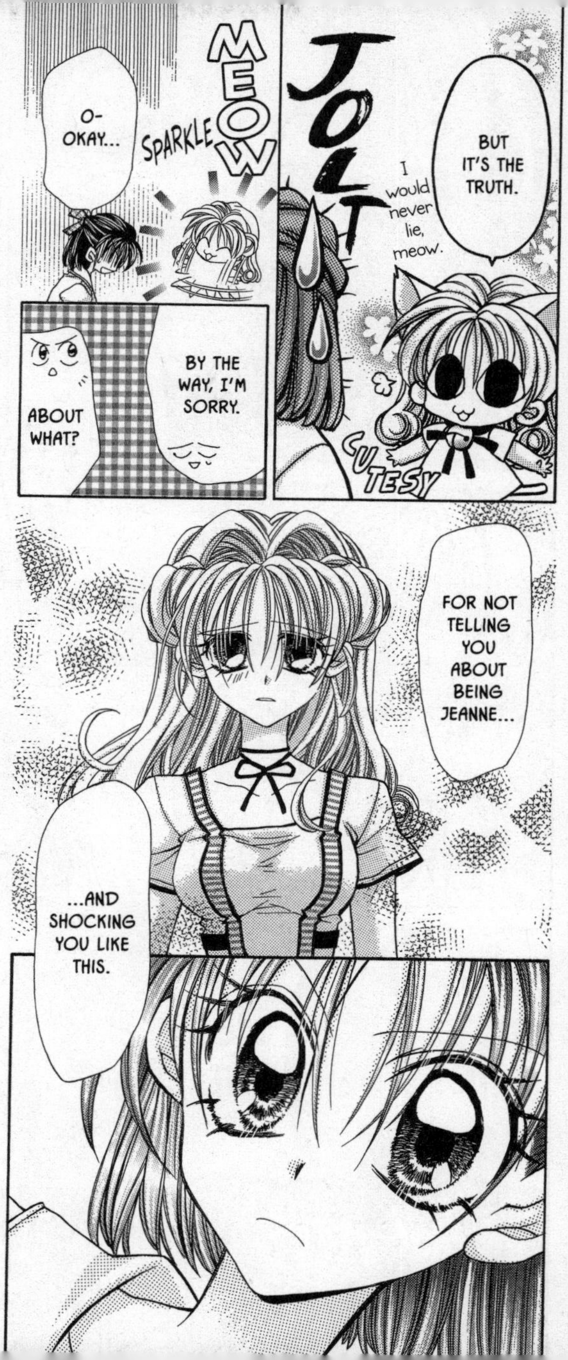
BUT IT'S THE TRUTH.
I would never lie, meow.
JOLT
CUTESY
MEOW
SPARKLE
O-OKAY...
BY THE WAY, I'M SORRY.
ABOUT WHAT?
FOR NOT TELLING YOU ABOUT BEING JEANNE...
...AND SHOCKING YOU LIKE THIS.

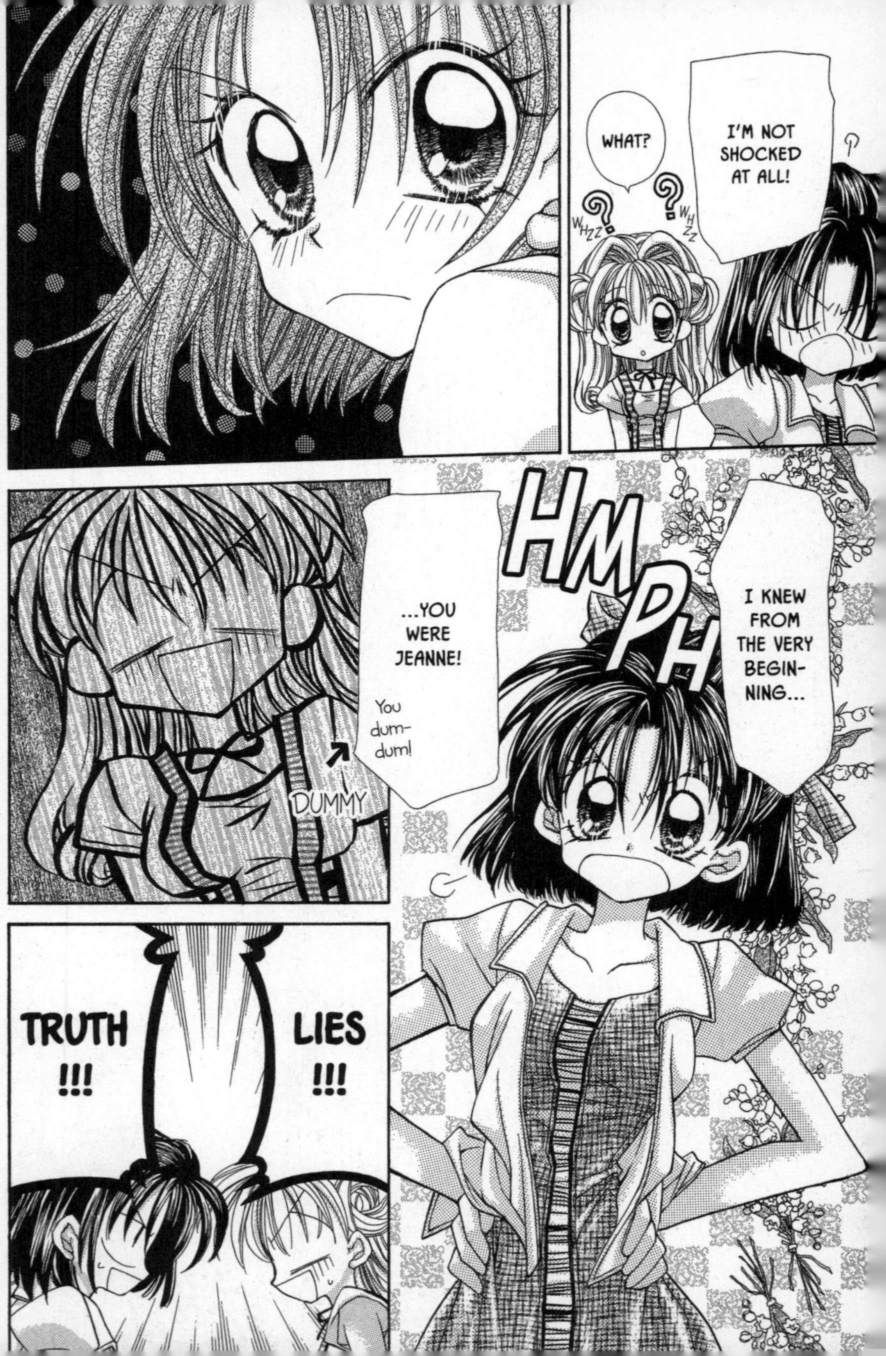
I'M NOT SHOCKED AT ALL!
WHAT?
WHZZ
WHZZ
HMPH
I KNEW FROM THE VERY BEGIN-NING...
...YOU WERE JEANNE!
You dum-dum!
DUMMY
LIES !!!
TRUTH !!!

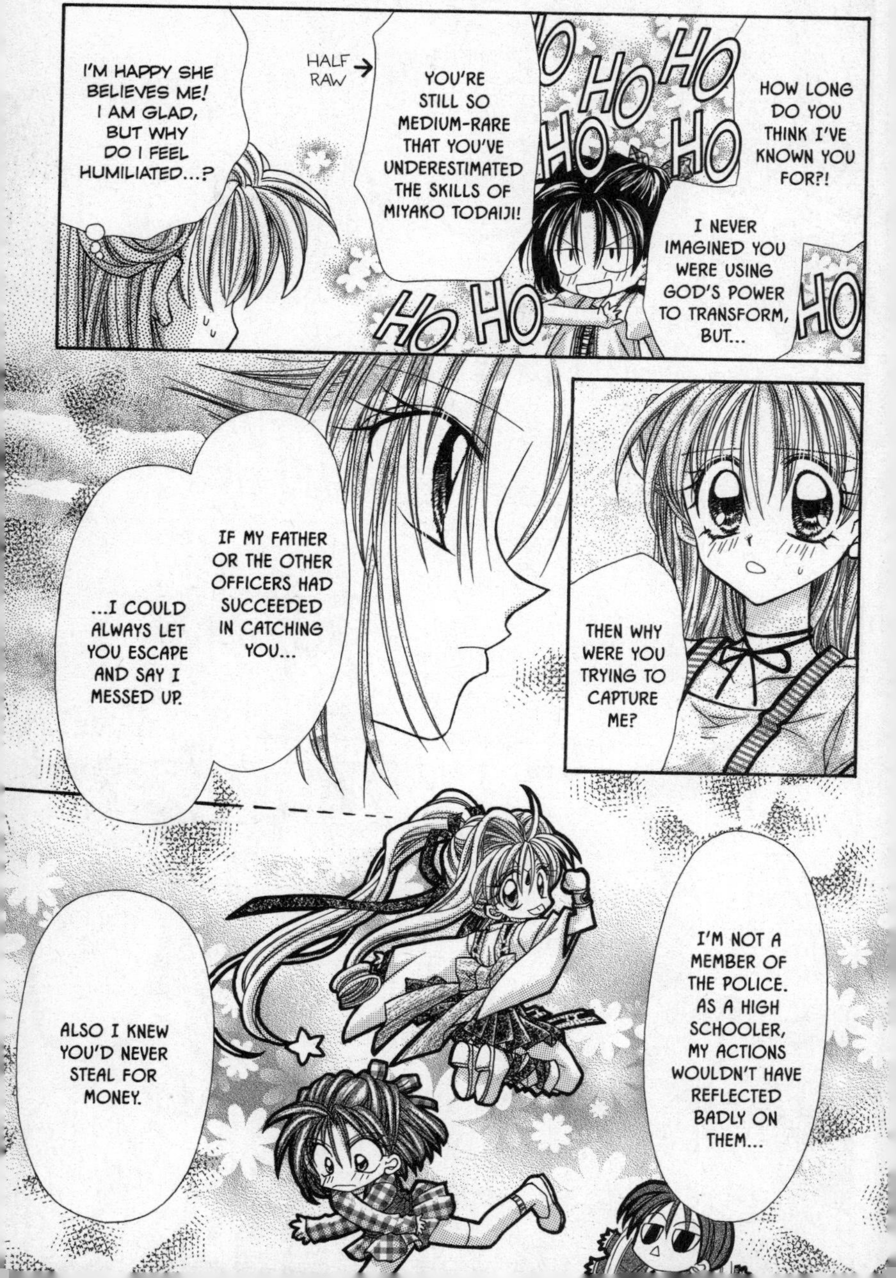
HO HO HO HO HO HO HO
HOW LONG DO YOU THINK I'VE KNOWN YOU FOR?!
I NEVER IMAGINED YOU WERE USING GOD'S POWER TO TRANSFORM, BUT...
YOU'RE STILL SO MEDIUM-RARE THAT YOU'VE UNDERESTIMATED THE SKILLS OF MIYAKO TODAIJI!
HALF RAW
I'M HAPPY SHE BELIEVES ME! I AM GLAD, BUT WHY DO I FEEL HUMILIATED...?
THEN WHY WERE YOU TRYING TO CAPTURE ME?
IF MY FATHER OR THE OTHER OFFICERS HAD SUCCEEDED IN CATCHING YOU...
...I COULD ALWAYS LET YOU ESCAPE AND SAY I MESSED UP.
I'M NOT A MEMBER OF THE POLICE. AS A HIGH SCHOOLER, MY ACTIONS WOULDN'T HAVE REFLECTED BADLY ON THEM...
ALSO I KNEW YOU'D NEVER STEAL FOR MONEY.

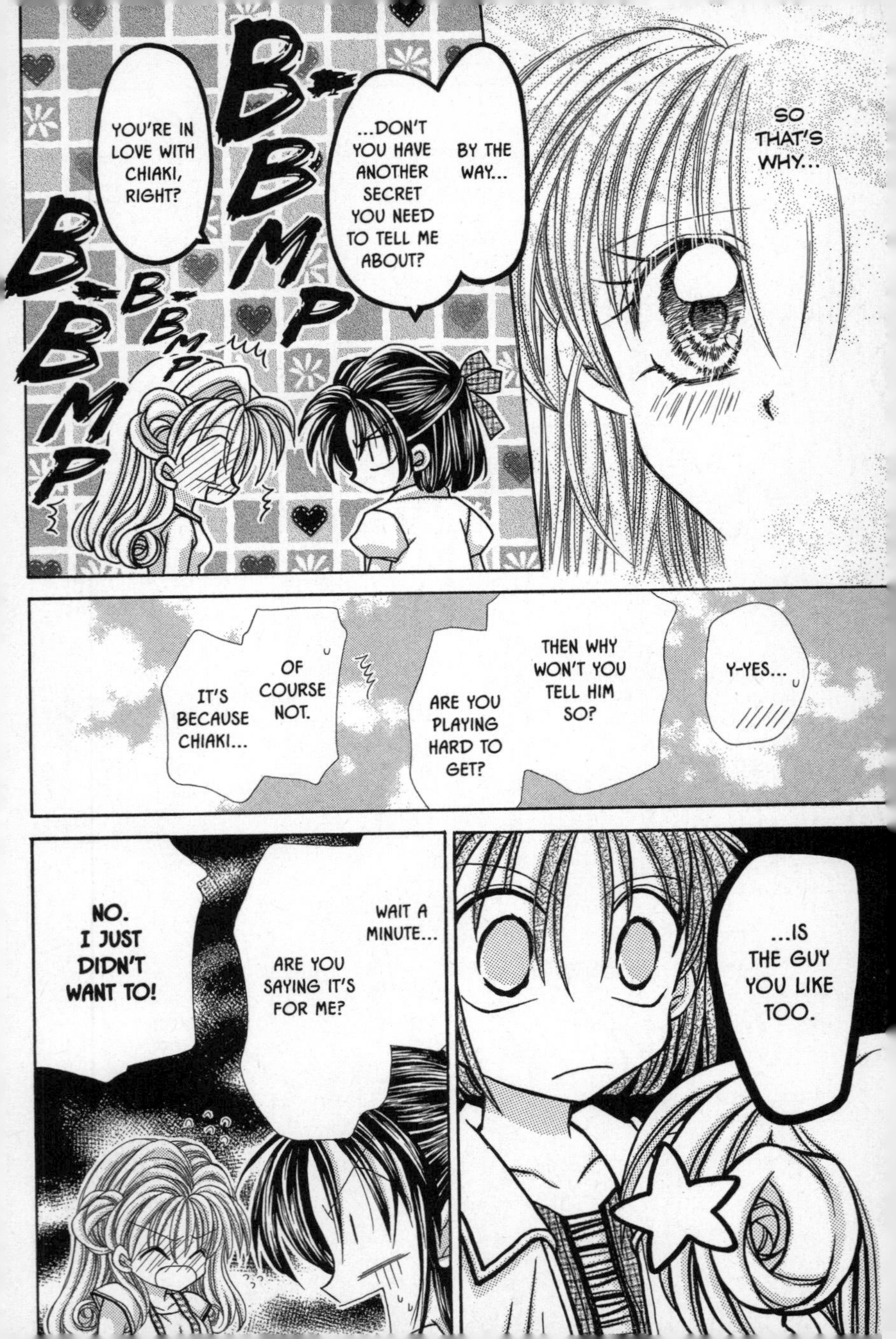
SO THAT'S WHY...
BY THE WAY...
...DON'T YOU HAVE ANOTHER SECRET YOU NEED TO TELL ME ABOUT?
B-BMP
YOU'RE IN LOVE WITH CHIAKI, RIGHT?
B-BMP
B-B-BMP
Y-YES...
THEN WHY WON'T YOU TELL HIM SO?
ARE YOU PLAYING HARD TO GET?
OF COURSE NOT.
IT'S BECAUSE CHIAKI...
...IS THE GUY YOU LIKE TOO.
WAIT A MINUTE...
ARE YOU SAYING IT'S FOR ME?
NO. I JUST DIDN'T WANT TO!

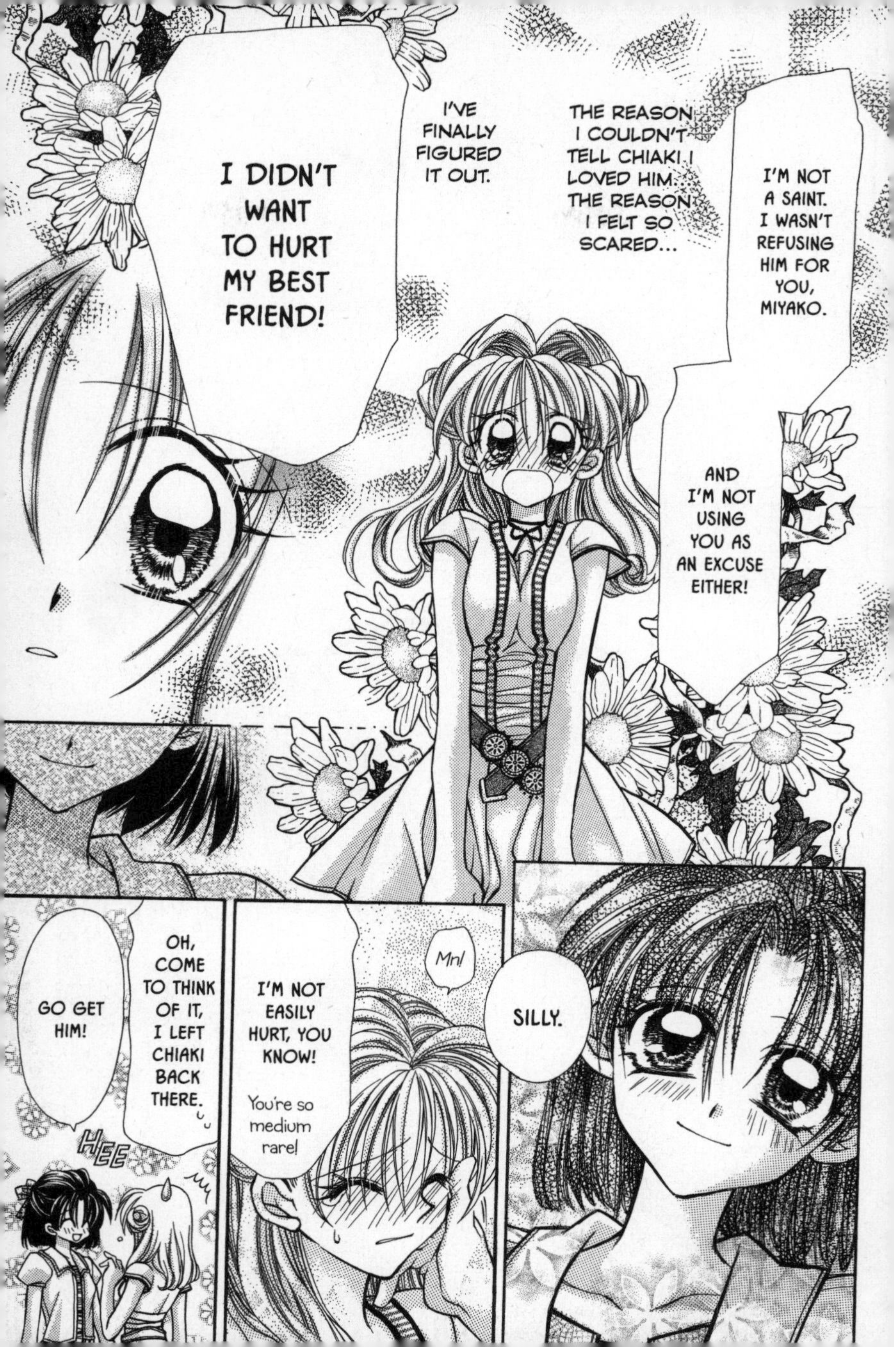
I'M NOT A SAINT. I WASN'T REFUSING HIM FOR YOU, MIYAKO.
AND I'M NOT USING YOU AS AN EXCUSE EITHER!
THE REASON I COULDN'T TELL CHIAKI I LOVED HIM. THE REASON I FELT SO SCARED...
I'VE FINALLY FIGURED IT OUT.
I DIDN'T WANT TO HURT MY BEST FRIEND!
SILLY.
Mn!
I'M NOT EASILY HURT, YOU KNOW!
You're so medium rare!
OH, COME TO THINK OF IT, I LEFT CHIAKI BACK THERE.
GO GET HIM!
HEE

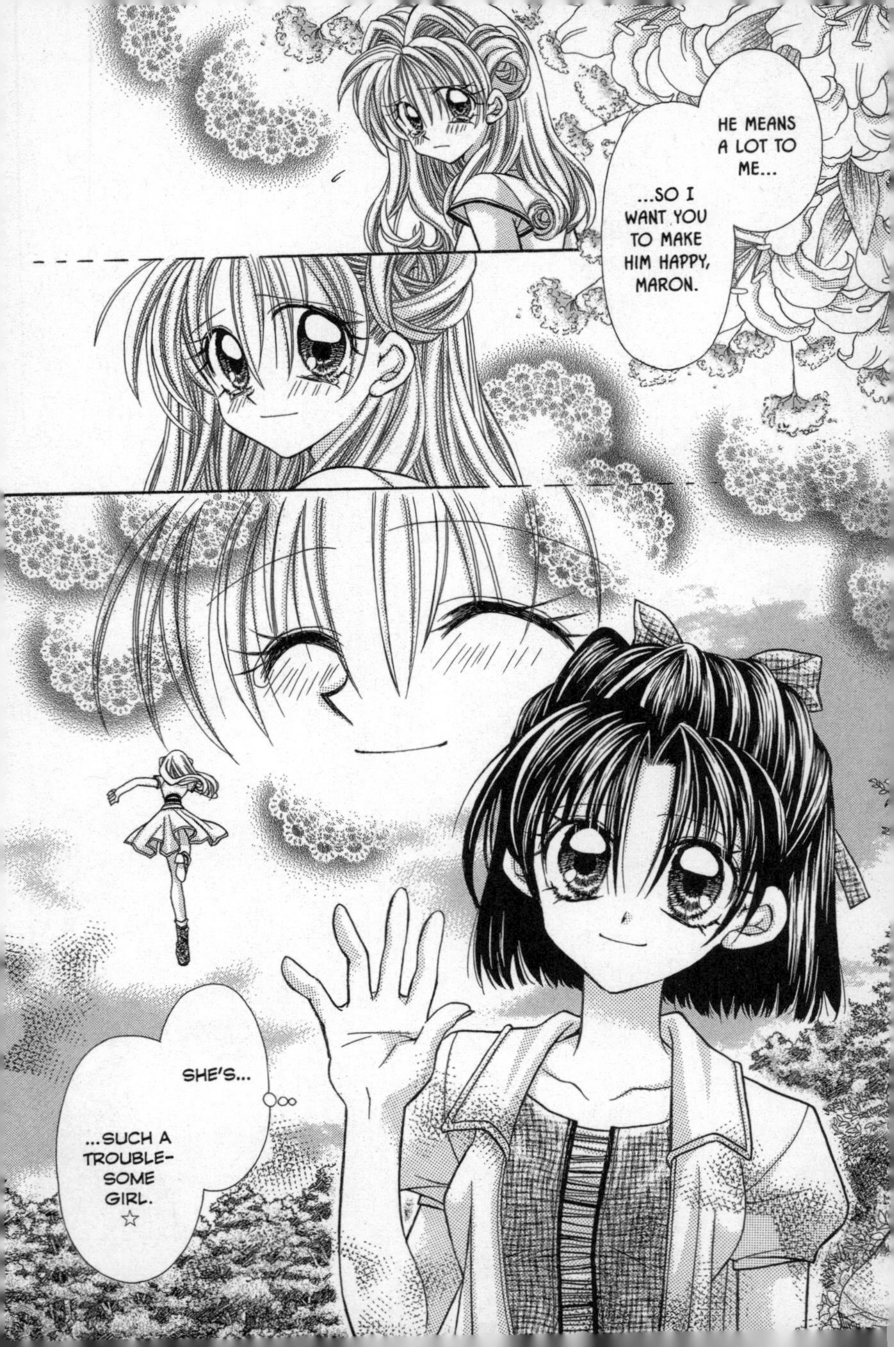
HE MEANS A LOT TO ME...
...SO I WANT YOU TO MAKE HIM HAPPY, MARON.
SHE'S...
...SUCH A TROUBLE-SOME GIRL. ☆

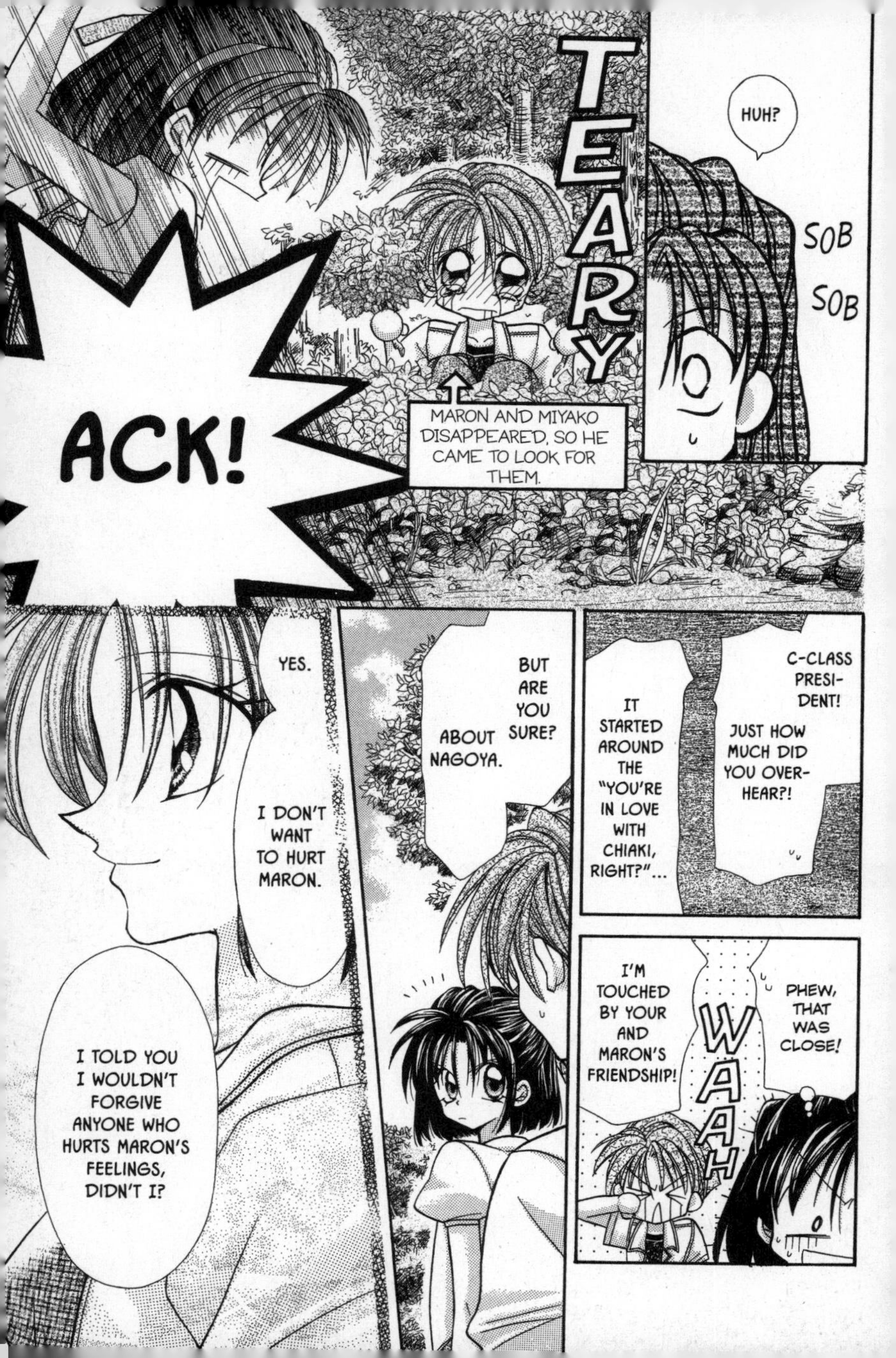
HUH?
SOB
SOB
TEARY
MARON AND MIYAKO DISAPPEARED, SO HE CAME TO LOOK FOR THEM.
ACK!
C-CLASS PRESI-DENT!
JUST HOW MUCH DID YOU OVER-HEAR?!
IT STARTED AROUND THE "YOU'RE IN LOVE WITH CHIAKI, RIGHT?"...
PHEW, THAT WAS CLOSE!
WAAH
I'M TOUCHED BY YOUR AND MARON'S FRIENDSHIP!
BUT ARE YOU SURE?
ABOUT NAGOYA.
YES.
I DON'T WANT TO HURT MARON.
I TOLD YOU I WOULDN'T FORGIVE ANYONE WHO HURTS MARON'S FEELINGS, DIDN'T I?

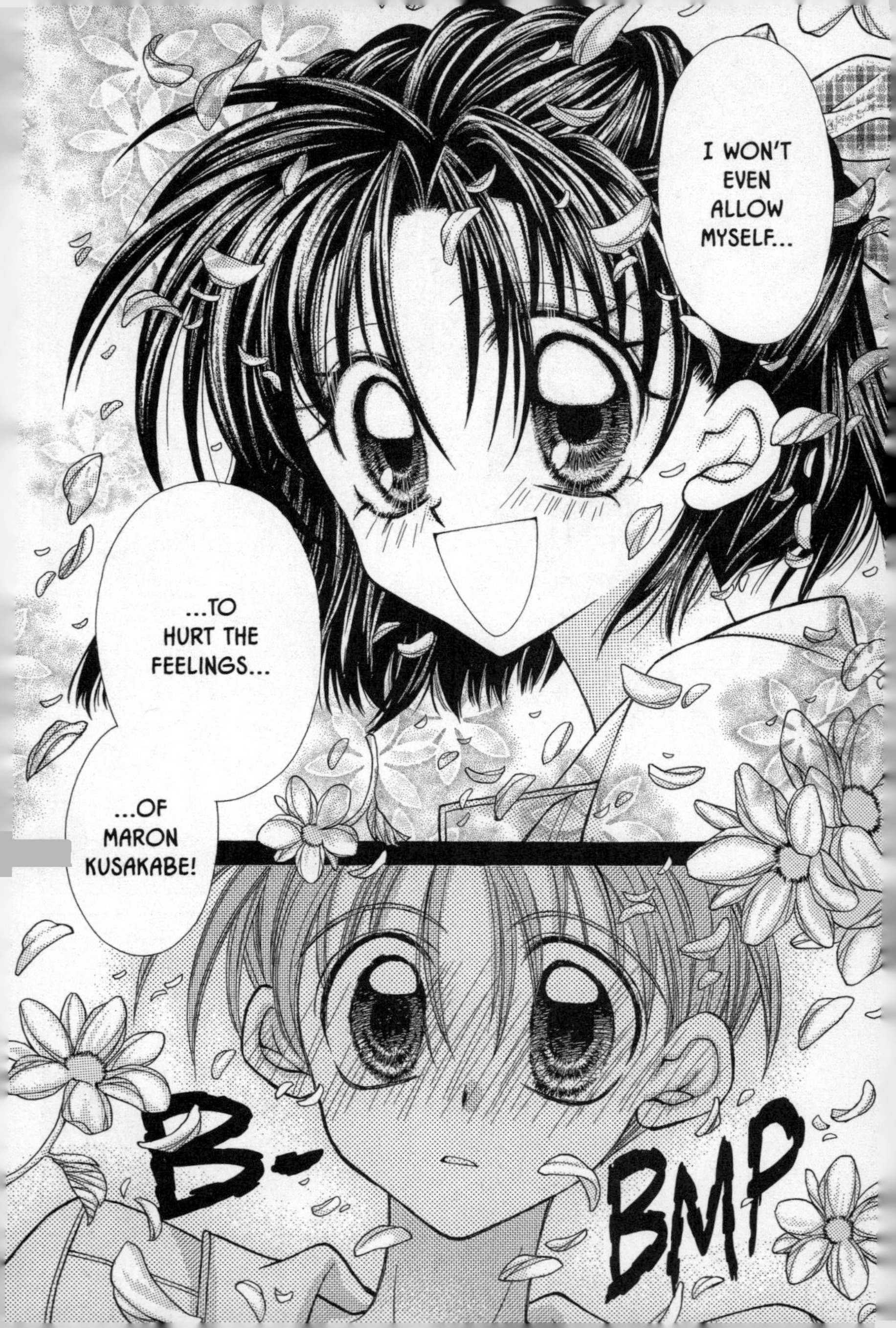
I WON'T EVEN ALLOW MYSELF...
...TO HURT THE FEELINGS...
...OF MARON KUSAKABE!
B-BMP

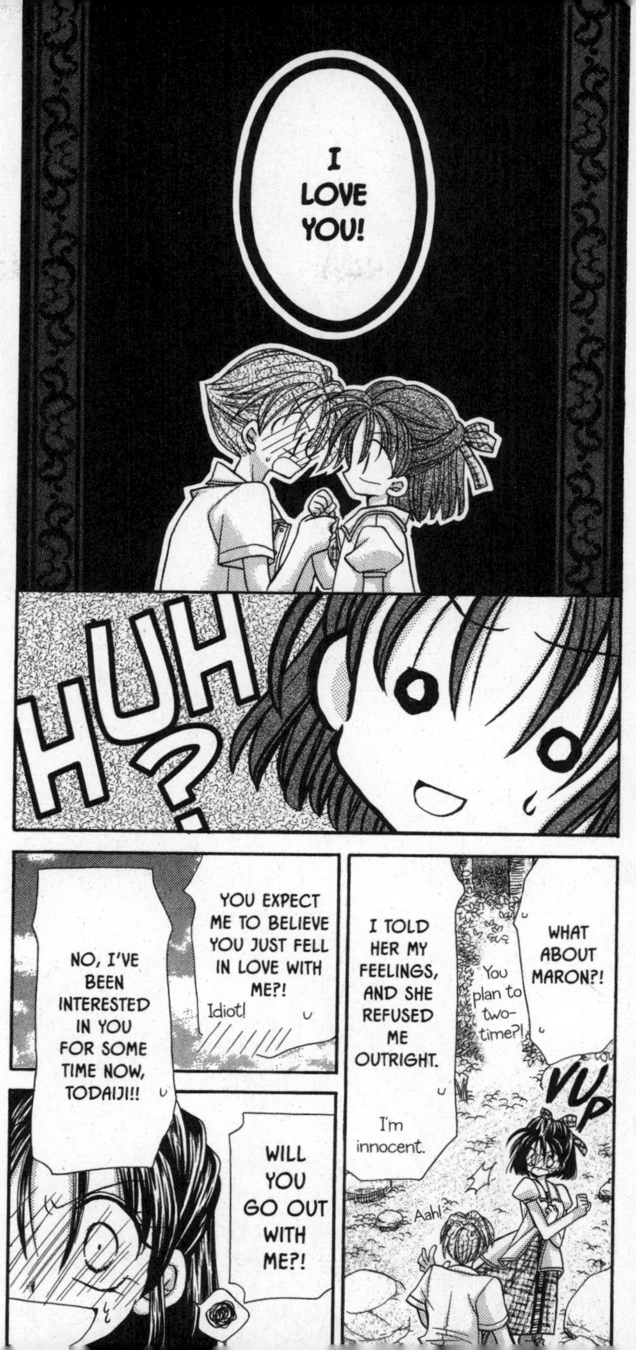
I LOVE YOU!
HUH?!
WHAT ABOUT MARON?!
You plan to two-time?!
I TOLD HER MY FEELINGS, AND SHE REFUSED ME OUTRIGHT.
I'm innocent.
VUP
Aah!
YOU EXPECT ME TO BELIEVE YOU JUST FELL IN LOVE WITH ME?!
Idiot!
NO, I'VE BEEN INTERESTED IN YOU FOR SOME TIME NOW, TODAIJI!!
WILL YOU GO OUT WITH ME?!

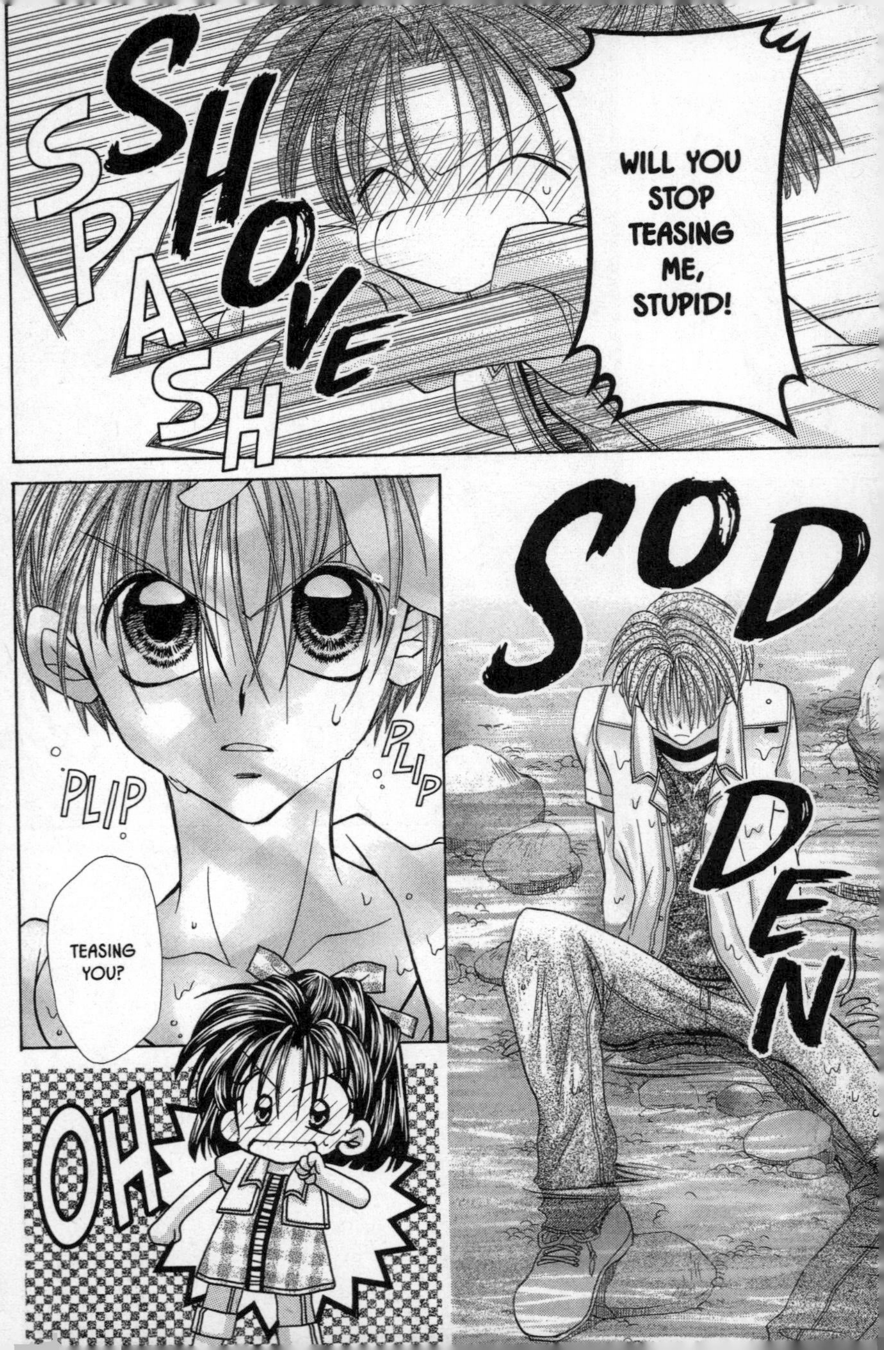
WILL YOU STOP TEASING ME, STUPID!
SHOVE
SPLASH
SODDEN
PLIP
PLIP
TEASING YOU?
OH

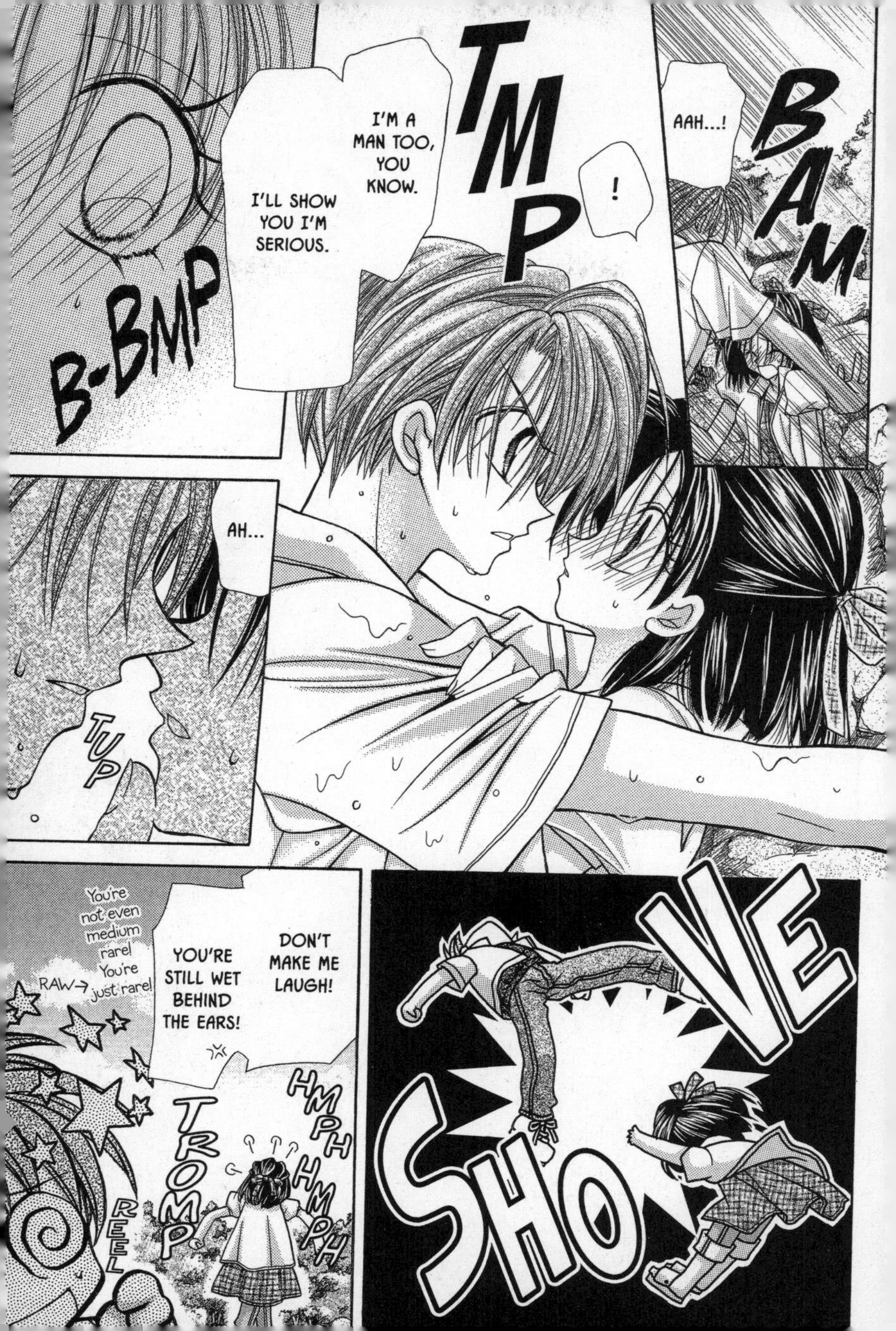
AAH...!
BAM
!
TMP
I'M A MAN TOO, YOU KNOW.
I'LL SHOW YOU I'M SERIOUS.
B-BMP
AH...
TUP
SHOVE
DON'T MAKE ME LAUGH!
YOU'RE STILL WET BEHIND THE EARS!
You're not even medium rare! You're just rare!
RAW→
HMPH HMPH
TROMP
REEL

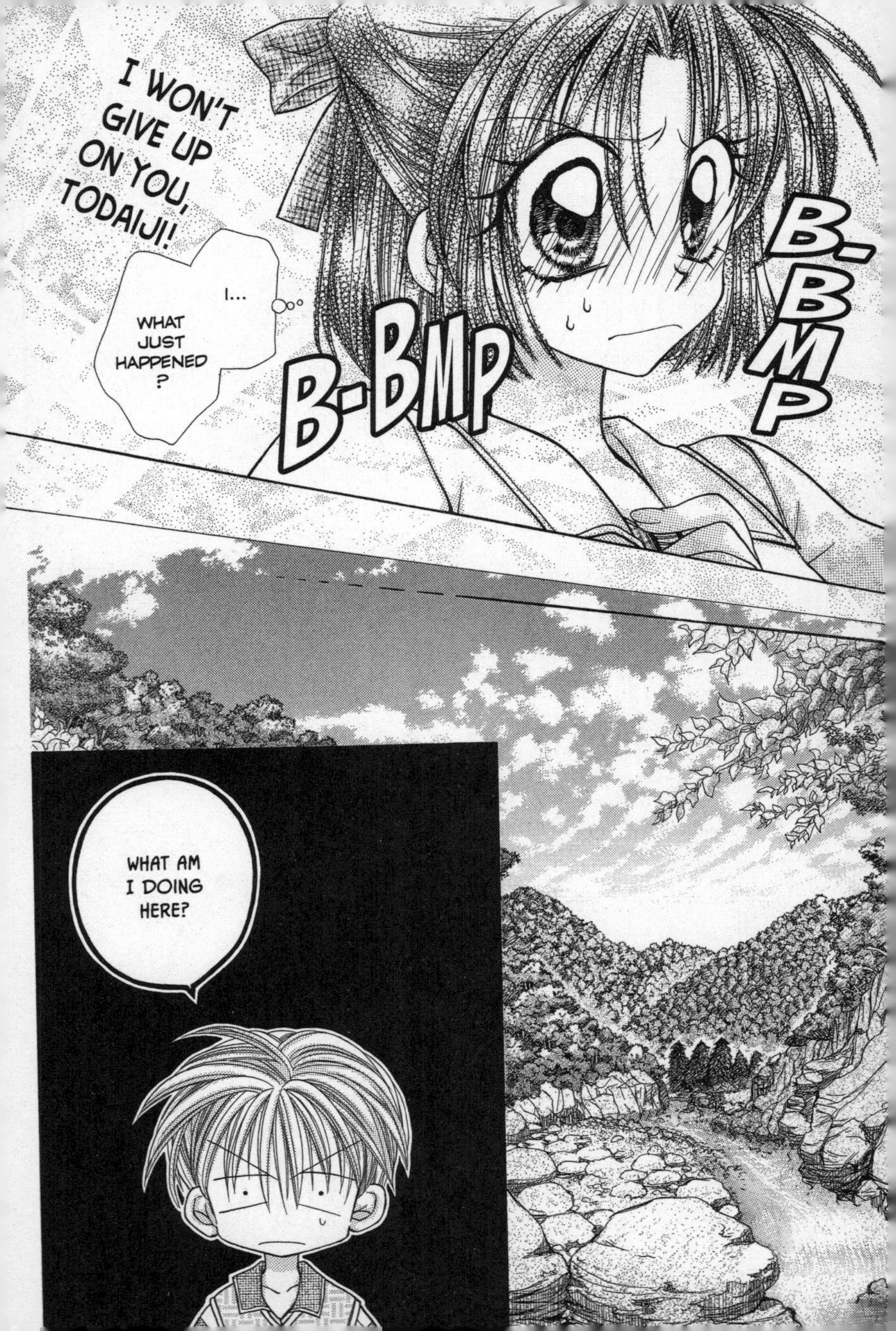

B-BMP
B-BMP
I WON'T GIVE UP ON YOU, TODAIJI!
I... WHAT JUST HAPPENED?
WHAT AM I DOING HERE?

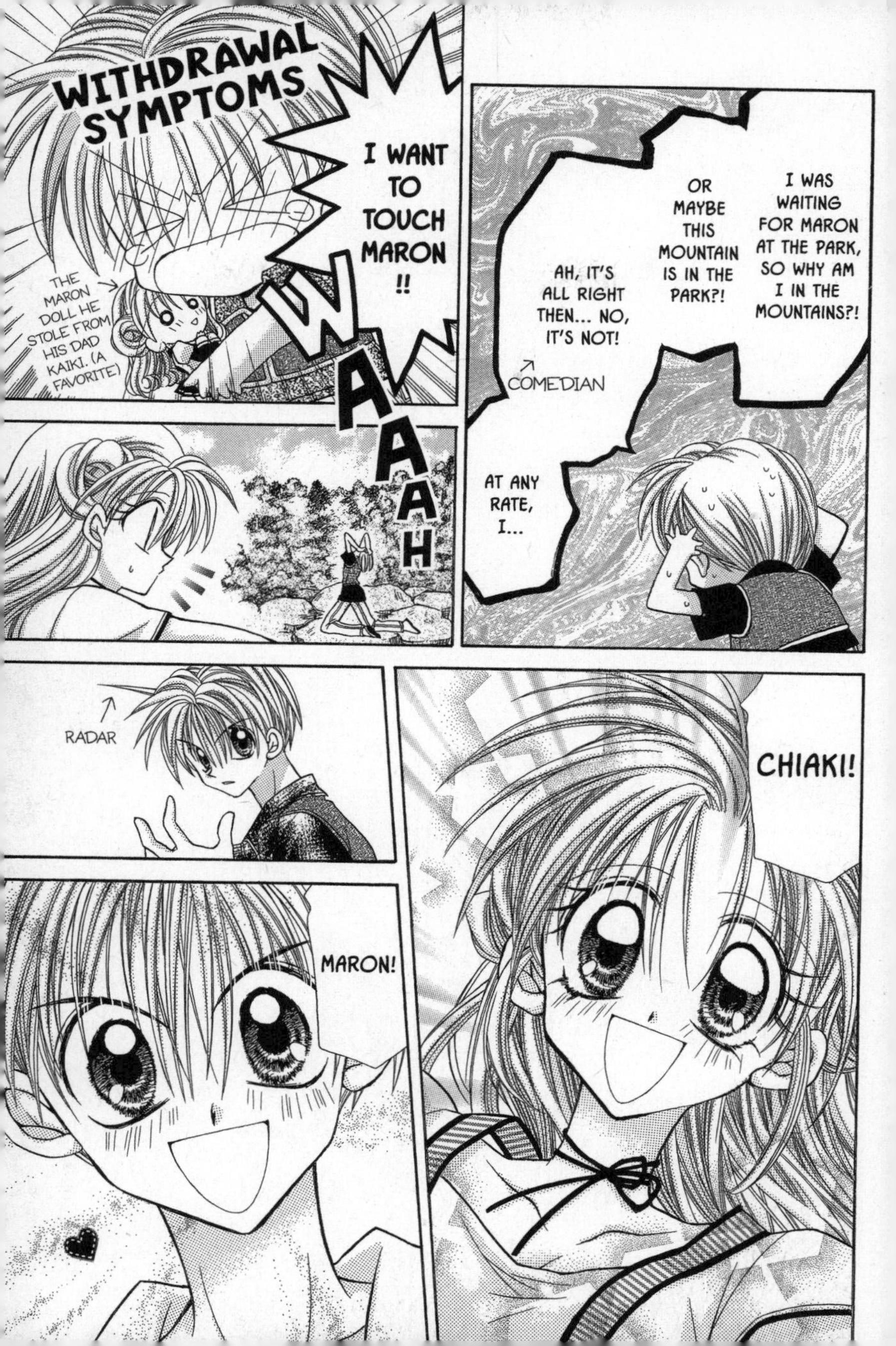
I WAS WAITING FOR MARON AT THE PARK, SO WHY AM I IN THE MOUNTAINS?!
OR MAYBE THIS MOUNTAIN IS IN THE PARK?!
AH, IT'S ALL RIGHT THEN... NO, IT'S NOT!
COMEDIAN
AT ANY RATE, I...
WITHDRAWAL SYMPTOMS
I WANT TO TOUCH MARON !!
THE MARON DOLL HE STOLE FROM HIS DAD KAIKI. (A FAVORITE)
WAAAAH
CHIAKI!
RADAR
MARON!

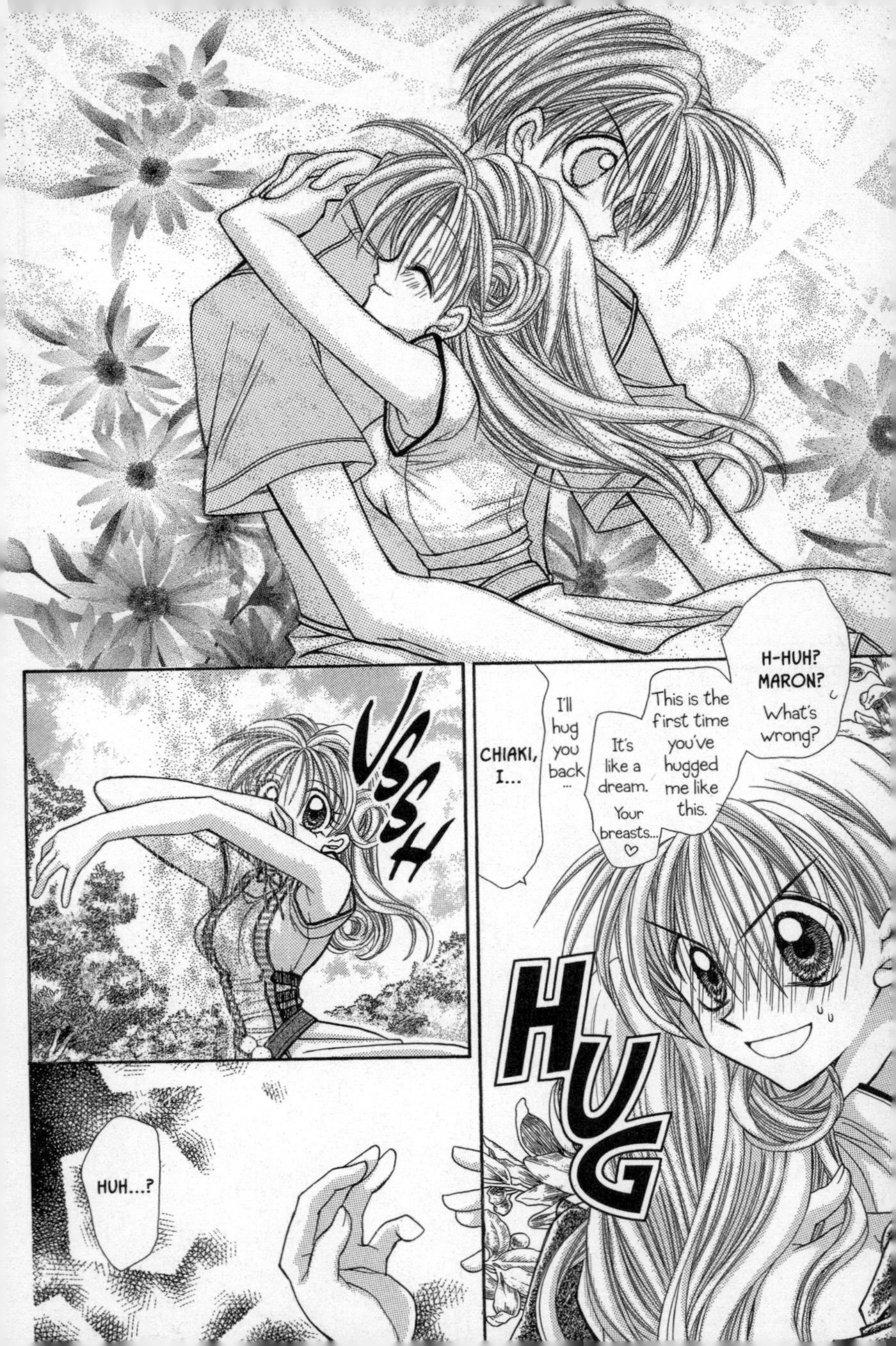
H-HUH? MARON? What's wrong?
This is the first time you've hugged me like this.
It's like a dream. Your breasts... ♡
I'll hug you back...
CHIAKI, I...
HUG
VSSH
HUH...?

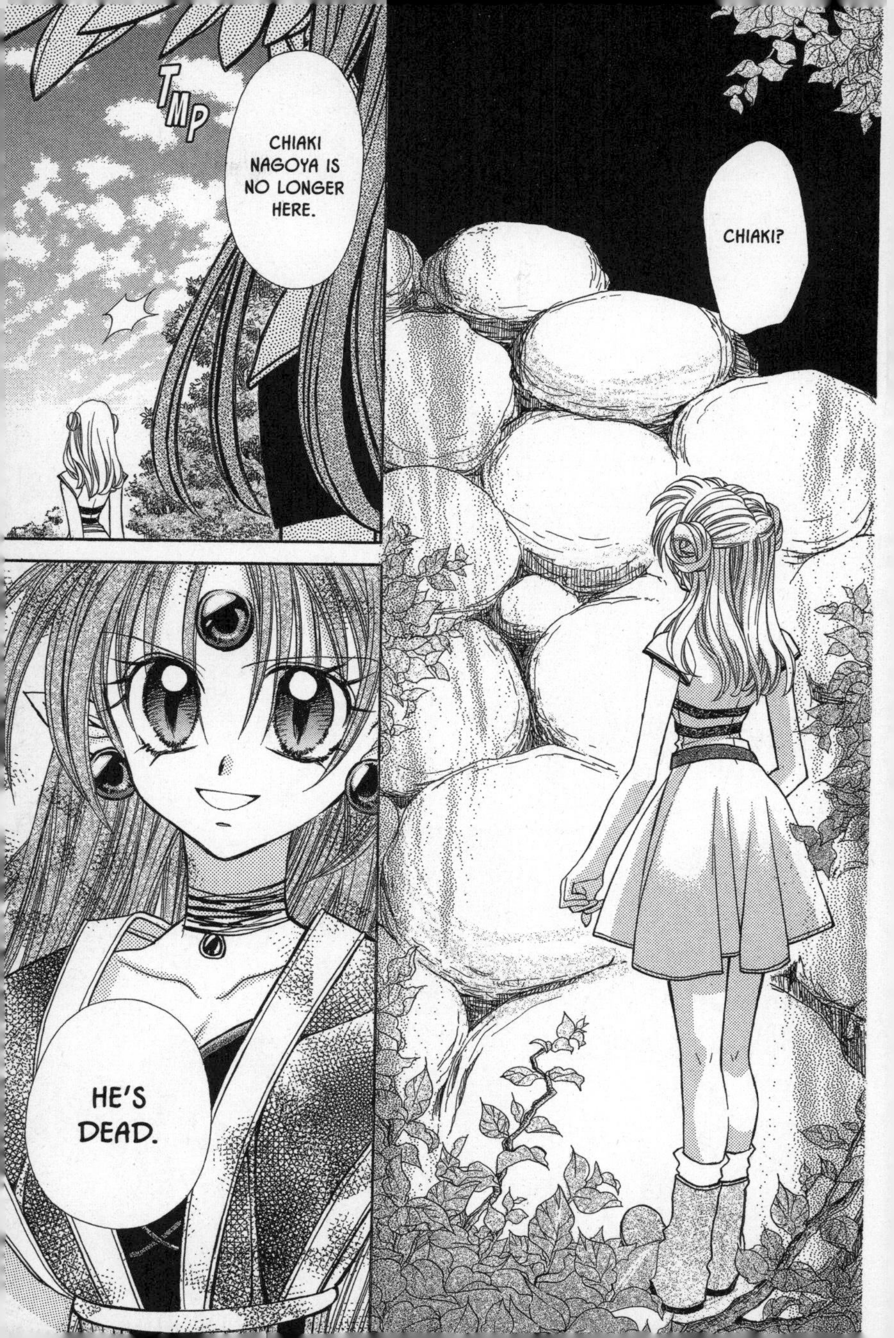
CHIAKI?
CHIAKI NAGOYA IS NO LONGER HERE.
TMP
HE'S DEAD.

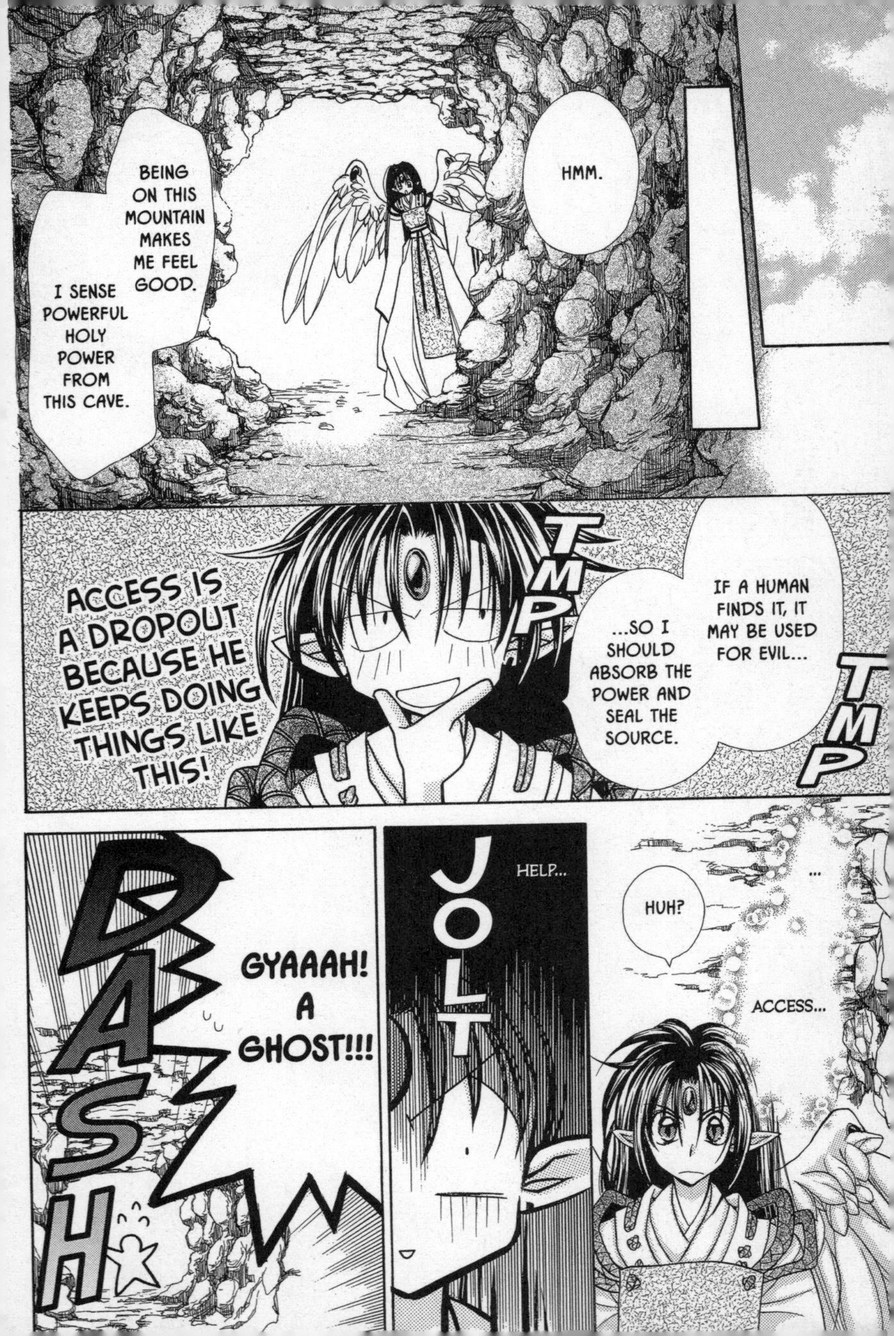
HMM.
BEING ON THIS MOUNTAIN MAKES ME FEEL GOOD.
I SENSE POWERFUL HOLY POWER FROM THIS CAVE.
TMP
IF A HUMAN FINDS IT, IT MAY BE USED FOR EVIL...
...SO I SHOULD ABSORB THE POWER AND SEAL THE SOURCE.
TMP
ACCESS IS A DROPOUT BECAUSE HE KEEPS DOING THINGS LIKE THIS!
...
HUH?
ACCESS...
HELP...
JOLT
GYAAAH! A GHOST!!!
DASH

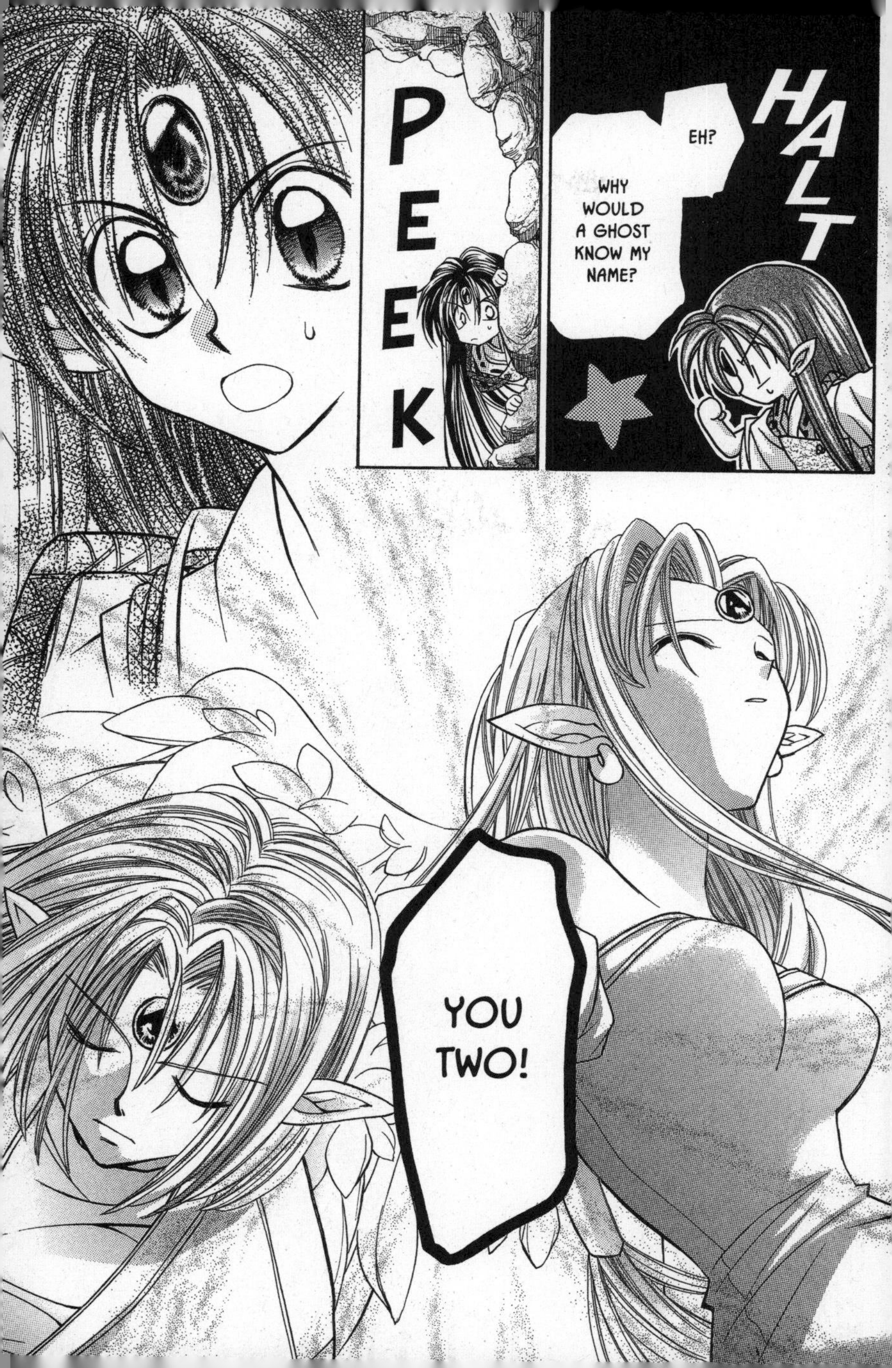
HALT
EH?
WHY WOULD A GHOST KNOW MY NAME?
PEEK
YOU TWO!

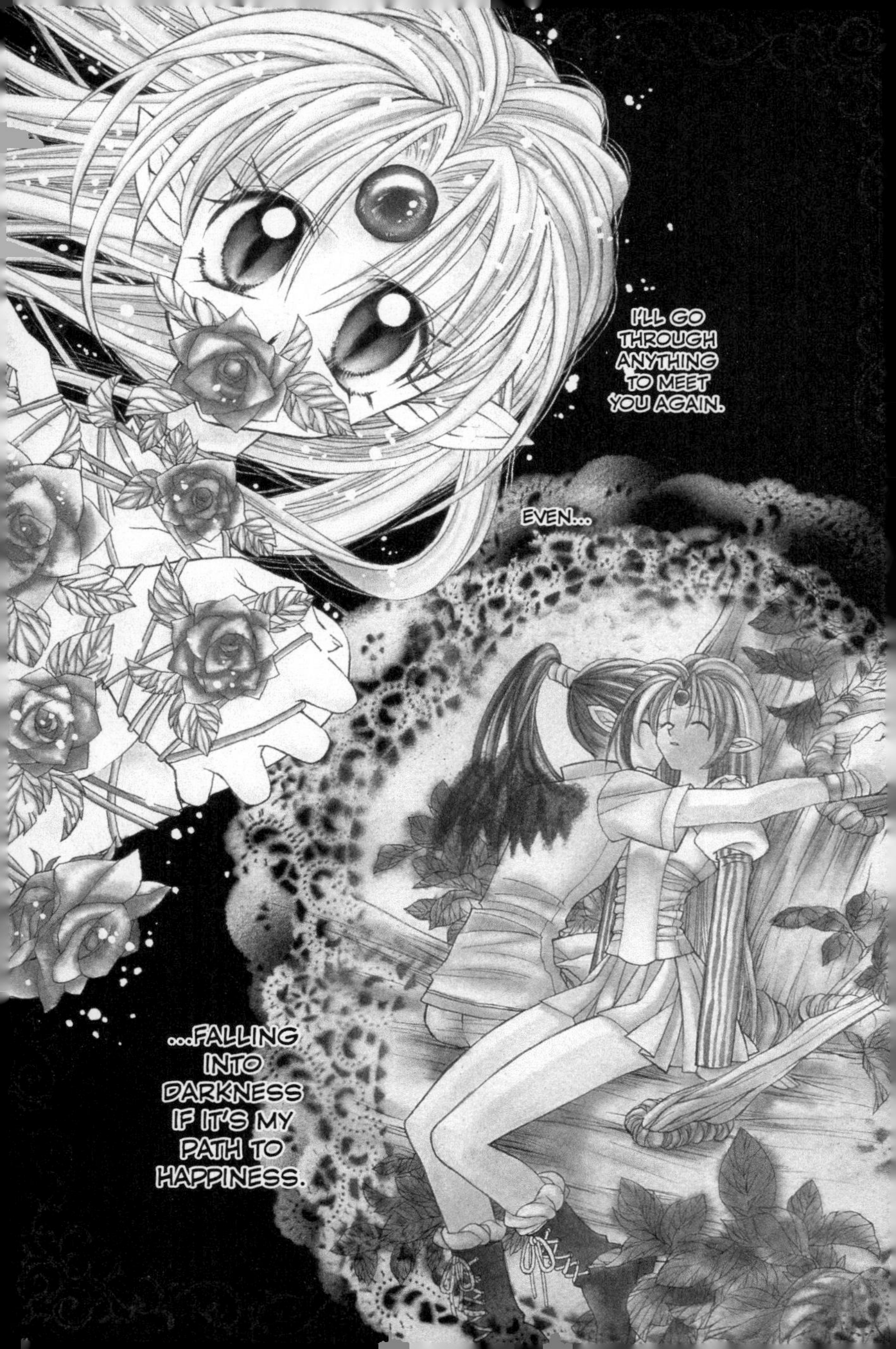
I'LL GO THROUGH ANYTHING TO MEET YOU AGAIN.
EVEN...
...FALLING INTO DARKNESS IF IT'S MY PATH TO HAPPINESS.

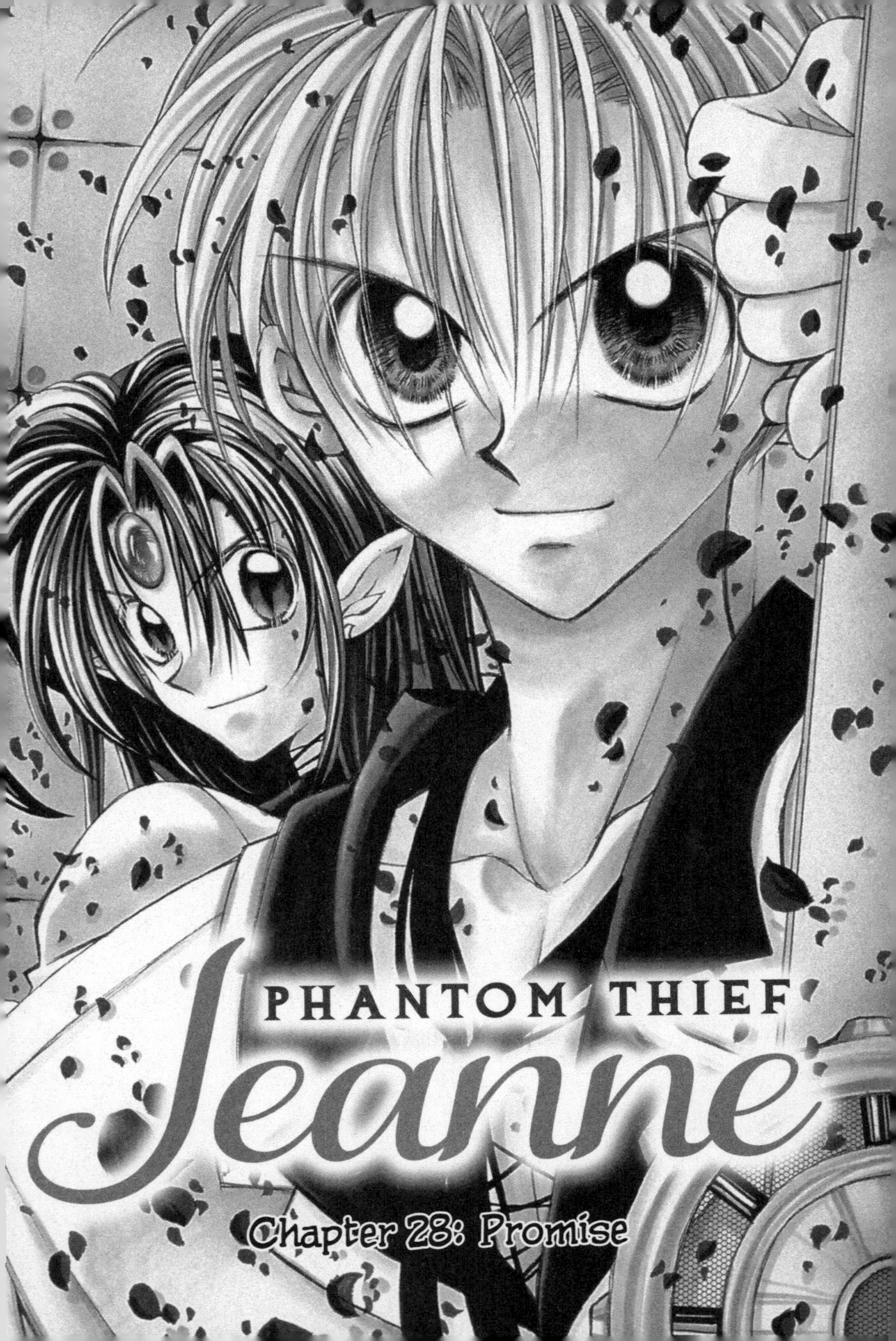
PHANTOM THIEF
Jeanne
Chapter 28: Promise

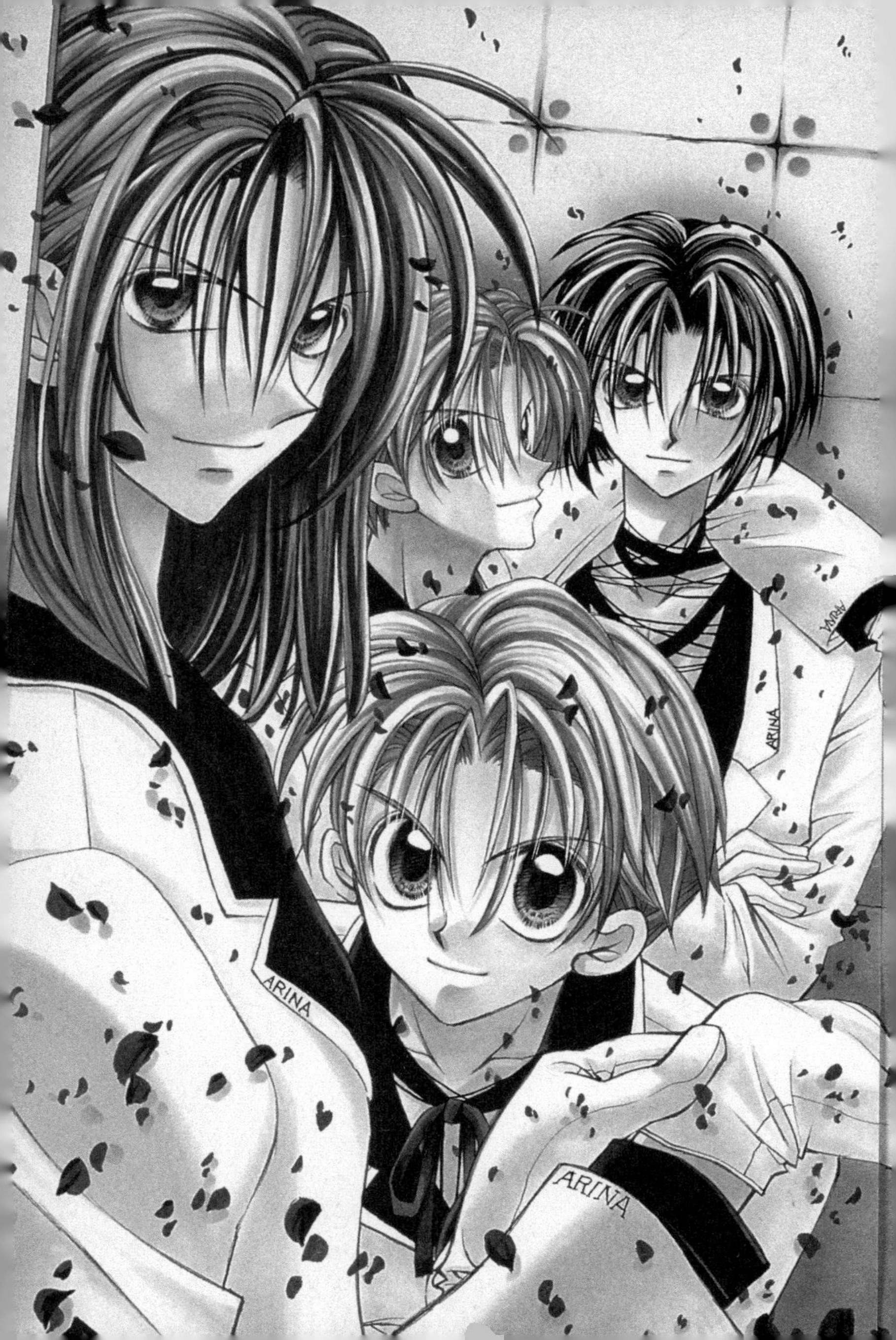
ARINA
ARINA
ARINA
ARINA

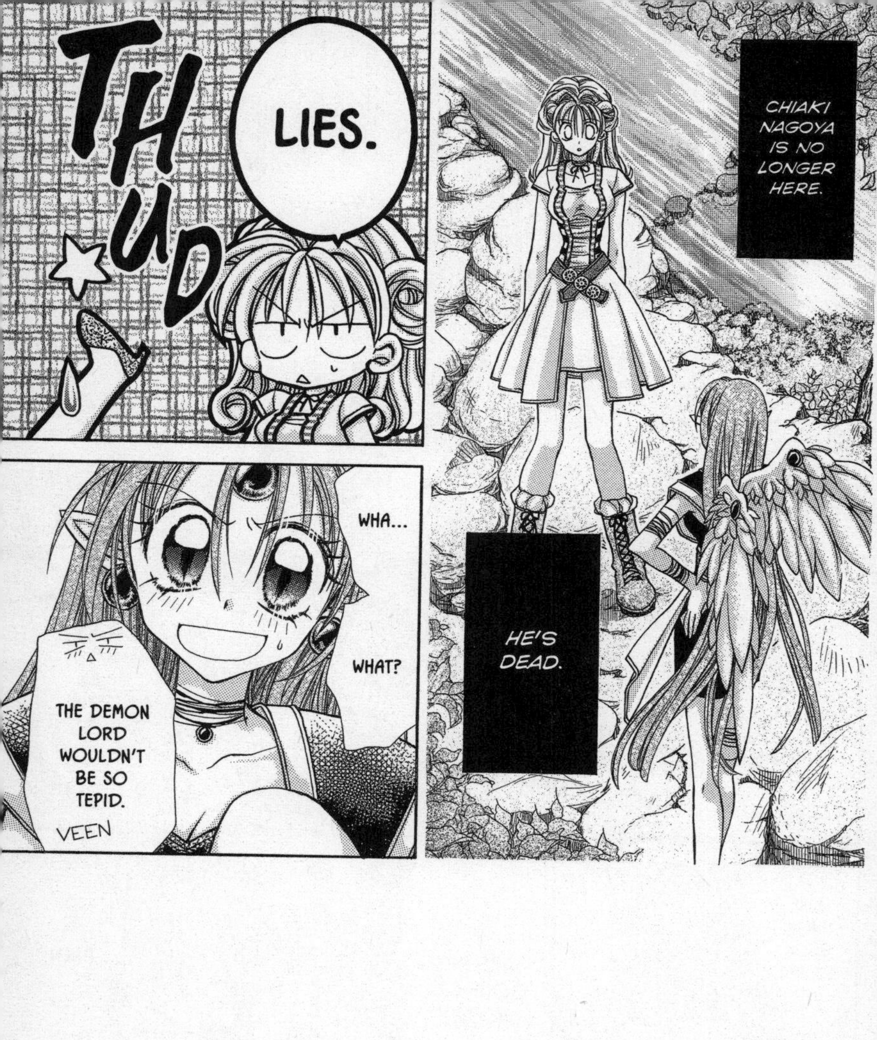
CHIAKI NAGOYA IS NO LONGER HERE.
HE'S DEAD.
THUD
LIES.
WHA...
WHAT?
THE DEMON LORD WOULDN'T BE SO TEPID.
VEEN

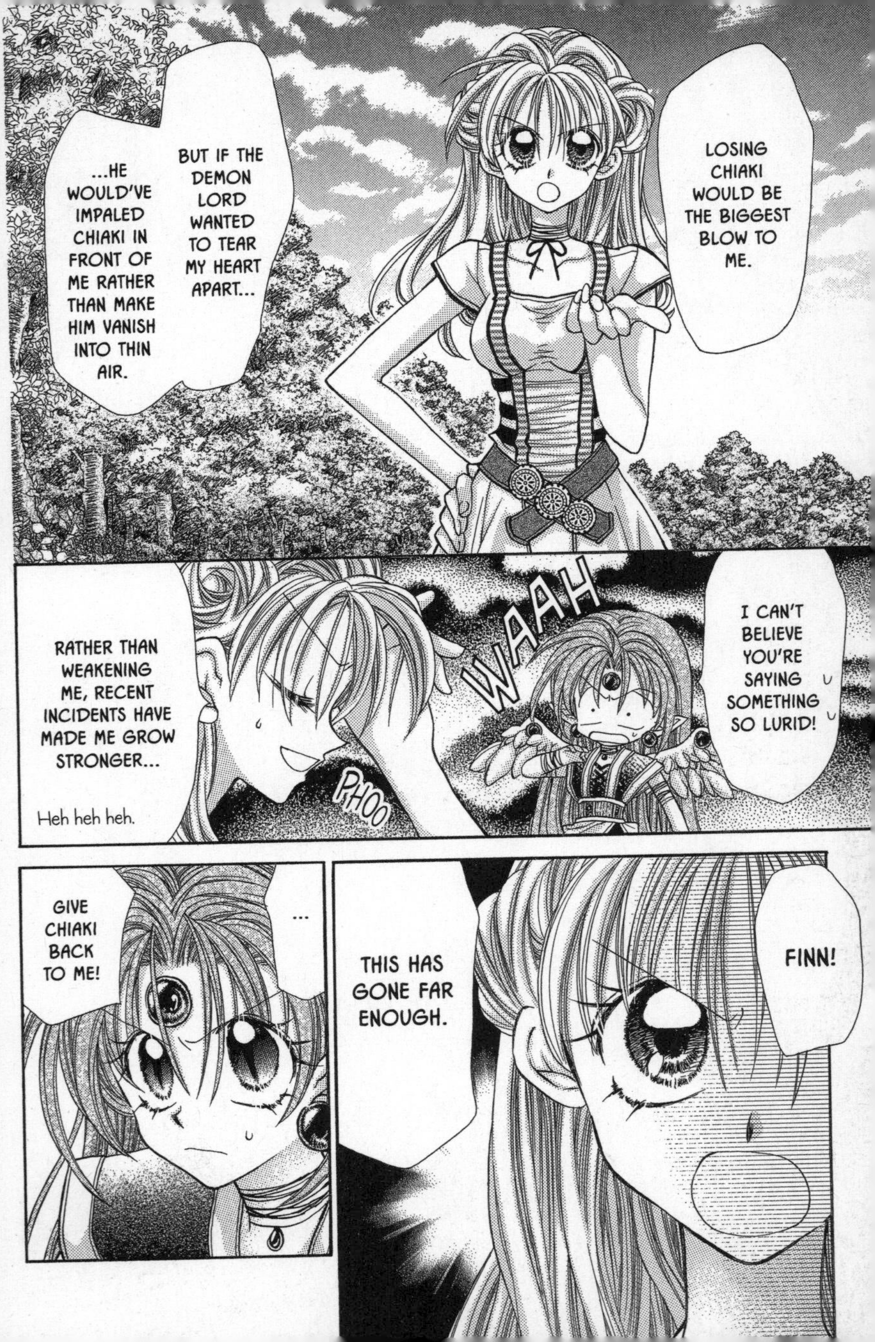
LOSING CHIAKI WOULD BE THE BIGGEST BLOW TO ME.
BUT IF THE DEMON LORD WANTED TO TEAR MY HEART APART...
...HE WOULD'VE IMPALED CHIAKI IN FRONT OF ME RATHER THAN MAKE HIM VANISH INTO THIN AIR.
I CAN'T BELIEVE YOU'RE SAYING SOMETHING SO LURID!
WAAH
PHOO
RATHER THAN WEAKENING ME, RECENT INCIDENTS HAVE MADE ME GROW STRONGER...
Heh heh heh.
FINN!
THIS HAS GONE FAR ENOUGH.
...
GIVE CHIAKI BACK TO ME!

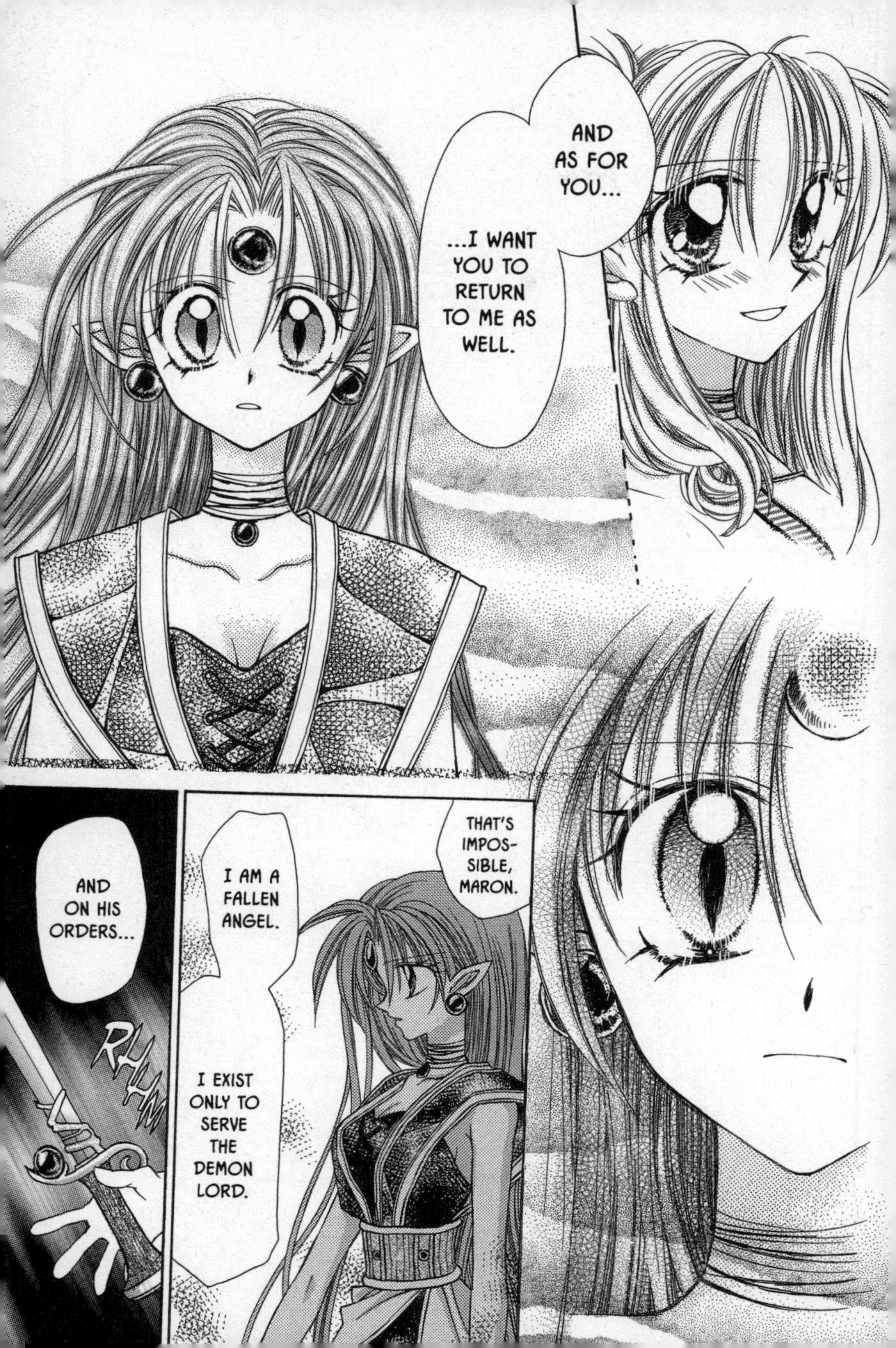
AND AS FOR YOU...
...I WANT YOU TO RETURN TO ME AS WELL.
THAT'S IMPOSSIBLE, MARON.
I AM A FALLEN ANGEL.
I EXIST ONLY TO SERVE THE DEMON LORD.
AND ON HIS ORDERS...
RHHM

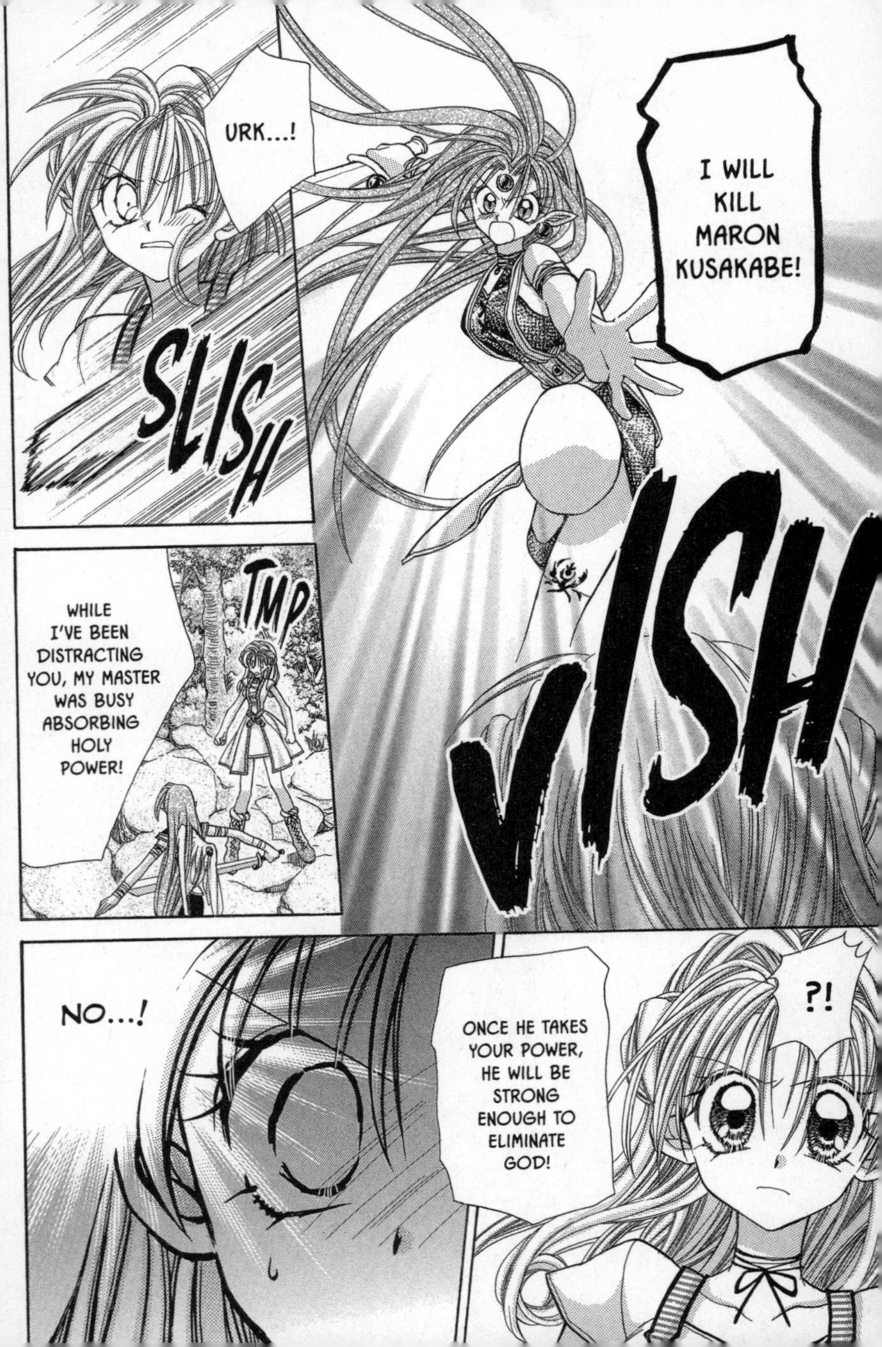
I WILL KILL MARON KUSAKABE!
VISH
URK...!
SLISH
TMP
WHILE I'VE BEEN DISTRACTING YOU, MY MASTER WAS BUSY ABSORBING HOLY POWER!
?!
ONCE HE TAKES YOUR POWER, HE WILL BE STRONG ENOUGH TO ELIMINATE GOD!
NO...!

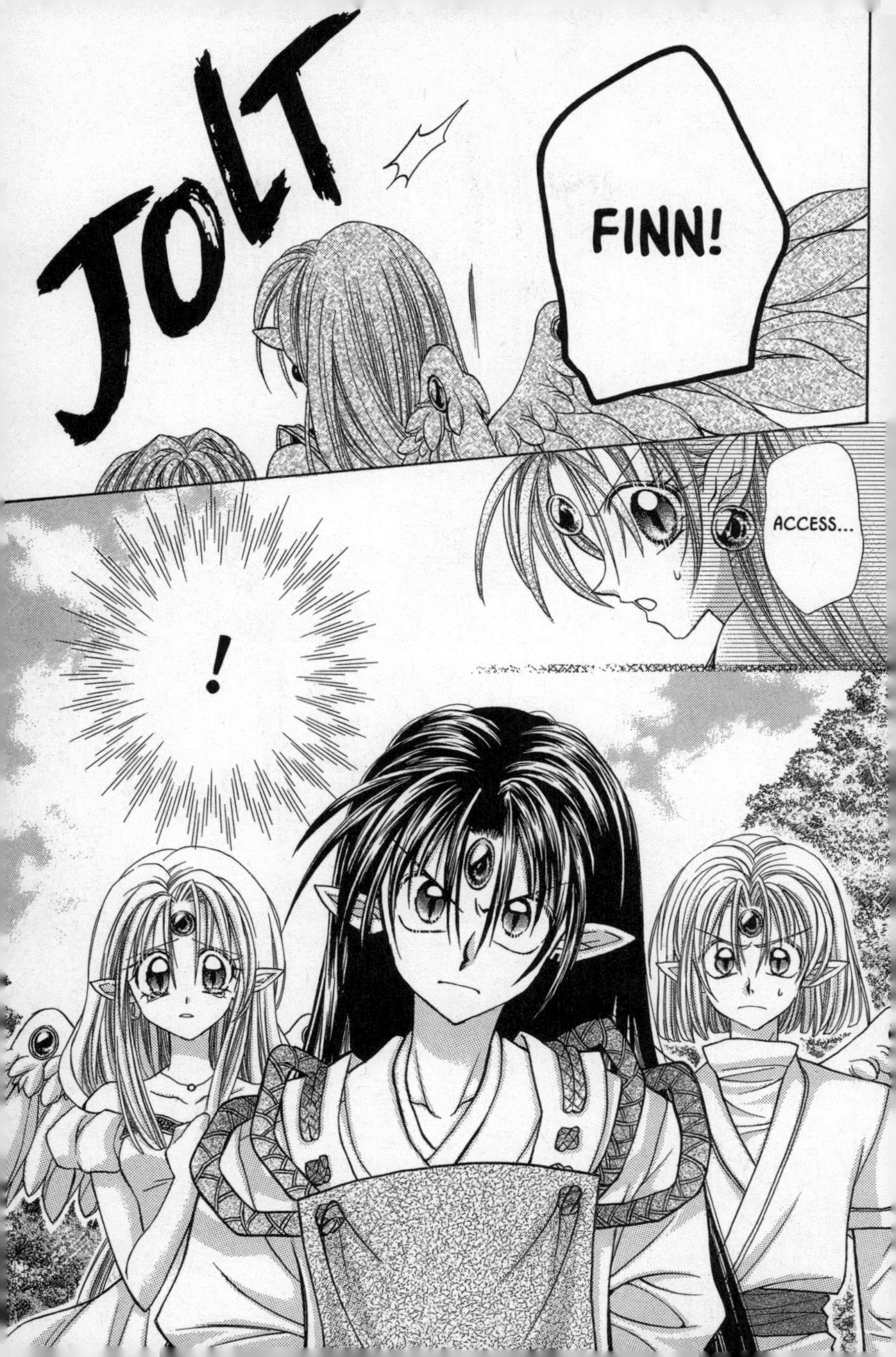
FINN!
JOLT
ACCESS...
!

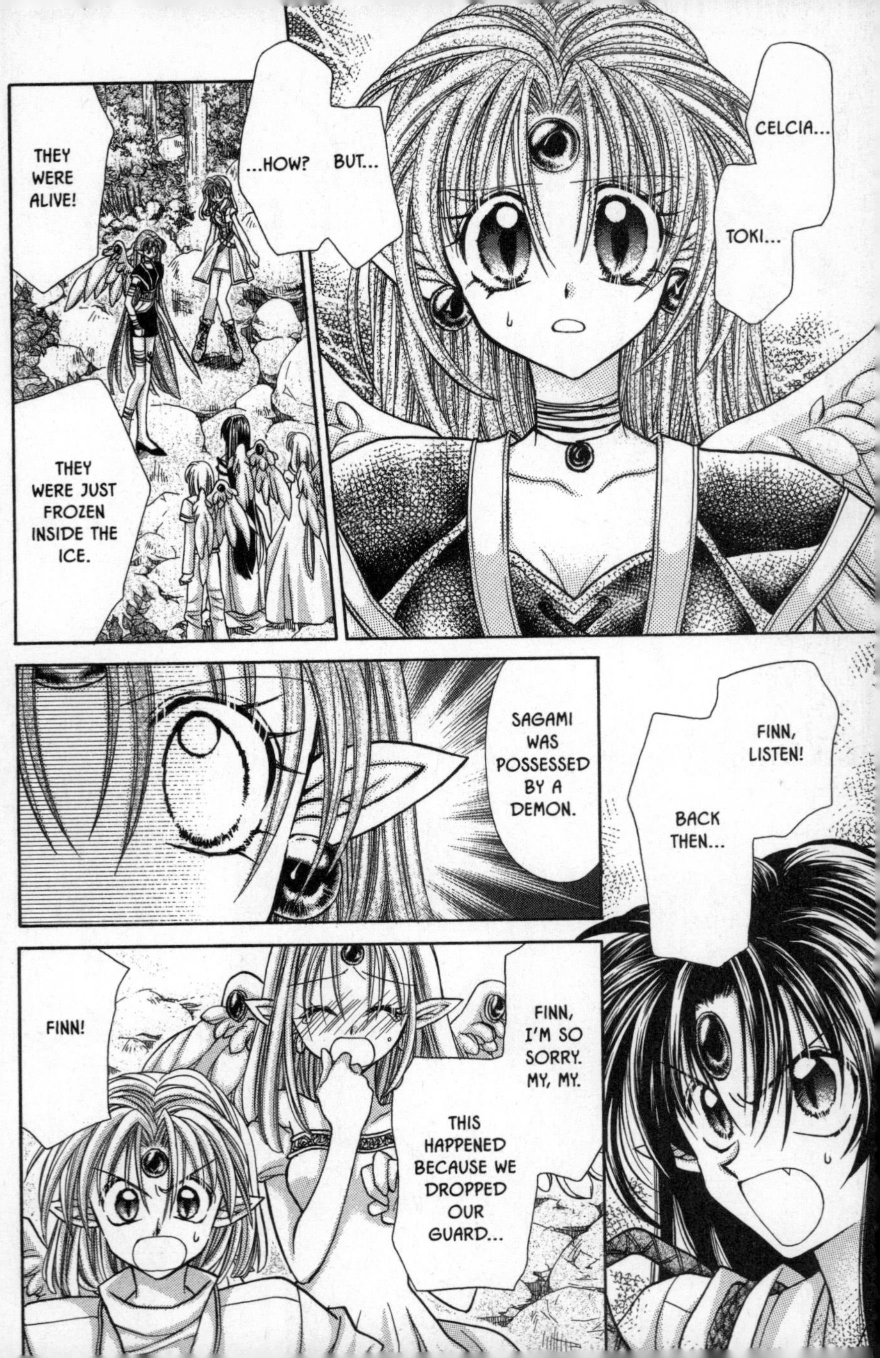
CELCIA...
TOKI...
BUT...
...HOW?
THEY WERE ALIVE!
THEY WERE JUST FROZEN INSIDE THE ICE.
FINN, LISTEN!
BACK THEN...
SAGAMI WAS POSSESSED BY A DEMON.
FINN, I'M SO SORRY. MY, MY.
THIS HAPPENED BECAUSE WE DROPPED OUR GUARD...
FINN!

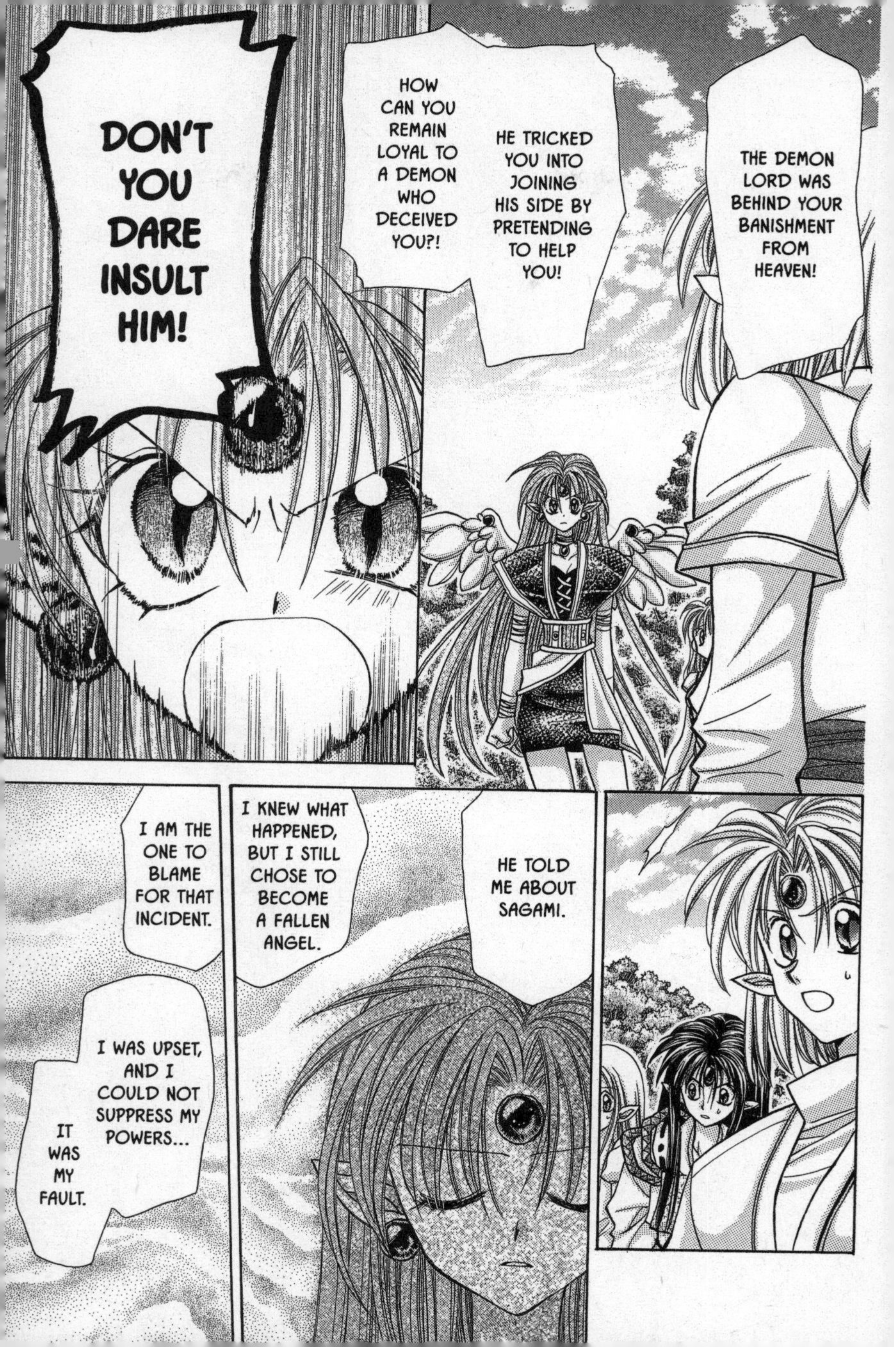
THE DEMON LORD WAS BEHIND YOUR BANISHMENT FROM HEAVEN!
HE TRICKED YOU INTO JOINING HIS SIDE BY PRETENDING TO HELP YOU!
HOW CAN YOU REMAIN LOYAL TO A DEMON WHO DECEIVED YOU?!
DON'T YOU DARE INSULT HIM!
HE TOLD ME ABOUT SAGAMI.
I KNEW WHAT HAPPENED, BUT I STILL CHOSE TO BECOME A FALLEN ANGEL.
I AM THE ONE TO BLAME FOR THAT INCIDENT.
I WAS UPSET, AND I COULD NOT SUPPRESS MY POWERS...
IT WAS MY FAULT.

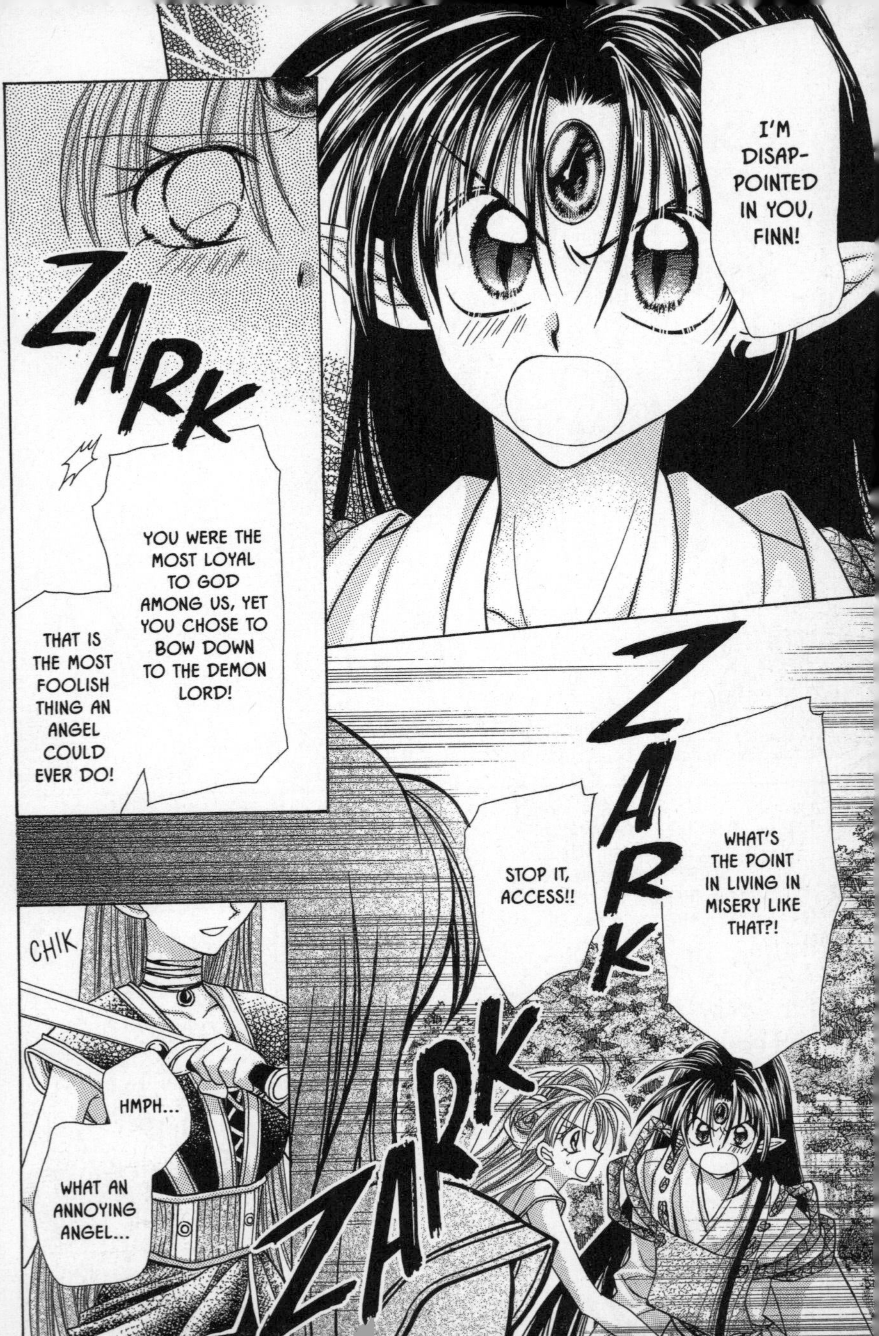

I'M DISAP-POINTED IN YOU, FINN!
ZARK
YOU WERE THE MOST LOYAL TO GOD AMONG US, YET YOU CHOSE TO BOW DOWN TO THE DEMON LORD!
THAT IS THE MOST FOOLISH THING AN ANGEL COULD EVER DO!
WHAT'S THE POINT IN LIVING IN MISERY LIKE THAT?!
ZARK
STOP IT, ACCESS!!
ZARK
CHIK
HMPH...
WHAT AN ANNOYING ANGEL...

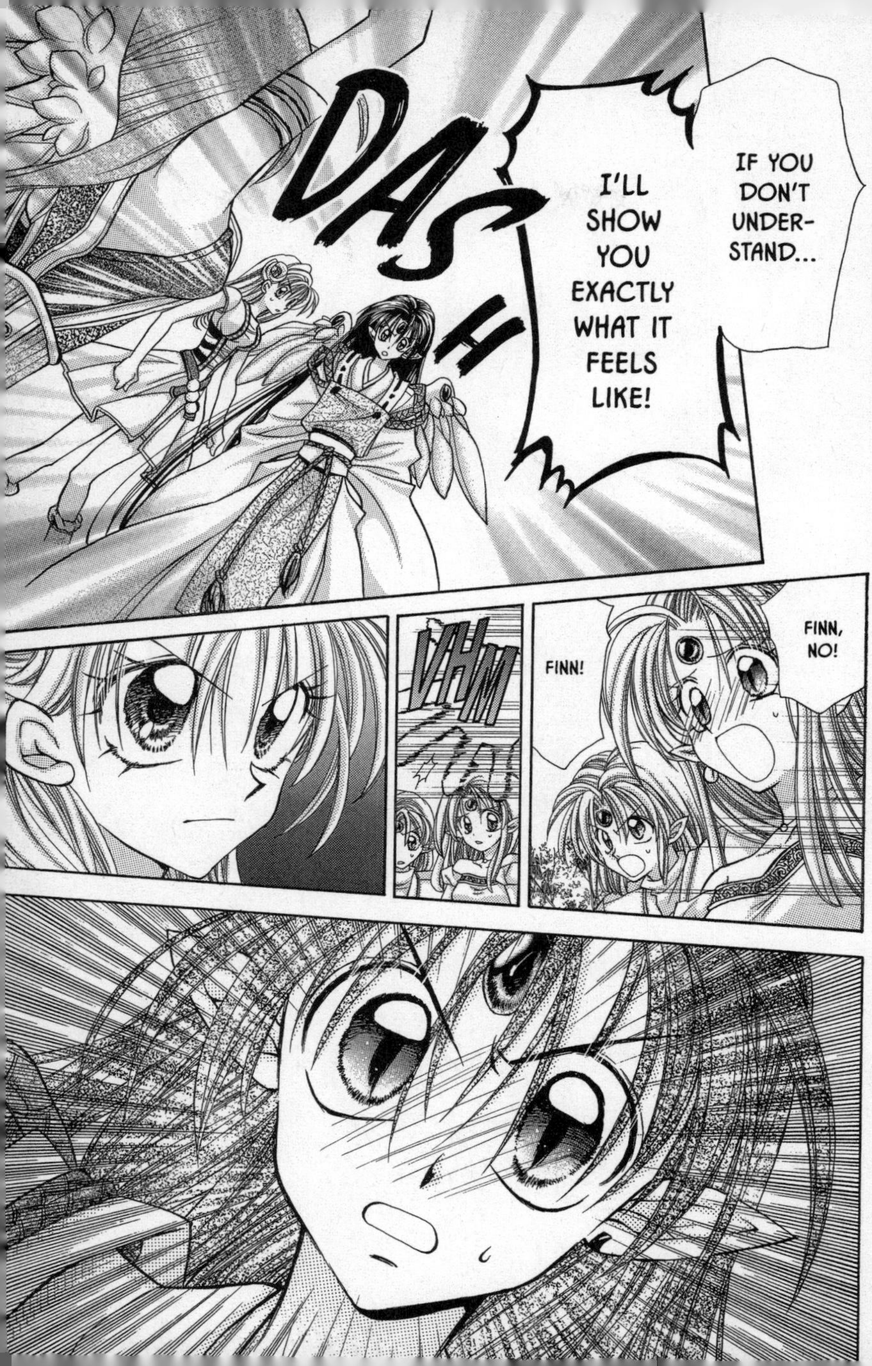
IF YOU DON'T UNDER-STAND...
I'LL SHOW YOU EXACTLY WHAT IT FEELS LIKE!
DASH
FINN, NO!
FINN!
VHM

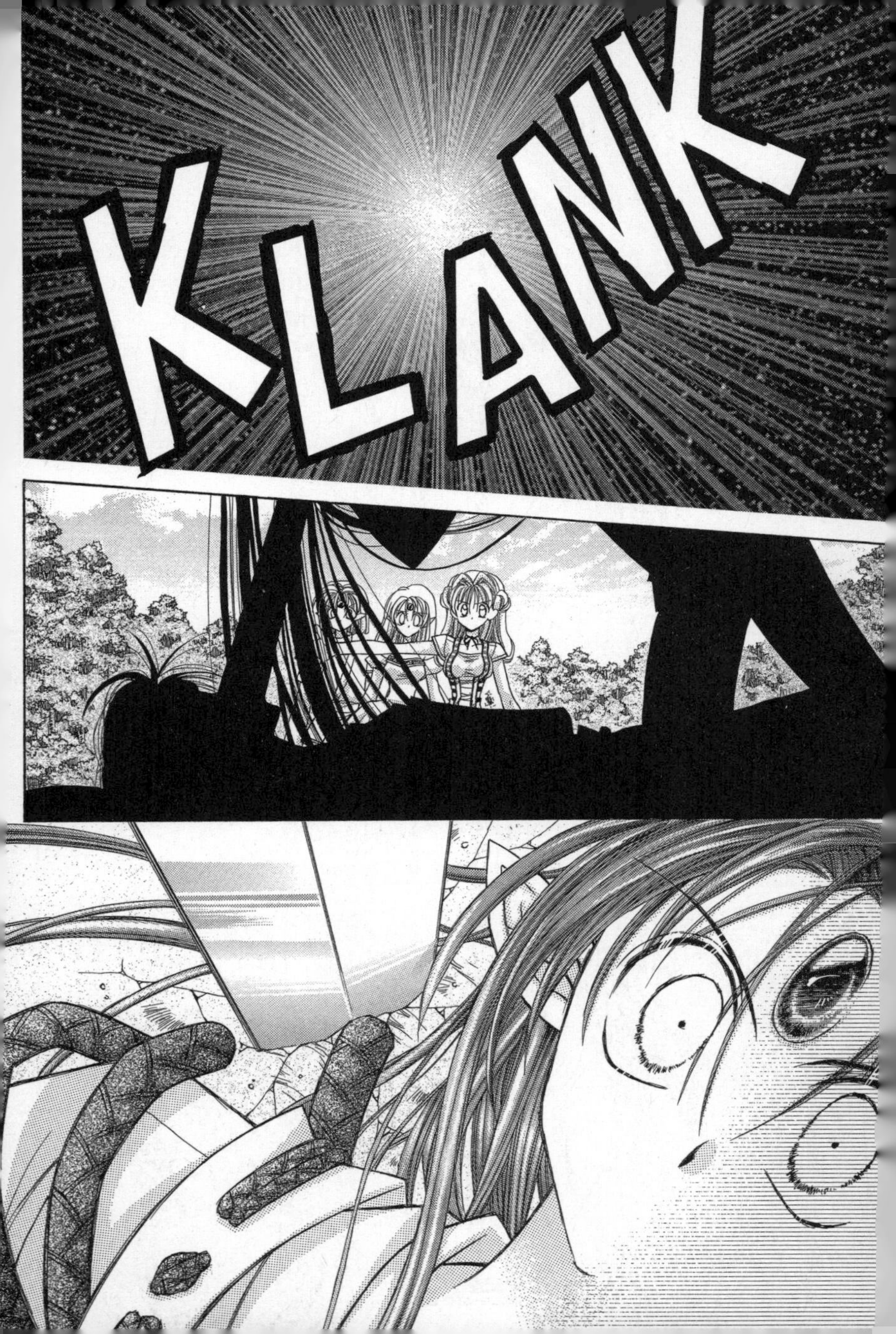
KLANK

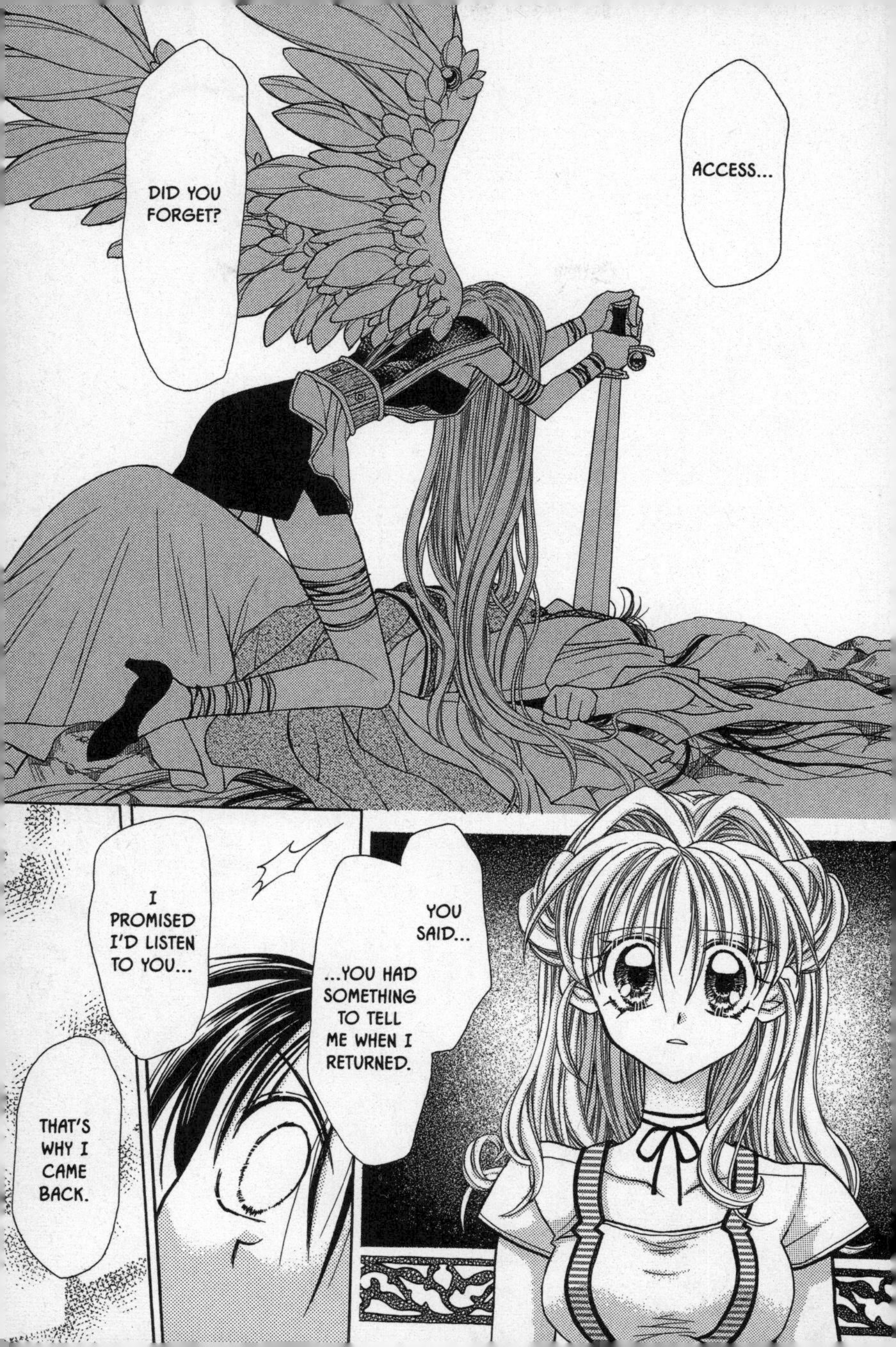
ACCESS...
DID YOU FORGET?
YOU SAID...
...YOU HAD SOMETHING TO TELL ME WHEN I RETURNED.
I PROMISED I'D LISTEN TO YOU...
THAT'S WHY I CAME BACK.

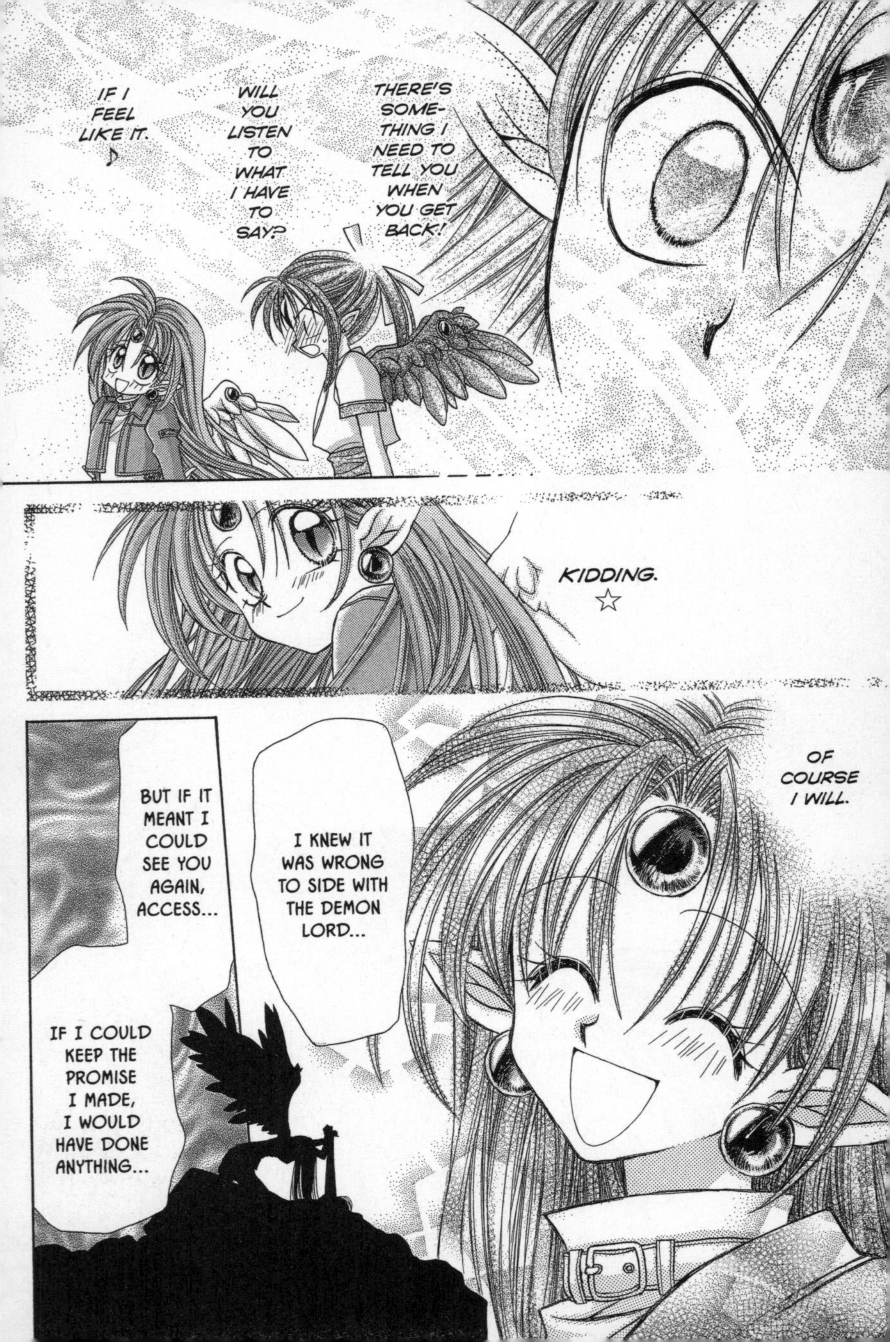
THERE'S SOMETHING I NEED TO TELL YOU WHEN YOU GET BACK!
WILL YOU LISTEN TO WHAT I HAVE TO SAY?
IF I FEEL LIKE IT. ♪
KIDDING. ☆
OF COURSE I WILL.
I KNEW IT WAS WRONG TO SIDE WITH THE DEMON LORD...
BUT IF IT MEANT I COULD SEE YOU AGAIN, ACCESS...
IF I COULD KEEP THE PROMISE I MADE, I WOULD HAVE DONE ANYTHING...

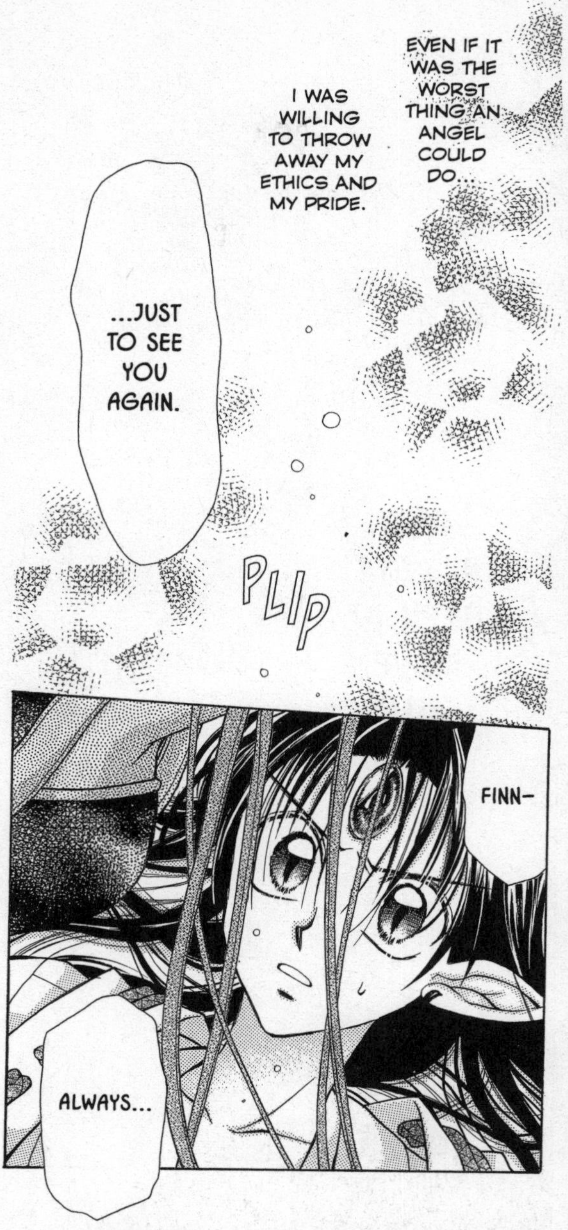
EVEN IF IT WAS THE WORST THING AN ANGEL COULD DO...
I WAS WILLING TO THROW AWAY MY ETHICS AND MY PRIDE.
...JUST TO SEE YOU AGAIN.
PLIP
FINN-
ALWAYS...

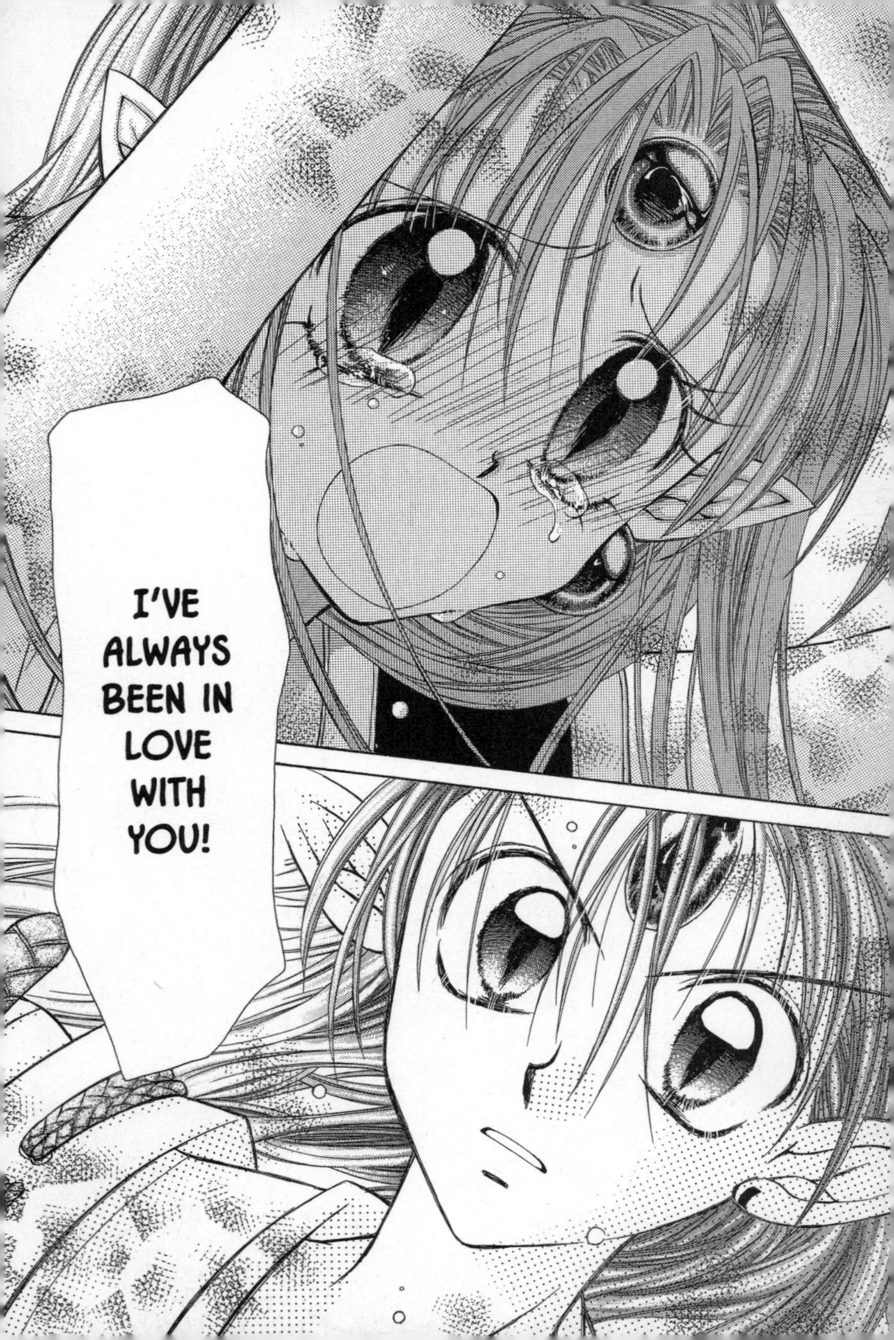
I'VE ALWAYS BEEN IN LOVE WITH YOU!

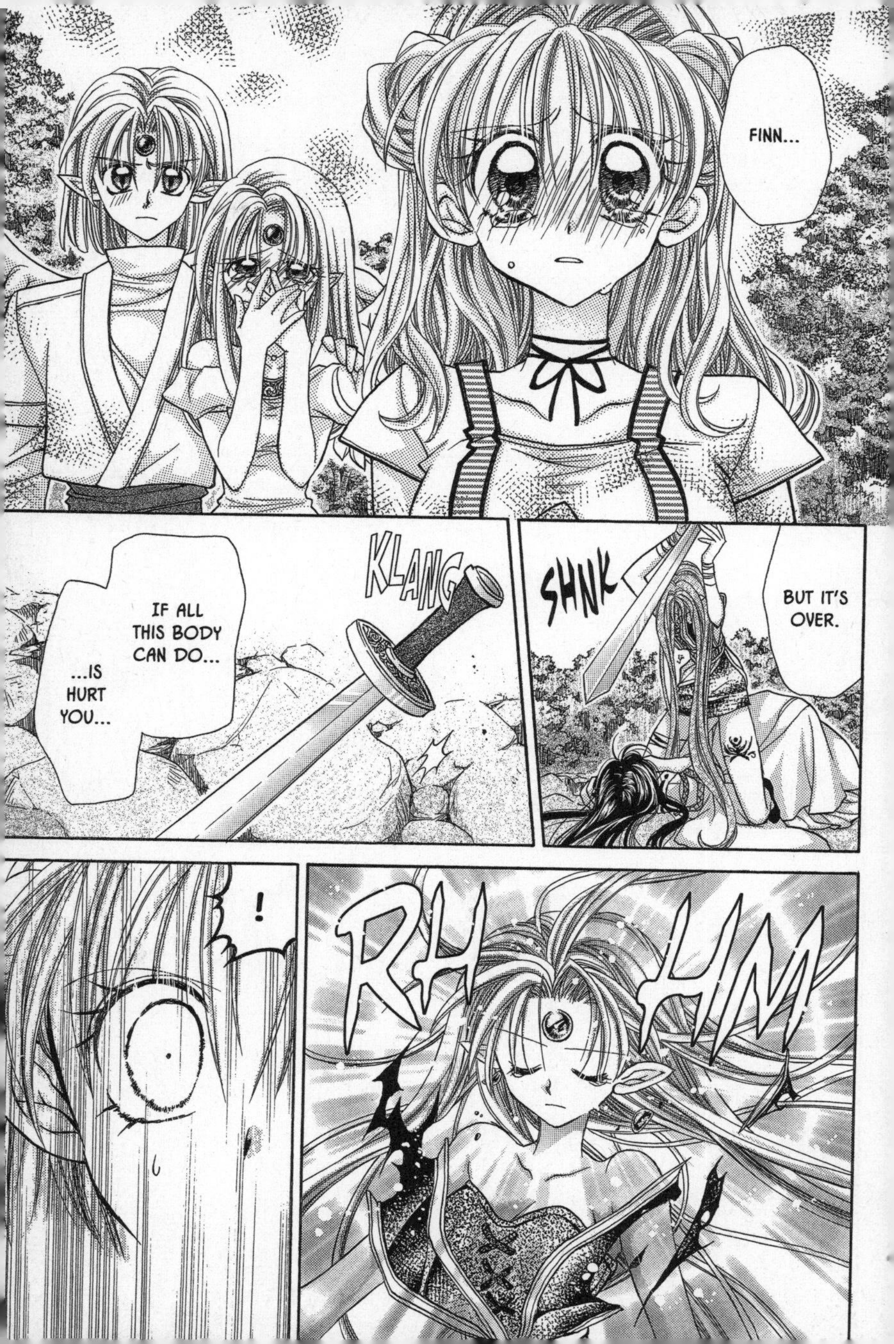
FINN...
SHNK
BUT IT'S OVER.
KLANG
IF ALL THIS BODY CAN DO...
...IS HURT YOU...
RHHM
!

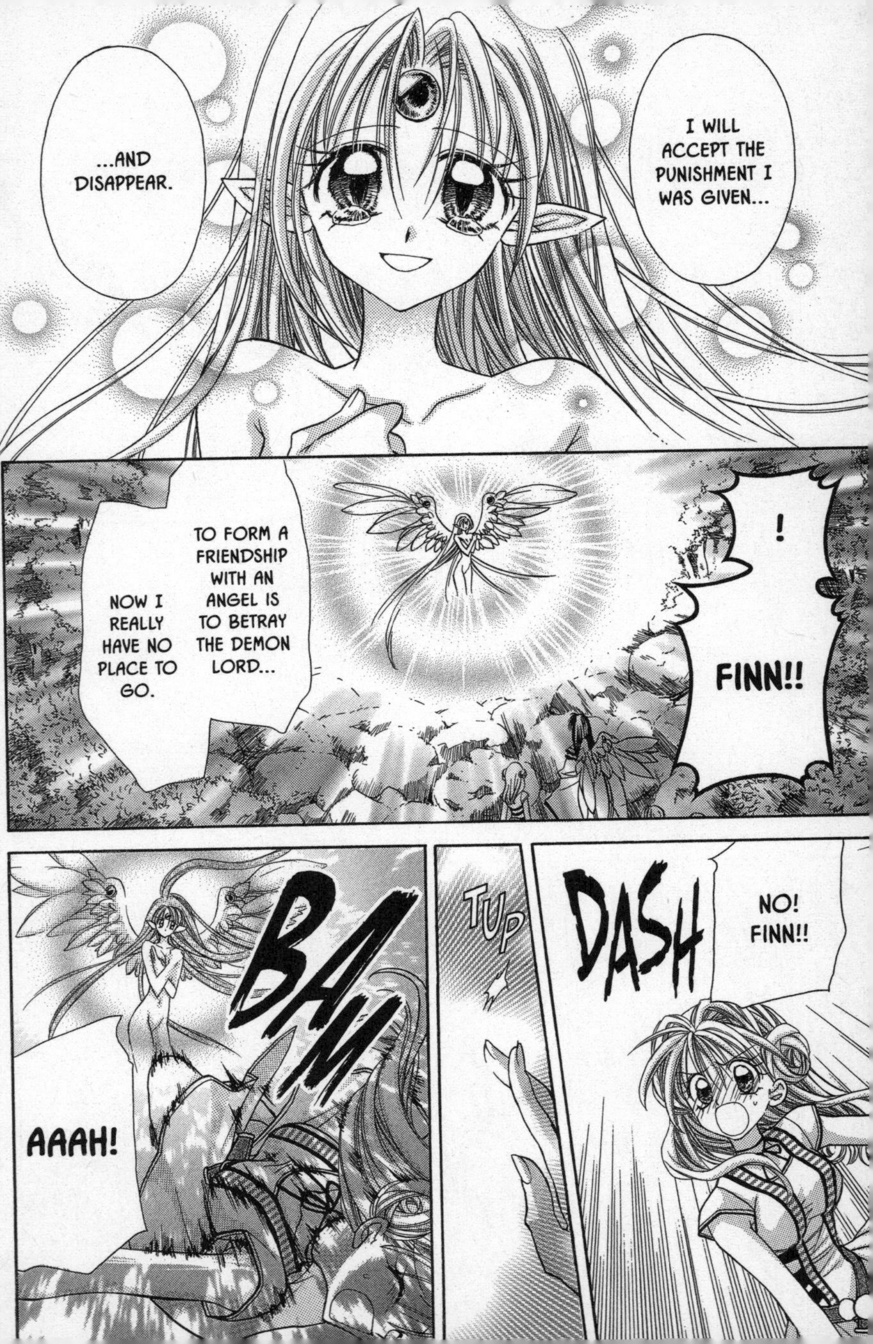
I WILL ACCEPT THE PUNISHMENT I WAS GIVEN...
...AND DISAPPEAR.
!
FINN!!
TO FORM A FRIENDSHIP WITH AN ANGEL IS TO BETRAY THE DEMON LORD...
NOW I REALLY HAVE NO PLACE TO GO.
NO! FINN!!
DASH
TUP
BAM
AAAH!

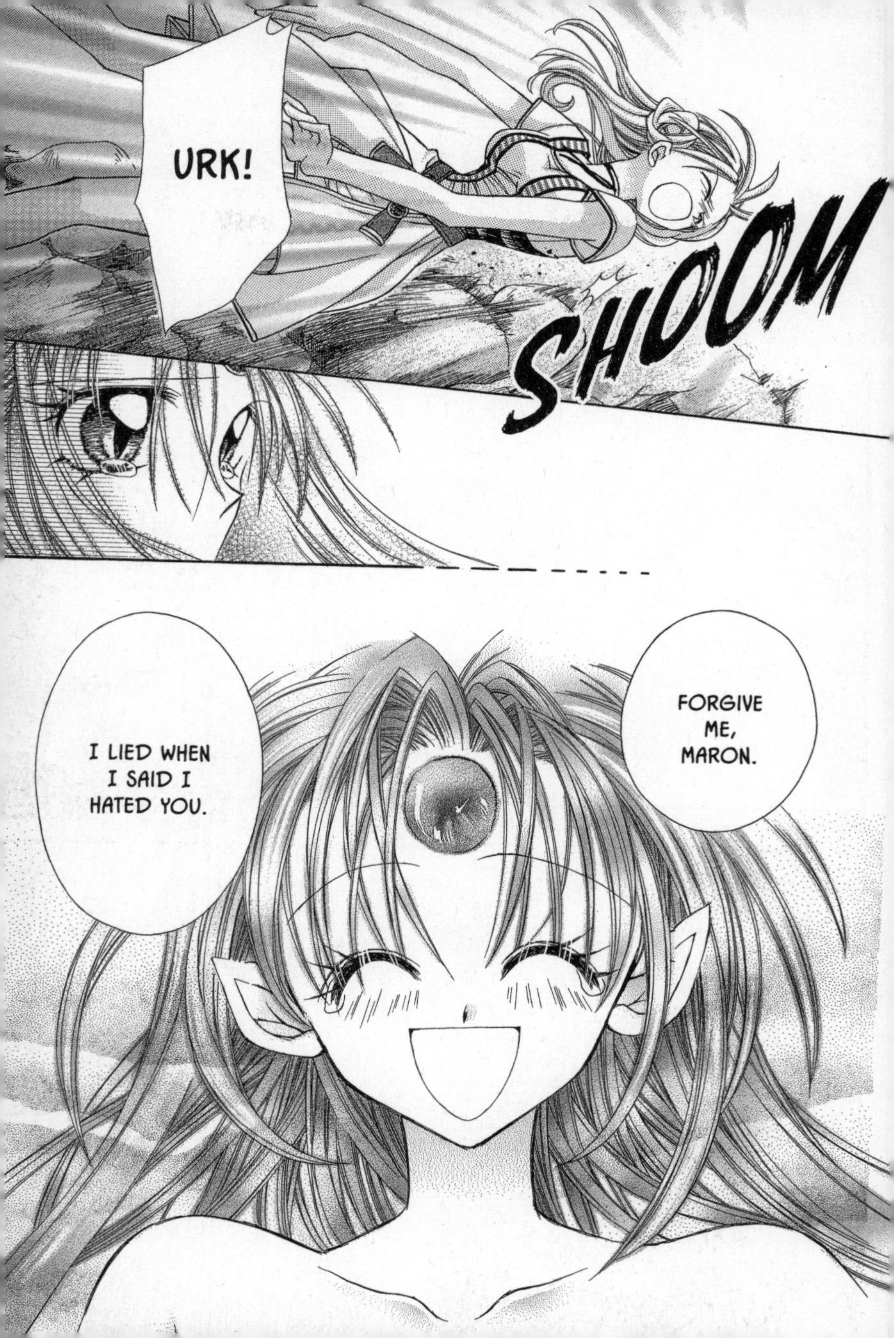
URK!
SHOOM
FORGIVE ME, MARON.
I LIED WHEN I SAID I HATED YOU.

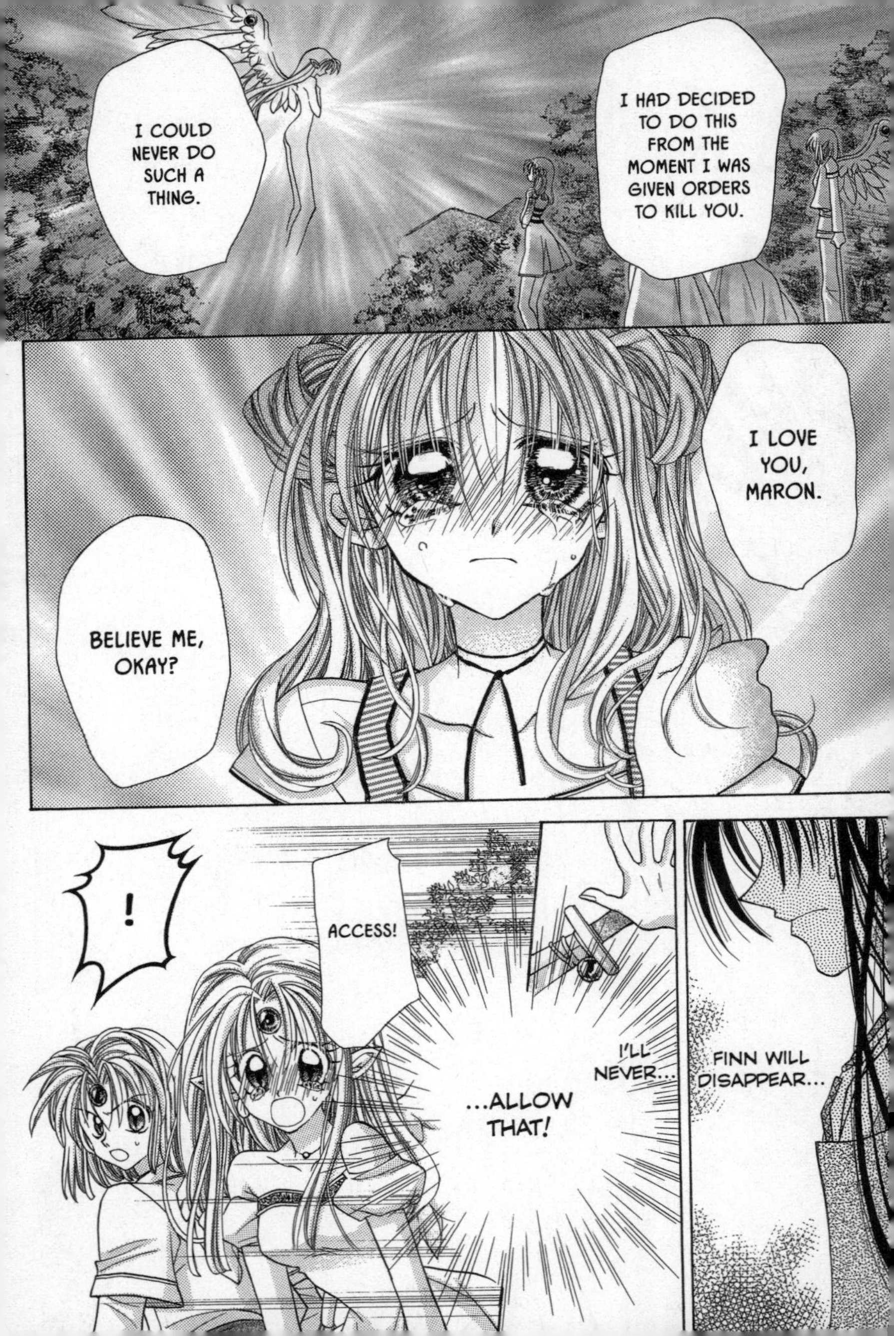
I HAD DECIDED TO DO THIS FROM THE MOMENT I WAS GIVEN ORDERS TO KILL YOU.
I COULD NEVER DO SUCH A THING.
I LOVE YOU, MARON.
BELIEVE ME, OKAY?
FINN WILL DISAPPEAR...
ACCESS!
!
I'LL NEVER...
...ALLOW THAT!

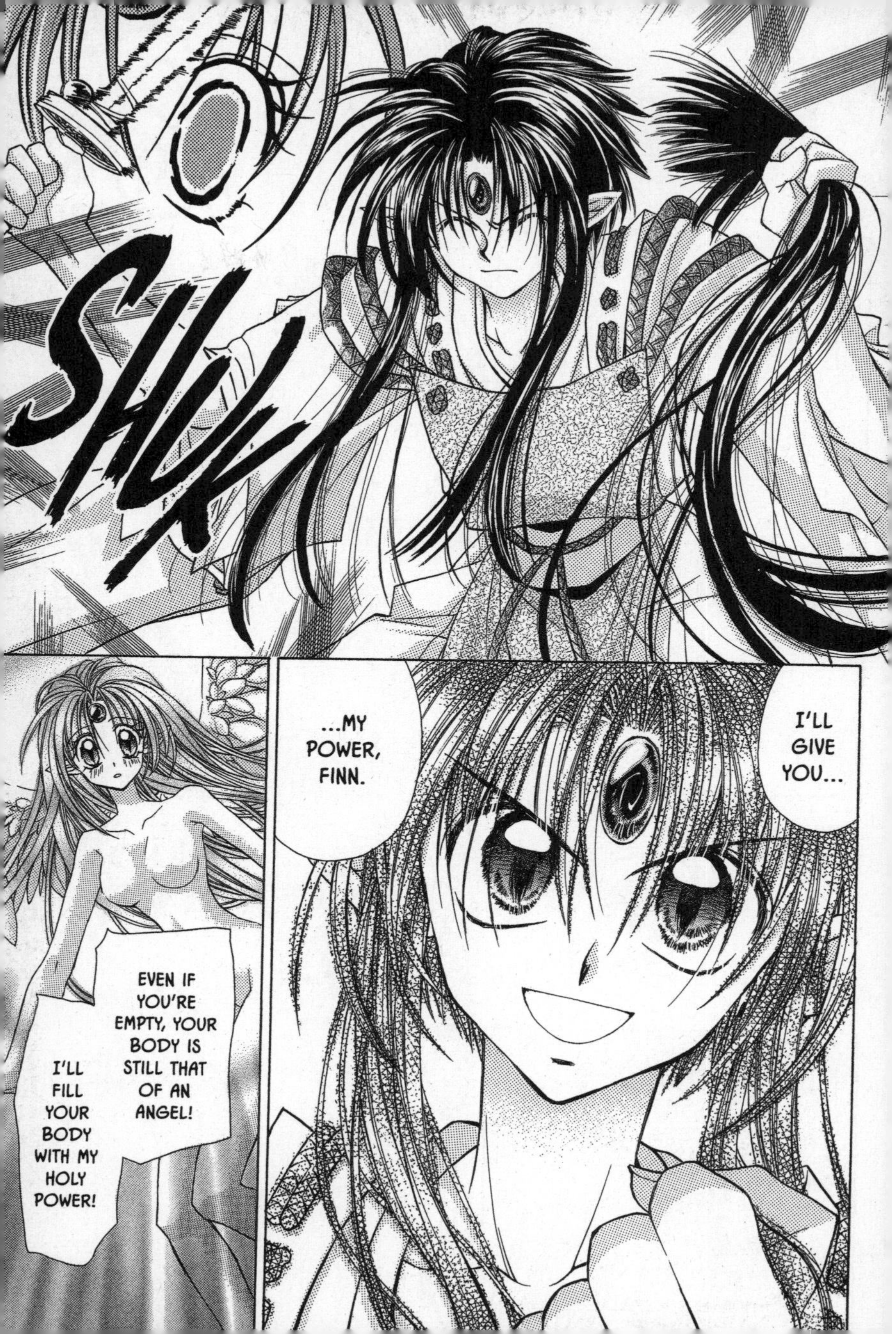
SHUK
I'LL GIVE YOU...
...MY POWER, FINN.
EVEN IF YOU'RE EMPTY, YOUR BODY IS STILL THAT OF AN ANGEL!
I'LL FILL YOUR BODY WITH MY HOLY POWER!

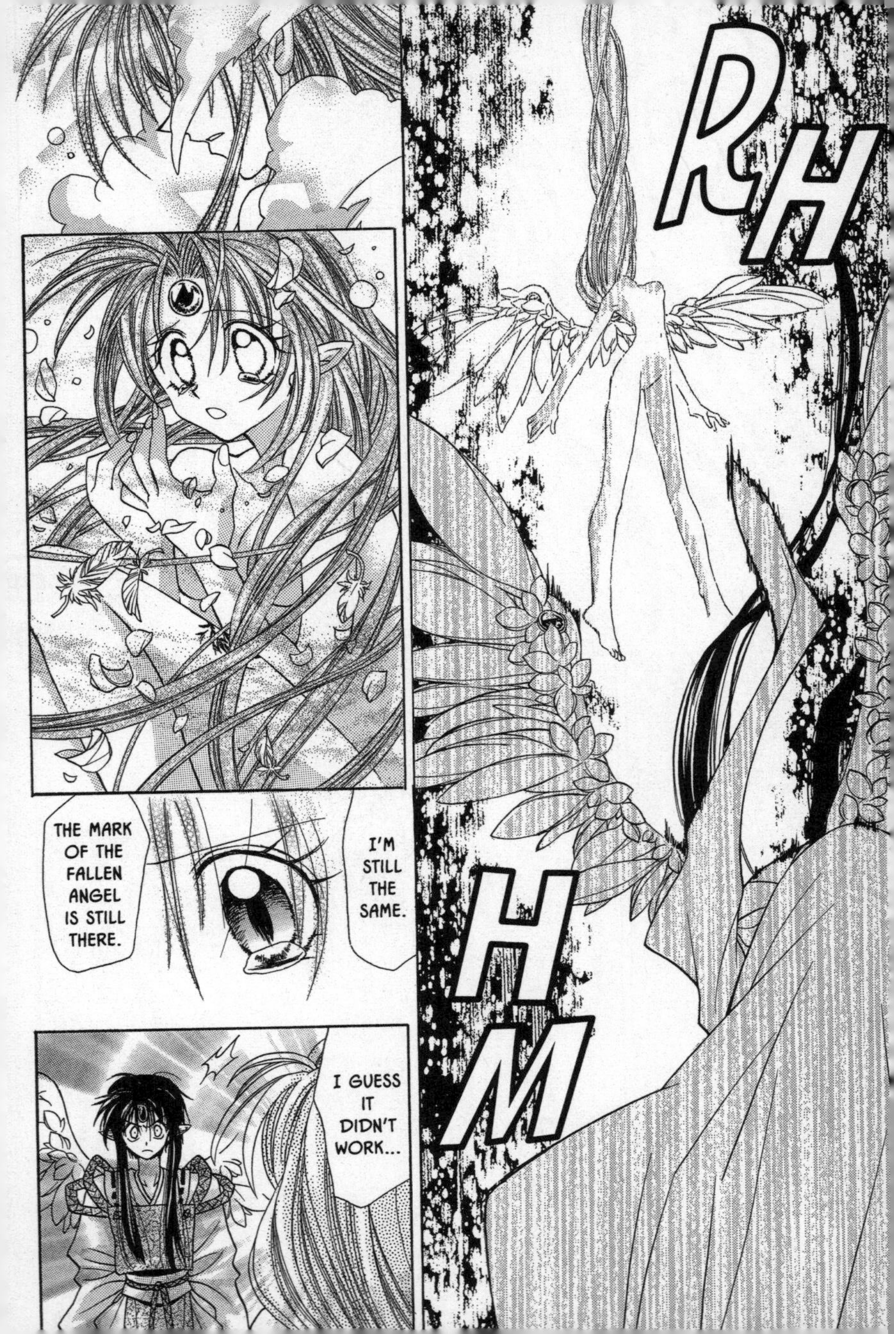
RH
HM
I'M STILL THE SAME.
THE MARK OF THE FALLEN ANGEL IS STILL THERE.
I GUESS IT DIDN'T WORK...

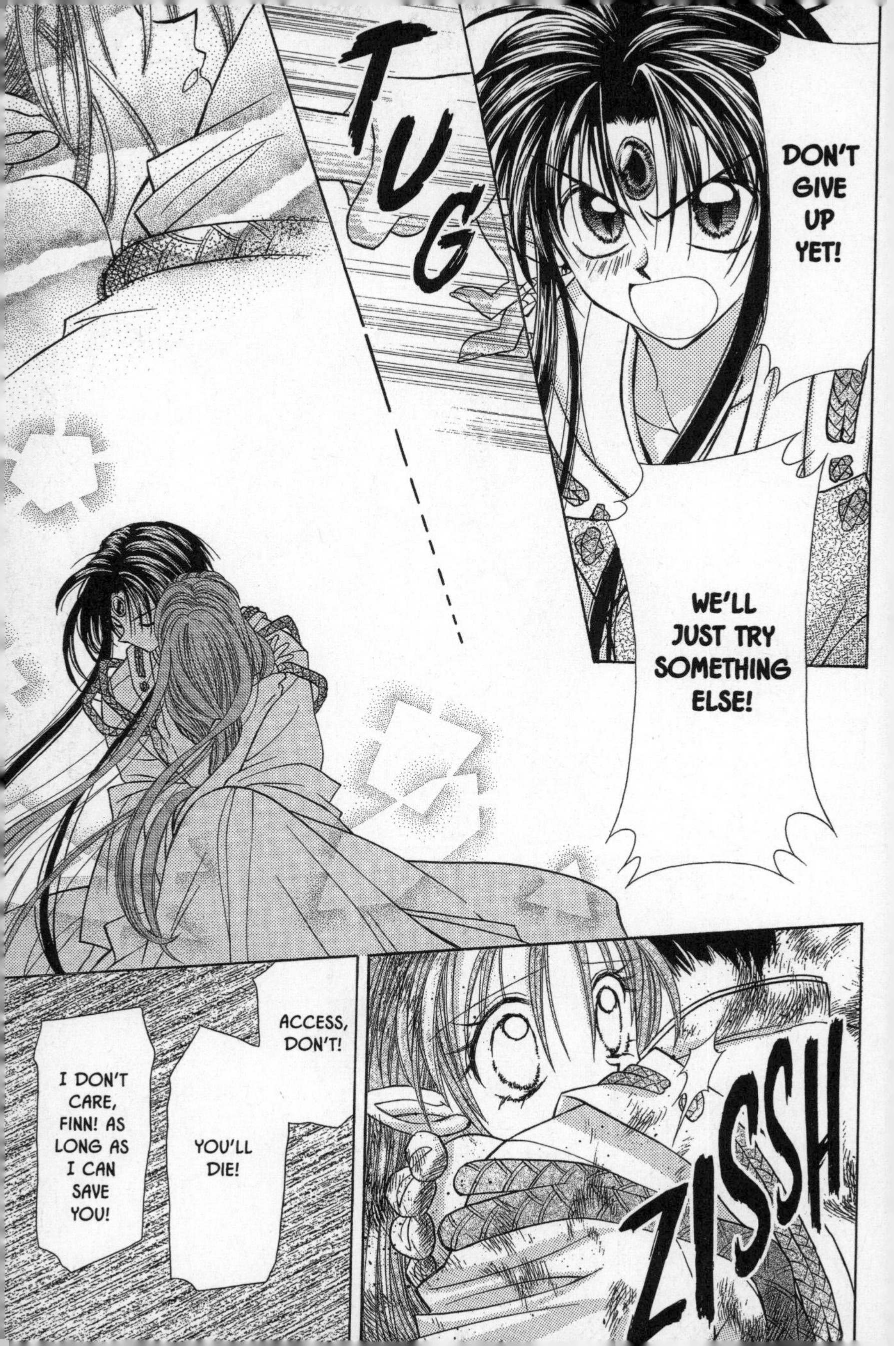
DON'T GIVE UP YET!
TUG
WE'LL JUST TRY SOMETHING ELSE!
ZISSH
ACCESS, DON'T!
YOU'LL DIE!
I DON'T CARE, FINN! AS LONG AS I CAN SAVE YOU!

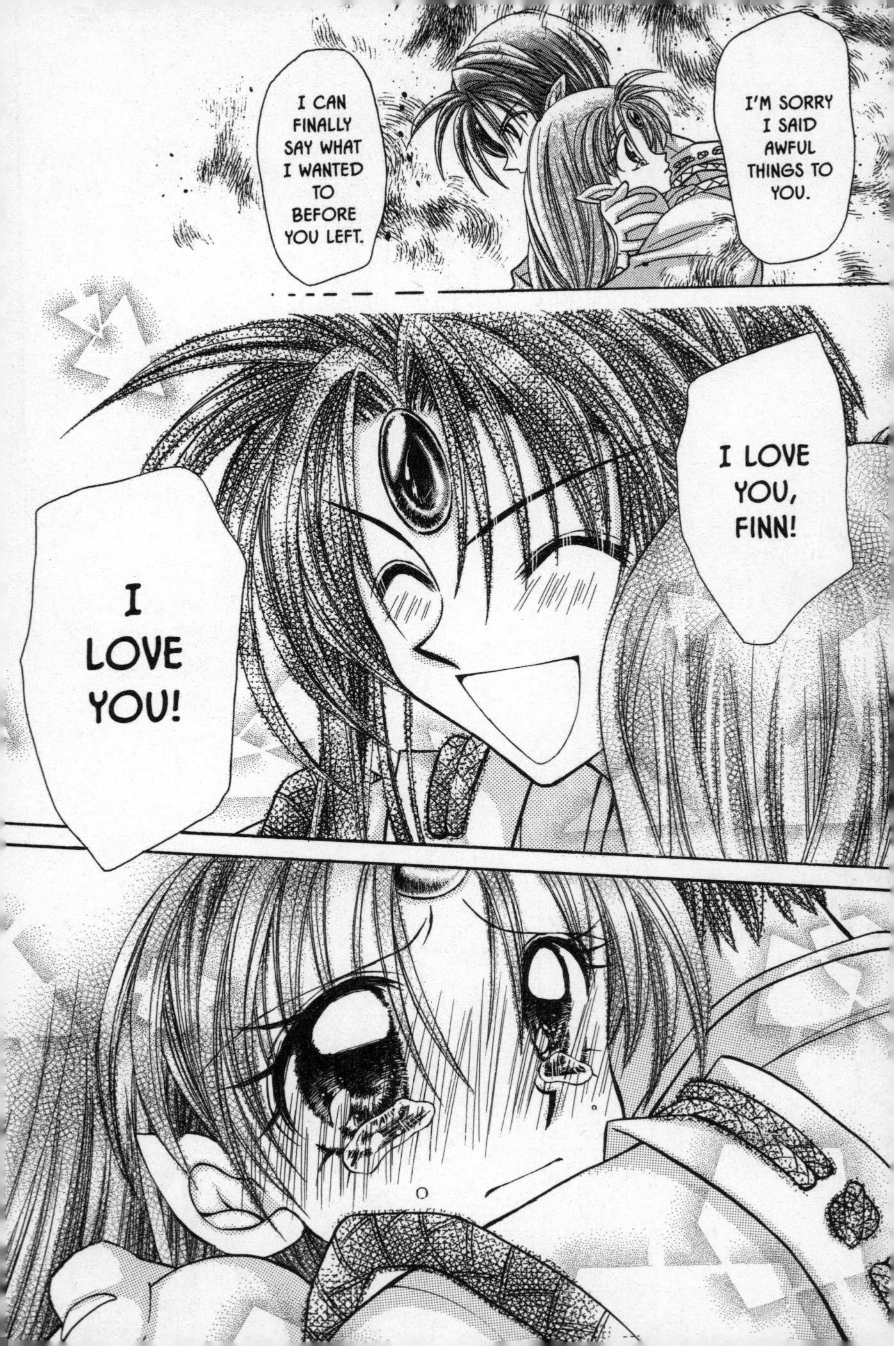
I'M SORRY I SAID AWFUL THINGS TO YOU.
I CAN FINALLY SAY WHAT I WANTED TO BEFORE YOU LEFT.
I LOVE YOU, FINN!
I LOVE YOU!

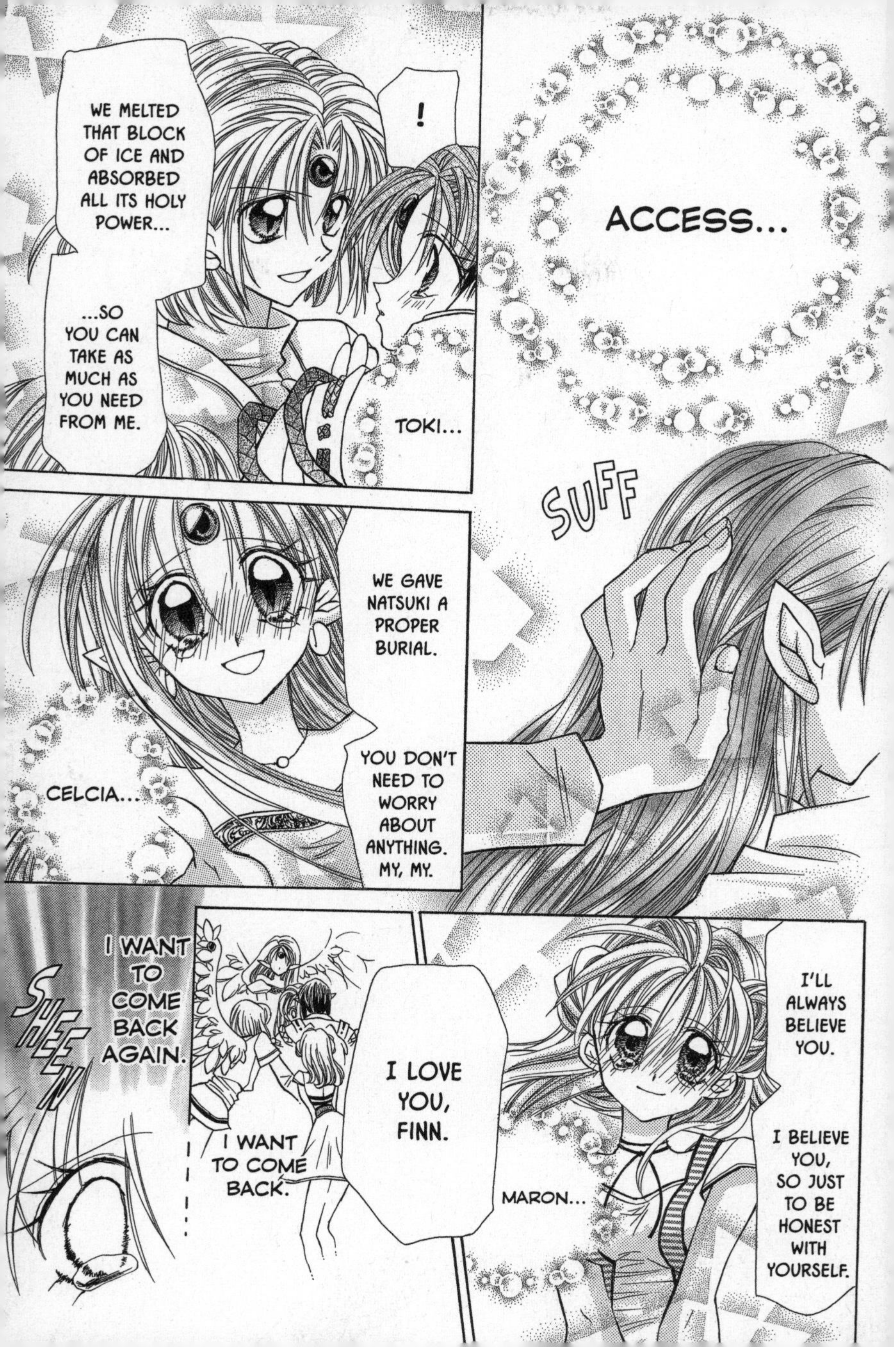

ACCESS...
SUFF
!
WE MELTED THAT BLOCK OF ICE AND ABSORBED ALL ITS HOLY POWER...
...SO YOU CAN TAKE AS MUCH AS YOU NEED FROM ME.
TOKI...
WE GAVE NATSUKI A PROPER BURIAL.
YOU DON'T NEED TO WORRY ABOUT ANYTHING. MY, MY.
CELCIA...
I'LL ALWAYS BELIEVE YOU.
I BELIEVE YOU, SO JUST TO BE HONEST WITH YOURSELF.
MARON...
I LOVE YOU, FINN.
I WANT TO COME BACK.
SHEEN
I WANT TO COME BACK AGAIN.

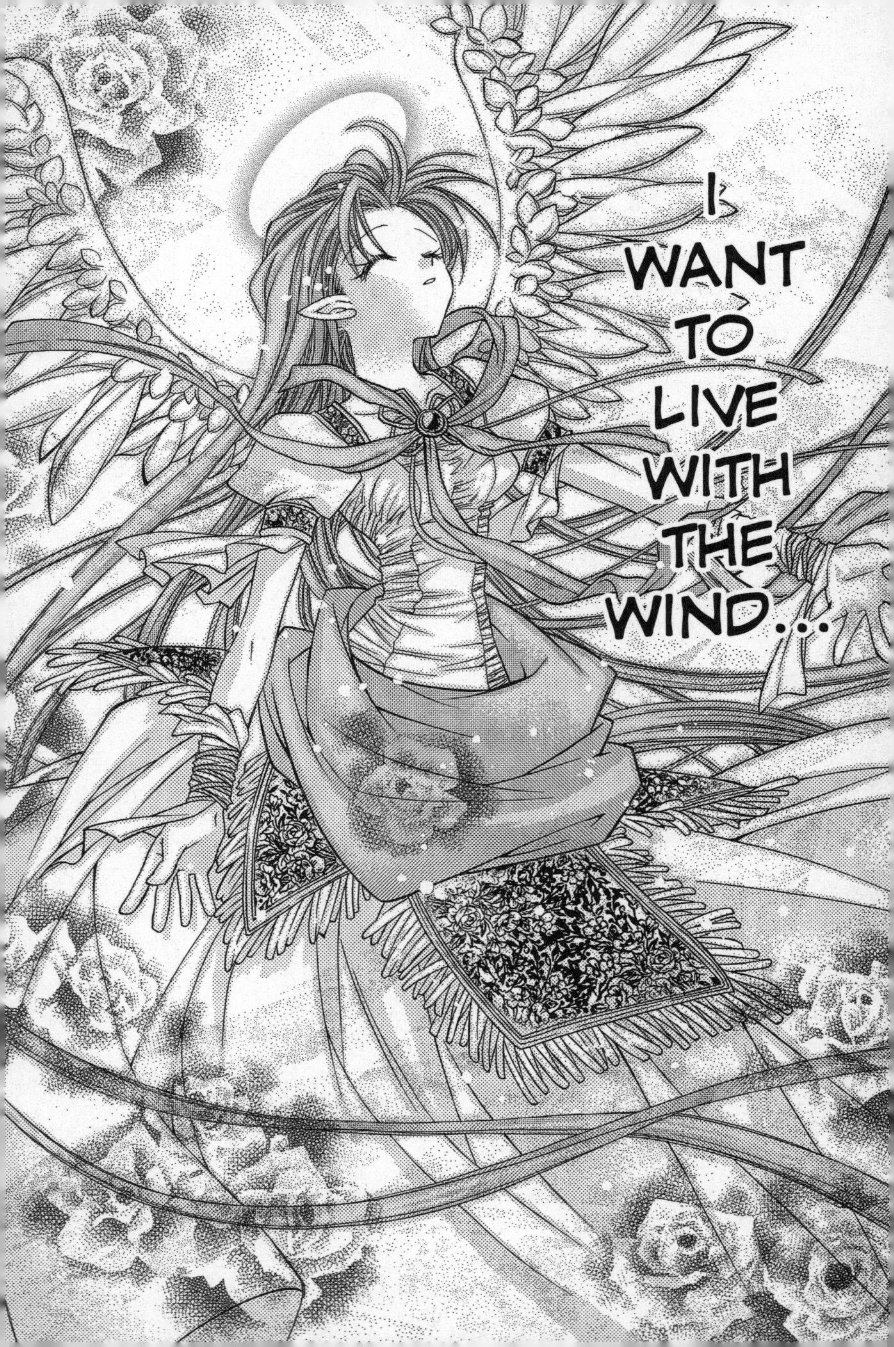
I WANT TO LIVE WITH THE WIND...

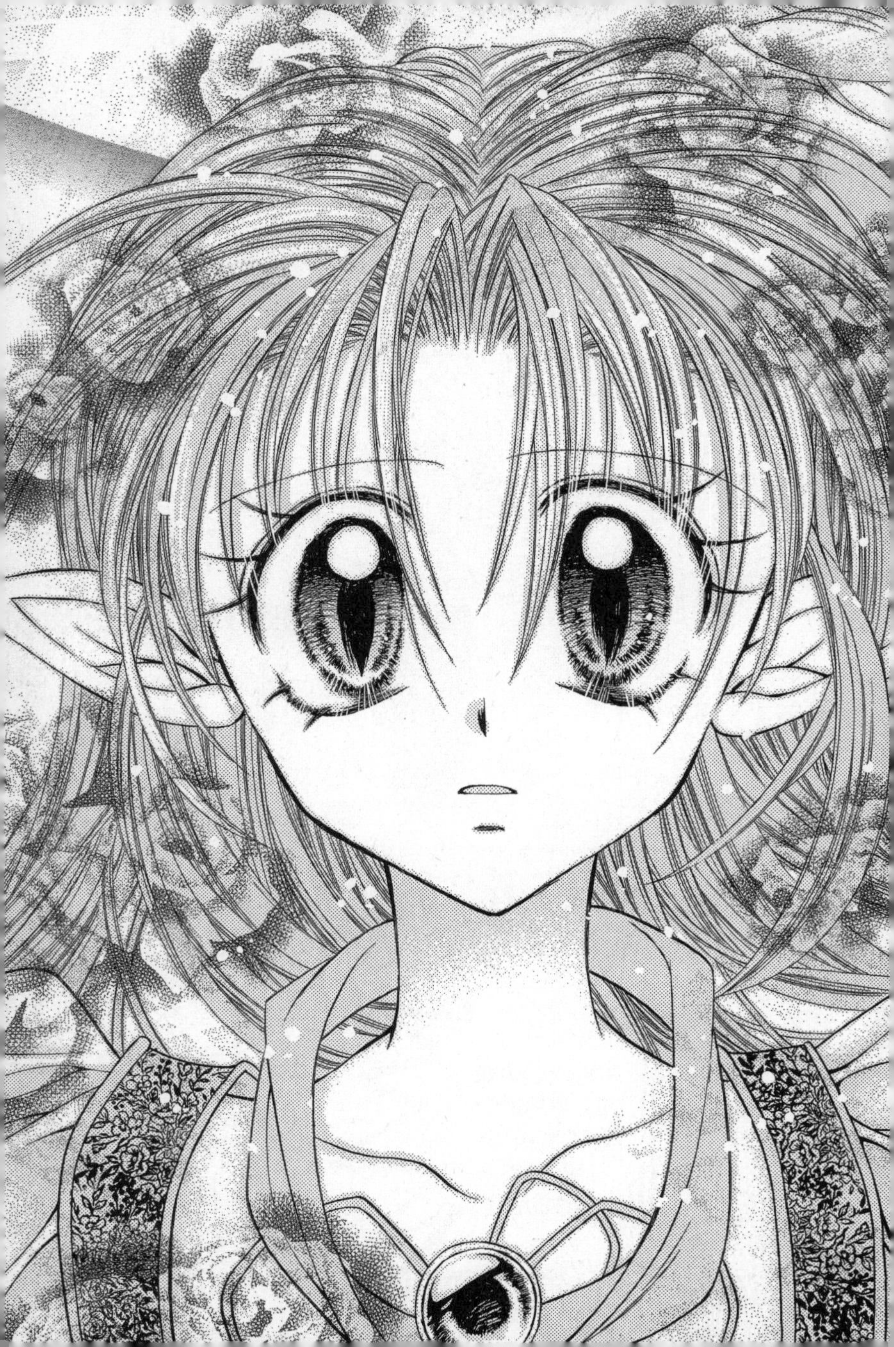

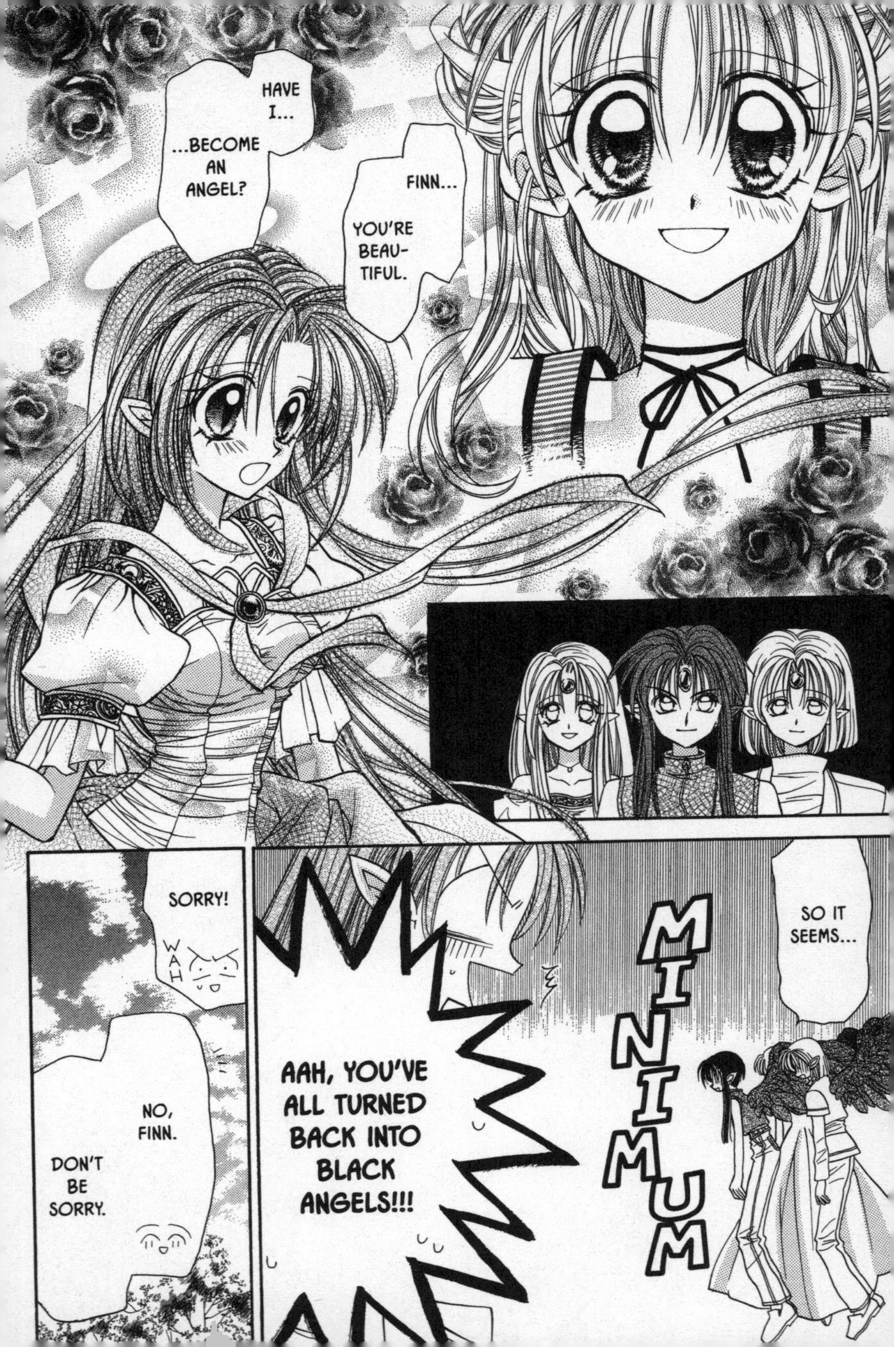
HAVE I... ...BECOME AN ANGEL?
FINN... YOU'RE BEAUTIFUL.
SO IT SEEMS...
MINIMUM
AAH, YOU'VE ALL TURNED BACK INTO BLACK ANGELS!!!
SORRY!
WAH
NO, FINN.
DON'T BE SORRY.

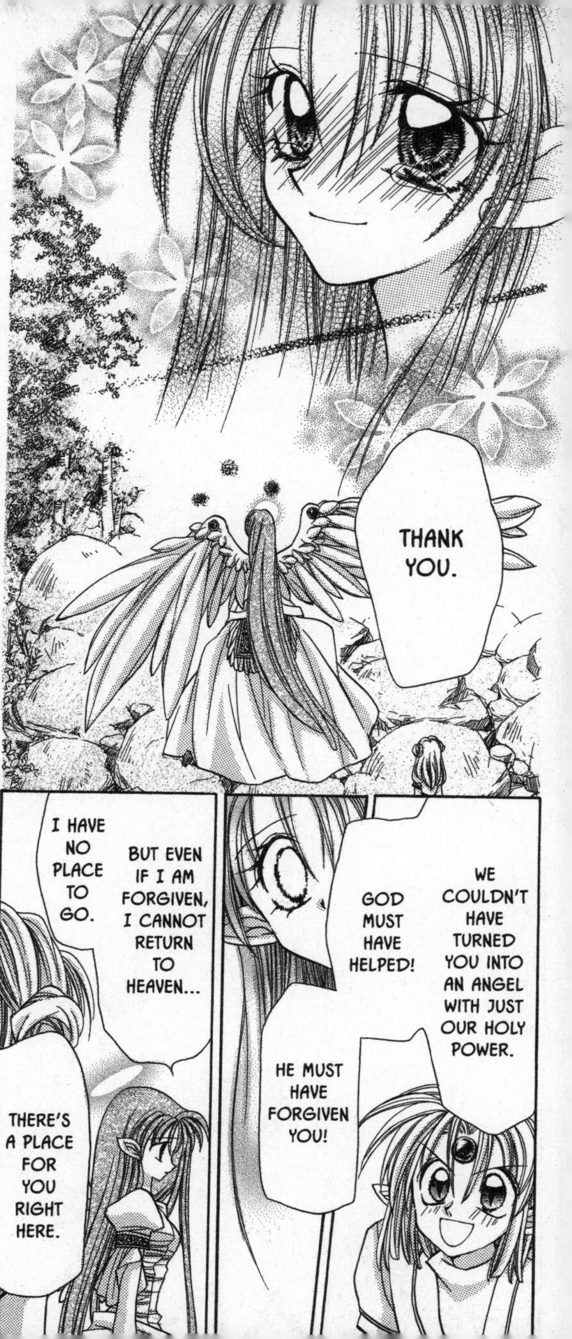
THANK YOU.
WE COULDN'T HAVE TURNED YOU INTO AN ANGEL WITH JUST OUR HOLY POWER.
GOD MUST HAVE HELPED!
HE MUST HAVE FORGIVEN YOU!
BUT EVEN IF I AM FORGIVEN, I CANNOT RETURN TO HEAVEN...
I HAVE NO PLACE TO GO.
THERE'S A PLACE FOR YOU RIGHT HERE.

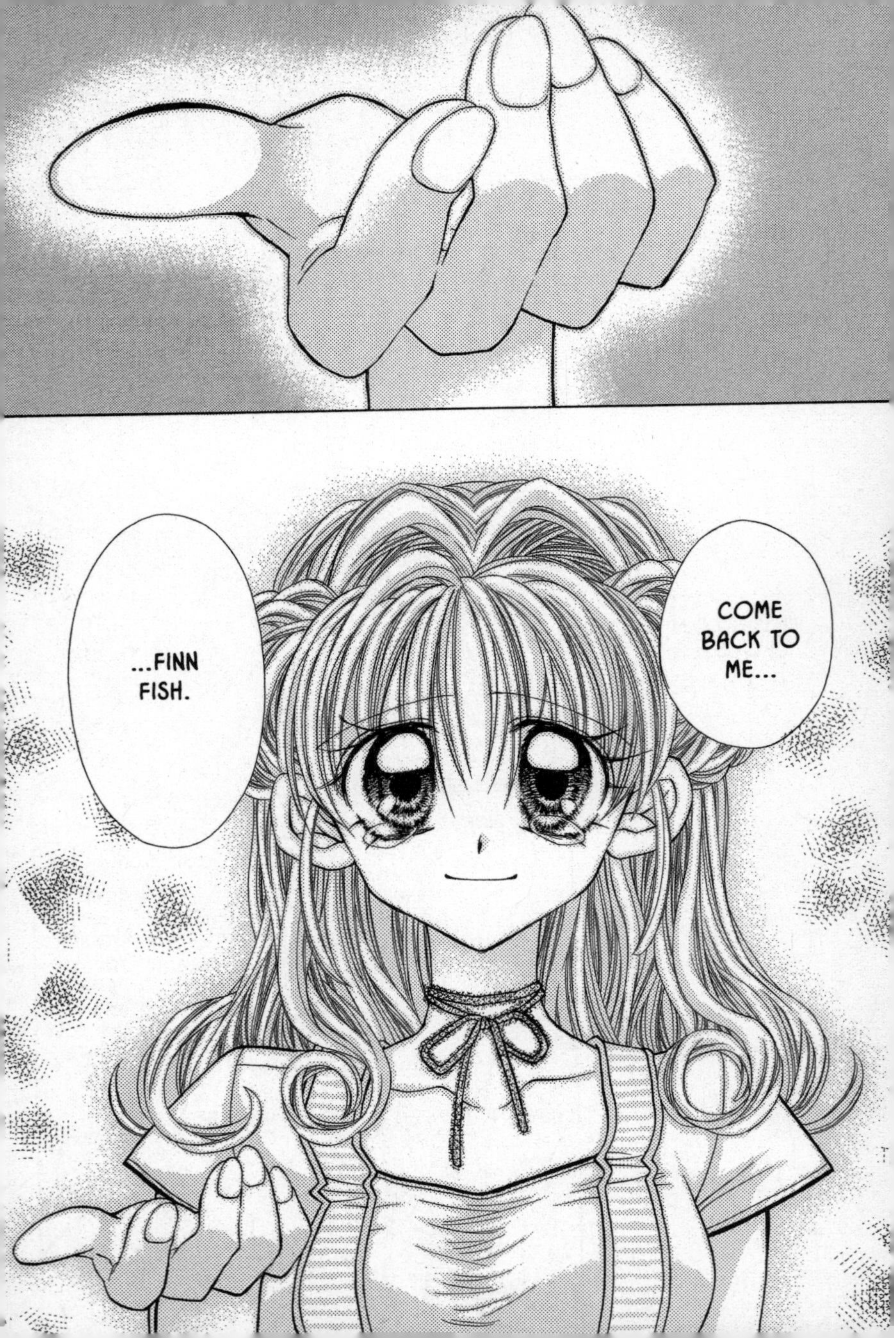
COME BACK TO ME...
...FINN FISH.

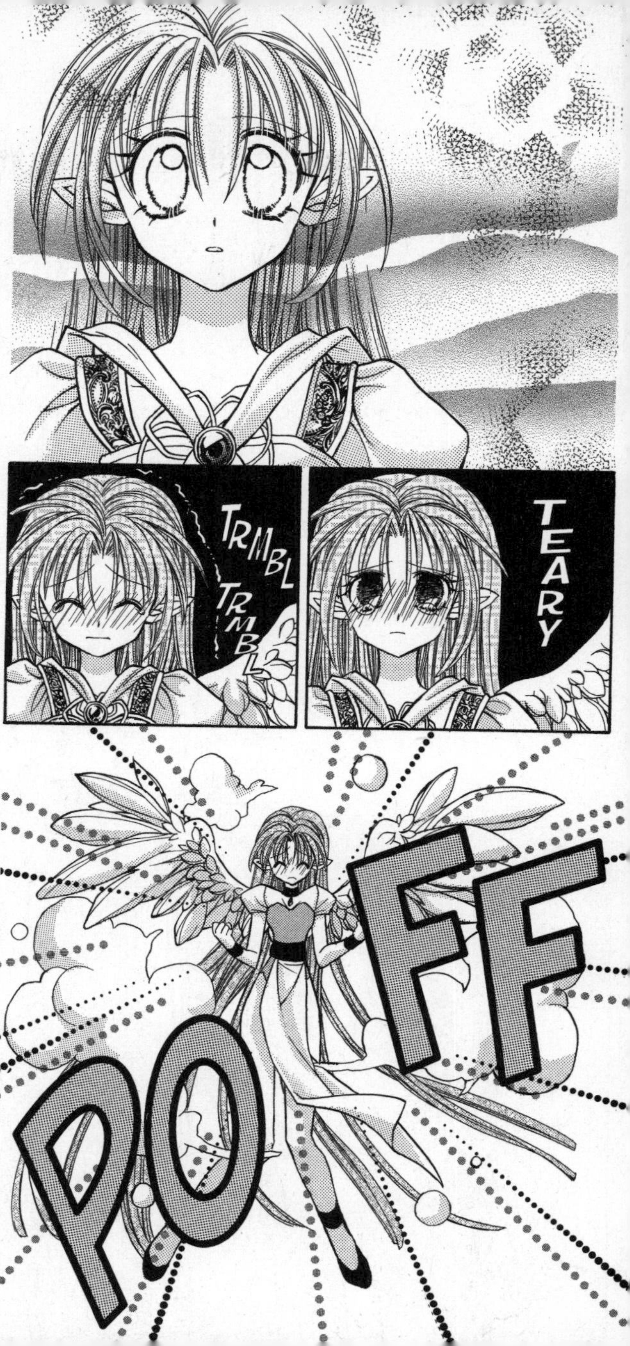
TEARY
TRMBL TRMBL
POOFF

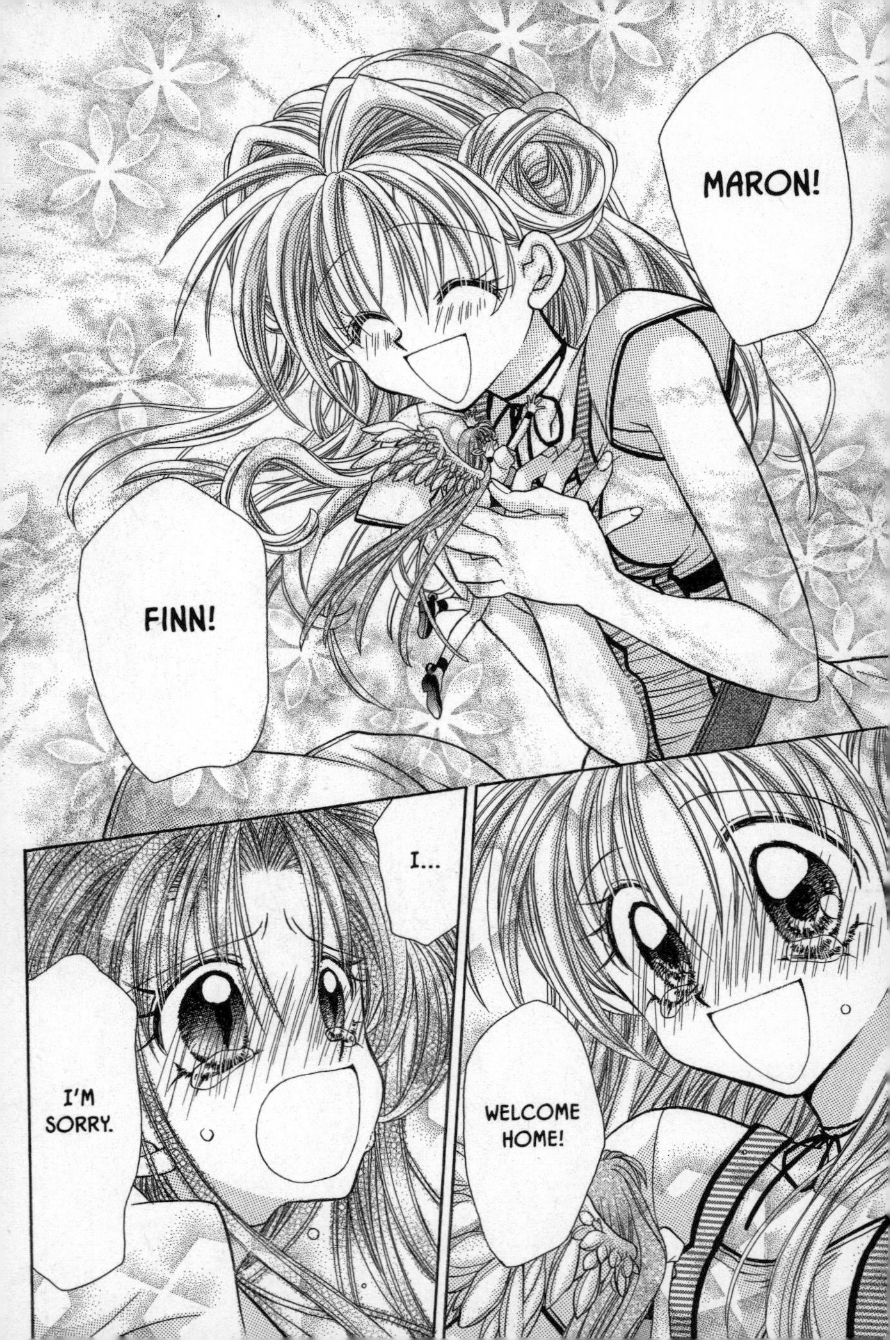
MARON!
FINN!
WELCOME HOME!
I...
I'M SORRY.

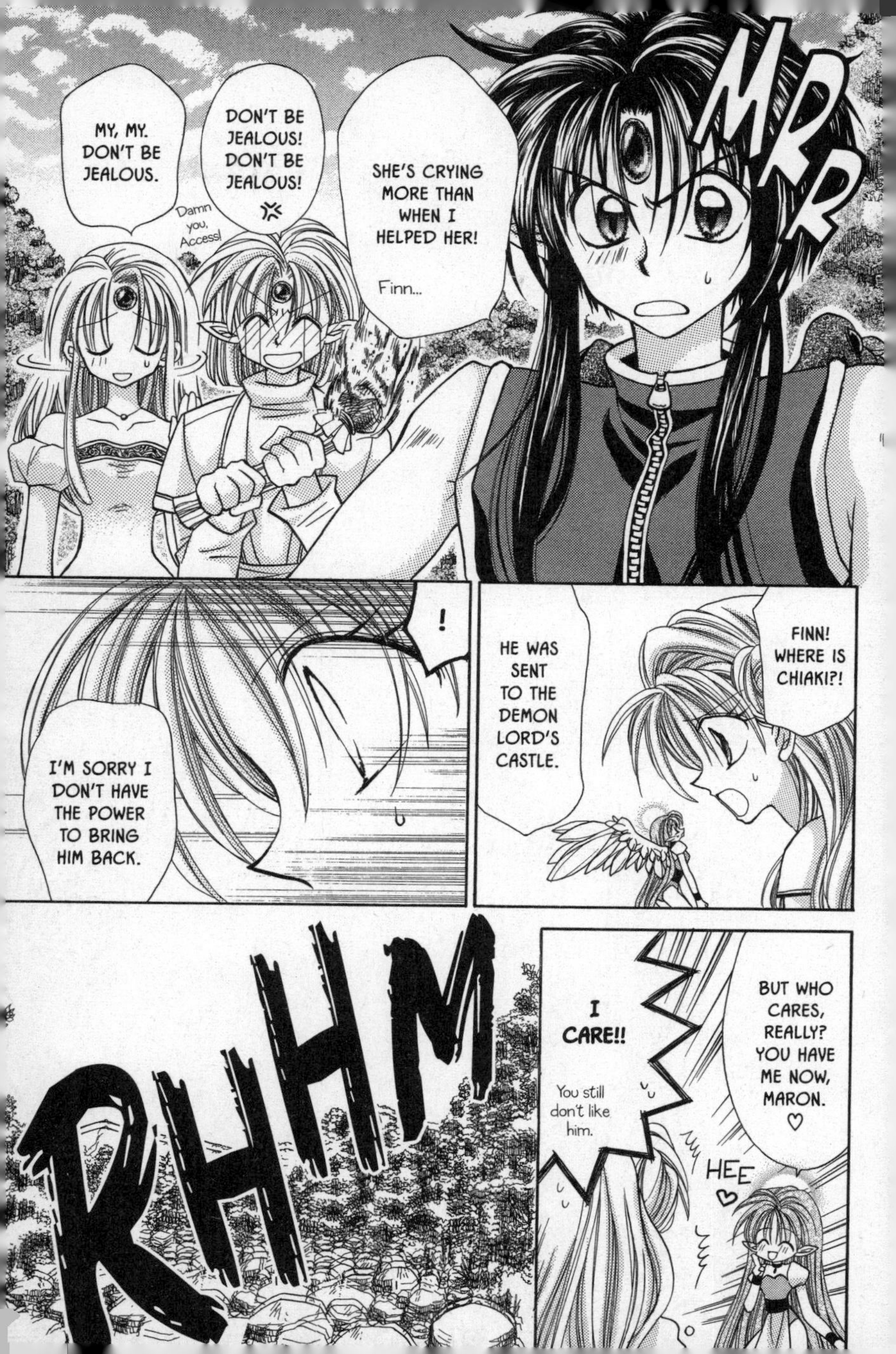
MRR
SHE'S CRYING MORE THAN WHEN I HELPED HER!
Finn...
DON'T BE JEALOUS! DON'T BE JEALOUS!
Damn you, Access!
MY, MY. DON'T BE JEALOUS.
FINN! WHERE IS CHIAKI?!
HE WAS SENT TO THE DEMON LORD'S CASTLE.
!
I'M SORRY I DON'T HAVE THE POWER TO BRING HIM BACK.
BUT WHO CARES, REALLY? YOU HAVE ME NOW, MARON. ♡
HEE ♡
I CARE!!
You still don't like him.
RHHM

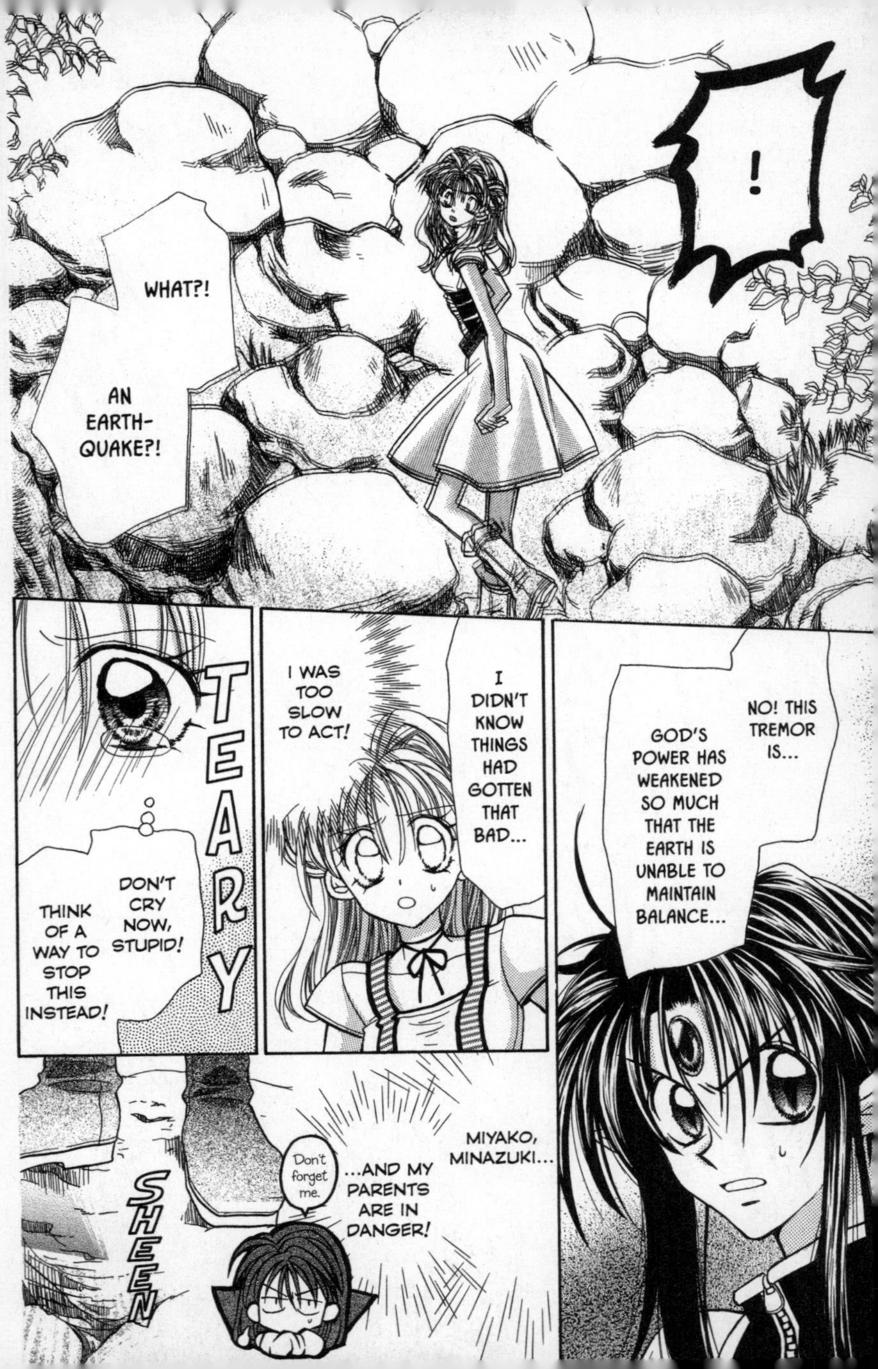
!
WHAT?!
AN EARTH-QUAKE?!
NO! THIS TREMOR IS...
GOD'S POWER HAS WEAKENED SO MUCH THAT THE EARTH IS UNABLE TO MAINTAIN BALANCE...
I DIDN'T KNOW THINGS HAD GOTTEN THAT BAD...
I WAS TOO SLOW TO ACT!
TEARY
DON'T CRY NOW, STUPID!
THINK OF A WAY TO STOP THIS INSTEAD!
MIYAKO, MINAZUKI...
...AND MY PARENTS ARE IN DANGER!
Don't forget me.
SHEEN

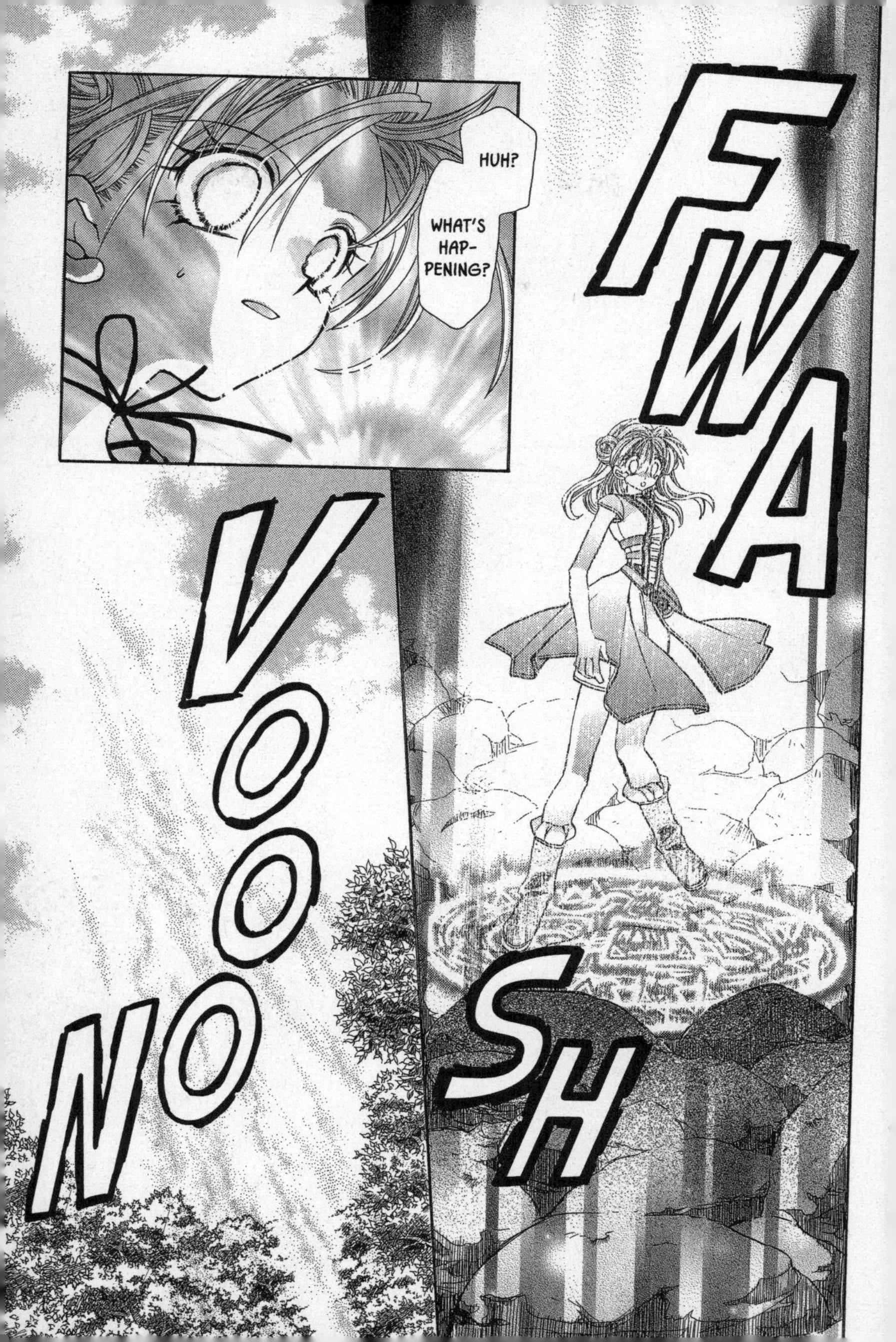
HUH?
WHAT'S HAP-PENING?
FWASH
VOOOON

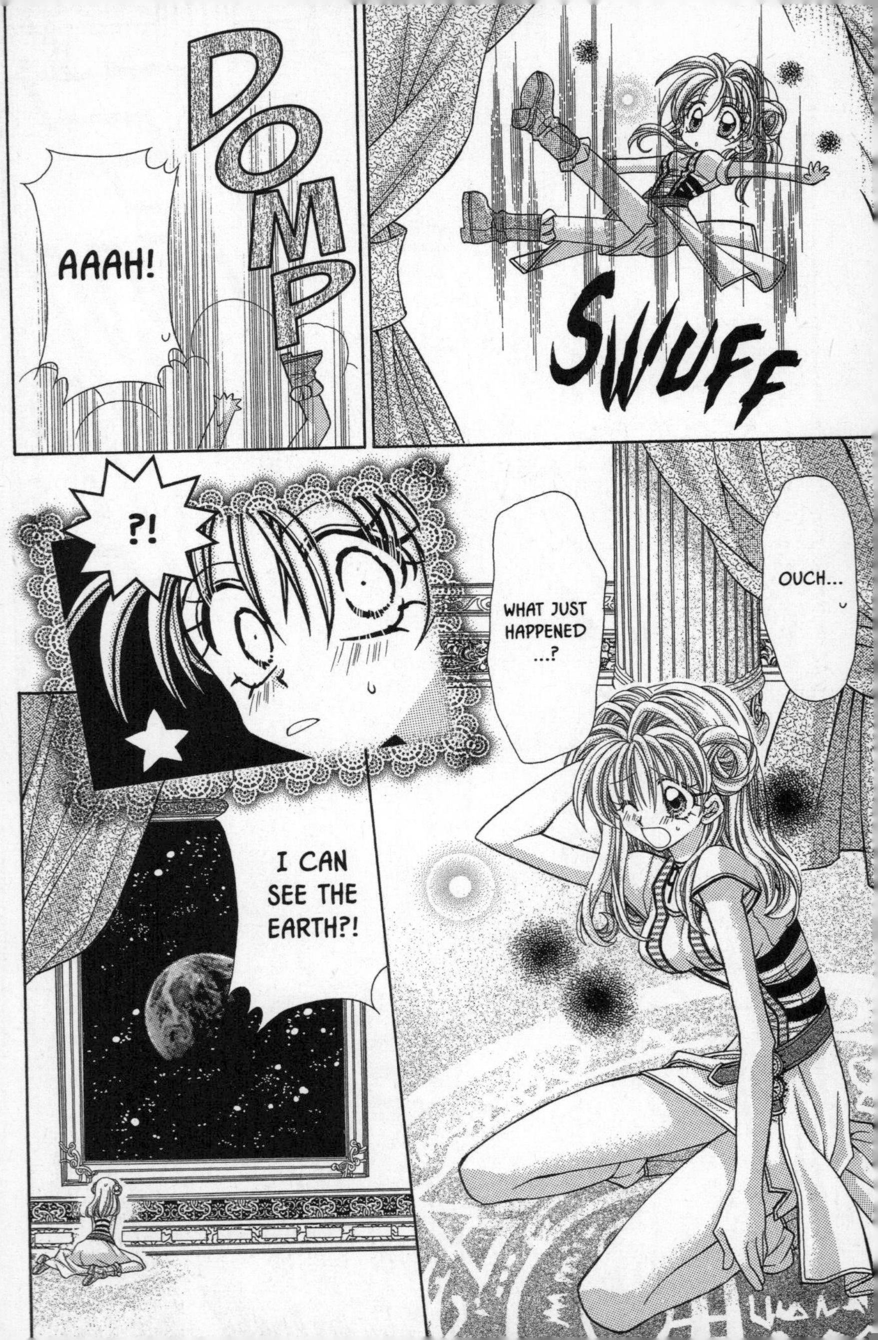
SWUFF
AAAH!
DOMP!
OUCH...
WHAT JUST HAPPENED ...?
?!
I CAN SEE THE EARTH?!

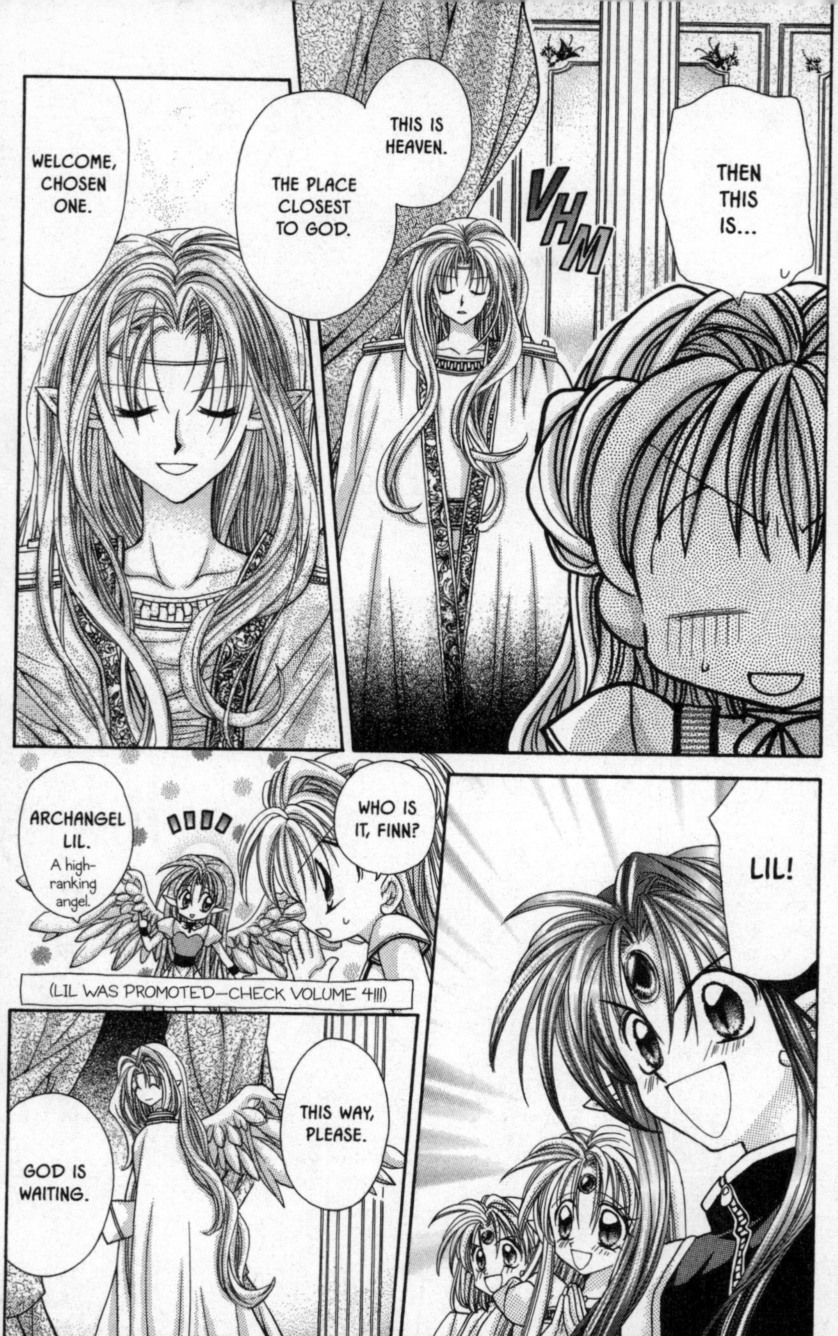
THEN THIS IS...
VHM
THIS IS HEAVEN.
THE PLACE CLOSEST TO GOD.
WELCOME, CHOSEN ONE.
LIL!
WHO IS IT, FINN?
ARCHANGEL LIL.
A high-ranking angel.
(LIL WAS PROMOTED—CHECK VOLUME 4!!!)
THIS WAY, PLEASE.
GOD IS WAITING.

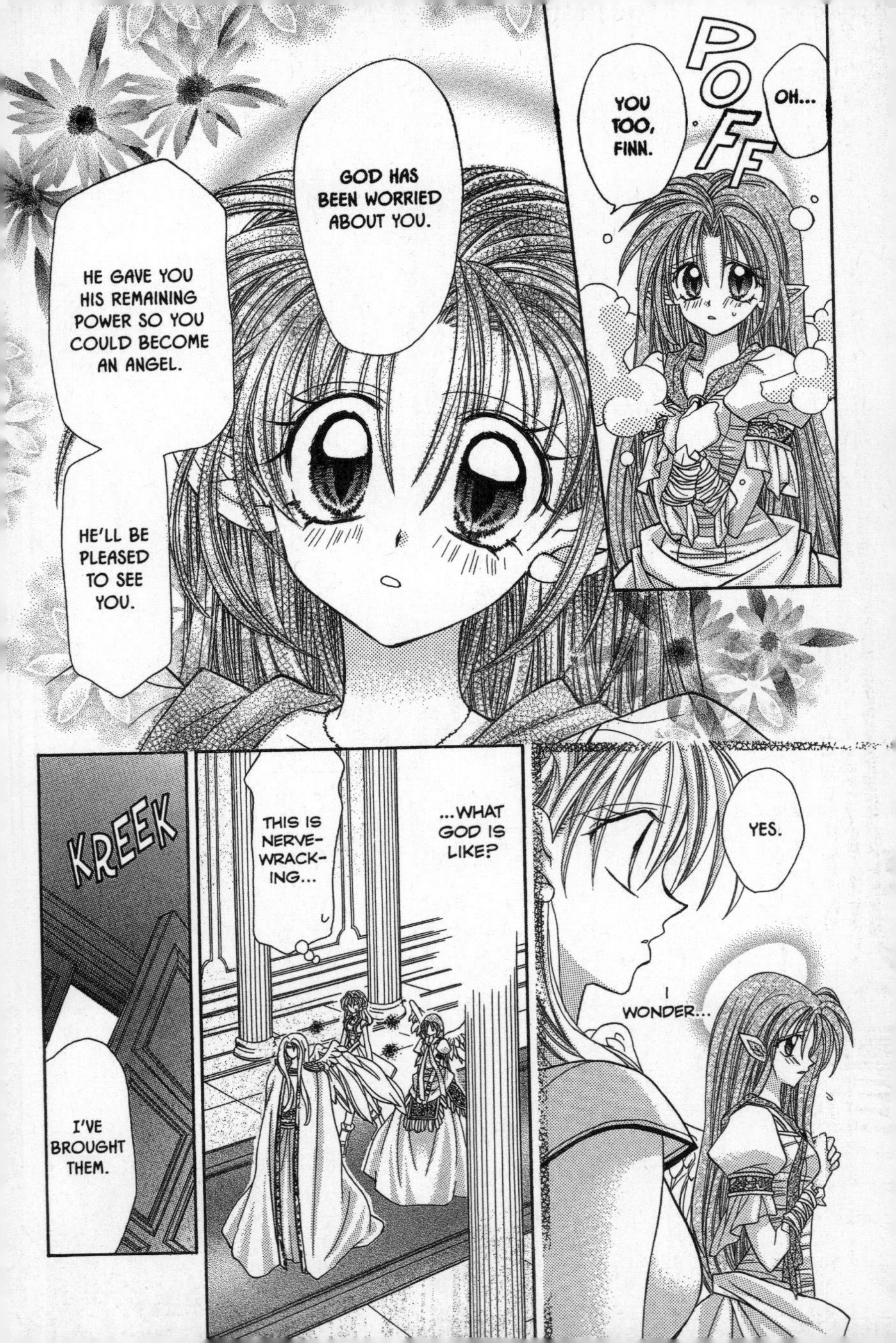
OH...
POFF
YOU TOO, FINN.
GOD HAS BEEN WORRIED ABOUT YOU.
HE GAVE YOU HIS REMAINING POWER SO YOU COULD BECOME AN ANGEL.
HE'LL BE PLEASED TO SEE YOU.
YES.
I WONDER...
...WHAT GOD IS LIKE?
THIS IS NERVE-WRACKING...
KREEK
I'VE BROUGHT THEM.

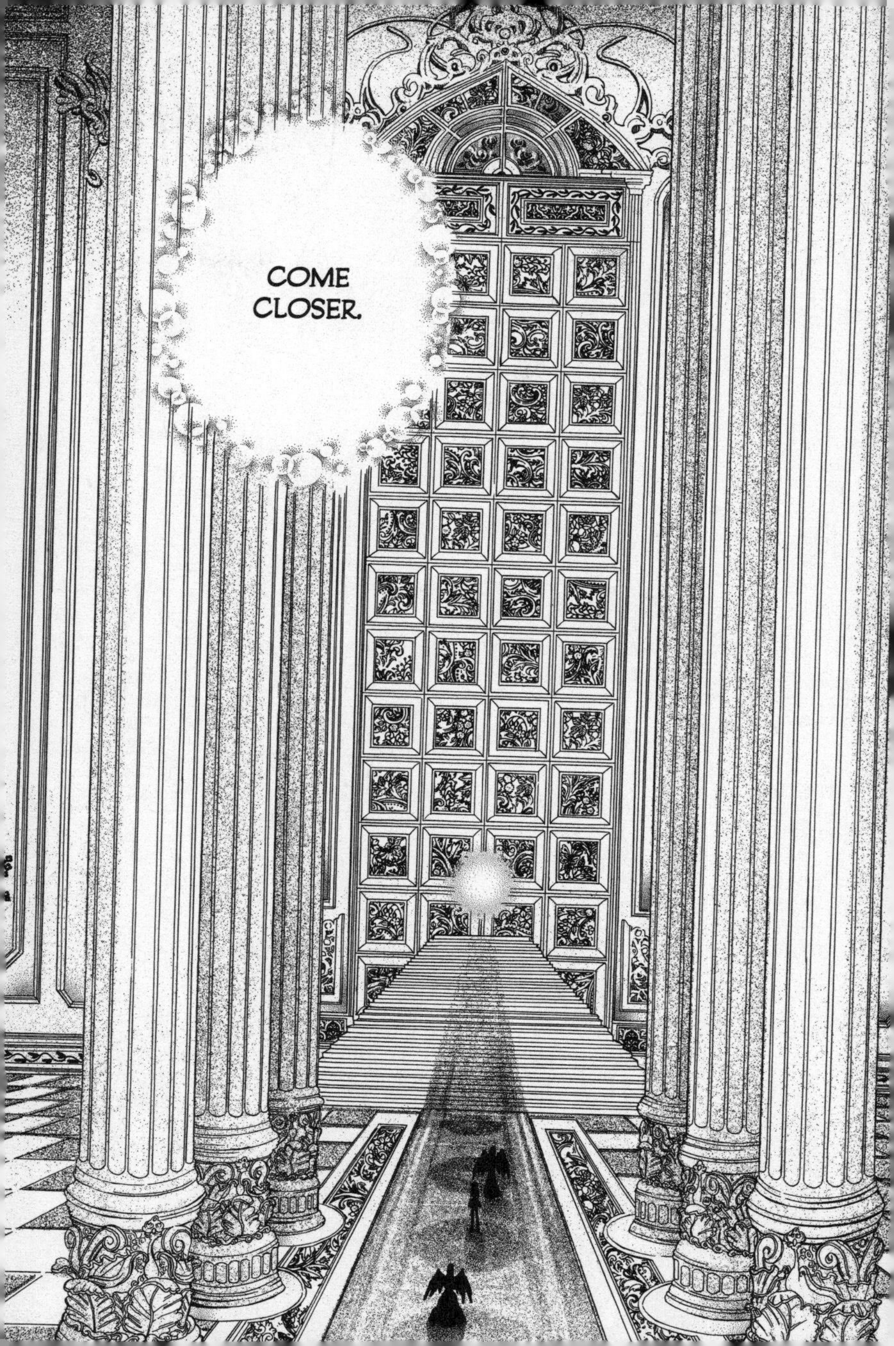
COME CLOSER.

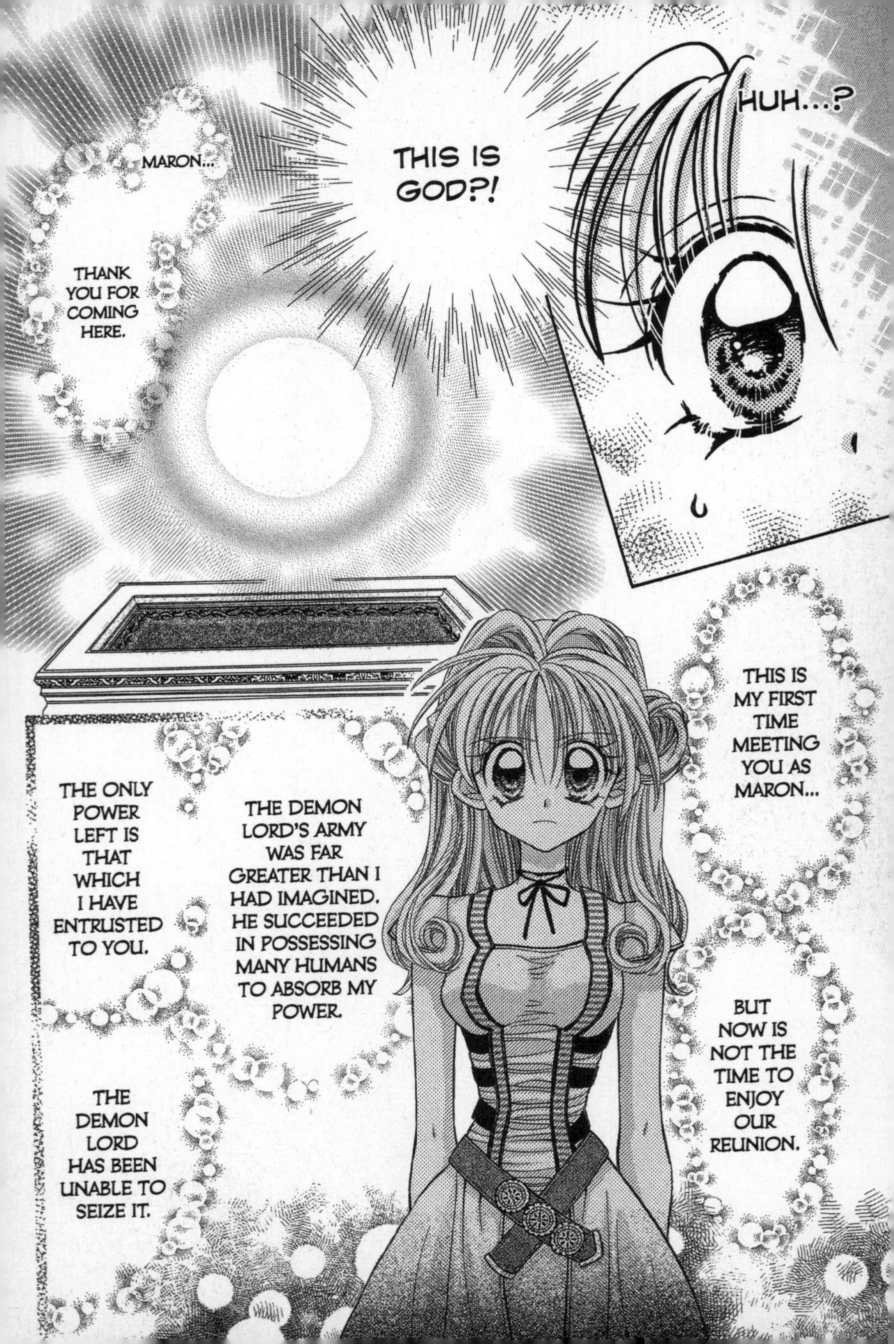
HUH...?
THIS IS GOD?!
MARON...
THANK YOU FOR COMING HERE.
THIS IS MY FIRST TIME MEETING YOU AS MARON...
BUT NOW IS NOT THE TIME TO ENJOY OUR REUNION.
THE DEMON LORD'S ARMY WAS FAR GREATER THAN I HAD IMAGINED. HE SUCCEEDED IN POSSESSING MANY HUMANS TO ABSORB MY POWER.
THE ONLY POWER LEFT IS THAT WHICH I HAVE ENTRUSTED TO YOU.
THE DEMON LORD HAS BEEN UNABLE TO SEIZE IT.

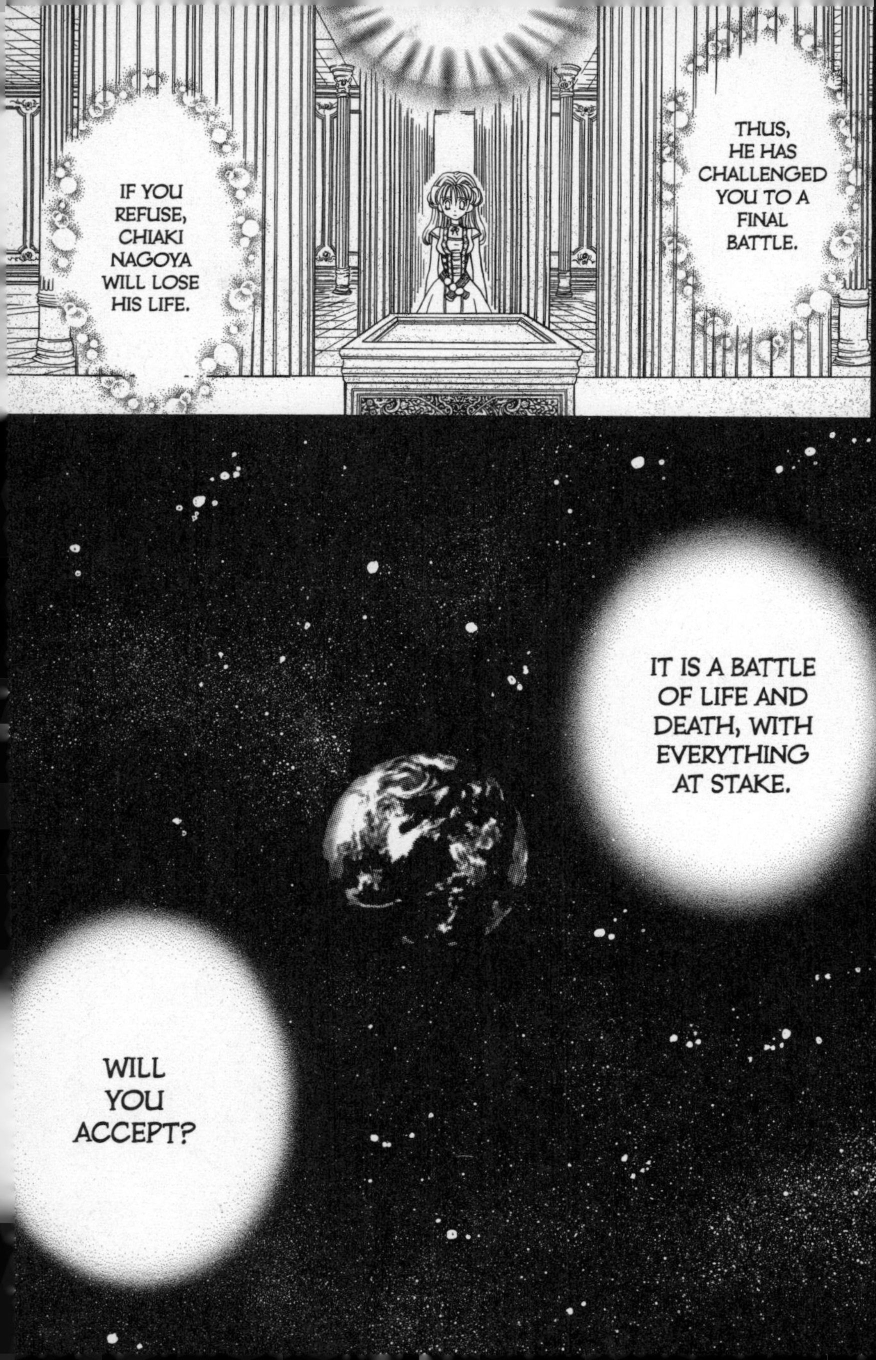
THUS, HE HAS CHALLENGED YOU TO A FINAL BATTLE.
IF YOU REFUSE, CHIAKI NAGOYA WILL LOSE HIS LIFE.
IT IS A BATTLE OF LIFE AND DEATH, WITH EVERYTHING AT STAKE.
WILL YOU ACCEPT?

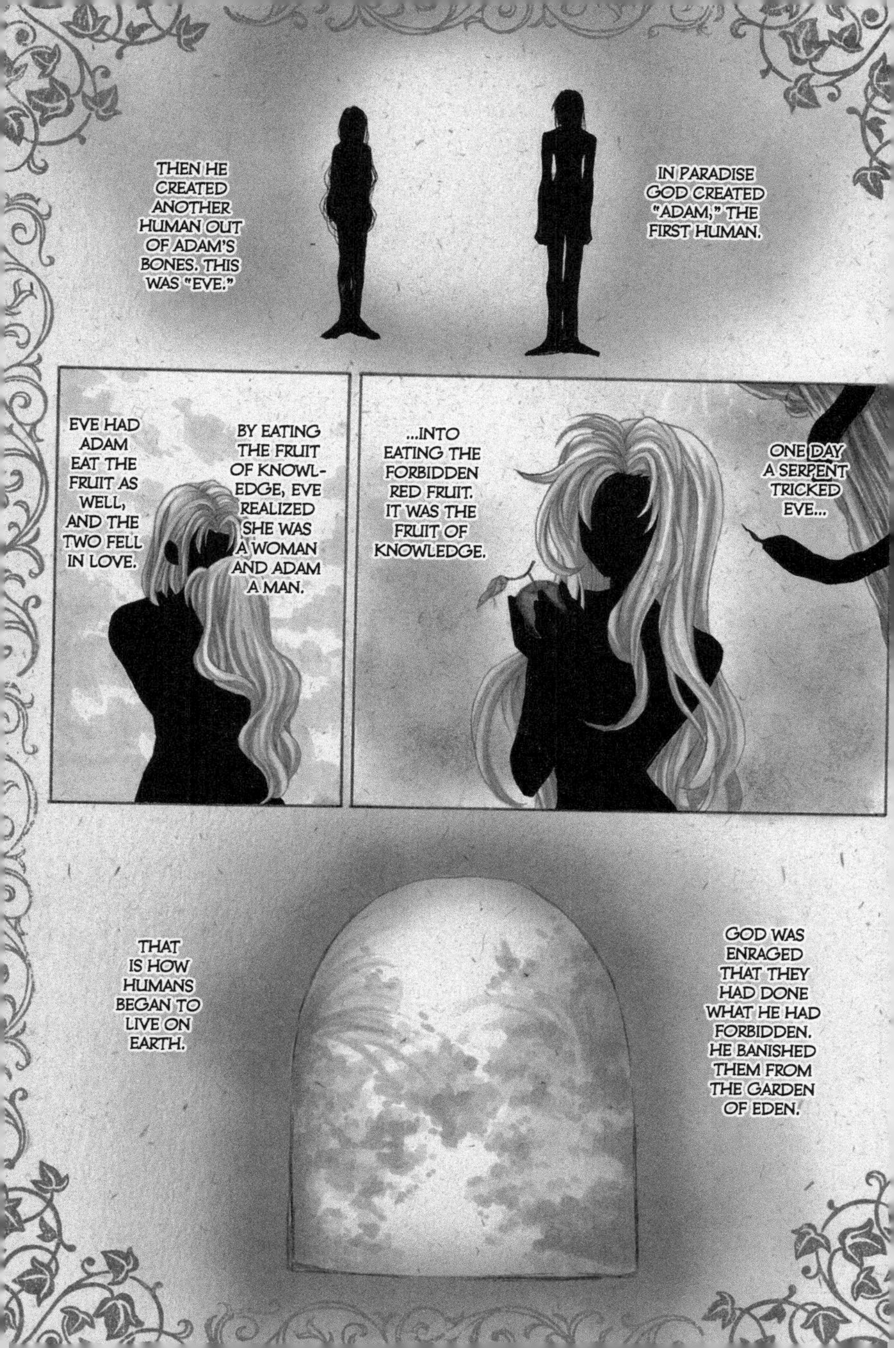
IN PARADISE GOD CREATED "ADAM," THE FIRST HUMAN.
THEN HE CREATED ANOTHER HUMAN OUT OF ADAM'S BONES. THIS WAS "EVE."
ONE DAY A SERPENT TRICKED EVE...
...INTO EATING THE FORBIDDEN RED FRUIT. IT WAS THE FRUIT OF KNOWLEDGE.
BY EATING THE FRUIT OF KNOWL-EDGE, EVE REALIZED SHE WAS A WOMAN AND ADAM A MAN.
EVE HAD ADAM EAT THE FRUIT AS WELL, AND THE TWO FELL IN LOVE.
GOD WAS ENRAGED THAT THEY HAD DONE WHAT HE HAD FORBIDDEN. HE BANISHED THEM FROM THE GARDEN OF EDEN.
THAT IS HOW HUMANS BEGAN TO LIVE ON EARTH.

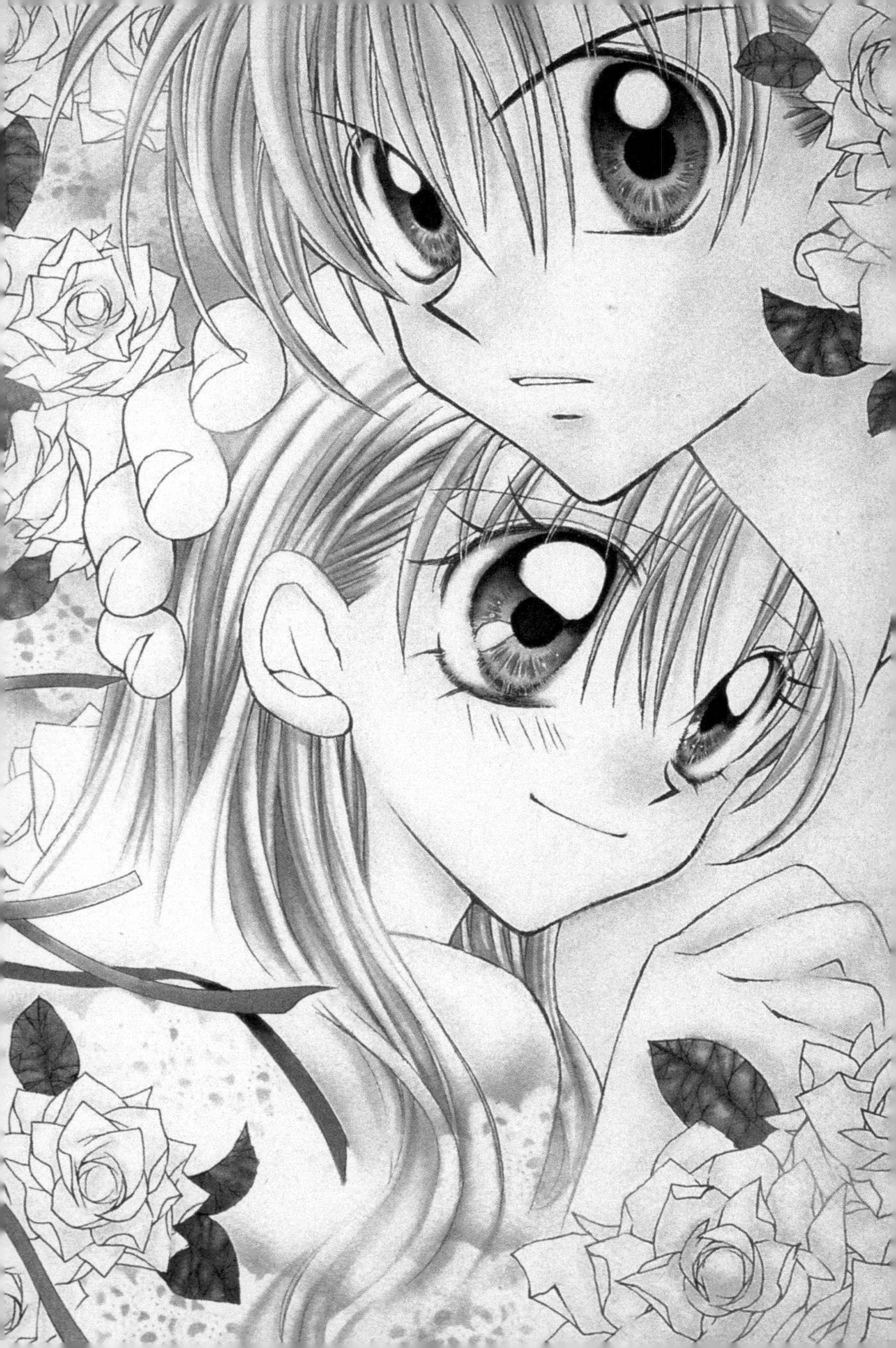

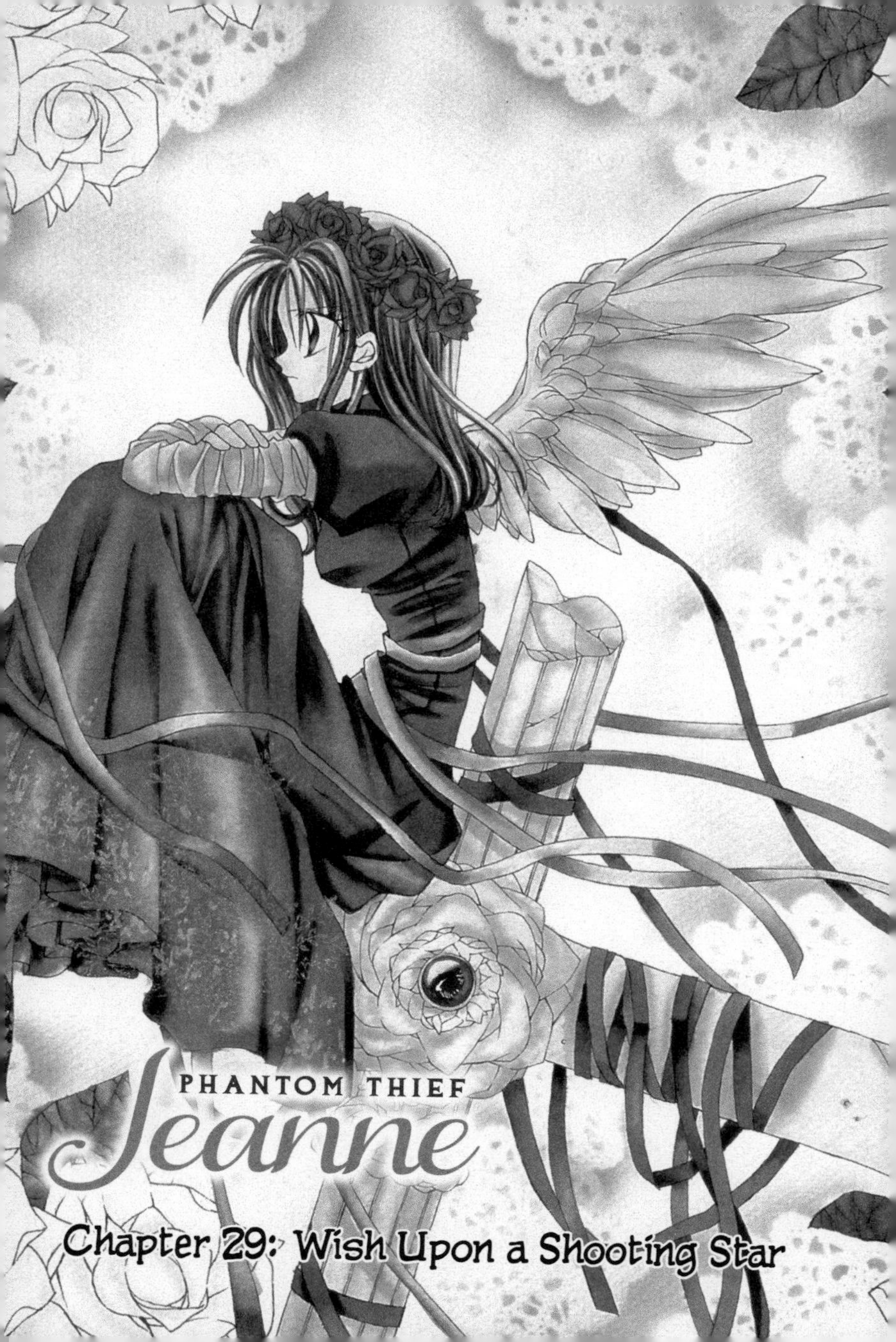
PHANTOM THIEF
Jeanne
Chapter 29: Wish Upon a Shooting Star

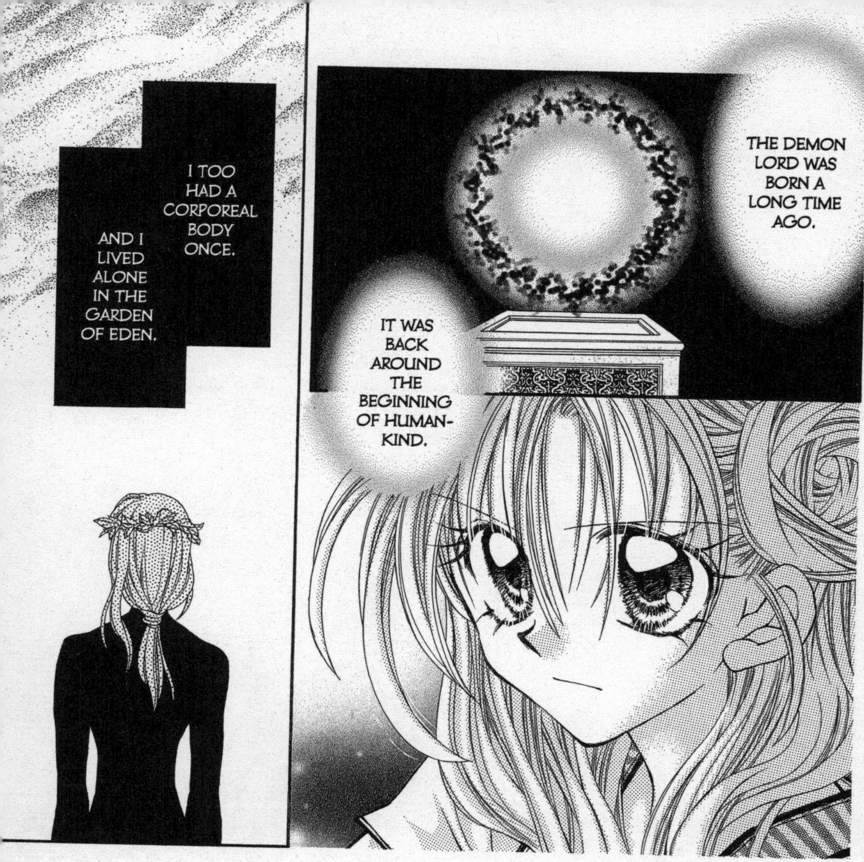
THE DEMON LORD WAS BORN A LONG TIME AGO.
IT WAS BACK AROUND THE BEGINNING OF HUMAN-KIND.
I TOO HAD A CORPOREAL BODY ONCE.
AND I LIVED ALONE IN THE GARDEN OF EDEN.

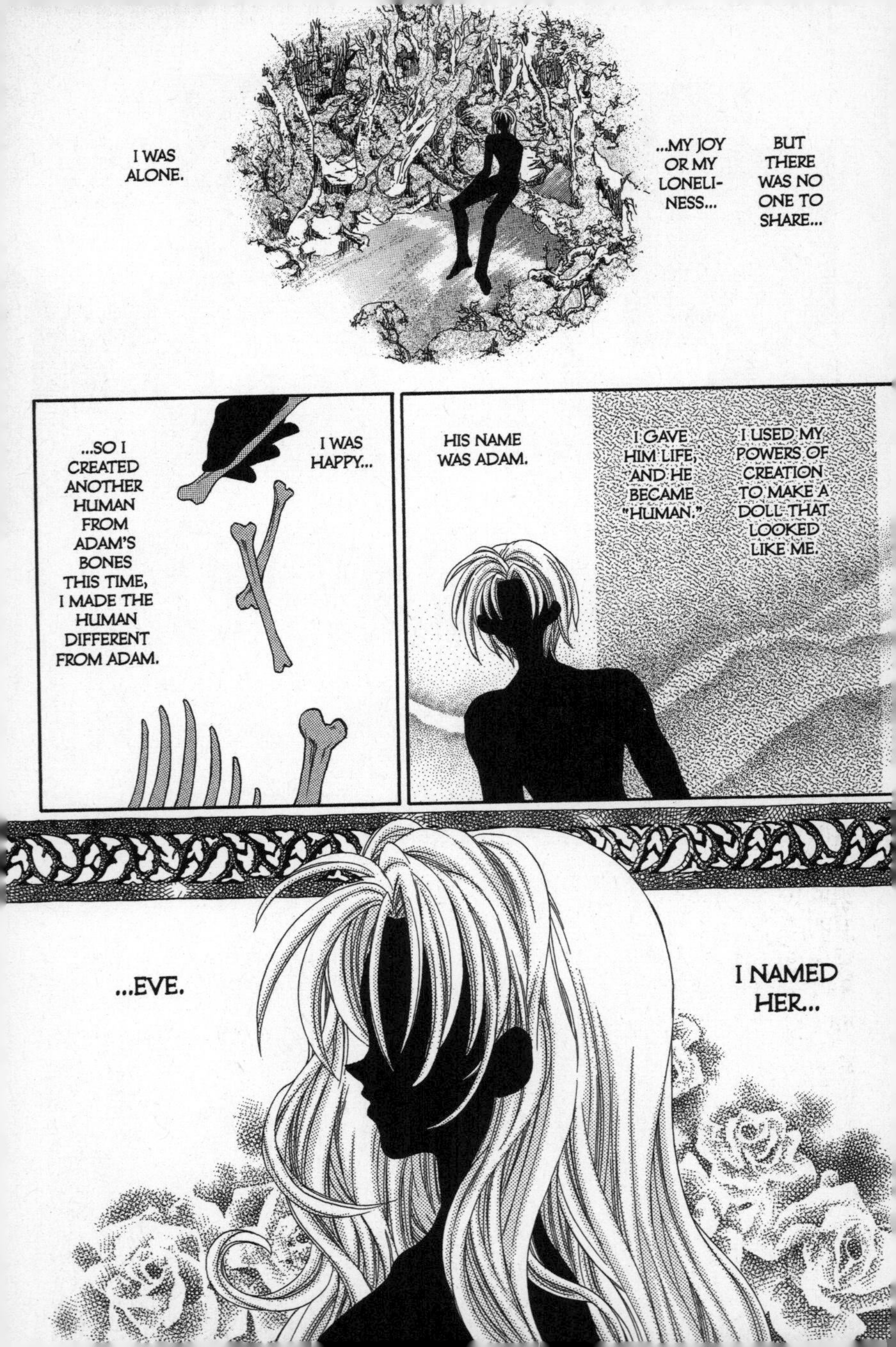
BUT THERE WAS NO ONE TO SHARE...
...MY JOY OR MY LONELINESS...
I WAS ALONE.
I USED MY POWERS OF CREATION TO MAKE A DOLL THAT LOOKED LIKE ME.
I GAVE HIM LIFE, AND HE BECAME "HUMAN."
HIS NAME WAS ADAM.
I WAS HAPPY...
...SO I CREATED ANOTHER HUMAN FROM ADAM'S BONES
THIS TIME, I MADE THE HUMAN DIFFERENT FROM ADAM.
I NAMED HER...
...EVE.

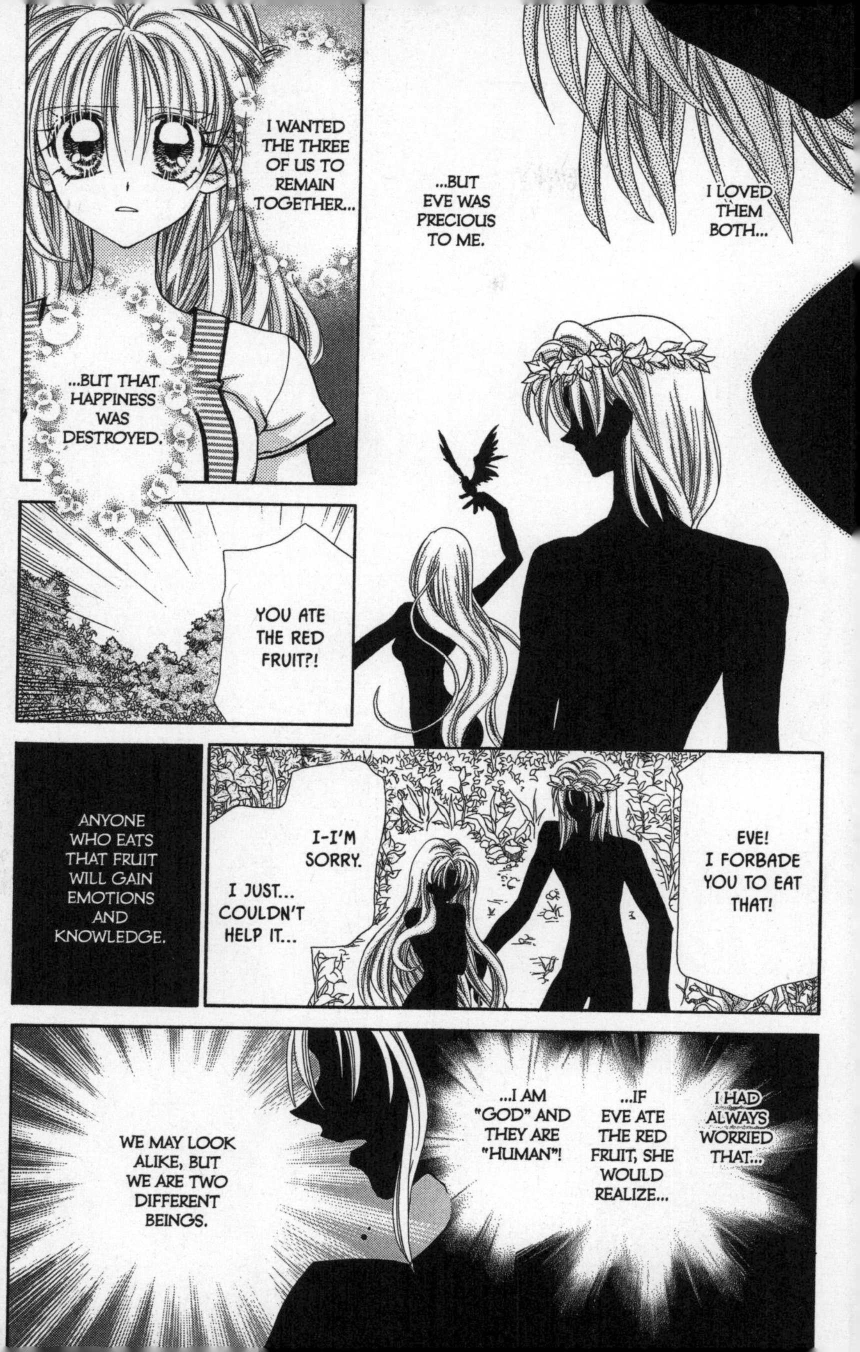
I LOVED THEM BOTH...
...BUT EVE WAS PRECIOUS TO ME.
I WANTED THE THREE OF US TO REMAIN TOGETHER...
...BUT THAT HAPPINESS WAS DESTROYED.
YOU ATE THE RED FRUIT?!
EVE! I FORBADE YOU TO EAT THAT!
I-I'M SORRY.
I JUST... COULDN'T HELP IT...
ANYONE WHO EATS THAT FRUIT WILL GAIN EMOTIONS AND KNOWLEDGE.
I HAD ALWAYS WORRIED THAT...
...IF EVE ATE THE RED FRUIT, SHE WOULD REALIZE...
...I AM "GOD" AND THEY ARE "HUMAN"!
WE MAY LOOK ALIKE, BUT WE ARE TWO DIFFERENT BEINGS.

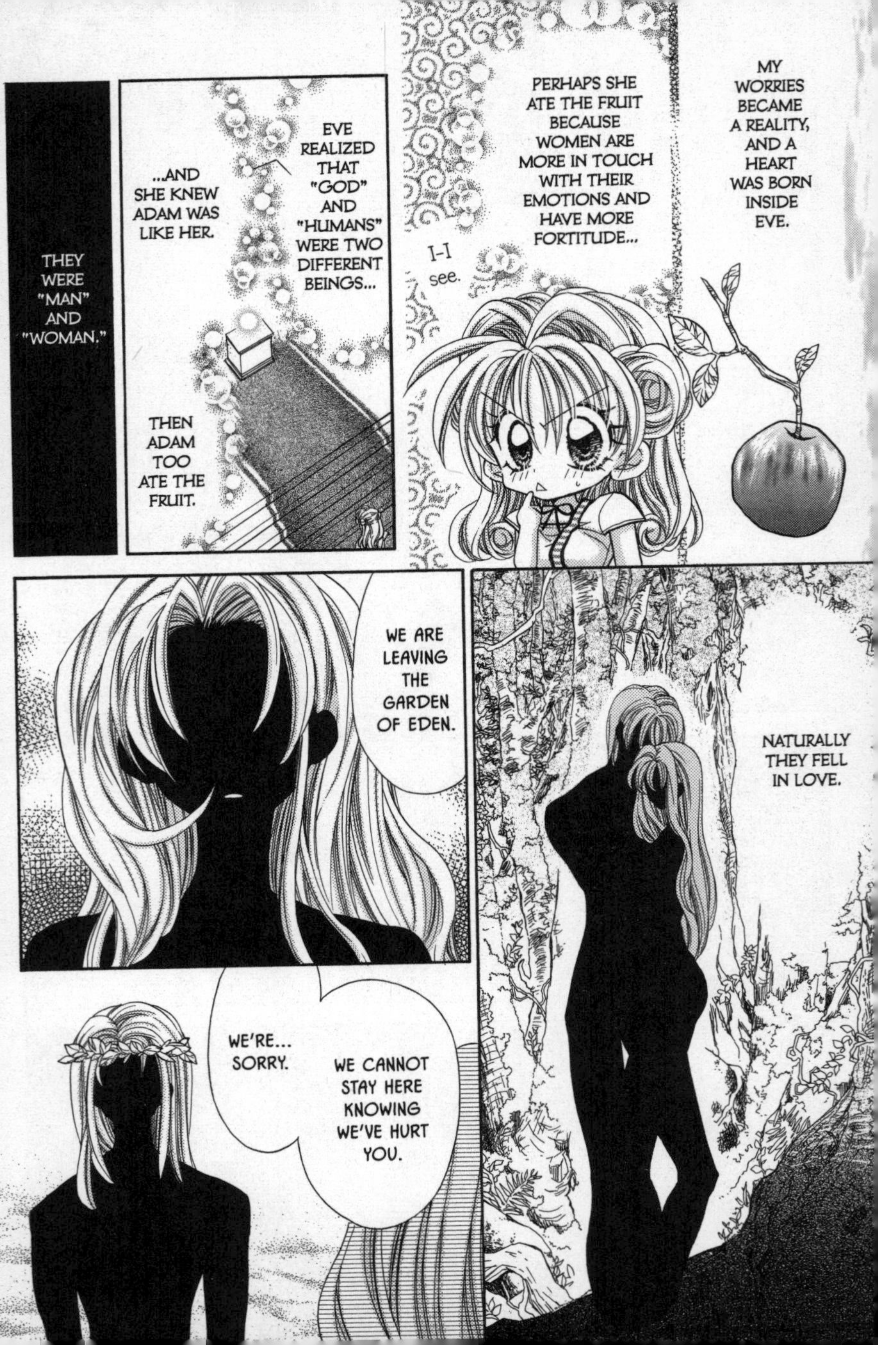
MY WORRIES BECAME A REALITY, AND A HEART WAS BORN INSIDE EVE.
PERHAPS SHE ATE THE FRUIT BECAUSE WOMEN ARE MORE IN TOUCH WITH THEIR EMOTIONS AND HAVE MORE FORTITUDE...
I-I see.
EVE REALIZED THAT "GOD" AND "HUMANS" WERE TWO DIFFERENT BEINGS...
...AND SHE KNEW ADAM WAS LIKE HER.
THEN ADAM TOO ATE THE FRUIT.
THEY WERE "MAN" AND "WOMAN."
NATURALLY THEY FELL IN LOVE.
WE ARE LEAVING THE GARDEN OF EDEN.
WE CANNOT STAY HERE KNOWING WE'VE HURT YOU.
WE'RE... SORRY.

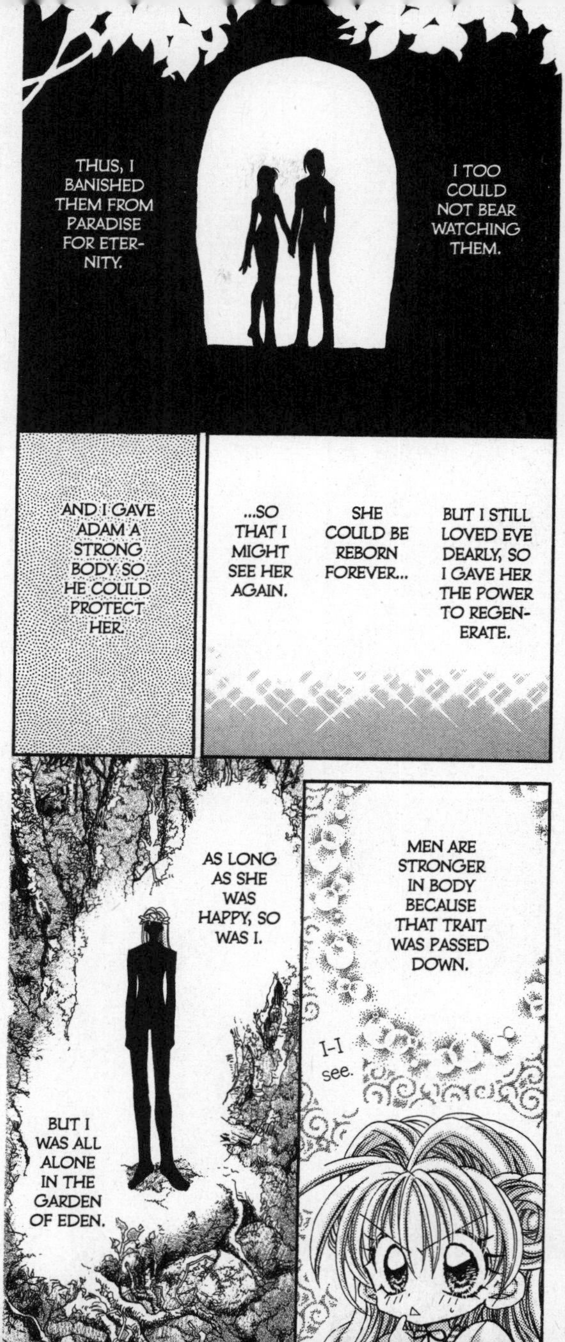
I TOO COULD NOT BEAR WATCHING THEM.
THUS, I BANISHED THEM FROM PARADISE FOR ETERNITY.
BUT I STILL LOVED EVE DEARLY, SO I GAVE HER THE POWER TO REGENERATE.
SHE COULD BE REBORN FOREVER...
...SO THAT I MIGHT SEE HER AGAIN.
AND I GAVE ADAM A STRONG BODY SO HE COULD PROTECT HER.
MEN ARE STRONGER IN BODY BECAUSE THAT TRAIT WAS PASSED DOWN.
I-I see.
AS LONG AS SHE WAS HAPPY, SO WAS I.
BUT I WAS ALL ALONE IN THE GARDEN OF EDEN.

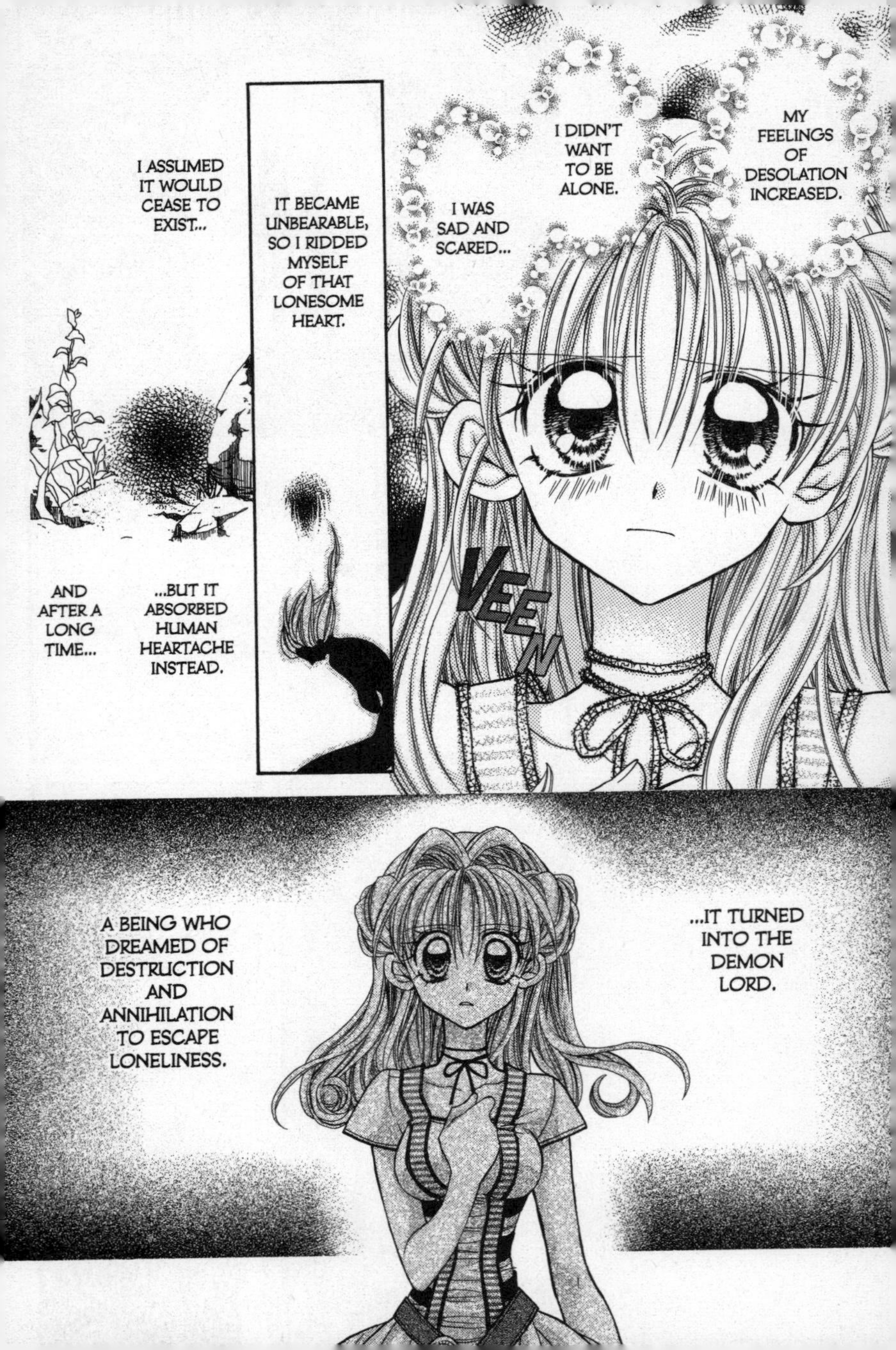
MY FEELINGS OF DESOLATION INCREASED.
I DIDN'T WANT TO BE ALONE.
I WAS SAD AND SCARED...
VEEN
IT BECAME UNBEARABLE, SO I RIDDED MYSELF OF THAT LONESOME HEART.
I ASSUMED IT WOULD CEASE TO EXIST...
...BUT IT ABSORBED HUMAN HEARTACHE INSTEAD.
AND AFTER A LONG TIME...
...IT TURNED INTO THE DEMON LORD.
A BEING WHO DREAMED OF DESTRUCTION AND ANNIHILATION TO ESCAPE LONELINESS.

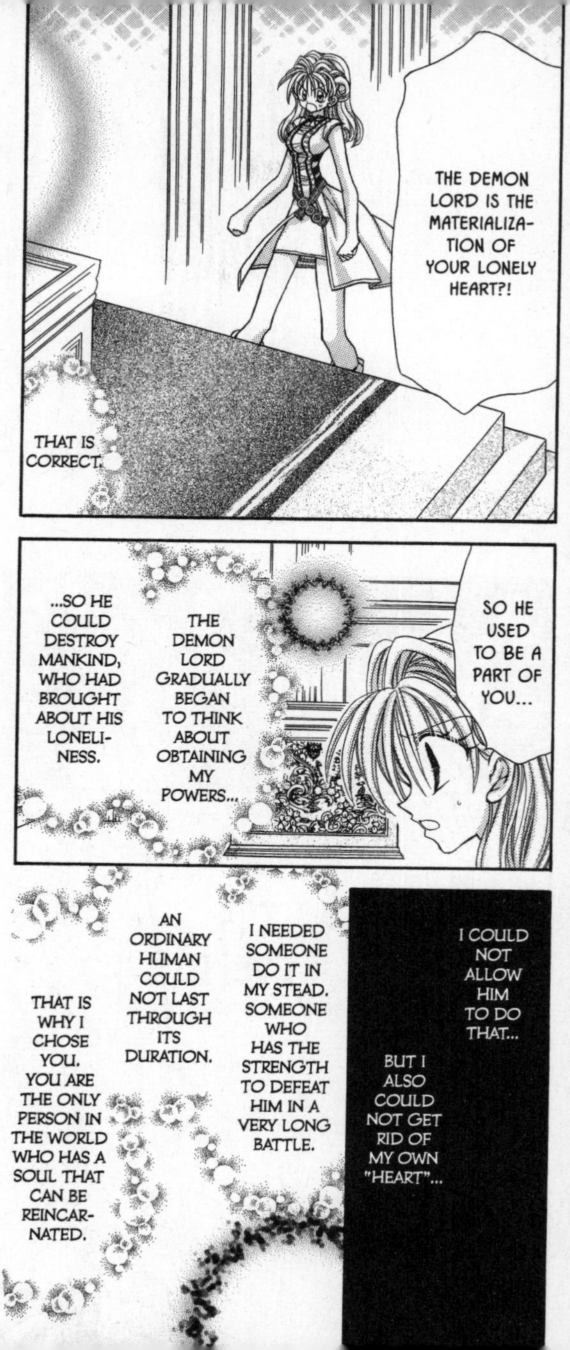
THE DEMON LORD IS THE MATERIALIZATION OF YOUR LONELY HEART?!
THAT IS CORRECT.
SO HE USED TO BE A PART OF YOU...
THE DEMON LORD GRADUALLY BEGAN TO THINK ABOUT OBTAINING MY POWERS...
...SO HE COULD DESTROY MANKIND, WHO HAD BROUGHT ABOUT HIS LONELINESS.
I COULD NOT ALLOW HIM TO DO THAT...
BUT I ALSO COULD NOT GET RID OF MY OWN "HEART"...
I NEEDED SOMEONE DO IT IN MY STEAD. SOMEONE WHO HAS THE STRENGTH TO DEFEAT HIM IN A VERY LONG BATTLE.
AN ORDINARY HUMAN COULD NOT LAST THROUGH ITS DURATION.
THAT IS WHY I CHOSE YOU. YOU ARE THE ONLY PERSON IN THE WORLD WHO HAS A SOUL THAT CAN BE REINCARNATED.

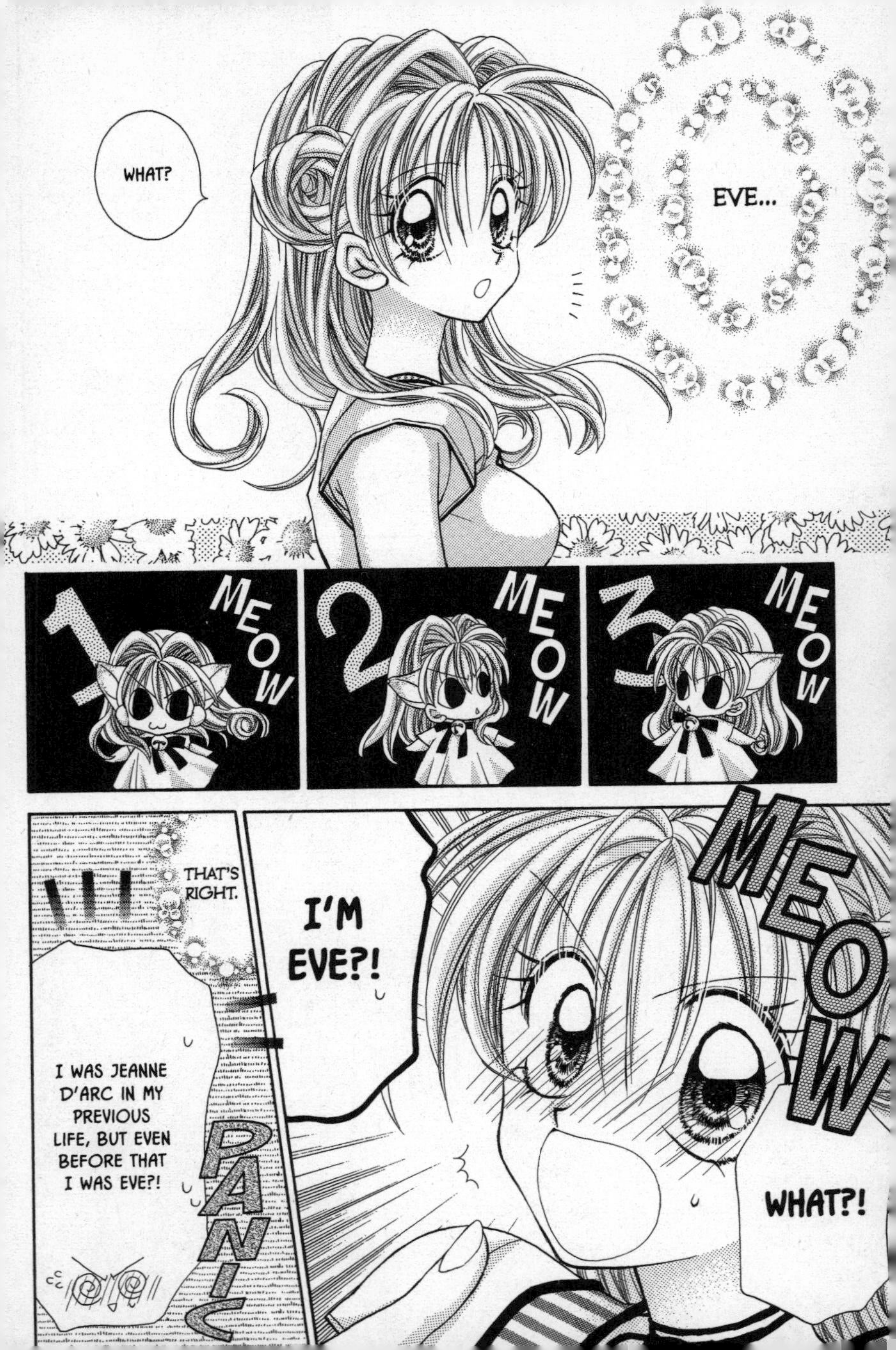
EVE...
WHAT?
3
MEOW
2
MEOW
1
MEOW
MEOW
WHAT?!
I'M EVE?!
THAT'S RIGHT.
I WAS JEANNE D'ARC IN MY PREVIOUS LIFE, BUT EVEN BEFORE THAT I WAS EVE?!
PANIC

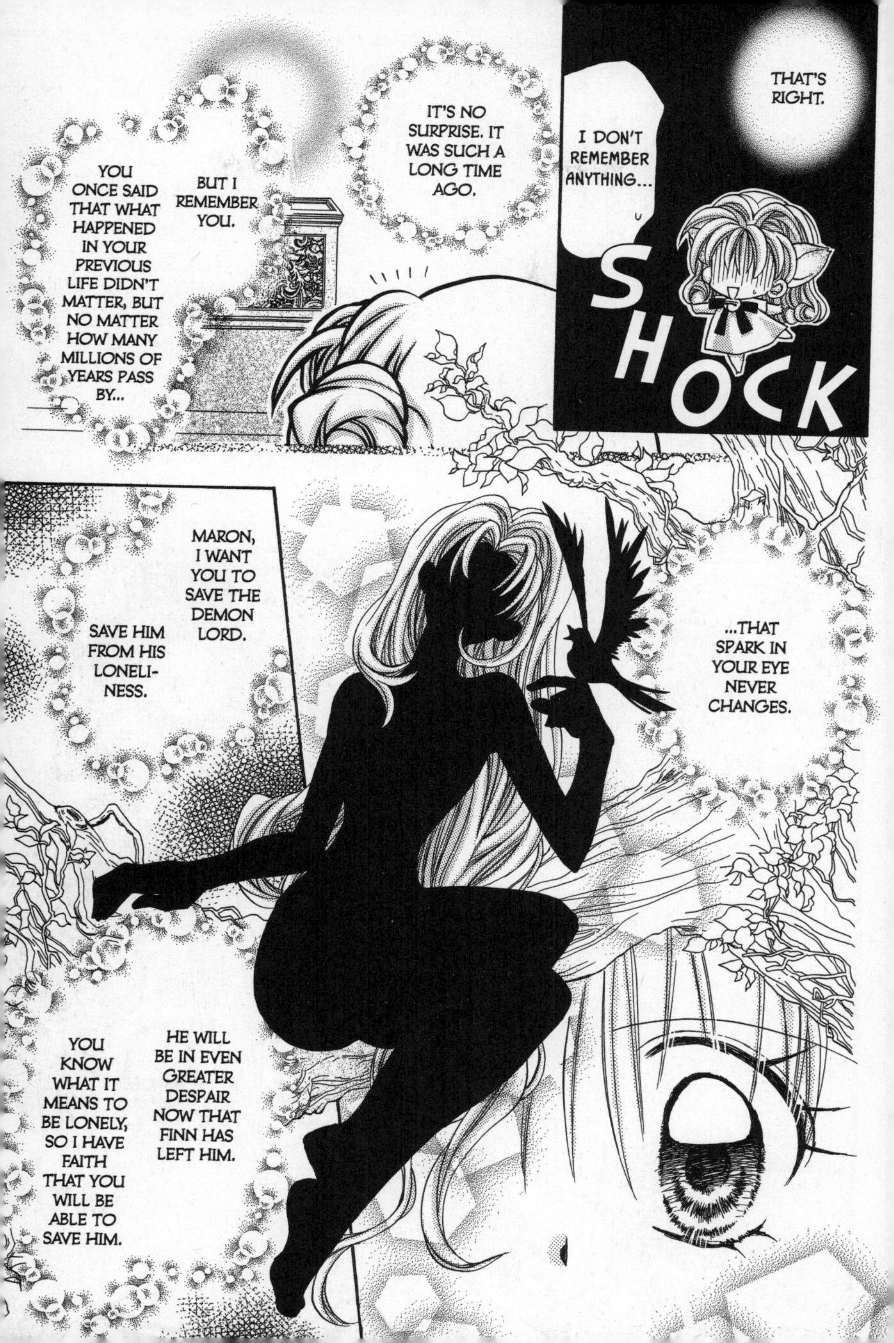
THAT'S RIGHT.
I DON'T REMEMBER ANYTHING...
SHOCK
IT'S NO SURPRISE. IT WAS SUCH A LONG TIME AGO.
BUT I REMEMBER YOU.
YOU ONCE SAID THAT WHAT HAPPENED IN YOUR PREVIOUS LIFE DIDN'T MATTER, BUT NO MATTER HOW MANY MILLIONS OF YEARS PASS BY...
...THAT SPARK IN YOUR EYE NEVER CHANGES.
MARON, I WANT YOU TO SAVE THE DEMON LORD.
SAVE HIM FROM HIS LONELI-NESS.
HE WILL BE IN EVEN GREATER DESPAIR NOW THAT FINN HAS LEFT HIM.
YOU KNOW WHAT IT MEANS TO BE LONELY, SO I HAVE FAITH THAT YOU WILL BE ABLE TO SAVE HIM.

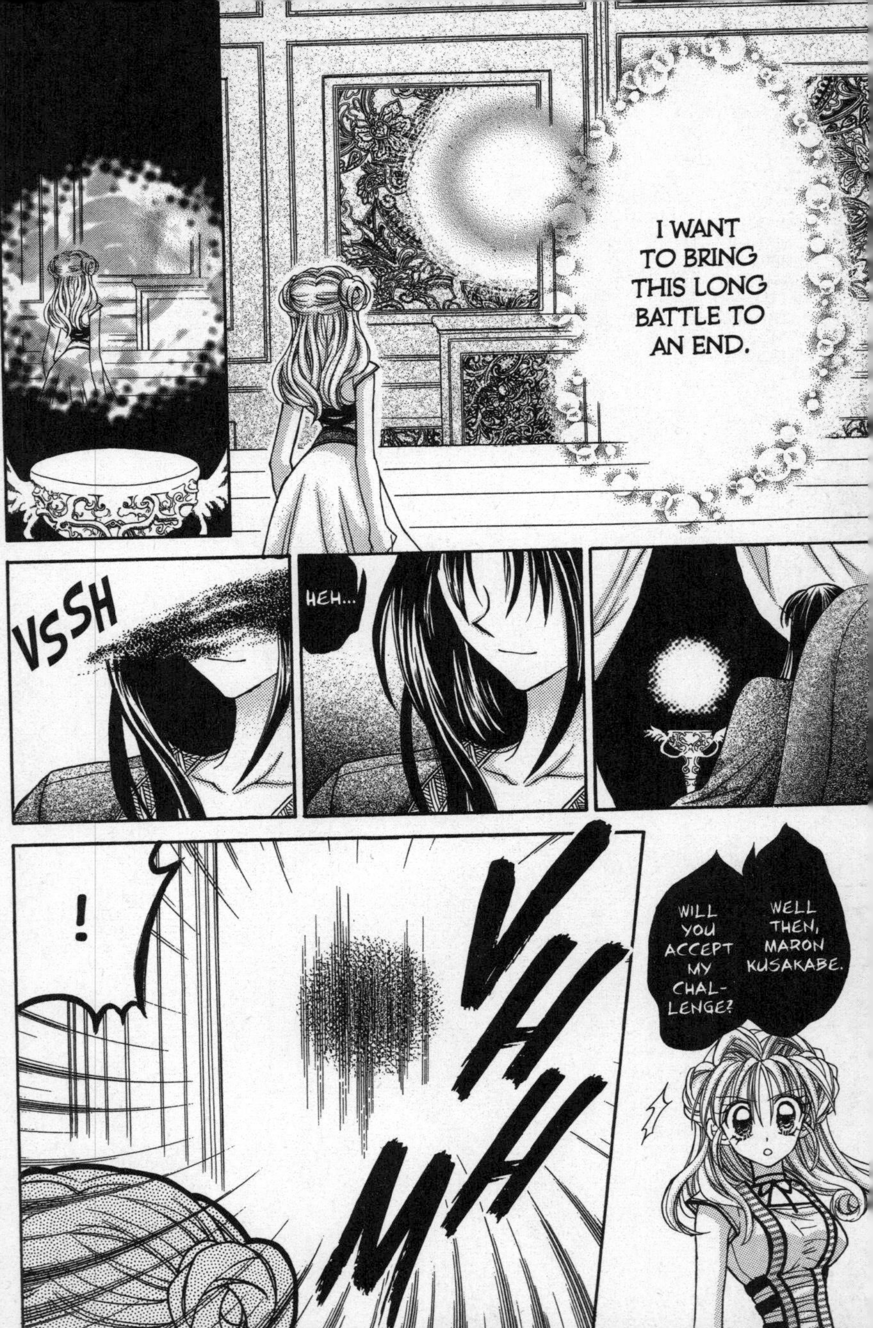
I WANT TO BRING THIS LONG BATTLE TO AN END.
HEH...
VSSH
WELL THEN, MARON KUSAKABE.
WILL YOU ACCEPT MY CHAL-LENGE?
VHHM
!

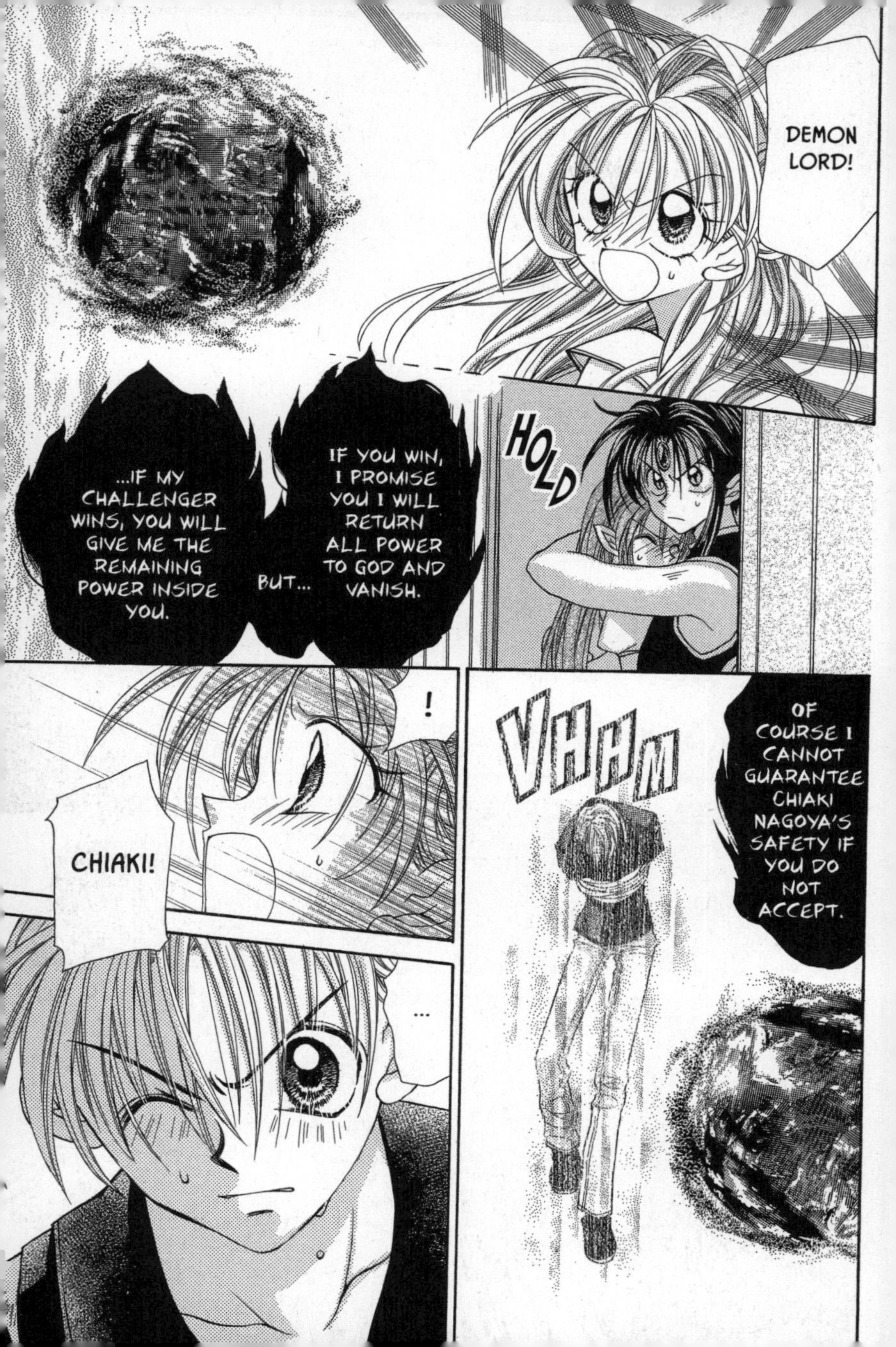

DEMON LORD!
HOLD
IF YOU WIN, I PROMISE YOU I WILL RETURN ALL POWER TO GOD AND VANISH.
BUT...
...IF MY CHALLENGER WINS, YOU WILL GIVE ME THE REMAINING POWER INSIDE YOU.
VHHM
OF COURSE I CANNOT GUARANTEE CHIAKI NAGOYA'S SAFETY IF YOU DO NOT ACCEPT.
!
CHIAKI!
...

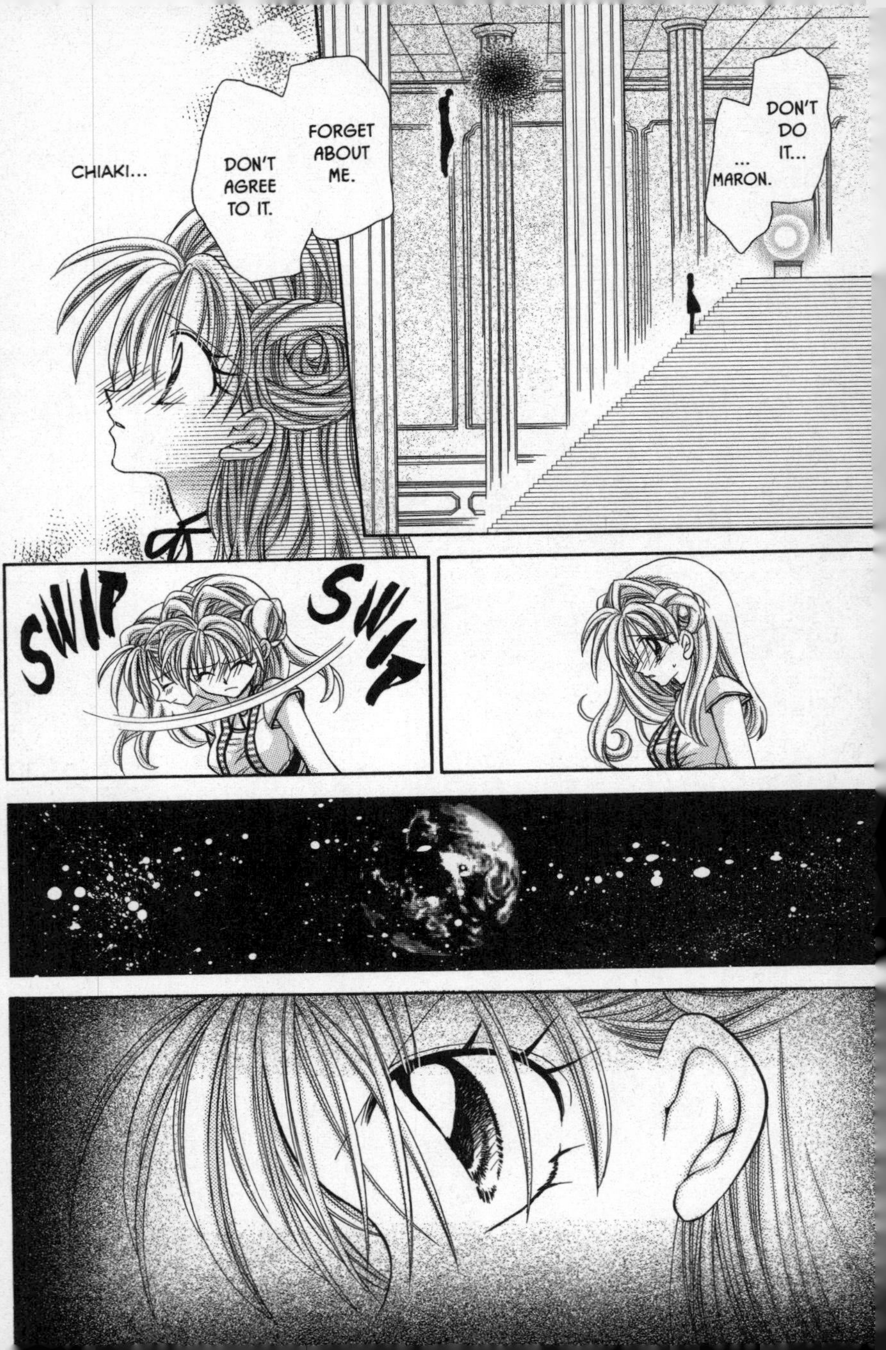
DON'T DO IT... ...MARON.
FORGET ABOUT ME. DON'T AGREE TO IT.
CHIAKI...
SWIP SWIP

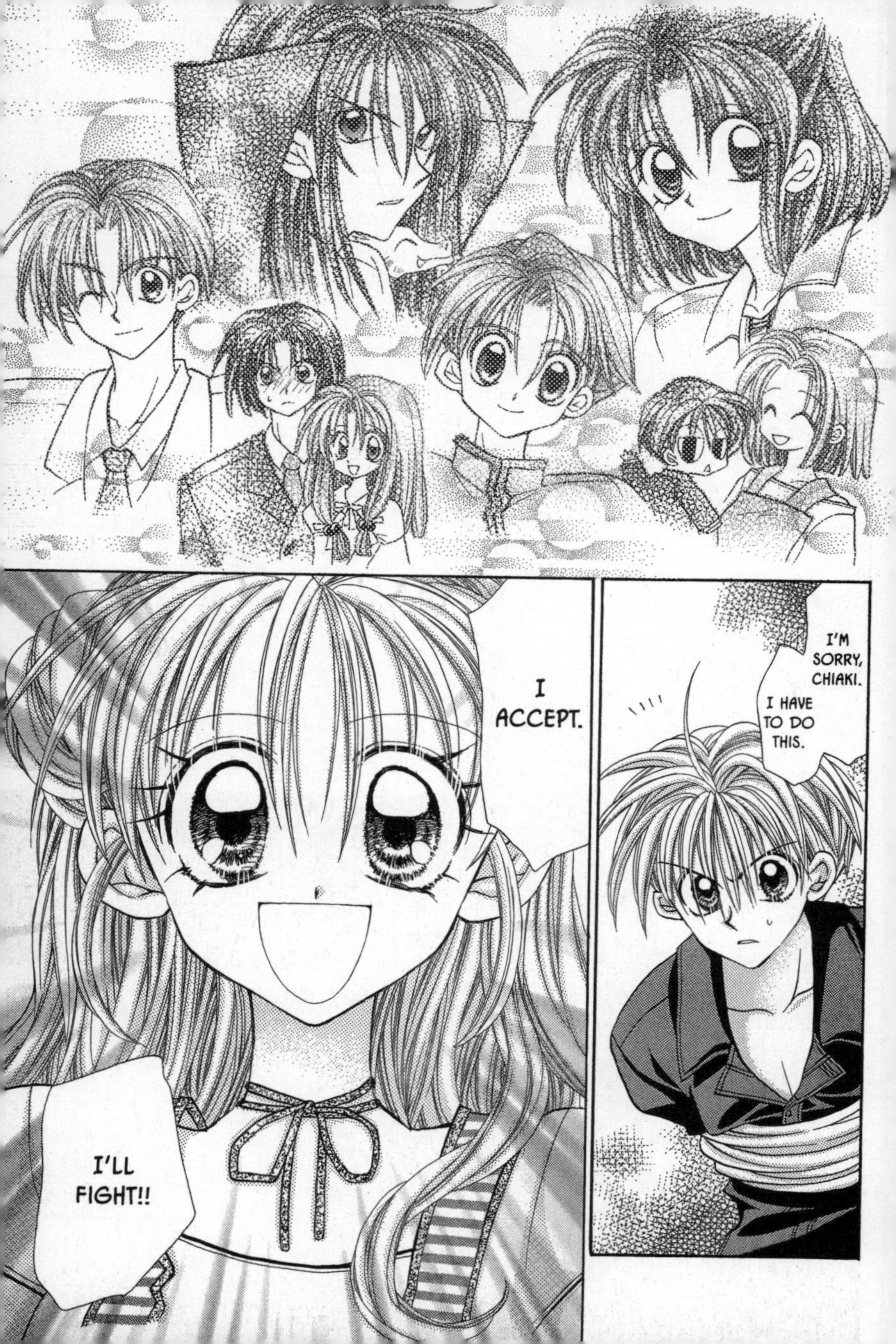
I'M SORRY, CHIAKI.
I HAVE TO DO THIS.
I ACCEPT.
I'LL FIGHT!!

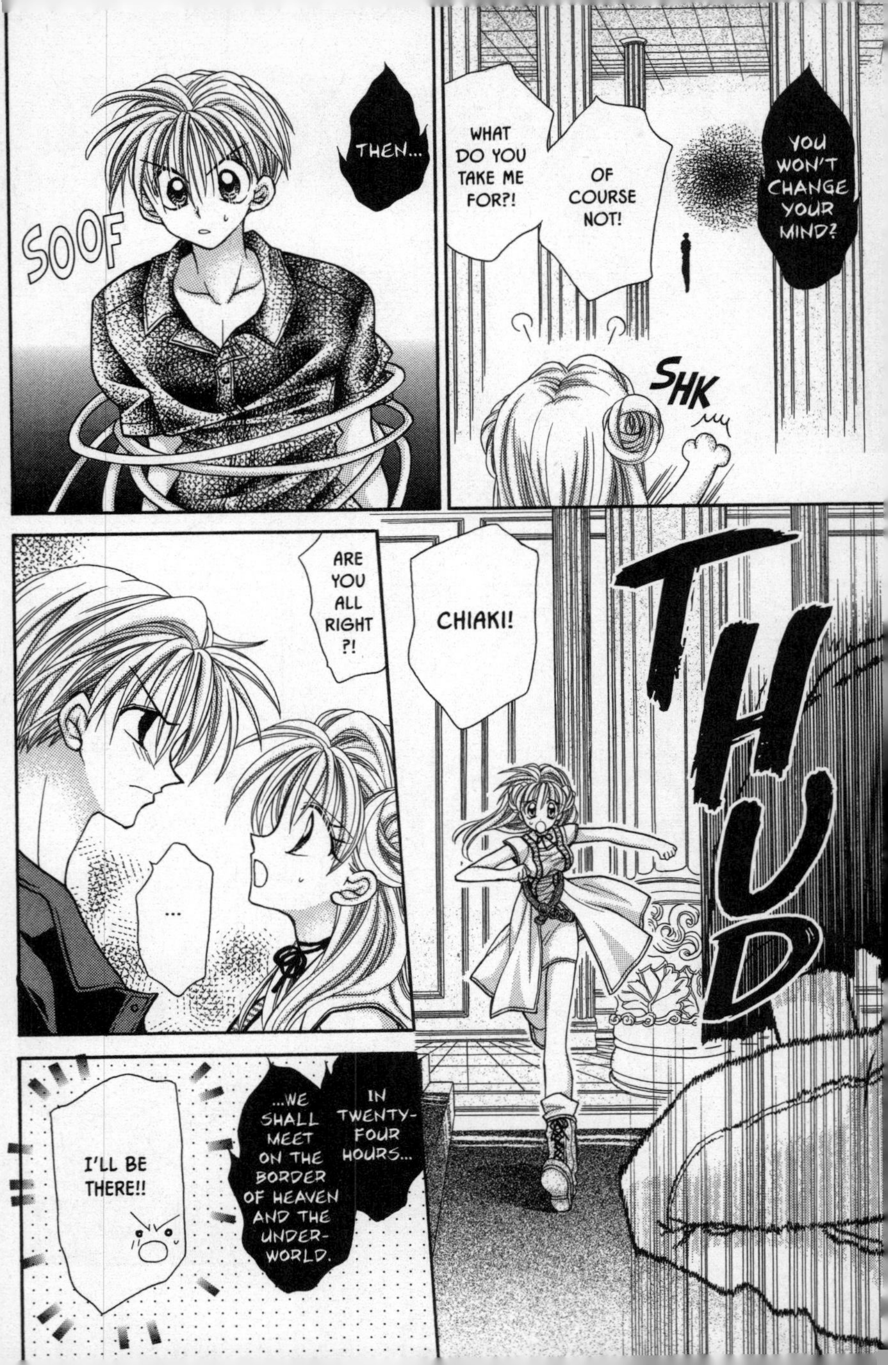
YOU WON'T CHANGE YOUR MIND?
OF COURSE NOT!
WHAT DO YOU TAKE ME FOR?!
SHK
THEN...
SOOF
THUD
CHIAKI!
ARE YOU ALL RIGHT?!
...
IN TWENTY-FOUR HOURS...
...WE SHALL MEET ON THE BORDER OF HEAVEN AND THE UNDER-WORLD.
I'LL BE THERE!!

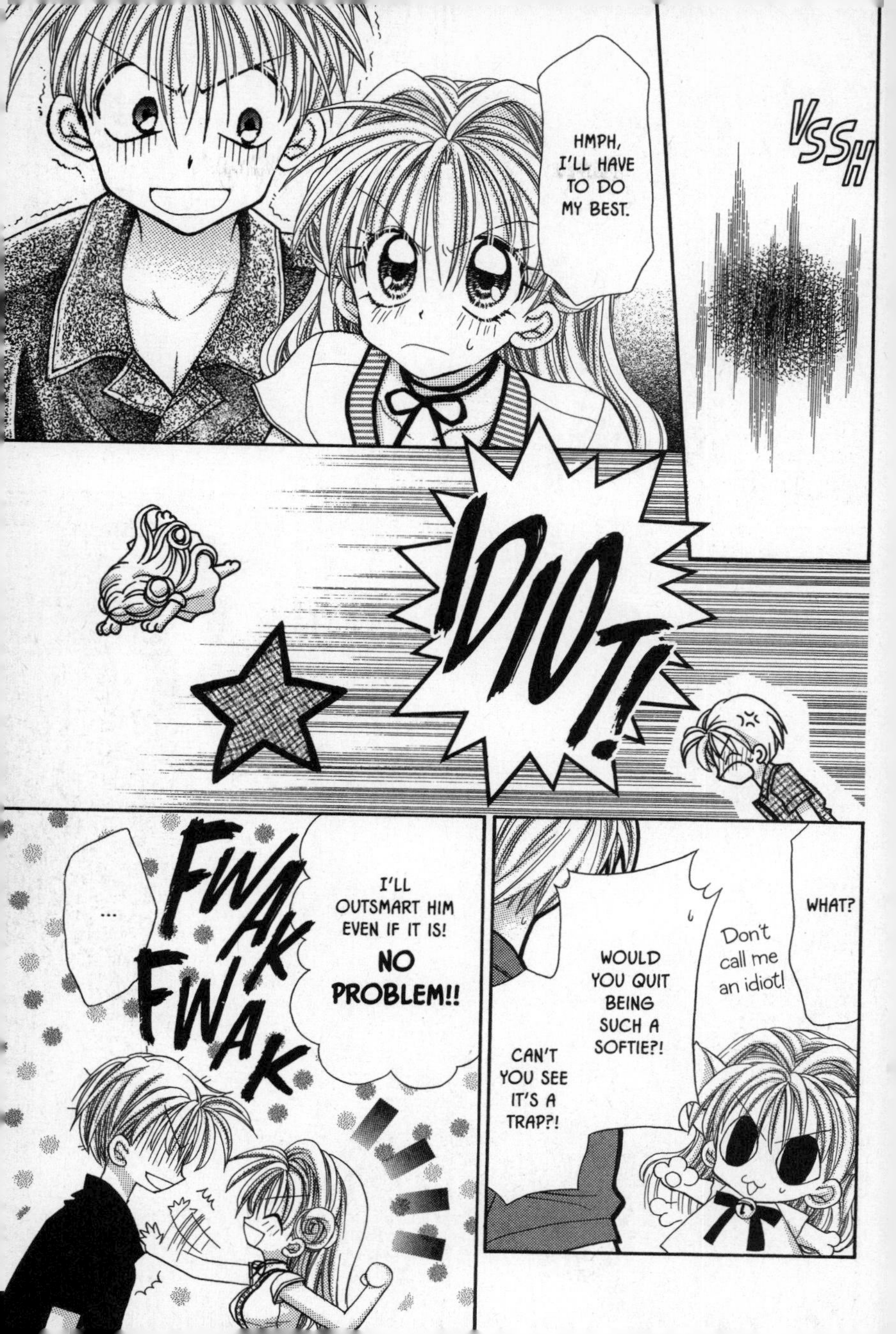
VSSH
HMPH, I'LL HAVE TO DO MY BEST.
IDIOT!
WHAT?
Don't call me an idiot!
WOULD YOU QUIT BEING SUCH A SOFTIE?!
CAN'T YOU SEE IT'S A TRAP?!
I'LL OUTSMART HIM EVEN IF IT IS! NO PROBLEM!!
FWAK FWAK
...

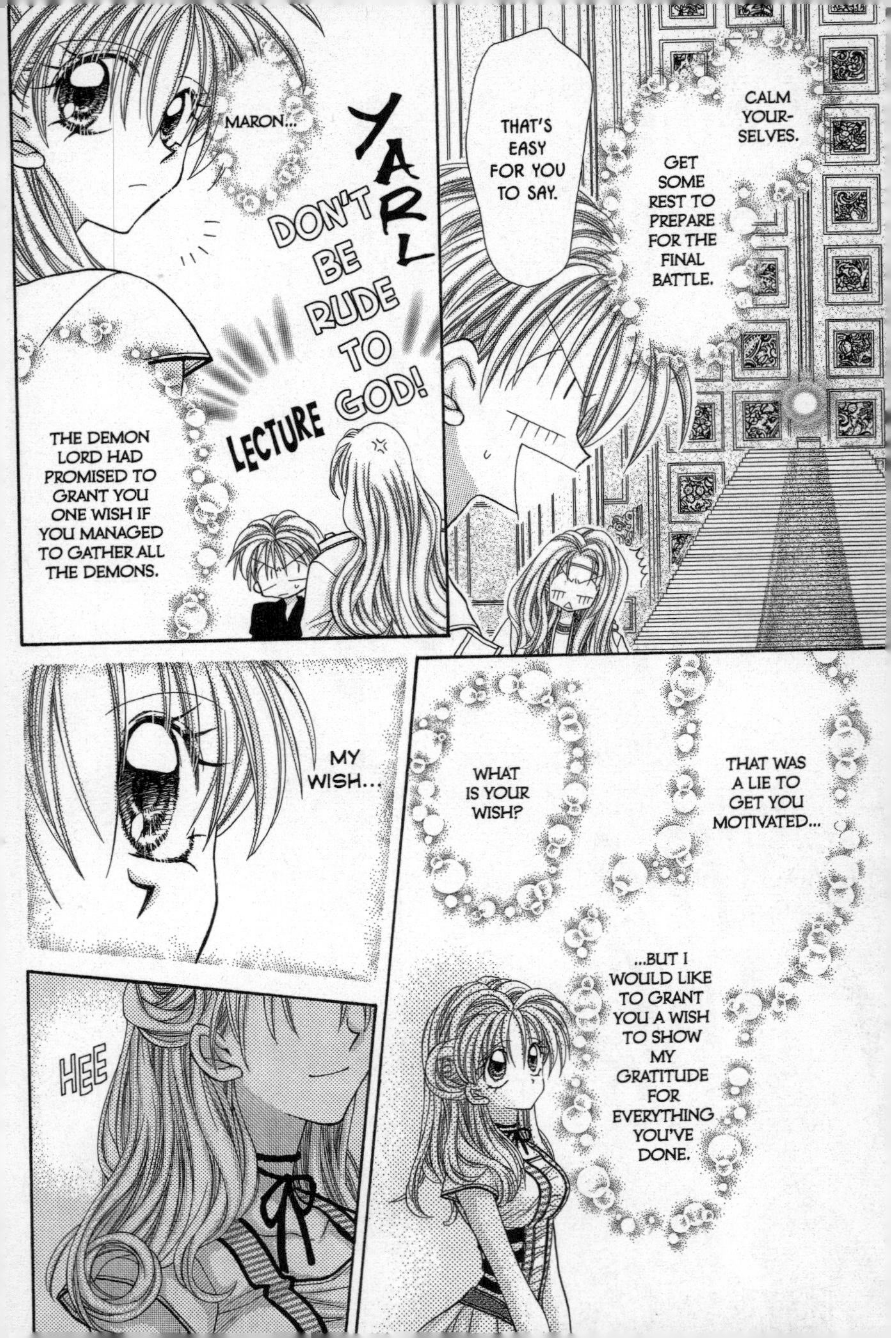
CALM YOUR-SELVES.
GET SOME REST TO PREPARE FOR THE FINAL BATTLE.
THAT'S EASY FOR YOU TO SAY.
YARL
DON'T BE RUDE TO GOD!
MARON...
LECTURE
THE DEMON LORD HAD PROMISED TO GRANT YOU ONE WISH IF YOU MANAGED TO GATHER ALL THE DEMONS.
THAT WAS A LIE TO GET YOU MOTIVATED...
...BUT I WOULD LIKE TO GRANT YOU A WISH TO SHOW MY GRATITUDE FOR EVERYTHING YOU'VE DONE.
WHAT IS YOUR WISH?
MY WISH...
HEE

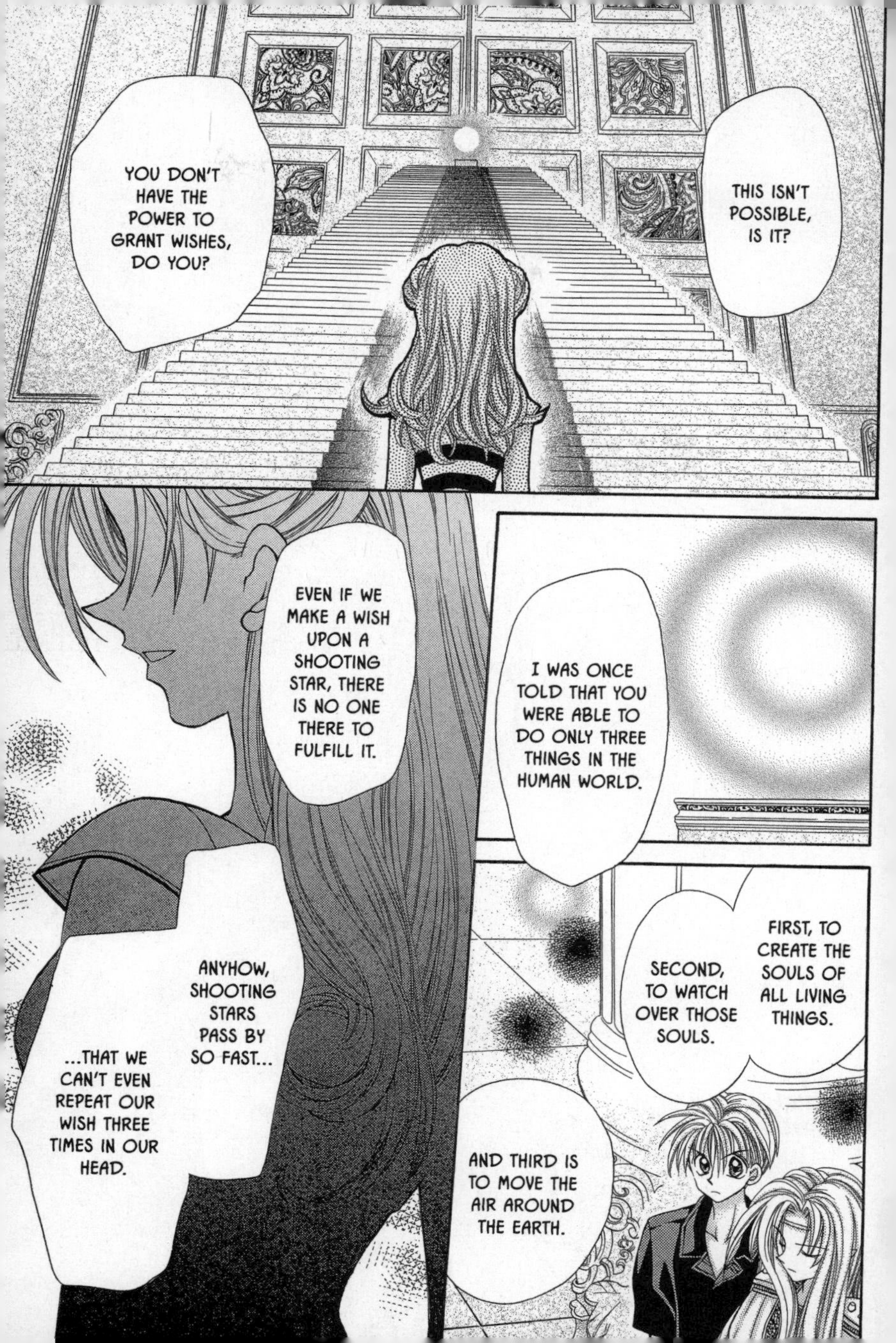
THIS ISN'T POSSIBLE, IS IT?
YOU DON'T HAVE THE POWER TO GRANT WISHES, DO YOU?
I WAS ONCE TOLD THAT YOU WERE ABLE TO DO ONLY THREE THINGS IN THE HUMAN WORLD.
FIRST, TO CREATE THE SOULS OF ALL LIVING THINGS.
SECOND, TO WATCH OVER THOSE SOULS.
AND THIRD IS TO MOVE THE AIR AROUND THE EARTH.
EVEN IF WE MAKE A WISH UPON A SHOOTING STAR, THERE IS NO ONE THERE TO FULFILL IT.
ANYHOW, SHOOTING STARS PASS BY SO FAST...
...THAT WE CAN'T EVEN REPEAT OUR WISH THREE TIMES IN OUR HEAD.

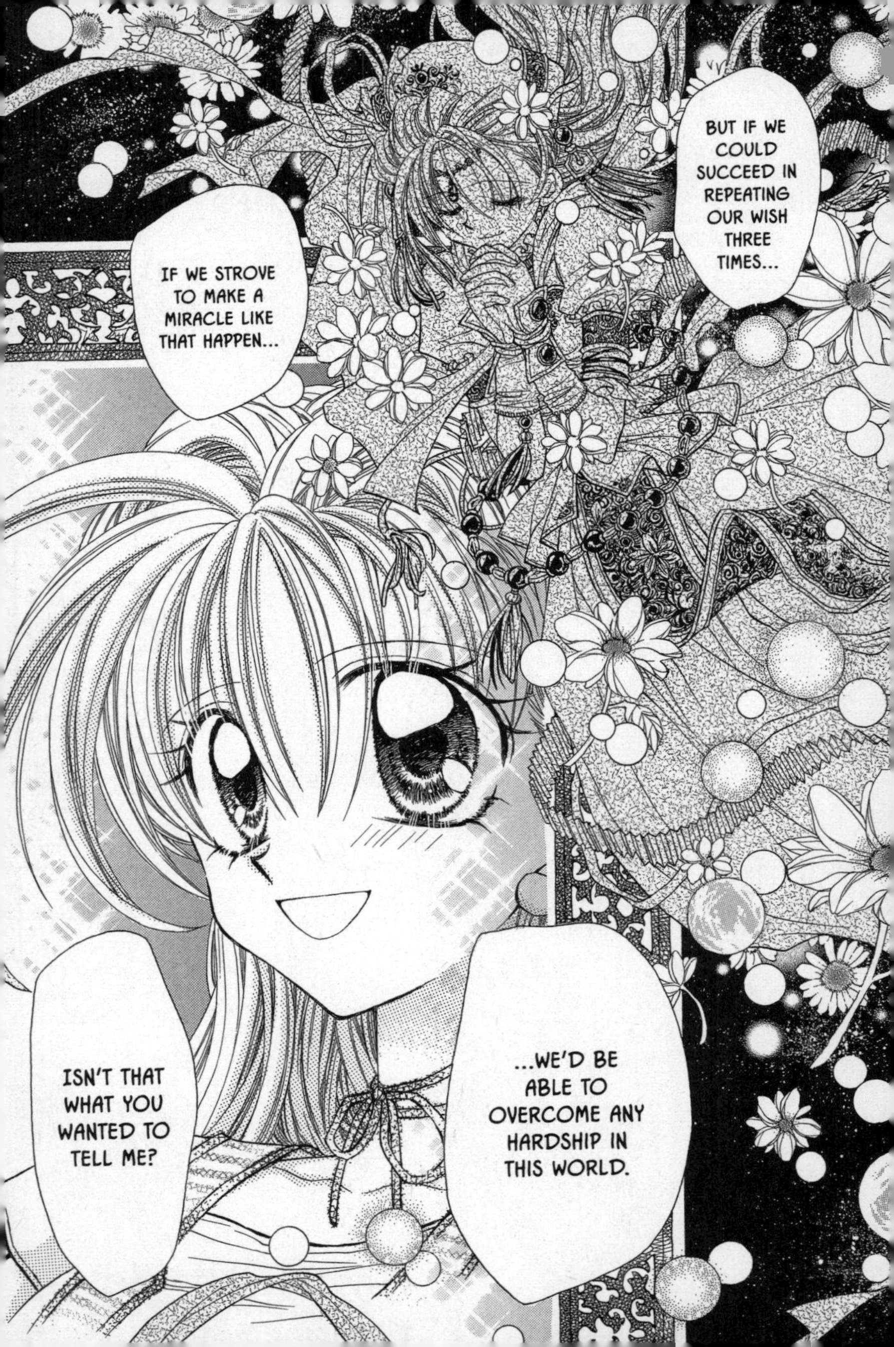
BUT IF WE COULD SUCCEED IN REPEATING OUR WISH THREE TIMES...
IF WE STROVE TO MAKE A MIRACLE LIKE THAT HAPPEN...
...WE'D BE ABLE TO OVERCOME ANY HARDSHIP IN THIS WORLD.
ISN'T THAT WHAT YOU WANTED TO TELL ME?

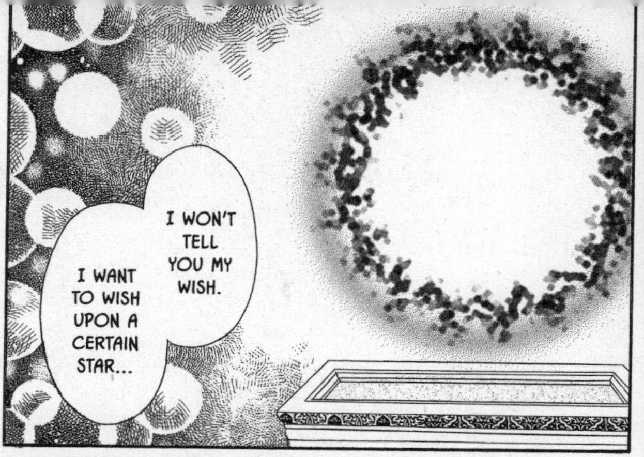
I WON'T TELL YOU MY WISH.
I WANT TO WISH UPON A CERTAIN STAR...

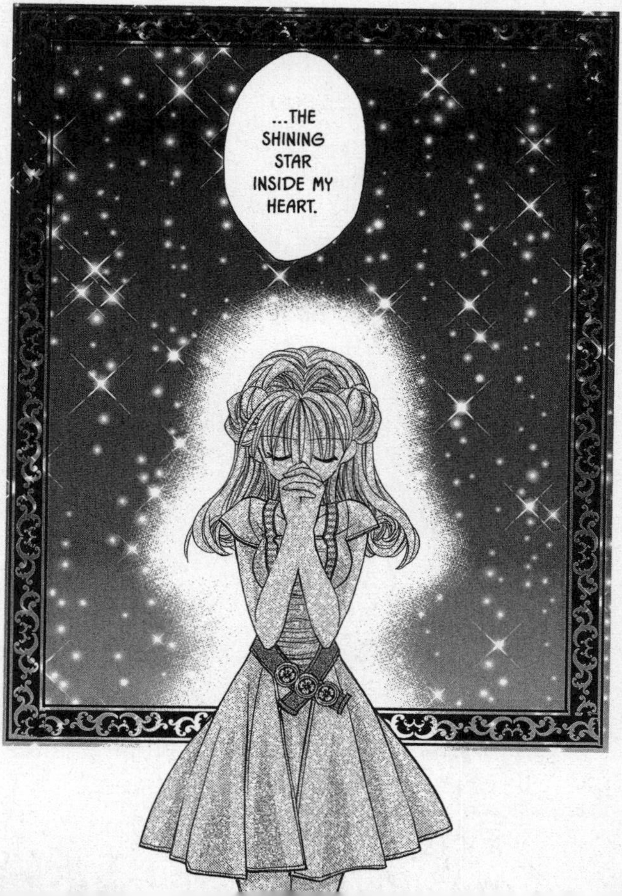
...THE SHINING STAR INSIDE MY HEART.

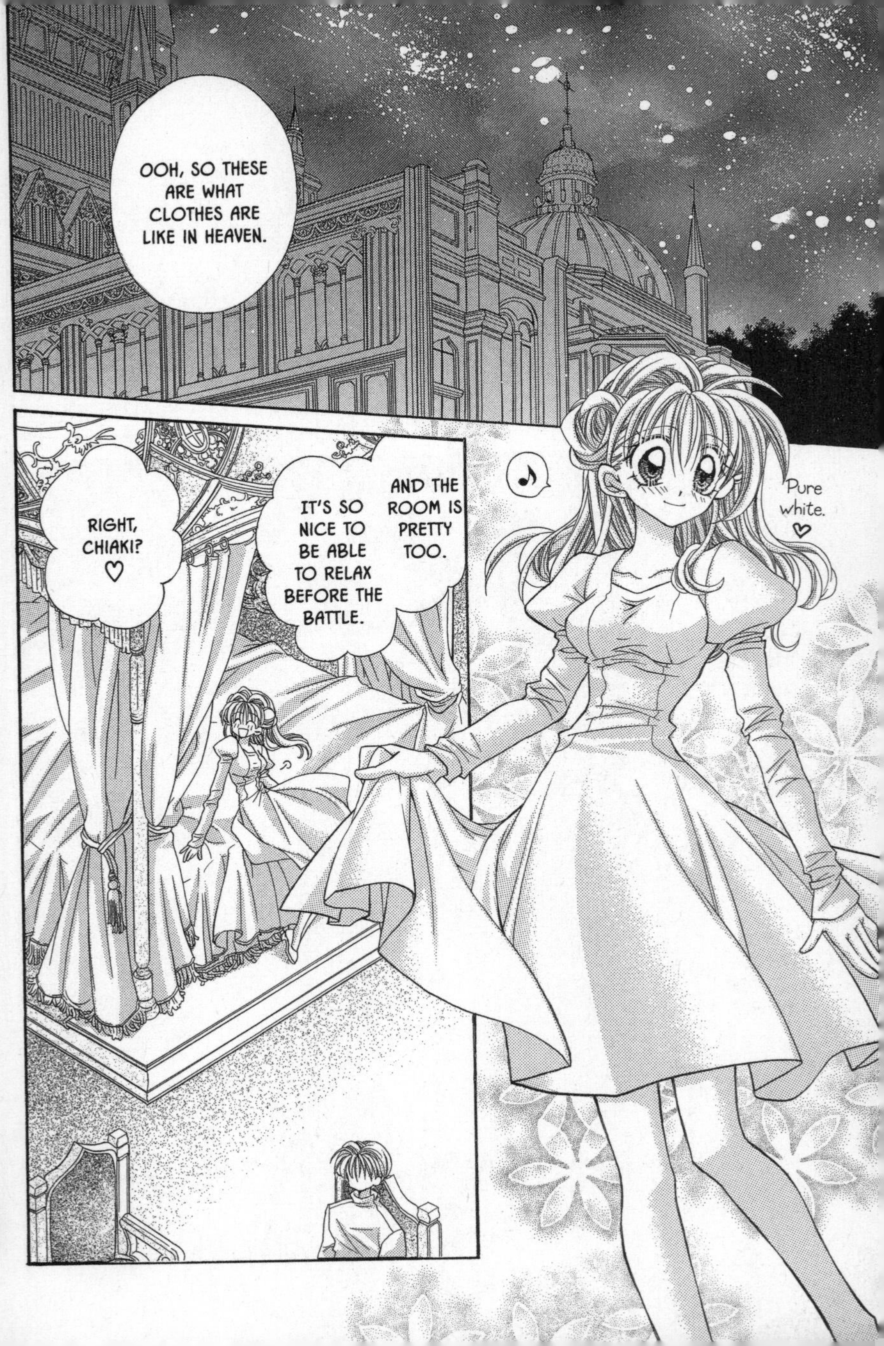
OOH, SO THESE ARE WHAT CLOTHES ARE LIKE IN HEAVEN.
♪
Pure white. ♡
AND THE ROOM IS PRETTY TOO.
IT'S SO NICE TO BE ABLE TO RELAX BEFORE THE BATTLE.
RIGHT, CHIAKI? ♡

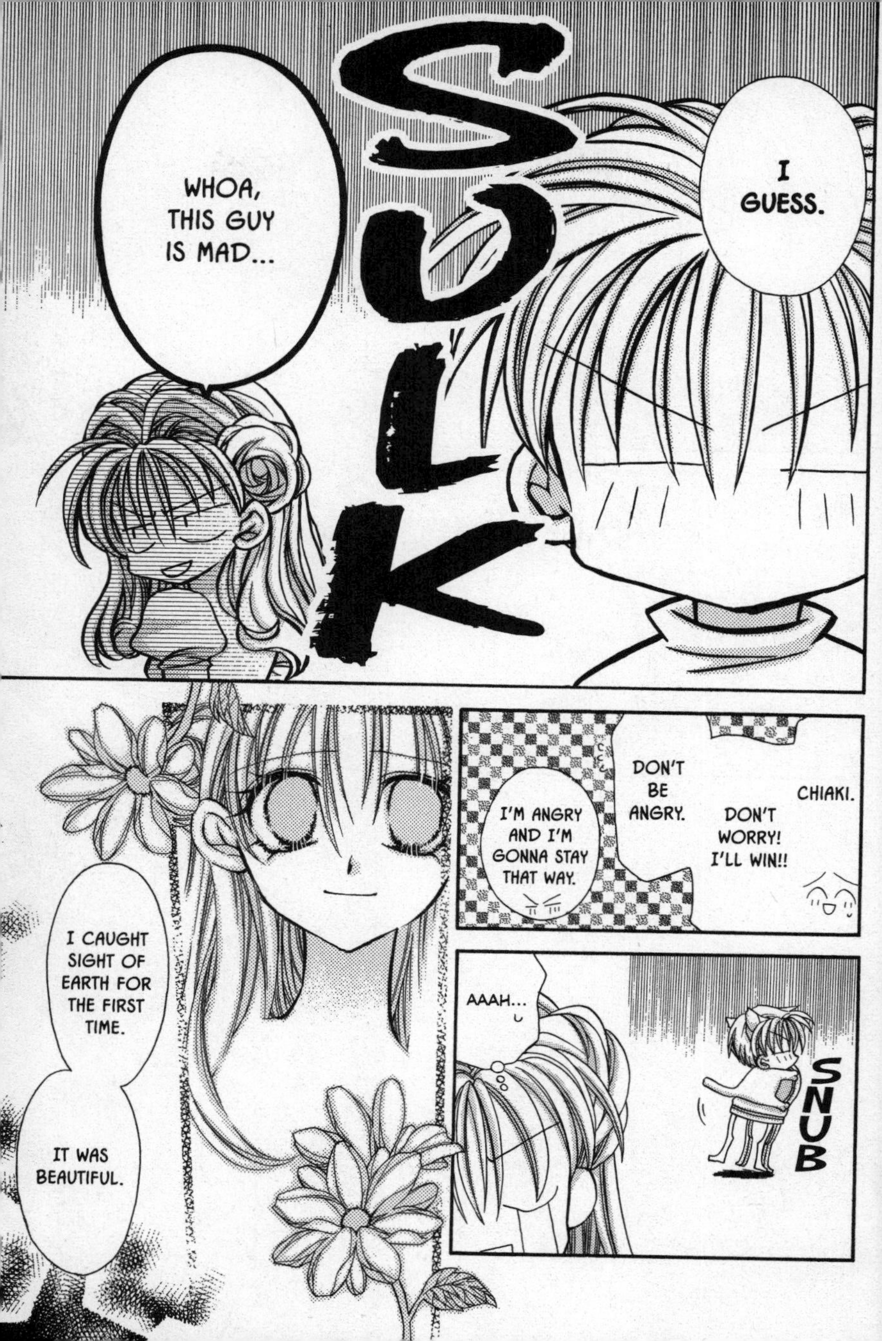
I GUESS.
SULK
WHOA, THIS GUY IS MAD...
CHIAKI.
DON'T WORRY! I'LL WIN!!
DON'T BE ANGRY.
I'M ANGRY AND I'M GONNA STAY THAT WAY.
SNUB
AAAH...
I CAUGHT SIGHT OF EARTH FOR THE FIRST TIME.
IT WAS BEAUTIFUL.

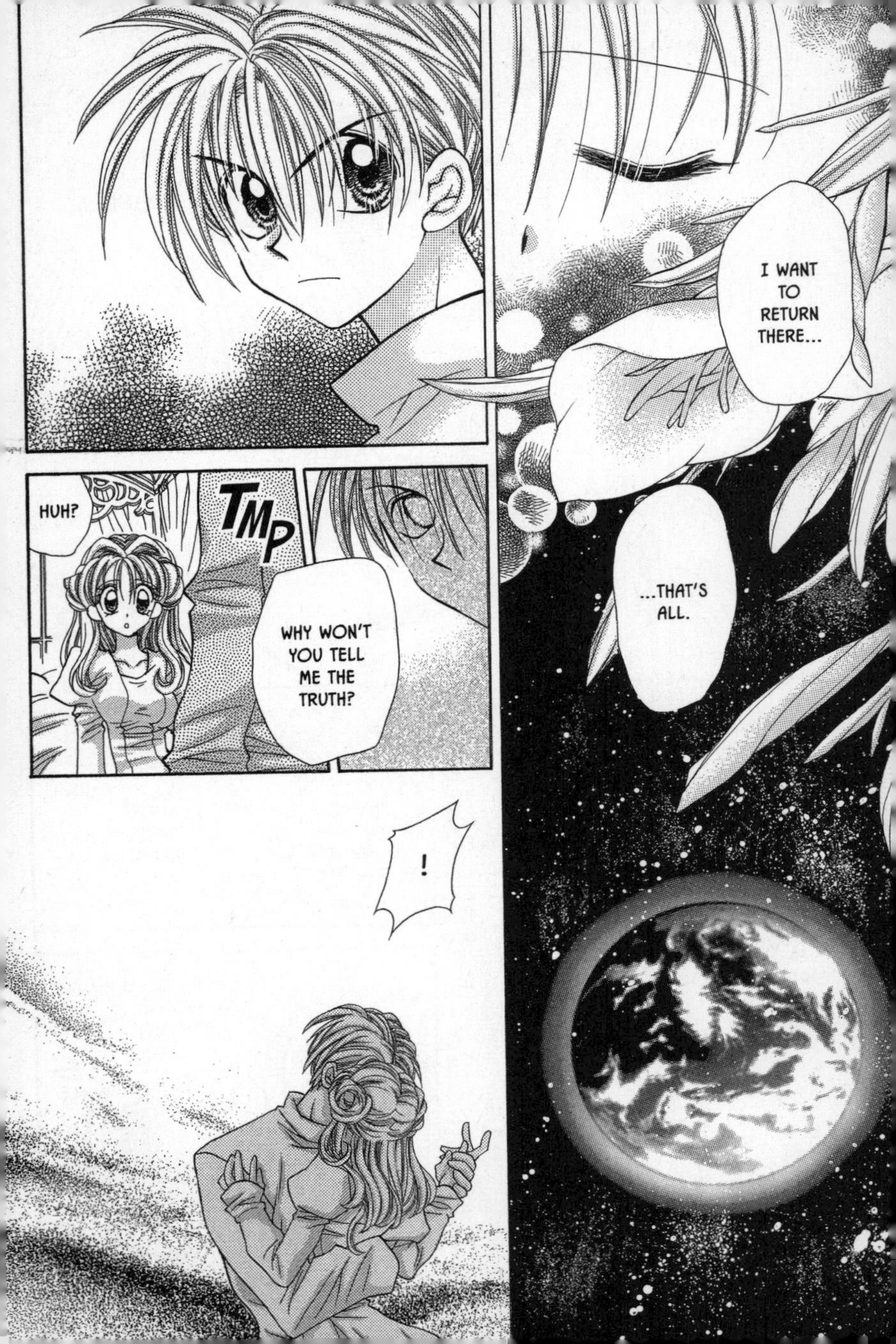
I WANT TO RETURN THERE...
...THAT'S ALL.
WHY WON'T YOU TELL ME THE TRUTH?
TMP
HUH?
!

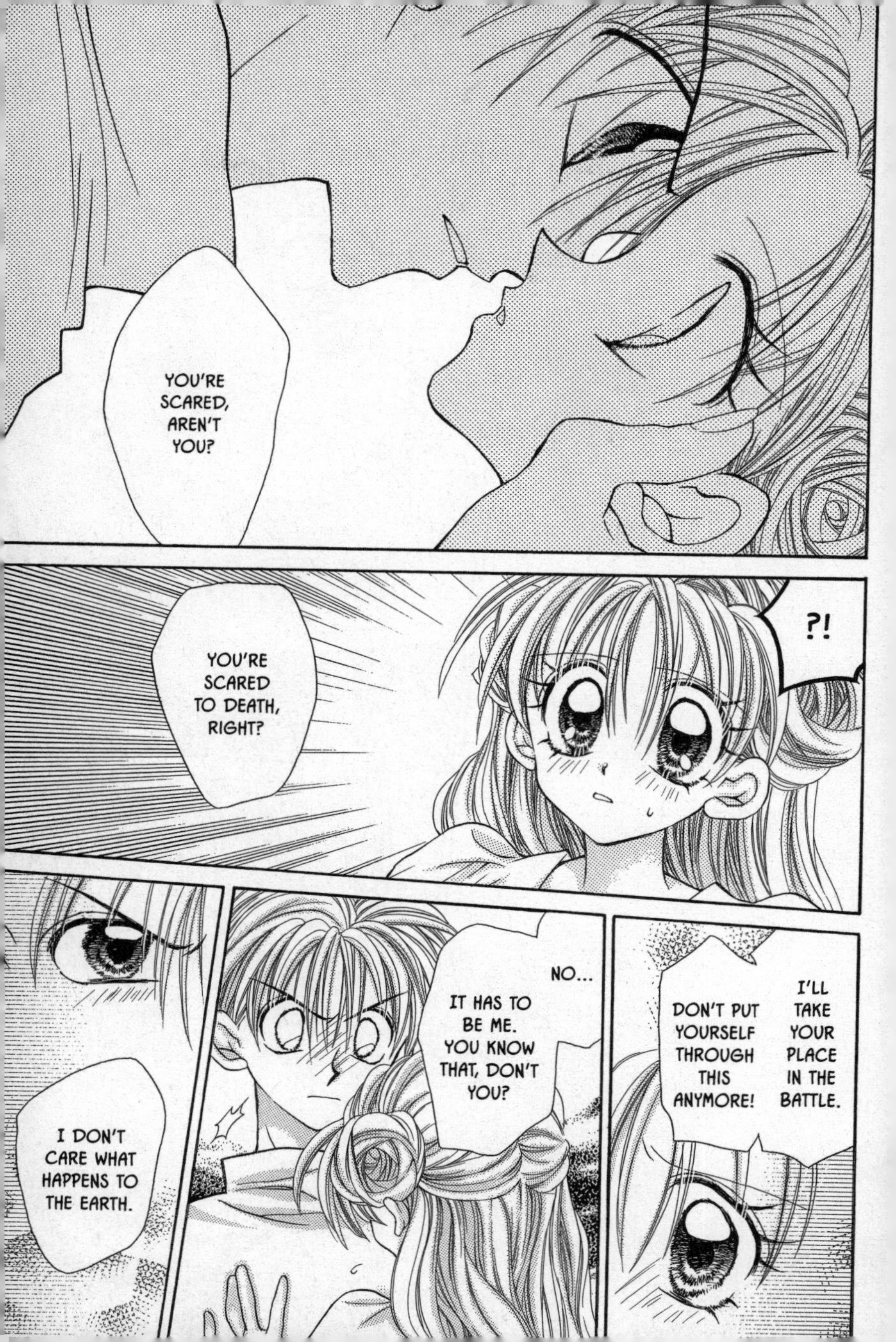
YOU'RE SCARED, AREN'T YOU?
?!
YOU'RE SCARED TO DEATH, RIGHT?
I'LL TAKE YOUR PLACE IN THE BATTLE.
DON'T PUT YOURSELF THROUGH THIS ANYMORE!
NO...
IT HAS TO BE ME. YOU KNOW THAT, DON'T YOU?
I DON'T CARE WHAT HAPPENS TO THE EARTH.

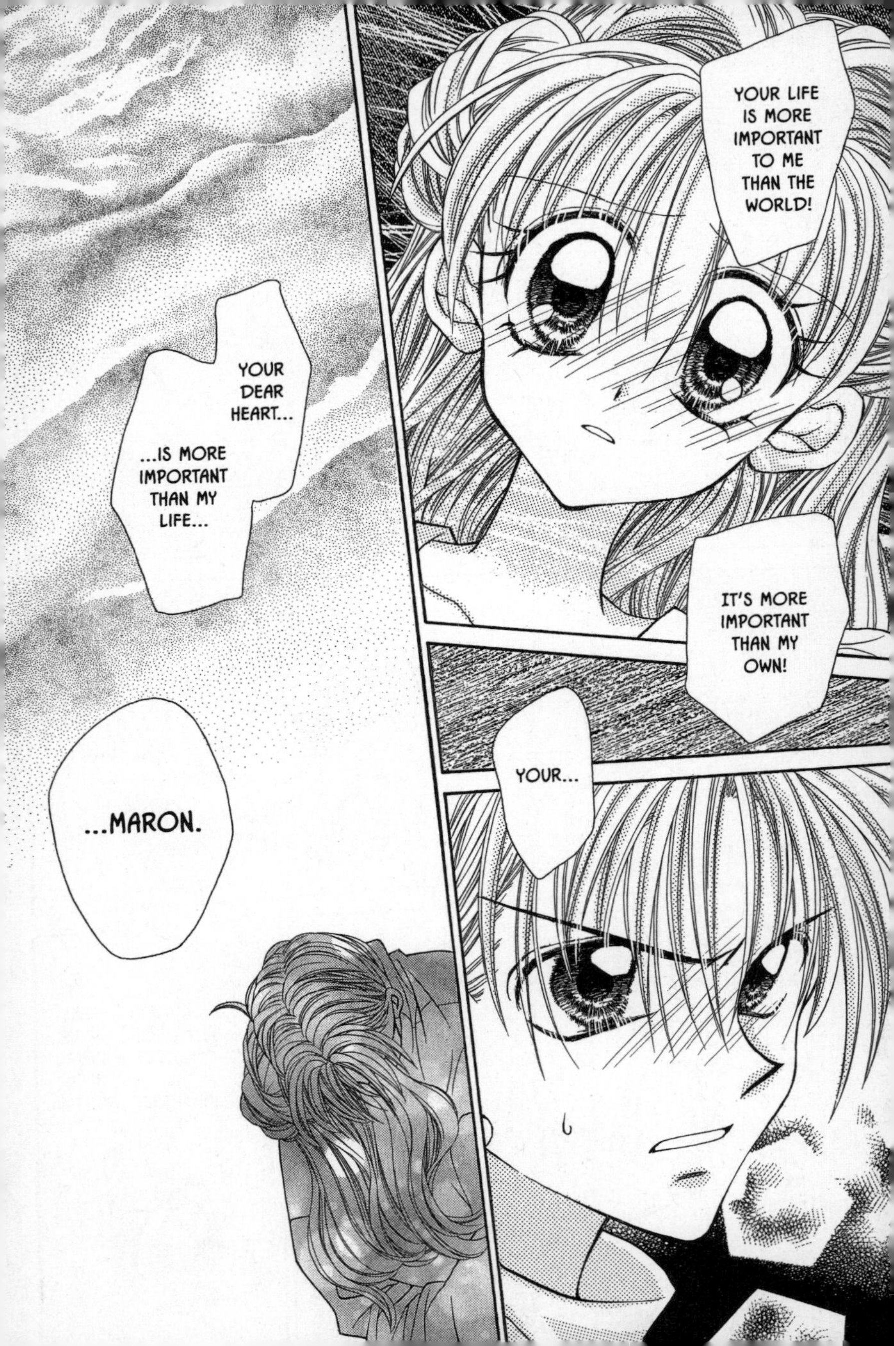
YOUR LIFE IS MORE IMPORTANT TO ME THAN THE WORLD!
IT'S MORE IMPORTANT THAN MY OWN!
YOUR...
YOUR DEAR HEART...
...IS MORE IMPORTANT THAN MY LIFE...
...MARON.

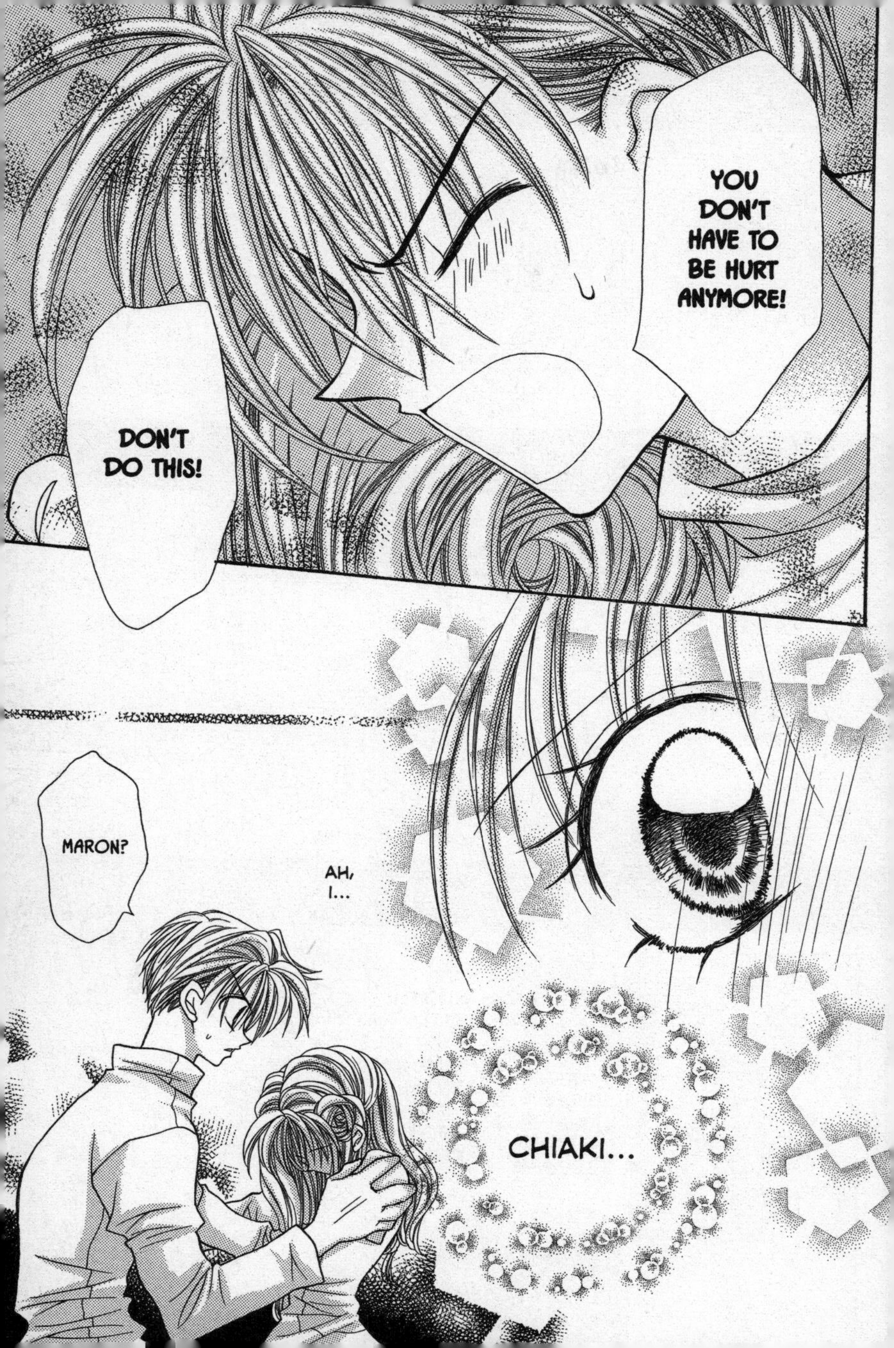
YOU DON'T HAVE TO BE HURT ANYMORE!
DON'T DO THIS!
AH, I...
CHIAKI...
MARON?

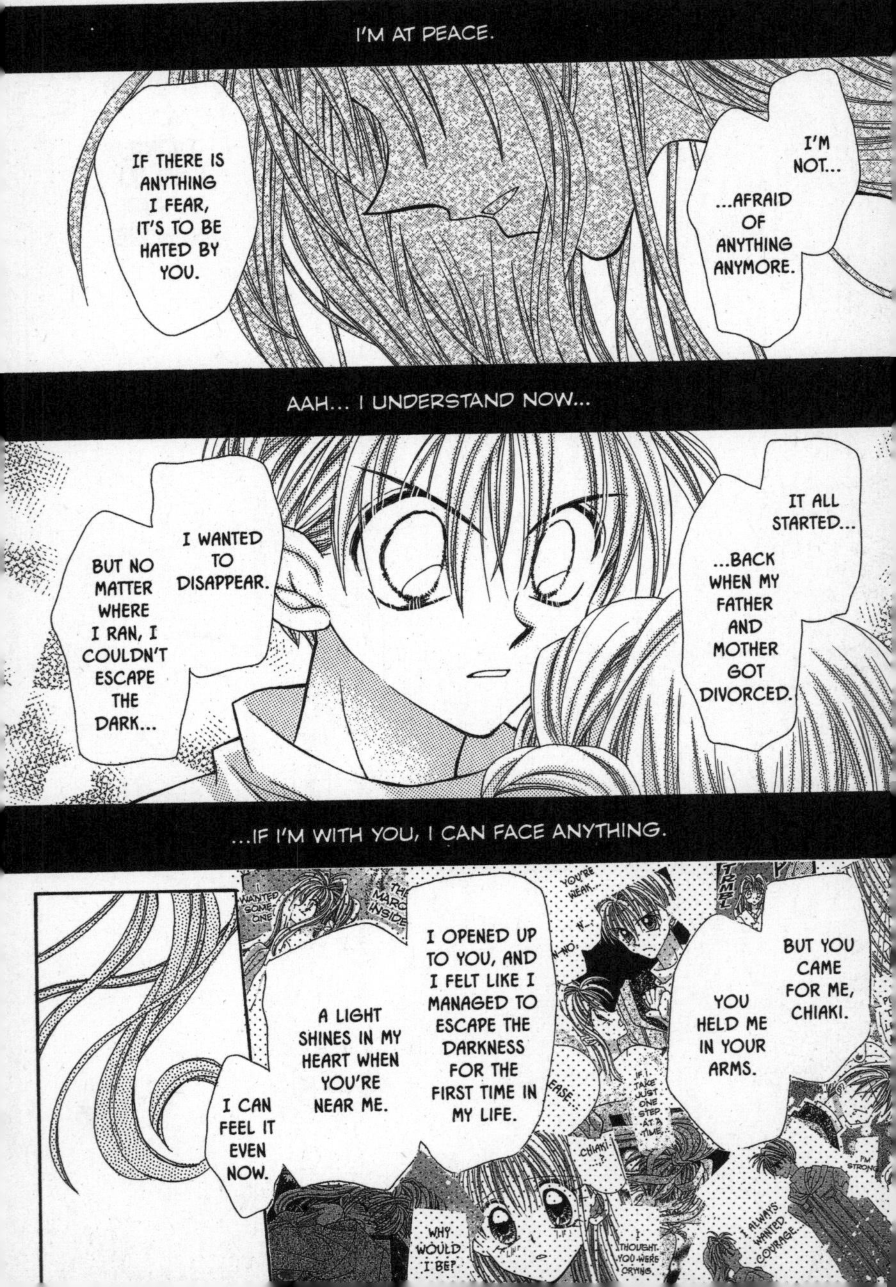
I'M AT PEACE.
I'M NOT...
...AFRAID OF ANYTHING ANYMORE.
IF THERE IS ANYTHING I FEAR, IT'S TO BE HATED BY YOU.
AAH... I UNDERSTAND NOW...
IT ALL STARTED...
...BACK WHEN MY FATHER AND MOTHER GOT DIVORCED.
I WANTED TO DISAPPEAR.
BUT NO MATTER WHERE I RAN, I COULDN'T ESCAPE THE DARK...
...IF I'M WITH YOU, I CAN FACE ANYTHING.
BUT YOU CAME FOR ME, CHIAKI.
YOU HELD ME IN YOUR ARMS.
YOU'RE WEAK...
N-NO.
I ALWAYS WANTED COURAGE.
I'M STRONG
IF I TAKE JUST ONE STEP AT A TIME...
CHIAKI?
I THOUGHT YOU WERE CRYING.
WHY WOULD I BE?
I OPENED UP TO YOU, AND I FELT LIKE I MANAGED TO ESCAPE THE DARKNESS FOR THE FIRST TIME IN MY LIFE.
I WANTED SOME ONE
A LIGHT SHINES IN MY HEART WHEN YOU'RE NEAR ME.
I CAN FEEL IT EVEN NOW.

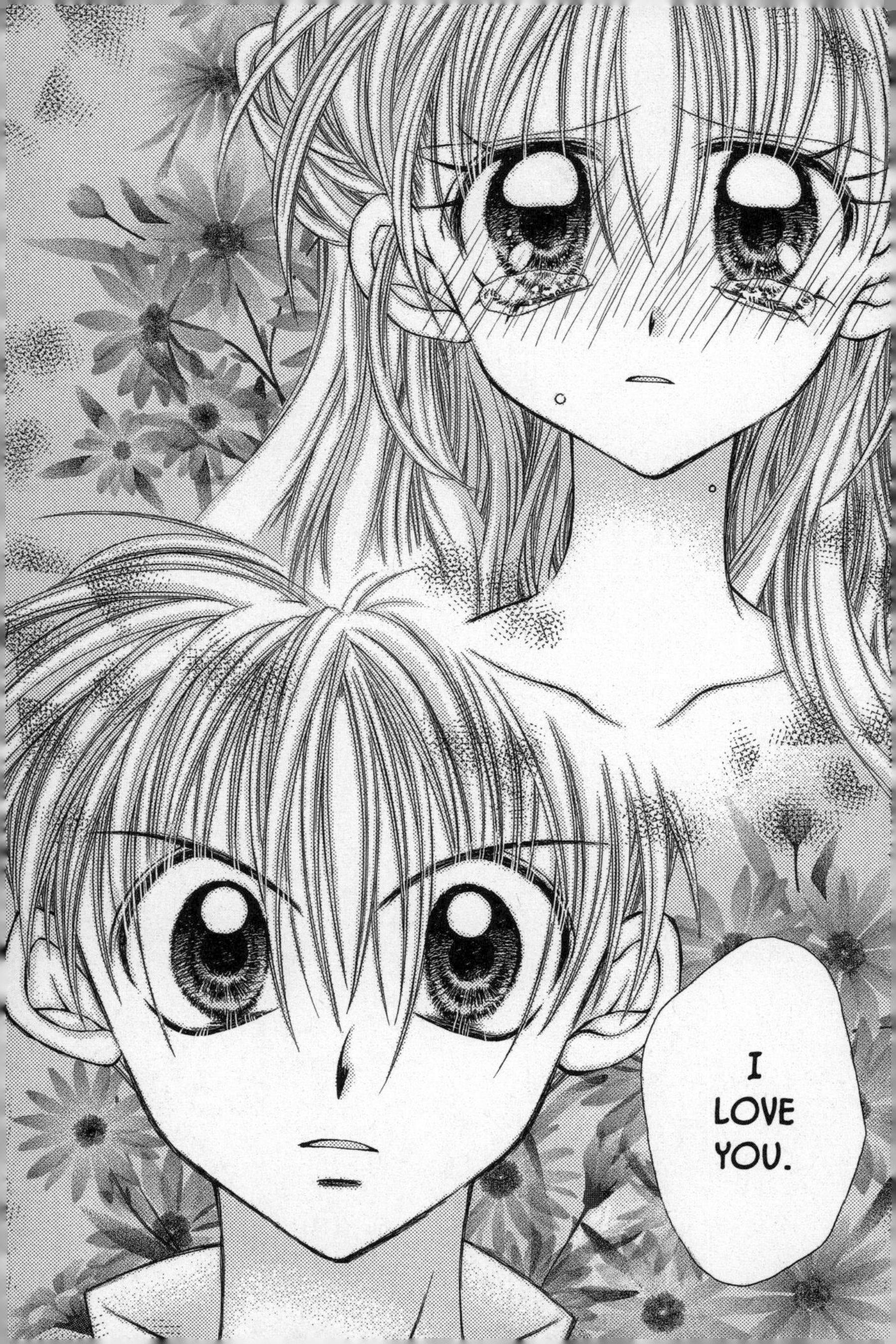
I LOVE YOU.

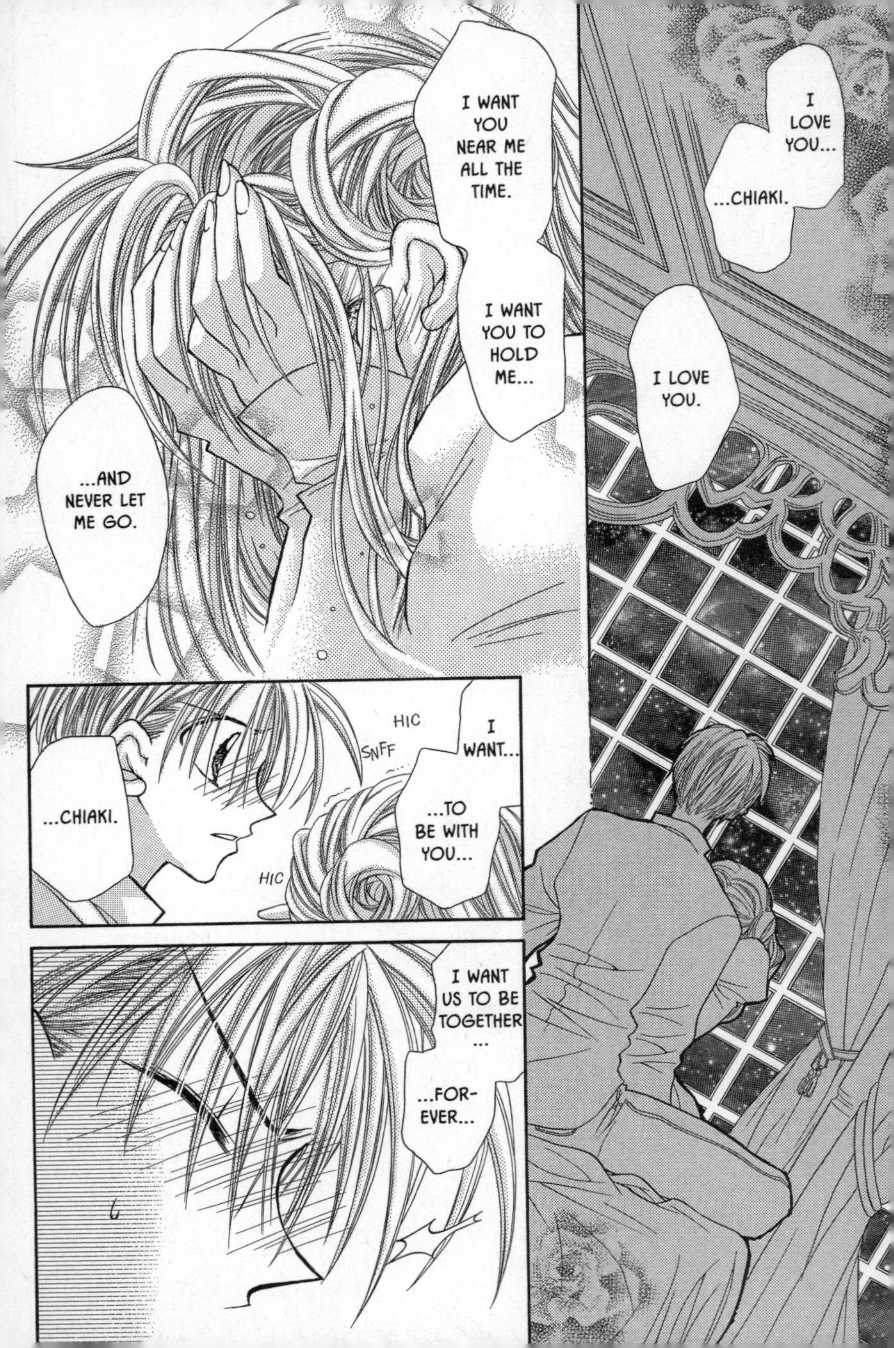
I LOVE YOU...
...CHIAKI.
I LOVE YOU.
I WANT YOU NEAR ME ALL THE TIME.
I WANT YOU TO HOLD ME...
...AND NEVER LET ME GO.
I WANT...
HIC
SNFF
...TO BE WITH YOU...
...CHIAKI.
HIC
I WANT US TO BE TOGETHER...
...FOR-EVER...

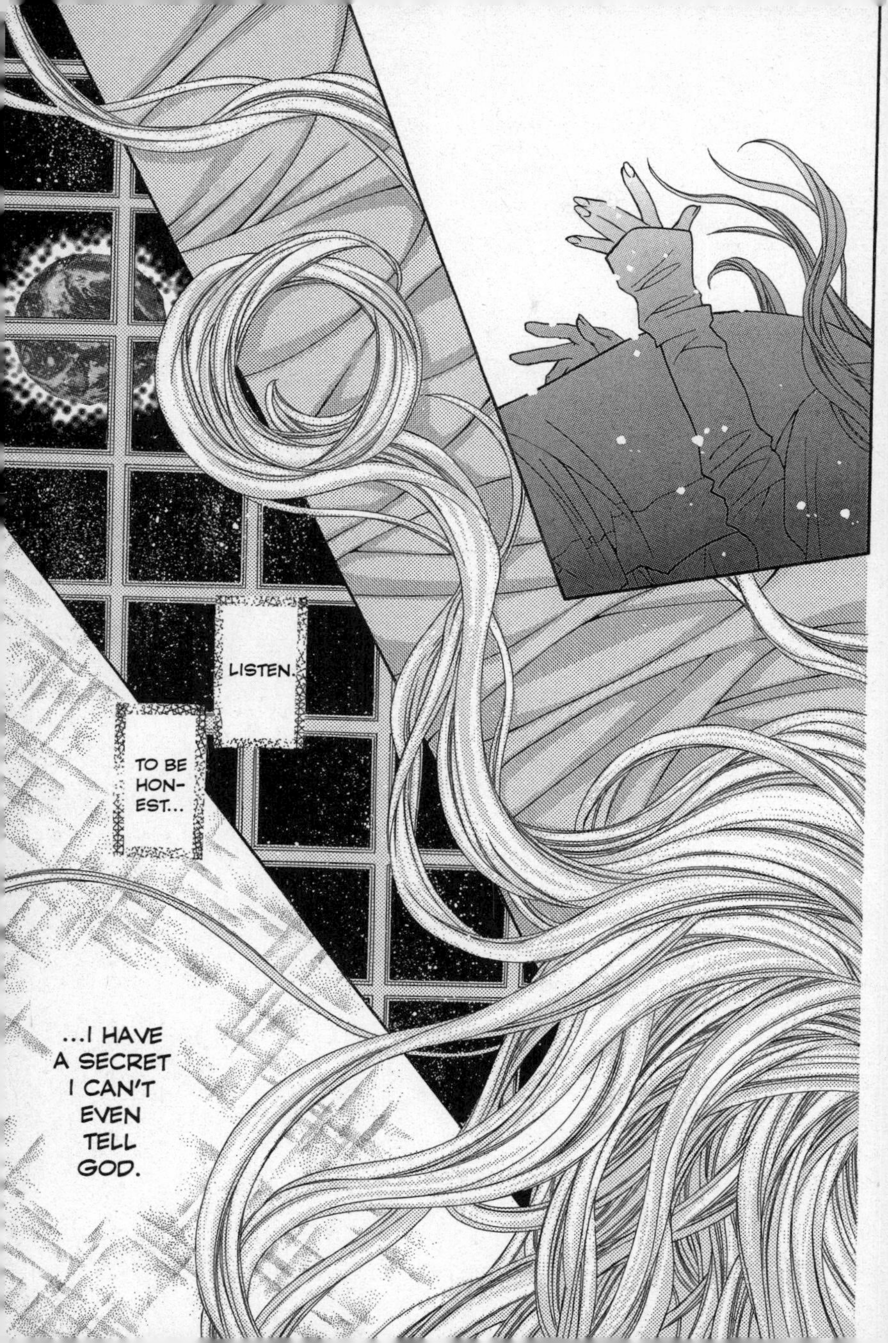
LISTEN.
TO BE HON-EST...
...I HAVE A SECRET I CAN'T EVEN TELL GOD.

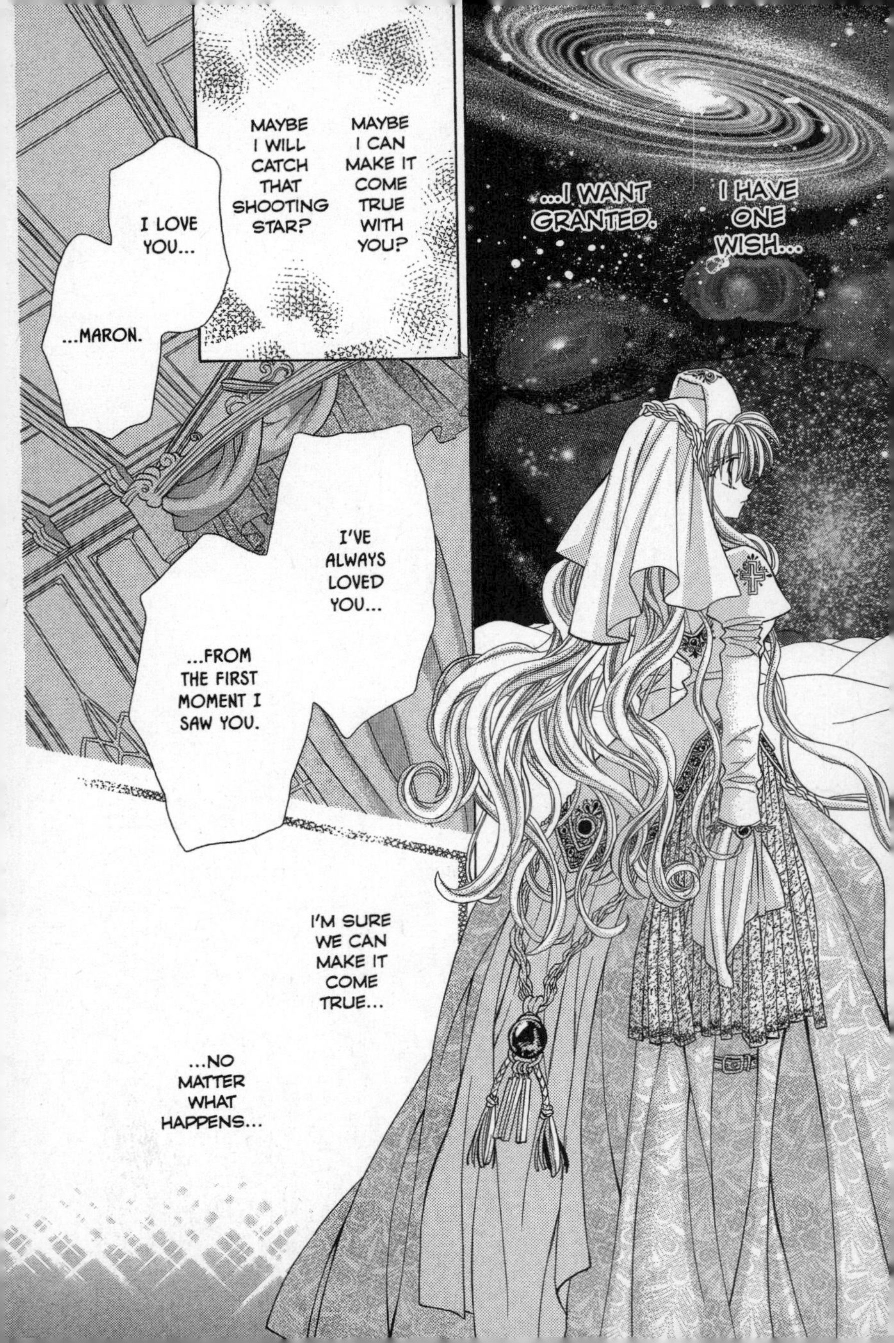
I HAVE ONE WISH...
...I WANT GRANTED.
MAYBE I CAN MAKE IT COME TRUE WITH YOU?
MAYBE I WILL CATCH THAT SHOOTING STAR?
I LOVE YOU... ...MARON.
I'VE ALWAYS LOVED YOU...
...FROM THE FIRST MOMENT I SAW YOU.
I'M SURE WE CAN MAKE IT COME TRUE...
...NO MATTER WHAT HAPPENS...

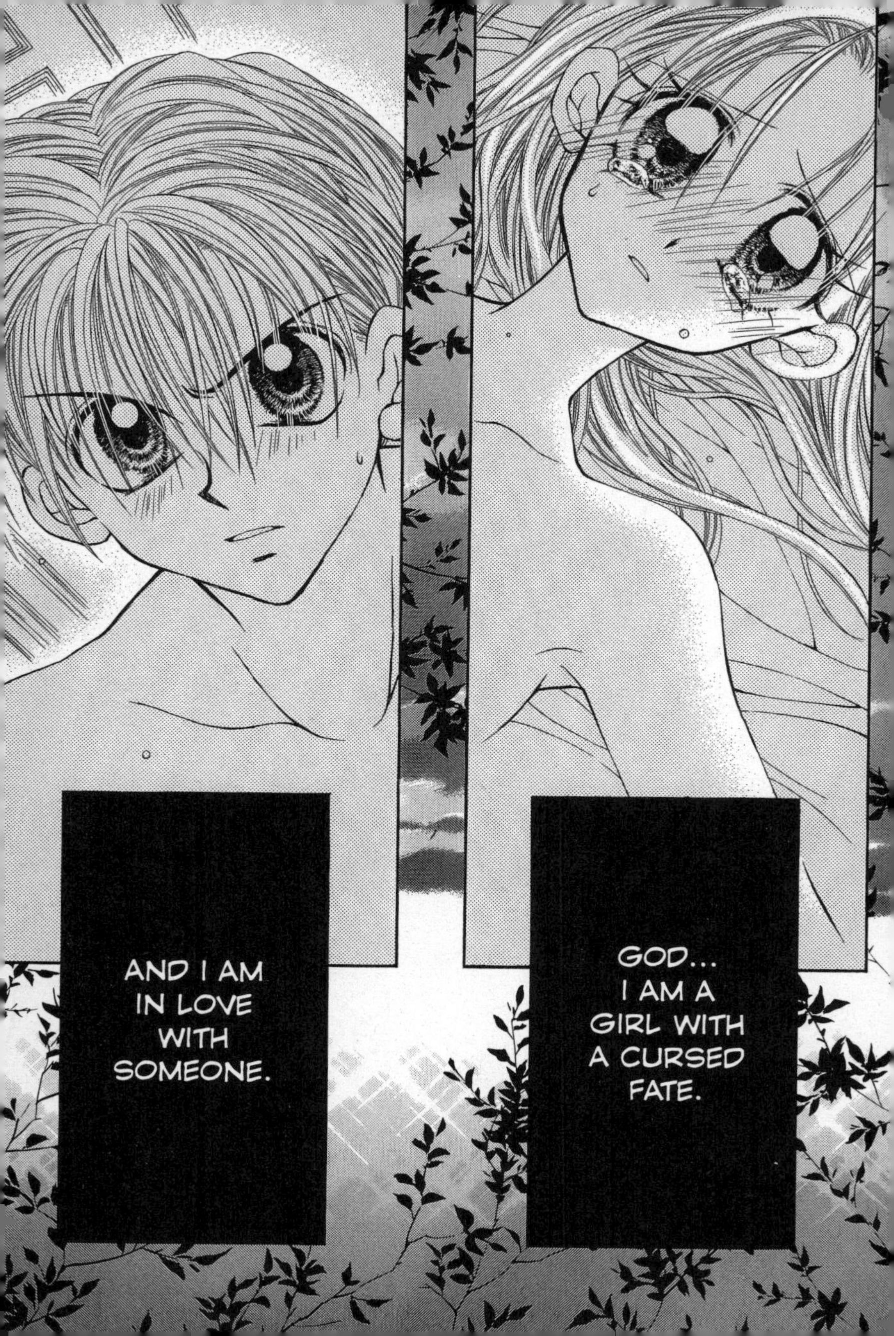
GOD... I AM A GIRL WITH A CURSED FATE.
AND I AM IN LOVE WITH SOMEONE.

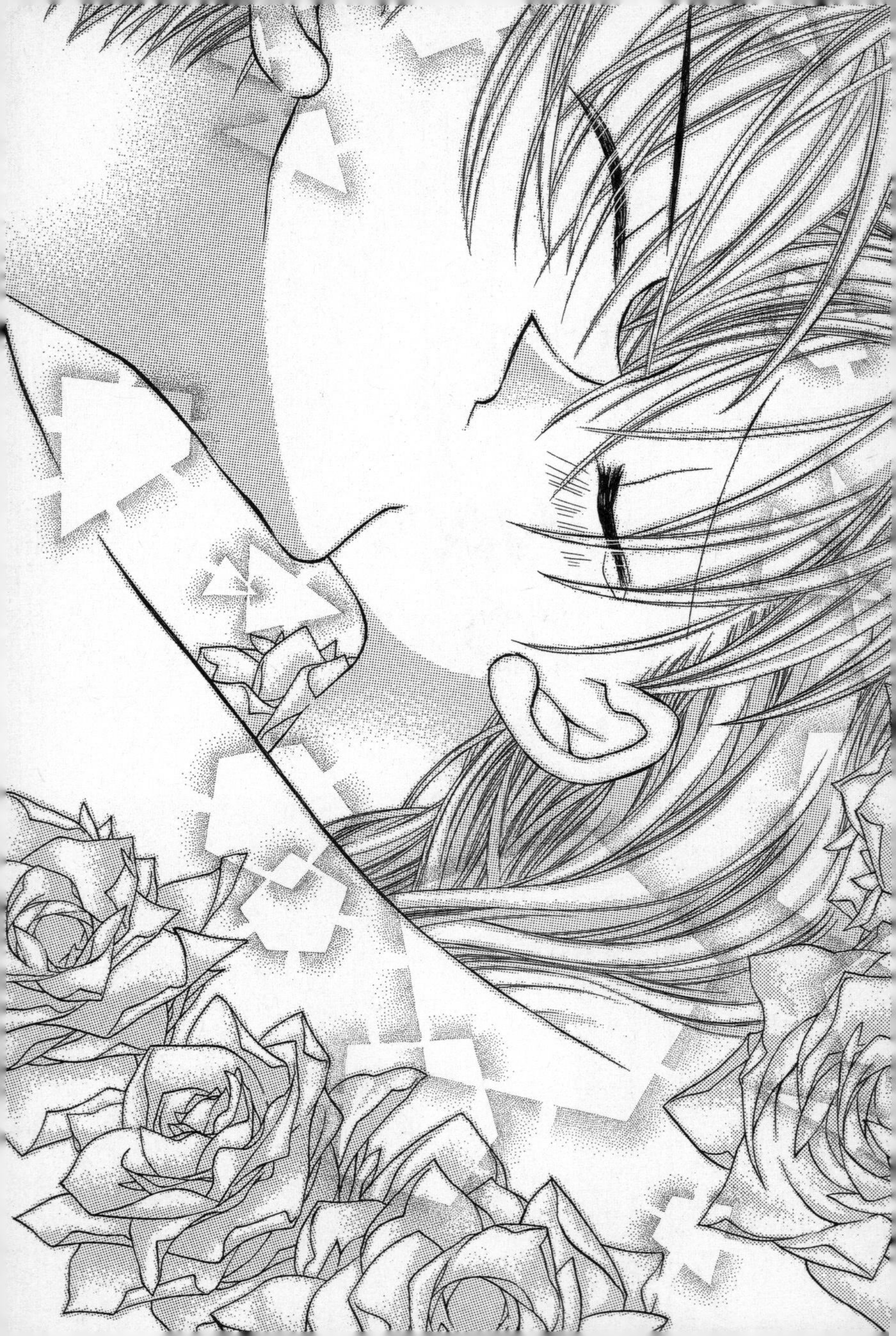

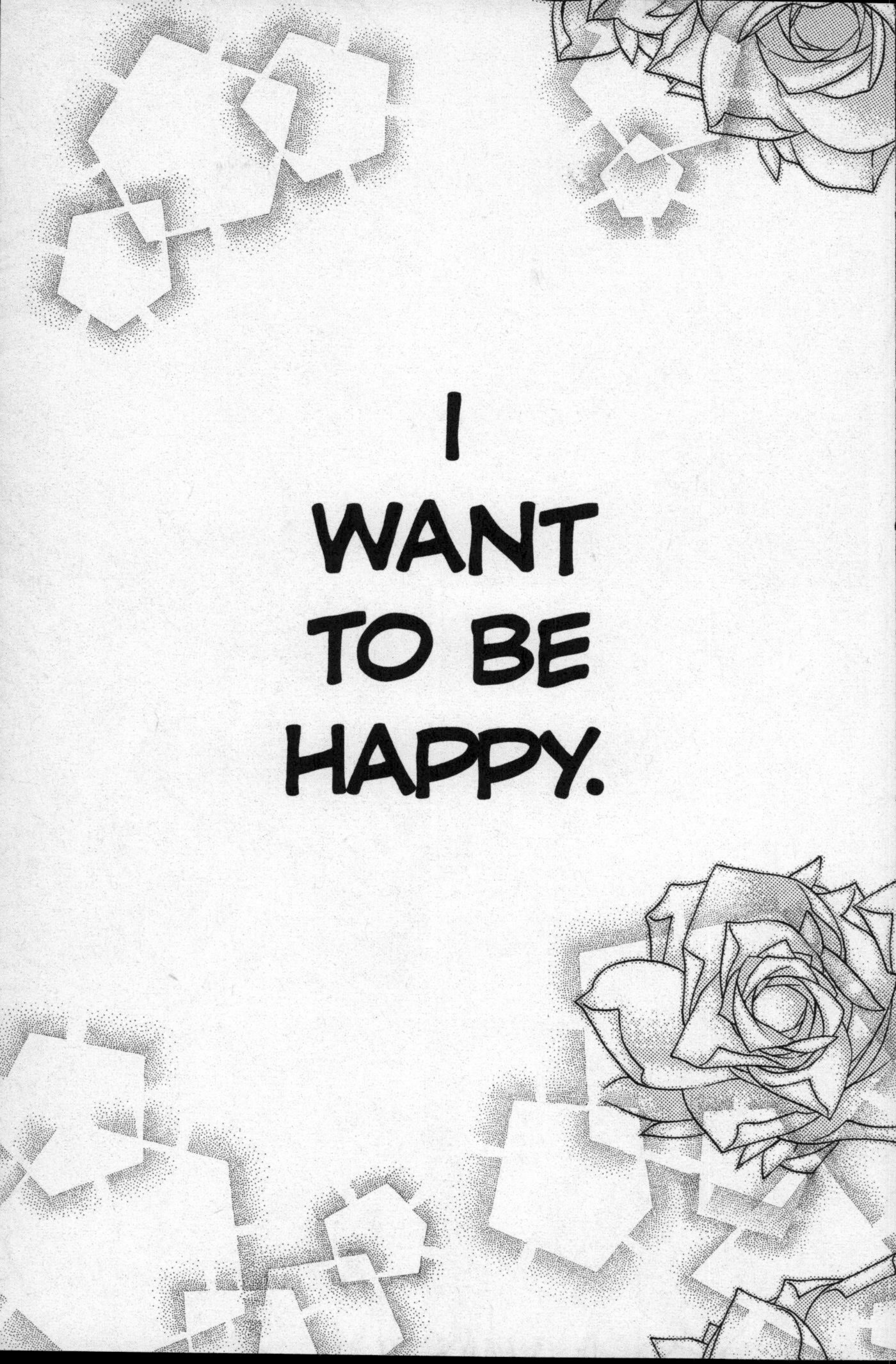
I WANT TO BE HAPPY.

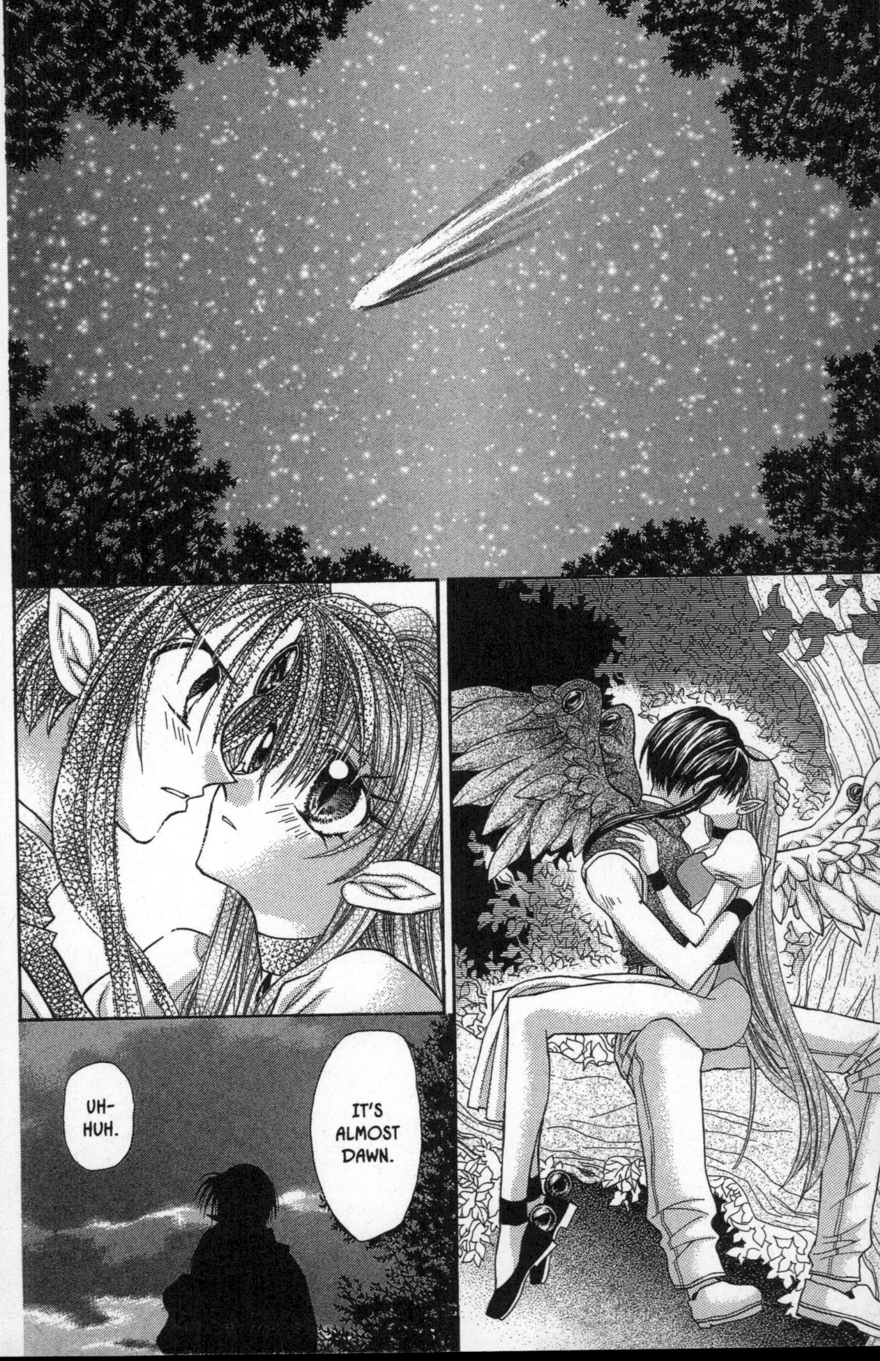
IT'S ALMOST DAWN.
UH-HUH.

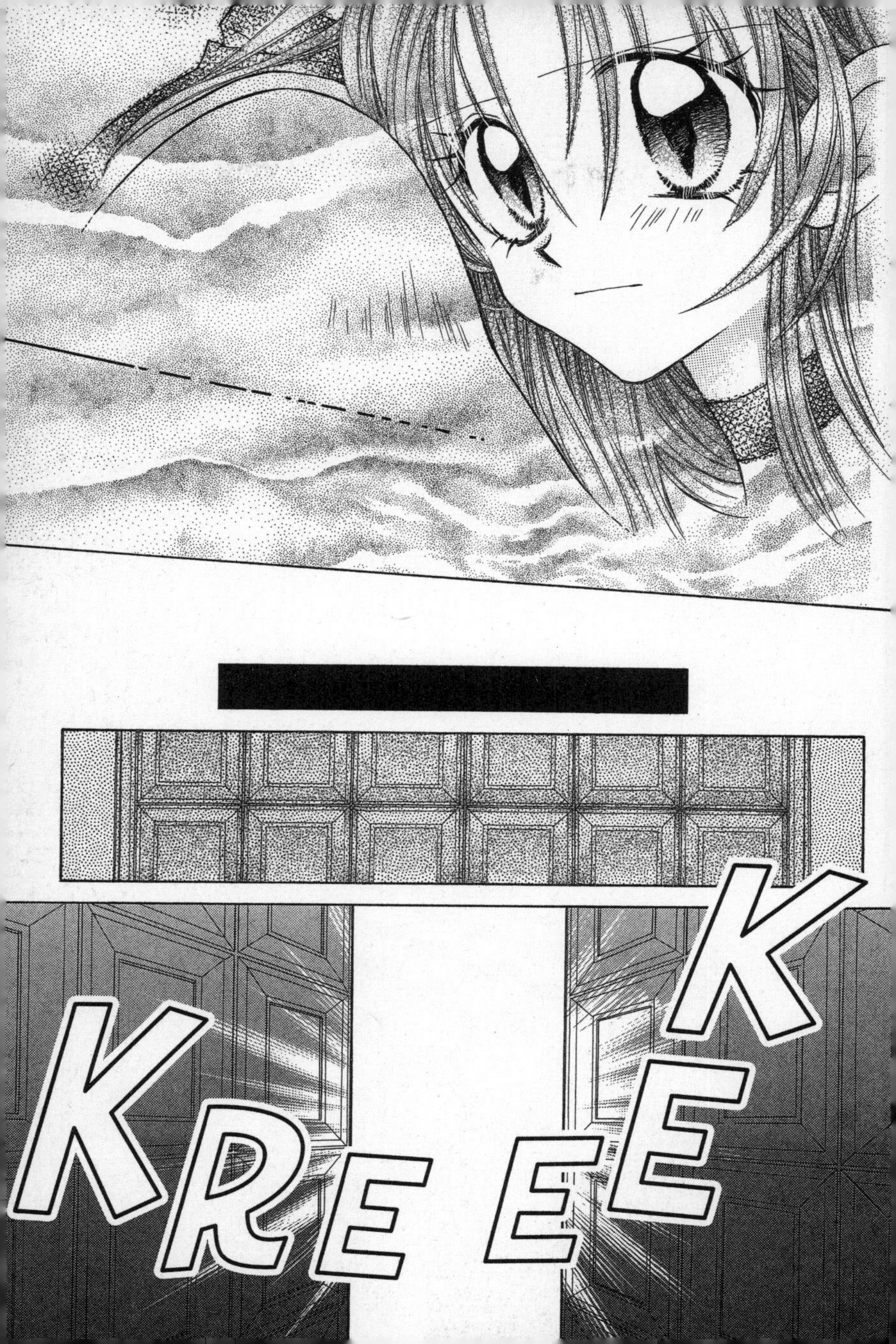
KREEEK

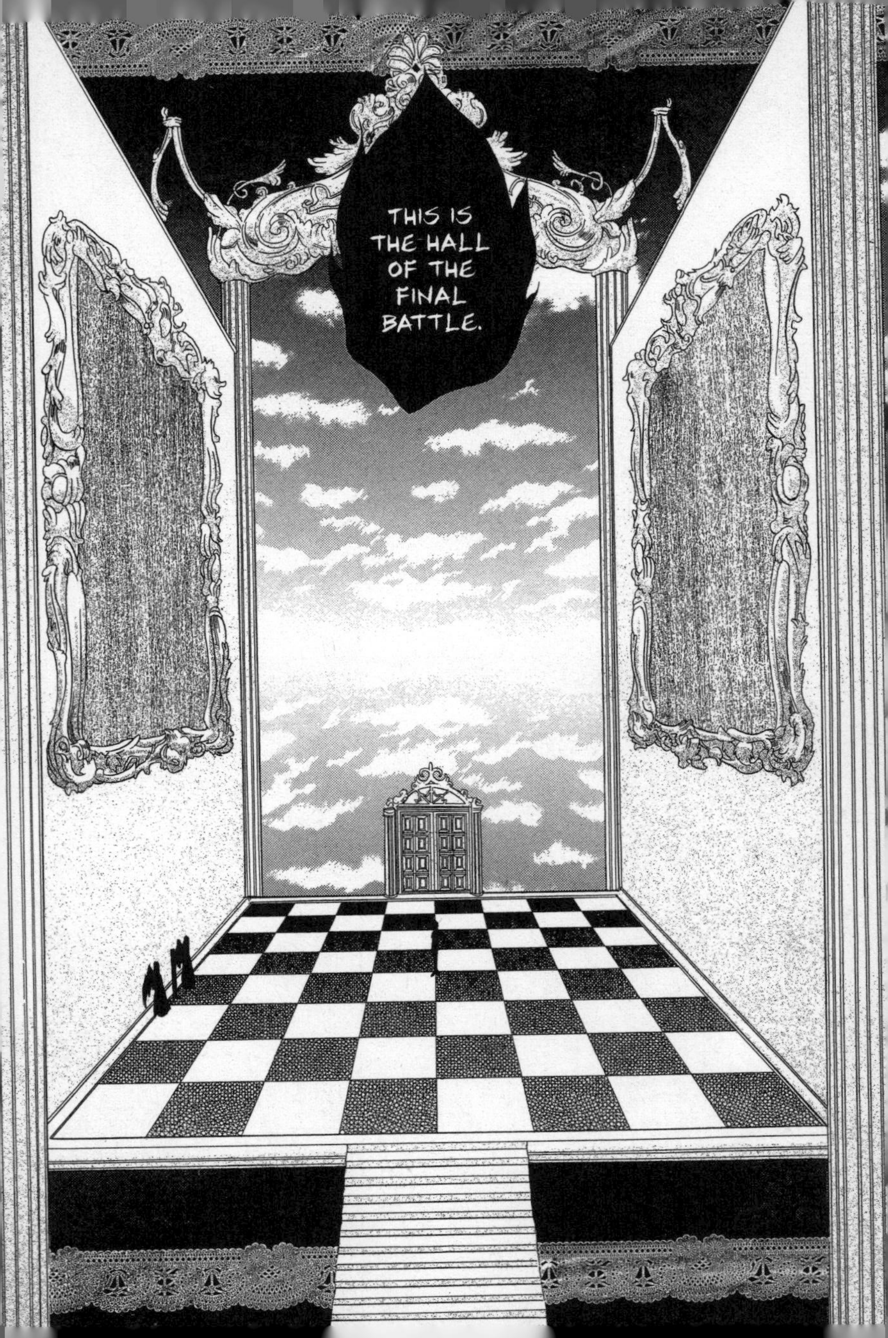
THIS IS THE HALL OF THE FINAL BATTLE.

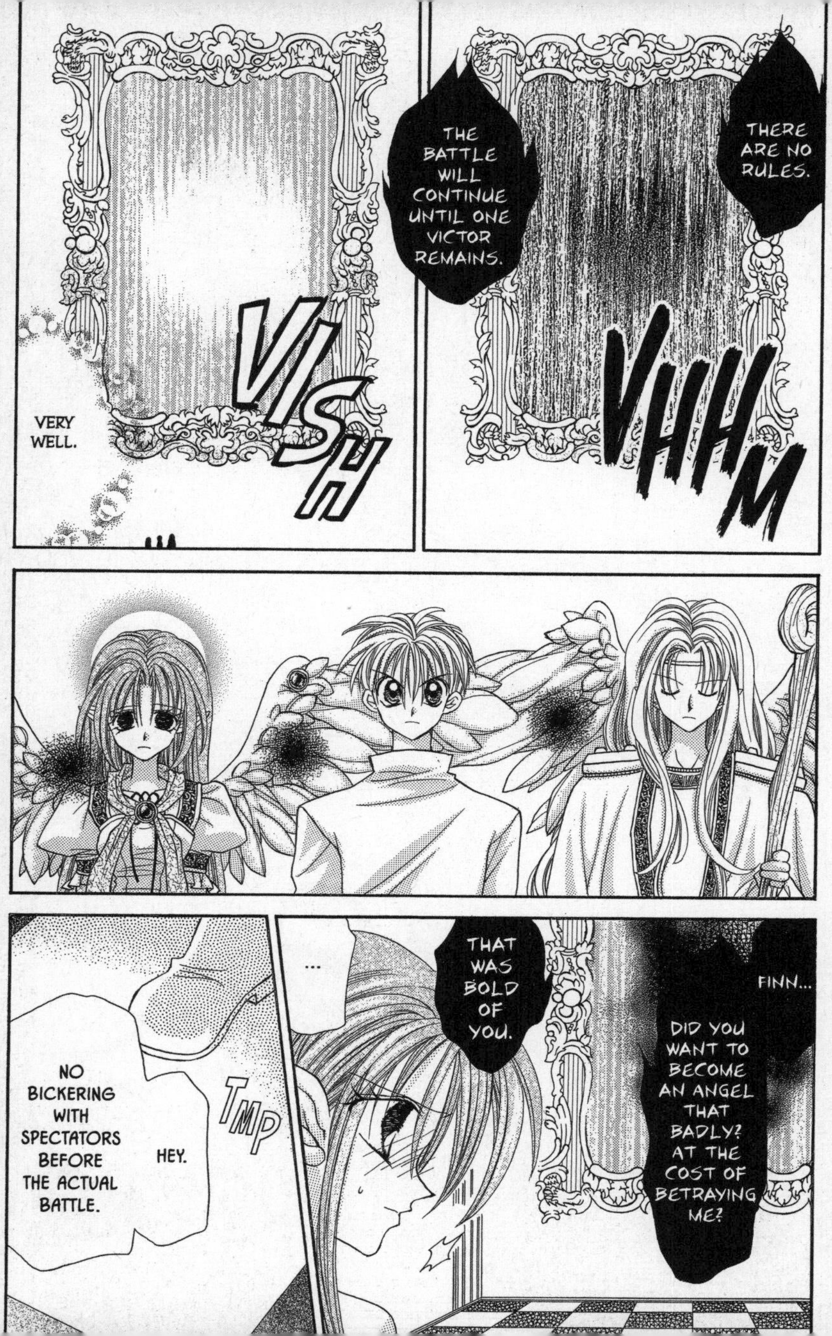
THERE ARE NO RULES.
THE BATTLE WILL CONTINUE UNTIL ONE VICTOR REMAINS.
VHHM
VISH
VERY WELL.
FINN...
DID YOU WANT TO BECOME AN ANGEL THAT BADLY? AT THE COST OF BETRAYING ME?
THAT WAS BOLD OF YOU.
...
TMP
HEY.
NO BICKERING WITH SPECTATORS BEFORE THE ACTUAL BATTLE.

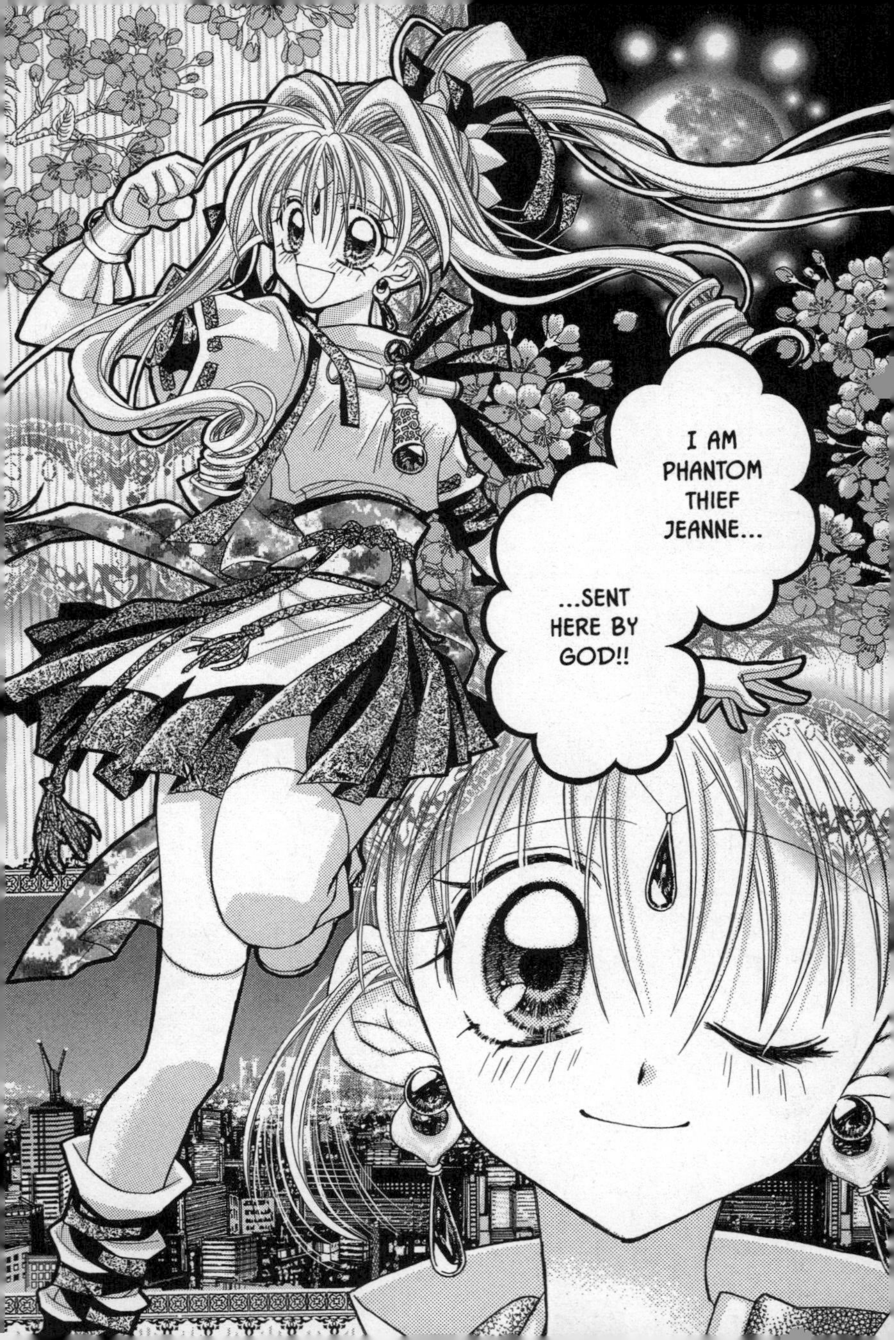
I AM PHANTOM THIEF JEANNE...
...SENT HERE BY GOD!!

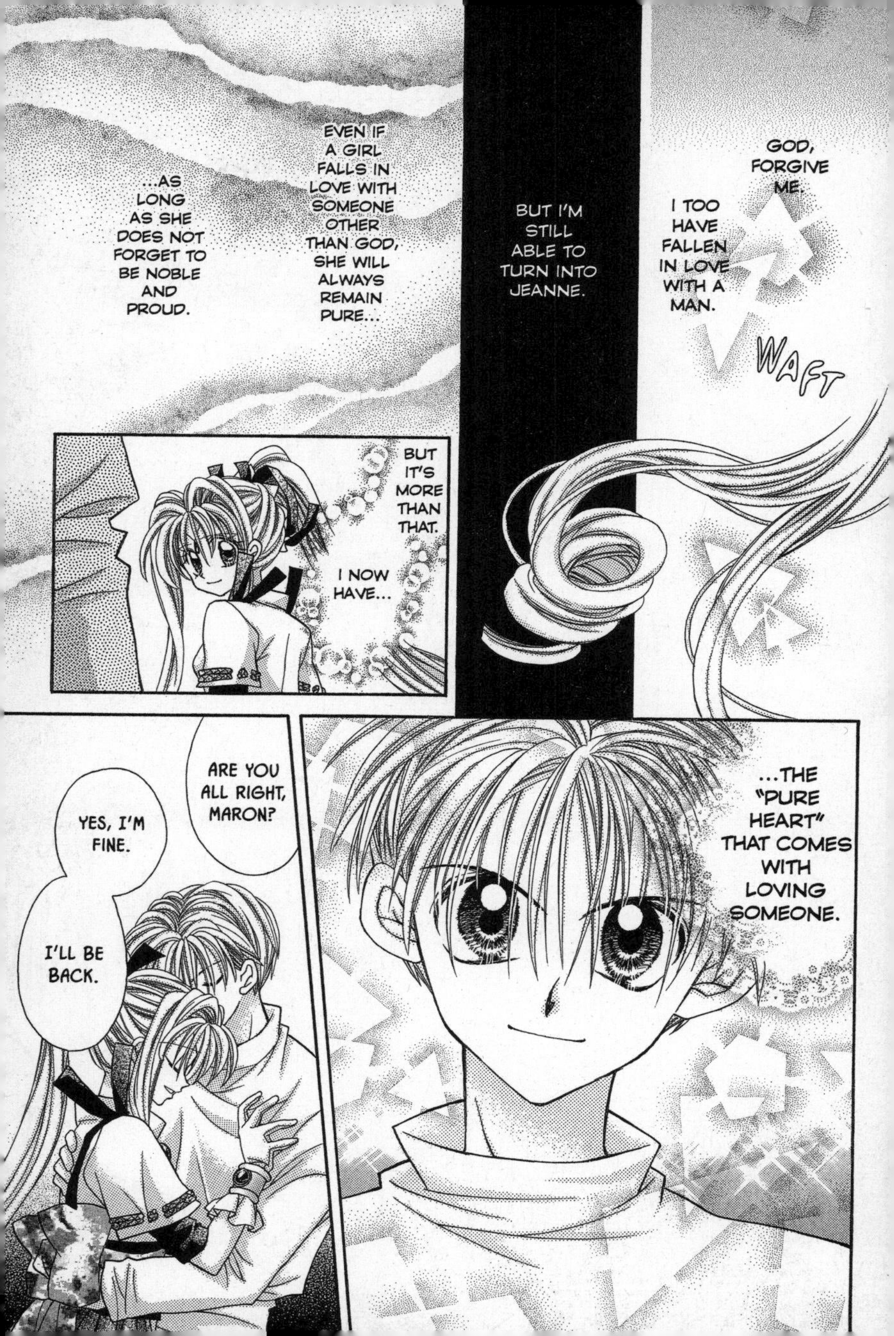
GOD, FORGIVE ME.
I TOO HAVE FALLEN IN LOVE WITH A MAN.
WAFT
BUT I'M STILL ABLE TO TURN INTO JEANNE.
EVEN IF A GIRL FALLS IN LOVE WITH SOMEONE OTHER THAN GOD, SHE WILL ALWAYS REMAIN PURE...
...AS LONG AS SHE DOES NOT FORGET TO BE NOBLE AND PROUD.
BUT IT'S MORE THAN THAT.
I NOW HAVE...
...THE "PURE HEART" THAT COMES WITH LOVING SOMEONE.
ARE YOU ALL RIGHT, MARON?
YES, I'M FINE.
I'LL BE BACK.

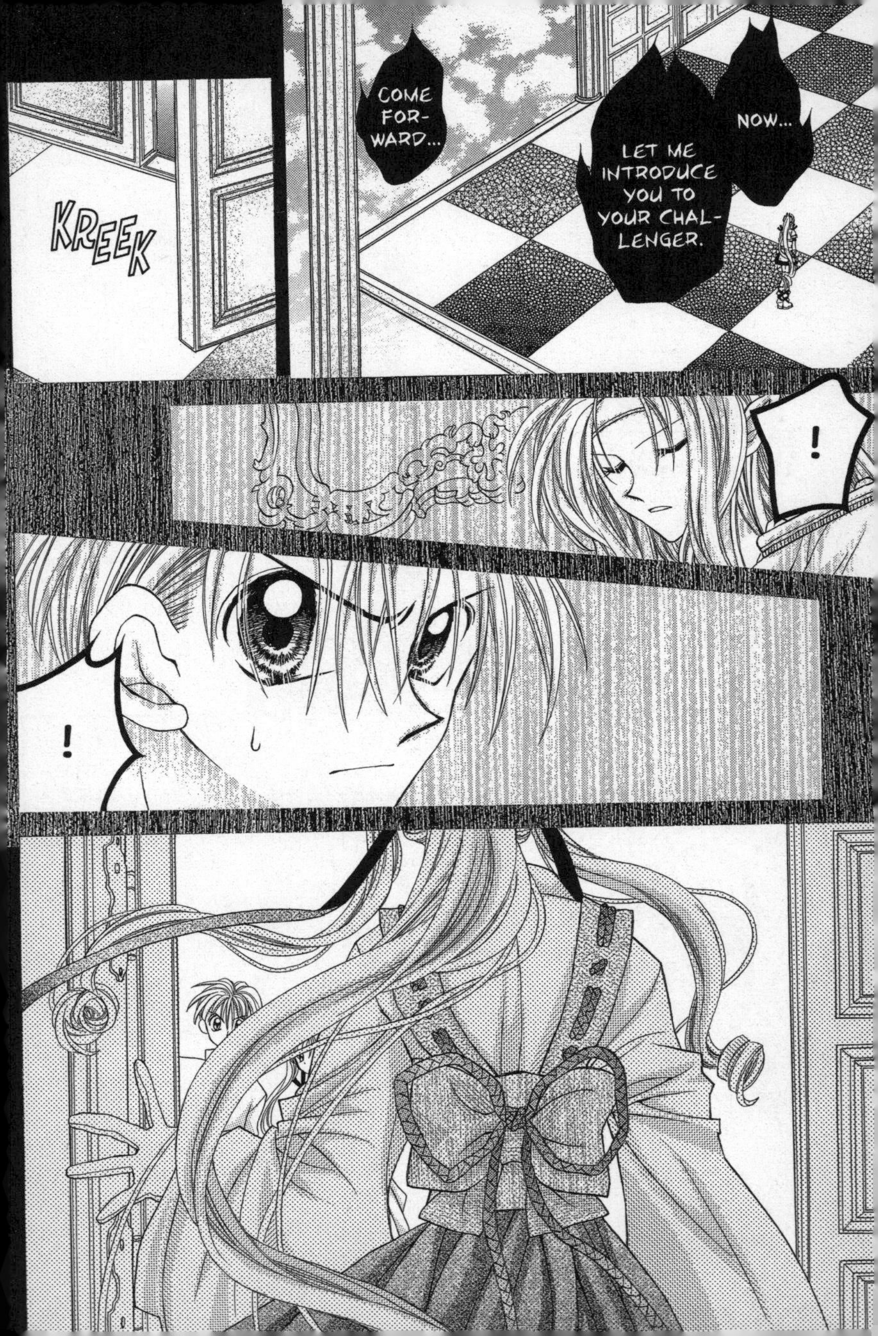
NOW...
LET ME INTRODUCE YOU TO YOUR CHAL-LENGER.
COME FOR-WARD...
KREEK
!
!

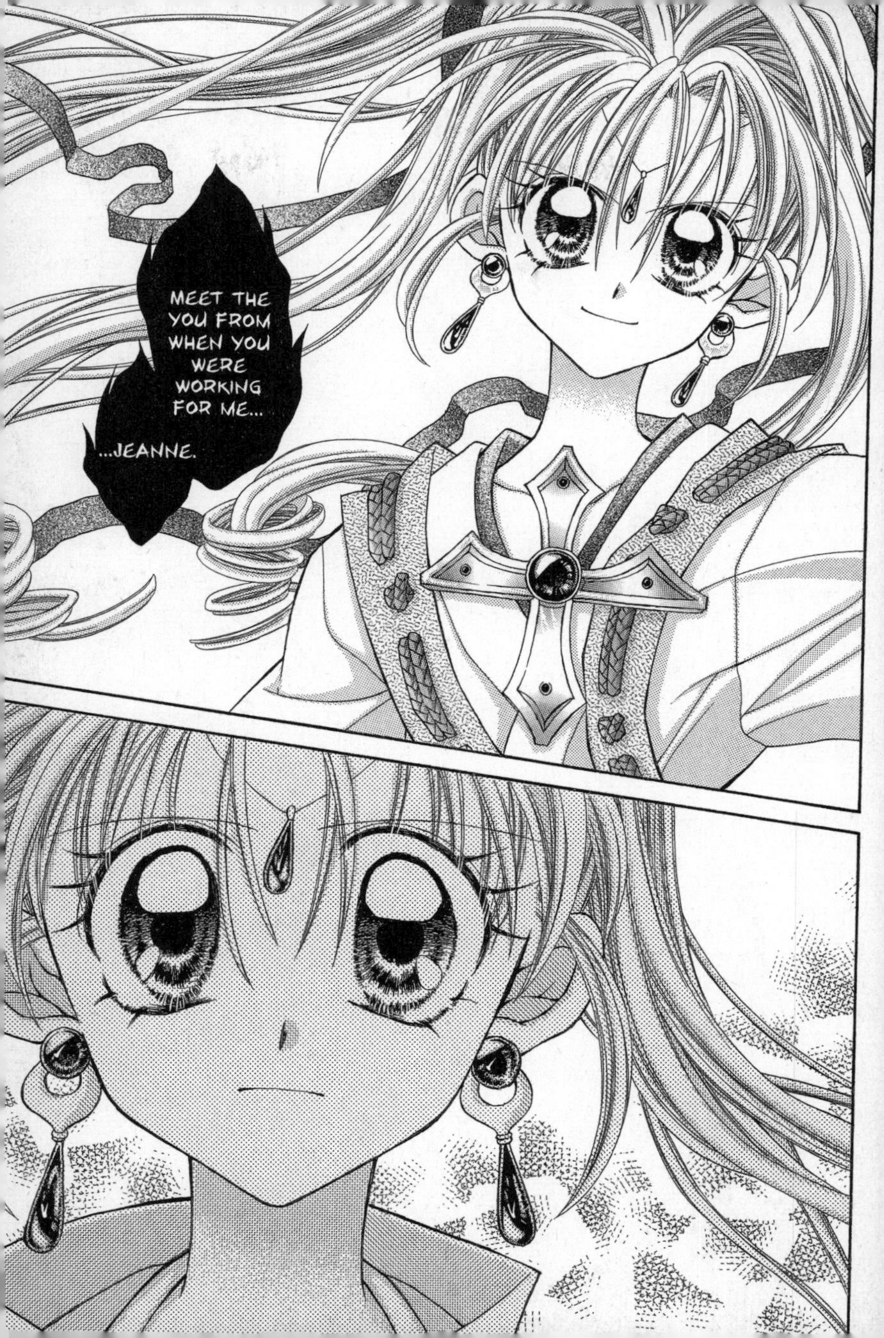
MEET THE YOU FROM WHEN YOU WERE WORKING FOR ME...
...JEANNE.

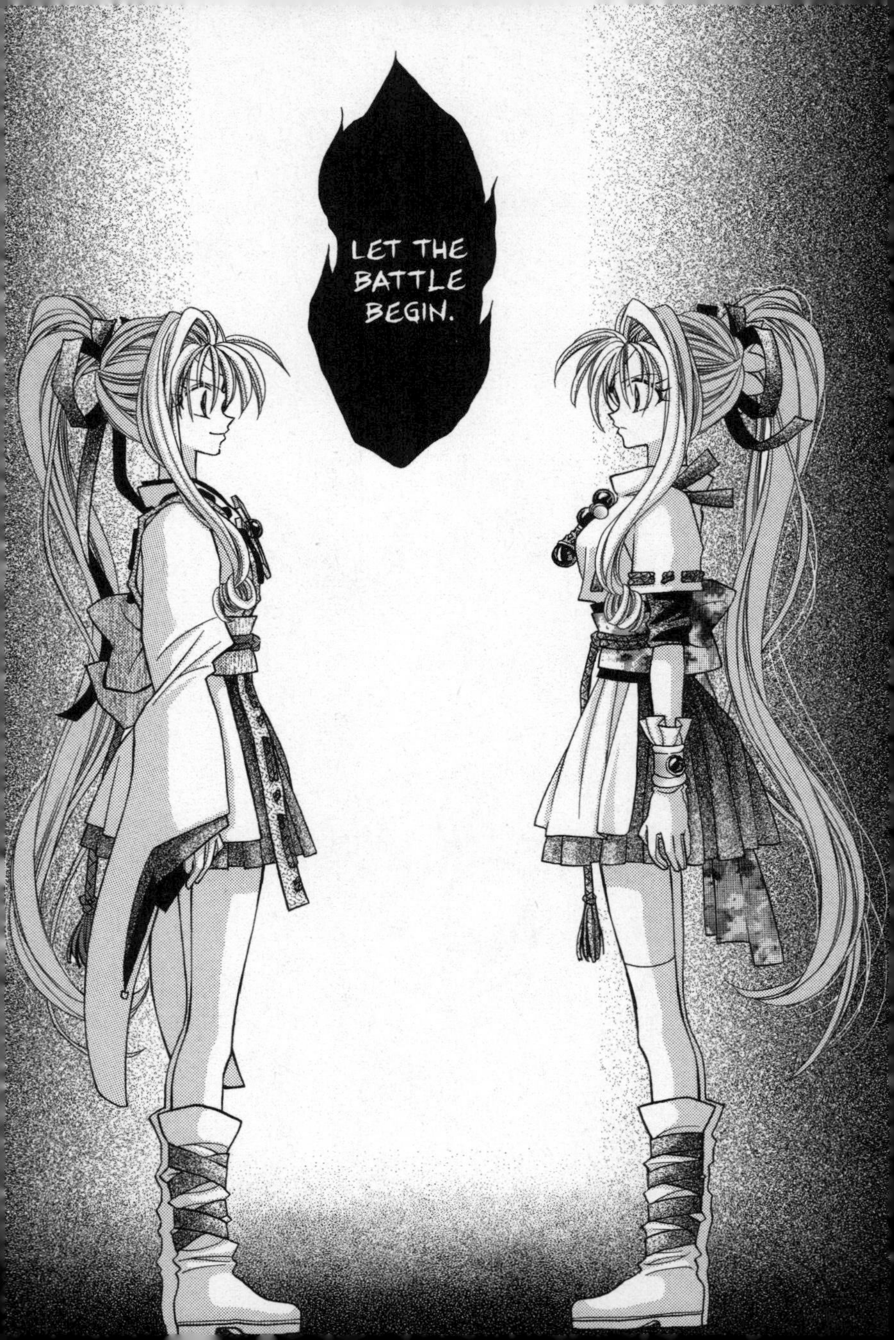
LET THE BATTLE BEGIN.

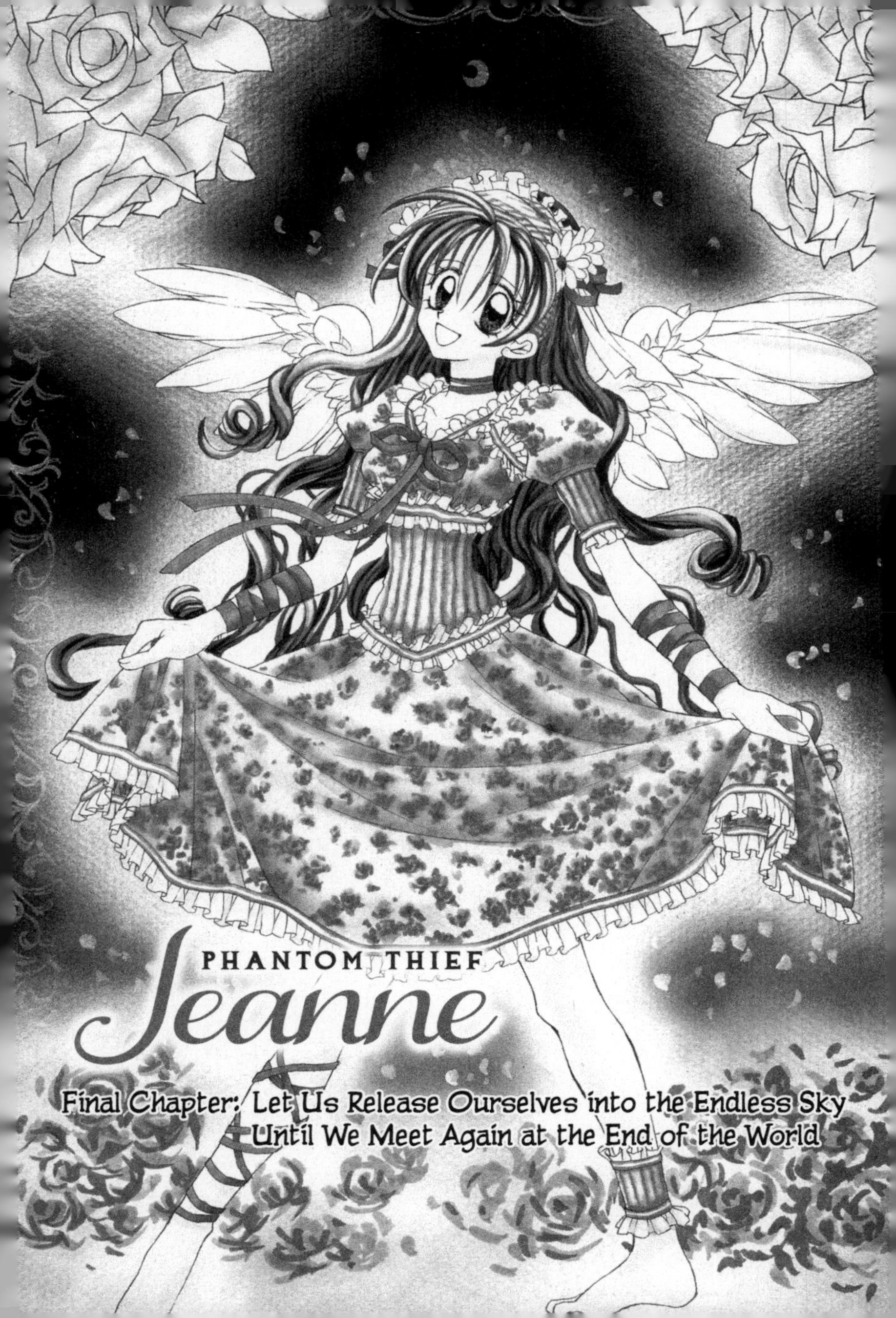
PHANTOM THIEF
Jeanne
Final Chapter: Let Us Release Ourselves into the Endless Sky
Until We Meet Again at the End of the World

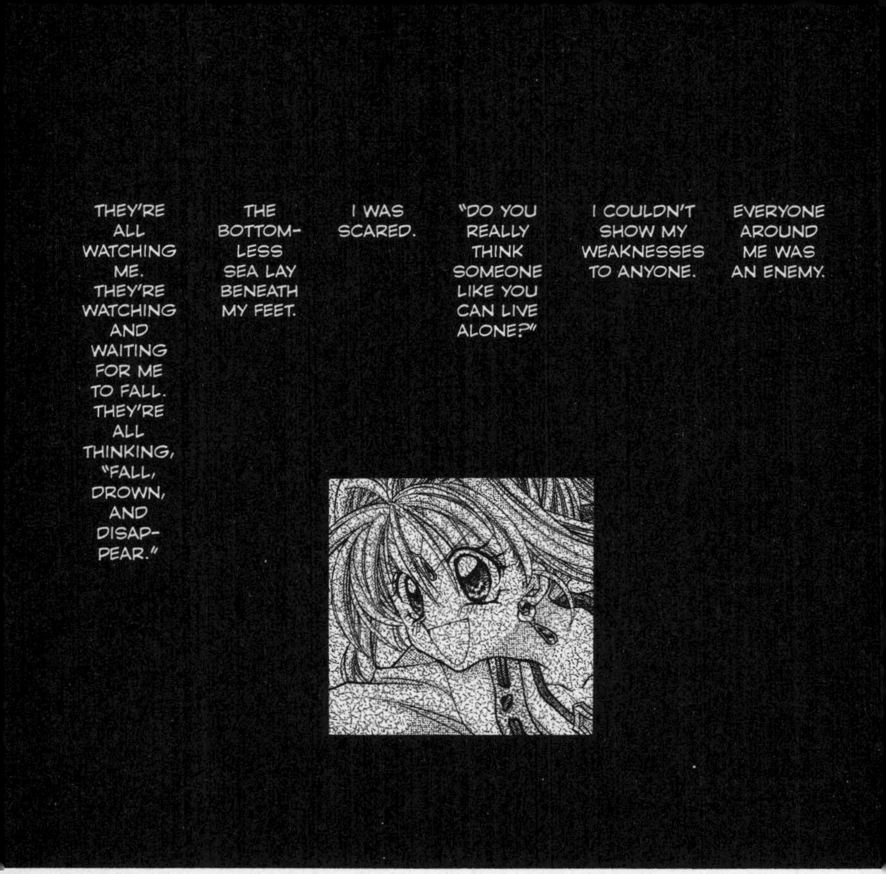
EVERYONE AROUND ME WAS AN ENEMY.
I COULDN'T SHOW MY WEAKNESSES TO ANYONE.
"DO YOU REALLY THINK SOMEONE LIKE YOU CAN LIVE ALONE?"
I WAS SCARED.
THE BOTTOM-LESS SEA LAY BENEATH MY FEET.
THEY'RE ALL WATCHING ME. THEY'RE WATCHING AND WAITING FOR ME TO FALL. THEY'RE ALL THINKING, "FALL, DROWN, AND DISAP-PEAR."

PHANTOM
THIEF
JEANNE

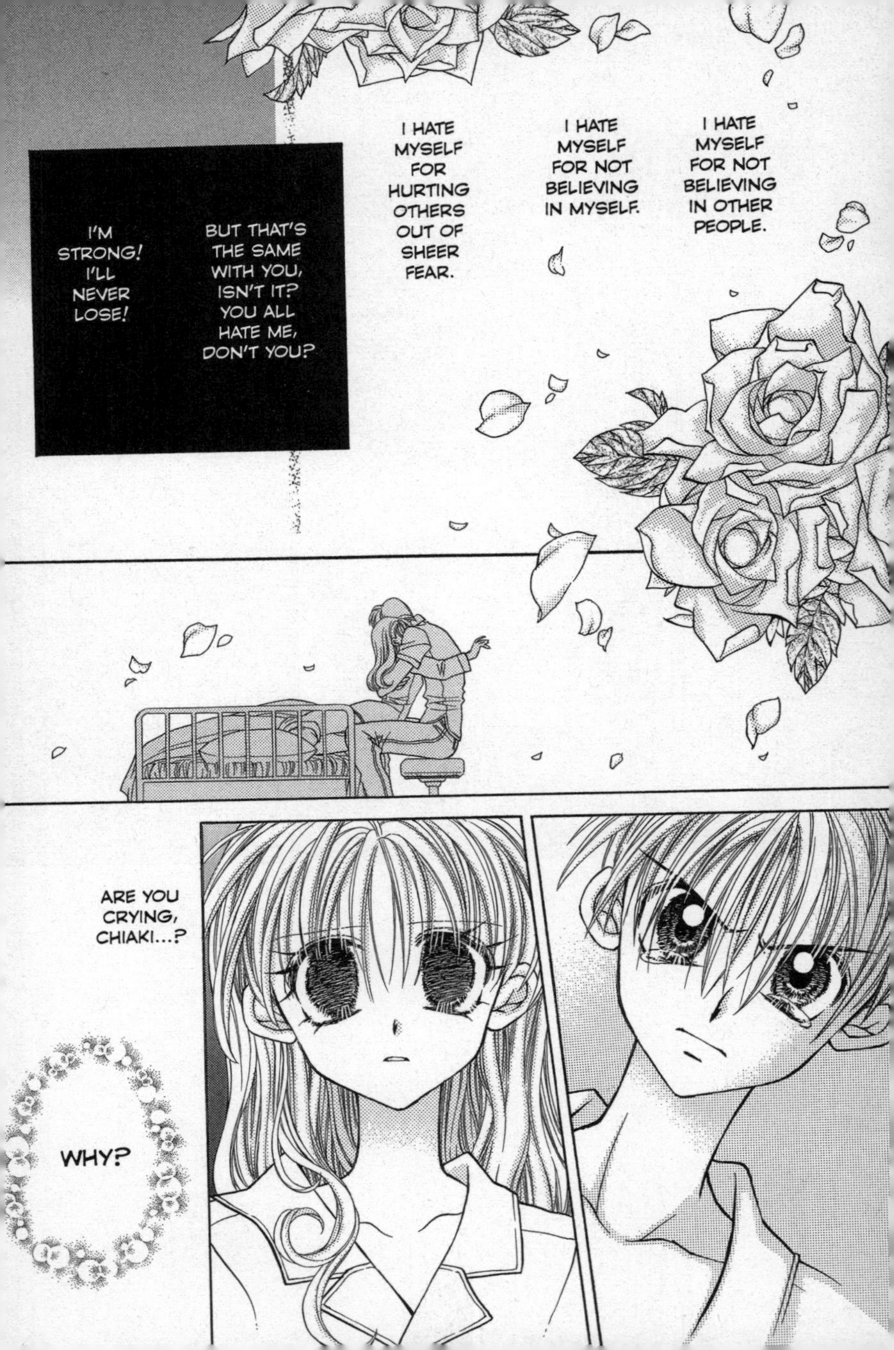
I HATE MYSELF FOR NOT BELIEVING IN OTHER PEOPLE.
I HATE MYSELF FOR NOT BELIEVING IN MYSELF.
I HATE MYSELF FOR HURTING OTHERS OUT OF SHEER FEAR.
BUT THAT'S THE SAME WITH YOU, ISN'T IT? YOU ALL HATE ME, DON'T YOU?
I'M STRONG! I'LL NEVER LOSE!
ARE YOU CRYING, CHIAKI...?
WHY?

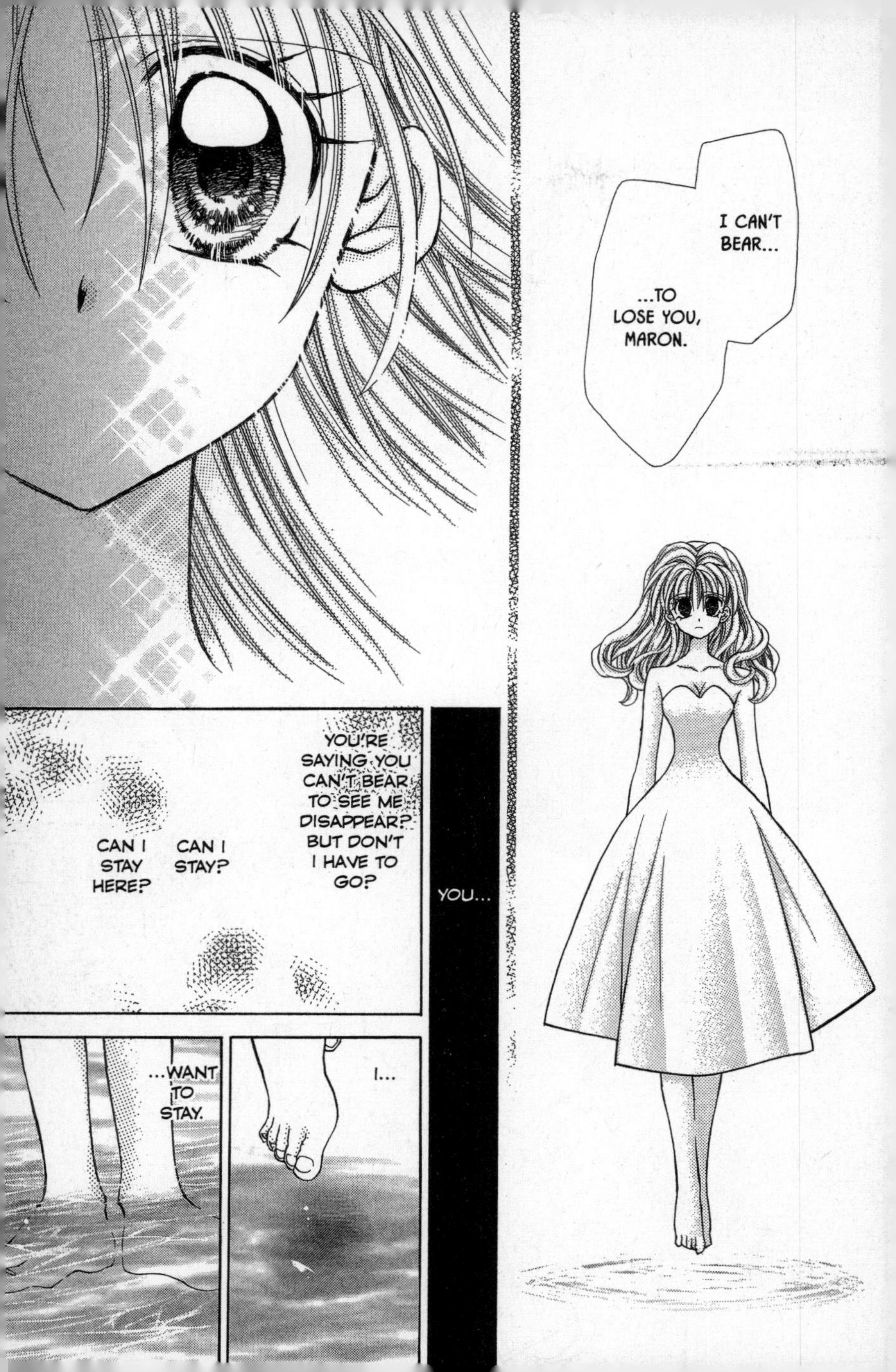
I CAN'T BEAR...
...TO LOSE YOU, MARON.
YOU...
YOU'RE SAYING YOU CAN'T BEAR TO SEE ME DISAPPEAR? BUT DON'T I HAVE TO GO?
CAN I STAY?
CAN I STAY HERE?
I...
...WANT TO STAY.

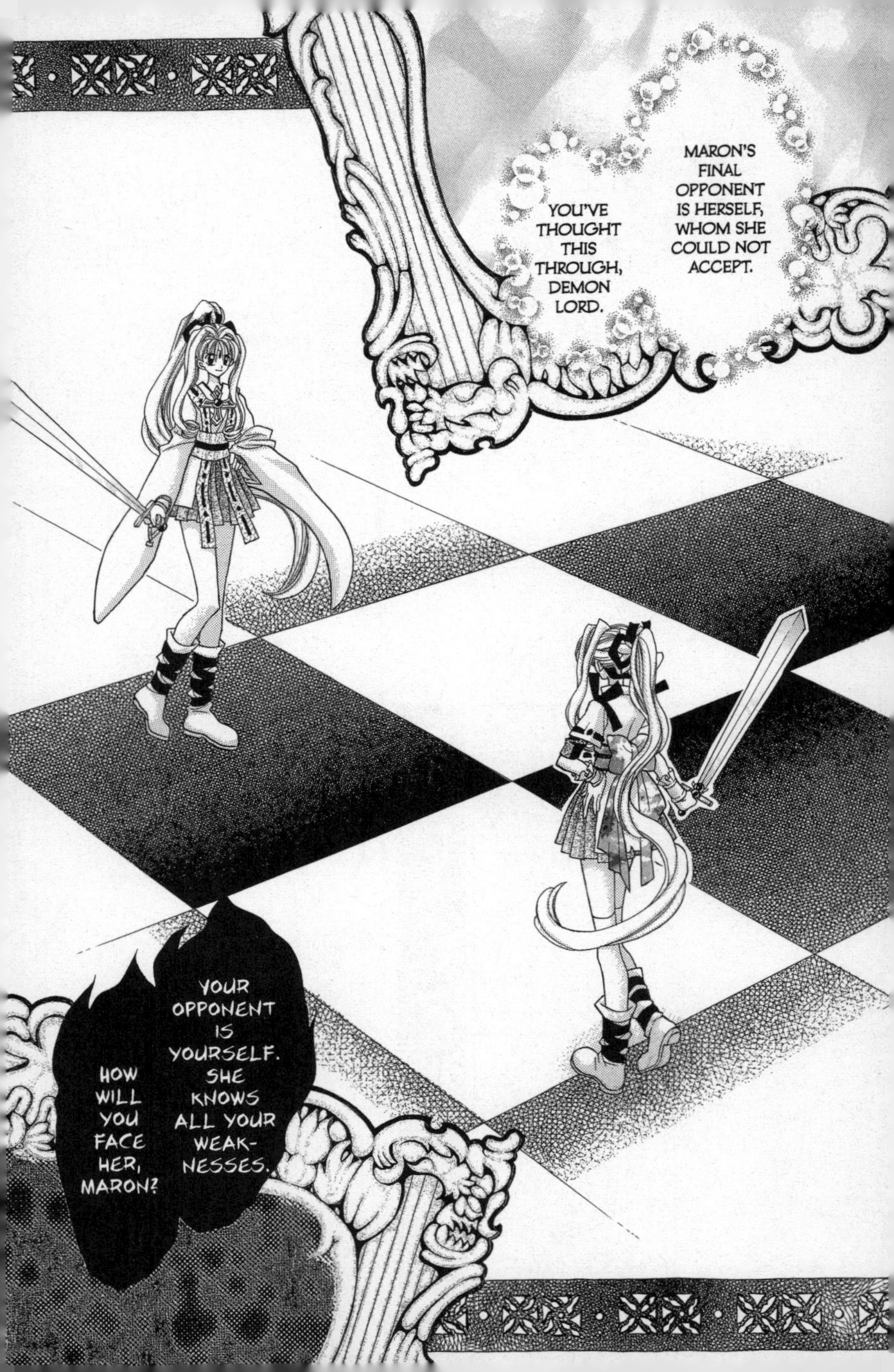
MARON'S FINAL OPPONENT IS HERSELF, WHOM SHE COULD NOT ACCEPT.
YOU'VE THOUGHT THIS THROUGH, DEMON LORD.
YOUR OPPONENT IS YOURSELF. SHE KNOWS ALL YOUR WEAK-NESSES.
HOW WILL YOU FACE HER, MARON?

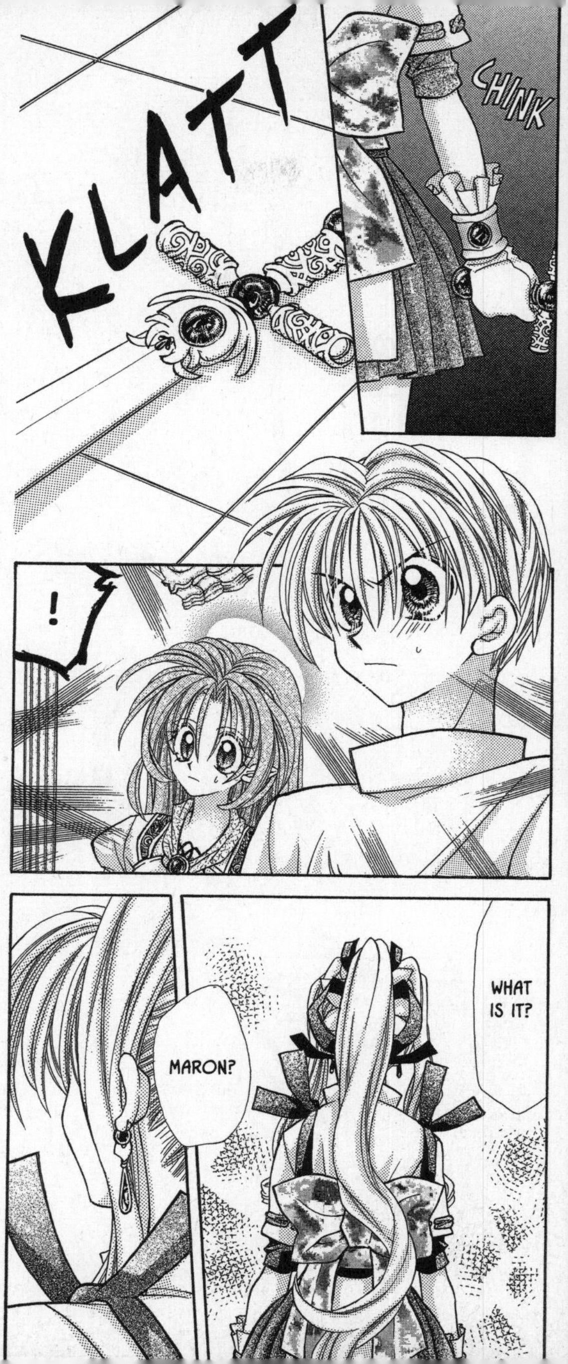
CHINK
KLATT
!
WHAT IS IT?
MARON?

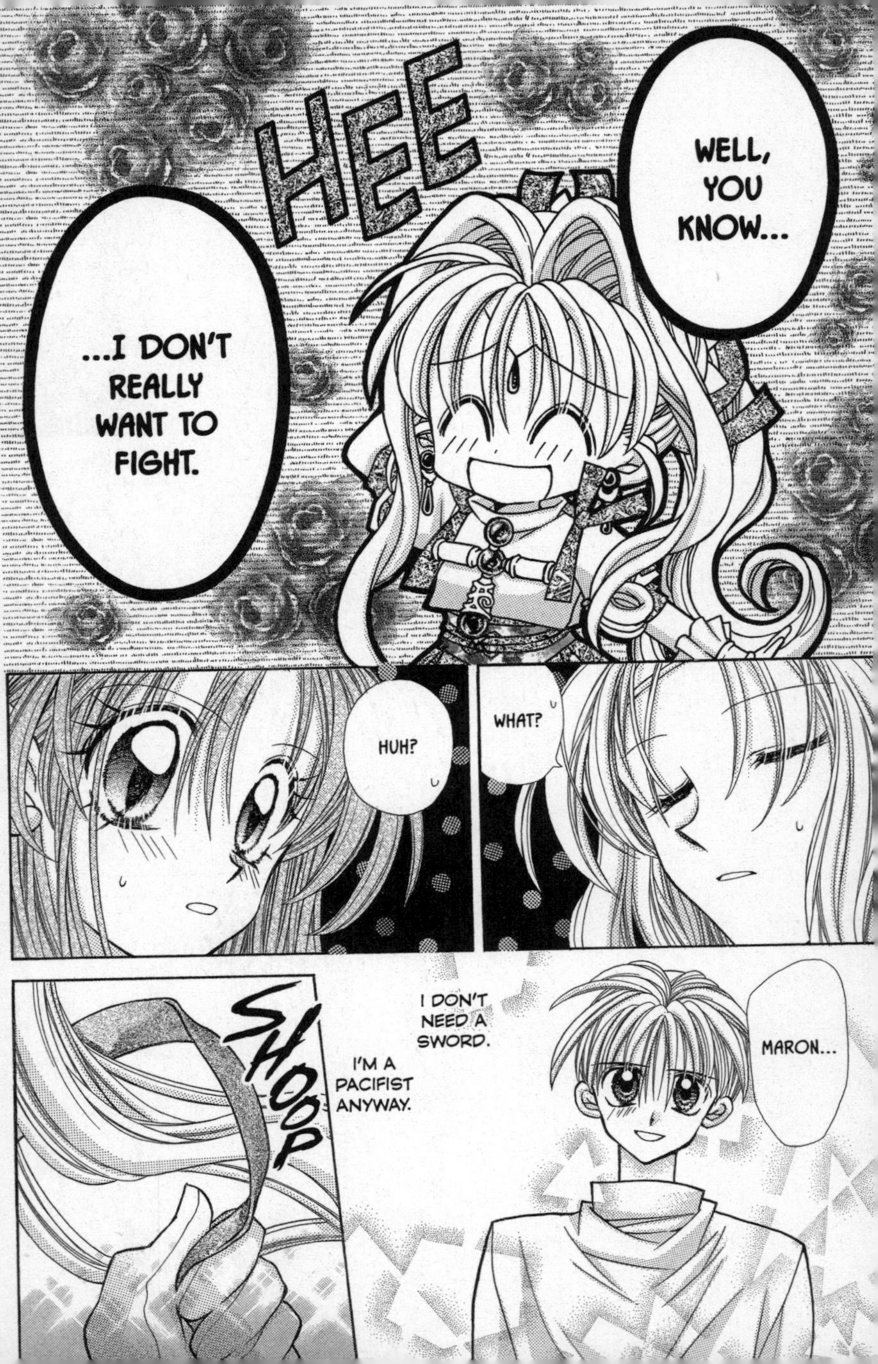
WELL, YOU KNOW...
HEE
...I DON'T REALLY WANT TO FIGHT.
WHAT?
HUH?
MARON...
I DON'T NEED A SWORD.
I'M A PACIFIST ANYWAY.
SHOOP

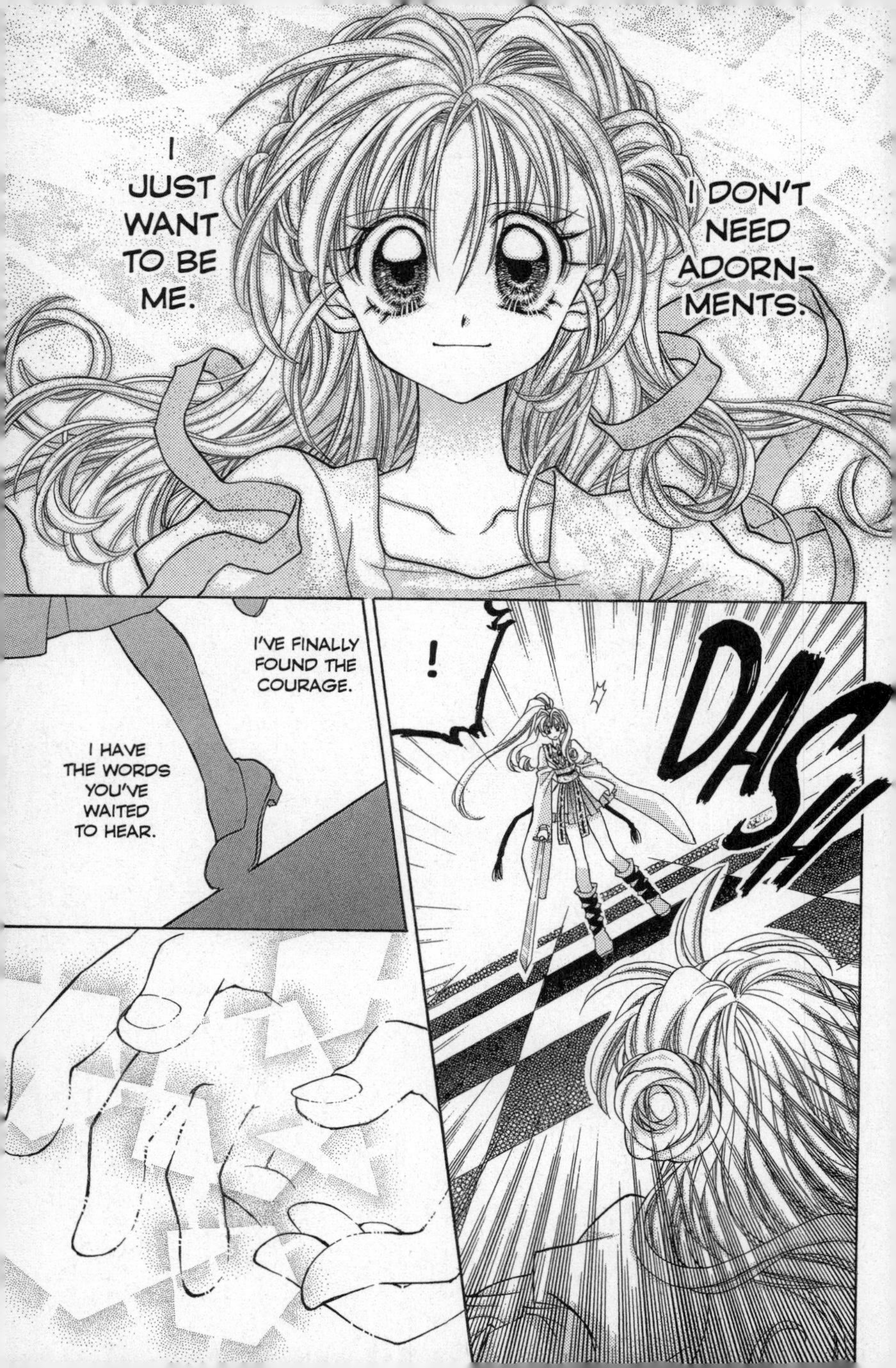
I DON'T NEED ADORN-MENTS.
I JUST WANT TO BE ME.
!
DASH
I'VE FINALLY FOUND THE COURAGE.
I HAVE THE WORDS YOU'VE WAITED TO HEAR.

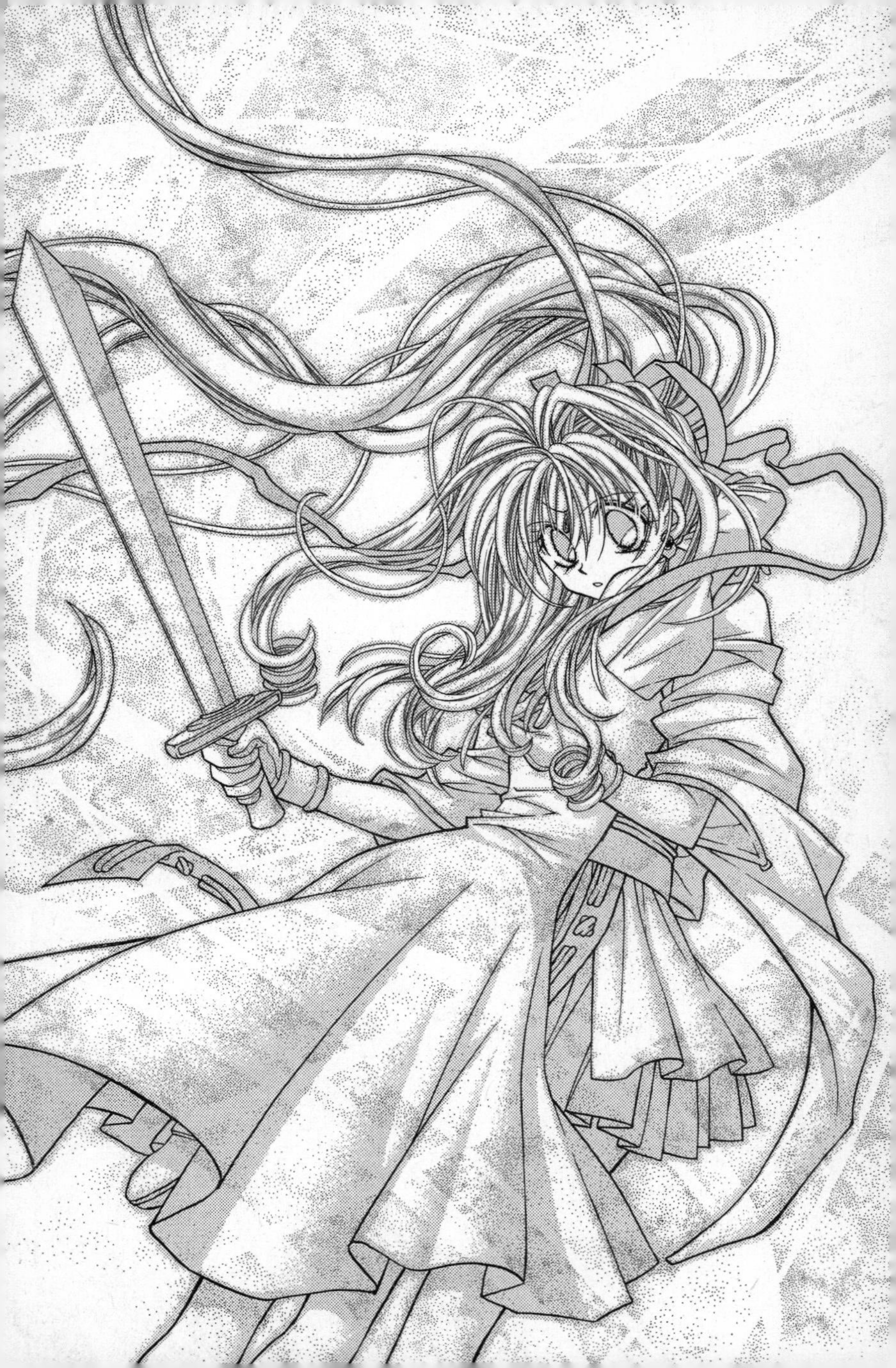

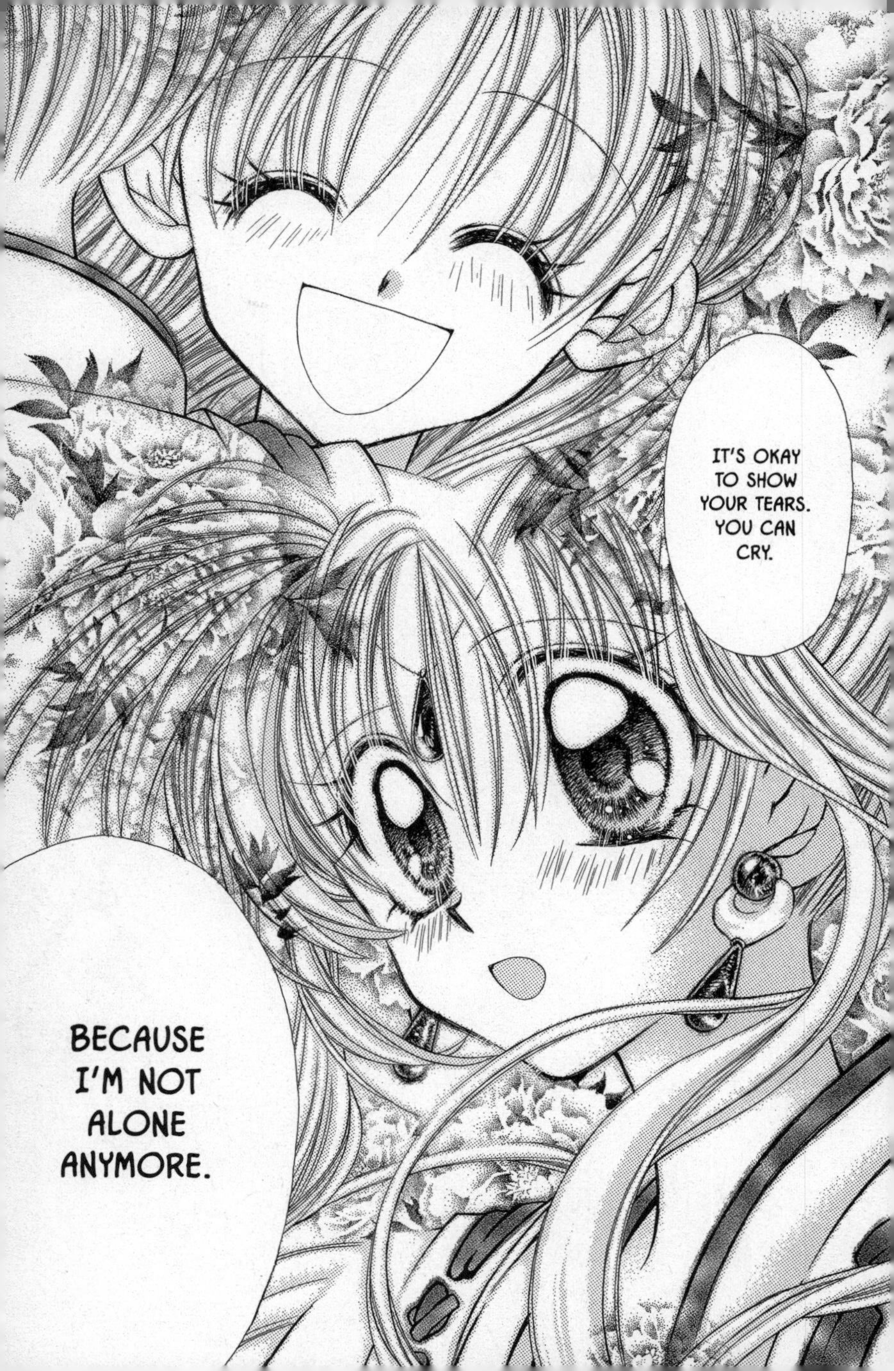
IT'S OKAY TO SHOW YOUR TEARS. YOU CAN CRY.
BECAUSE I'M NOT ALONE ANYMORE.

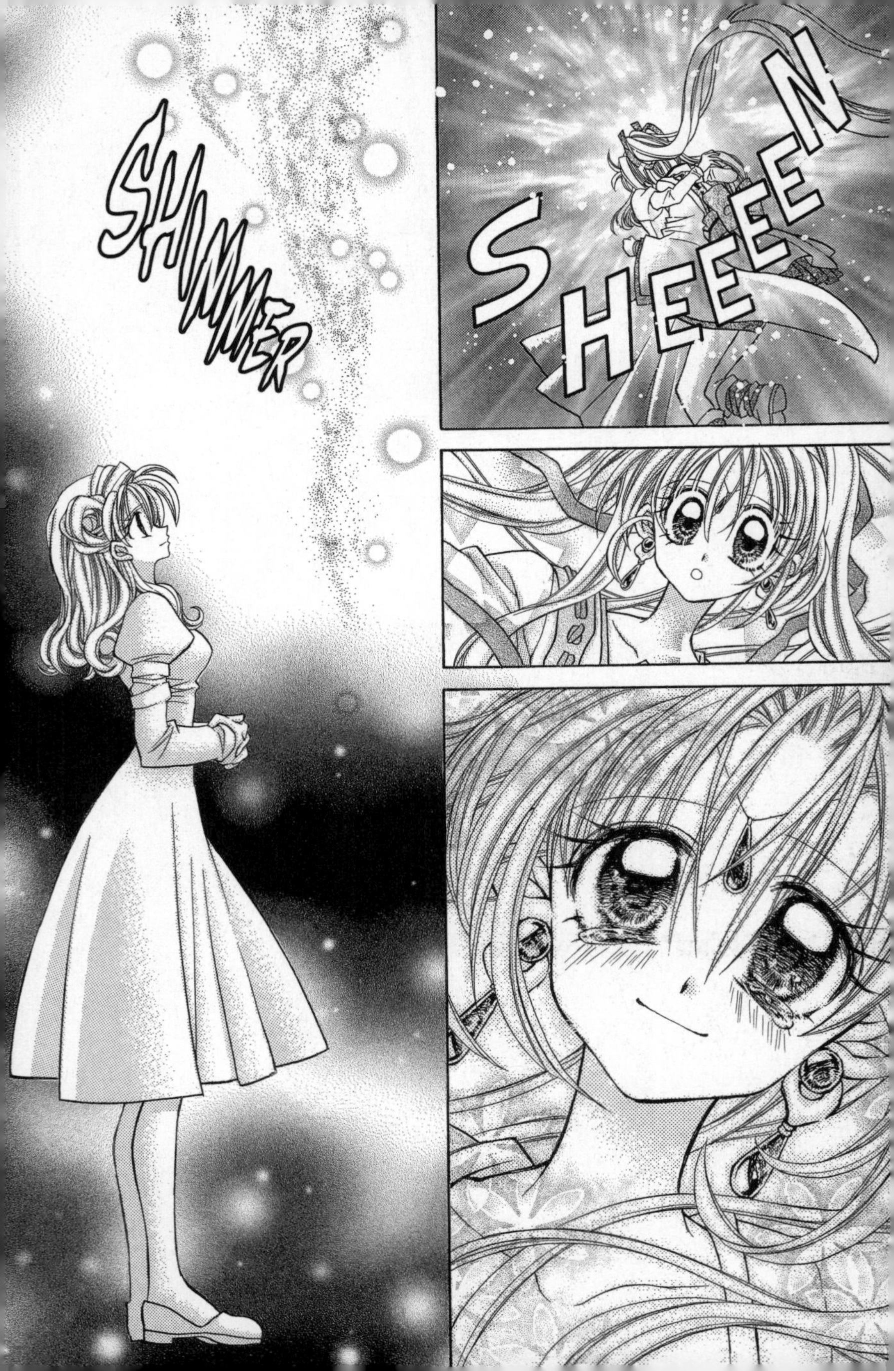
SHEEEEN
SHIMMER

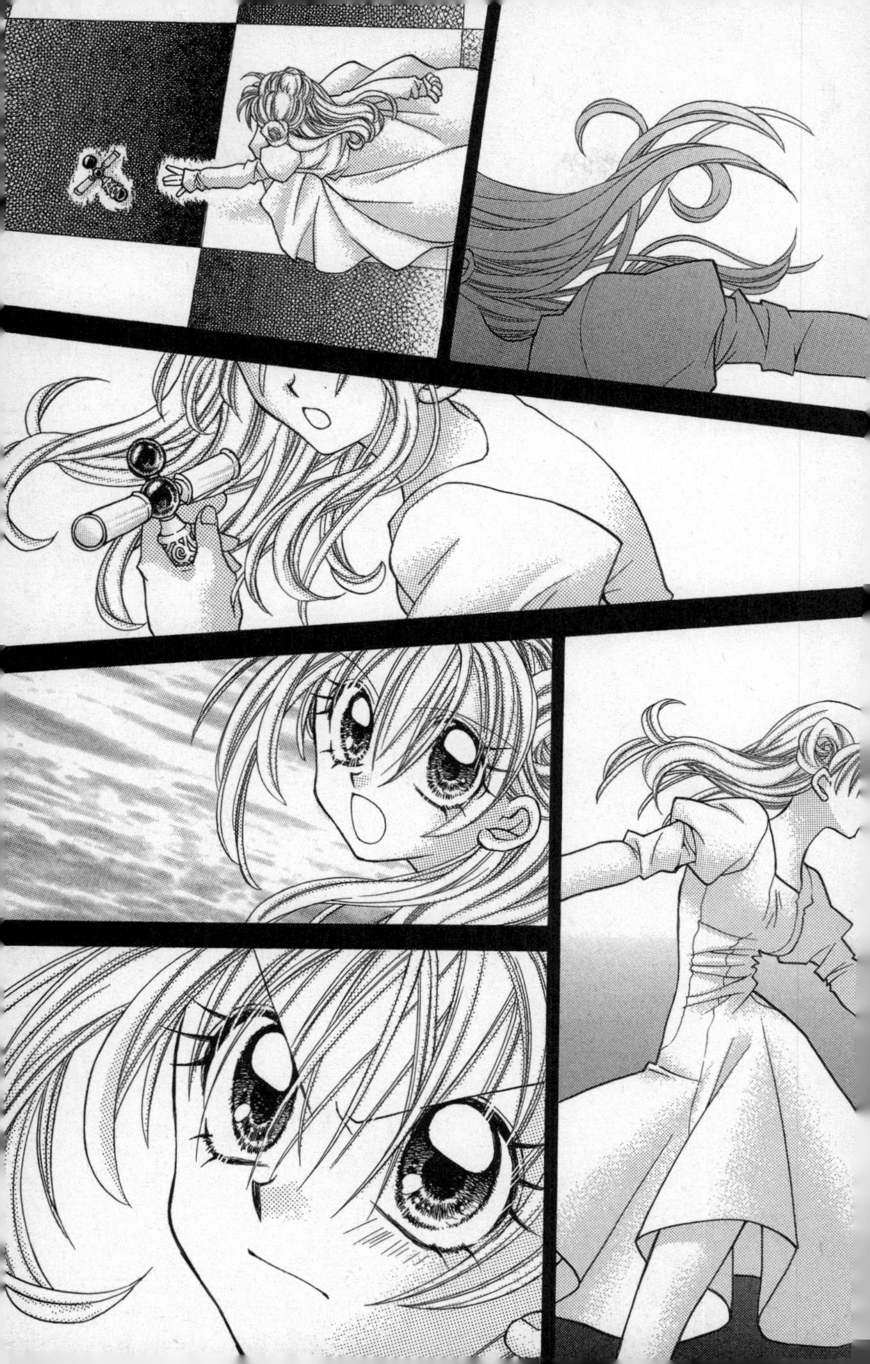

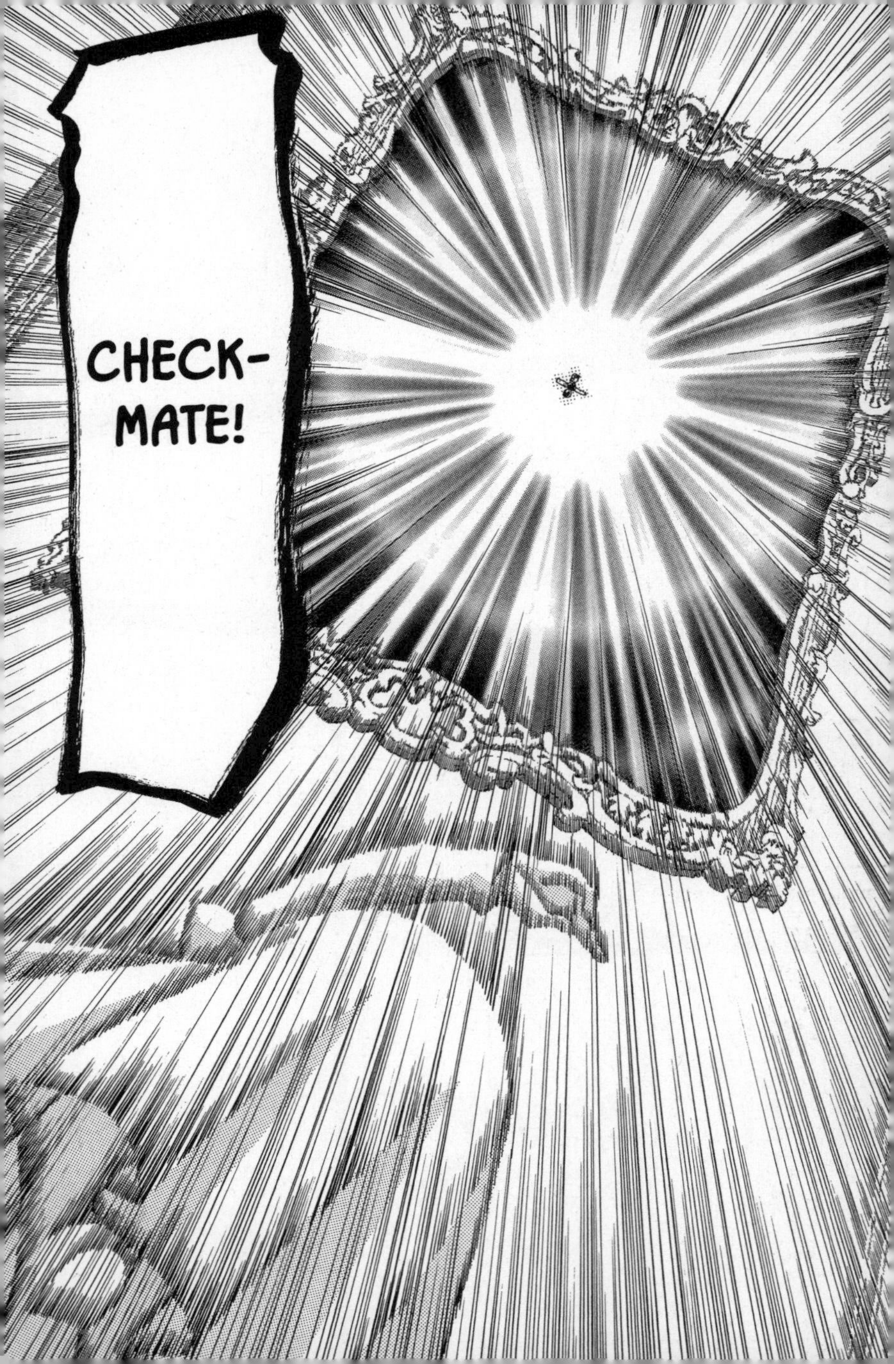
CHECK-
MATE!

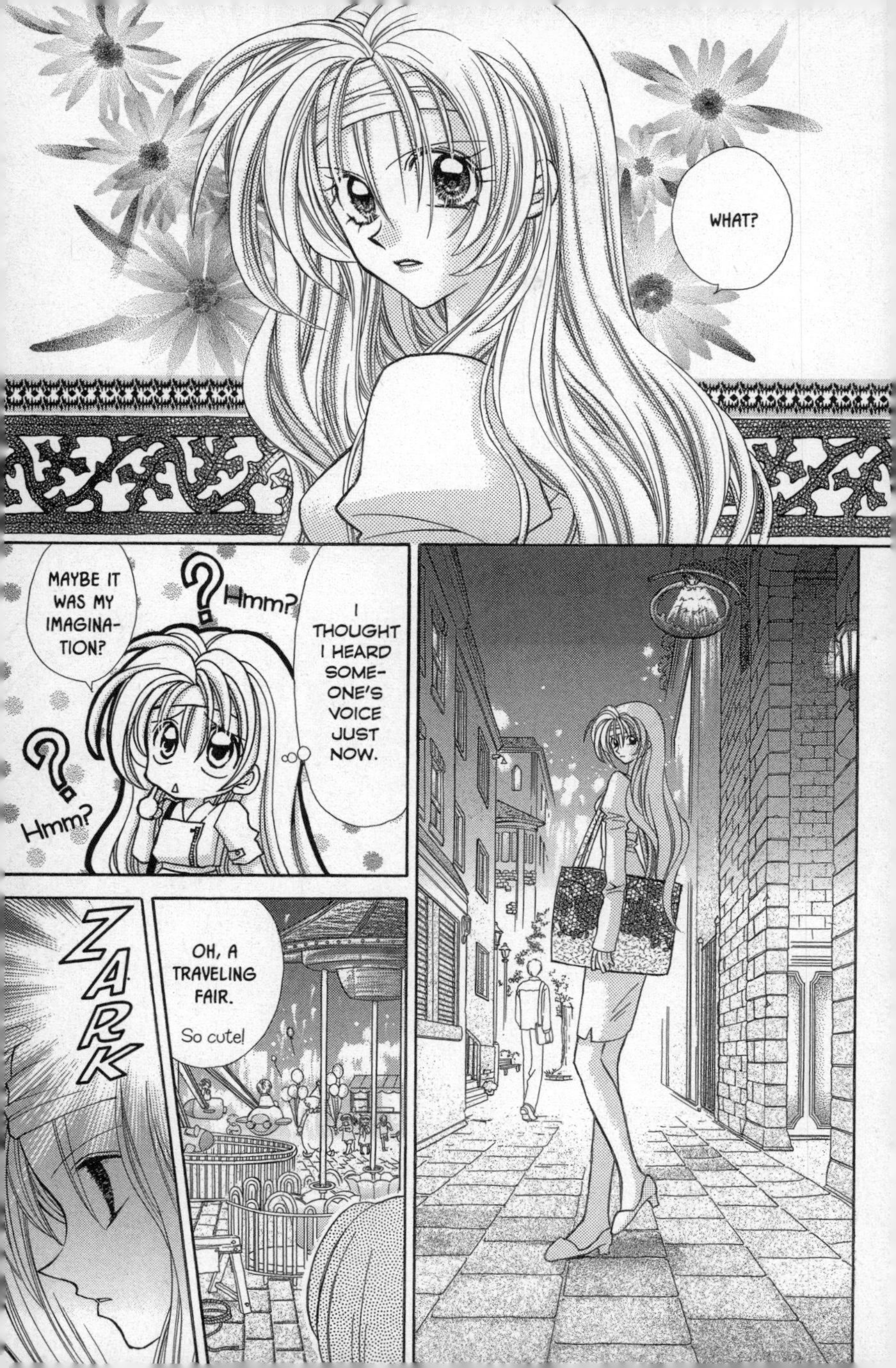
WHAT?
I THOUGHT I HEARD SOME-ONE'S VOICE JUST NOW.
Hmm?
MAYBE IT WAS MY IMAGINA-TION?
Hmm?
OH, A TRAVELING FAIR.
So cute!
ZARK

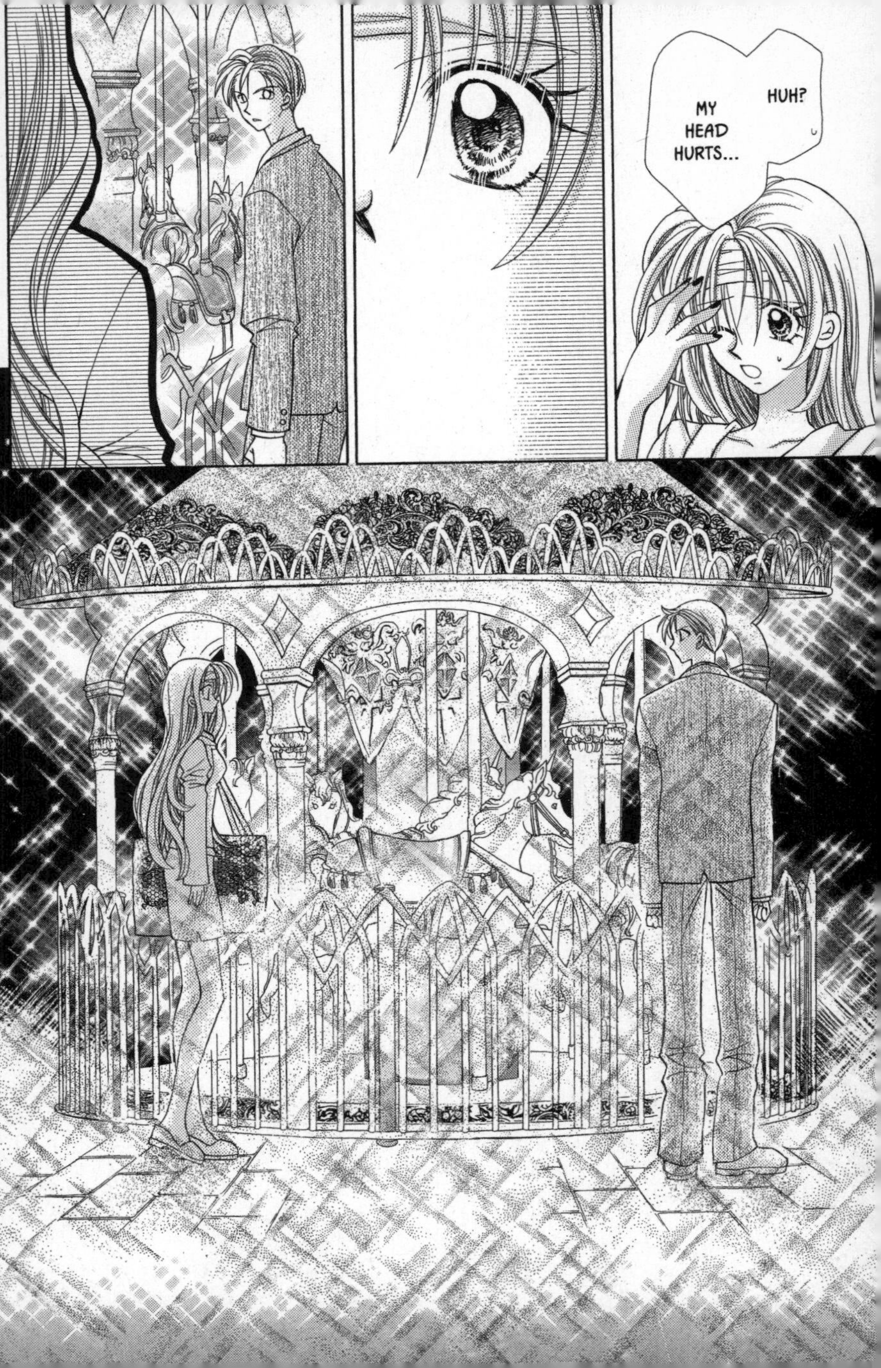
HUH?
MY HEAD HURTS...

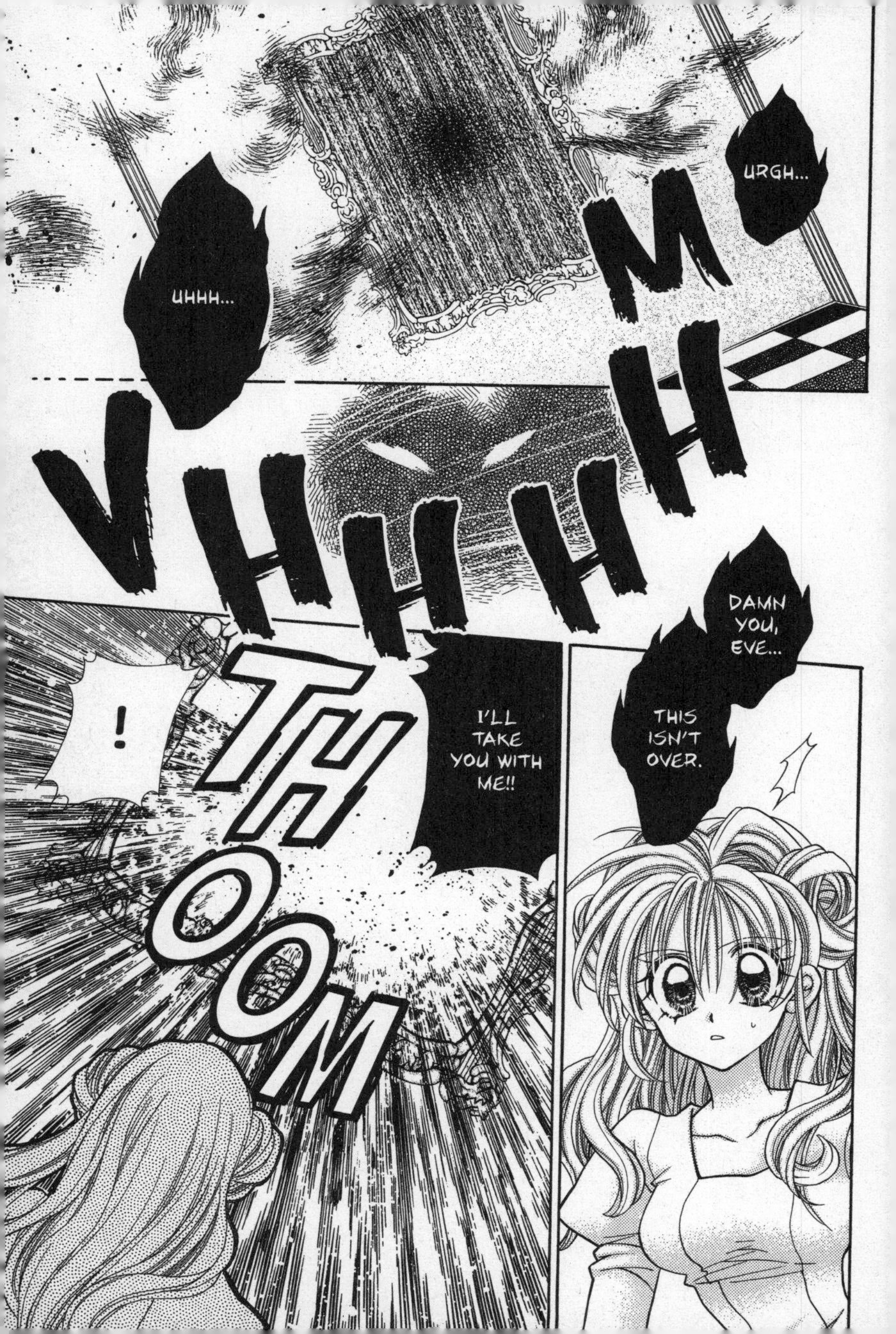
URGH...
UHHH...
VHHHHM
DAMN YOU, EVE...
THIS ISN'T OVER.
I'LL TAKE YOU WITH ME!!
THOOM
!

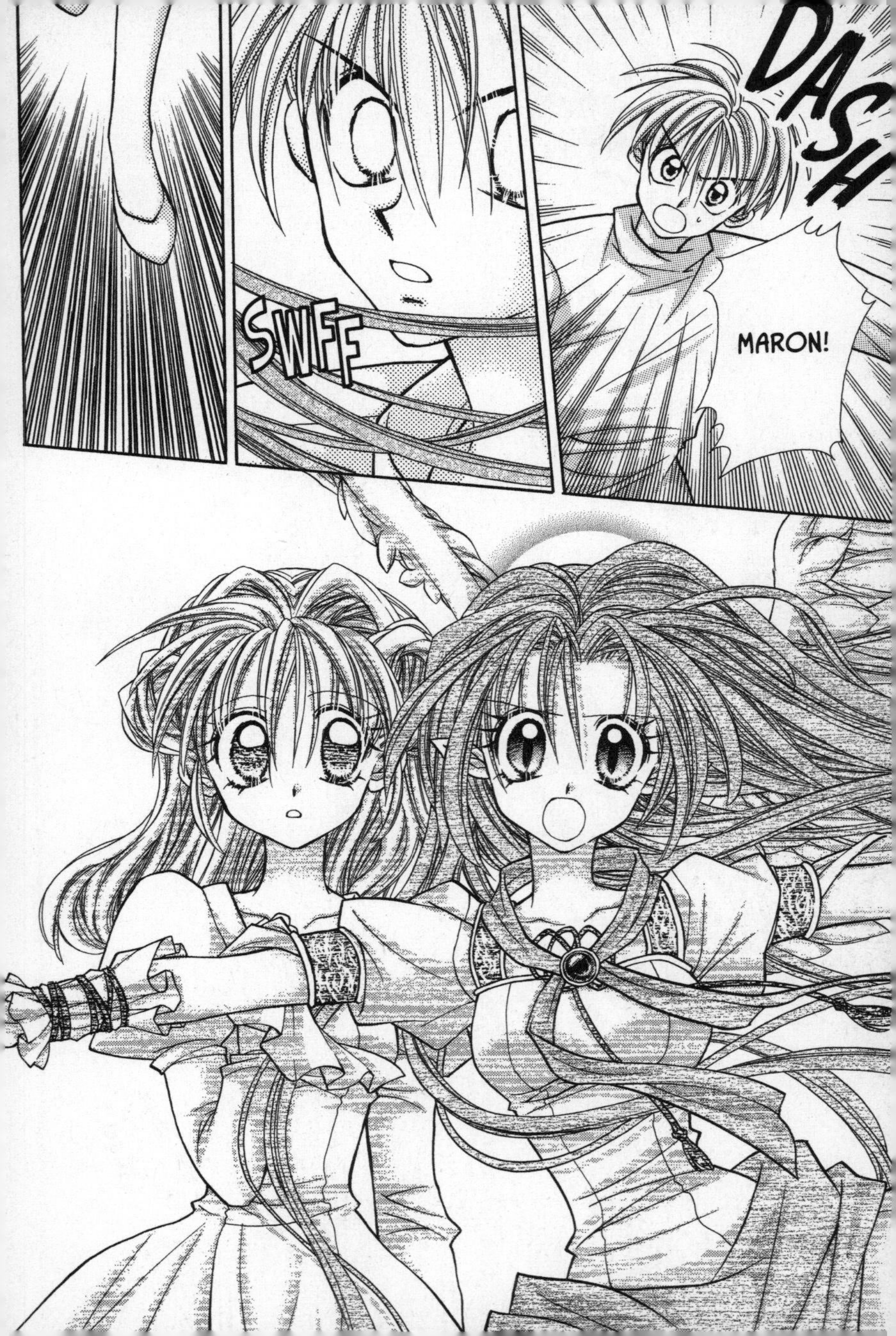
DASH
MARON!
SWFF

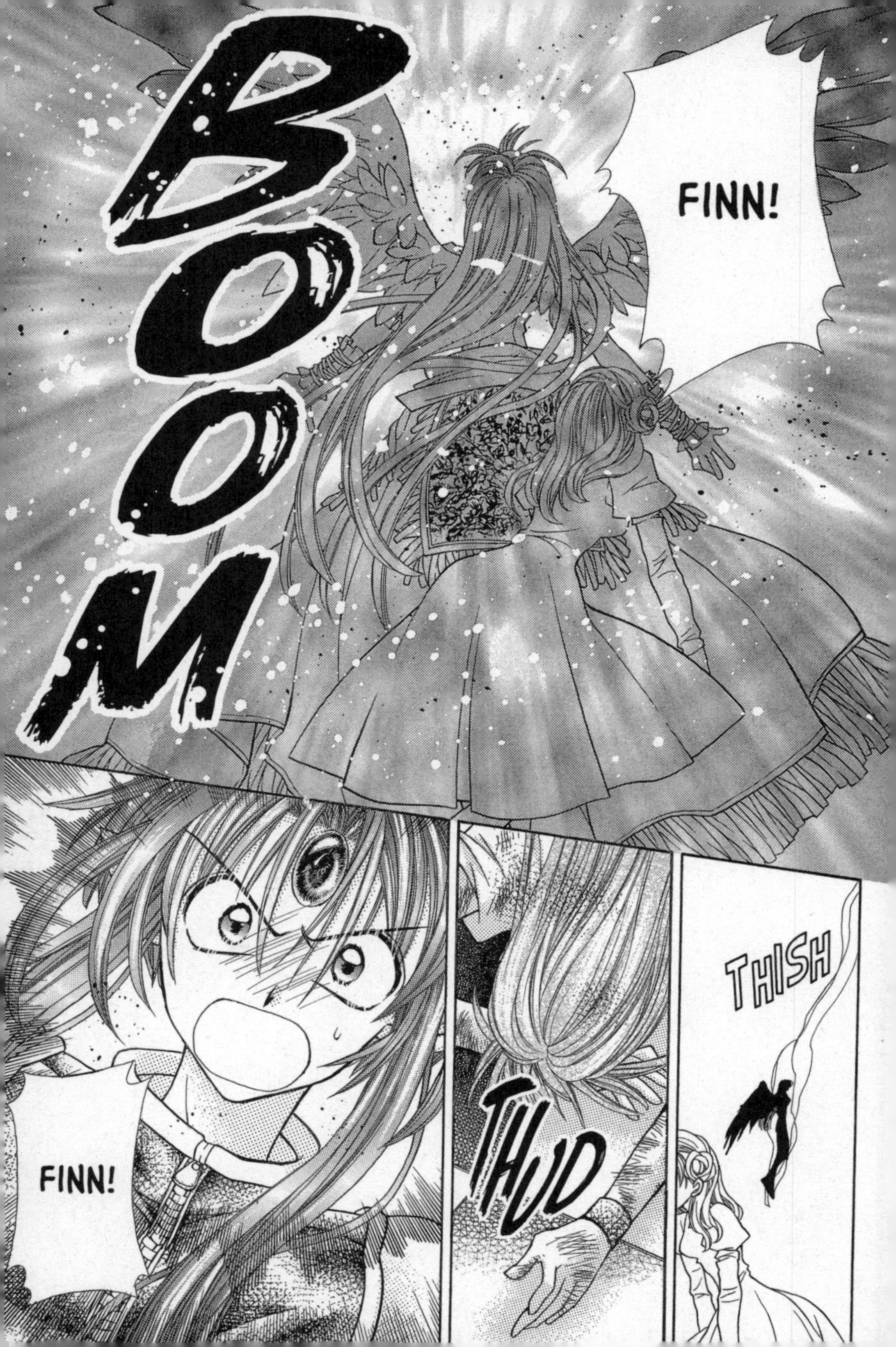
FINN!
BOOM
THISH
THUD
FINN!

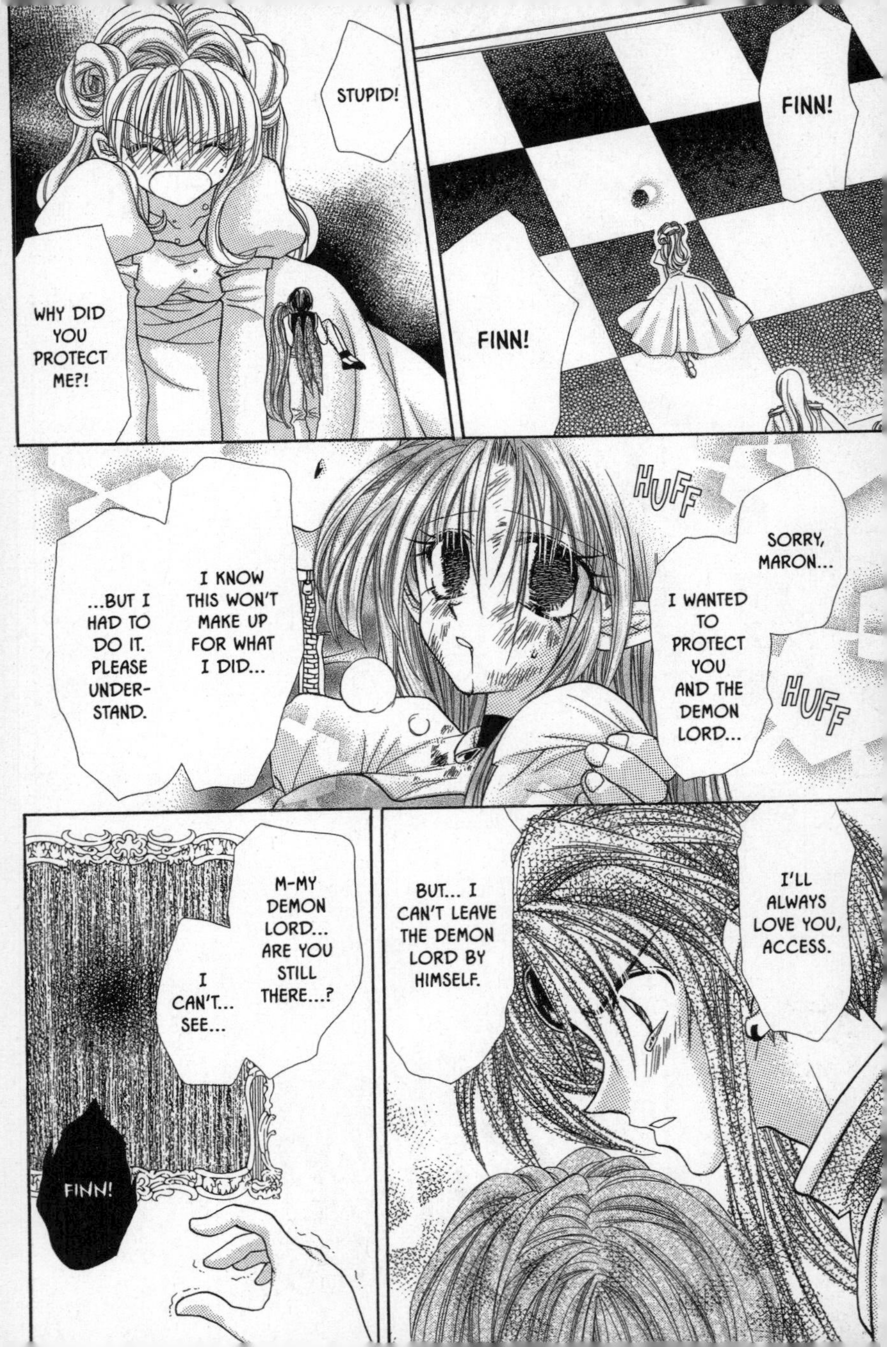
FINN!
FINN!
STUPID!
WHY DID YOU PROTECT ME?!
HUFF
SORRY, MARON...
I WANTED TO PROTECT YOU AND THE DEMON LORD...
HUFF
I KNOW THIS WON'T MAKE UP FOR WHAT I DID...
...BUT I HAD TO DO IT. PLEASE UNDER-STAND.
I'LL ALWAYS LOVE YOU, ACCESS.
BUT... I CAN'T LEAVE THE DEMON LORD BY HIMSELF.
M-MY DEMON LORD... ARE YOU STILL THERE...?
I CAN'T... SEE...
FINN!

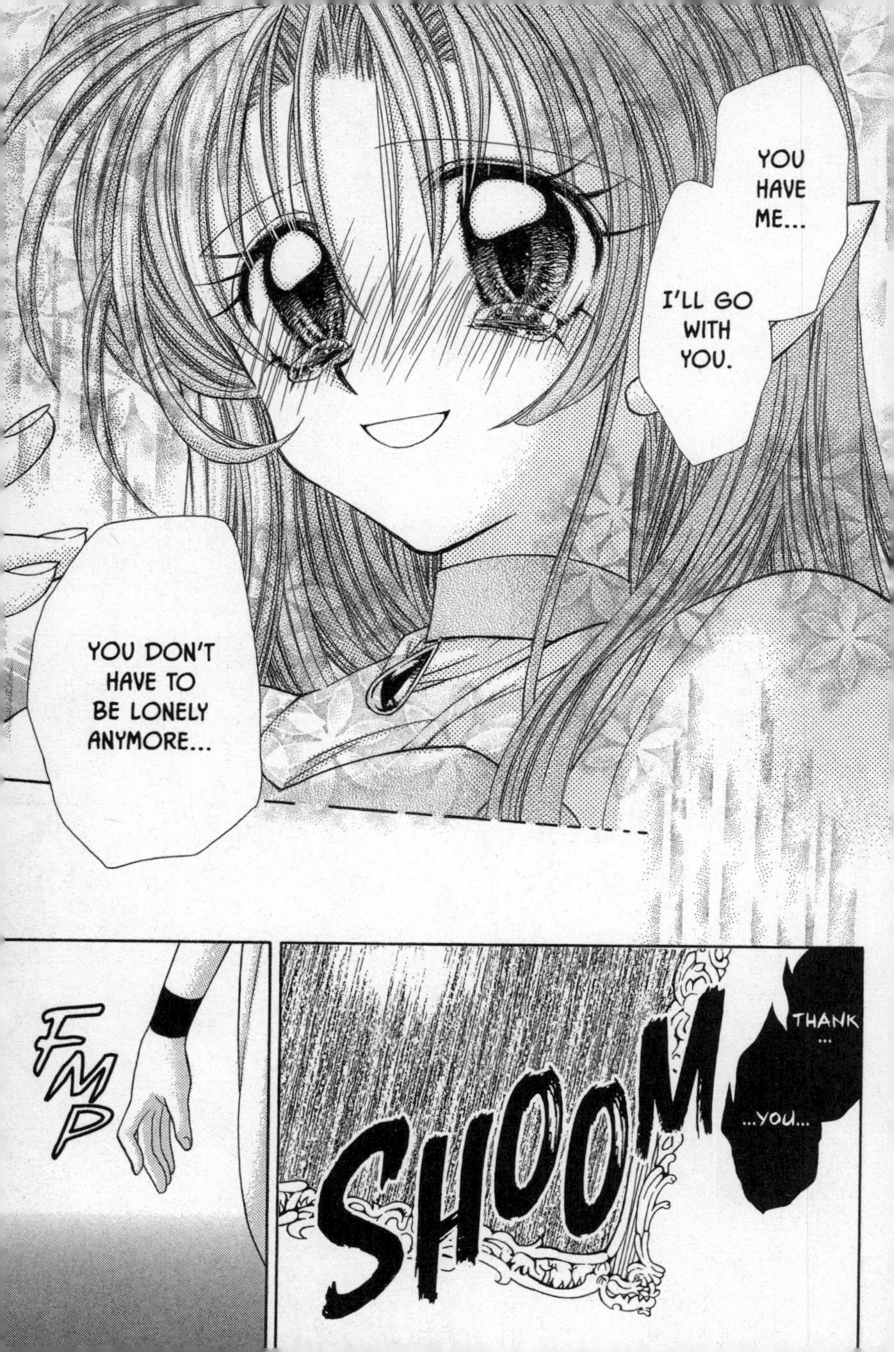
YOU HAVE ME... I'LL GO WITH YOU.
YOU DON'T HAVE TO BE LONELY ANYMORE...
THANK... ...YOU...
SHOOM
FMP

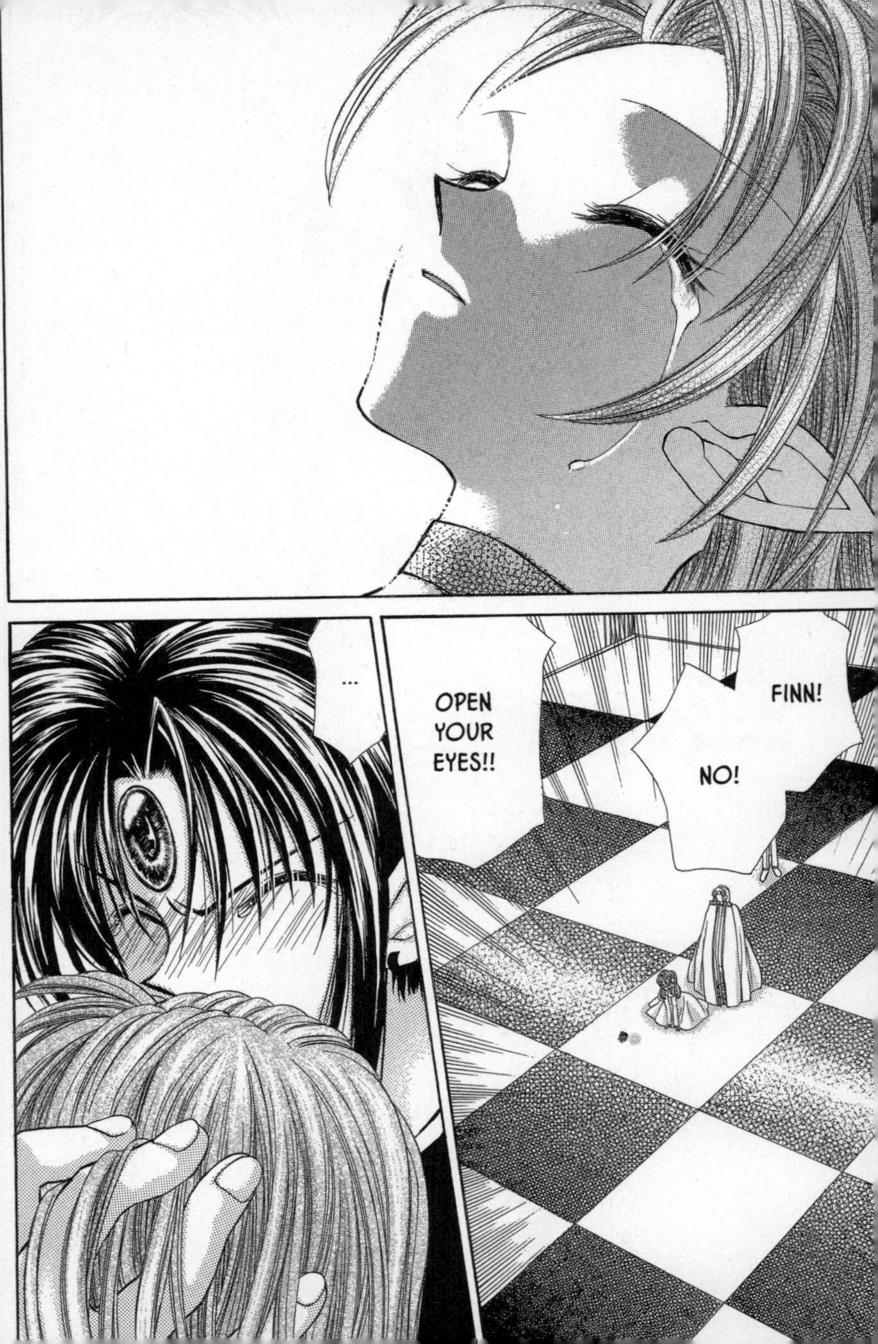
FINN!
NO!
OPEN YOUR EYES!!
...

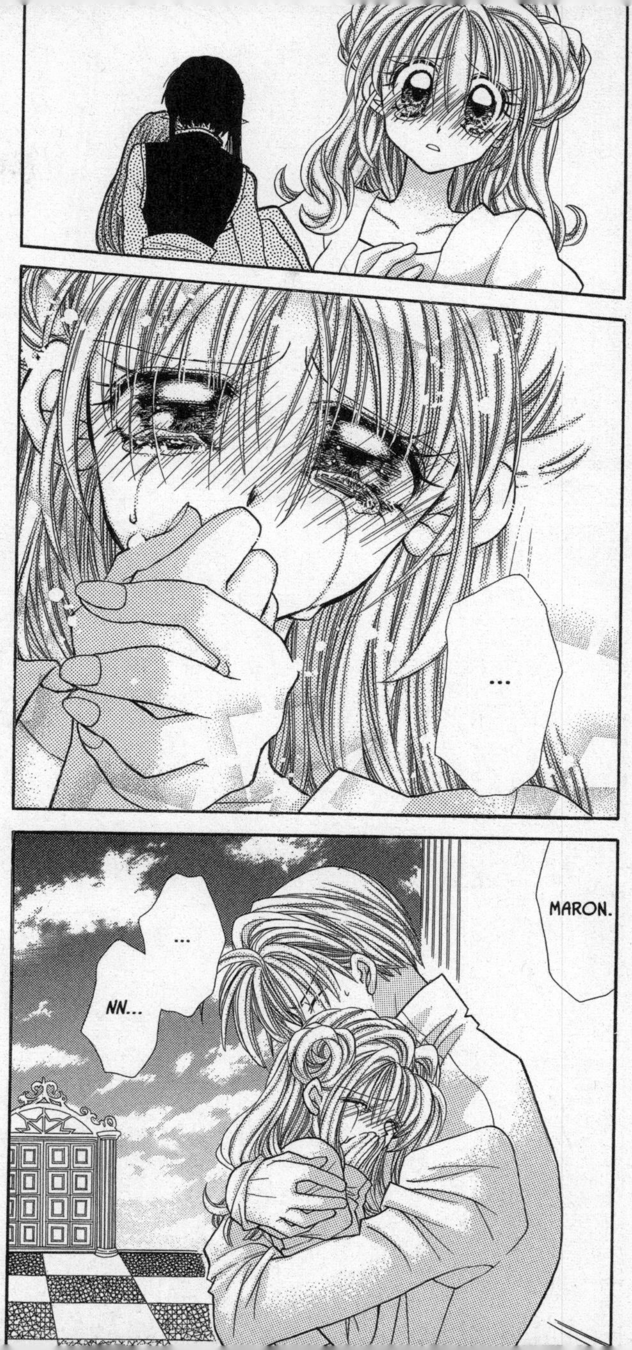
...
MARON.
...
NN...

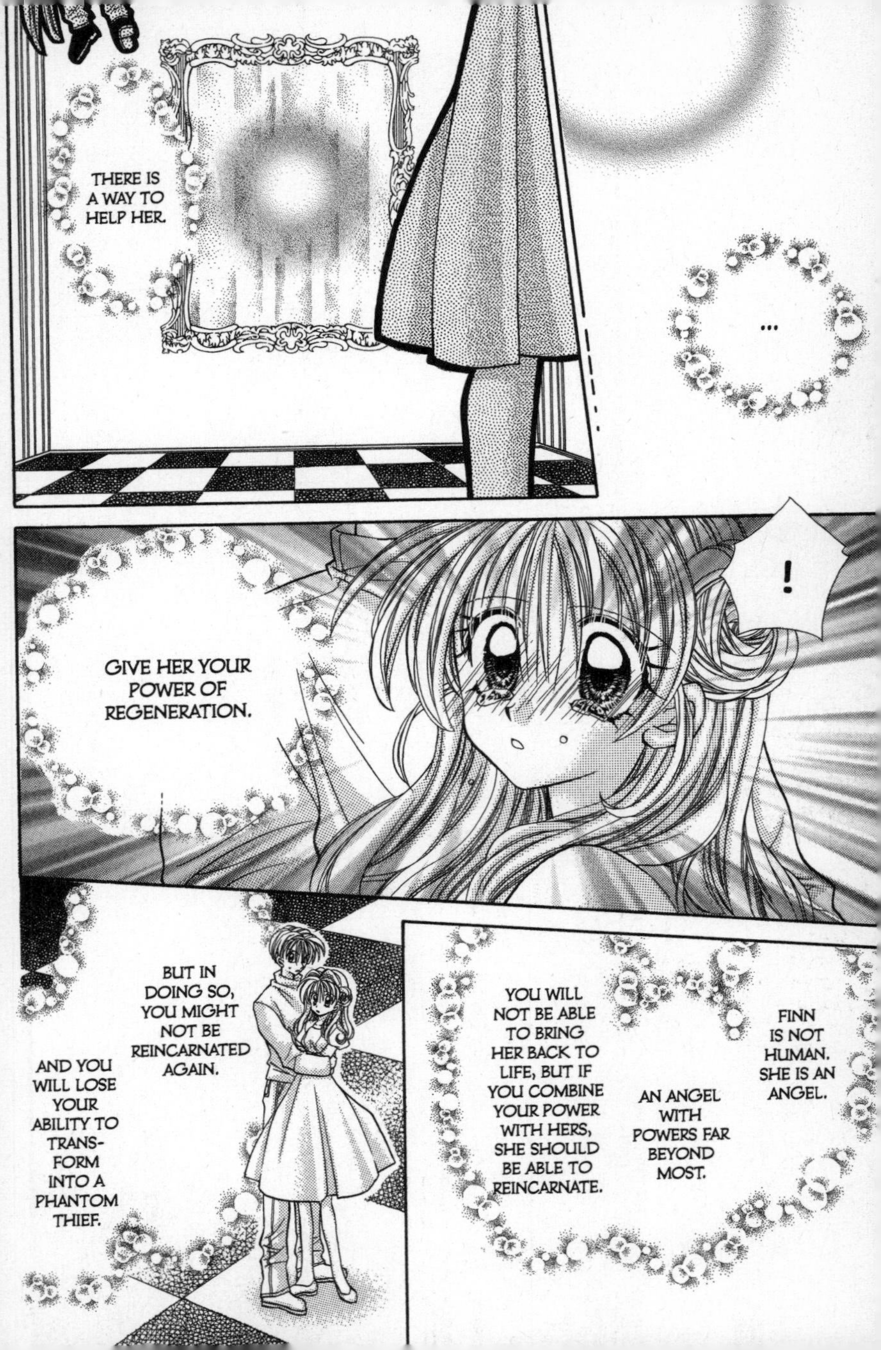

...
THERE IS A WAY TO HELP HER.
!
GIVE HER YOUR POWER OF REGENERATION.
FINN IS NOT HUMAN. SHE IS AN ANGEL.
AN ANGEL WITH POWERS FAR BEYOND MOST.
YOU WILL NOT BE ABLE TO BRING HER BACK TO LIFE, BUT IF YOU COMBINE YOUR POWER WITH HERS, SHE SHOULD BE ABLE TO REINCARNATE.
BUT IN DOING SO, YOU MIGHT NOT BE REINCARNATED AGAIN.
AND YOU WILL LOSE YOUR ABILITY TO TRANS-FORM INTO A PHANTOM THIEF.

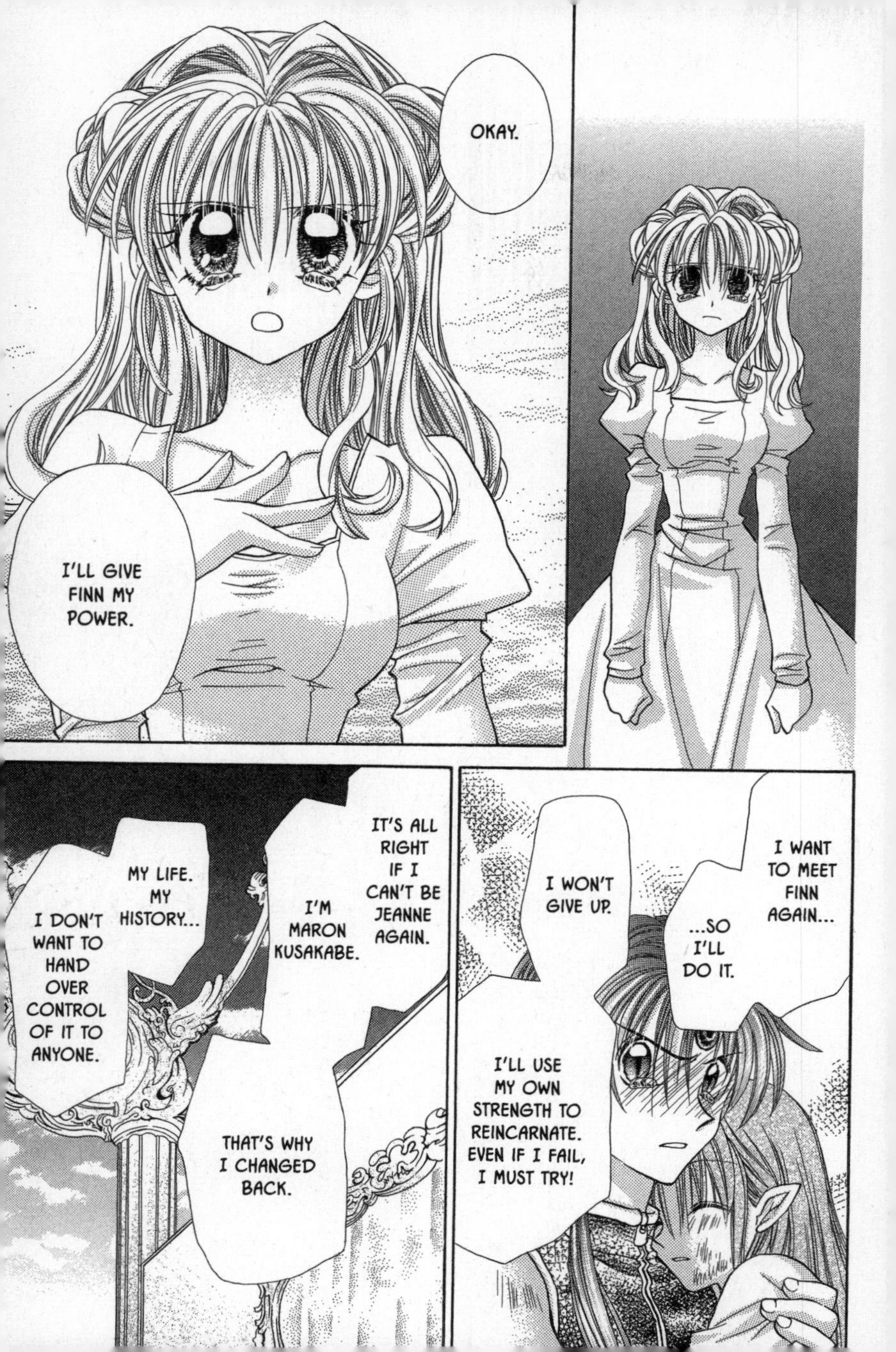
OKAY.
I'LL GIVE FINN MY POWER.
I WANT TO MEET FINN AGAIN...
...SO I'LL DO IT.
I WON'T GIVE UP.
I'LL USE MY OWN STRENGTH TO REINCARNATE. EVEN IF I FAIL, I MUST TRY!
IT'S ALL RIGHT IF I CAN'T BE JEANNE AGAIN.
I'M MARON KUSAKABE.
MY LIFE. MY HISTORY...
I DON'T WANT TO HAND OVER CONTROL OF IT TO ANYONE.
THAT'S WHY I CHANGED BACK.

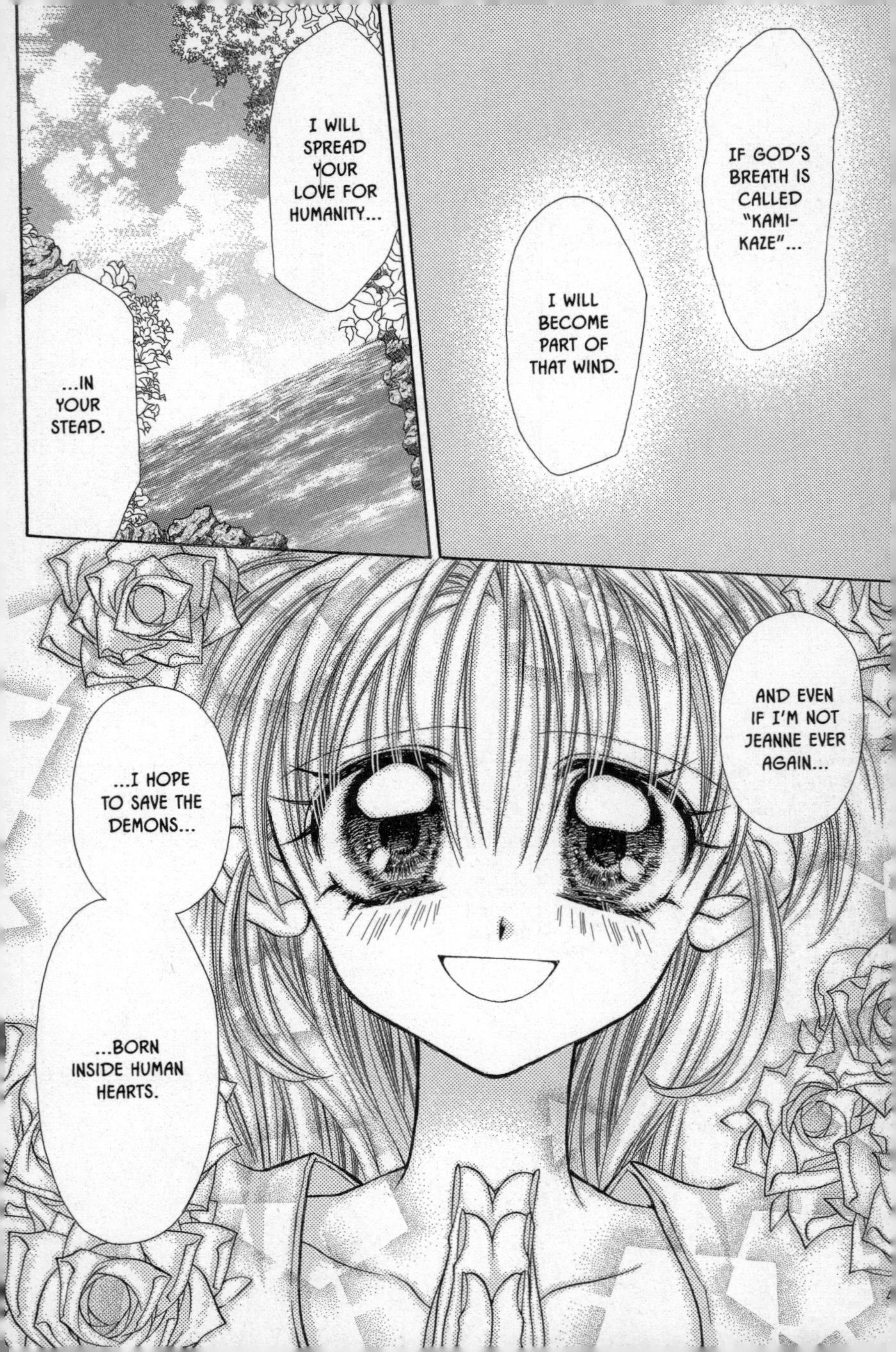

IF GOD'S BREATH IS CALLED "KAMI-KAZE"...
I WILL BECOME PART OF THAT WIND.
I WILL SPREAD YOUR LOVE FOR HUMANITY...
...IN YOUR STEAD.
AND EVEN IF I'M NOT JEANNE EVER AGAIN...
...I HOPE TO SAVE THE DEMONS...
...BORN INSIDE HUMAN HEARTS.

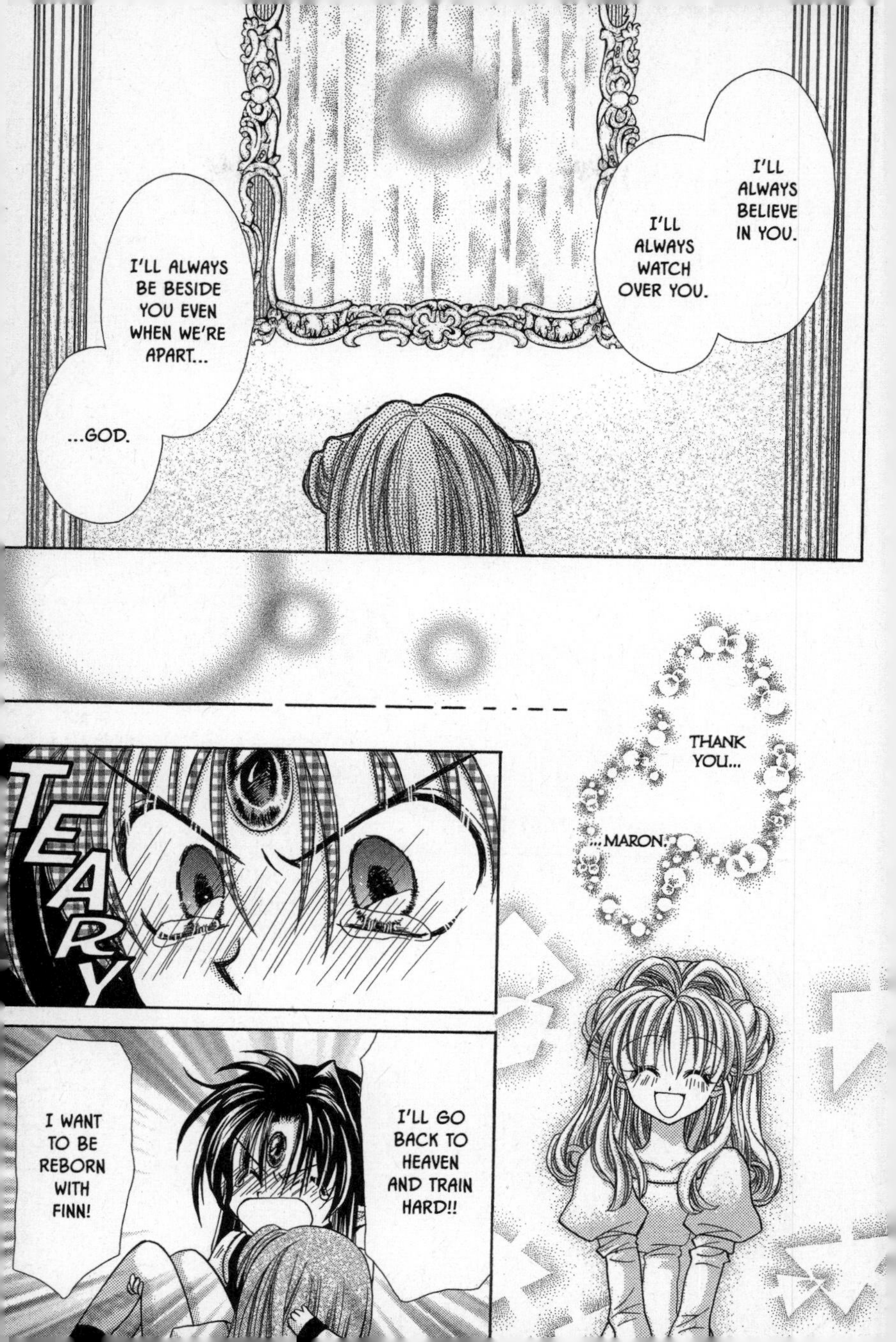
I'LL ALWAYS BELIEVE IN YOU.
I'LL ALWAYS WATCH OVER YOU.
I'LL ALWAYS BE BESIDE YOU EVEN WHEN WE'RE APART...
...GOD.
THANK YOU...
...MARON.
TEARY
I'LL GO BACK TO HEAVEN AND TRAIN HARD!!
I WANT TO BE REBORN WITH FINN!

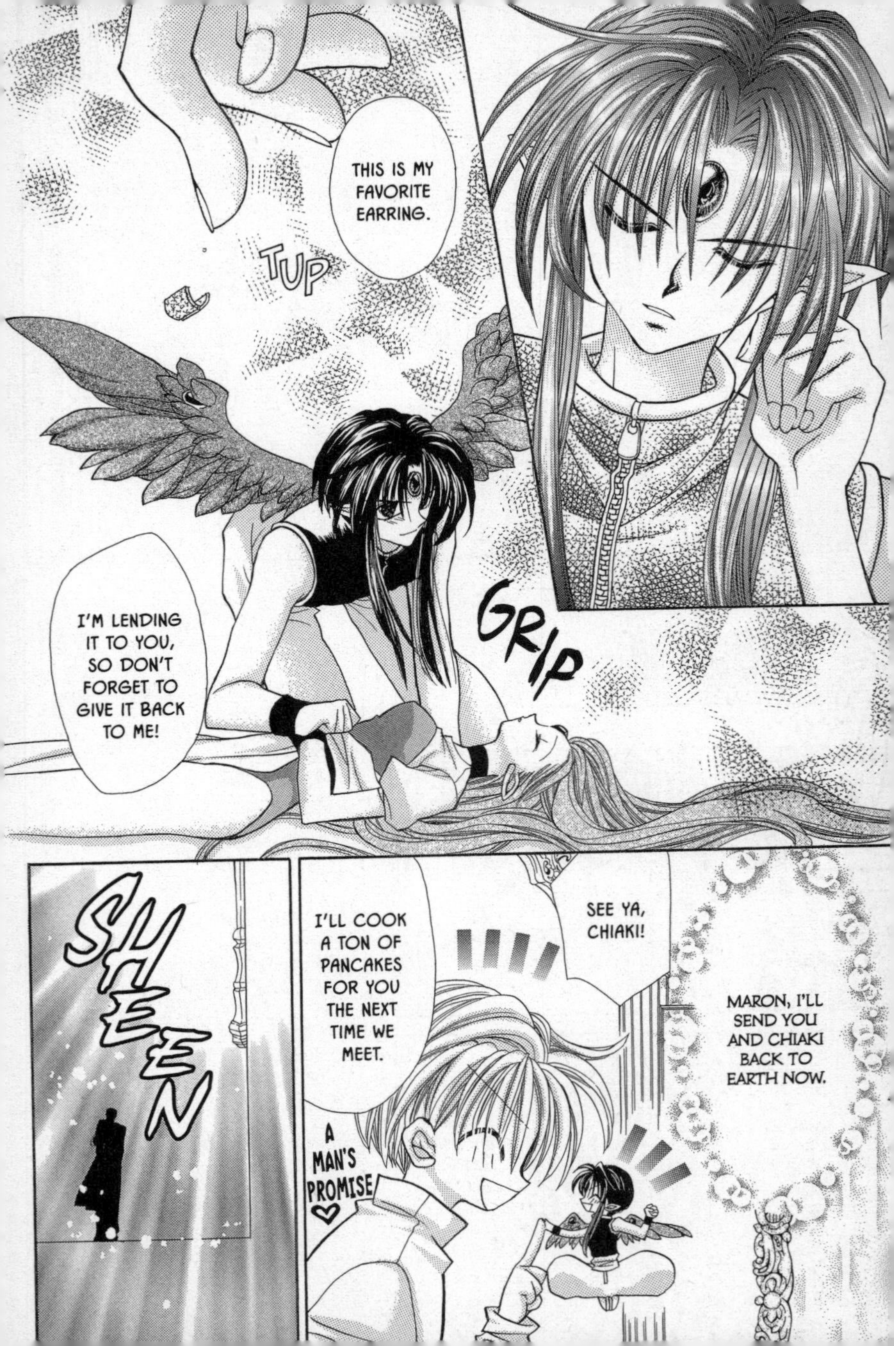
THIS IS MY FAVORITE EARRING.
TUP
GRIP
I'M LENDING IT TO YOU, SO DON'T FORGET TO GIVE IT BACK TO ME!
MARON, I'LL SEND YOU AND CHIAKI BACK TO EARTH NOW.
SEE YA, CHIAKI!
I'LL COOK A TON OF PANCAKES FOR YOU THE NEXT TIME WE MEET.
A MAN'S PROMISE
SHEEN

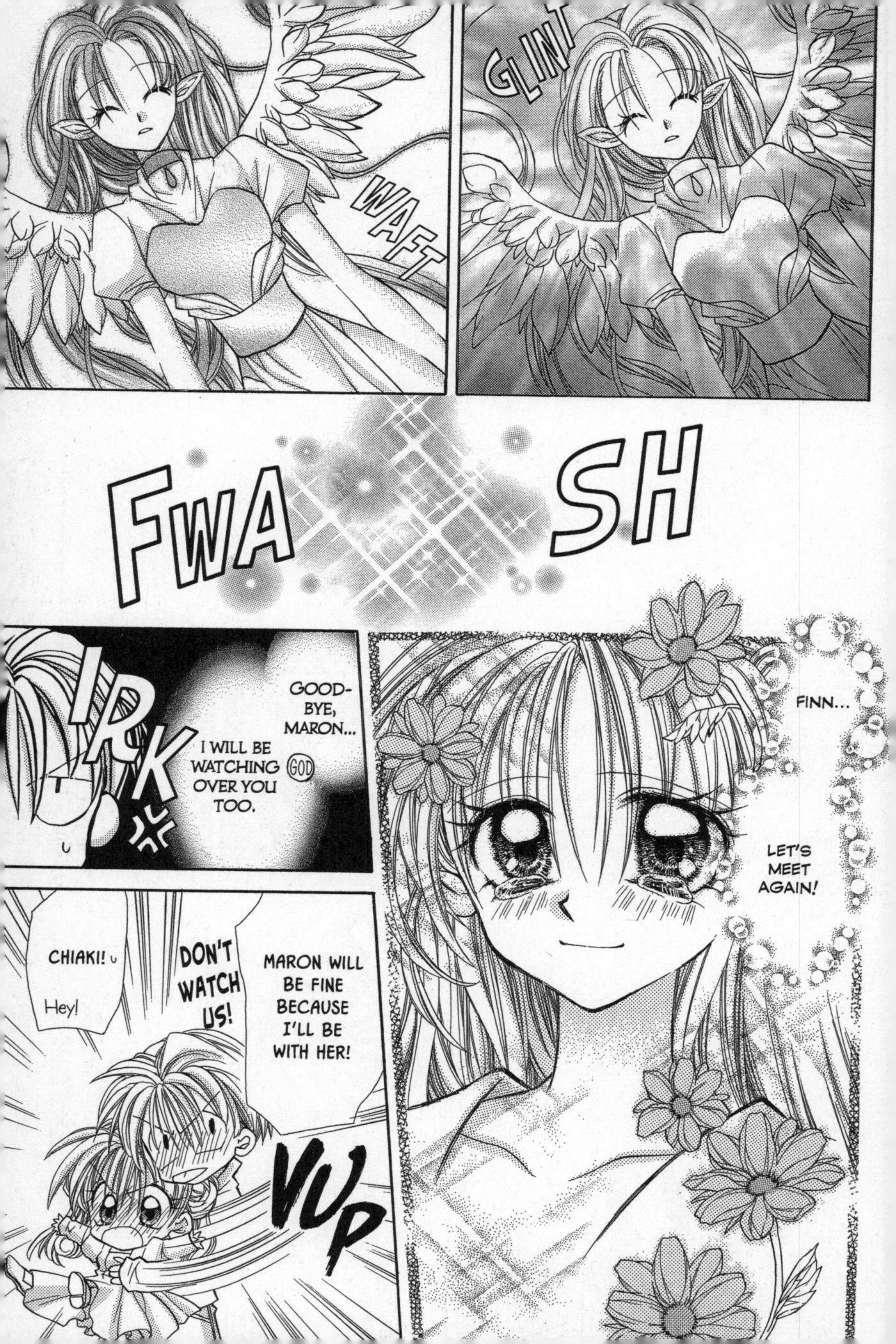
GLINT
WAFT
FWASH
FINN...
LET'S MEET AGAIN!
GOOD-BYE, MARON...
I WILL BE WATCHING OVER YOU TOO.
GOD
IRK
MARON WILL BE FINE BECAUSE I'LL BE WITH HER!
DON'T WATCH US!
CHIAKI!
Hey!
VUP

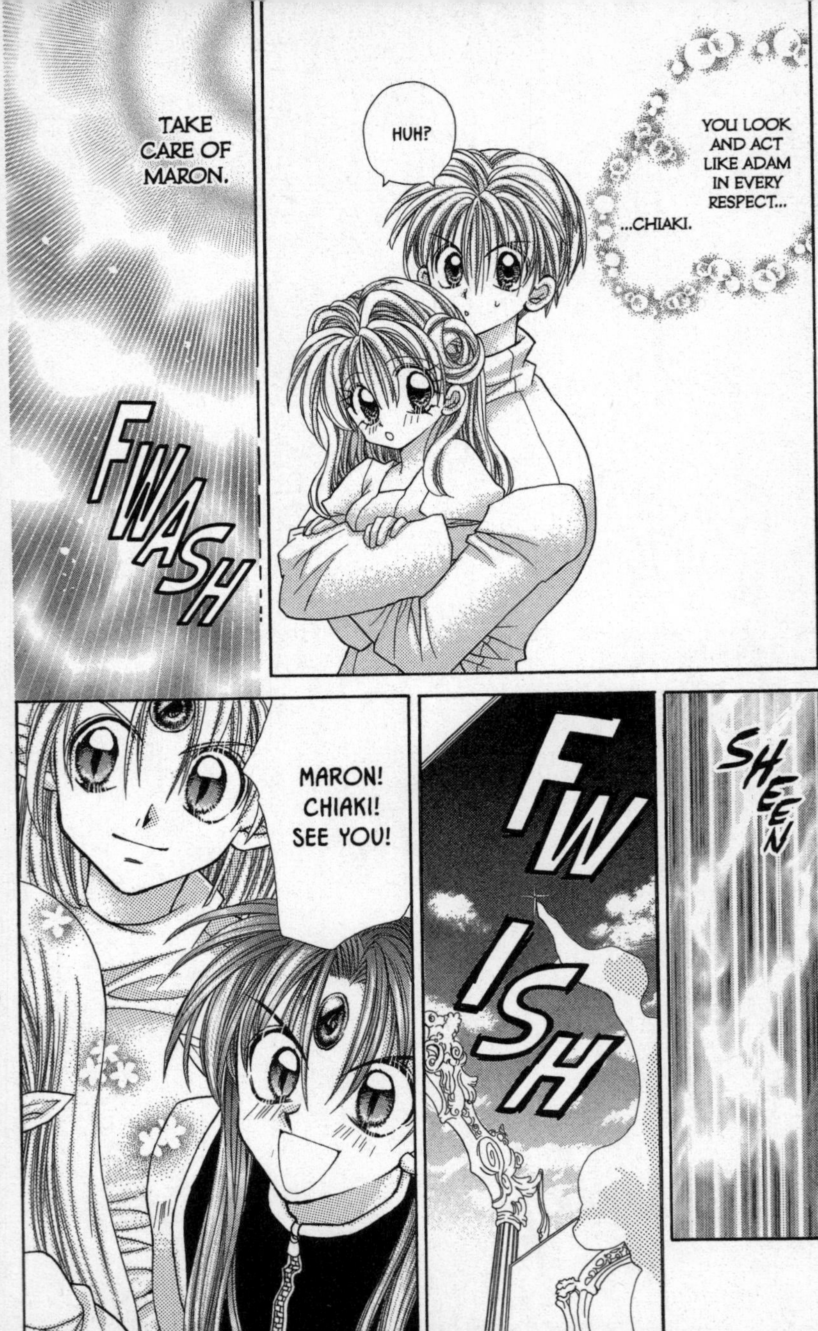
YOU LOOK AND ACT LIKE ADAM IN EVERY RESPECT...
...CHIAKI.
HUH?
TAKE CARE OF MARON.
FWASH
SHEEN
FWISH
MARON! CHIAKI! SEE YOU!

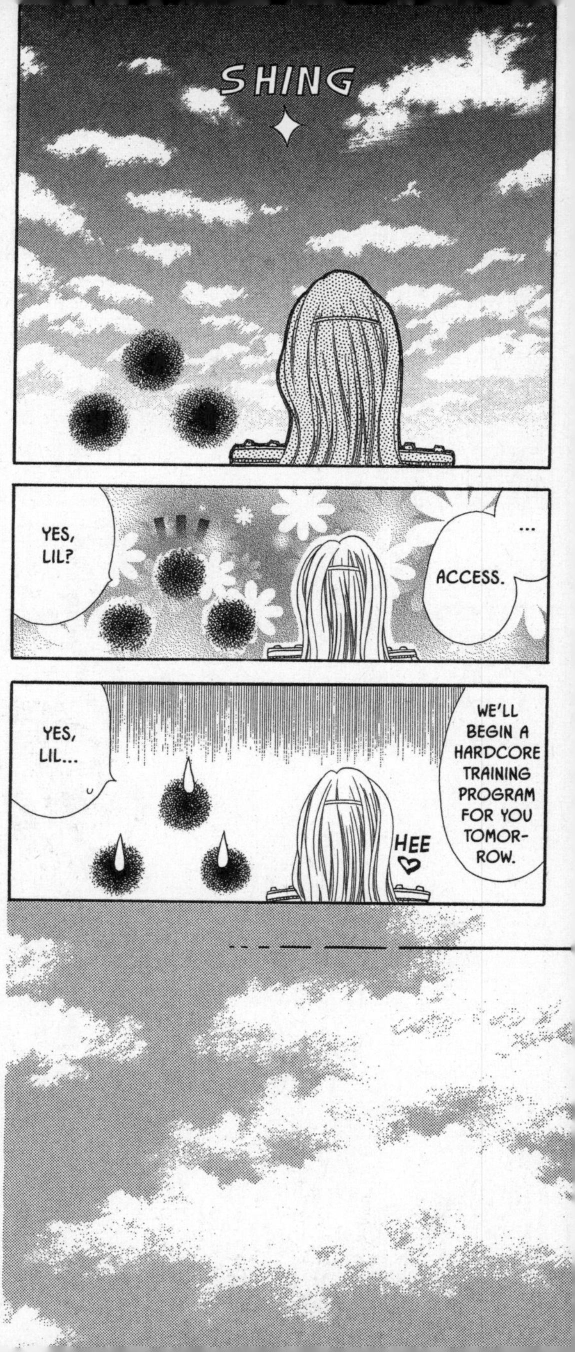
SHING
... ACCESS.
YES, LIL?
WE'LL BEGIN A HARDCORE TRAINING PROGRAM FOR YOU TOMOR-ROW.
HEE ♡
YES, LIL...

PHANTOM THIEF JEANNE

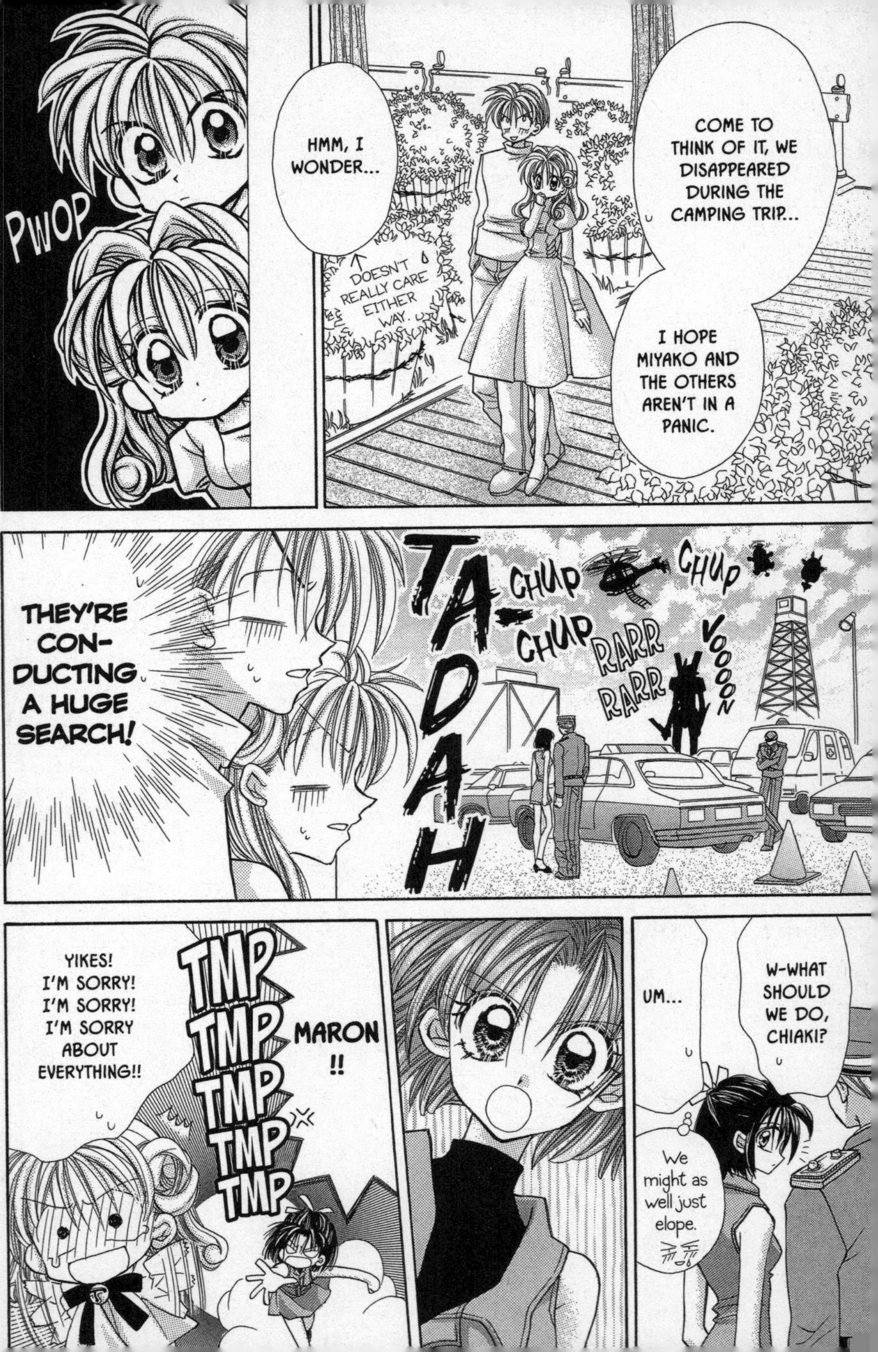
COME TO THINK OF IT, WE DISAPPEARED DURING THE CAMPING TRIP...
I HOPE MIYAKO AND THE OTHERS AREN'T IN A PANIC.
HMM, I WONDER...
DOESN'T REALLY CARE EITHER WAY.
PWOP
CHUP
CHUP
VOOOOON
CHUP
RARR RARR
TA-DAH
THEY'RE CON-DUCTING A HUGE SEARCH!
W-WHAT SHOULD WE DO, CHIAKI?
UM...
We might as well just elope.
MARON!!
TMP TMP TMP TMP TMP TMP
YIKES! I'M SORRY! I'M SORRY! I'M SORRY ABOUT EVERYTHING!!

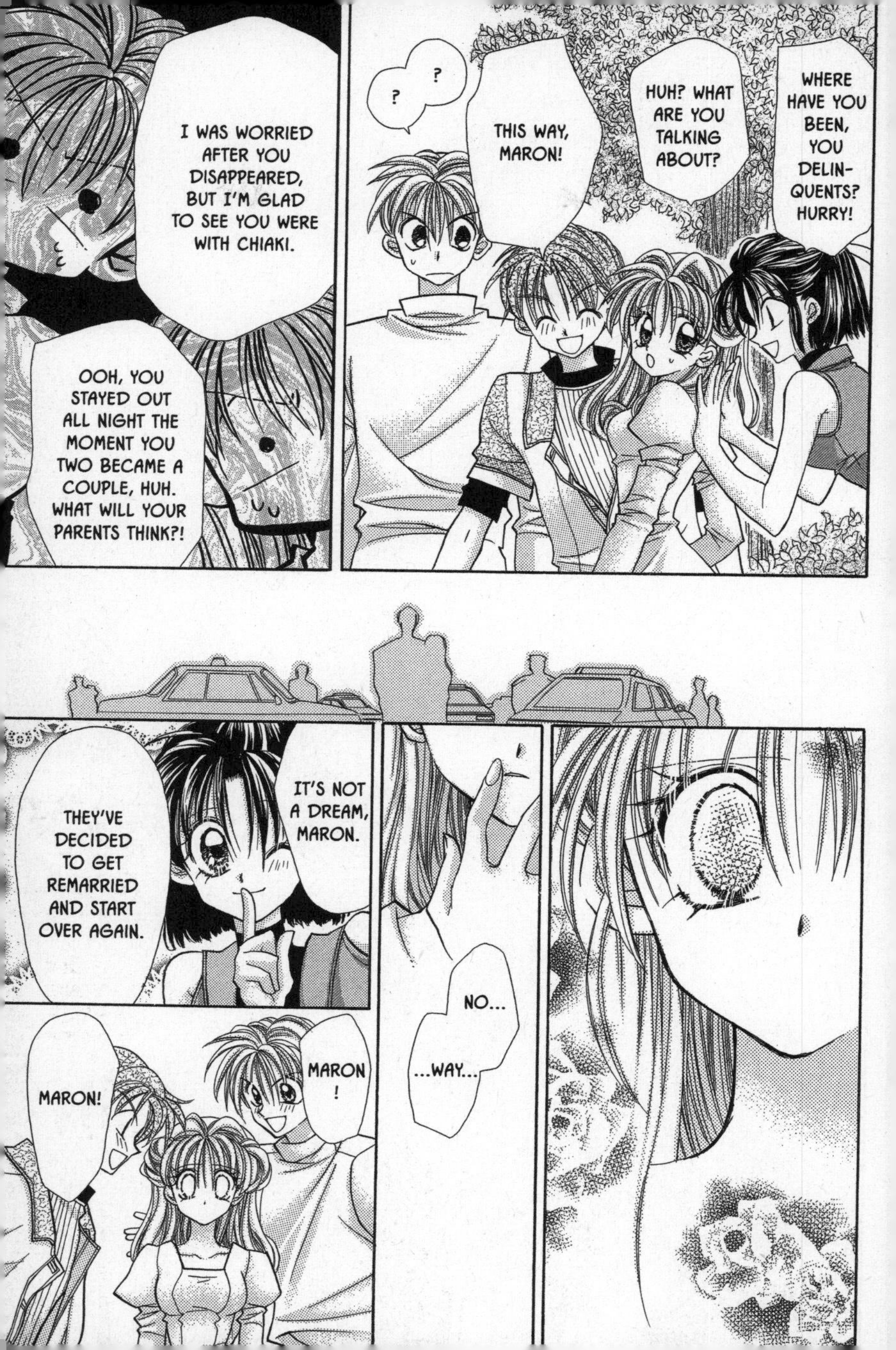
WHERE HAVE YOU BEEN, YOU DELIN-QUENTS? HURRY!
HUH? WHAT ARE YOU TALKING ABOUT?
THIS WAY, MARON!
? ?
I WAS WORRIED AFTER YOU DISAPPEARED, BUT I'M GLAD TO SEE YOU WERE WITH CHIAKI.
OOH, YOU STAYED OUT ALL NIGHT THE MOMENT YOU TWO BECAME A COUPLE, HUH. WHAT WILL YOUR PARENTS THINK?!
NO...
...WAY...
IT'S NOT A DREAM, MARON.
THEY'VE DECIDED TO GET REMARRIED AND START OVER AGAIN.
MARON!
MARON!

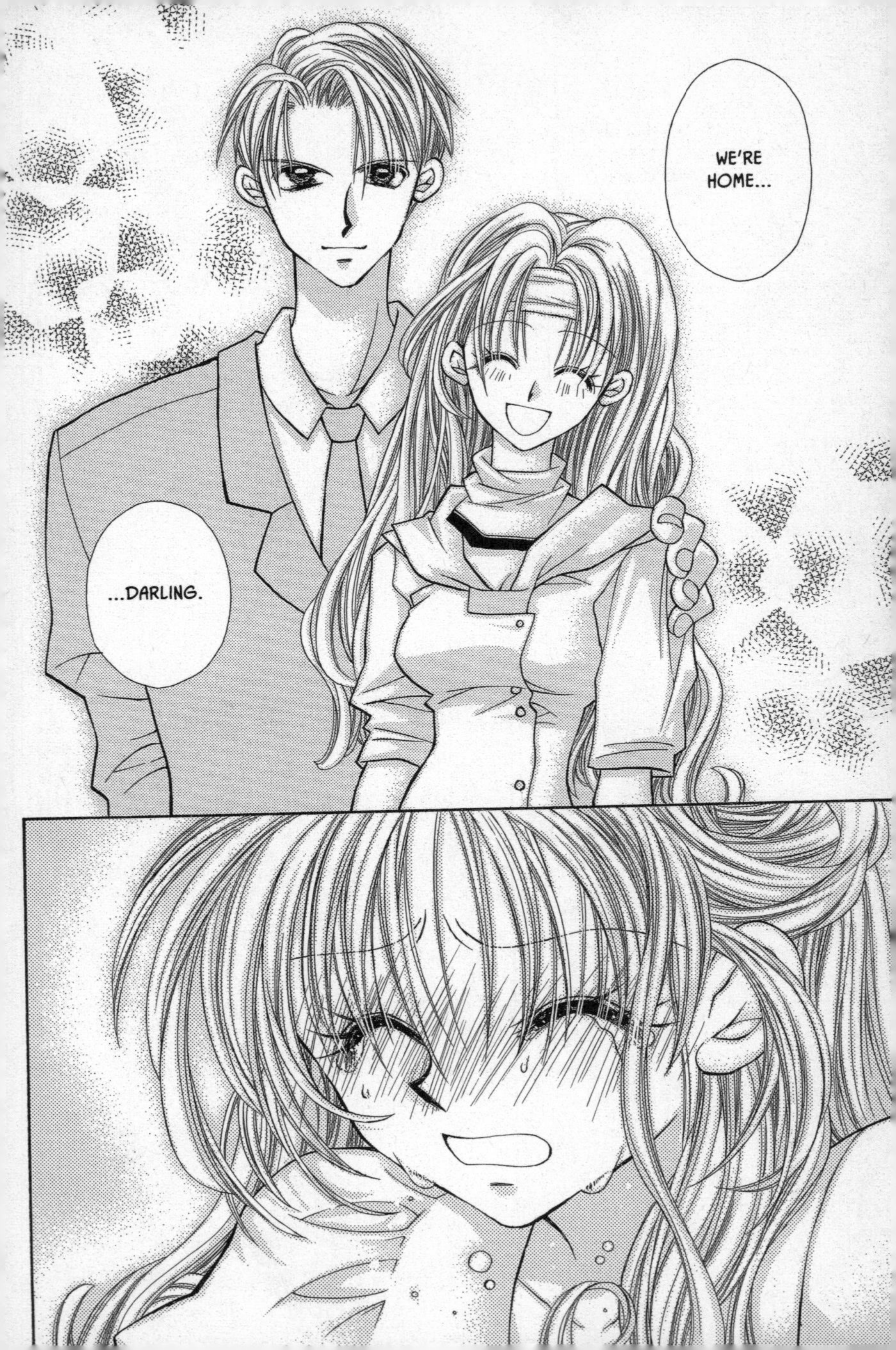
WE'RE HOME...
...DARLING.

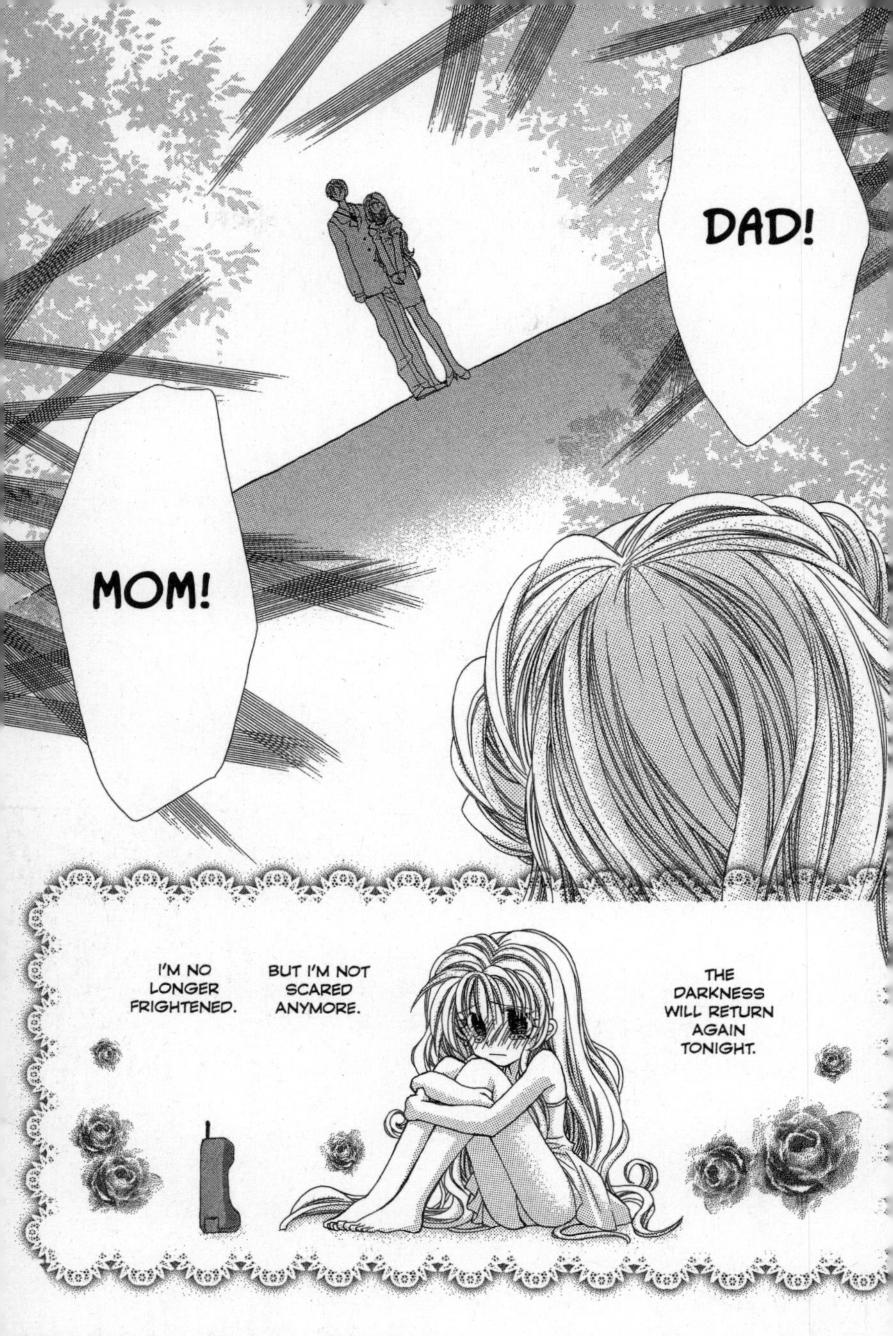
DAD!
MOM!
THE DARKNESS WILL RETURN AGAIN TONIGHT.
BUT I'M NOT SCARED ANYMORE.
I'M NO LONGER FRIGHTENED.

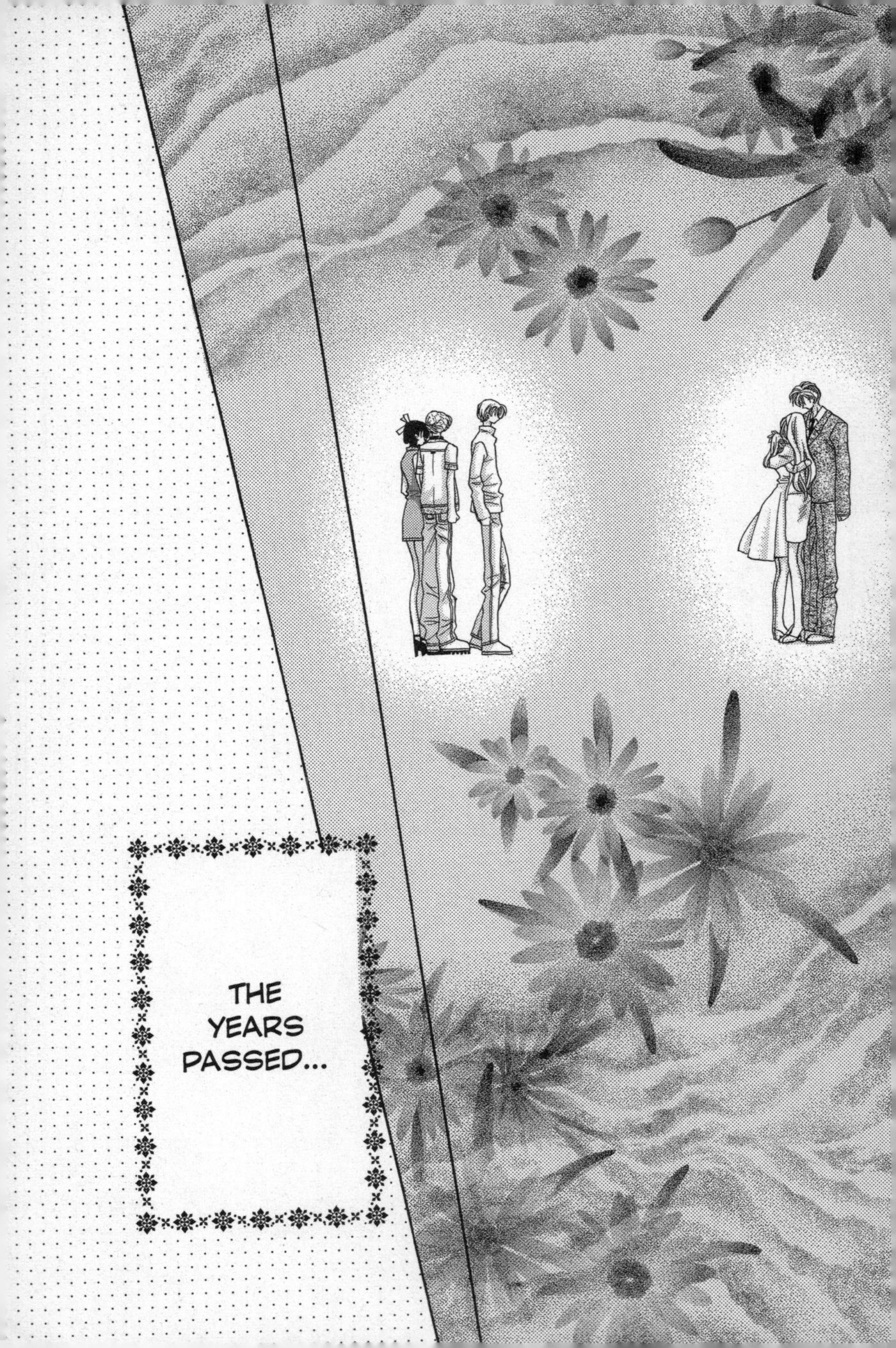
THE YEARS PASSED...

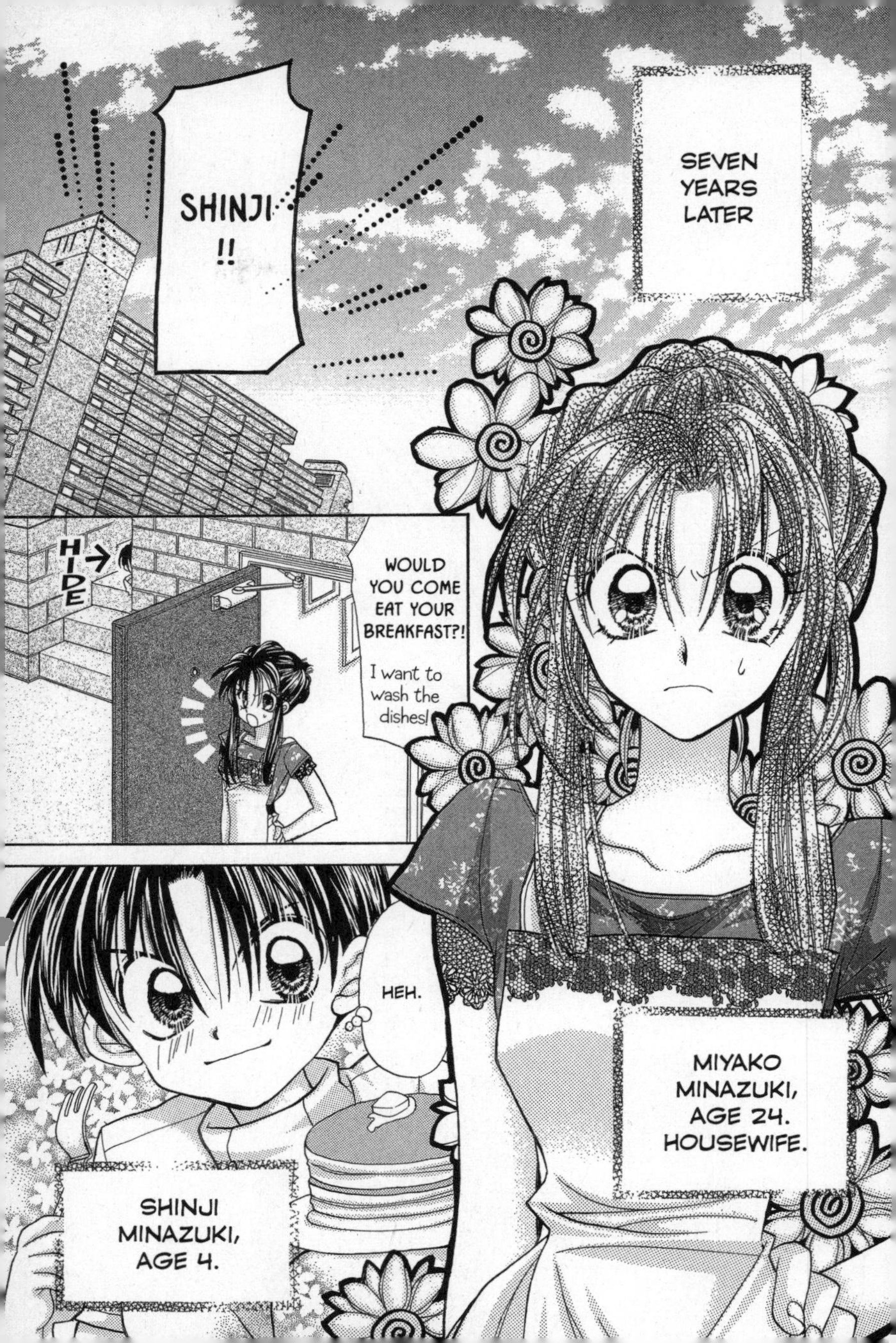
SEVEN YEARS LATER
SHINJI!!
MIYAKO MINAZUKI, AGE 24. HOUSEWIFE.
WOULD YOU COME EAT YOUR BREAKFAST?!
I want to wash the dishes!
HIDE
HEH.
SHINJI MINAZUKI, AGE 4.

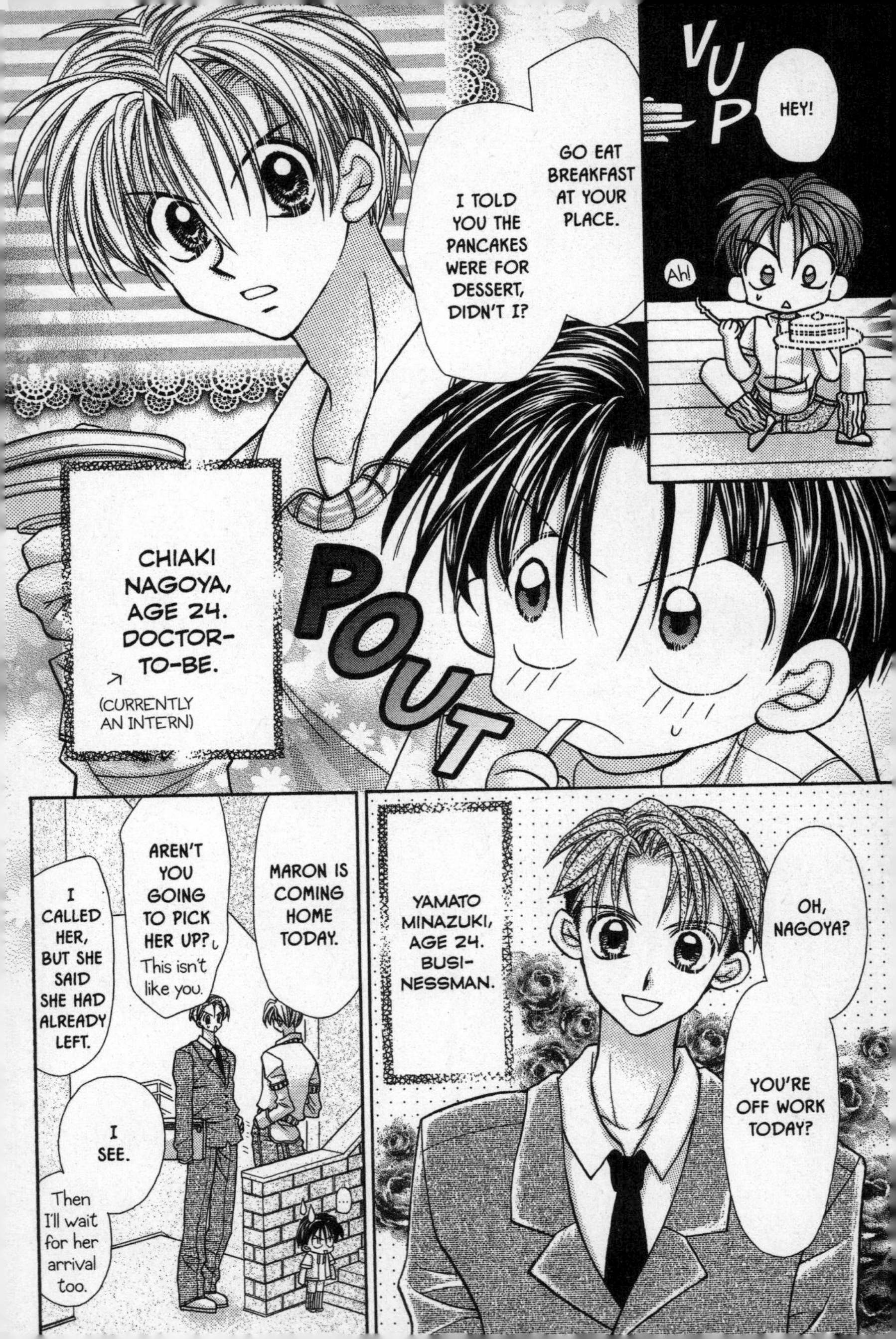
VUP
HEY!
Ah!
GO EAT BREAKFAST AT YOUR PLACE.
I TOLD YOU THE PANCAKES WERE FOR DESSERT, DIDN'T I?
POUT
CHIAKI NAGOYA, AGE 24. DOCTOR-TO-BE.
(CURRENTLY AN INTERN)
OH, NAGOYA?
YOU'RE OFF WORK TODAY?
YAMATO MINAZUKI, AGE 24. BUSI-NESSMAN.
MARON IS COMING HOME TODAY.
AREN'T YOU GOING TO PICK HER UP?
This isn't like you.
I CALLED HER, BUT SHE SAID SHE HAD ALREADY LEFT.
I SEE.
Then I'll wait for her arrival too.

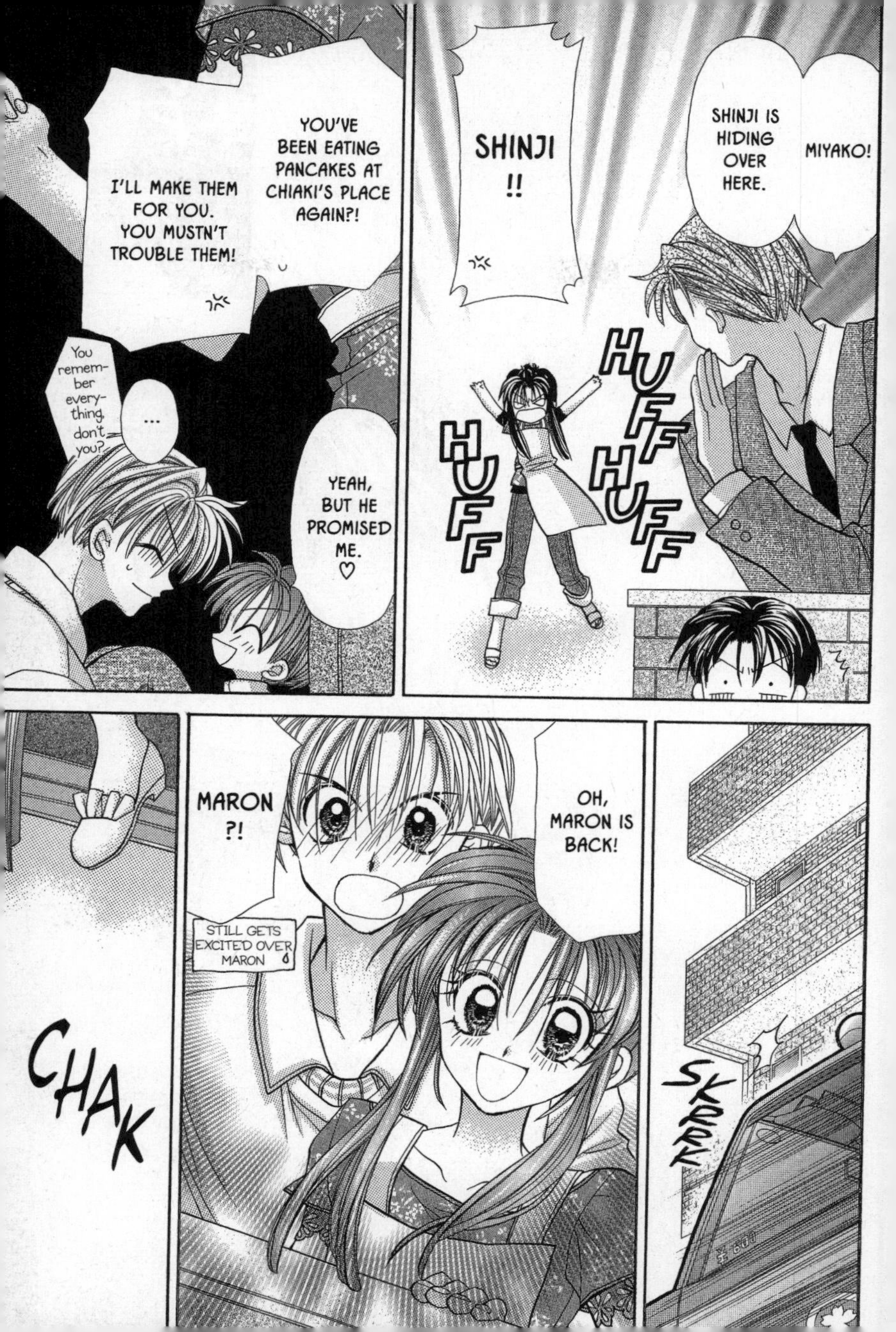
MIYAKO!
SHINJI IS HIDING OVER HERE.
SHINJI !!
HUFF HUFF HUFF HUFF
YOU'VE BEEN EATING PANCAKES AT CHIAKI'S PLACE AGAIN?!
I'LL MAKE THEM FOR YOU. YOU MUSTN'T TROUBLE THEM!
YEAH, BUT HE PROMISED ME. ♡
...
You remember everything, don't you?
SKRRK
OH, MARON IS BACK!
MARON ?!
STILL GETS EXCITED OVER MARON
CHAK

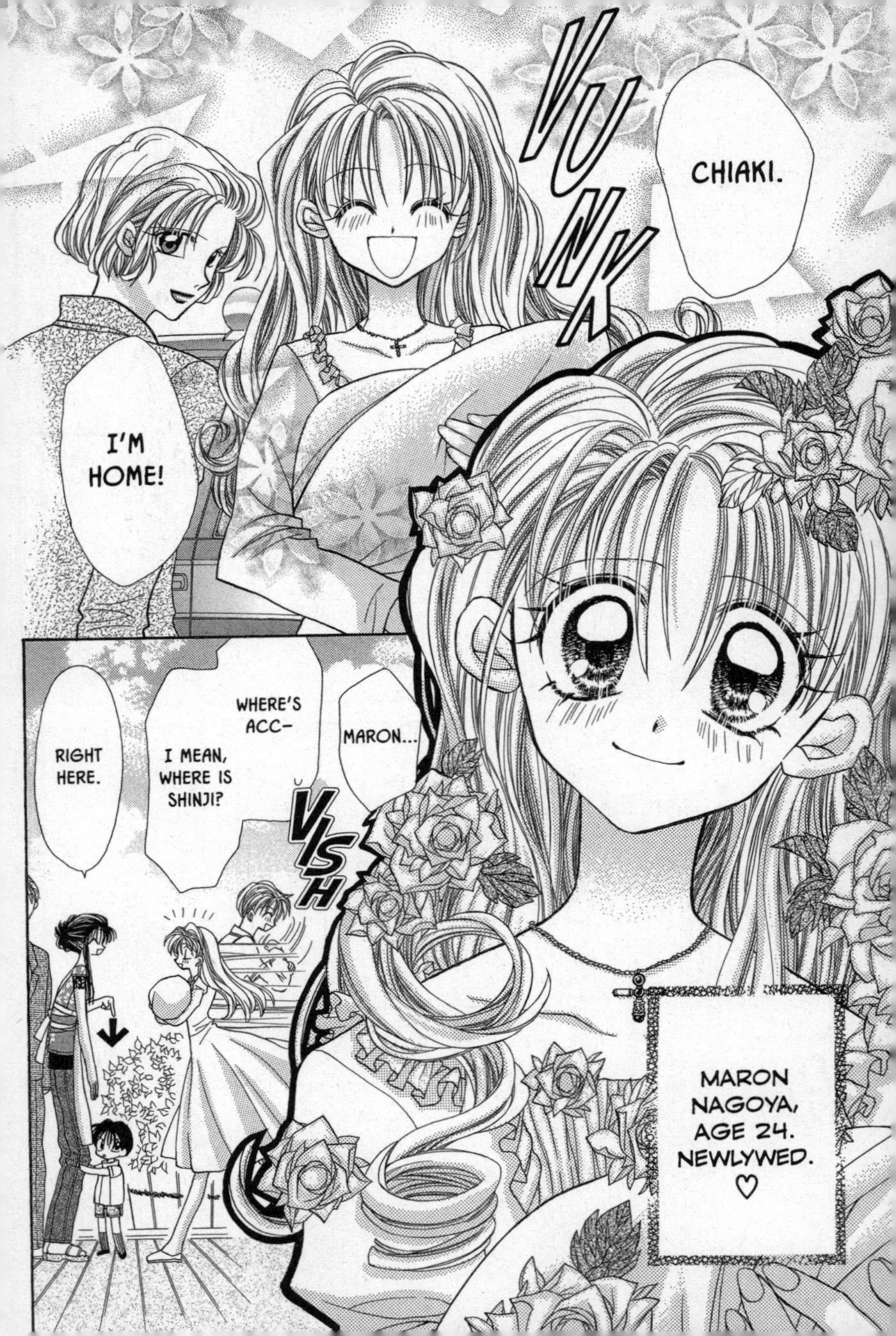
VUNK
CHIAKI.
I'M HOME!
MARON NAGOYA, AGE 24. NEWLYWED. ♡
MARON...
WHERE'S ACC–
I MEAN, WHERE IS SHINJI?
VISH
RIGHT HERE.

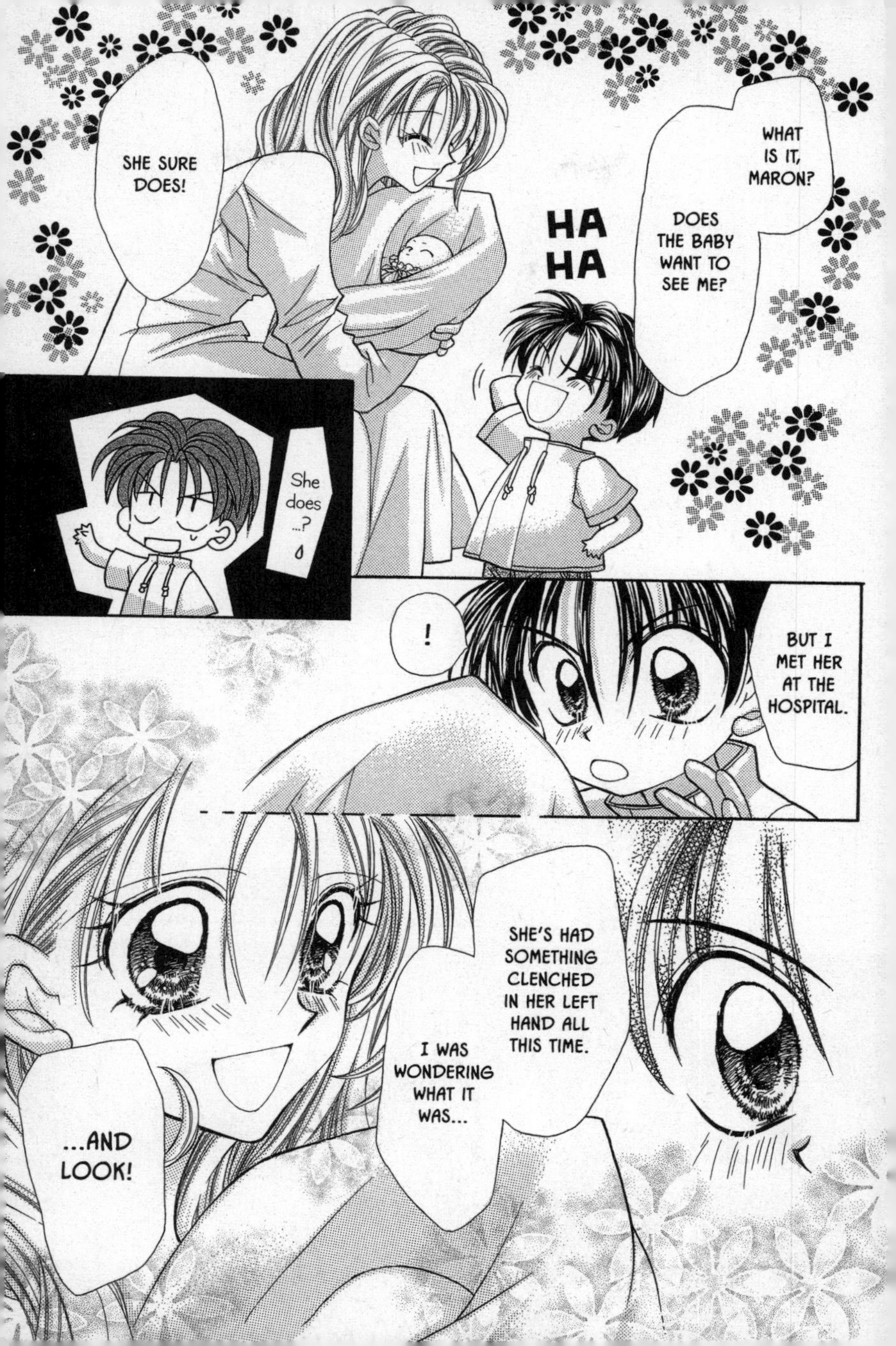
WHAT IS IT, MARON?
DOES THE BABY WANT TO SEE ME?
HA HA
SHE SURE DOES!
She does ...?
BUT I MET HER AT THE HOSPITAL.
!
SHE'S HAD SOMETHING CLENCHED IN HER LEFT HAND ALL THIS TIME.
I WAS WONDERING WHAT IT WAS...
...AND LOOK!

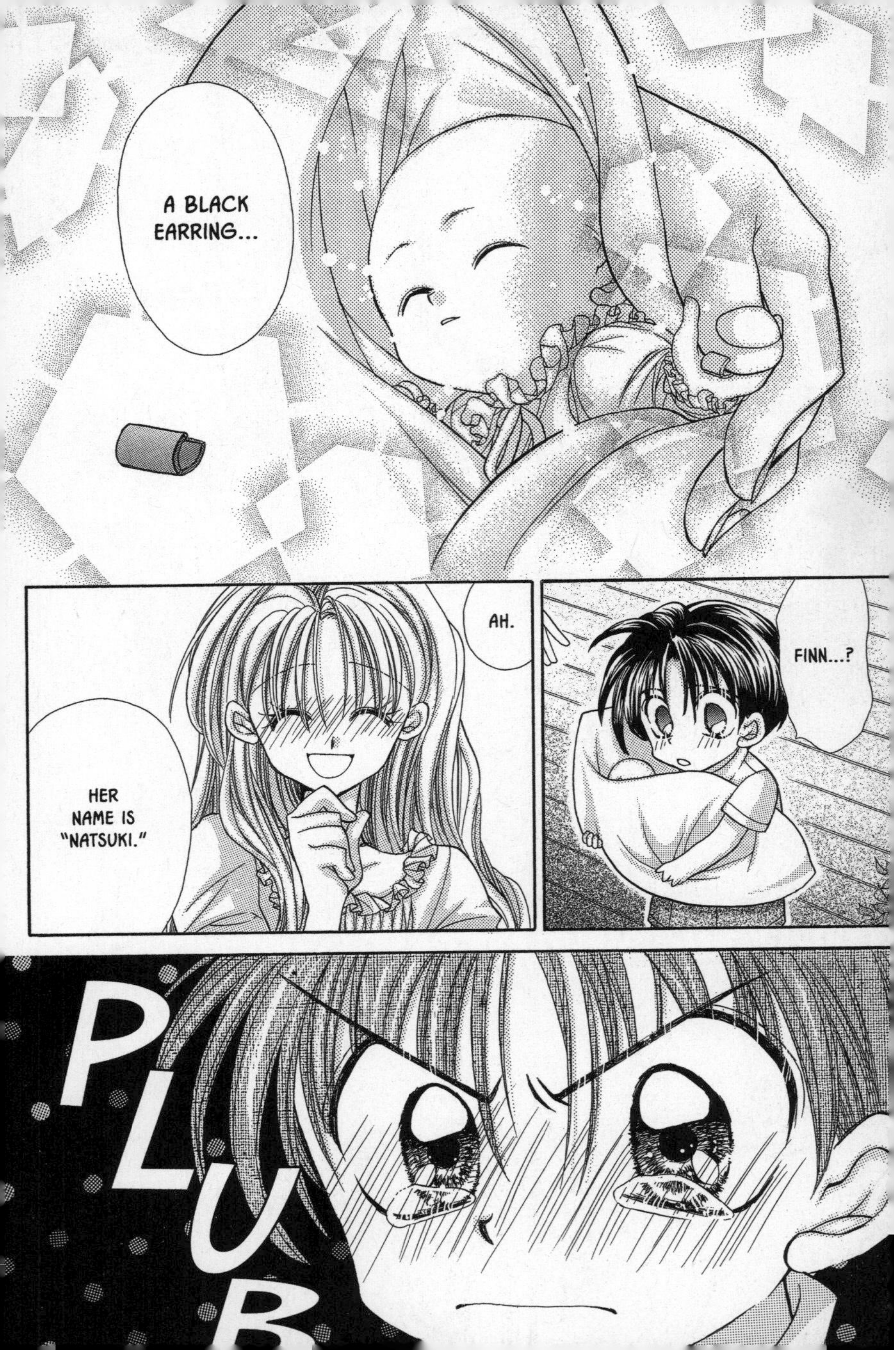
A BLACK EARRING...
FINN...?
AH.
HER NAME IS "NATSUKI."
PLUB

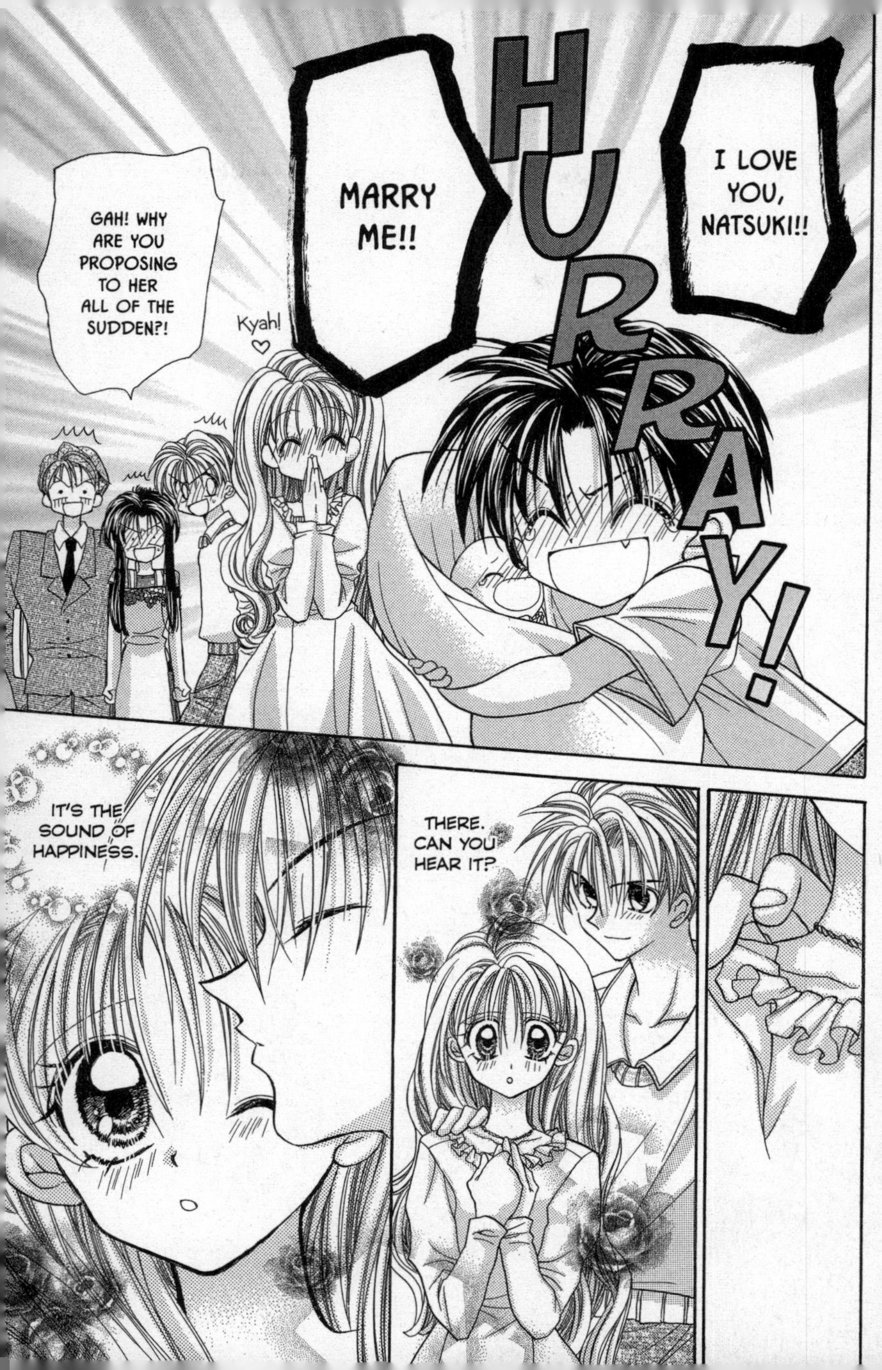
I LOVE YOU, NATSUKI!!
HURRAY!
MARRY ME!!
Kyah!
GAH! WHY ARE YOU PROPOSING TO HER ALL OF THE SUDDEN?!
THERE. CAN YOU HEAR IT?
IT'S THE SOUND OF HAPPINESS.

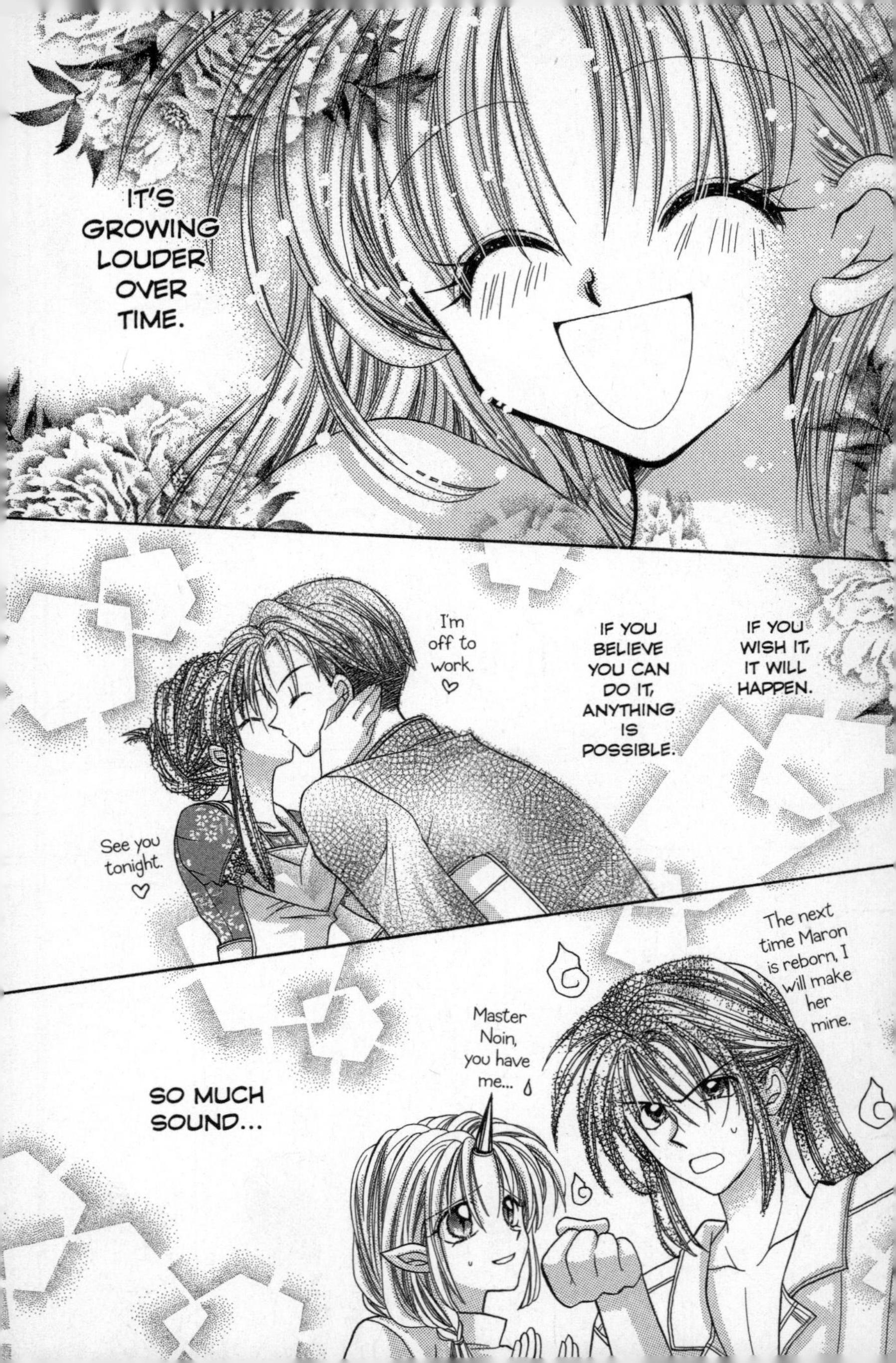
IT'S GROWING LOUDER OVER TIME.
IF YOU WISH IT, IT WILL HAPPEN.
IF YOU BELIEVE YOU CAN DO IT, ANYTHING IS POSSIBLE.
I'm off to work. ♡
See you tonight. ♡
The next time Maron is reborn, I will make her mine.
Master Noin, you have me...
SO MUCH SOUND...

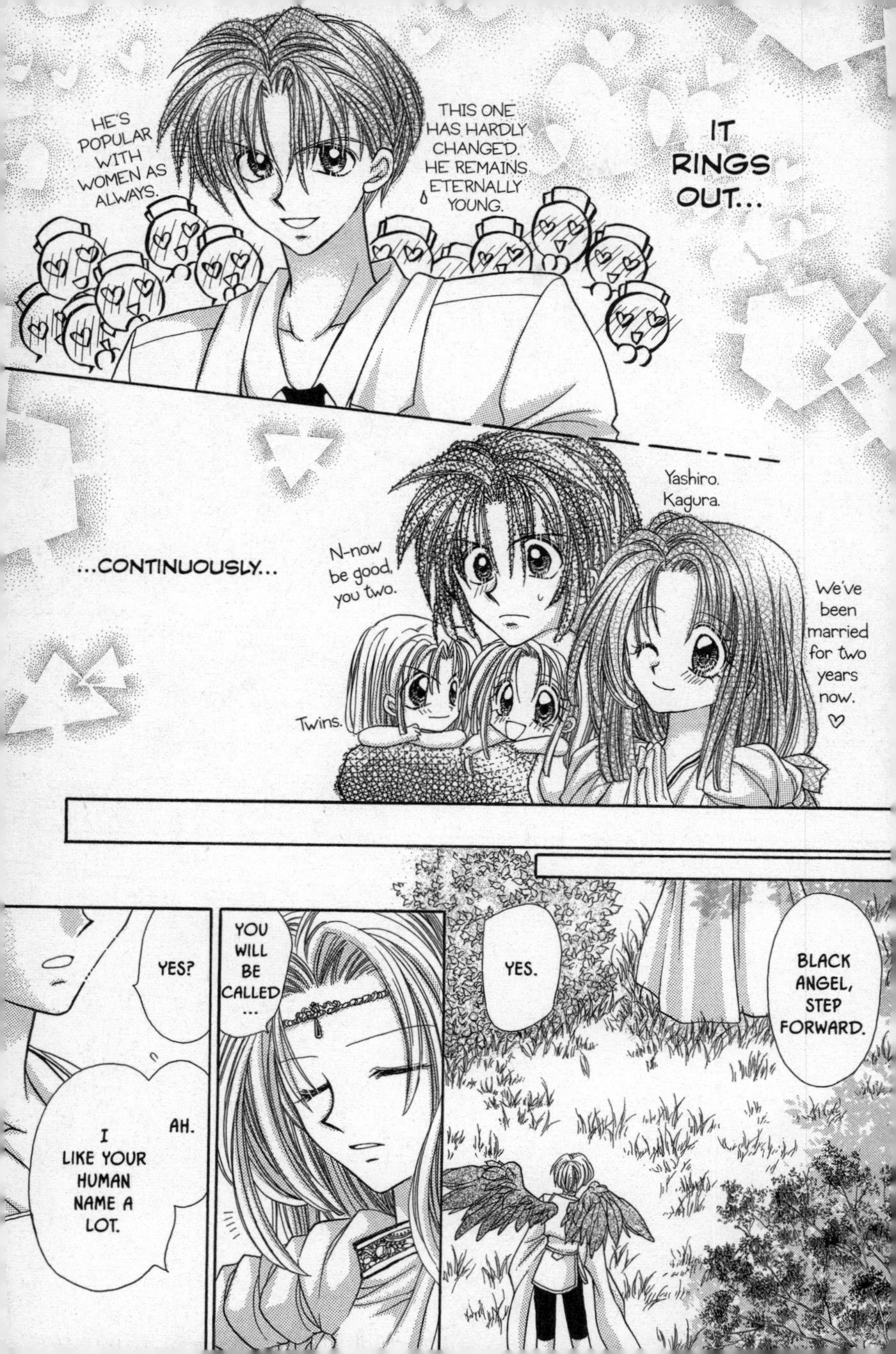

IT RINGS OUT...
THIS ONE HAS HARDLY CHANGED. HE REMAINS ETERNALLY YOUNG.
HE'S POPULAR WITH WOMEN AS ALWAYS.
Yashiro. Kagura.
We've been married for two years now. ♡
N-now be good, you two.
...CONTINUOUSLY...
Twins.
BLACK ANGEL, STEP FORWARD.
YES.
YOU WILL BE CALLED ...
YES?
AH.
I LIKE YOUR HUMAN NAME A LOT.

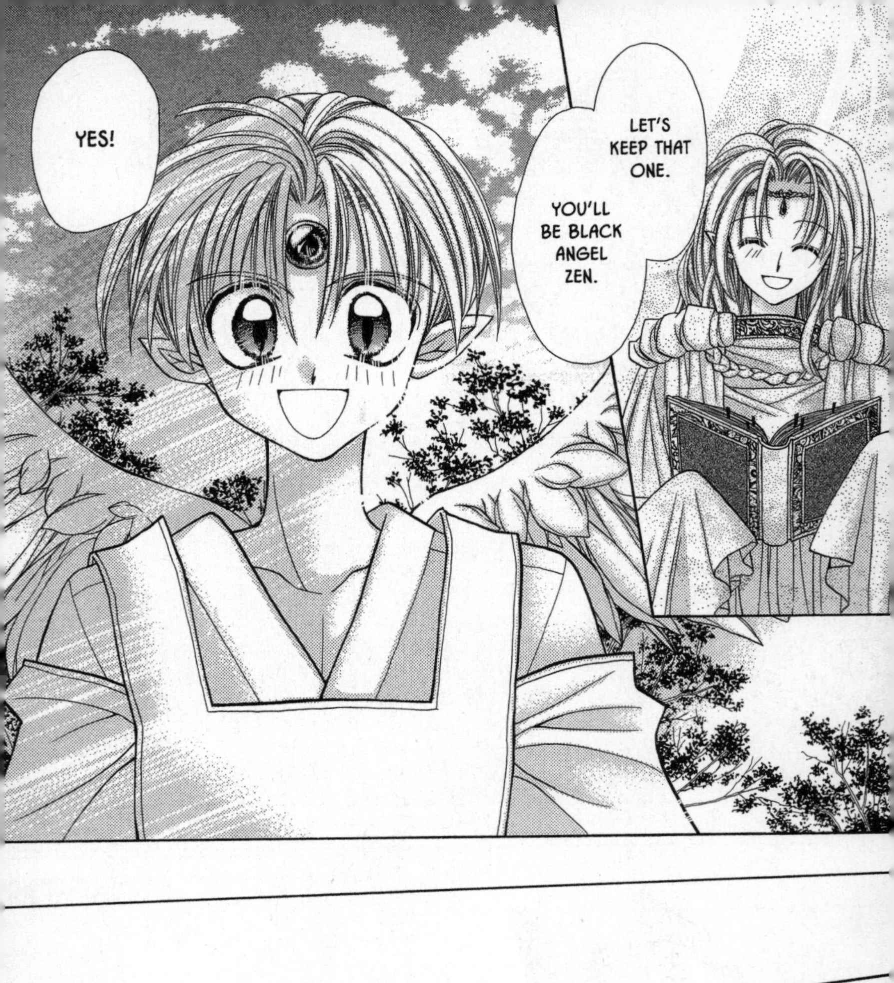
LET'S KEEP THAT ONE.
YOU'LL BE BLACK ANGEL ZEN.
YES!

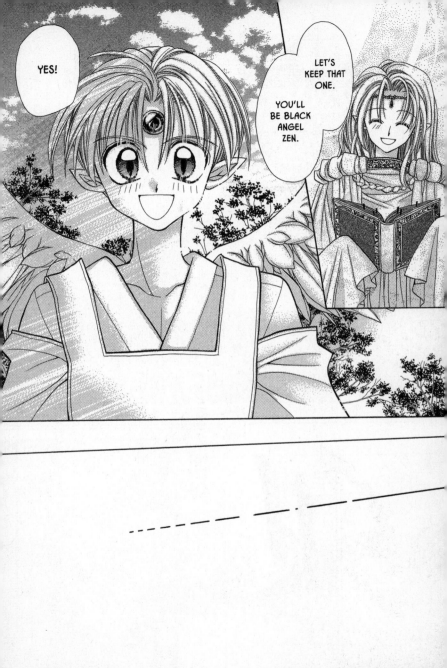

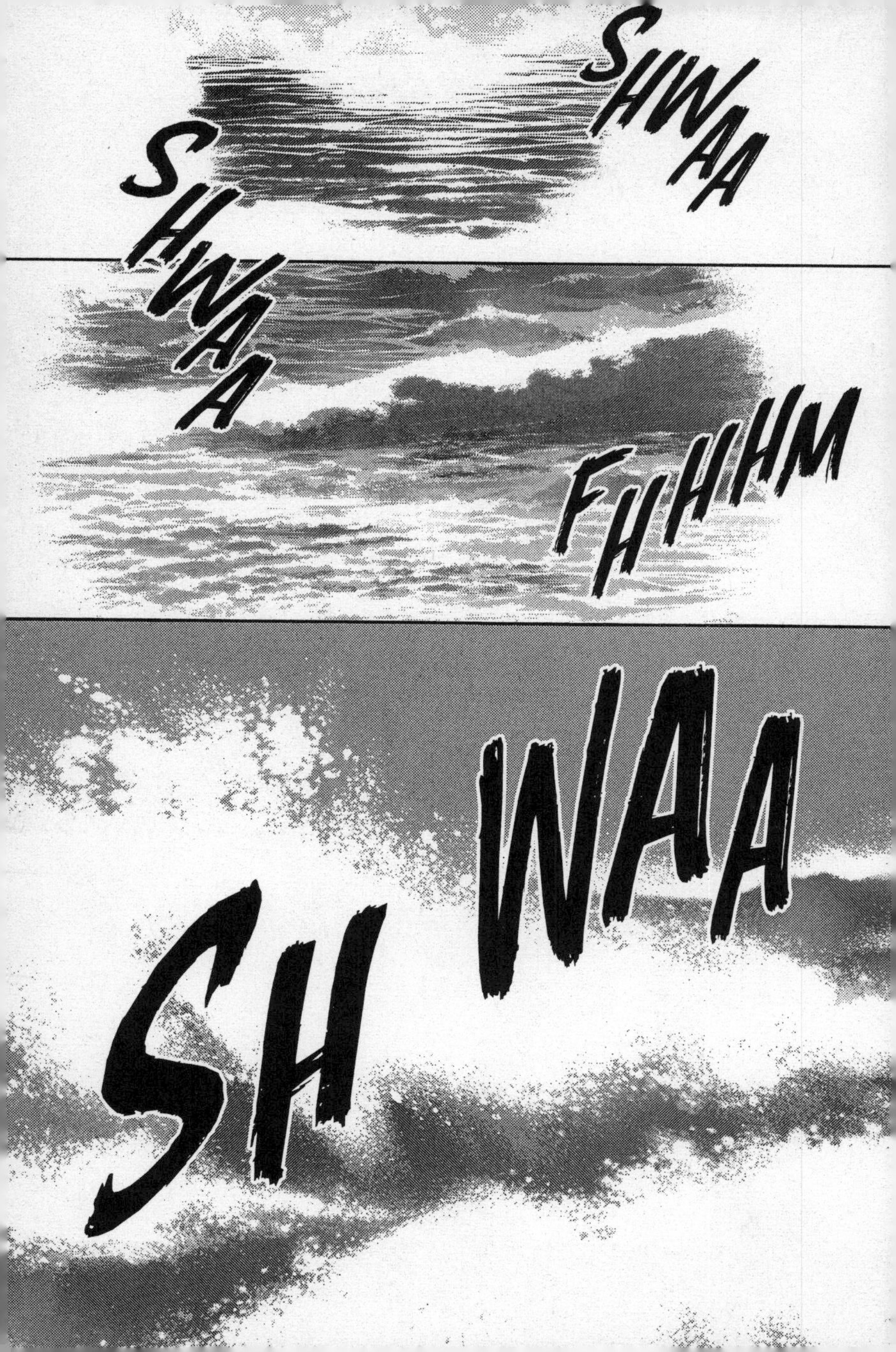
SHWAA
SHWAA
FHHHHM
SHWAA

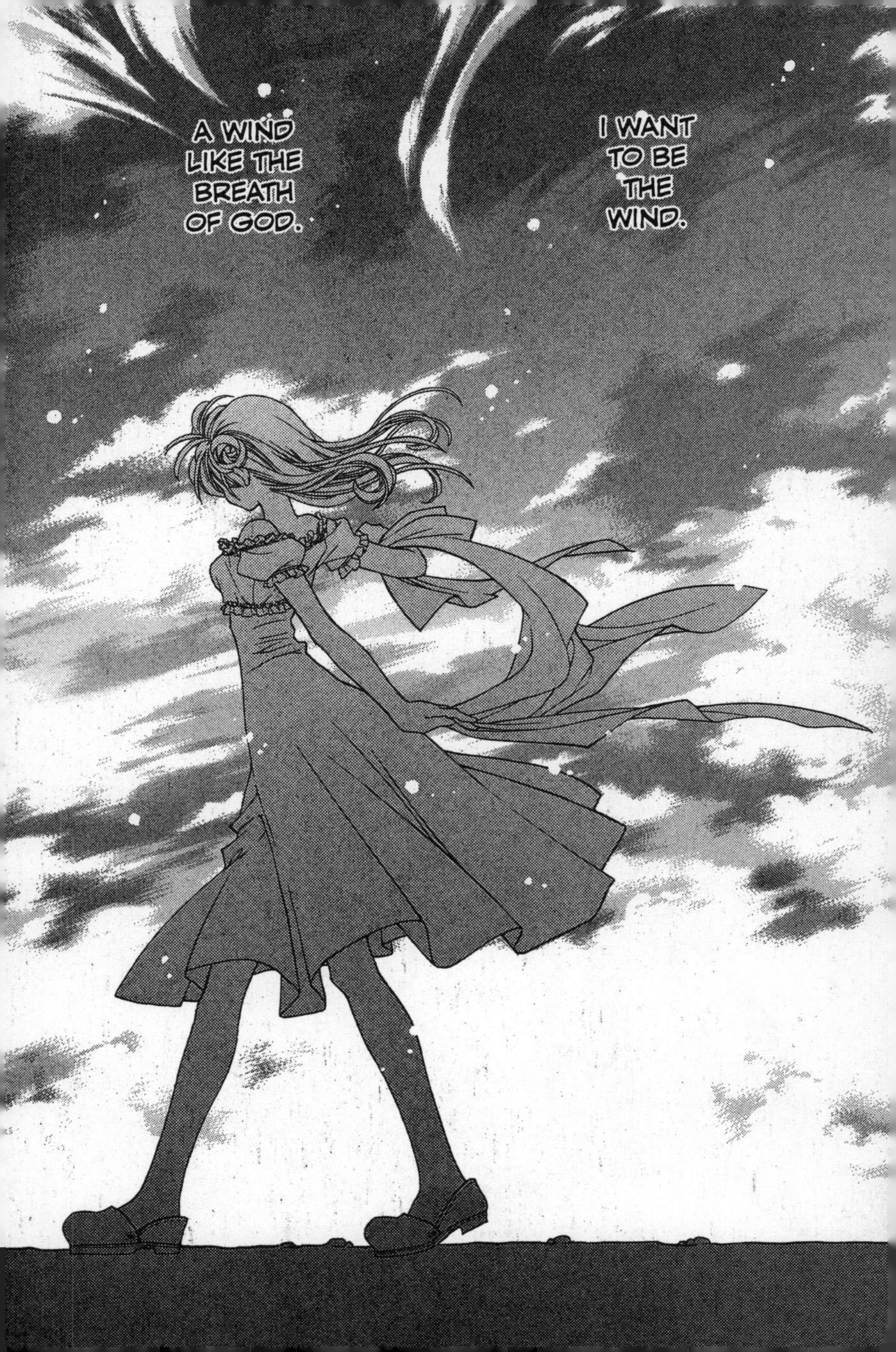
I WANT TO BE THE WIND.
A WIND LIKE THE BREATH OF GOD.

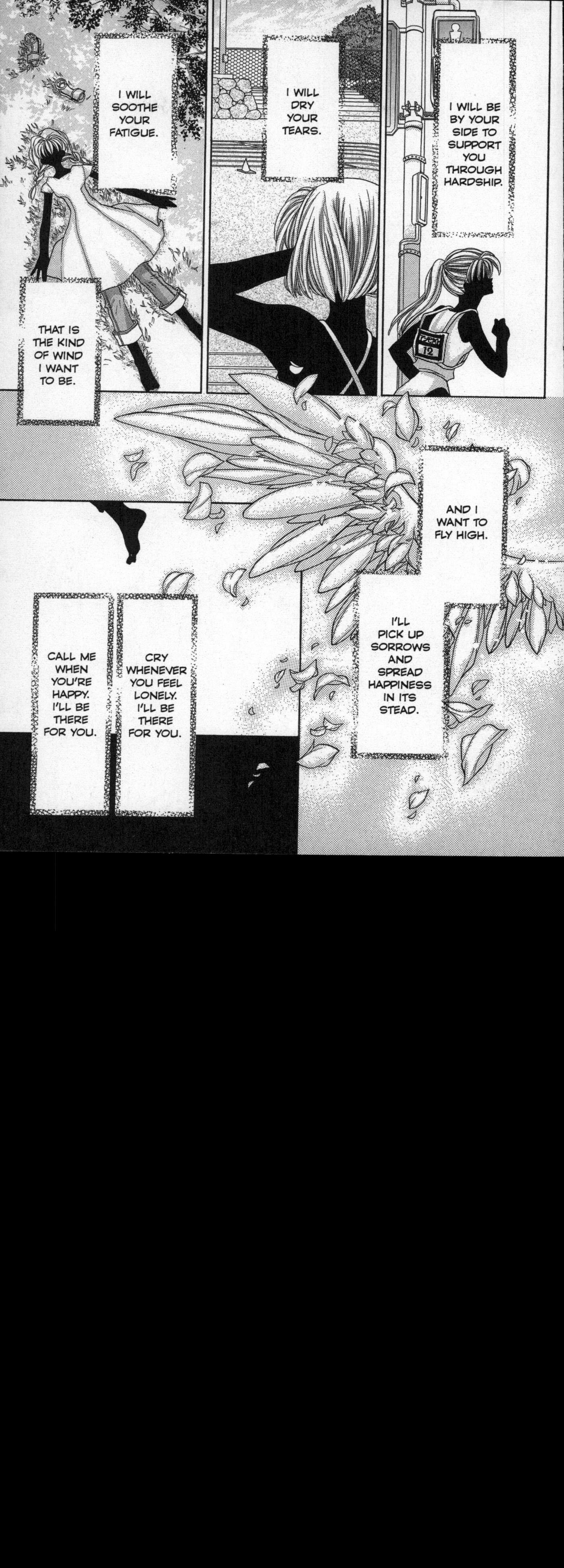
I WILL BE BY YOUR SIDE TO SUPPORT YOU THROUGH HARDSHIP.
I WILL DRY YOUR TEARS.
I WILL SOOTHE YOUR FATIGUE.
THAT IS THE KIND OF WIND I WANT TO BE.
AND I WANT TO FLY HIGH.
I'LL PICK UP SORROWS AND SPREAD HAPPINESS IN ITS STEAD.
CRY WHENEVER YOU FEEL LONELY. I'LL BE THERE FOR YOU.
CALL ME WHEN YOU'RE HAPPY. I'LL BE THERE FOR YOU.

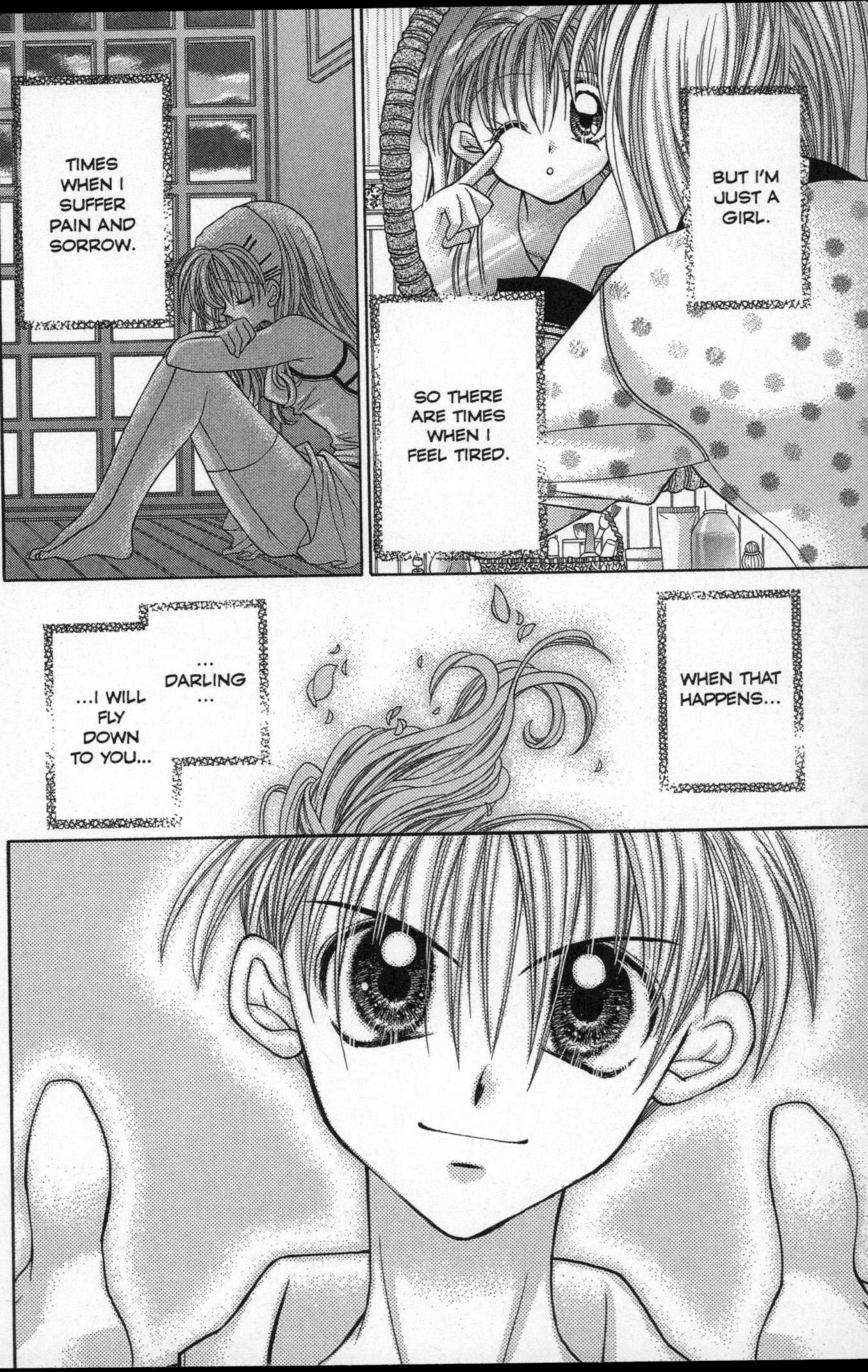
BUT I'M JUST A GIRL.
SO THERE ARE TIMES WHEN I FEEL TIRED.
TIMES WHEN I SUFFER PAIN AND SORROW.
WHEN THAT HAPPENS...
...DARLING...
...I WILL FLY DOWN TO YOU...

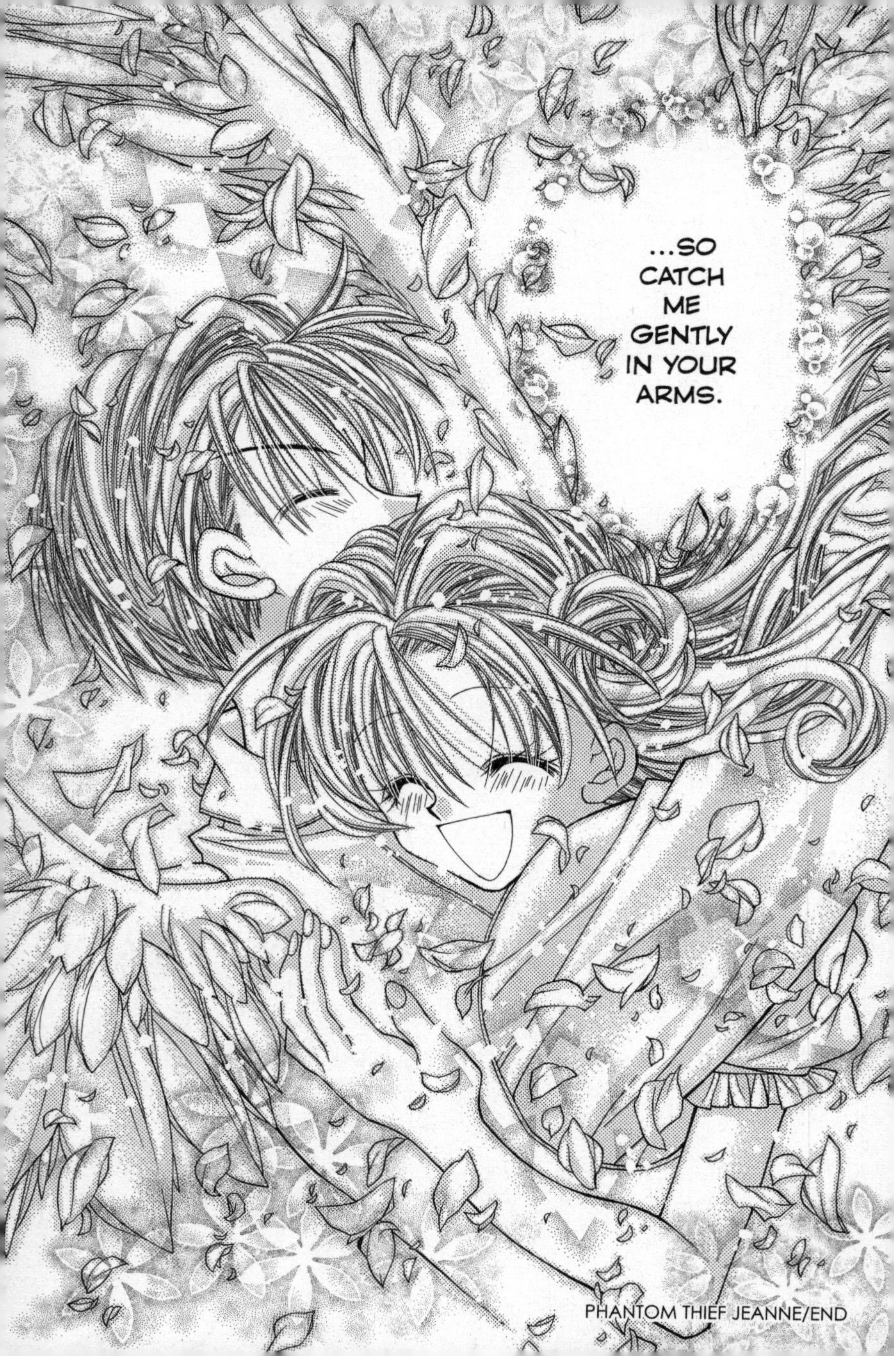
...SO CATCH ME GENTLY IN YOUR ARMS.
PHANTOM THIEF JEANNE/END

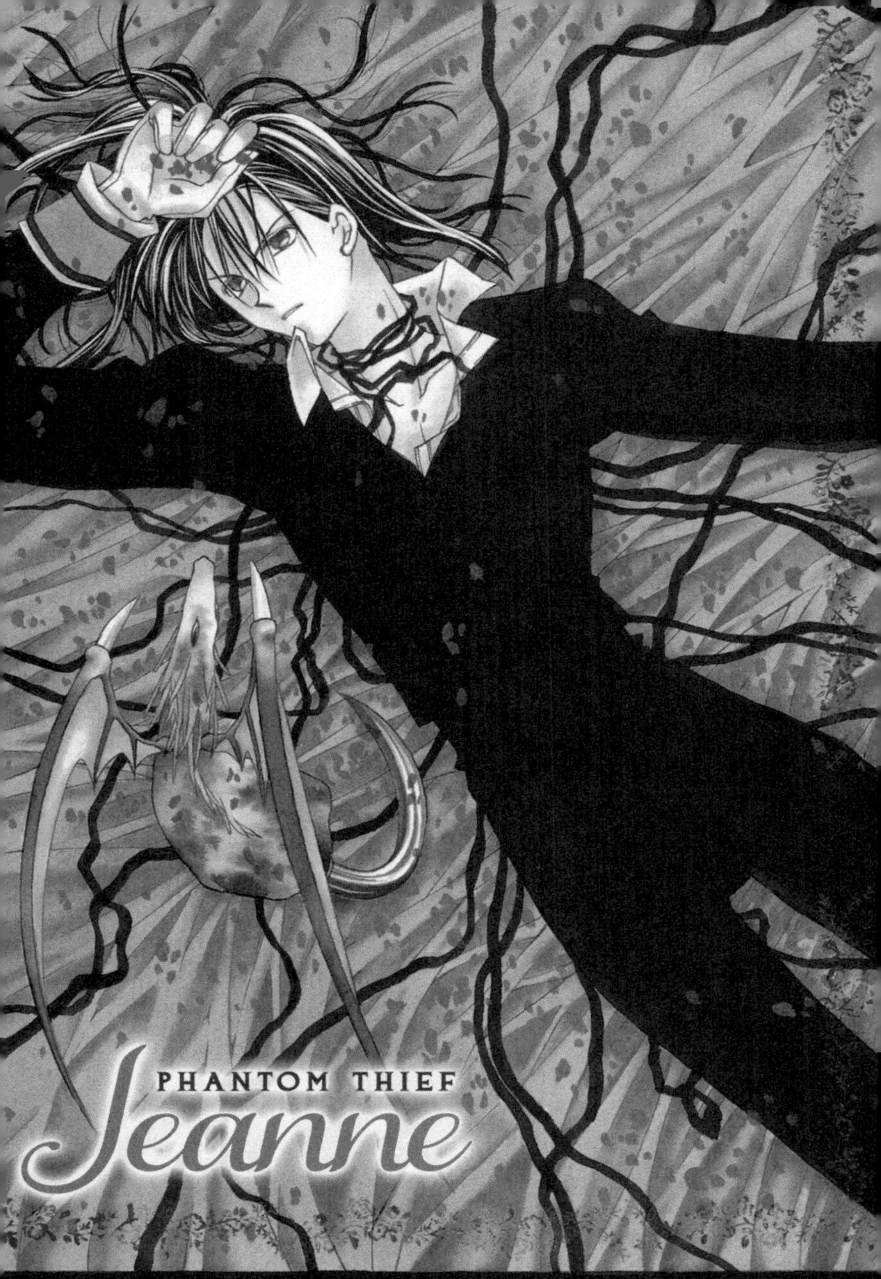
PHANTOM THIEF
Jeanne

Bonus Story: Let's Go, Silk Road ★

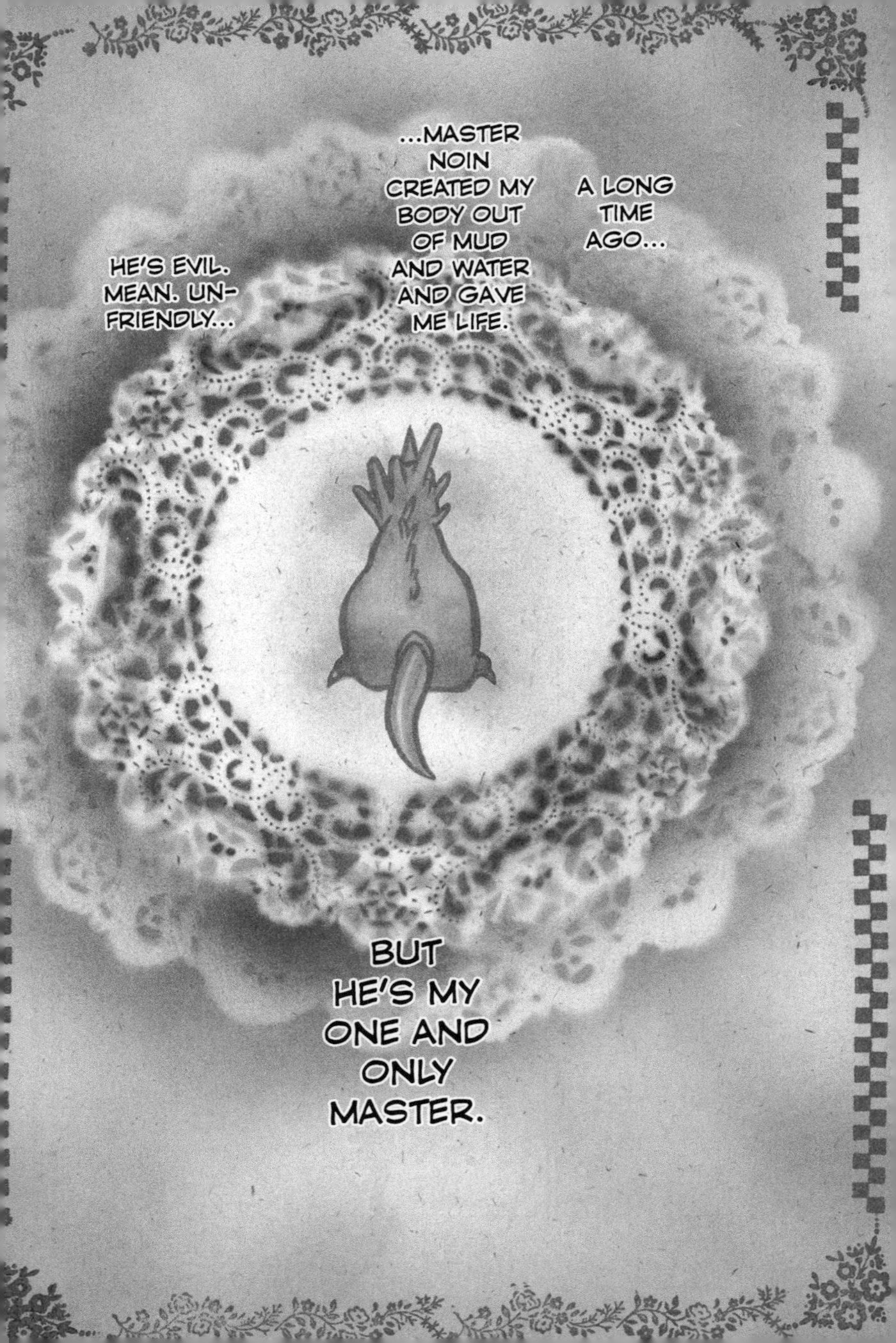
A LONG TIME AGO...
...MASTER NOIN CREATED MY BODY OUT OF MUD AND WATER AND GAVE ME LIFE.
HE'S EVIL. MEAN. UN-FRIENDLY...
BUT HE'S MY ONE AND ONLY MASTER.

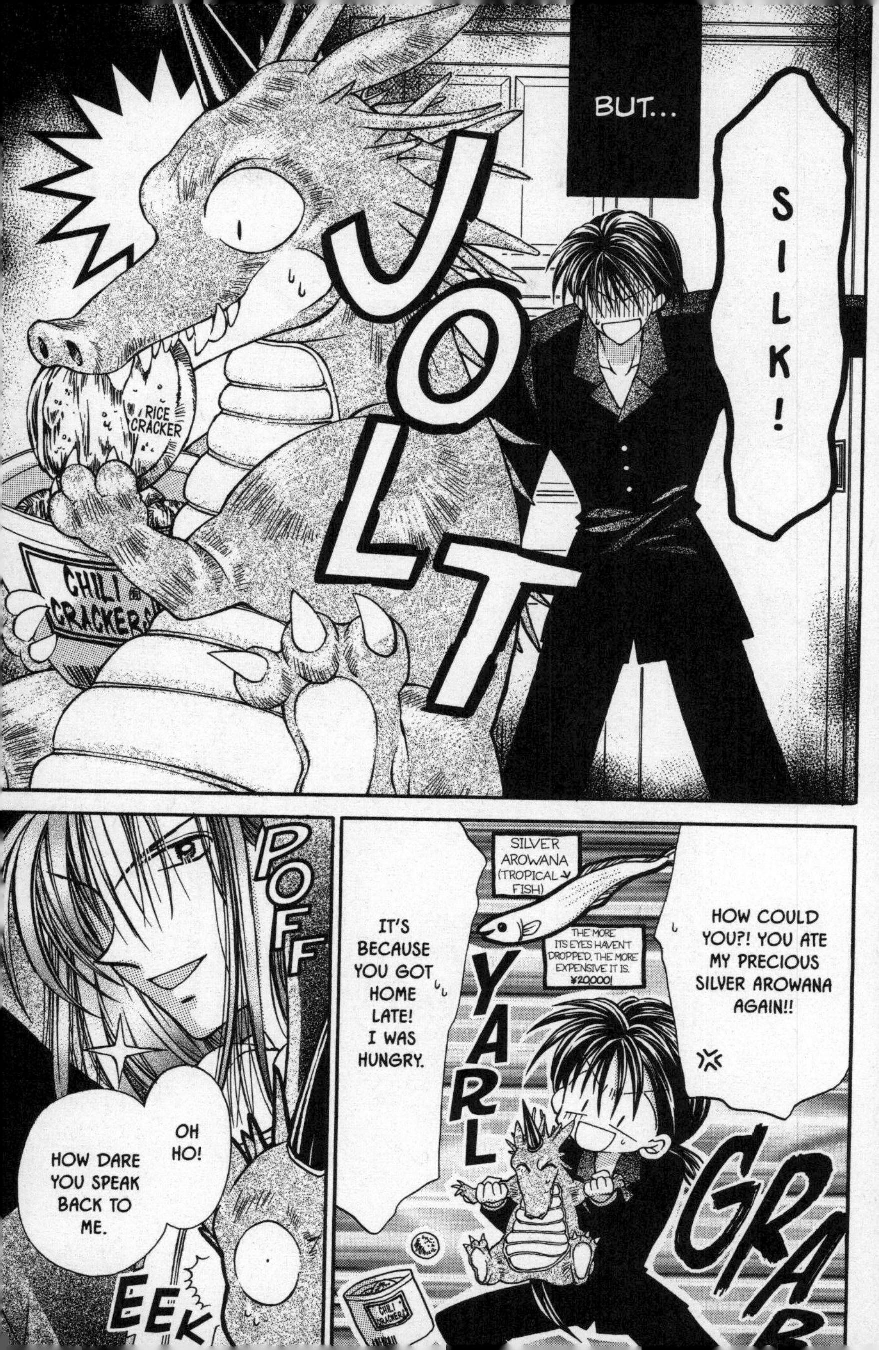
BUT...
SILK!
JOLT
RICE CRACKER
CHILI CRACKERS
SILVER AROWANA (TROPICAL FISH)
HOW COULD YOU?! YOU ATE MY PRECIOUS SILVER AROWANA AGAIN!!
THE MORE ITS EYES HAVEN'T DROPPED, THE MORE EXPENSIVE IT IS. ¥20,000!
IT'S BECAUSE YOU GOT HOME LATE! I WAS HUNGRY.
YARL
GRA
CHILI CRACKERS
POFF
OH HO!
HOW DARE YOU SPEAK BACK TO ME.
EEK

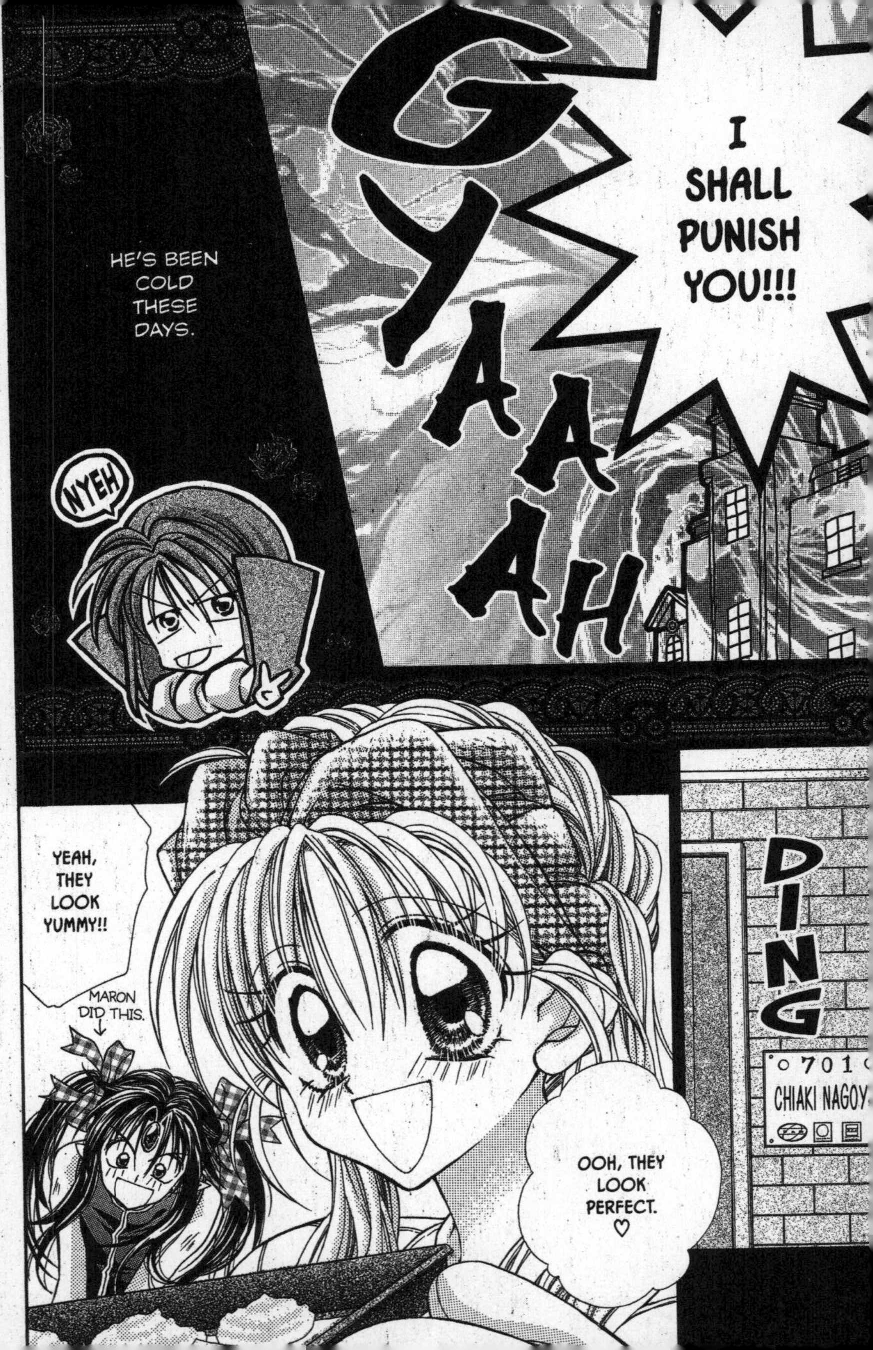
I SHALL PUNISH YOU!!!
GYAAAH
HE'S BEEN COLD THESE DAYS.
NYEH
DING
701
CHIAKI NAGOY
OOH, THEY LOOK PERFECT. ♡
YEAH, THEY LOOK YUMMY!!
MARON DID THIS.

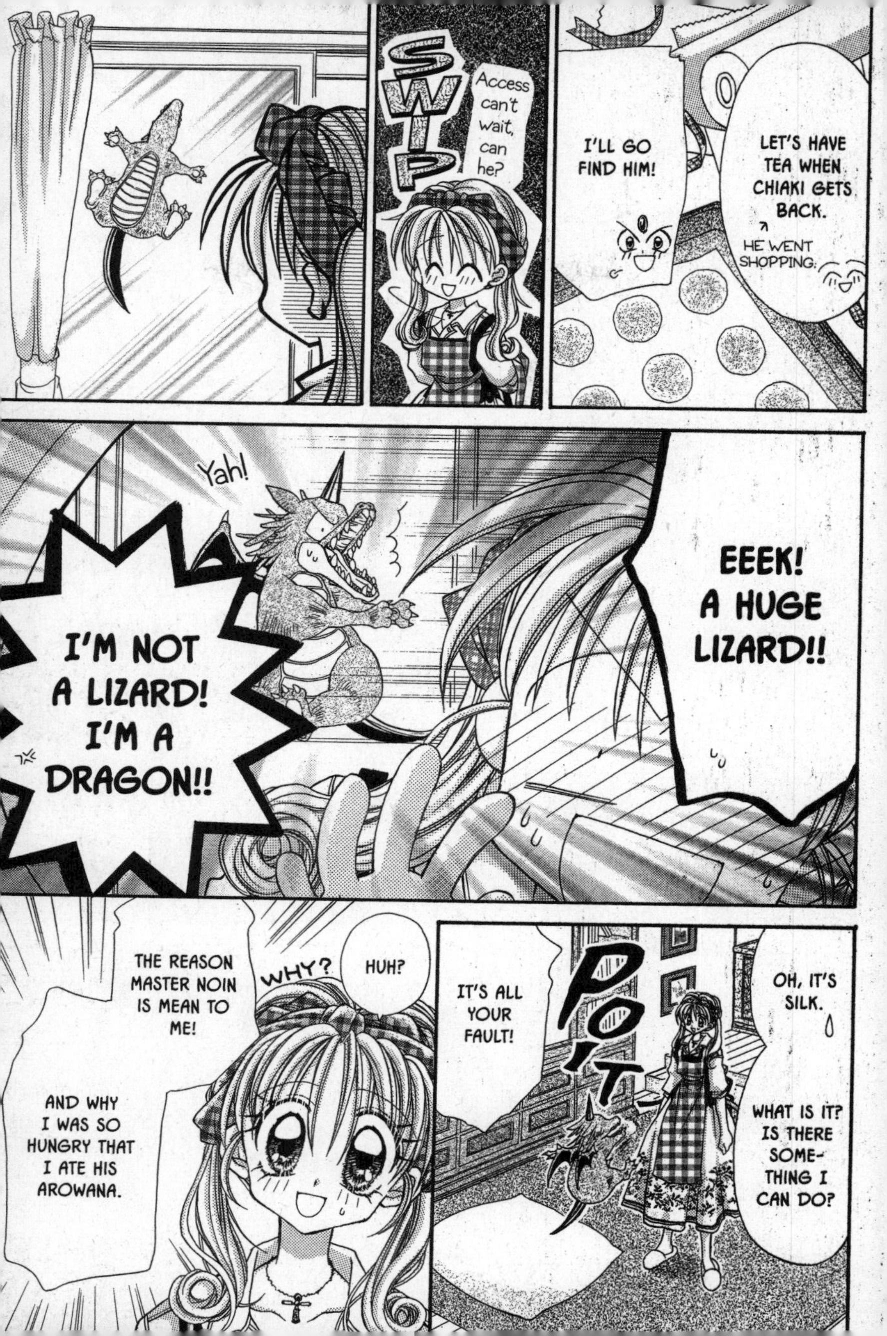
LET'S HAVE TEA WHEN CHIAKI GETS BACK.
HE WENT SHOPPING.
I'LL GO FIND HIM!
SWIP
Access can't wait, can he?
EEEK! A HUGE LIZARD!!
Yah!
I'M NOT A LIZARD! I'M A DRAGON!!
OH, IT'S SILK.
WHAT IS IT? IS THERE SOME-THING I CAN DO?
POIT
IT'S ALL YOUR FAULT!
HUH?
WHY?
THE REASON MASTER NOIN IS MEAN TO ME!
AND WHY I WAS SO HUNGRY THAT I ATE HIS AROWANA.

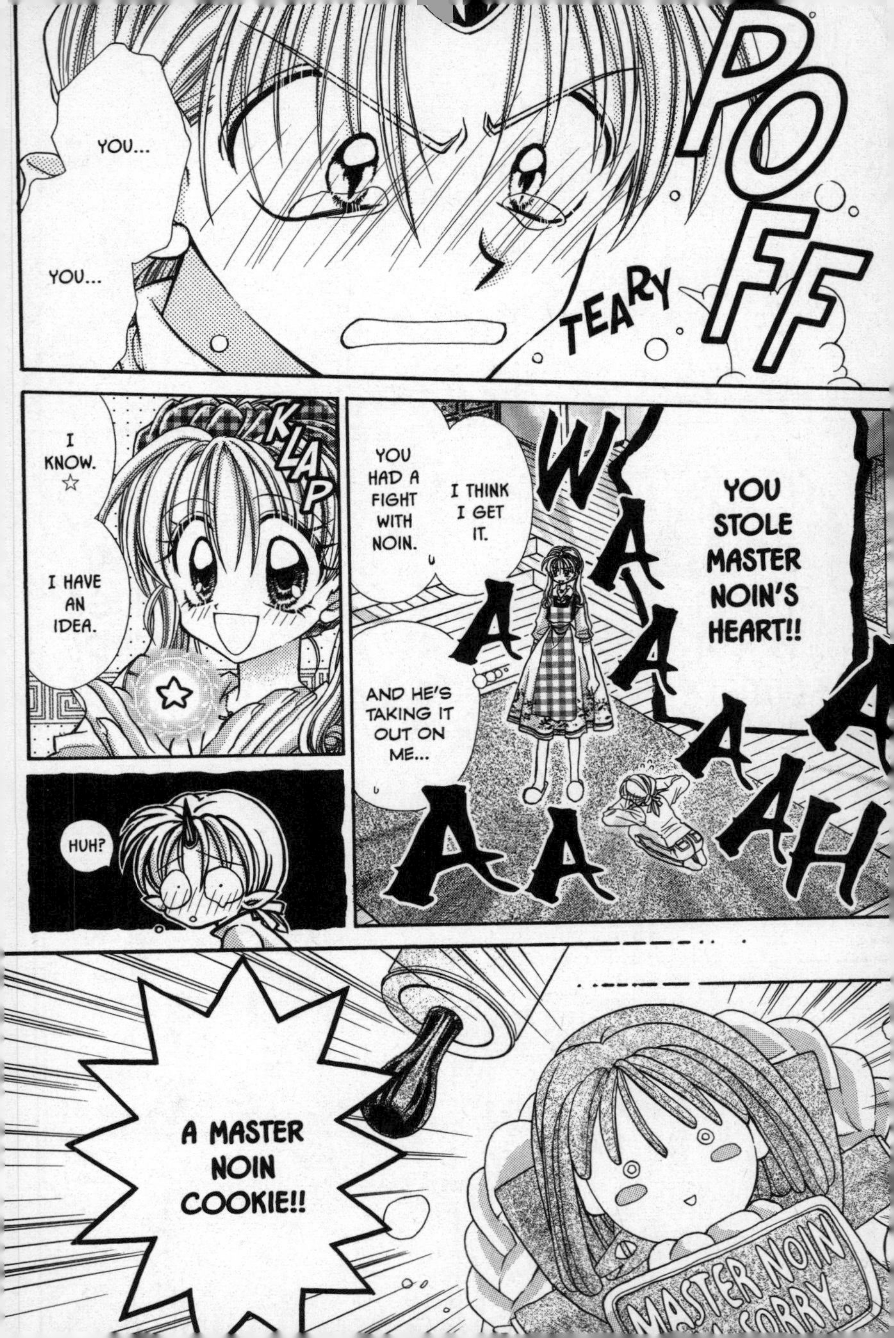
POFFF
YOU...
YOU...
TEARY
YOU STOLE MASTER NOIN'S HEART!!
WAAAAAAAAAH
I THINK I GET IT.
YOU HAD A FIGHT WITH NOIN.
AND HE'S TAKING IT OUT ON ME...
KLAP
I KNOW. ☆
I HAVE AN IDEA.
HUH?
A MASTER NOIN COOKIE!!
MASTER NOIN
SORRY

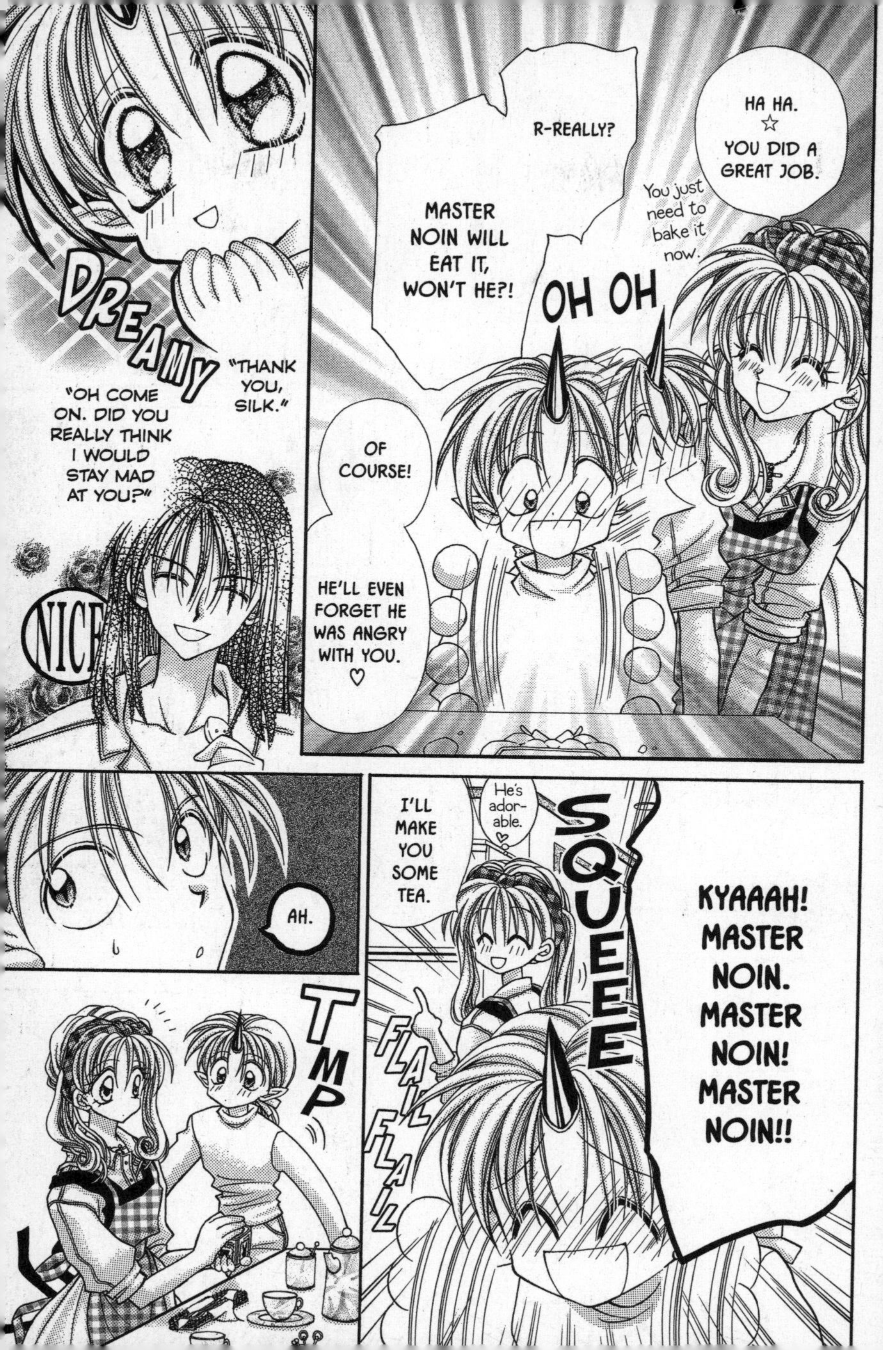
HA HA. ☆ YOU DID A GREAT JOB.
You just need to bake it now.
R-REALLY?
MASTER NOIN WILL EAT IT, WON'T HE?!
OH OH
OF COURSE!
HE'LL EVEN FORGET HE WAS ANGRY WITH YOU. ♡
DREAMY
"THANK YOU, SILK."
"OH COME ON. DID YOU REALLY THINK I WOULD STAY MAD AT YOU?"
NICE
KYAAAH! MASTER NOIN. MASTER NOIN! MASTER NOIN!!
SQUEEE
He's adorable. ♡
I'LL MAKE YOU SOME TEA.
FLAIL
FLAIL
AH.
TMP

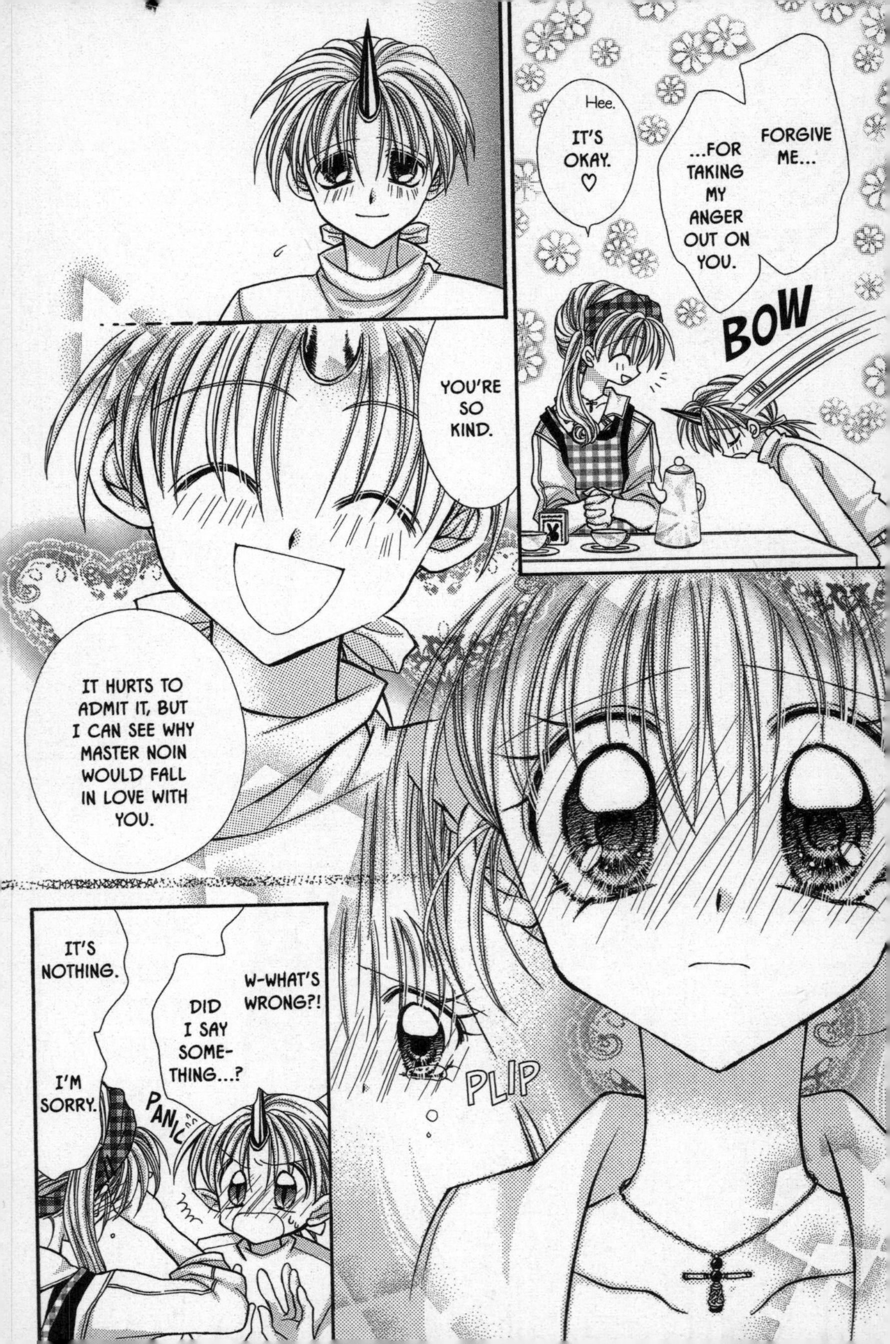
FORGIVE ME... ...FOR TAKING MY ANGER OUT ON YOU.
BOW
Hee.
IT'S OKAY. ♡
YOU'RE SO KIND.
IT HURTS TO ADMIT IT, BUT I CAN SEE WHY MASTER NOIN WOULD FALL IN LOVE WITH YOU.
PLIP
W-WHAT'S WRONG?!
DID I SAY SOME-THING...?
PANIC
IT'S NOTHING.
I'M SORRY.

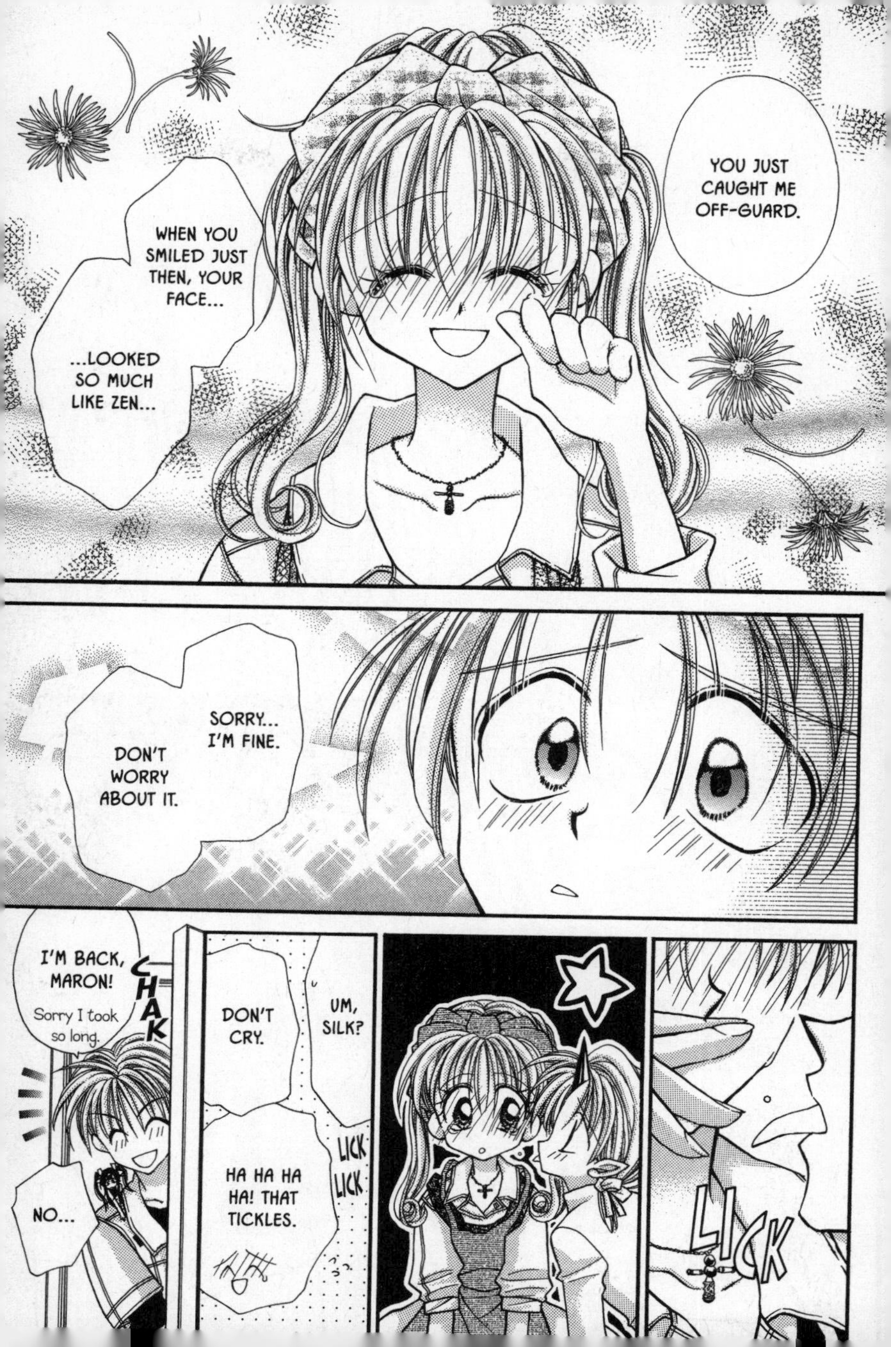
YOU JUST CAUGHT ME OFF-GUARD.
WHEN YOU SMILED JUST THEN, YOUR FACE...
...LOOKED SO MUCH LIKE ZEN...
SORRY... I'M FINE.
DON'T WORRY ABOUT IT.
LICK
UM, SILK?
DON'T CRY.
LICK LICK
HA HA HA HA! THAT TICKLES.
CHAK
I'M BACK, MARON!
Sorry I took so long.
NO...

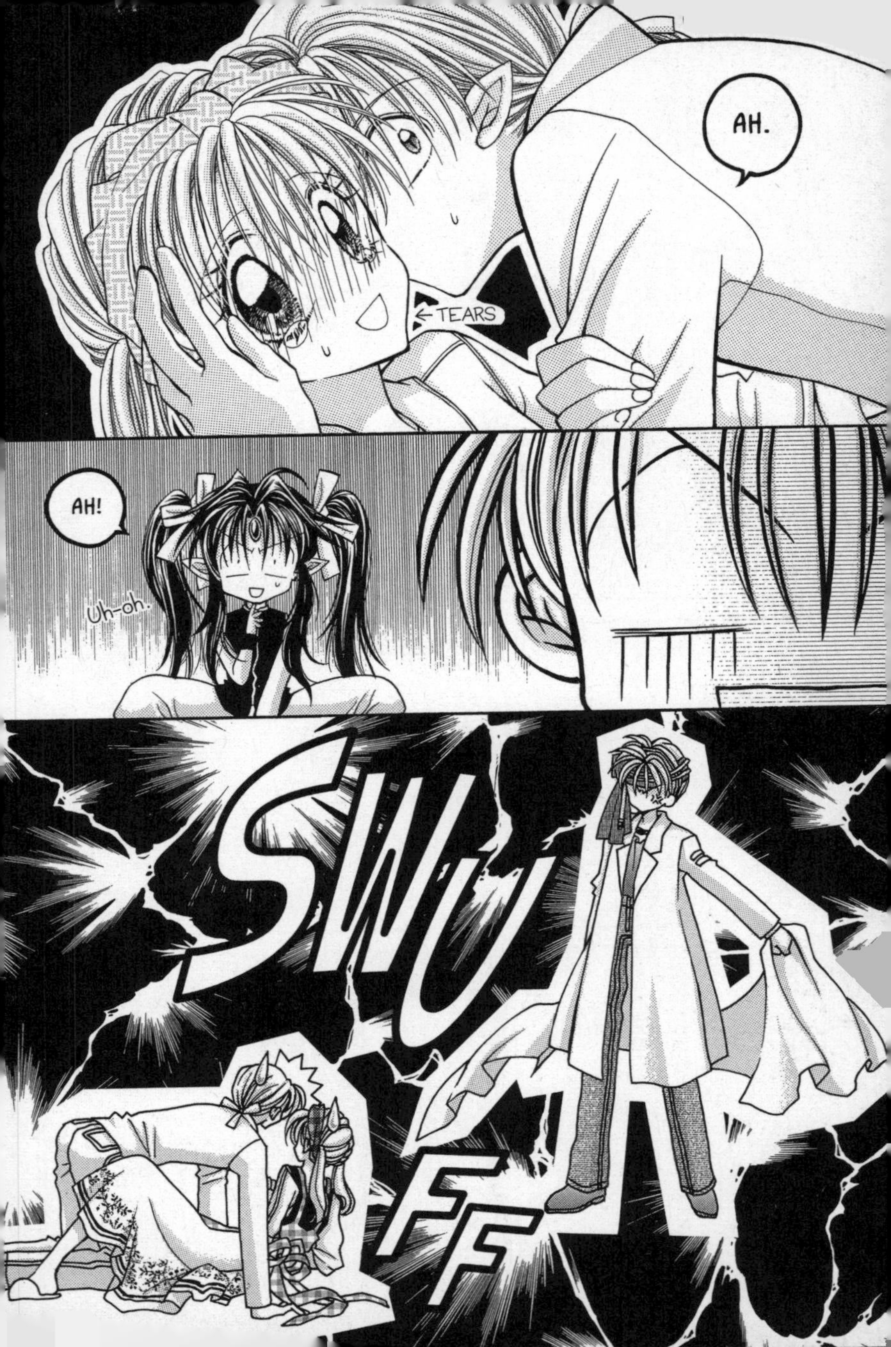
AH.
←TEARS
AH!
Uh-oh.
SWUFF

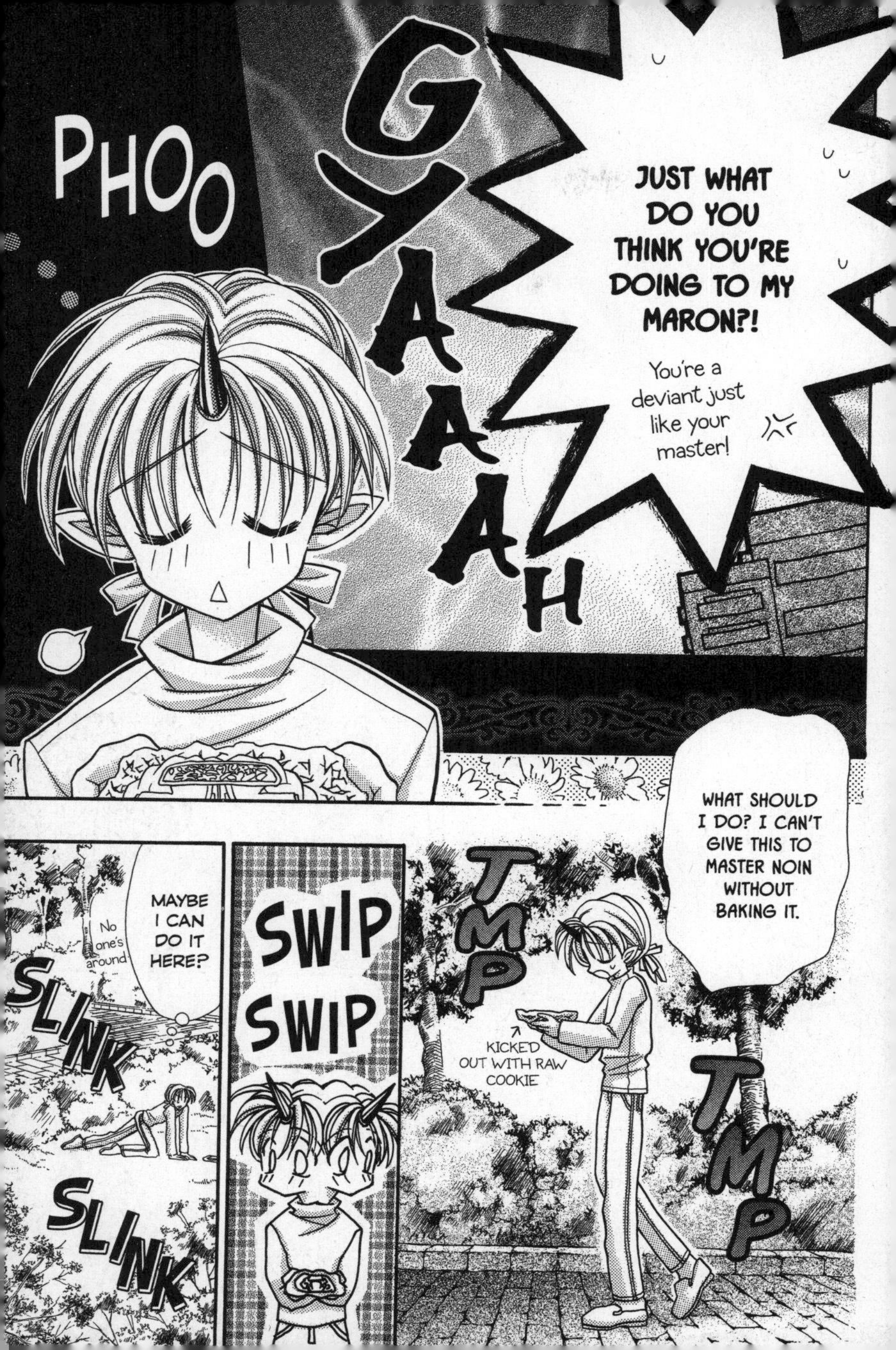
GYAAAAH
JUST WHAT DO YOU THINK YOU'RE DOING TO MY MARON?!
You're a deviant just like your master!
PHOO
WHAT SHOULD I DO? I CAN'T GIVE THIS TO MASTER NOIN WITHOUT BAKING IT.
TMP
TMP
KICKED OUT WITH RAW COOKIE
SWIP SWIP
MAYBE I CAN DO IT HERE?
No one's around...
SLINK
SLINK

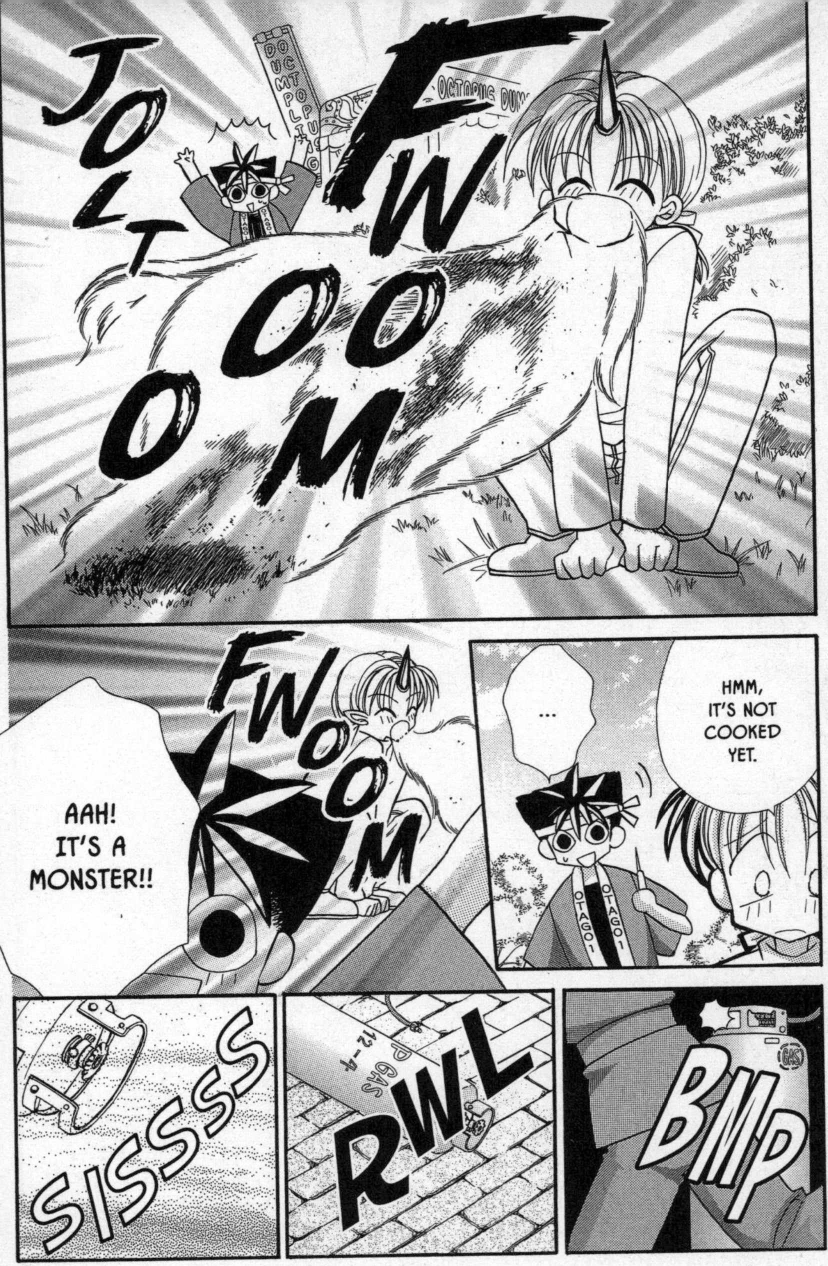
FWOOOOM
JOLT
...
HMM, IT'S NOT COOKED YET.
FWOOOM
AAH! IT'S A MONSTER!!
BMP
RWL
SISSSS

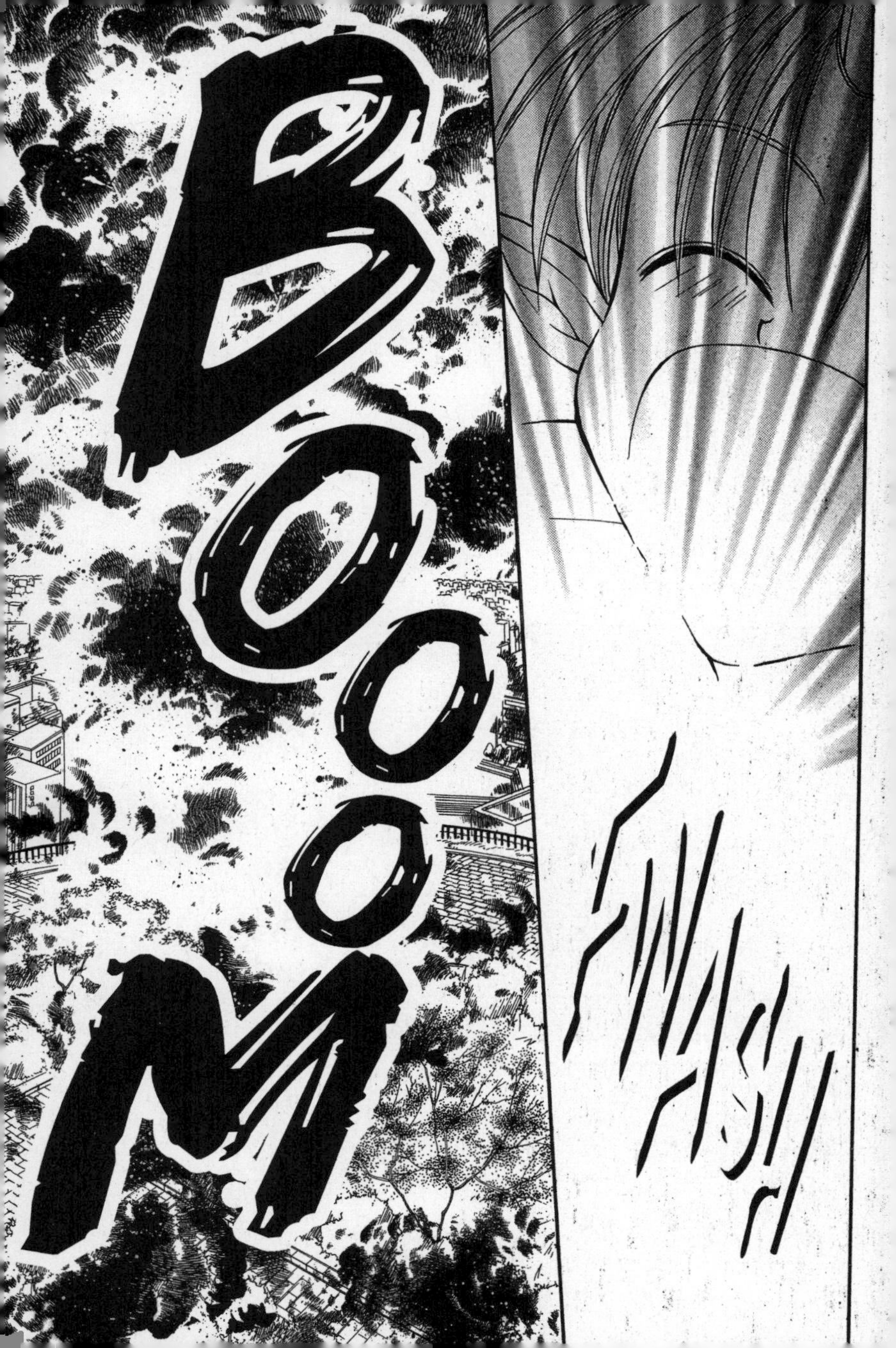
FLASH
BOOOM

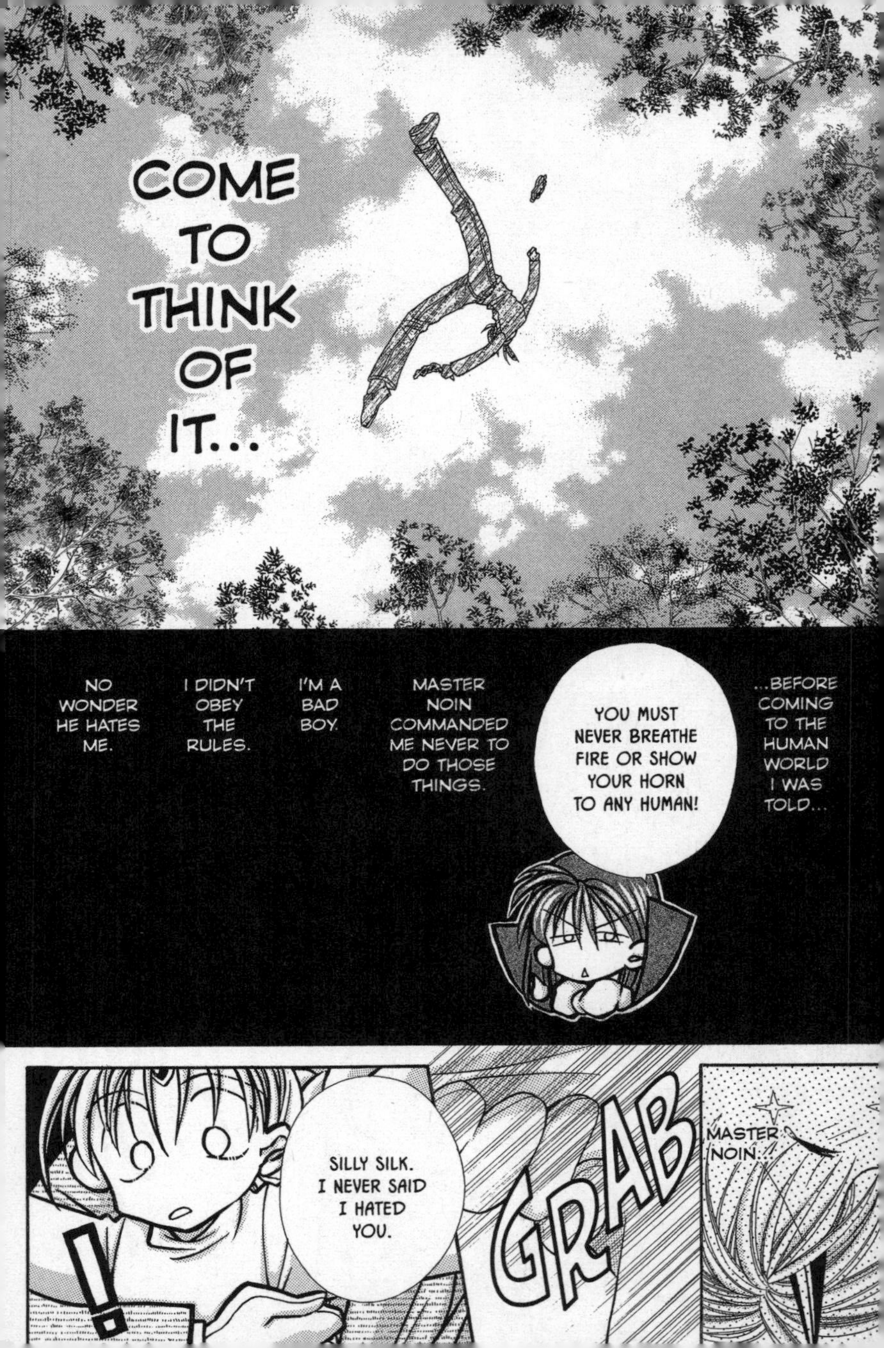
COME TO THINK OF IT...
...BEFORE COMING TO THE HUMAN WORLD I WAS TOLD...
YOU MUST NEVER BREATHE FIRE OR SHOW YOUR HORN TO ANY HUMAN!
MASTER NOIN COMMANDED ME NEVER TO DO THOSE THINGS.
I'M A BAD BOY.
I DIDN'T OBEY THE RULES.
NO WONDER HE HATES ME.
MASTER NOIN..!!
GRAB
SILLY SILK. I NEVER SAID I HATED YOU.
!

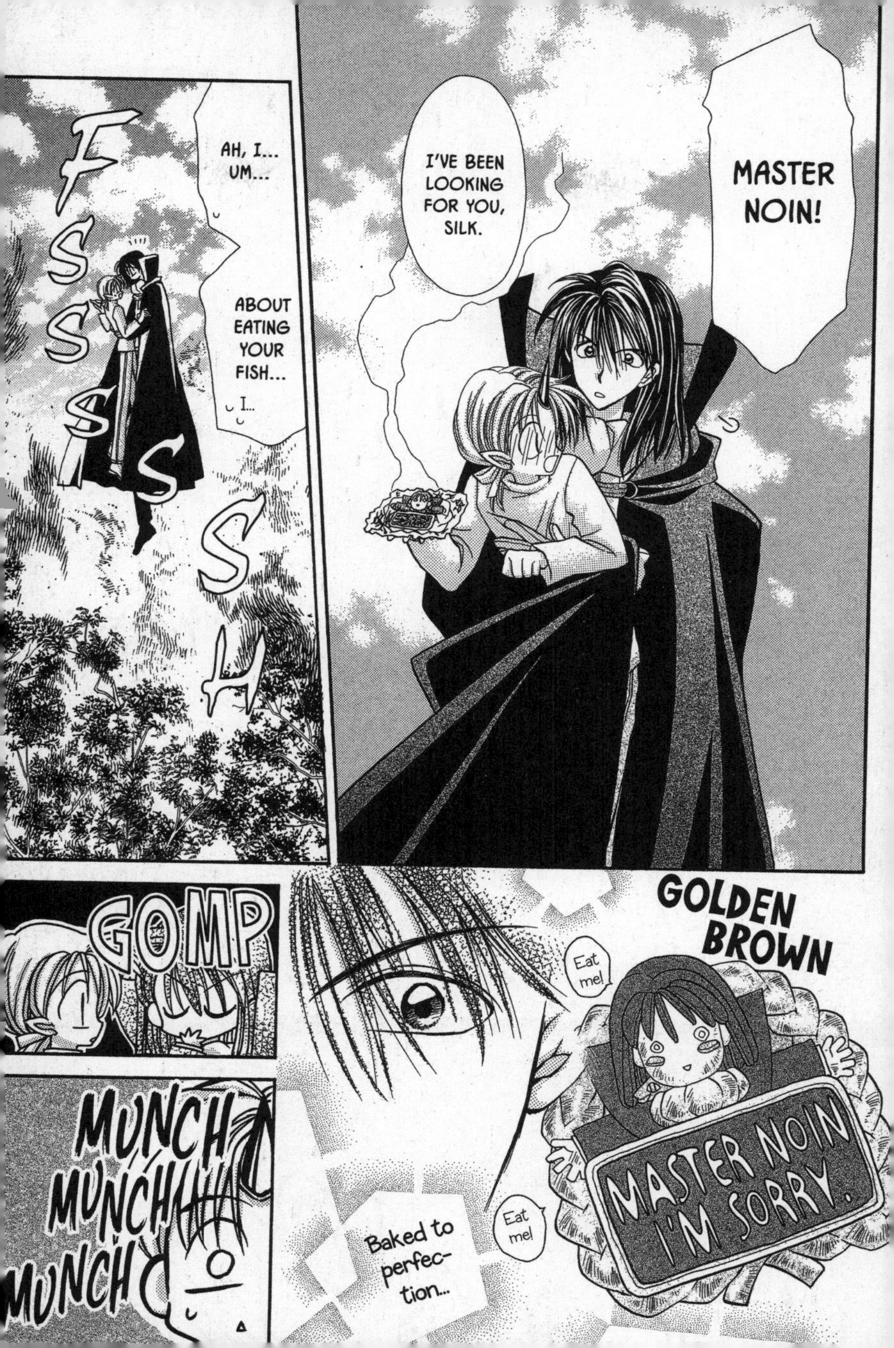
MASTER NOIN!
I'VE BEEN LOOKING FOR YOU, SILK.
AH, I... UM...
ABOUT EATING YOUR FISH... I...
FSSSSSH
GOLDEN BROWN
Eat me!
MASTER NOIN I'M SORRY.
Eat me!
Baked to perfection...
GOMP
MUNCH MUNCH MUNCH

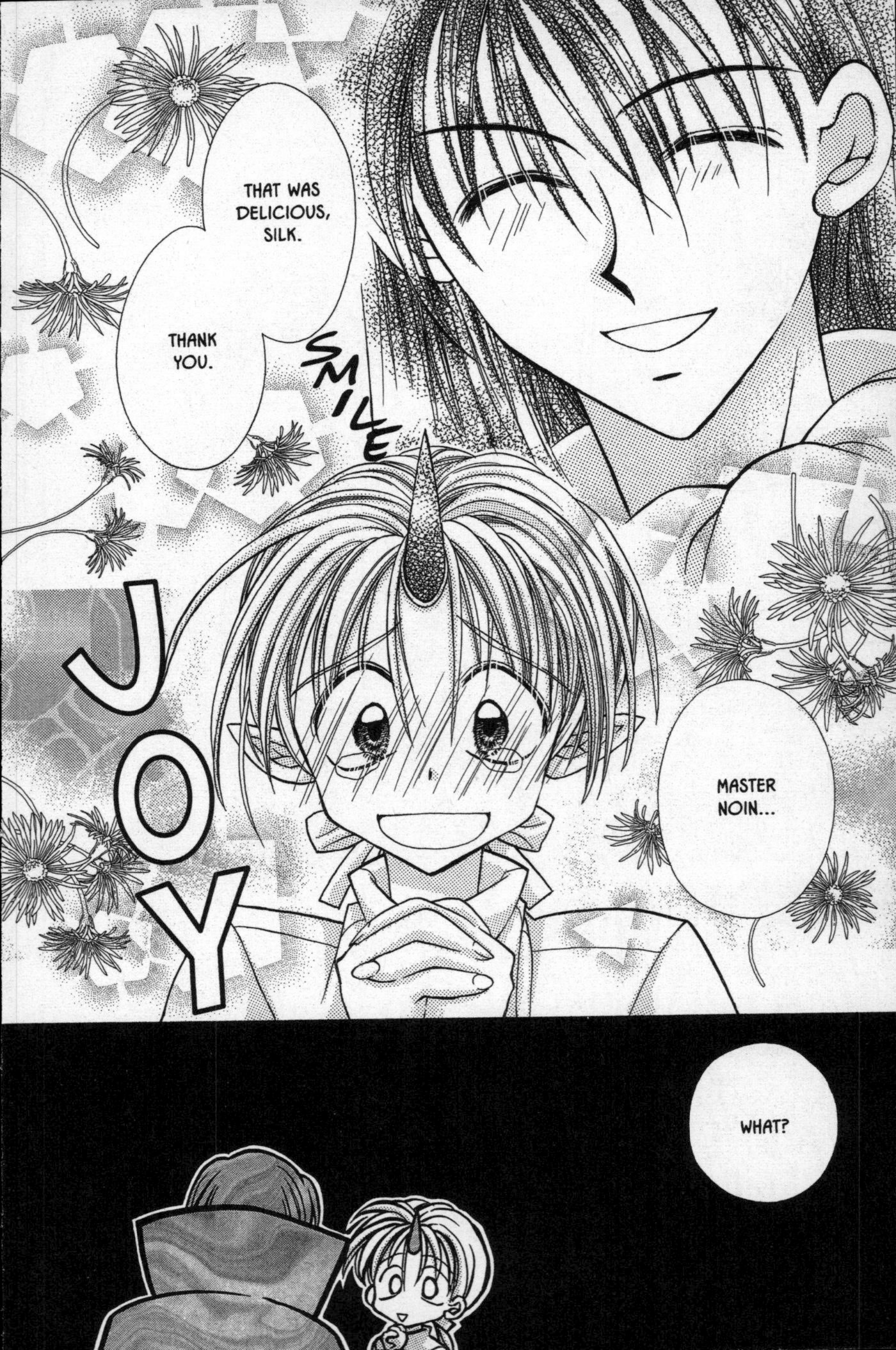
THAT WAS DELICIOUS, SILK.
THANK YOU.
SMILE
MASTER NOIN...
JOY
WHAT?

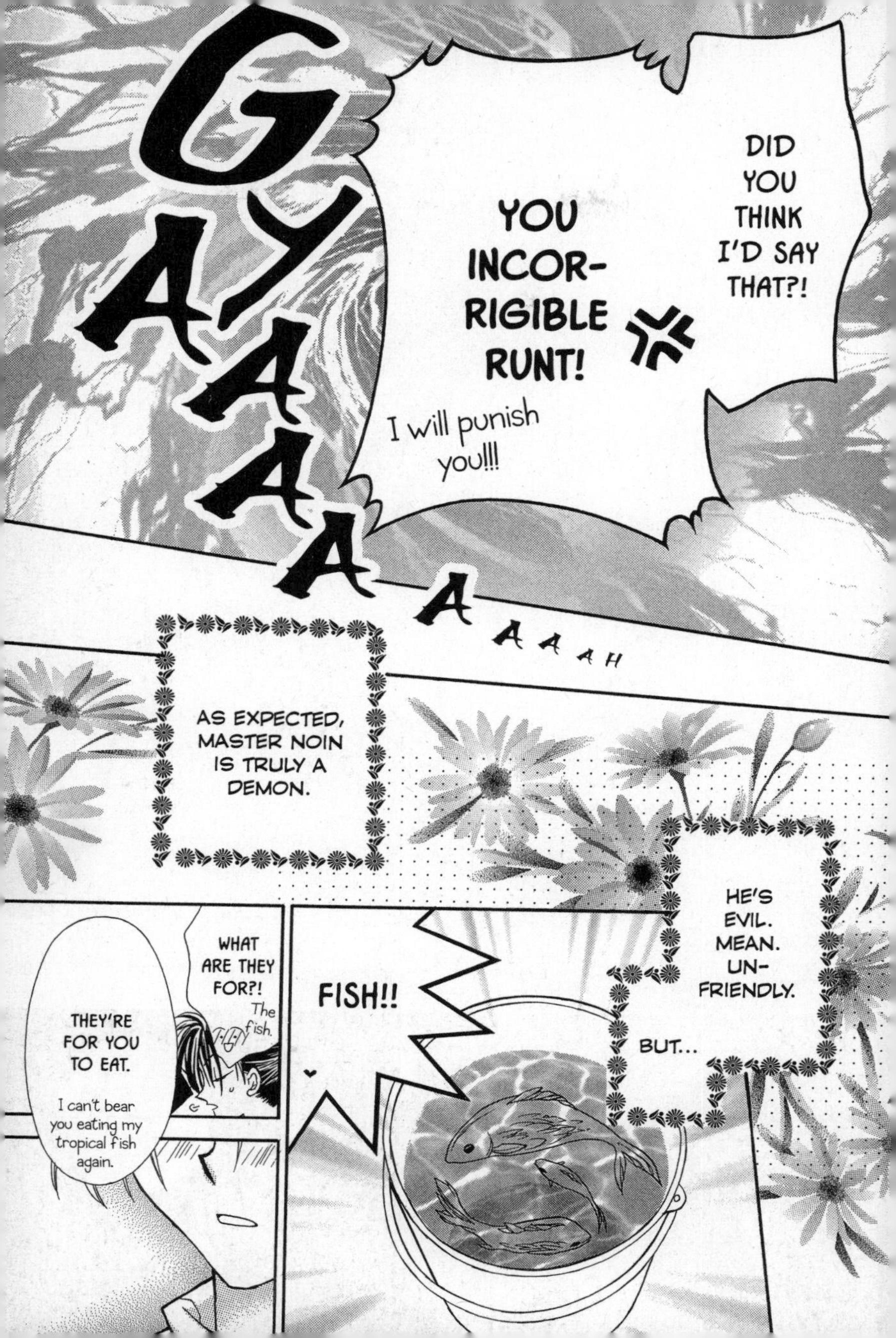
DID YOU THINK I'D SAY THAT?!
YOU INCORRIGIBLE RUNT!
I will punish you!!!
GYAAAAAAAAAH
AS EXPECTED, MASTER NOIN IS TRULY A DEMON.
HE'S EVIL. MEAN. UNFRIENDLY.
BUT...
FISH!!
WHAT ARE THEY FOR?!
The fish.
THEY'RE FOR YOU TO EAT.
I can't bear you eating my tropical fish again.

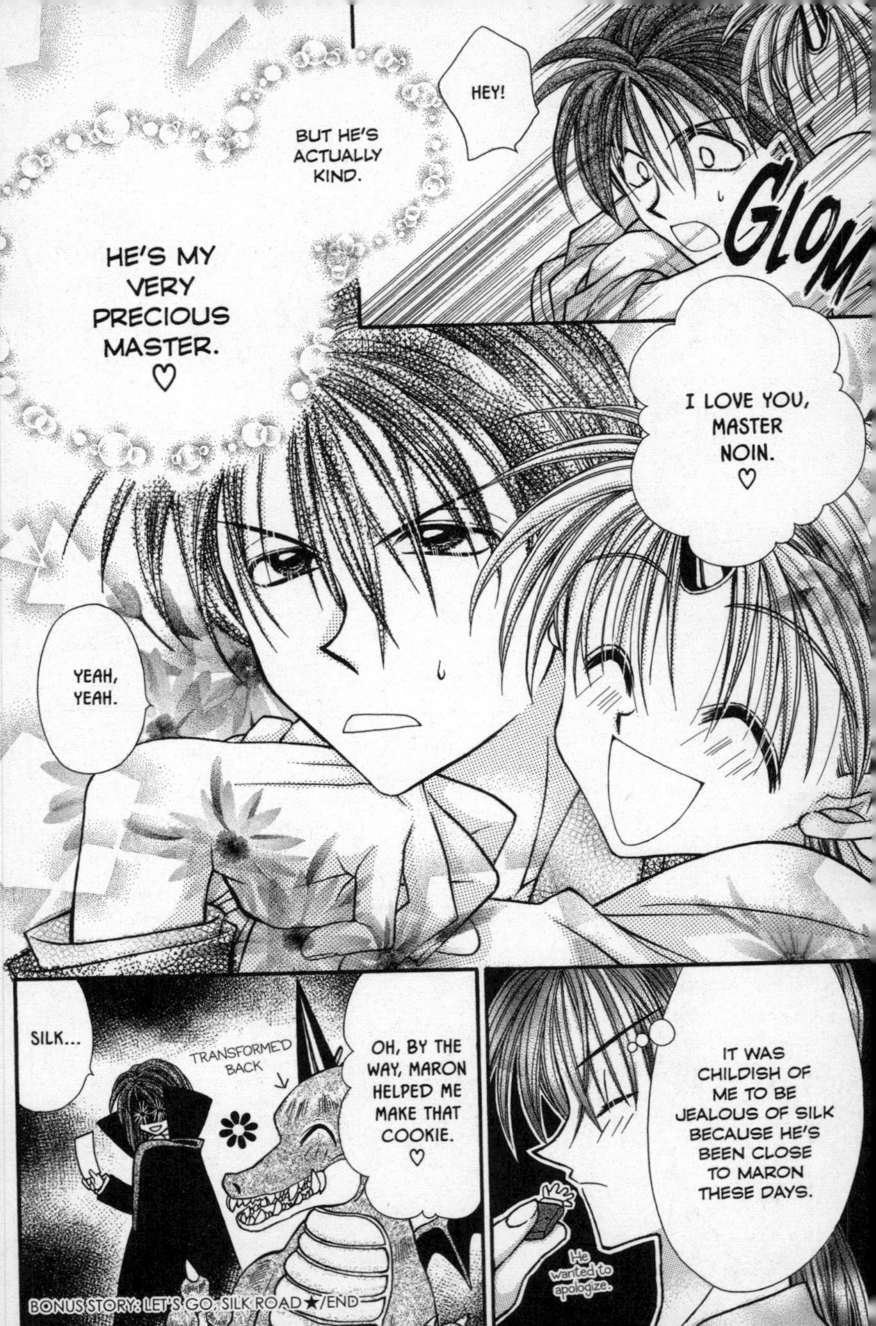
HEY!
GLOM
I LOVE YOU, MASTER NOIN. ♡
BUT HE'S ACTUALLY KIND.
HE'S MY VERY PRECIOUS MASTER. ♡
YEAH, YEAH.
IT WAS CHILDISH OF ME TO BE JEALOUS OF SILK BECAUSE HE'S BEEN CLOSE TO MARON THESE DAYS.
He wanted to apologize.
OH, BY THE WAY, MARON HELPED ME MAKE THAT COOKIE. ♡
TRANSFORMED BACK
SILK...
BONUS STORY: LET'S GO, SILK ROAD★/END

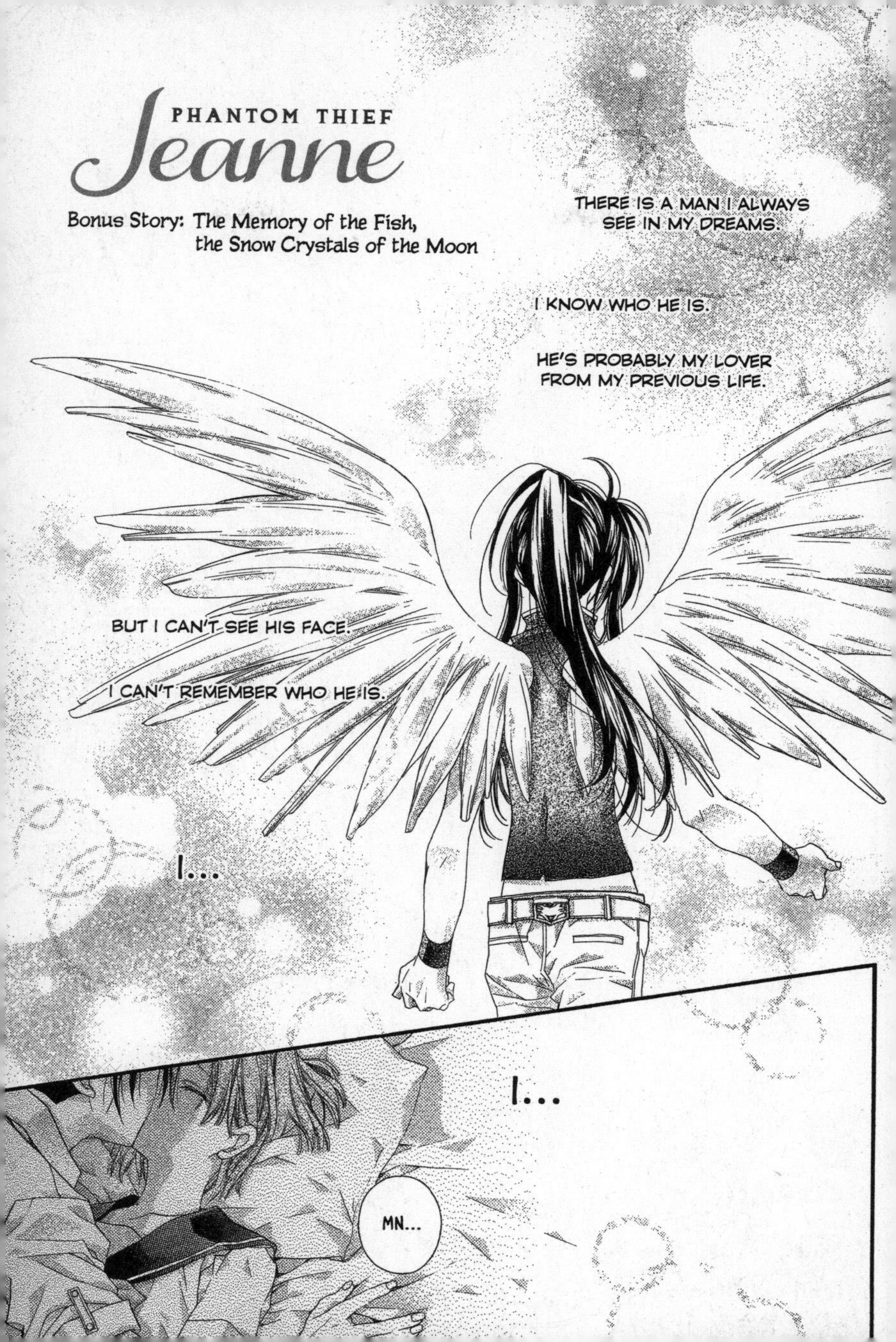

PHANTOM THIEF
Jeanne
Bonus Story: The Memory of the Fish, the Snow Crystals of the Moon
THERE IS A MAN I ALWAYS SEE IN MY DREAMS.
I KNOW WHO HE IS.
HE'S PROBABLY MY LOVER FROM MY PREVIOUS LIFE.
BUT I CAN'T SEE HIS FACE.
I CAN'T REMEMBER WHO HE IS.
I...
I...
MN...

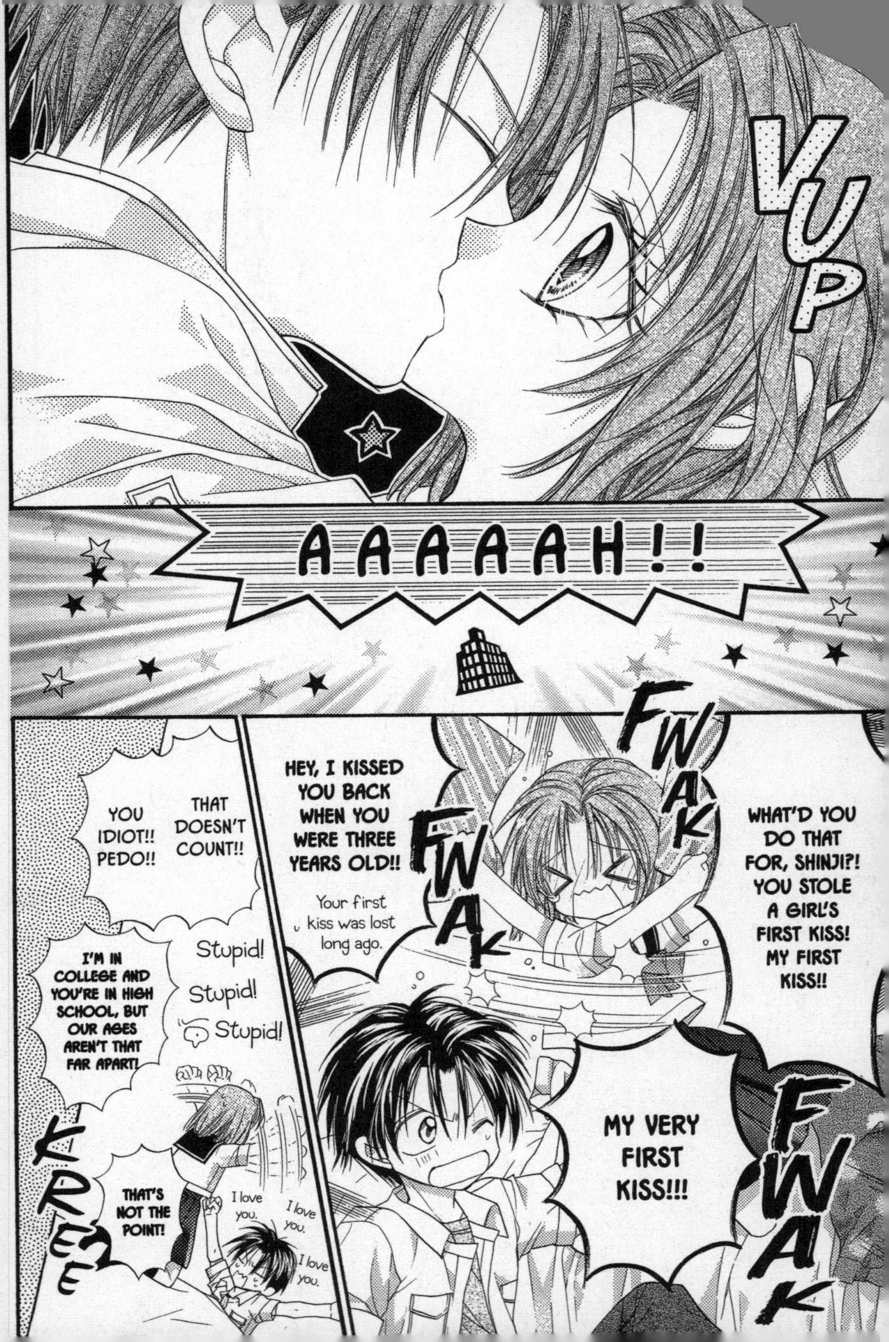
VUP
AAAAAH!!
FWAK
WHAT'D YOU DO THAT FOR, SHINJI?! YOU STOLE A GIRL'S FIRST KISS! MY FIRST KISS!!
FWAK
HEY, I KISSED YOU BACK WHEN YOU WERE THREE YEARS OLD!!
Your first kiss was lost long ago.
MY VERY FIRST KISS!!!
FWAK
THAT DOESN'T COUNT!!
YOU IDIOT!! PEDO!!
Stupid!
Stupid!
Stupid!
I'M IN COLLEGE AND YOU'RE IN HIGH SCHOOL, BUT OUR AGES AREN'T THAT FAR APART!
KREEE
THAT'S NOT THE POINT!
I love you.
I love you.
I love you.

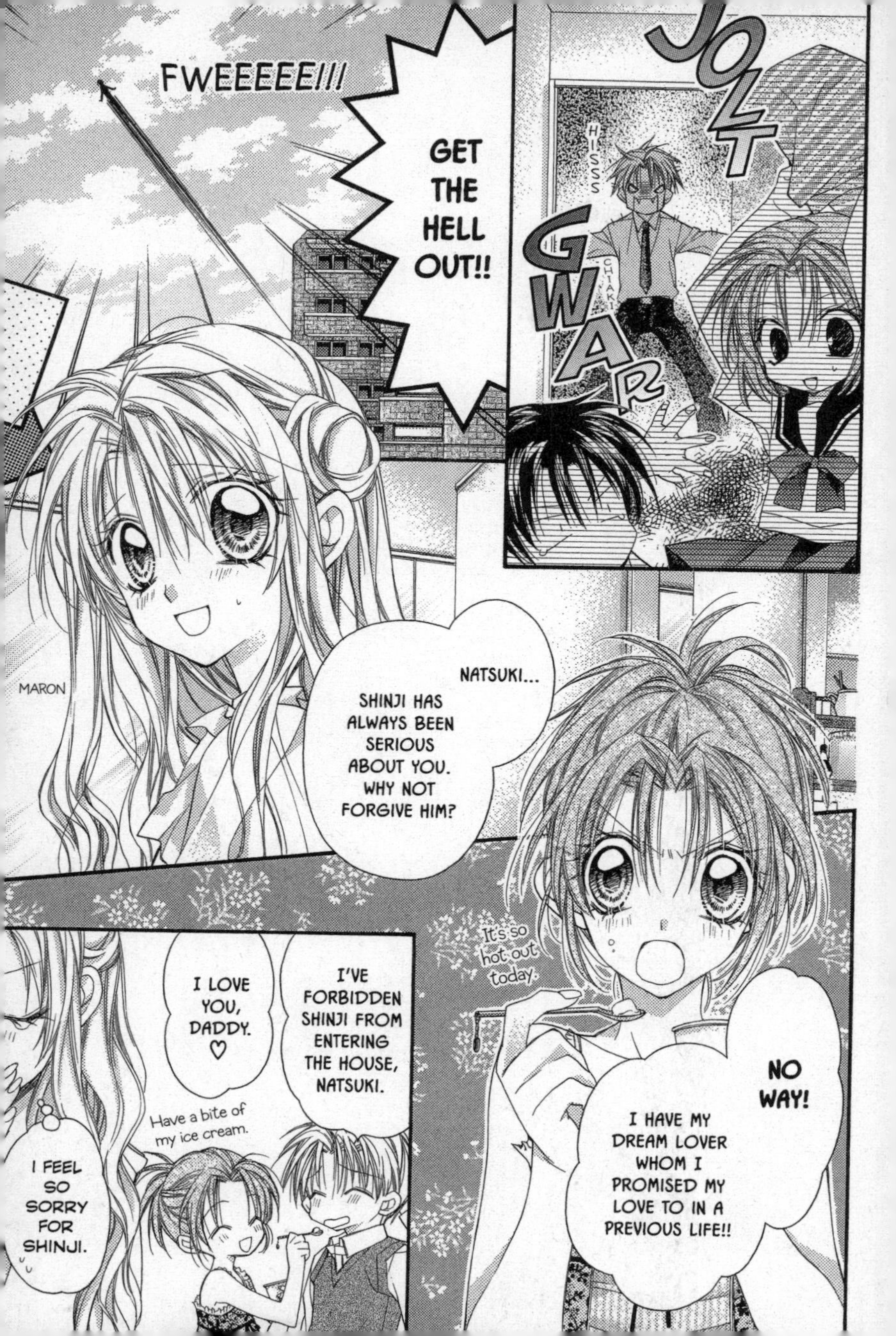
JOLT
HISSS
CHIAKI
GWAR
FWEEEEEE!!!
GET THE HELL OUT!!
MARON
NATSUKI... SHINJI HAS ALWAYS BEEN SERIOUS ABOUT YOU. WHY NOT FORGIVE HIM?
It's so hot out today.
NO WAY!
I HAVE MY DREAM LOVER WHOM I PROMISED MY LOVE TO IN A PREVIOUS LIFE!!
I'VE FORBIDDEN SHINJI FROM ENTERING THE HOUSE, NATSUKI.
I LOVE YOU, DADDY. ♡
Have a bite of my ice cream.
I FEEL SO SORRY FOR SHINJI.

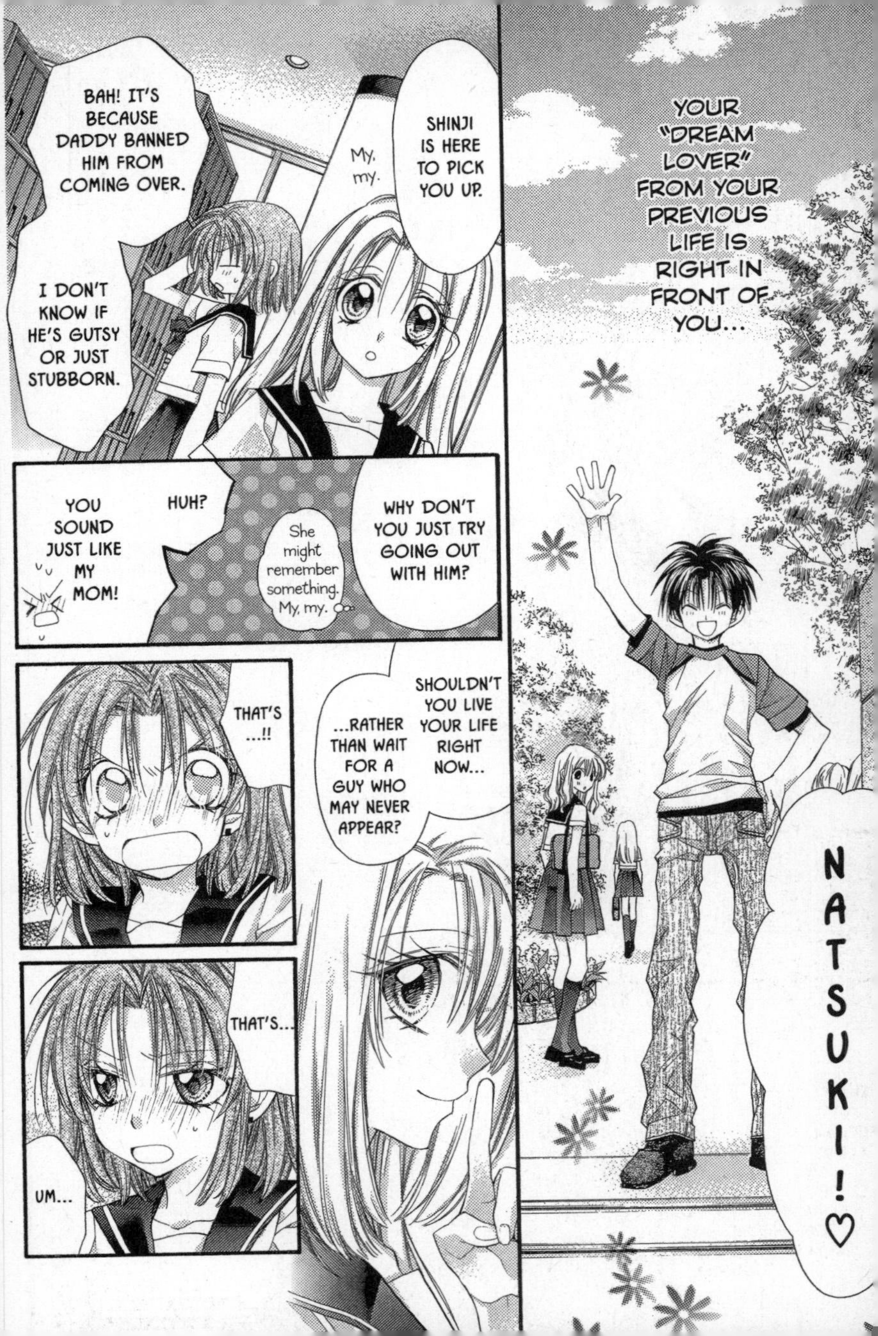
YOUR "DREAM LOVER" FROM YOUR PREVIOUS LIFE IS RIGHT IN FRONT OF YOU...
NATSUKI!♡
SHINJI IS HERE TO PICK YOU UP.
My, my.
BAH! IT'S BECAUSE DADDY BANNED HIM FROM COMING OVER.
I DON'T KNOW IF HE'S GUTSY OR JUST STUBBORN.
WHY DON'T YOU JUST TRY GOING OUT WITH HIM?
She might remember something. My, my.
HUH?
YOU SOUND JUST LIKE MY MOM!
SHOULDN'T YOU LIVE YOUR LIFE RIGHT NOW...
...RATHER THAN WAIT FOR A GUY WHO MAY NEVER APPEAR?
THAT'S ...!!
THAT'S...
UM...

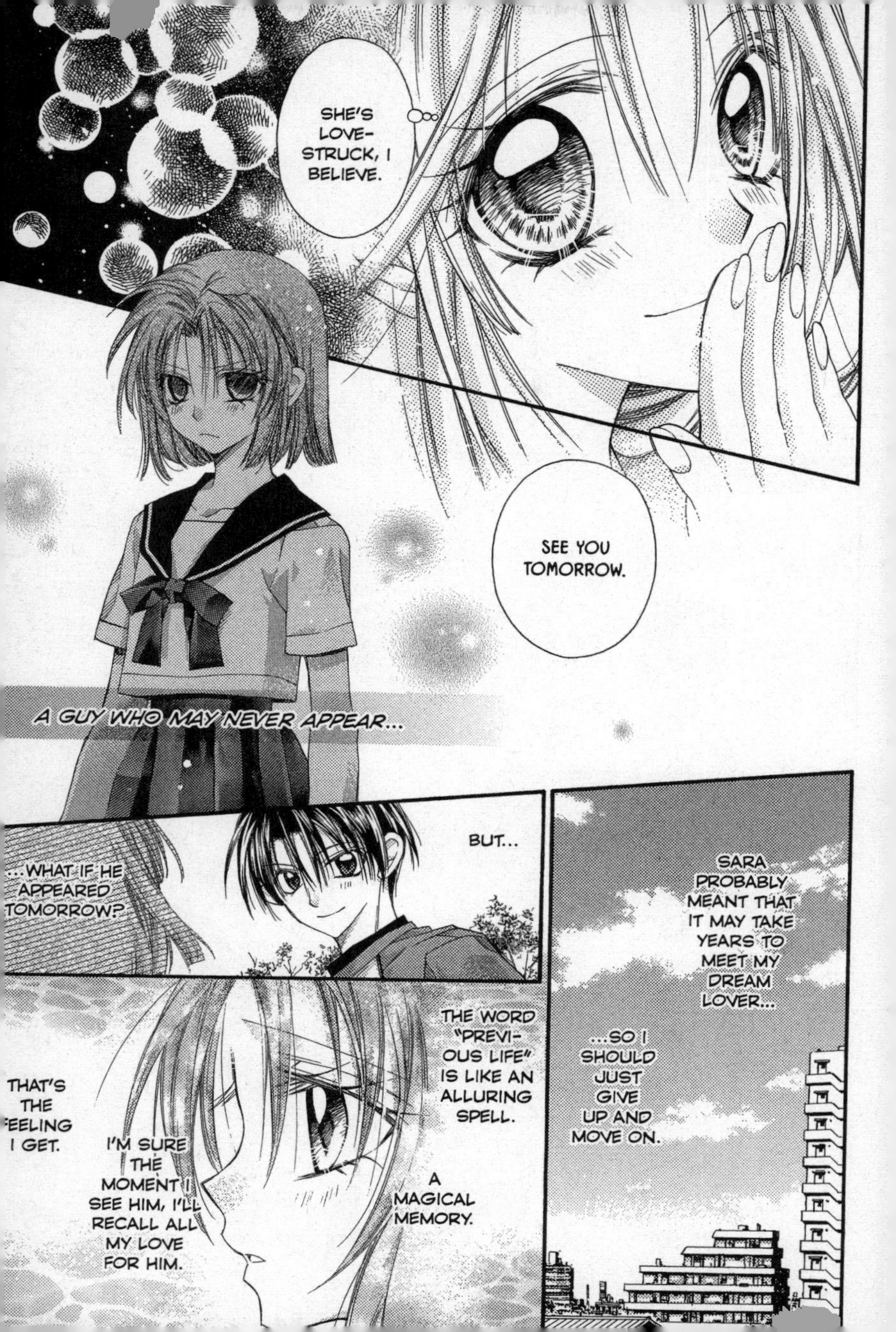
SHE'S LOVE-STRUCK, I BELIEVE.
SEE YOU TOMORROW.
A GUY WHO MAY NEVER APPEAR...
SARA PROBABLY MEANT THAT IT MAY TAKE YEARS TO MEET MY DREAM LOVER...
...SO I SHOULD JUST GIVE UP AND MOVE ON.
BUT...
...WHAT IF HE APPEARED TOMORROW?
THE WORD "PREVIOUS LIFE" IS LIKE AN ALLURING SPELL.
A MAGICAL MEMORY.
I'M SURE THE MOMENT I SEE HIM, I'LL RECALL ALL MY LOVE FOR HIM.
THAT'S THE FEELING I GET.

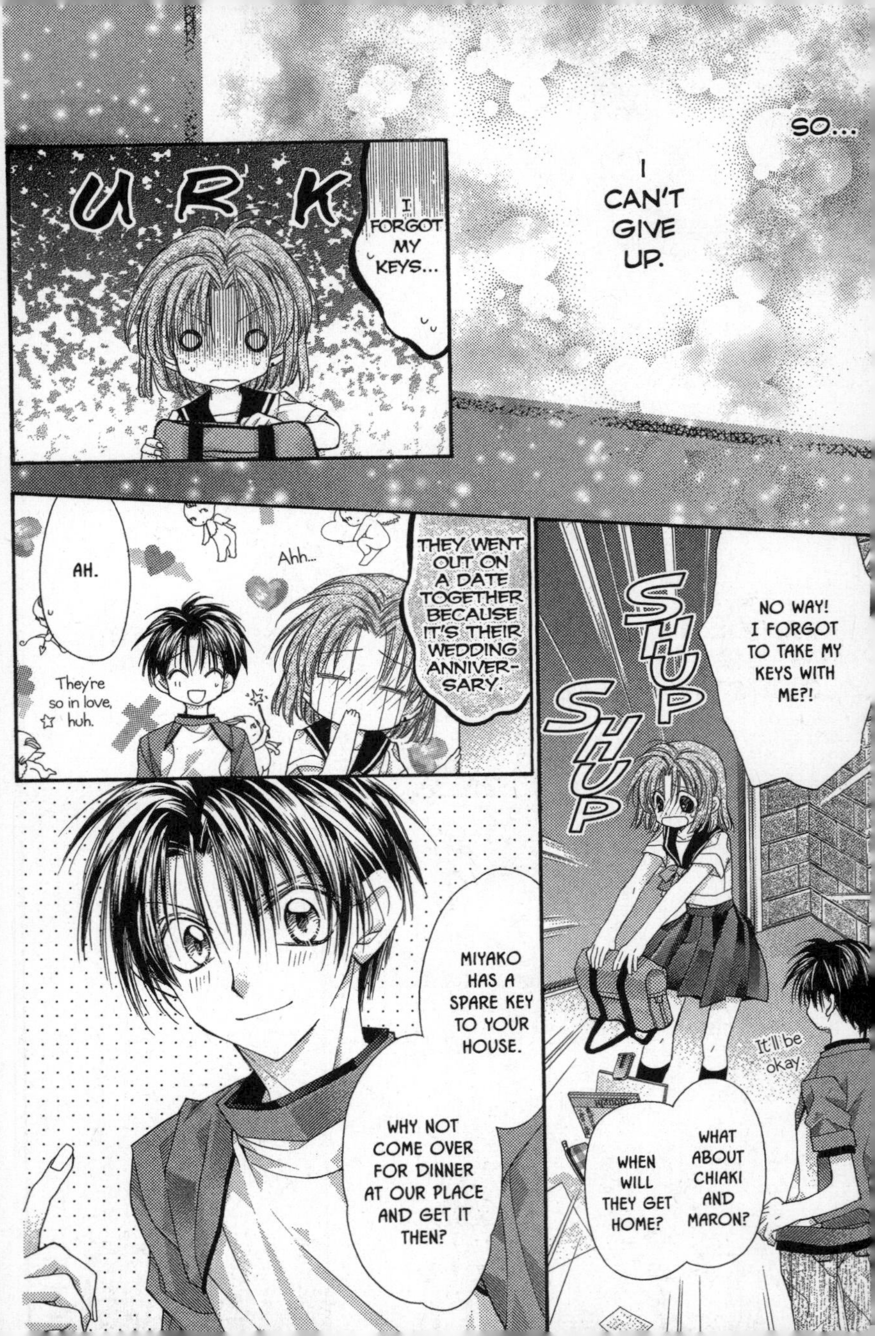
SO...
I CAN'T GIVE UP.
URK
I FORGOT MY KEYS...
SHUP SHUP
NO WAY! I FORGOT TO TAKE MY KEYS WITH ME?!
It'll be okay.
WHAT ABOUT CHIAKI AND MARON?
WHEN WILL THEY GET HOME?
THEY WENT OUT ON A DATE TOGETHER BECAUSE IT'S THEIR WEDDING ANNIVER-SARY.
Ahh...
AH.
They're so in love, huh.
MIYAKO HAS A SPARE KEY TO YOUR HOUSE.
WHY NOT COME OVER FOR DINNER AT OUR PLACE AND GET IT THEN?

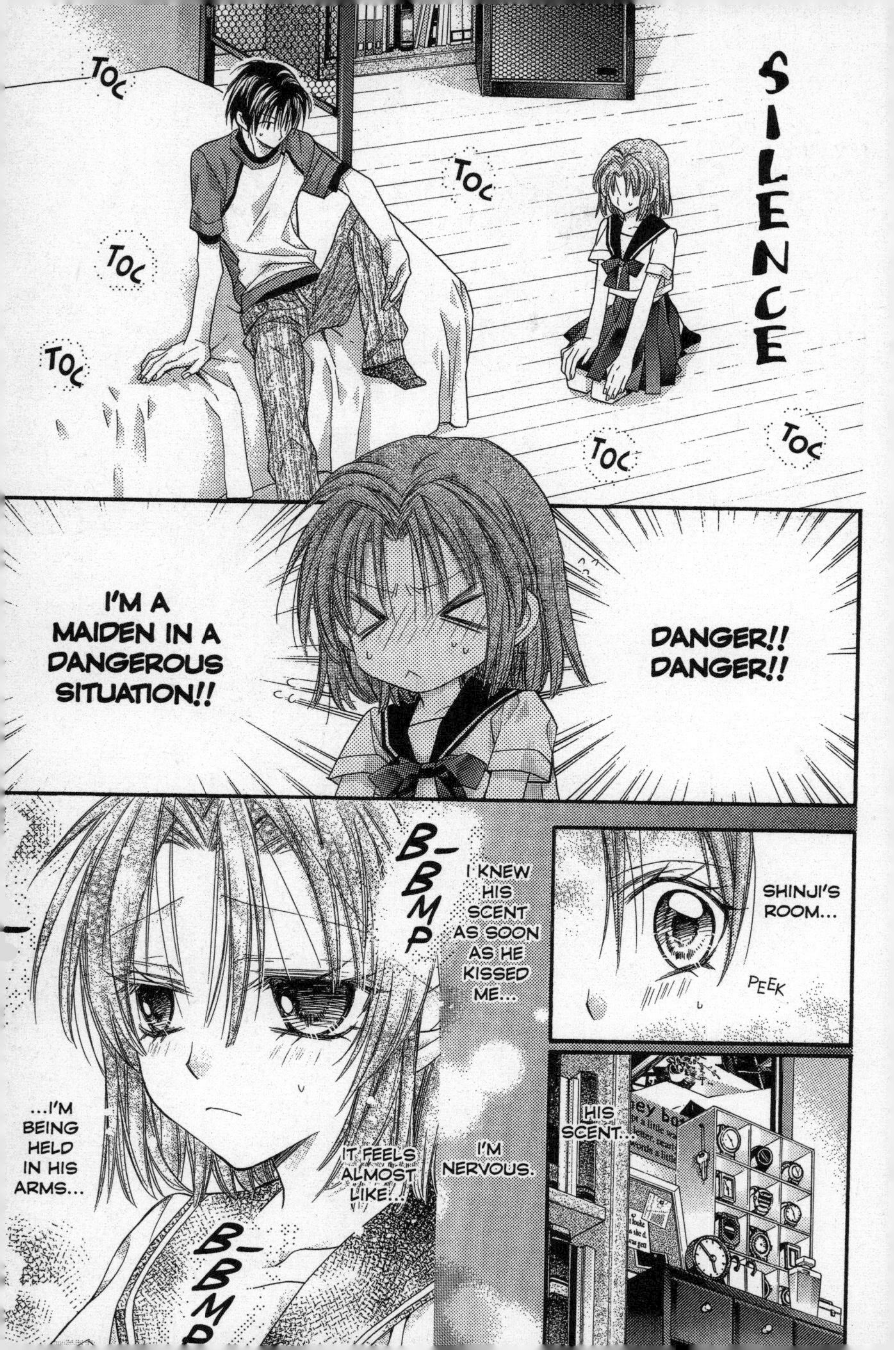
SILENCE
TOC
TOC
TOC
TOC
TOC
TOC
DANGER!! DANGER!!
I'M A MAIDEN IN A DANGEROUS SITUATION!!
SHINJI'S ROOM...
PEEK
HIS SCENT...
B-BMP
I KNEW HIS SCENT AS SOON AS HE KISSED ME...
I'M NERVOUS.
IT FEELS ALMOST LIKE...
...I'M BEING HELD IN HIS ARMS...
B-BMP

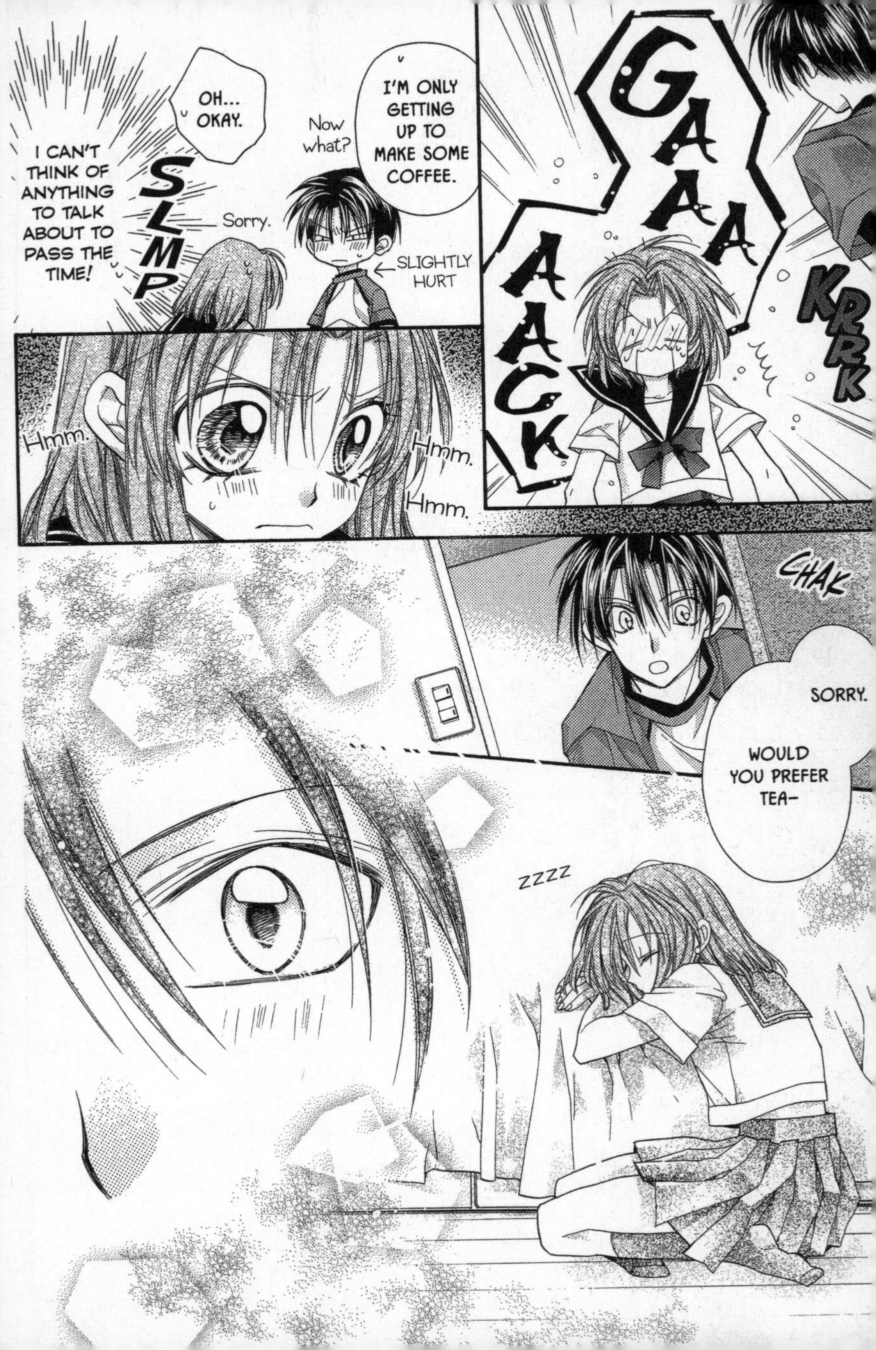
GAAAAACK
KRRK
I'M ONLY GETTING UP TO MAKE SOME COFFEE.
Now what?
OH... OKAY.
I CAN'T THINK OF ANYTHING TO TALK ABOUT TO PASS THE TIME!
SLMP
Sorry.
SLIGHTLY HURT
Hmm.
Hmm.
Hmm.
CHAK
SORRY.
WOULD YOU PREFER TEA-
ZZZZ

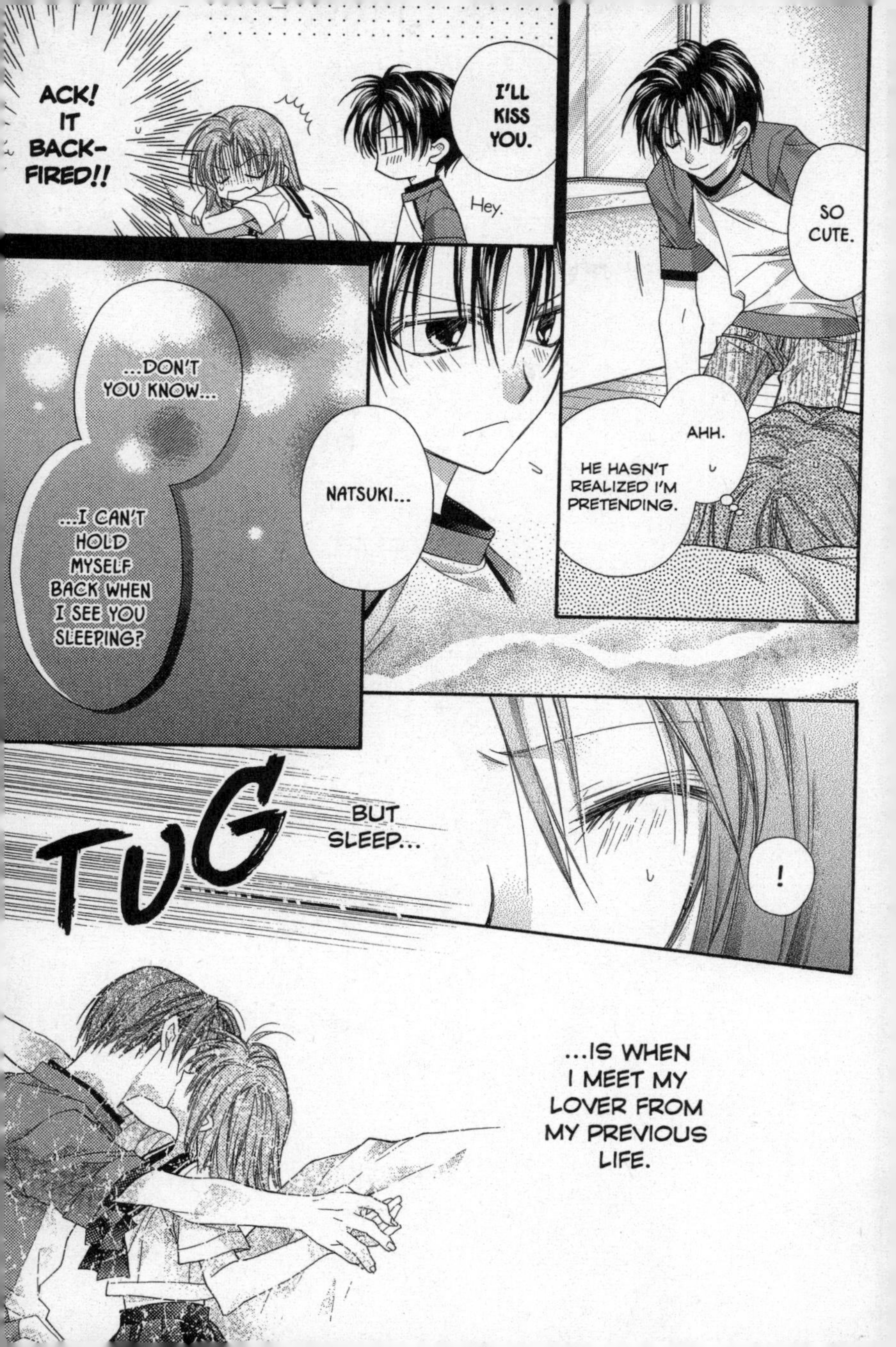
SO CUTE.
AHH.
HE HASN'T REALIZED I'M PRETENDING.
I'LL KISS YOU.
Hey.
ACK! IT BACK-FIRED!!
NATSUKI...
...DON'T YOU KNOW...
...I CAN'T HOLD MYSELF BACK WHEN I SEE YOU SLEEPING?
!
BUT SLEEP...
TUG
...IS WHEN I MEET MY LOVER FROM MY PREVIOUS LIFE.

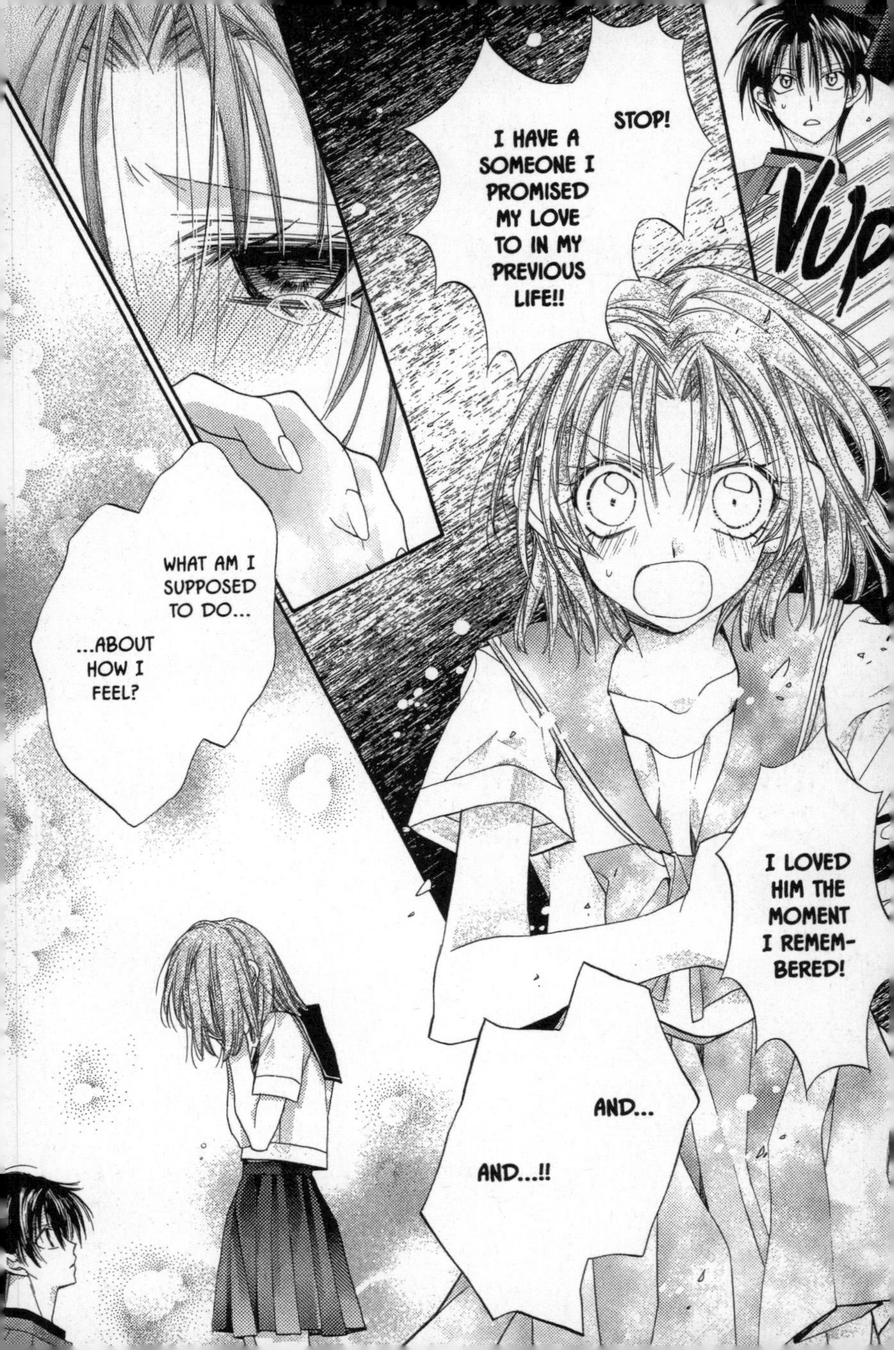
VUP
STOP!
I HAVE A SOMEONE I PROMISED MY LOVE TO IN MY PREVIOUS LIFE!!
I LOVED HIM THE MOMENT I REMEM-BERED!
AND...
AND...!!
WHAT AM I SUPPOSED TO DO...
...ABOUT HOW I FEEL?

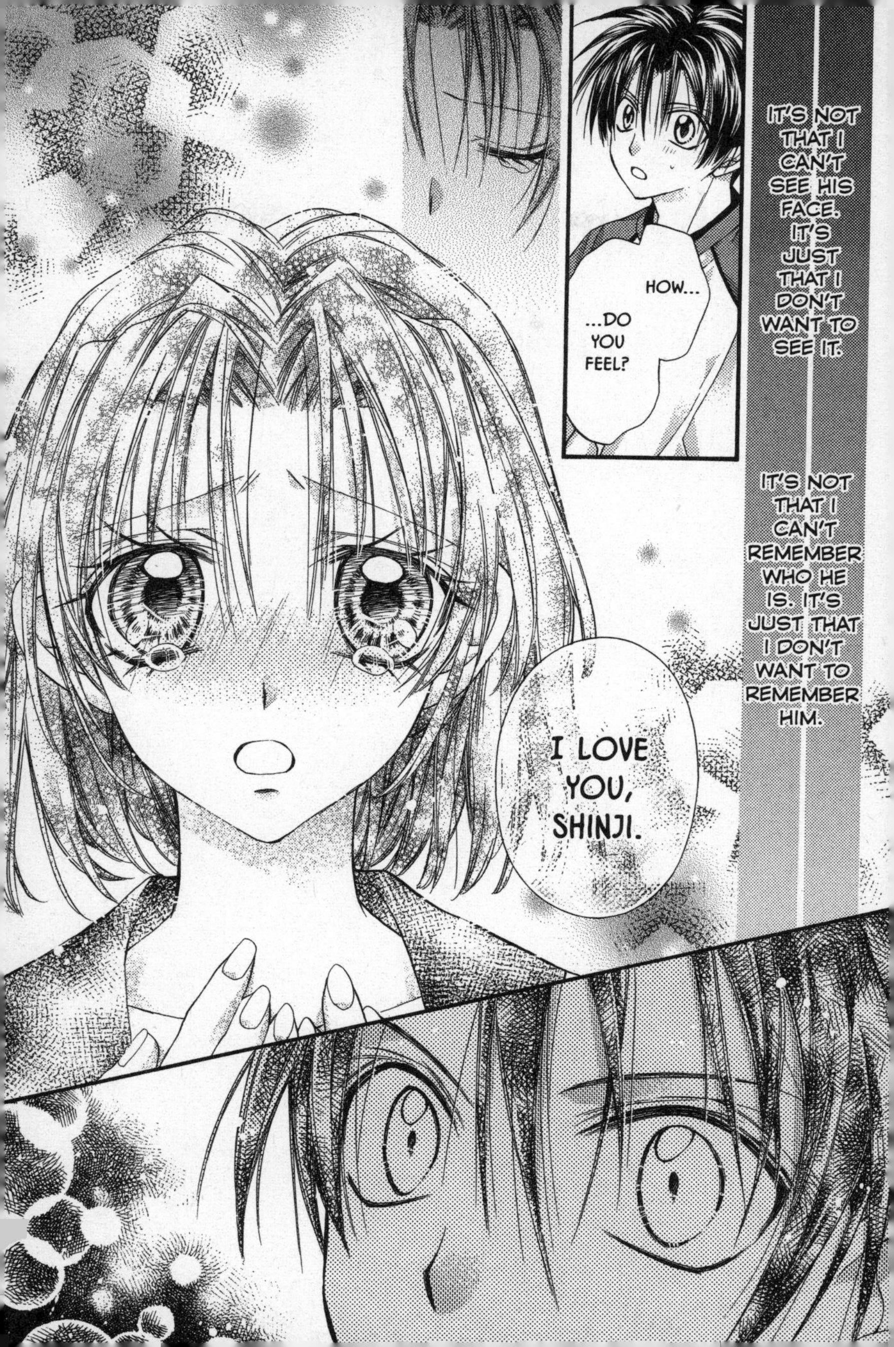
IT'S NOT THAT I CAN'T SEE HIS FACE. IT'S JUST THAT I DON'T WANT TO SEE IT.
HOW...
...DO YOU FEEL?
IT'S NOT THAT I CAN'T REMEMBER WHO HE IS. IT'S JUST THAT I DON'T WANT TO REMEMBER HIM.
I LOVE YOU, SHINJI.

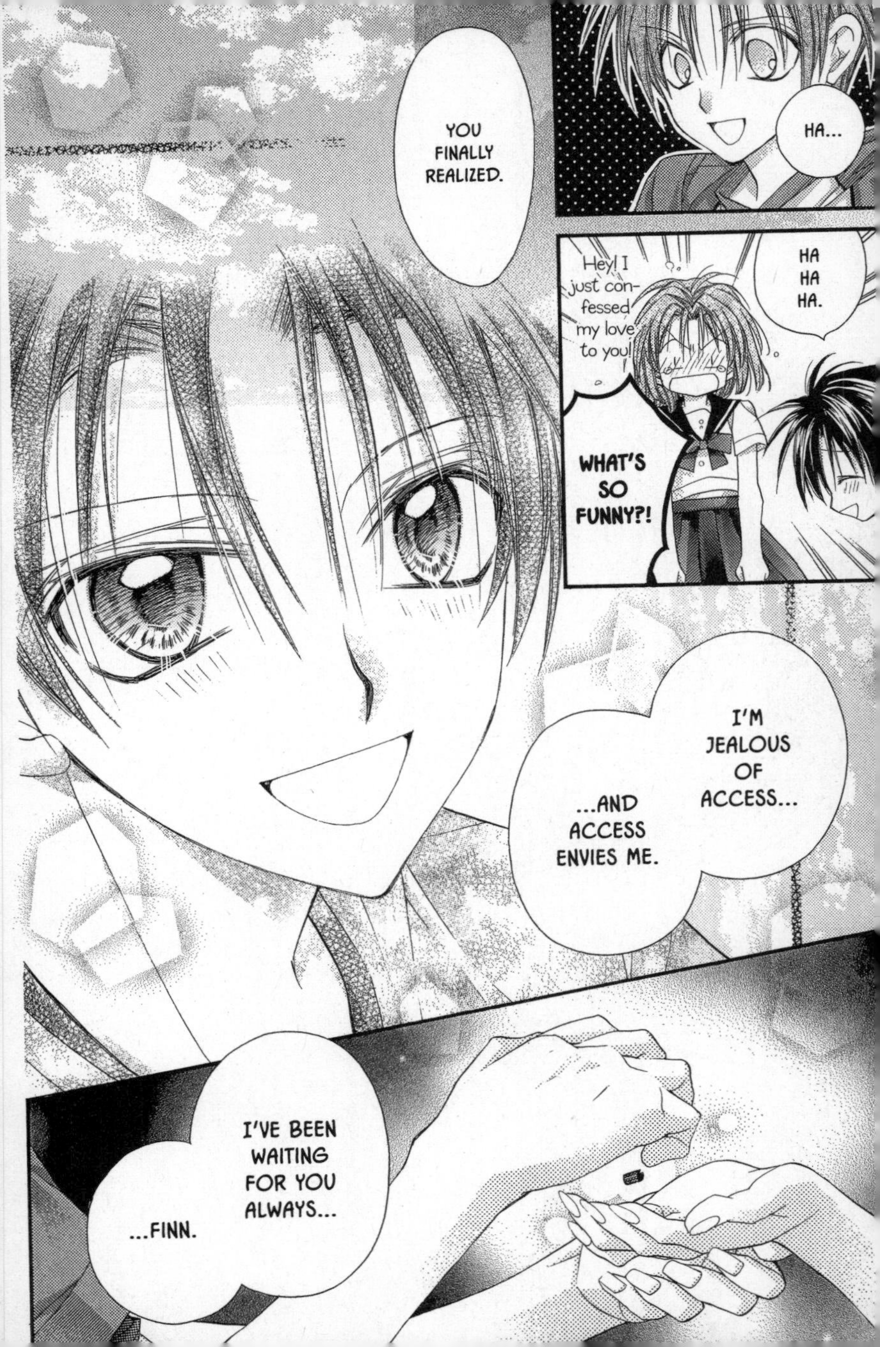
HA...
HA HA HA.
Hey! I just confessed my love to you!
WHAT'S SO FUNNY?!
YOU FINALLY REALIZED.
I'M JEALOUS OF ACCESS...
...AND ACCESS ENVIES ME.
I'VE BEEN WAITING FOR YOU ALWAYS...
...FINN.

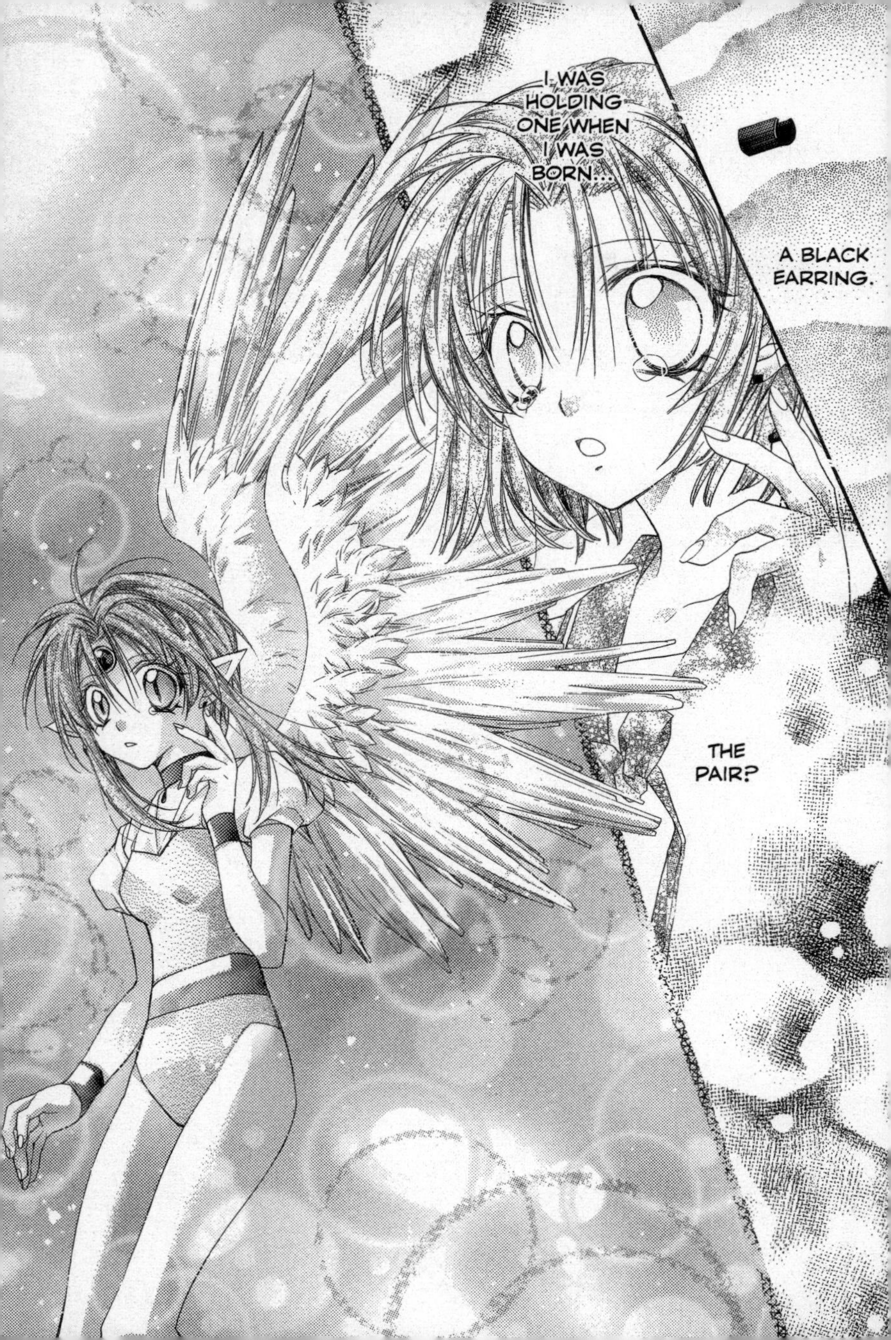
I WAS HOLDING ONE WHEN I WAS BORN...
A BLACK EARRING.
THE PAIR?

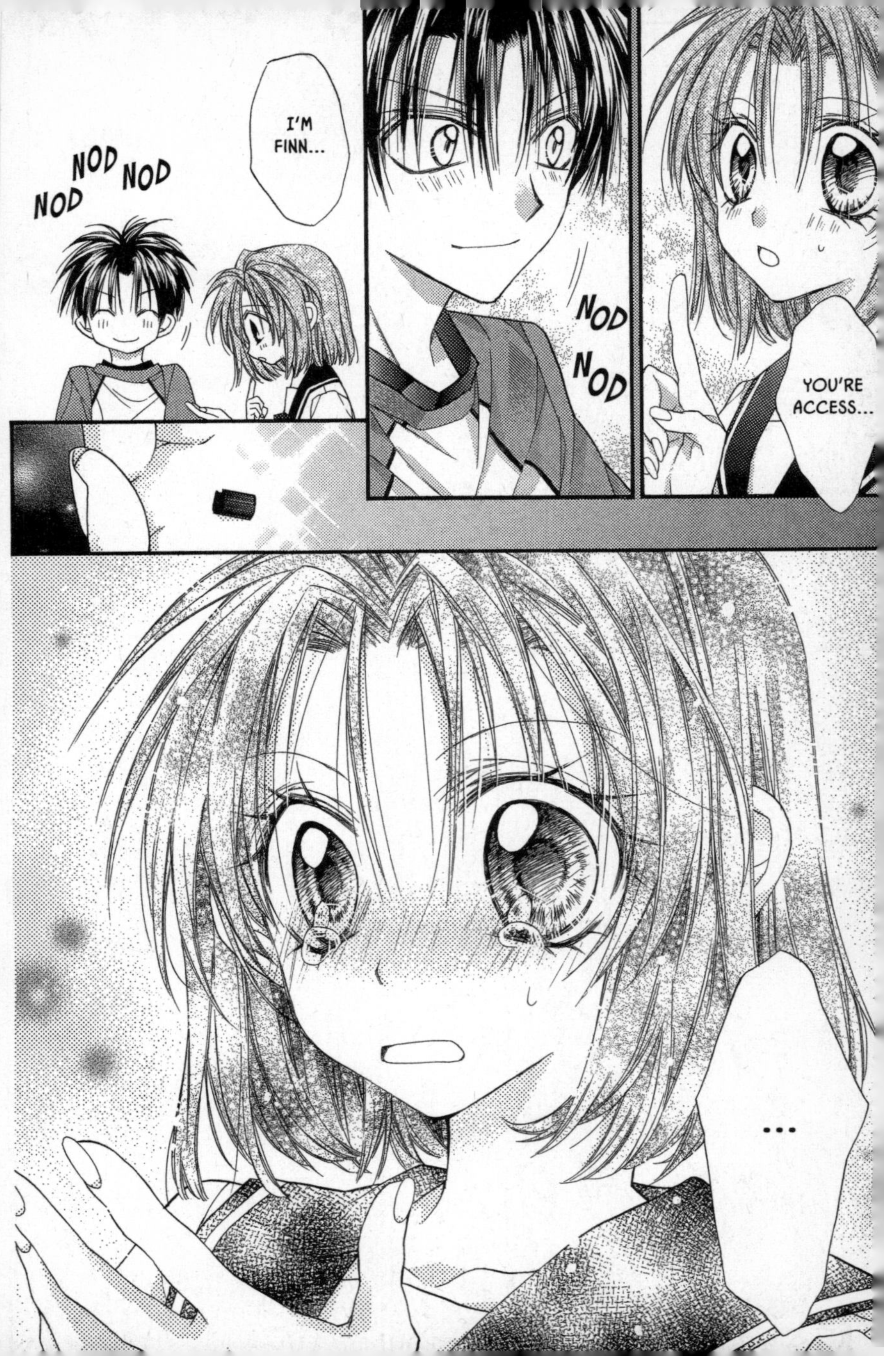
YOU'RE ACCESS...
NOD NOD
I'M FINN...
NOD NOD NOD
...

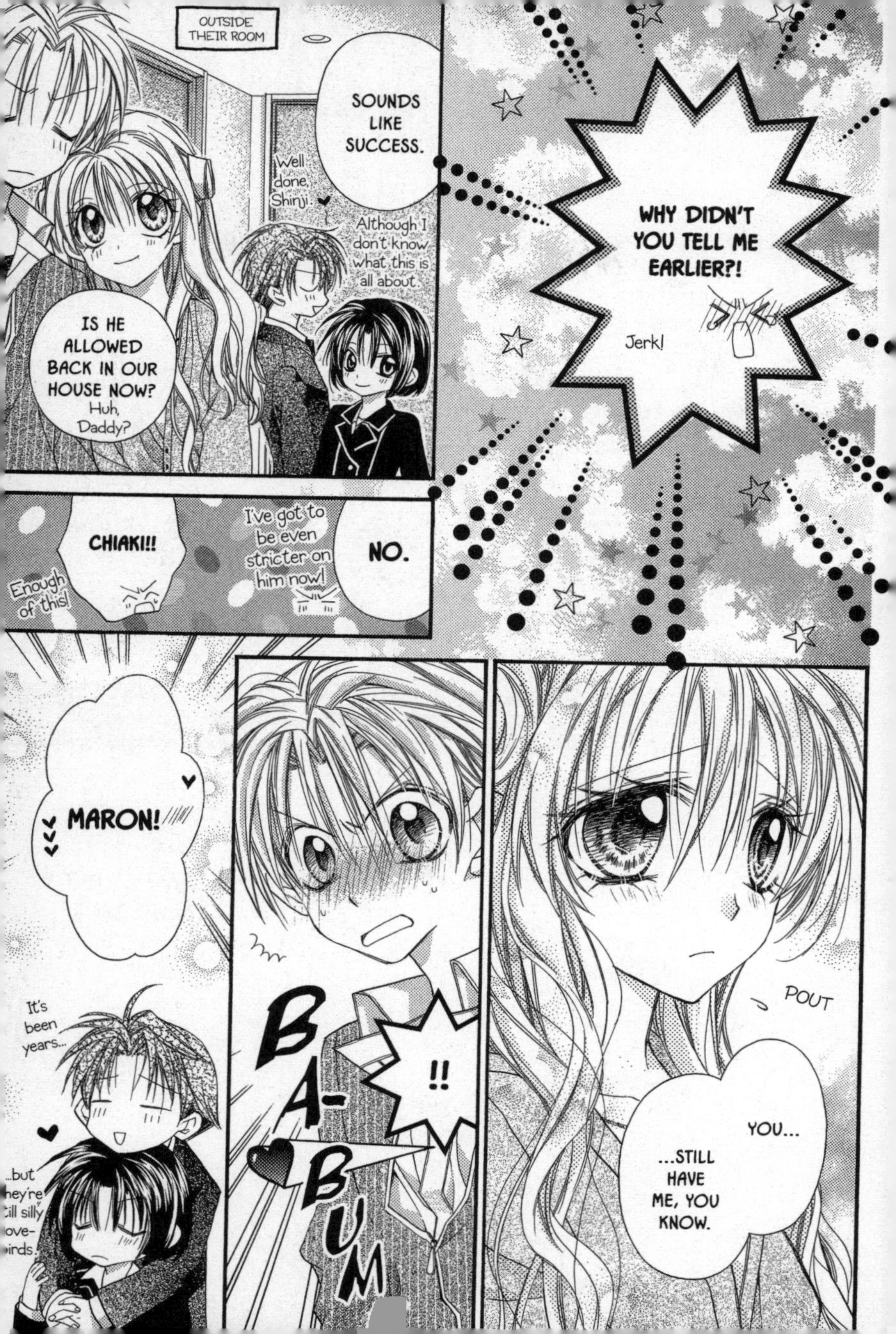
WHY DIDN'T YOU TELL ME EARLIER?!
Jerk!
OUTSIDE THEIR ROOM
SOUNDS LIKE SUCCESS.
Well done, Shinji.
Although I don't know what this is all about.
IS HE ALLOWED BACK IN OUR HOUSE NOW?
Huh, Daddy?
NO.
I've got to be even stricter on him now!
CHIAKI!!
Enough of this!
POUT
YOU...
...STILL HAVE ME, YOU KNOW.
!!
BA-BUM
MARON!
It's been years...
...but hey're till silly ove-irds.

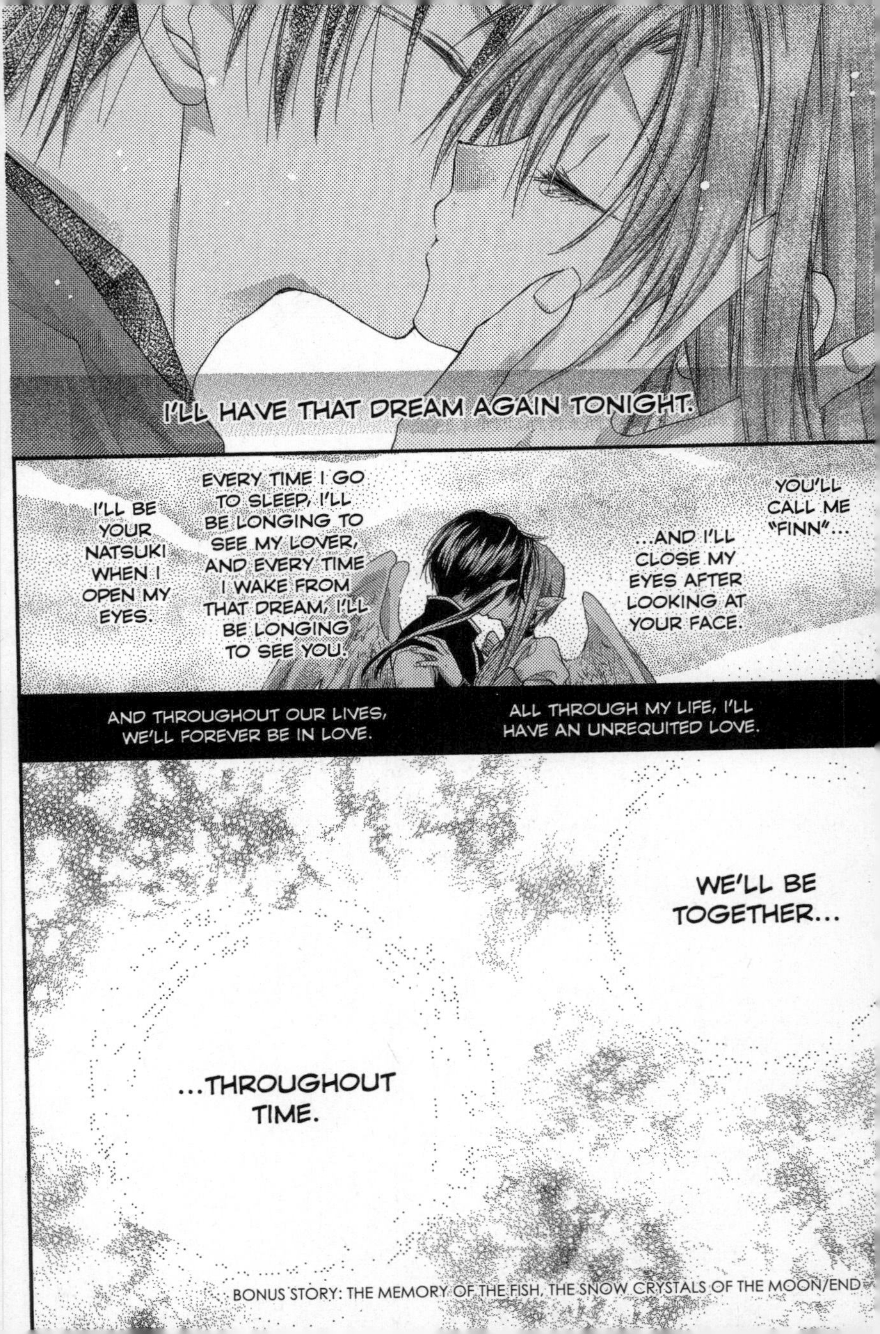
I'LL HAVE THAT DREAM AGAIN TONIGHT.
YOU'LL CALL ME "FINN"...
...AND I'LL CLOSE MY EYES AFTER LOOKING AT YOUR FACE.
EVERY TIME I GO TO SLEEP, I'LL BE LONGING TO SEE MY LOVER, AND EVERY TIME I WAKE FROM THAT DREAM, I'LL BE LONGING TO SEE YOU.
I'LL BE YOUR NATSUKI WHEN I OPEN MY EYES.
ALL THROUGH MY LIFE, I'LL HAVE AN UNREQUITED LOVE.
AND THROUGHOUT OUR LIVES, WE'LL FOREVER BE IN LOVE.
WE'LL BE TOGETHER...
...THROUGHOUT TIME.
BONUS STORY: THE MEMORY OF THE FISH, THE SNOW CRYSTALS OF THE MOON/END

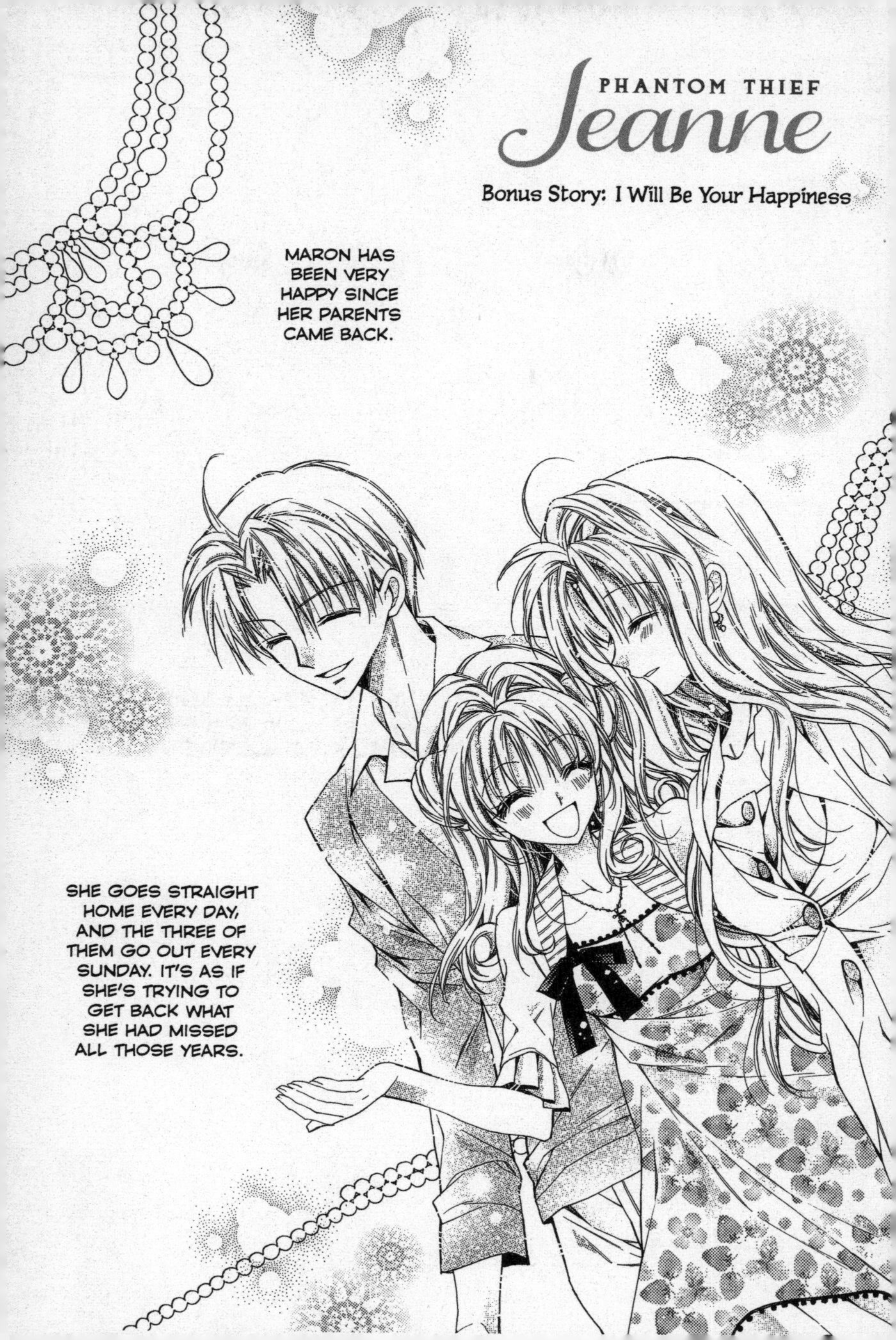
PHANTOM THIEF
Jeanne
Bonus Story: I Will Be Your Happiness
MARON HAS BEEN VERY HAPPY SINCE HER PARENTS CAME BACK.
SHE GOES STRAIGHT HOME EVERY DAY, AND THE THREE OF THEM GO OUT EVERY SUNDAY. IT'S AS IF SHE'S TRYING TO GET BACK WHAT SHE HAD MISSED ALL THOSE YEARS.

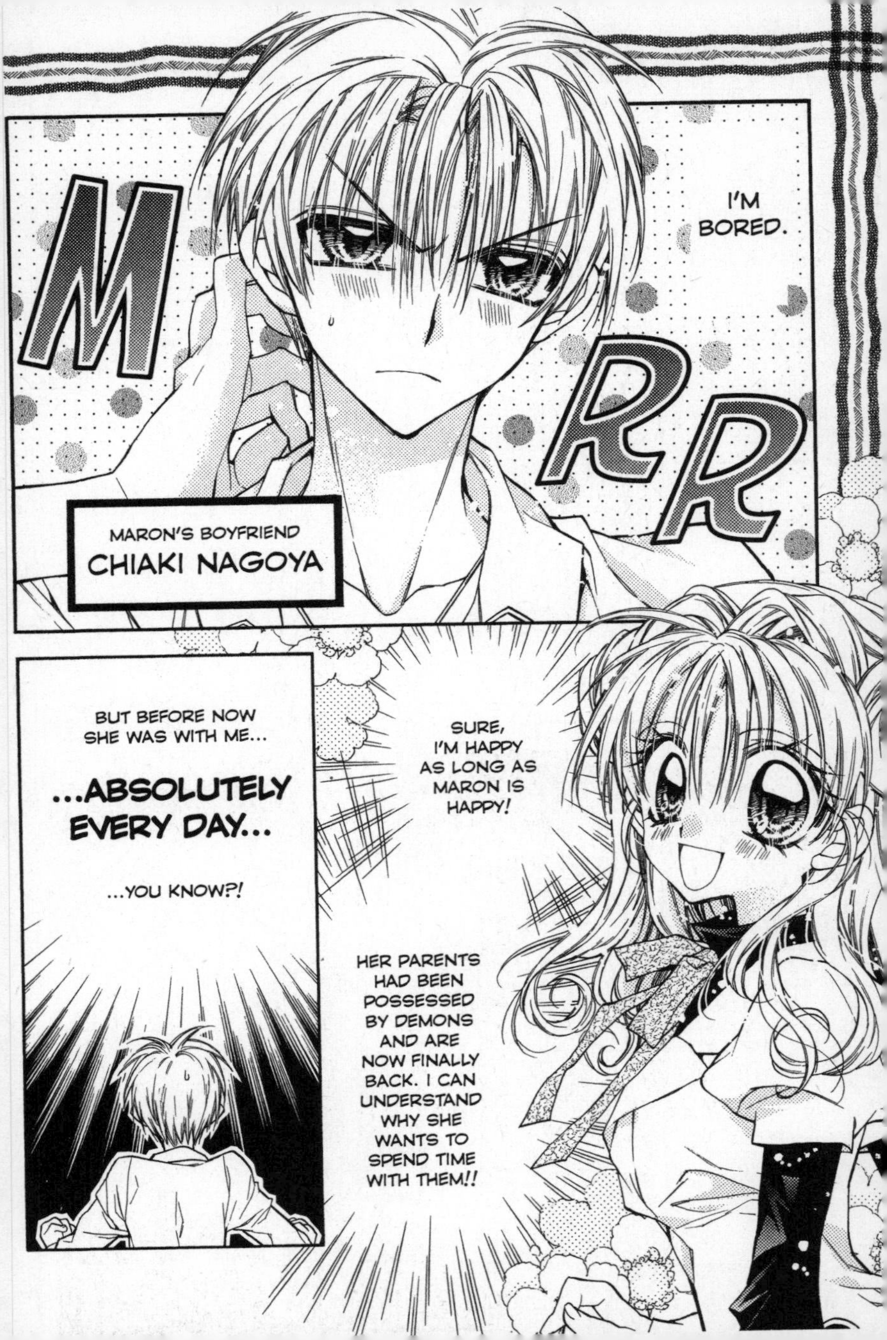
I'M BORED.
MRR
MARON'S BOYFRIEND
CHIAKI NAGOYA
SURE, I'M HAPPY AS LONG AS MARON IS HAPPY!
HER PARENTS HAD BEEN POSSESSED BY DEMONS AND ARE NOW FINALLY BACK. I CAN UNDERSTAND WHY SHE WANTS TO SPEND TIME WITH THEM!!
BUT BEFORE NOW SHE WAS WITH ME...
...ABSOLUTELY EVERY DAY...
...YOU KNOW?!

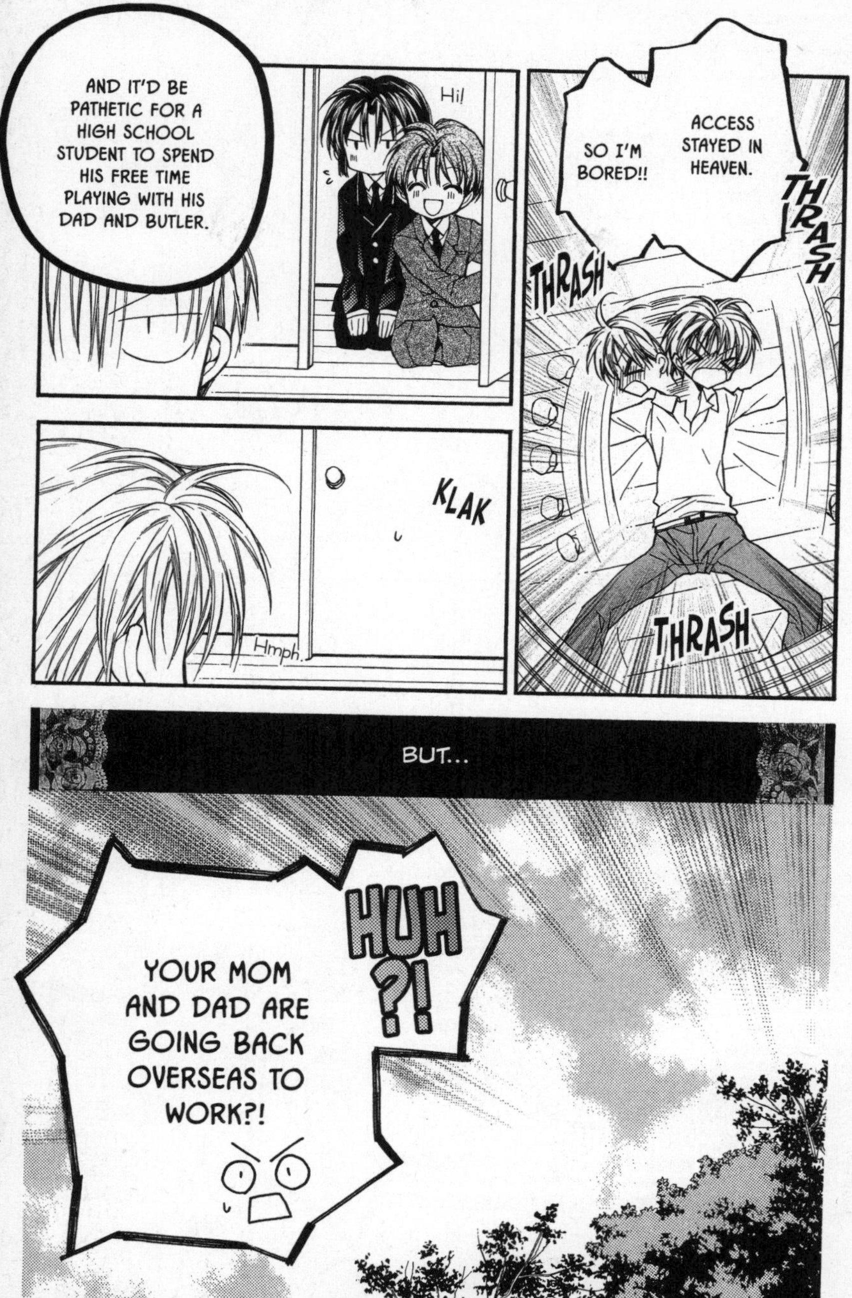
ACCESS STAYED IN HEAVEN.
SO I'M BORED!!
THRASH
THRASH
THRASH
AND IT'D BE PATHETIC FOR A HIGH SCHOOL STUDENT TO SPEND HIS FREE TIME PLAYING WITH HIS DAD AND BUTLER.
Hi!
KLAK
Hmph.
BUT...
HUH ?!
YOUR MOM AND DAD ARE GOING BACK OVERSEAS TO WORK?!

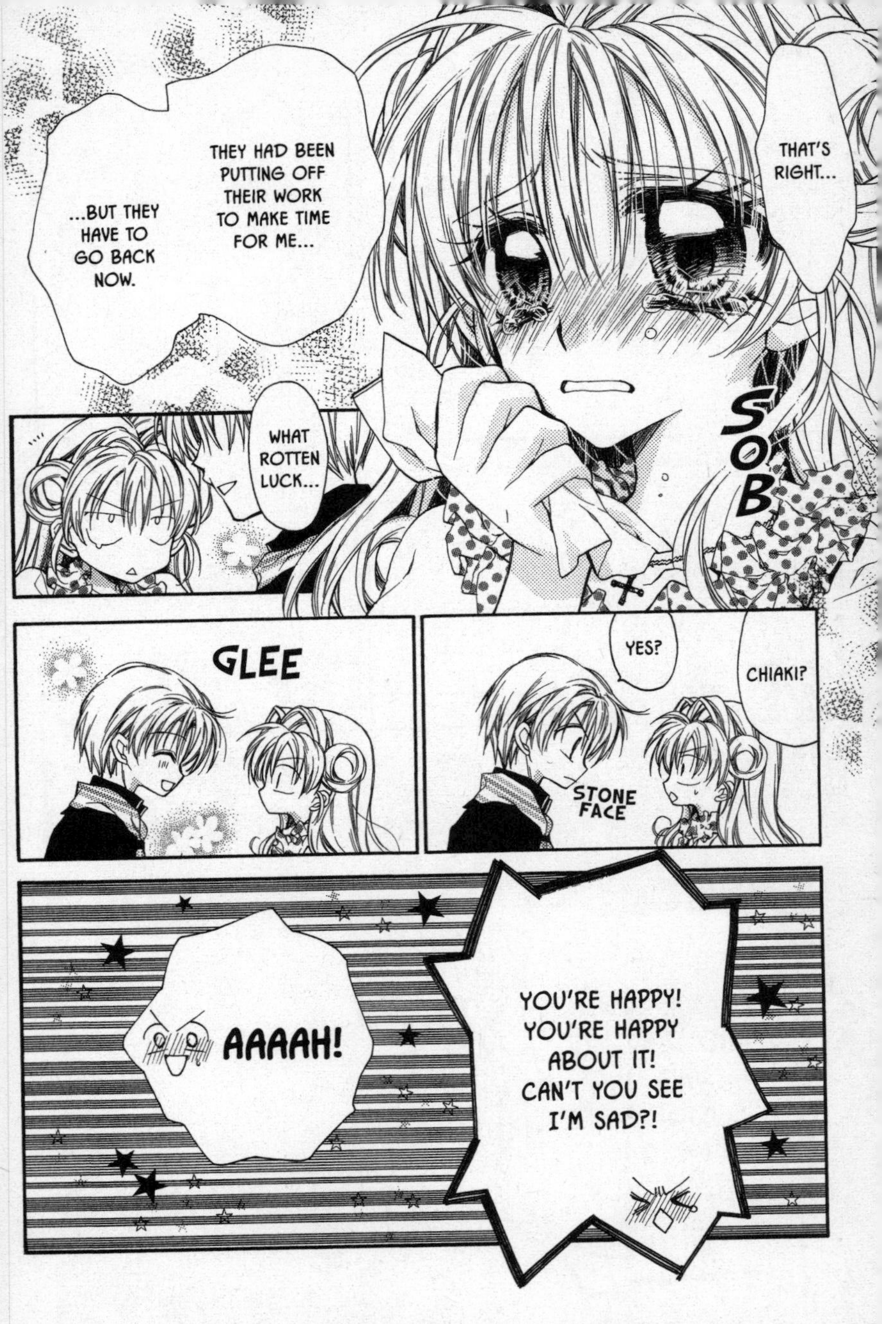
THAT'S RIGHT...
THEY HAD BEEN PUTTING OFF THEIR WORK TO MAKE TIME FOR ME...
...BUT THEY HAVE TO GO BACK NOW.
SOB
WHAT ROTTEN LUCK...
CHIAKI?
YES?
STONE FACE
GLEE
YOU'RE HAPPY! YOU'RE HAPPY ABOUT IT! CAN'T YOU SEE I'M SAD?!
AAAAH!

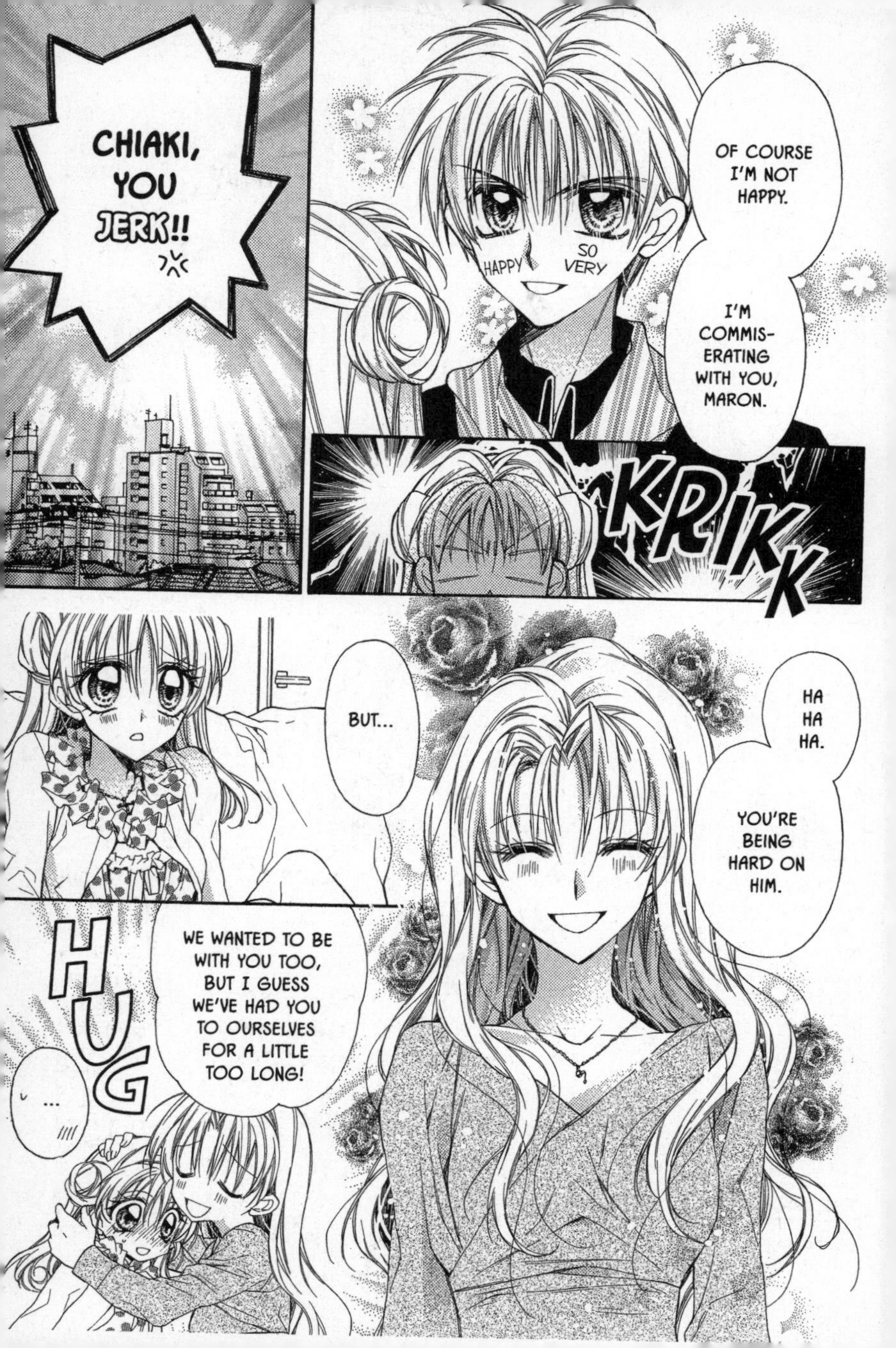
OF COURSE I'M NOT HAPPY.
SO VERY HAPPY
I'M COMMIS-ERATING WITH YOU, MARON.
KRIKK
CHIAKI, YOU JERK!!
HA HA HA.
YOU'RE BEING HARD ON HIM.
BUT...
WE WANTED TO BE WITH YOU TOO, BUT I GUESS WE'VE HAD YOU TO OURSELVES FOR A LITTLE TOO LONG!
HUG
...

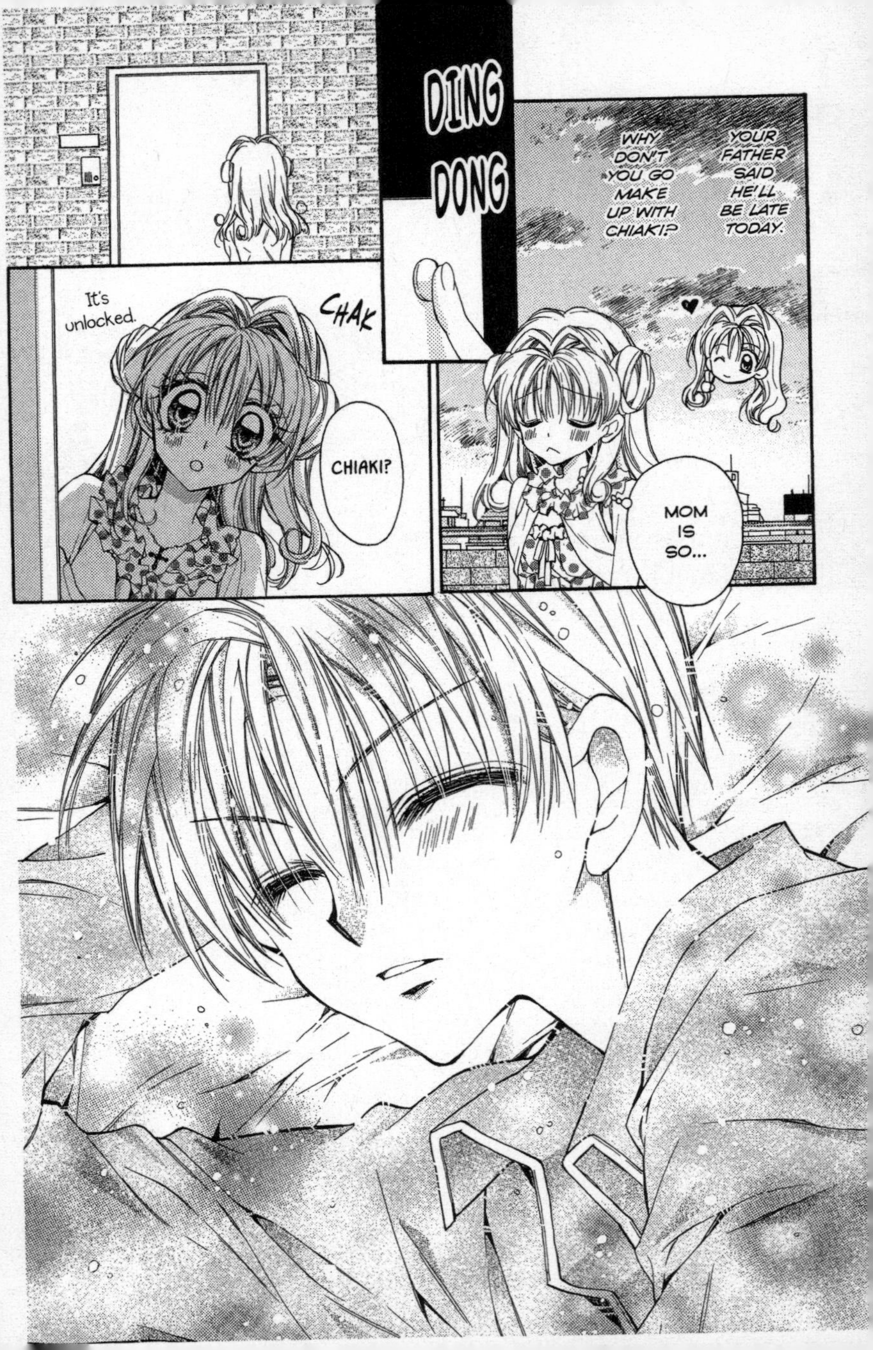
YOUR FATHER SAID HE'LL BE LATE TODAY.
WHY DON'T YOU GO MAKE UP WITH CHIAKI?
MOM IS SO...
DING DONG
CHAK
It's unlocked.
CHIAKI?

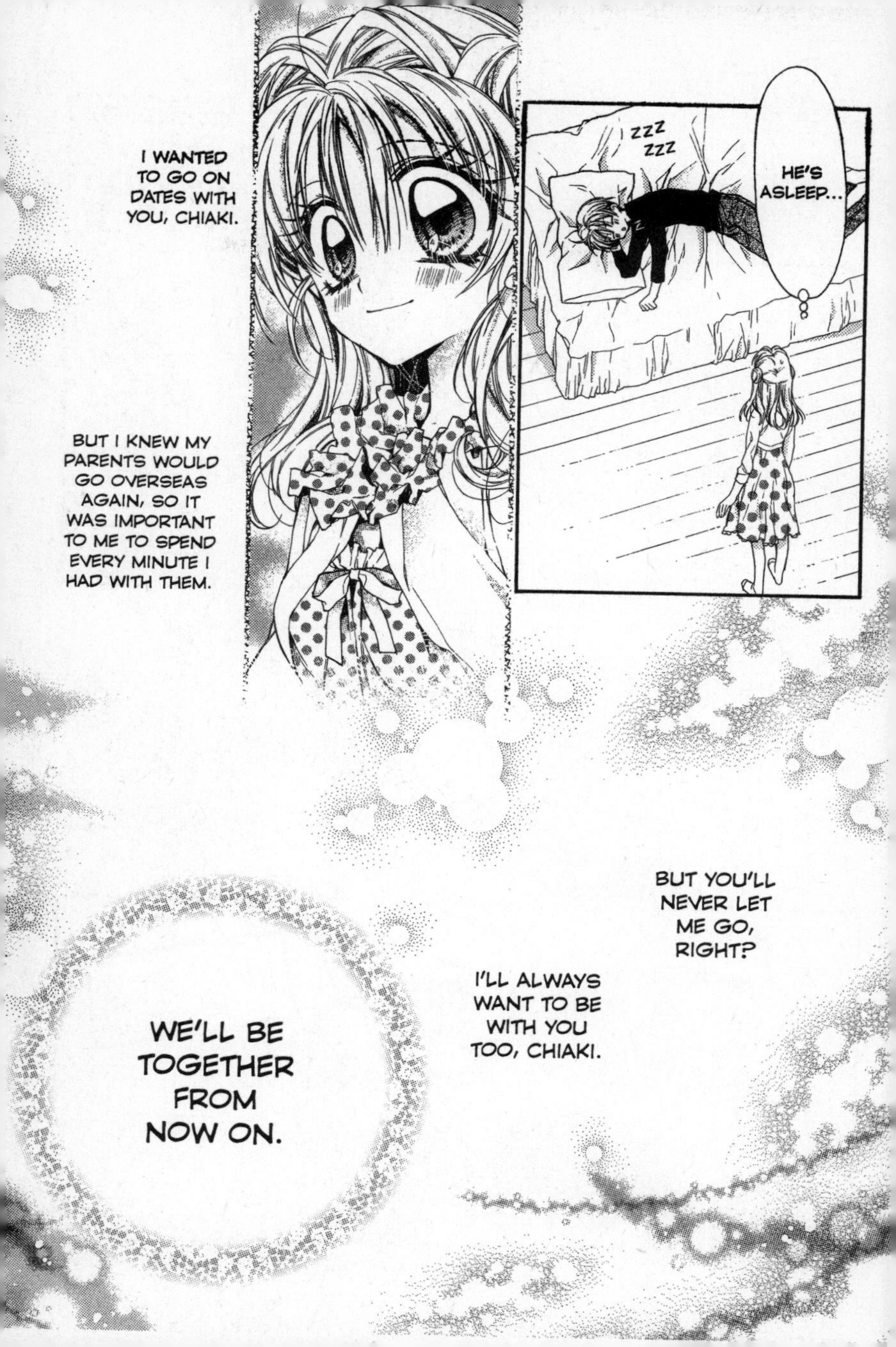
HE'S ASLEEP...
ZZZ ZZZ
I WANTED TO GO ON DATES WITH YOU, CHIAKI.
BUT I KNEW MY PARENTS WOULD GO OVERSEAS AGAIN, SO IT WAS IMPORTANT TO ME TO SPEND EVERY MINUTE I HAD WITH THEM.
BUT YOU'LL NEVER LET ME GO, RIGHT?
I'LL ALWAYS WANT TO BE WITH YOU TOO, CHIAKI.
WE'LL BE TOGETHER FROM NOW ON.

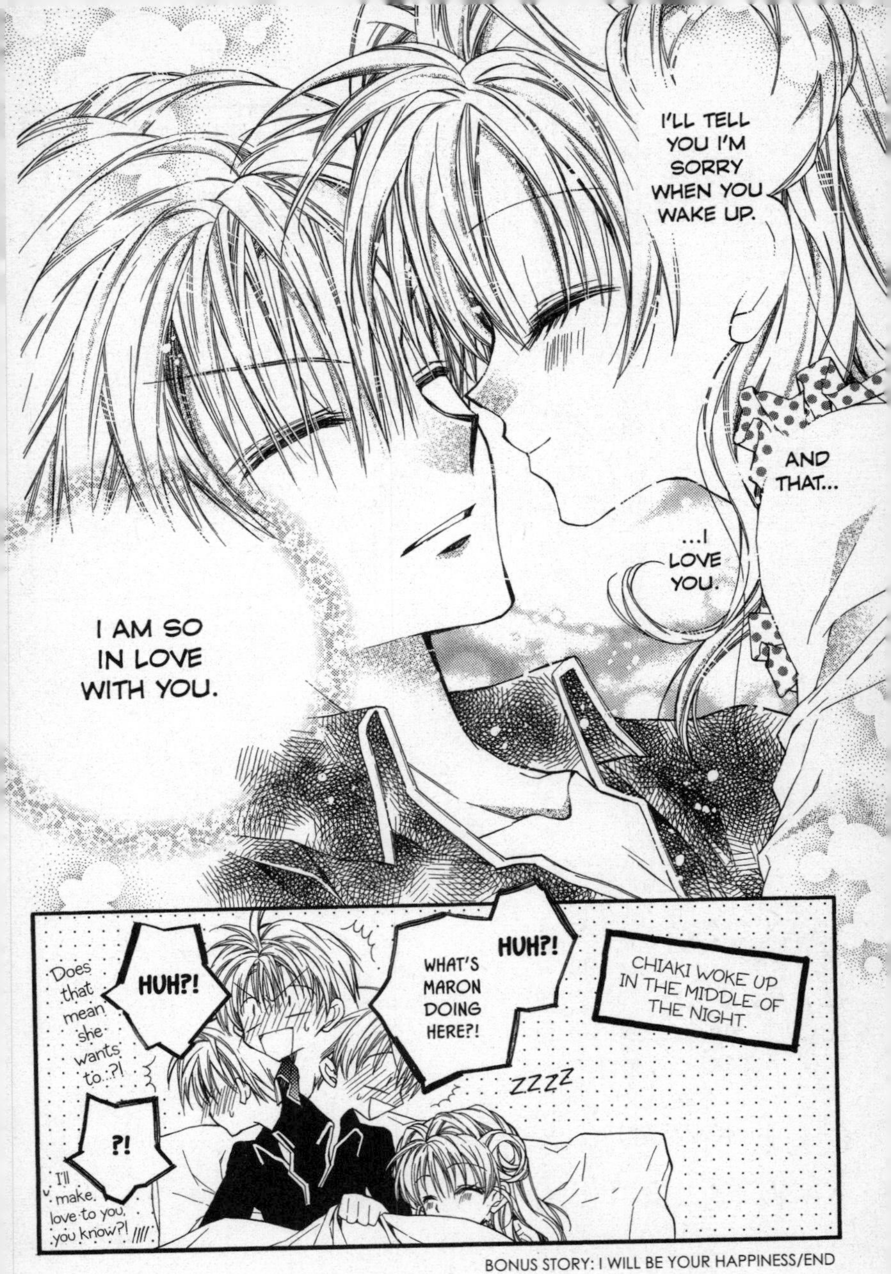
I'LL TELL YOU I'M SORRY WHEN YOU WAKE UP.
AND THAT...
...I LOVE YOU.
I AM SO IN LOVE WITH YOU.
CHIAKI WOKE UP IN THE MIDDLE OF THE NIGHT.
HUH?!
WHAT'S MARON DOING HERE?!
ZZZZ
HUH?!
Does that mean she wants to..?!
?!
I'll make love to you, you know?!

BONUS STORY: I WILL BE YOUR HAPPINESS/END

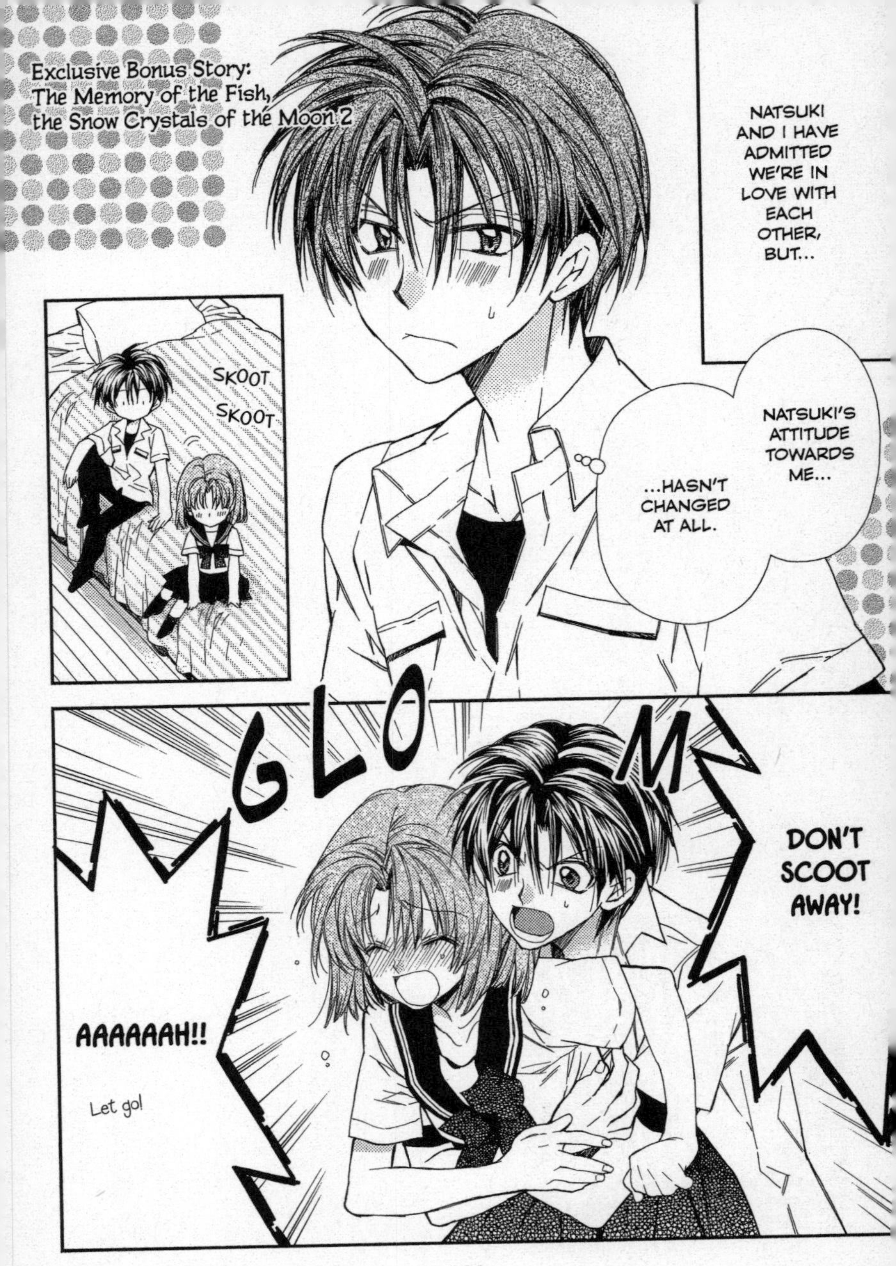
Exclusive Bonus Story:
The Memory of the Fish, the Snow Crystals of the Moon 2
NATSUKI AND I HAVE ADMITTED WE'RE IN LOVE WITH EACH OTHER, BUT...
NATSUKI'S ATTITUDE TOWARDS ME...
...HASN'T CHANGED AT ALL.
SKOOT
SKOOT
GLOM
DON'T SCOOT AWAY!
AAAAAAH!!
Let go!

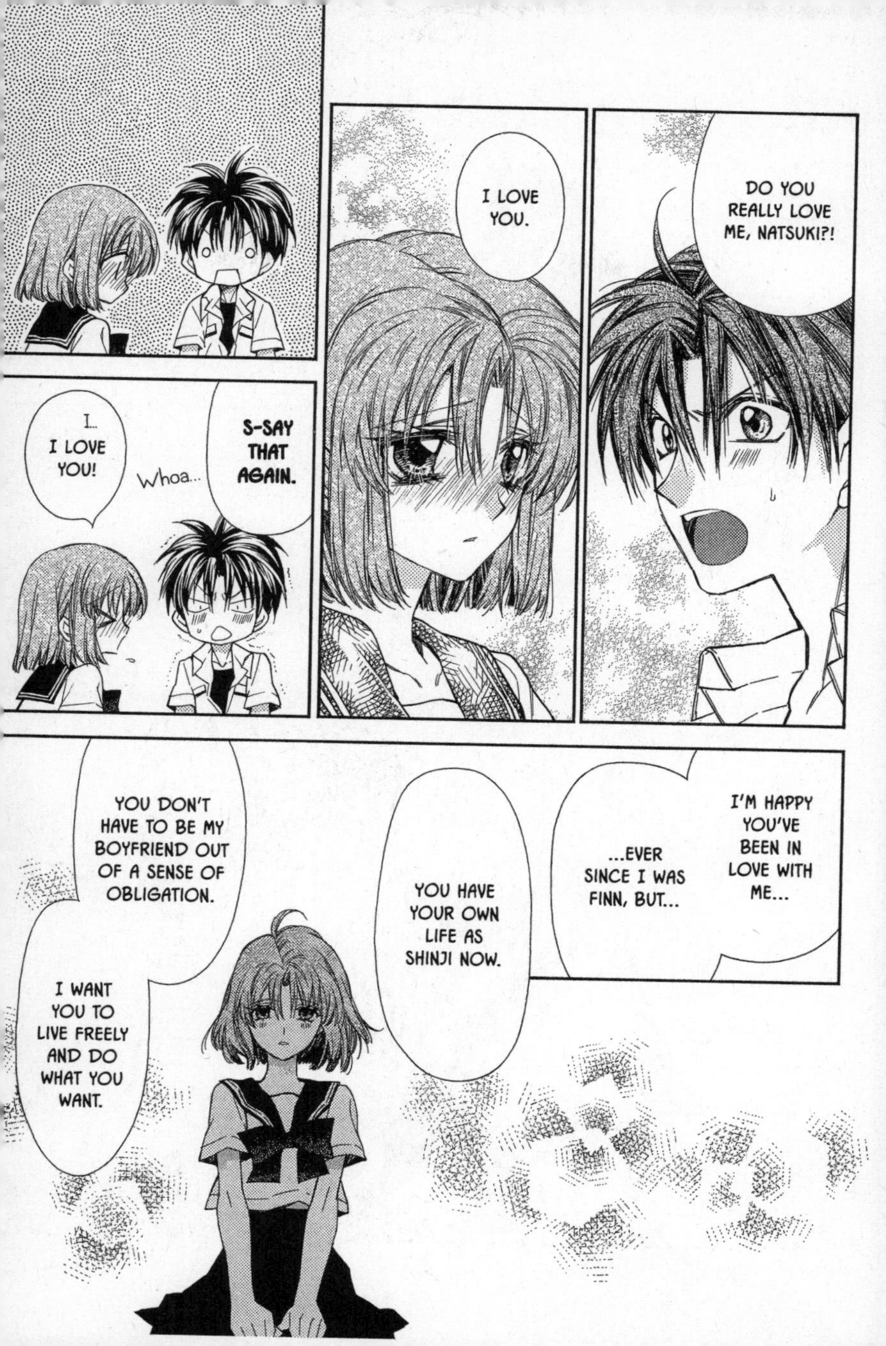
DO YOU REALLY LOVE ME, NATSUKI?!
I LOVE YOU.
S-SAY THAT AGAIN.
Whoa...
I... I LOVE YOU!
I'M HAPPY YOU'VE BEEN IN LOVE WITH ME...
...EVER SINCE I WAS FINN, BUT...
YOU HAVE YOUR OWN LIFE AS SHINJI NOW.
YOU DON'T HAVE TO BE MY BOYFRIEND OUT OF A SENSE OF OBLIGATION.
I WANT YOU TO LIVE FREELY AND DO WHAT YOU WANT.

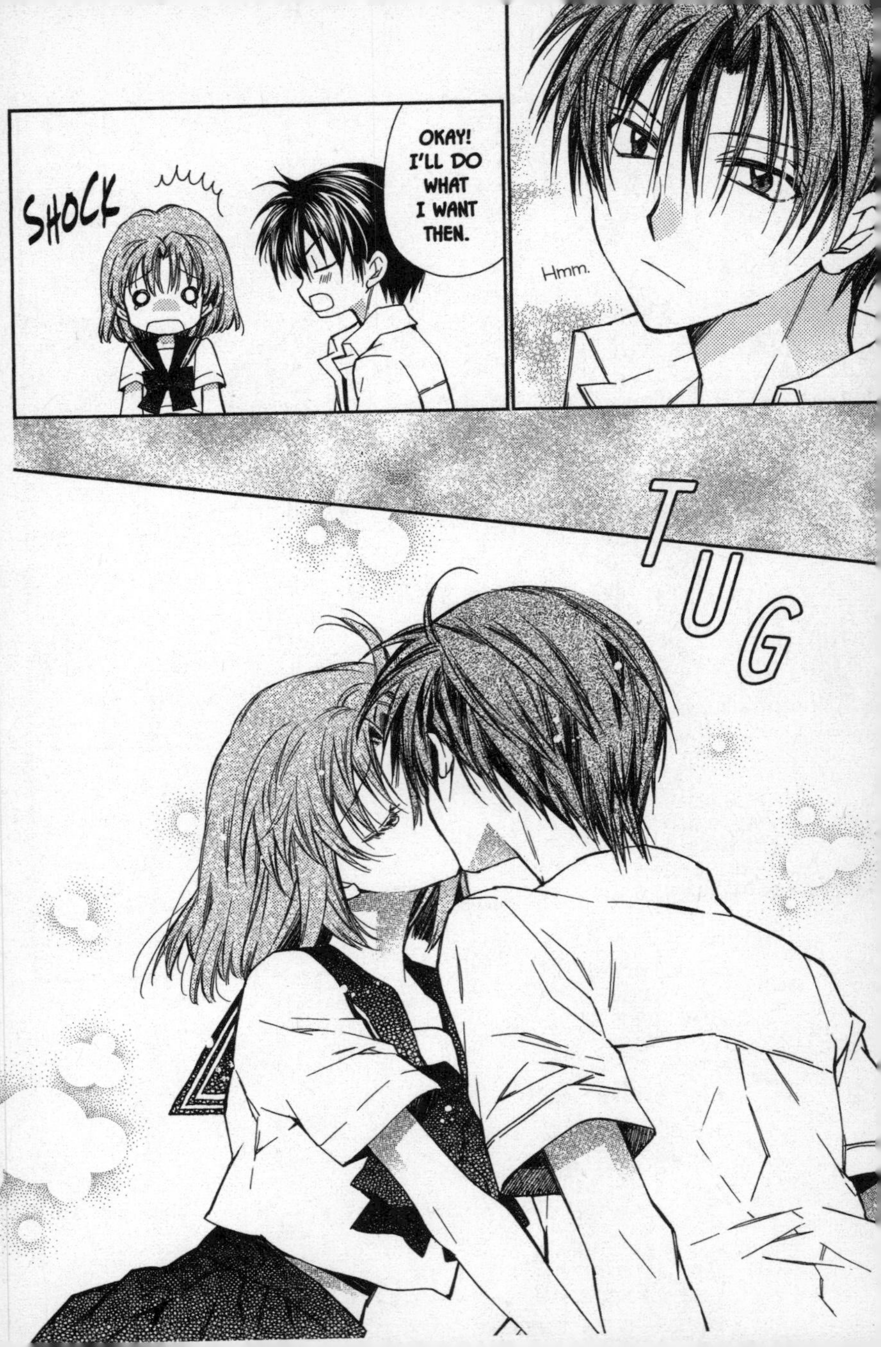
Hmm.
OKAY! I'LL DO WHAT I WANT THEN.
SHOCK
TUG

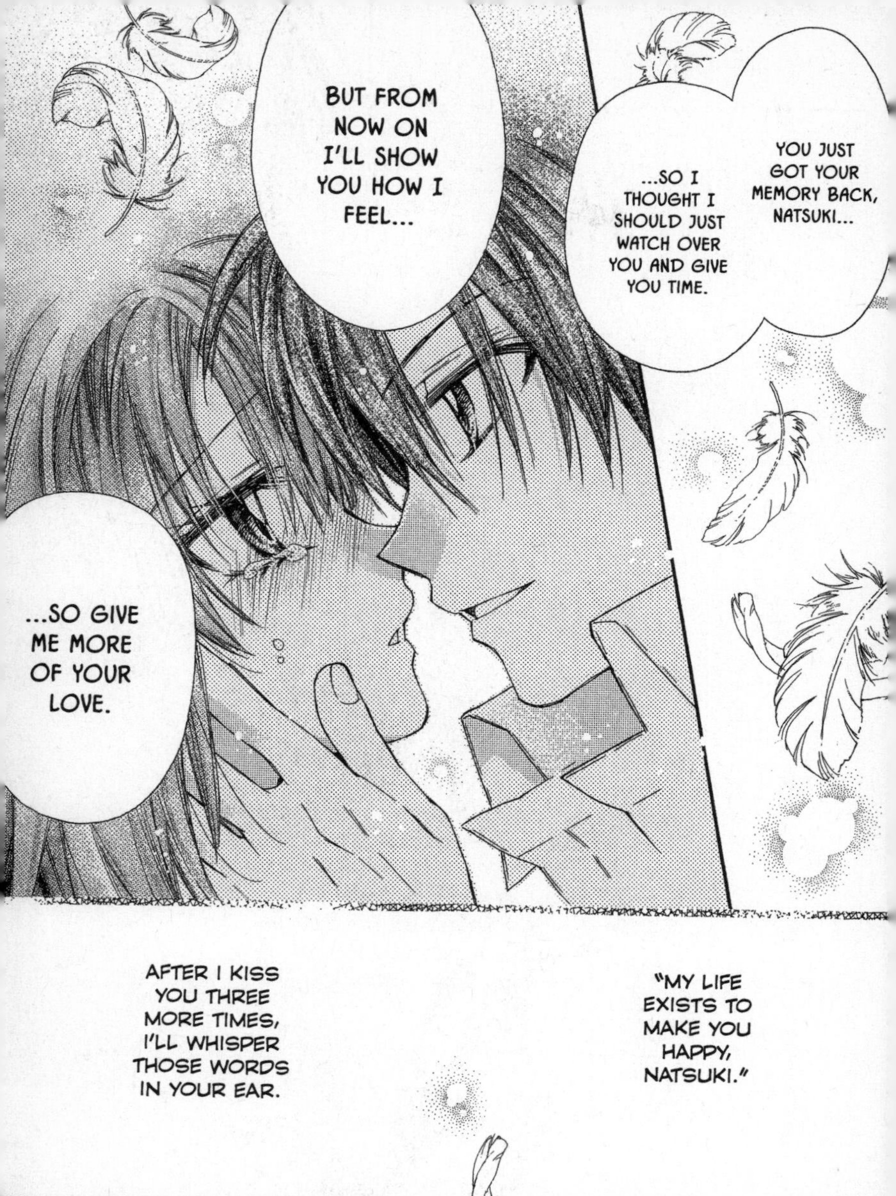
YOU JUST GOT YOUR MEMORY BACK, NATSUKI...
...SO I THOUGHT I SHOULD JUST WATCH OVER YOU AND GIVE YOU TIME.
BUT FROM NOW ON I'LL SHOW YOU HOW I FEEL...
...SO GIVE ME MORE OF YOUR LOVE.
"MY LIFE EXISTS TO MAKE YOU HAPPY, NATSUKI."
AFTER I KISS YOU THREE MORE TIMES, I'LL WHISPER THOSE WORDS IN YOUR EAR.

EXCLUSIVE BONUS STORY:
THE MEMORY OF THE FISH, THE SNOW CRYSTALS OF THE MOON 2

ARINA TANEMURA

Arina Tanemura began her manga career in 1996 when her short stories debuted in *Ribon* magazine. She gained fame with the 1997 publication of *I•O•N*, and ever since her debut Tanemura has been a major force in shojo manga with popular series *Phantom Thief Jeanne, Time Stranger Kyoko, Full Moon,* and *The Gentlemen's Alliance †*. Both *Phantom Thief Jeanne* and *Full Moon* have been adapted into animated TV series.

PHANTOM THIEF
Jeanne

VOLUME 5
SHOJO BEAT EDITION

STORY AND ART BY Arina Tanemura

TRANSLATION Tetsuichiro Miyaki
TOUCH-UP ART & LETTERING Inori Fukuda Trant
DESIGN Shawn Carrico
EDITOR Nancy Thistlethwaite

Published by VIZ Media, LLC
P.O. Box 77010
San Francisco, CA 94107

10 9 8 7 6 5 4 3 2 1
First printing, November 2014

www.viz.com

www.shojobeat.com

STOP! You may be reading the wrong way!

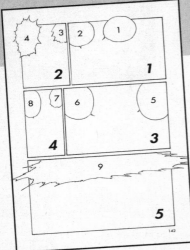

It's true: In keeping with the original Japanese comic format, this book reads from right to left—so action, sound effects, and word balloons are completely reversed. This preserves the orientation of the original artwork—plus, it's fun! Check out the diagram shown here to get the hang of things, and then turn to the other side of the book to get started!